Forty Years of Stock Car Racing
The Beginning
1949-1958
Revised Edition

First of a Four Volume Series

By Greg Fielden

Also by Greg Fielden
The Forty Years of Stock Car Racing Series
Vol. II - The Superspeedway Boom 1959-1964
'Vol. III - Big Bucks and Boycotts 1965-1971
Vol. IV' - The Modern Era - 1972-1989
Rumblin' Ragtops - The History of NASCAR's Fabulous Convertible Division
High Speed At Low Tide

The Galfield Press
P.O. Box 15009
Surfside Beach, S.C. 29587

Author Greg Fielden, right, with fellow historian Bob Latford at Daytona International Speedway.

About the Author...

Born in Charlotte, N.C., the 40 year-old author, Greg Fielden, is recognized as one of the premier historians of NASCAR Winston Cup Grand National stock car racing.

He has served as Historian and Statistician in the TV broadcast booths for all major networks as well as many cable stations during the past decade.

Fielden has written the *Forty Years of Stock Car Racing* series to provide racing fans with a chronicle of the history of the sport. This series has been acclaimed by motorsports writers as a most important contribution to the literature of motorsports.

The author resides in Surfside Beach, South Carolina.

Forty Years of Stock Car Racing, Volume I, The Beginning, 1949-1958

First Printing, February 1988
Second Printing, May 1988
Third Printing, February 1989
Fourth Printing, November 1989
Revised Edition, April 1990
Second Printing Revised Edition, March 1992
Third Printing Revised Edition, April 1993

Copyright © 1992 by Gregory Lawrence Fielden

ISBN   0-9621580-2-X

Published by the Galfield Press
Manufactured in the United States of America

Cover Photo: Marshall Teague #6 and Herb Thomas #92 with first and second place trophies proudly mounted on the hoods of the Fabulous Hudson Hornets on the shores of Daytona Beach in February, 1952. *Courtesy of Fletcher Williams.*

Dedication

This series of books is dedicated to those individuals who paid the ultimate price in NASCAR Winston Cup Grand National stock car racing -- the sport they loved.

Larry Mann	Buren Skeen
Frank Arford	Harold Kite
Lou Figaro	Billy Foster
John McVitty	Talmadge Prince
Clint McHugh	Friday Hassler
Cotton Priddy	Larry Smith
Bobby Myers	Tiny Lund
Gwyn Staley	Ricky Knotts
Joe Weatherly	Terry Schoonover
Fireball Roberts	Bruce Jacobi
Jimmy Pardue	Grant Adcox
Billy Wade	J.D. McDuffie

Credits

The author wishes to extend a special thanks to P.J. Hollebrand for editorial content, and Fletcher Williams and the NASCAR photo department for providing photographs.

Elizabeth Baker	Larry Fielden	Houston Lawing
Fred Bince	Patricia Fielden	Jeanie Metcalfe
Allan E. Brown	Tim Flock	Morris Metcalfe
Ken Clapp	Frances Flock	Danny Myers
Richard Cole	Gene Granger	Don O'Reilly
Irma Combs	Andy Hall	Doris Roberts
Phil Combs	Betty Harb	Hank Schoolfield
Bob Costanzo	Fred Harb	Mitzi Teague
Paul Dalton	Bill Hennecy	Paul Vinson
Dorothy Davis	Ned Jarrett	Bob Weeks
Larry Eanes	Larry Jendras	Chip Williams
Chris Economaki	Kenny Kane	
	Bob Latford	

Table of Contents

The 1949 Season
The Day It All Began --
June 19, 1949

Volume one of a four volume series . . . . . . The Beginning 1949 - 1958

1949

On December 14, 1947, in a smoke-filled room at the Streamline Hotel in Daytona Beach, Florida, thirty-five men sat at a table and laid the ground work for a national sanctioning body to tie up the loose threads and govern the sport of stock car racing.

Chairman of the meeting on that Sunday afternoon was Big Bill France, who had directed stock car races in the South in 1947. In the next three days a set of by-laws, rules and guidelines were drawn up.

France had begun the 1947 season as director of the National Championship Stock Car Circuit (NCSCC), a

sanctioning body he founded that used the slogan, "Where The Fastest That Run, Run the Fastest". The young promoter also staged events under the Stock Car Auto Racing Society, but the call letters spelled SCARS so that idea was quickly scrapped.

Red Vogt, renowned mechanic from Atlanta and one of those attending the meeting has generally been given credit for coming up with the name for the new organization; and on February 21, 1948, the National Association for Stock Car Auto Racing was incorporated.

France was elected President of NASCAR with E.G. "Cannonball" Baker of Indianapolis as National Commissioner. Eddie Bland of Jacksonville was the new Vice-president; Bill Tuthill of Hartford, Secretary; and

The meeting at the Streamline Hotel where the groundwork was laid for the National Association of Stock Car Auto Racing.

race driver Marshall Teague, Treasurer. "The purpose of this association is to unite all stock car racing under one set of rules; to set up a benevolent fund and a national point standings system whereby only one stock car driver will be crowned national champion," declared France. "Every track and every area has a 'national champion' of every type of racing. This has so confused the sports writers that they give up in disgust after trying to give the public an accurate picture."

NASCAR proposed the sanctioning of three different divisions in 1948, and curiously the "Strictly Stock" class was listed as the headlining attraction. Support divisions were the Modified Stocks and Roadsters.

The Strictly Stocks, which would eventually become the Winston Cup Grand National Tour, never made it off the ground in 1948.

No new cars had been built from 1942 to 1946, and the auto manufacturers were still trying to "catch up" on the shortage. A race fan would not stand for the idea of new showroom cars being beat up on a race track while he was still driving the old 1940 clunker. There was an influx of old pre-war coupes which was the "meat" of stock car racing. The Roadsters fizzled out soon thereafter, and France had to rely on the Modifieds to make his bread and butter. He did, however, permit the late model Strictly Stocks to compete in Modified races. They were driven sparingly.

Fifty-two championship Modified meets comprised the 1948 slate, and Red Byron of Atlanta was crowned national champion.

France had the ball rolling, but his concept of having one set of rules to determine one national champion was not entirely a success. In

Bill France -- the man who made it all happen.

1949, NASCAR had to rival the National Stock Car Racing Association (NSCRA), the United Stock Car Racing Association (USCRA), the National Auto Racing League (NARL), and the American Stock Car Racing Association (ASCRA) for supremacy in the stock car field. All had point systems which would determine a "national champion" and the journalists still had to juggle several names in the sport sections when penning stories about stock car racing titlists.

The sport was getting nowhere fast.

France tried to revitalize the Strictly Stocks, a class of racing designed for the late model family sedan. He figured the racing enthusiast would be interested in a division which featured automobiles the general public was buying off the showroom floor. Besides, no other sanctioning body had utilized the idea, and it might substantiate NASCAR's claim of having a true "national champion".

On February 27, 1949, an experimental Strictly Stock race was staged at the Broward Speedway, a massive two-mile paved track in Southern Florida. The five lap, 10-mile race was the "novice" event of a three-race card, falling in behind the top billing of a 100-mile National Grand Prix Roadster race and a 25-mile European Sports Car race.

Most of the "name" drivers participated in the 100-miler for low-slung, chopped-up Roadsters, a classification France was also trying to rebuild for the 1949 season.

The event was won by Bob Flock of Atlanta. Future Indianapolis 500 champion Jim Rathmann finished second. Tom Demetry won the Sports Car event

Glenn Dunnaway's #25 Ford was flagged the winner, but was disqualified several hours later.

and Benny Georgeson of Fort Lauderdale, Florida, captured the very first Strictly Stock race in a Buick. Eddie Mitchell of Defiance, Ohio came in second in a Mercury.

It was difficult for France to evaluate the impact of the Strictly Stocks since it was merely a supplementary event at Broward. For the most part, everyone forgot about it.

However, early in 1949, NASCAR found itself being challenged by the NSCRA, a fledgling operation directed by Olin Bruton Smith, now Chairman of Charlotte Motor Speedway. Both NASCAR and NSCRA were fighting for the same cars and drivers in the same general area. Smith's new organization was a threat to France, who hurriedly prepared to stage another Strictly Stock race in the early summer.

This time, however, the Strictly Stocks would be the main attraction, and a "marathon" 150-miler would be presented in Charlotte on June 19, 1949, with a purse of $5,000 on the line.

Zack Mosely inserted news about the Charlotte race in his comic strip "Smilin' Jack'.

The surprise announcement caught nearly everyone off guard, but France was not worried about attracting a full field of cars since Strictly Stocks were just that. And anyone who owned a full size American made passenger car was eligible to enter. He felt confident the 33-car field would be filled when the green flag was waved.

The battleground was a rough three-quarter mile dirt track surrounded by scraggly fences of undressed lumber misappropriating the name "speedway". The track, built by Harvey and Pat Charles on property leased from Mr. & Mrs. C.C. Allison, had opened on July 11, 1948, and had hosted Modified races for parts of two seasons.

Most of the Modified hotshots showed up with late model sedans. There were, however, four top drivers who were not permitted to enter for reasons NASCAR listed as "actions detrimental to auto racing".

During his short tenure as Treasurer of NASCAR, Teague noticed that the gate receipts at some tracks were substantially greater than the guaranteed purse which was posted. He wanted NASCAR to adopt a policy used by the American Automobile Association which paid 40-percent of the gate receipts into the purse for the Indy Car drivers whenever and wherever they raced. Teague withdrew from two spring NASCAR races in protest.

Buddy Shuman, Speedy Thompson and Ed Samples were not allowed to compete because they had allegedly deposited a few hundred thumb tacks on a track before a NASCAR Modified meet a couple of weeks earlier. Jimmy Thompson had been cleared of similar charges, placed on a one-year probation period, and was granted permission to compete.

Qualifying trials were held on Saturday, June 18th. Bob Flock, a man with majestic blue eyes and a volatile temper, posted the quickest lap of 67.958 miles per hour in the Davis Brothers '46 Hudson. Tim Flock, a fidgety, nervous youngster, was second in the Buddy Elliott '49 Oldsmobile; and Red Byron, the original Huckleberry Finn of racing, was third fastest in the Parks Novelty Co. '49 Olds. Otis Martin, a scraggly mountaineer wearing farmer's overalls, qualified fourth in a '48 Ford, and smiling jokester Fonty Flock was fifth in a '49 Hudson. The Flock Brothers were doing very well.

Other qualifiers included Curtis Turner, a womanizing lumberjack in a '46 Buick Roadmaster; Hubert Westmoreland, an eccentric moonshiner in a '47 Ford; and Bill Blair, a laid-back greasy little fellow who put a Lincoln through the timing lights.

Lining up 12th was Jim Roper, who had hauled his Lincoln all the way from Great Bend, Kansas. Roper

Jim Roper's #34 Lincoln finished second in Charlotte's 150-miler, but was elevated to first place when NASCAR disqualified the winning car.

had become aware of the race from the syndicated "Smilin' Jack" comic strip authored by Zack Mosely, an auto racing fan who often slipped racing news into his art work.

Another notable in the field was Sara Christian, who

*Otis Martin #19 leads Red Byron #22 down front chute in inaugural NASCAR Strictly Stock
race at Charlotte Speedway. Jim Roper of Great Bend, KS won the race and earned a spot in stock car racing history.*

was regarded as "The Leading Woman Stock Car Driver in the Country" in early NASCAR press releases.

Christian qualified 13th in a '47 Ford, one spot ahead of Sam Rice, a quiet and polite man whose trademark was a full-brimmed hat.

Others in the field included Jim Paschal, tatooed up to his armpits with ships and anchors; Herb Thomas, a skinny tobacco farmer; Jack Smith, a portly Georgia boy with a pure leather neck; and Buck Baker, a big-eared ex-door-to-door milk man. All these would eventually be represented in the National Motorsports Press Association Hall of Fame.

Nine different makes of automobiles would go to the post: Lincoln, Hudson, Ford Olds, Cadillac, Buick, Chrysler, Kaiser and Mercury.

The gates were scheduled to open at noon on June 19th, but with an unexpectedly long line of cars and spectators leading into the speedway grounds, France began letting them in several minutes early.

Crowd estimates by Houston A. Lawing, NASCAR's first Publicity Director, were as high as 22,500, but France later said about 13,000 had paid to get in. It was a healthy turnout. Maybe the Strictly Stocks could support themselves after all.

The field of 33 cars snarled around the track three times behind the pace car. The crowd, full of anticipation, were on their collective feet for this historic occasion. Seventeen rows were filled by cars with unimaginative color schemes - some not painted at all. Lots of black cars, a couple of red ones, a gray one. And then there was a bright green flag in the hands of Starter Alvin Hawkins.

Into the first turn they sped - the leaders disappearing into clouds of billowing dust which rose well above the undressed wooden fence. Wheel to wheel, hub to hub they came. Fenders popping. Throttles snapping. Spectators cheering.

For five dusty trips around, Bob Flock's bulky Hudson led the way. Then a black Lincoln with five-foot, six-inch Bill Blair peeping over the steering wheel took command, skimming past Flock as they roared down the backstretch.

Greasy little Bill Blair, broadsliding over the bumps and chuck-holes, left his comrades choking on the dust from his whitewall heels.

*Lee Petty's '46 Buick Roadmaster was banged up after a spill on lap 107.
Jimmy Thompson, #36, passes on track.*

Bob Flock was one of the first drivers out of the race. His Hudson retired to the pit area and was parked in a pool of oil that had oozed from his motor. He then accepted relief driving chores for Sara Christian, who climbed out of her Ford after 30 or so punishing miles.

Blair continued to tackle the gently banked corners with reckless abandon, passing each and every car with bold, daring thrusts. Meanwhile, as the half-way point rolled around, perhaps a dozen or more cars were motionless in the unmanicured pit area. Drivers, with helmet in hand, studied geysers of steam shooting skyward from tortured, overheated engines.

On Lap 107, Lee Petty, a new face to the racing game, found himself holding on for dear life as his Buick -- a vehicle he drove from Level Cross, North Carolina to Charlotte two days earlier -- tumbled endlessly through the third turn, coming to rest on all four wheels. Petty unbuckled his seat belt, got out of the car and sat down on the upper crest of the track, staring out over the countryside in a dejected muse. "I was just sitting there thinking about having to go back home and explain to my wife where I'd been with the car," Petty said later. It was the first and to be the only crash of the afternoon, and Petty suffered nothing more serious than a cut on his cheek.

Bill Blair pressed on, lapping the rapidly fading field at least once. His sights were set on the black and which checkered flag and the $2,000 that went to the driver who got there first.

But the casualty epidemic struck Blair's fleet Lincoln 50 laps from paydirt. He brought his R.B. McIntosh-owned car down the grassy pit lane, steam whining as it gushed from the radiator, his quest for racing immortality ruined by mechanical problems.

Blair's misfortune allowed Glenn Dunnaway to pick up first place on lap 151. The Gastonia, North Carolina driver arrived trackside Sunday morning without a ride. But Hubert Westmoreland let Dunnaway, the more experienced pedal-pusher, tighten the seat belt at race time.

Funny page reader Jim Roper moved up to second place, but overheating problems forced him to slacken his pace. He finished the race slowly, cruising the inside of the track.

Dunnaway's Ford breezed across the finish line three full laps ahead of Roper's ailing Lincoln. He was congratulated by all. The handful of newspaper writers wrote their stories accordingly.

But as twilight descended on Charlotte, Major Al Crisler, NASCAR's first Technical Inspector was summoned to conduct a teardown of Dunnaway's winning Ford. Some officials had wondered about the apparent stability of the car as it passed through the bumpy turns.

Crisler said the Westmoreland-Dunnaway Ford was equipped with "altered rear springs" and therefore it did not fit the guidelines of the Strictly Stocks. No modifications of any kind were allowed except for a reinforcing steel plate on the right front wheel in the interest of safety to prevent lug nuts from pulling through the rims on conventional wheels.

The '47 Ford was a bootlegger car designed to haul heavy loads of illegal moonshine, and "spreading the springs" was common in vehicles used for that purpose.

Westmoreland howled like a coyote when NASCAR disqualified his car and awarded the $2,000 first prize to Roper, who had completed 197 of the scheduled 200 laps. Westmoreland was so incensed that he filed a lawsuit for $10,000 in damages against NASCAR.

But Judge John J. Hayes threw the case out of Greensboro, North Carolina court. NASCAR had prevailed in all aspects of the inaugural Strictly Stock race.

Fonty Flock got credit for finishing second and picked up a check for $1,000. Had Roper been forced to complete the full 200 laps running at a snail's pace, Flock very well may have won the race. Red Byron wound up third and collected $500. Sam Rice finished fourth for $300, and Tim Flock got fifth and $200.

Rounding out the top ten were Archie Smith in a Ford, Sterling Long in a Hudson, the Olds of Slick Smith, Curtis Turner's Buick, and a Chrysler manned by Jimmy Thompson.

Blair got credit for 12th place, and Bob Flock, in relief of Sara Christian, was 14th.

The Charlotte race was a monumental success, and France organized a slate of seven additional races in 1949. Within eight months the newly named Grand National Division would replace the Modifieds as the premier class of NASCAR.

The principals on that sunny, muggy afternoon in Charlotte were an outlandish cast of characters with a sense for adventure. The meek did not inherit the confines of this small acreage of earth. It was a circus of carefree performers who were neither stylized nor synchronized, but the collection of odd-balls at center stage commenced the theatre of Winston Cup Grand National racing, which opened for a long run.

1949 Season
Strictly Stock Race No. 1
200 Laps at Charlotte Speedway
Charlotte, NC
150 Miles on 3/4-mile Dirt Track

June 19, 1949

Fin	St	No.	Driver	Team / Car	Laps	Money	Status
1	12	34	Jim Roper	Mecklenburg Motors '49 Lincoln	197	$2,000	Running
2	5	47	Fonty Flock	Grady Cole-Bruce Griffin '49 Hudson		1,000	Running
3	3	22	Red Byron	Parks Novelty '49 Olds 88		500	Running
4	14	2	Sam Rice	Rice Racing '49 Olds 88		300	Running
5	2	90	Tim Flock	Buddy Elliott '49 Olds 88		200	Running
6			Archie Smith	Smith '46 Ford		175	
7		31	Sterling Long	Long Racing '46 Hudson		150	
8			Slick Smith	'49 Olds 88		125	
9	6	41	Curtis Turner	'46 Buick Roadmaster		100	
10		36	Jimmy Thompson	'46 Chrysler		75	
11		87	Buck Baker	Penny Mullis '48 Kaiser		50	
12	8	44	Bill Blair	R.B. McIntosh '49 Lincoln	150	50	Overheating
13			Jack Smith	Bishop Brothers '48 Ford		50	Overheating
14	13	71	Sara Christian *	Frank Christian '47 Ford		50	Overheating
15			John Barker	'47 Kaiser		50	
16		0	Jimmie Lewallen	'46 Ford		25	
17	9	38	Lee Petty	Petty '46 Buick Roadmaster	105	25	Crash
18		11	Skimp Hersey	'47 Ford		25	
19		25	Bob Smith	Lane's Motor Co. '49 Olds 88		25	
20	4	19	Otis Martin	'48 Ford		25	Overheating
21		37	Frank Smith	Smith Racing '47 Chrysler		---	
22		16	Bill Snowden	Snowden Racing '48 Mercury		---	Overheating
23			Jim Paschal	'46 Ford		---	Overheating
24		1	B.E. Renfro	'49 Hudson		---	
25		10	Fred Johnson			---	
26			George Mantooth			---	
27		5	Felix Wilkes	'49 Lincoln		---	Overheating
28	10		Pee Wee Martin	'49 Olds		---	
29		93	Herb Thomas	Thomas Racing '47 Ford		---	Springs
30		4	Frank Mundy	Sam Rice '49 Cadillac		---	
31		29	Clarence Benton	'49 Ford		---	
32	1	7	Bob Flock	Davis Brothers '46 Hudson	38	---	Engine
33	7	25	Glenn Dunnaway **	Hubert Westmoreland '47 Ford	200	---	Disqualified

  * Relieved by Bob Flock
  ** Glenn Dunnaway flagged winner; disqualified for illegal use of rear springs
 *** Drivers listed in positions 21-32 are not necessarily in correct finish order
    Time of Race:
    Average Speed:
    Pole Winner: Bob Flock - 67.958 mph
    Lap Leaders: Bob Flock 1-5, Bill Blair 6-150, Jim Roper 151-197
    Cautions:
    Margin of Victory:
    Attendance: 13,000

Race No. 2

Byron Nabs Daytona With Late Race Pass

Strictly Stock Race No. 2
40 Laps at Beach & Road Course
Daytona Beach, FL
166 Miles on 4.15-mile Beach & Road Course
July 10, 1949

Red Byron won Daytona event in final six laps.

DAYTONA BEACH, FL. (July 10) -- Red Byron of Atlanta took the lead from Gober Sosebee with six laps remaining and went on to win the 166-mile NASCAR Strictly Stock race on the sands of the 4.15-mile Daytona Beach and Road Course. Sosebee, who had taken the lead from Joe Littlejohn just after the drop of the green flag, appeared to be headed for the $2,000 victory, but his Oldsmobile bobbled as he negotiated the North Turn in the 34th lap of the 49-lap contest.

Byron put his Raymond Parks-owned Oldsmobile into the lead at that point and led the rest of the way.

Fin	St	No.	Driver	Team / Car	Laps	Money	Status
1	2	22	Red Byron	Parks Novelty '49 Olds	40	$2,000	Running
2	90		Tim Flock	Buddy Elliott '49 Olds	40	1,000	Running
3		5	Frank Mundy	Sam Rice '49 Olds	40	500	Running
4	4	7	Joe Littlejohn	Littlejohn '49 Olds	40	300	Running
5	5	44	Bill Blair	McIntosh/Roper '49 Lincoln	40	200	Running
6		37	Frank Christian	Christian '49 Olds		175	Running
7		16	Bill Snowden	Snowden '49 Mercury		150	Running
8	1	50	Gober Sosebee	Davis Brothers '49 Olds		125	Running
9		36	Jimmy Thompson	'47 Chrysler		100	Running
10		15	Jack Etheridge	Etheridge '49 Mercury		75	Running
11		91	Ethel Mobley	Charles Mobley '48 Cadillac		50	Running
12		9	Herb Thomas	'49 Ford		50	
13		29	Slick Smith	'48 Buick		50	
14	6	6	Marshall Teague	Bill Appleton '49 Hudson		50	
15	3	8	Billy Carden	David Chester '47 Ford		50	
16			Howard Elder			25	
17		12	Woodrow Wilson	Wilson '49 Mercury		25	
18		17	Sara Christian	Ruby Flock '49 Ford		25	
19		47	Fonty Flock	Gene Horne '49 Hudson		25	
20		94	Louise Smith	Smith '47 Ford		25	
21		71	Buckshot Morris	Sara Christian '47 Ford		---	Crash
22		14	Bob Flock	Parks Novelty '46 Ford		---	Shocks
23		87	Buck Baker	Buzzy Boehmen '47 Kaiser		---	
24		34	Sam Marshall	Jax Hudson '49 Hudson		---	
25		41	Curtis Turner	Turner '48 Buick		---	
26		10	Fred Johnson	Johnson '47 Ford		---	
27		64	Benny Georgeson	Georgeson '49 Buick		---	
28		35	Glenn Dunnaway	'49 Lincoln		---	

Time of Race: 2 hours, 3 minutes, 13 seconds
Average Speed: 80.883 mph
Pole Winner: Gober Sosebee
Lap Leaders: Gober Sosebee 1-34, Red Byron 35-40
Cautions: None   Margin of Victory: 1 minute, 51 seconds   Attendance: 5,000

Tim Flock, Frank Mundy and Littlejohn captured positions two through four as Oldsmobiles swept the top four places. Bill Blair's Lincoln nabbed fifth spot.

Twenty-eight cars started the race with 21 running at the finish. Byron averaged 80.883 mph as the race was uninterrupted by caution flags.

Louise Smith, one of three female drivers at the starting line, flipped her Ford in the North turn early in the race. With the help of several spectators who uprighted her machine, Smith continued in the event and placed 20th. Ethel Mobley finished 11th in her Cadillac, and Sara Christian came in 18th in a Ford.

Sosebee, who led 34 of the 40 laps, recovered from his near spin, but fell to eighth in the final rundown. A crowd of 5,000 watched as Byron beat Flock by one minute and 51 seconds.

Riley "Buckshot" Morris, noted mechanic, was assigned to drive a Ford owned by Sara Christian. Morris, of Atlanta, crashed late in the race.

Bob Flock, Glenn Dunnaway and Curtis Turner were three pre-race favorites who ran into trouble and did not finish.

Red Byron #22 cuts inside of Bob Flock in North turn en route to victory at Daytona.

Race No. 3

Crash Depletes Hillsboro Field; Bob Flock Wins

HILLSBORO, NC (August 7) -- Bob Flock scored his first win of the season in the 200-mile Strictly Stock race at Hillsboro's Occoneechee Speedway, giving Oldsmobile its second straight victory.

Flock outdistanced runner-up Gober Sosebee to collect the $2,000 first prize. Third place went to Glenn Dunnaway, Fonty Flock took fourth, and Bill Snowden fifth.

Tim Flock was pressuring brother Bob in the late stages, but a broken right-front spindle sent his Oldsmobile to the sidelines with ten laps to go. The younger Flock got credit for seventh in the final rundown.

Bob Smith's Oldsmobile plunges over bank at Hillsboro's Occoneechee Speedway.

The race was spiced by a wild collision, triggered by Sara Christian. The highly regarded lady driver looped her Ford after losing the right front wheel in the 38th lap. As she tried to steer her car toward the pit area, a Lincoln driven by Felix Wilkes clobbered her. Both cars spun to a halt on the home stretch completely blocking the track. Red Byron, point leader in the Strictly Stock series, whipped off the fourth turn and collected Wilkes' car.

Bob Smith's Olds was also kayoed in a solo crash. There were no driver injuries in any of the mishaps.

A crowd of 17,500 watched as Flock averaged 76.8 mph on the low-banked, one-mile dirt oval.

After the first three NASCAR Strictly Stock races, Bill France and other officials of the new-born association were elated. It was clear that France's dream was accepted by the fans.

Strictly Stock Race No. 3
200 Laps at Occoneechee Speedway
Hillsboro, NC
200 Miles on 1-mile Dirt Track
August 7, 1949

Fin	St	No.	Driver	Team / Car	Laps	Money	Status
1		7	Bob Flock	Bob Flock Garage '48 Olds 88	200	$2,000	Running
2		50	Gober Sosebee	Cherokee Garage '49 Olds 88		1,000	Running
3		55	Glenn Dunnaway	Dunnaway '49 Olds 88		500	Running
4		47	Fonty Flock	Ed Lawrence '47 Buick		300	Running
5		3	Bill Snowden	Al Wagoner '49 Chevrolet		200	Running
6		44	Bill Blair	R.B. McIntosh '49 Olds 88		175	
7		90	Tim Flock	Buddy Elliott '49 Olds 88	190	150	Spindle
8		19	Otis Martin	'48 Ford		125	
9		42	Lee Petty	Petty Brothers '49 Plymouth		100	
10		28	Buddy Helms	Helms '47 Hudson		75	
11		21	Bobby Greene	Greene '48 Ford		50	
12			J.D. Edwards			50	
13		11	Bob Apperson	Apperson '47 Ford		50	
14			Frank Smith			50	
15		34	Jim Roper	Millard Clothier '49 Lincoln		50	
16			Bill Harrison			25	
17		1	B.E. Renfro	'49 Hudson		25	
18			Garland Smith			25	
19			Jim Carruso			25	
20		41	Curtis Turner	'46 Buick Roadmaster		25	
21		25	Bob Smith	Lane's Motor Co. '49 Olds		---	Crash
22		22	Red Byron	Parks Novelty '49 Olds 88	39	---	Crash
23		71	Sara Christian	Frank Christian '47 Ford	38	---	Crash
24		5	Felix Wilkes	'49 Lincoln	38	---	Crash
25		2	Jimmie Lewallen	'49 Lincoln		---	
26			Herb Thomas	Thomas '47 Ford		---	
27		94	Louise Smith	Smith Auto Parts '47 Ford		---	
28		31	Sterling Long	'46 Hudson		---	

Time of Race:
Average Speed: 76.8 mph
Pole Winner:
Lap Leaders: - - - - - - - - - - Bob Flock -200
Cautions: Margin of Victory: Attendance: 17,500

Fonty Flock sits in his big Buick Roadmaster which he drove to a 4th place finish in 200-miler at Occoneechee Speedway.

Race No. 4

Turner Wins Langhorne; Sara Shines

LANGHORNE, PA (Sept 11) -- Curtis Turner, the "Blond Blizzard" out of Roanoke, Virginia, outdueled Bob Flock and came home first in the celebrated 200-mile Strictly Stock race at the famed circular Langhorne Speedway before 20,000 spectators.

Sara Christian, leading female driver out of Atlanta, finished sixth in a sterling performance. Her effort in the grueling 200-lapper prompted race officials to escort her to victory lane to join winner Turner in the ceremonies.   Turner drove his Oldsmobile into the

Red Byron #22 and Gober Sosebee, wheeling a pair of Oldsmobiles, lead the charge at Langhorne Speedway.

lead in the 141st lap when Bob Flock went to the pits for a tire change. Turner led the rest of the way to pocket the $2,250 first prize. Flock scampered out of the pits and finished second, 20 seconds behind the winner. Third place went to point leader Red Byron as Oldsmobiles finished 1-2-3. Frank Mundy and Bill Blair rounded out the top five, both driving Cadillacs.

Strictly Stock Race No. 4
200 Laps at Langhorne Speedway
Langhorne, PA
200 Miles on 1-mile Dirt Track
September 11, 1949

Fin	St	No.	Driver	Team / Car	Laps	Money	Status
1	11	41	Curtis Turner	Westmoreland '49 Olds	200	$2,250	Running
2	6	7	Bob Flock	Bob Flock Garage '49 Olds	200	1,000	Running
3	1	22	Red Byron	Parks Novelty '49 Olds	199	800	Running
4	33	44	Frank Mundy	Sam Rice '49 Cadillac	196	500	Running
5	4	46	Bill Blair	'49 Cadillac	196	350	Running
6	21	71	Sara Christian	Frank Christian '49 Olds	190	300	Running
7	25	42	Lee Petty	Petty Brothers '49 Plymouth	188	250	Running
8	22	89	Al Keller	W.O. Taylor '49 Ford	185	200	Running
9	17	6	Al Bonnell	Don Rogalla '48 Olds	183	150	Running
10	34	52	Lou Volk	'47 Buick	182	125	Running
11	41	61	Bill Bennett	'49 Kaiser	181	100	
12	30	39	Budd Olsen	'49 Mercury	180	75	
13	26	14	Dick Zimmerman	'47 Mercury	178	50	
14	23	59	Bill Rexford	Julian Buesink '49 Ford	177	50	
15	40	23	Erwin Blatt	'46 Ford	176	50	
16	38	94	Louise Smith	Smith '47 Ford	175	50	
17	44	4	Don Cecchini	'49 Nash 600	173	50	
18	28	48	Lee Schmidt	'49 Buick	171	50	Crash
19	2	50	Gober Sosebee	Cherokee Garage '49 Olds	170	100	
20	9	25	Ken Marriott	Moyer Co. Special '49 Lincoln	169	50	
21	12	62	Ed Tyson	'49 Ford	169	50	
22	37	77	Ken Schroeder	'49 Buick	168	50	
23	24	91	Tommy Coates	W.O. Taylor '49 Ford	167	50	
24	8	8	Wally Campbell	'49 Olds	166	25	
25	31	86	Harvey Hilligas	'49 Ford	162	25	
26	35	20	Dick Linder	La Belle Motor Co. '49 Kaiser	162	25	
27	39	31	Ben Cannaziaro	'46 Ford	159	25	
28	45	9	Len Brown	'47 Ford Convertible	158	25	
29	19	13	Pat Kirkwood	'49 Olds		---	
30	14	2	Jimmie Lewallen	'49 Lincoln		---	
31	5	90	Tim Flock	Buddy Elliott '49 Olds		---	Wheel
32	13	32	Jim Rathmann	'49 Olds		---	
33	15	88	P Cunningham	Cunningham '49 Lincoln	134	---	Crash
34	32	35	John Belgard	'47 Ford		---	
35	10	27	Buckshot Morris	'49 Olds		---	
36	7	3	Johnny Rogers	'49 Olds		---	
37	36	69	Chick DiNatale	'46 Ford	96	---	Crash
38	18	51	Jack O'Brien	'47 Buick		---	
39	27	79	Tony Ganeva	'47 Hudson			
40	43	11	Jim Delaney	'49 Ford		---	
41	20	5	Felix Wilkes	'49 Lincoln		---	
42	29	43	Jack Russell	'48 Ford		---	
43	16	49	Walter Minx	'49 Buick	25	---	Crash
44	42	92	Ethel Mobley	'48 Cadillac		---	
45	3	47	Fonty Flock	Ed Lawrence '49 Buick	2	---	Engine

Time of Race: 2 hours, 52 minutes, 54.12 seconds
Average Speed 69.403 mph
Pole Winner: Red Byron - 77.482 mph
Fastest Qualifier: Fonty Flock - 80.140
Lap Leaders: - - - - - -, Bob Flock -140, Curtis Turner 141-200
Cautions: Margin of Victory: 20 seconds   Attendance: 20,000

Sara Christian leads Al Bonnell and Len Brown in front of packed grandstands in Langhorne 200.

Forty-five new Strictly Stock automobiles went to the starting post, the most cars to start a race in the 1949 season. Turner averaged 69.403 mph.

Byron and Gober Sosebee earned the front row starting positions in qualifying. Fonty Flock, however, registered the fastest time in "Speed Trials" with a 80.140 fast lap. Fonty challenged Byron and Sosebee at the start, but the engine in his Buick blew after three laps. Sosebee struggled with tire problems and wound up 19th.

Len Brown drove a '47 Ford Convertible in the 200-mile championship chase -- the first person to drive an open-top vehicle on the premier NASCAR stock car racing tour. Brown managed to come home 28th -- earning $25 for his day of work.

Accidents took out Pepper Cunningham, Walter Minx and Chick DiNatale. Tim Flock was a contender for victory until sidelined by a lost wheel.

nated by Northern drivers.

White sailed into the lead when erstwhile leader Glenn Dunnaway lost a wheel on his Olds, forcing him out of the race in the 134th lap. With Dunnaway out of the way, White was able to hold off Ray Erickson to take the $1,500 top prize. Billy Rafter wound up third, Mike Eagan was fourth and Bill Rexford took fifth.

Dunnaway, disqualified from victory in the season opener at Charlotte in June, appeared to be headed for an easy win until his misfortune. His 134 laps completed gave him ninth in the final rundown in the field of sixteen cars.

A sell-out crowd of 11,733 jammed the wooden grandstands to watch the fifth event of the year in NASCAR's new Strictly Stock division.

Race No. 5

Yankee Jack White Wins at Hamburg Before 11,733

HAMBURG, NY   (Sept 18) -- Young Jack White drove a Lincoln to victory in the 100-mile Strictly Stock race at Hamburg Speedway in an event domi-

*A standing room only crowd watches start of
the 100-mile Strictly Stock event at Martinsville Speedway.*

Strictly Stock Race No. 5
200 Laps at Hamburg Speedway
Hamburg, NY
100 Miles on Half-mile Dirt Track
September 18, 1949

Fin	St	No.	Driver	Team / Car	Laps	Money	Status
1		25	Jack White	Moyer Co. '49 Lincoln	200	$1,500	Running
2		5	Ray Erickson	Ed Hastings '49 Mercury	200	750	Running
3			Billy Rafter	'49 Ford		400	Running
4			Mike Eagan	'49 Mercury		300	Running
5		59	Bill Rexford	Julian Buesink '49 Ford		175	Running
6			Frankie Schneider	'49 Ford		150	
7		43	Jack Russell	'49 Ford		100	
8			Charles Muscatel	'49 Ford		75	
9		55	Glenn Dunnaway	Dunnaway '49 Olds	134	50	Wheel
10			Ellis Pearce			50	
11		93	Ted Chamberlain	Chamberlain '49 Plymouth		50	
12			Sam Rider			50	
13			Frank Matthews			50	
14			Bob Cameron			50	
15		11	Bob Apperson	Apperson '47 Ford		50	
16		77	Chuck Mahoney	Brooks Motors '49 Mercury		---	

Time of Race:
Average Speed:
Pole Winner:
Lap Leaders: - - - - - - Glenn Dunnaway   -134, Jack White 135-200
Cautions: Margin of Victory: Attendance: 11,733

Race No. 6

Byron Romps in Martinsville 200

MARTINSVILLE, VA (Sept. 25) -- Red Byron all but wrapped up the 1949 Strictly Stock championship with an overwhelming triumph in the 100-miler at Martinsville Speedway. The 33 year old veteran out of Atlanta, drove his Oldsmobile into the lead on lap 104 and led the rest of the way.

Finishing second, three laps behind Byron, was Lee Petty's Plymouth. Ray Erickson finished third, Clyde

Minter fourth and Bill Blair fifth.

Pole sitter Curtis Turner led the opening 18 laps, but gave way to the hard-charging Fonty Flock, who started fourth. Flock was pacing the field when his Buick lost a right front wheel and crashed into Slick Smith's Hudson. Byron took the lead when Flock departed and was never seriously challenged the rest of the way.

Turner faded after leading early and wound up ninth, 29 laps off the pace.

Strictly Stock Race No. 6
200 Laps at Martinsville Speedway
Martinsville, VA
100 Miles on Half-mile Dirt Track
September 25, 1949

Fin	St	No.	Driver	Team / Car	Laps	Money	Status
1	3	22	Red Byron	Parks Novelty '49 Olds	200	$1,500	Running
2	8	42	Lee Petty	Petty Brothers '49 Plymouth	197	750	Running
3	5	5	Ray Erickson	Ed Hastings '49 Mercury	197	400	Running
4	7	19	Clyde Minter	'46 Ford	187	300	Running
5	11	2	Bill Blair	'49 Chevrolet	186	175	Running
6	12	16	Bill Snowden	Snowden '49 Ford	182	150	
7	6	55	Glenn Dunnaway	Dunnaway '49 Olds	178	100	
8	13	3	Al Wagoner	Wagoner '49 Chevrolet	178	75	
9	1	41	Curtis Turner	Frank Christian '49 Olds	171	50	
10	15	36	Archie Smith	Frank Smith '47 Chrysler	161	50	
11	10	15	Ken Wagner	Moyer Co. Special '49 Lincoln	129	50	
12	4	47	Fonty Flock	Ed Lawrence '47 Buick	103	50	Wheel
13	14	28	Slick Smith	'47 Hudson	103	50	Crash
14	2	7	Bob Flock	Bob Flock Garage '49 Olds	90	50	
15	9	4	Otis Martin	'48 Buick	16	50	

Time of Race:
Average Speed:
Pole Winner: Curtis Turner -
Lap Leaders: Curtis Turner 1-18, Fonty Flock 19-103, Red Byron 104-200
Cautions: Margin of Victory: 3-plus laps   Attendance: 10,000

Race No. 7

Lee Petty Triumphs in Lightweight Plymouth

PITTSBURGH, PA (Oct. 2) -- In the first Strictly Stock event in Charlotte in June, Lee Petty entered a bulky Buick Roadmaster. The enormous automobile was fast on the straights, but it wobbled like a tank through the turns. Just past the halfway point, Petty rolled the the Buick a number of times. After dismounting the mangled mass of metal, the North Carolina speedster vowed never to drive a heavy vehicle in competition again.

In the 100-mile event at Heidelberg Speedway, Petty, driving his number 42 lightweight Plymouth, was five full laps ahead of his nearest competitor. "We figured the lighter car would get through the turns better," said Petty. "It would also be easier on the suspension parts. We knew we could win one with the Plymouth."

The big triumph at Heidelberg was the largest winning margin of any NASCAR Strictly Stock race in 1949. Dick Linder's Kaiser finished second, but was in no position to challenge the fleet Petty.

Bill Rexford finished third, Sam Rice's Chevrolet was fourth with relief driver Glenn Dunnaway at the helm. Fifth place went to Sara Christian, the first time a female driver has cracked the top five in a premier NASCAR event. She was 10 laps off the pace in her '49 Ford.

Al Bonnell, a driver of open wheel fame, qualified for the pole with a speed of 61.475 mph. However, Bonnell's Olds was the first car out of the race, and he was placed at the end of the 23 car field in the final rundown. Bonnell then relieved Don Rogalla and carried his Ford to 10th at the finish. Petty averaged 57.458 mph.

Strictly Stock Race No. 7
200 Laps at Heidelberg Speedway
Pittsburgh, PA
100 Miles on Half-mile Dirt Track
October 2, 1949

Fin	St	No.	Driver	Team / Car	Laps	Money	Status
1		42	Lee Petty	Petty Bros '49 Plymouth	200	$1,500	Running
2		8	Dick Linder	La Belle Motor Co. Kaiser	195	750	Running
3		4	Bill Rexford	'49 Ford	193	400	Running
4		2	Sam Rice *	'49 Chevrolet	192	300	Running
5		1	Sara Christian	'49 Ford	190	175	Running
6		21	Lloyd Moore	Julian Buesink '49 Ford	186	150	
7		18	John Wright	'49 Ford	179	100	
8		43	Jack Russell	'49 Ford	178	75	
9		23	George Lewis	'49 Kaiser	168	50	
10		20	Don Rogalla **	'49 Ford	167	50	
11		111	Clarence Burris	'49 Ford	165	50	
12		69	Joe Merola	'49 Ford	161	50	
13		14	Ted Chamberlain	'46 Ford	148	50	
14		7	Nick Garin	'48 Ford	142	50	
15		5	Ray Erickson	Ed Hastings '49 Mercury	122	50	
16		15	Ken Wagner	'49 Lincoln	118	---	
17		16	Jack O'Brien	'47 Buick	115	---	
18		55	Glenn Dunnaway	'49 Cadillac	82	---	
19		11	Curt Foss	'49 Olds 88	68	---	
20		17	Jim Carruso	'48 Nash	67	---	
21		12	Ralph Zrimsek	'49 Studebaker	59	---	
22		10	John Riggi	'47 Olds	33	---	
23	1	19	Al Bonnell	Don Rogalla '49 Olds 88	---		

* Relieved by Glenn Dunnaway on Lap 85
** Relieved by Al Bonnell on Lap 30
Time of Race: 1 hour, 44 minutes, 25.42 seconds
Average Speed: 57.458 mph
Pole Winner: Al Bonnell - 61.475 mph
Lap Leaders: - - - - - - - - - - - - - - - - - - Lee Petty -200.
Cautions: Margin of Victory: 5 laps plus   Attendance:

Race No. 8

Bob Flock Edges Petty in Finale; Red Byron Champ

N. WILKESBORO, NC (Oct. 16) -- Bob Flock took the lead in the closing stages when mechanical problems kayoed Bill Blair and edged Lee Petty to win the season finale at North Wilkesboro Speedway.

It was the eighth and final point race of the year, although two additional non-point events were staged by Sam Nunis at Atlanta's Lakewood Speedway. Red Byron, finishing 16th, was crowned Strictly Stock Champion in 1949 by a margin of 117.5 points over Petty.

Blair, wheeling Sam Rice's Cadillac, started second on the grid and jumped out to the lead at the drop of the green flag. The diminutive High Point, NC star led the first 180 laps, but a souring engine robbed him once again of certain victory.

Flock's Oldsmobile nipped Petty's Plymouth by a mere 100 yards in the finish. Fonty Flock, Clyde Minter and Herb Thomas rounded out the top five.

Strictly Stock Race No. 8
200 Laps at N. Wilkesboro Speedway
North Wilkesboro, NC
100 Miles on Half-mile Dirt Track
October 16, 1949

Fin	St	No.	Driver	Team / Car	Laps	Money	Status
1		7	Bob Flock	Bob Flock Garage '49 Olds	200	$1,500	Running
2		42	Lee Petty	Petty Bros '49 Plymouth	200	750	Running
3		47	Fonty Flock	Ed Lawrence '47 Buick	199	400	Running
4		19	Clyde Minter	'47 Ford	199	300	Running
5		92	Herb Thomas	'49 Ford	197	175	Running
6		14	Roy Hall	'49 Olds 88	196	150	
7		5	Ray Erickson	Ed Hastings '49 Mercury	194	100	
8		9	Raymond Lewis	Robert Dixon '49 Cadillac	194	75	
9		41	Curtis Turner	Frank Christian '49 Olds 88	193	50	
10	2	44	Bill Blair	Sam Rice '49 Cadillac	191	50	Engine
11		11	Bob Apperson	'47 Ford	191	50	
12		71	Sara Christian	Frank Christian '49 Olds 88	188	50	
13		28	Slick Smith	Buddy Helms '47 Hudson	174	50	
14		20	H.F. Stickleather	'48 Lincoln	167	50	
15	1	15	Ken Wagner	Moyer Co. '49 Lincoln	165	50	
16		22	Red Byron	Parks Novelty Olds 88	155	---	
17		21	Bobby Greene	'48 Ford	148	---	
18		1	Bill Greever	'48 Mercury	134	---	
19		90	Tim Flock	Buddy Elliott '49 Olds 88	117	---	
20		8	Dick Linder	La Belle Motors '49 Kaiser	59	---	
21		4	Otis Martin	'47 Buick	50	---	
22		2	Frank Mundy	'49 Ford	38	---	

Time of Race: 1 hour, 52 minutes, 26 seconds
Average Speed: 53.364 mph
Pole Winner: Ken Wagner - 31.27 seconds, 57.563 mph
Lap Leaders: Bill Blair 1-180, Bob Flock 181-200
Cautions: Margin of Victory: 100 Yards   Attendance: 10,000

Robert "Red" Byron won the first NASCAR
Strictly Stock championship.

1949 NASCAR Season
Final Point Standings Strictly Stock Division

Rank	Driver	Points	Starts	Wins	Top 5	Top 10	Winnings
1	Red Byron	842.5	6	2	4	4	$5,800
2	Lee Petty	725.0	6	1	3	5	3,855
3	Bob Flock	704.0	6	2	3	3	4,870
4	Bill Blair	567.5	6	0	3	5	1,280
5	Fonty Flock	554.5	6	0	3	3	2,015
6	Curtis Turner	430.0	6	1	1	4	2,675
7	Ray Erickson	422.0	4	0	2	3	1,460
8	Tim Flock	421.0	5	0	2	3	1,510
9	Glenn Dunnaway	384.0	6	0	1	3	810
10	Frank Mundy	370.0	4	0	2	2	1,160
11	Bill Snowden	315.0	4	0	1	3	660
12	Bill Rexford	286.0	3	0	2	2	785
13	Sara Christian	282.0	6	0	1	2	760
14	Clyde Minter	280.0	2	0	2	2	760
15	Gober Sosebee	265.0	3	0	1	2	1,305
16	Jim Roper	253.0	2	1	1	1	2,130
17	Sam Rice	231.0	2	0	2	2	680
18	Jack White	200.0	1	1	1	1	1,580
19	Dick Linder	180.5	3	0	1	1	830
20	Billy Rafter	160.0	1	0	1	1	480
21	Archie Smith	145.0	2	0	0	1	225
22	Joe Littlejohn	140.0	1	0	1	1	300
	Jack Russell	140.0	3	0	0	2	175
	Mike Eagan	140.0	1	0	1	1	300
25	Herb Thomas	132.0	4	0	1	1	225
26	Sterling Long	100.0	2	0	0	1	150
	Frank Christian	100.0	1	0	0	1	175
	Frankie Schneider	100.0	1	0	0	1	150
	Lloyd Moore	100.0	1	0	0	1	150
	Roy Hall	100.0	1	0	0	1	150
31	Slick Smith	99.0	4	0	0	1	275
32	Al Keller	90.0	1	0	0	1	200
33	John Wright	80.0	2	0	0	1	100
	Al Bonnell	80.0	2	0	0	1	150
35	Otis Martin	69.5	4	0	0	1	200
36	Jimmy Thompson	65.0	2	0	0	2	175
37	Charles Muscatel	60.0	1	0	0	1	75
	Raymond Lewis	60.0	1	0	0	1	75
	Al Wagoner	60.0	1	0	0	1	75
40	George "Skip" Lewis	40.0	1	0	0	1	50
41	Lou Volk	30.0	2	0	0	1	125
42	Buddy Helms	27.5	1	0	0	1	75
43	Bob Apperson	25.0	3	0	0	0	150
44	Bill Bennett	24.0	1	0	0	0	100
	Ted Chamberlain	24.0	2	0	0	0	100
46	Buck Baker	20.0	2	0	0	0	50
	Jack Etheridge	20.0	1	0	0	1	75
	Ellis Pearce	20.0	1	0	0	1	50
49	Bobby Greene	19.5	2	0	0	0	50
50	Ken Wagner	19.0	3	0	0	0	100

The 1950 Season
Growing Pains
and   Growing Up
Volume one of a four volume series . . . . The Beginning 1949 - 1958

1950

Things were happening fast for Bill France as the calendar was flipped to 1950.

The Strictly Stock division was undergoing a name change -- and the new Grand Nationals took over the headlining role as NASCAR's premier series.

The name Grand National was derived from England's thoroughbred horse racing event. "Grand National indicates superior qualities," said a NASCAR statement. France felt the 'Strictly Stock' label was more of a guideline for rules; 'Grand National' was a dynamic title that would have more appeal to the general public.

Before the early 1950 Grand National schedule had been established, two races had already been run. Because they were staged between the end of the 1949 season and the beginning of the 1950 slate, they carried no championship points.

Sam Nunis, a promoter whose executive offices were located in Reading, PA, operated Atlanta's Lakewood Speedway. He directed Indianapolis-type championship races, Big Cars, Sprint Cars and Stock Cars. Nunis announced that Lakewood Speedway -- once tagged the "Indianapolis of the South" -- would host a 150-mile Strictly Stock race on October 23, 1949. The event was open to any driver who was 21 years of age and held a valid driver's license.

The 1949 NASCAR season had ended on October 16th at North Wilkesboro. Red Byron had been crowned champion of NASCAR's new-fangled late model circuit, and he stood to collect a $1,000 prize at NASCAR's victory dinner during Daytona's Speed Week in 1950.

Nunis' shotgun scheduling of the Lakewood event caught France off-guard, but he generously offered to assist Nunis in the direction of his 150-miler. He also indicated the door would then be opened for all NASCAR members to participate.

Attendance on that pleasant autumn afternoon was 33,452, an astonishing figure which was about 59 percent more than the highest number on hand during the

Otis Martin's Plymouth bounces over rough Beach and Road Course at Daytona.

1949 point season.

Tim Flock, youngest member of the Flyin' Flock gang, drove his Oldsmobile past Curtis Turner in the 127th lap and led the final 24 laps to win the 150-miler. He pocketed $1,650 for his efforts.

The event was marred by serious injuries to 11 year-old Buster Henley. Buster suffered fractures to both legs when a wheel came off Bob Flock's Oldsmobile and bounded into an area heavily populated by spectators.

The contest was so successful at the turnstyles that

Sara Christian's Olds lies upside down after crash at Lakewood.

Nunis scheduled another race for November 13th. Once again, France stepped in and assisted Nunis in the direction of the show.

Rain interrupted the Strictly Stock return to Lakewood, yet a crowd of 22,000 showed up. Fonty Flock led the first 22 laps from his pole position. On lap 23, Flock was gobbled up in a five car crash in the second turn.

Sara Christian, America's leading female race driver, collided with B.C. Speig and flipped her Oldsmobile on its roof. She suffered a "bruised chest" in the mishap, but her injuries were not serious. Speig broke his left hand in the crash. Other drivers involved were veteran Carson Dyer, who suffered head and hand lacerations, and Olin Allen, minor cuts and bruises. Allen Terrell was involved but escaped injury.

Curtis Turner picked up the lead, but a cloudburst halted the event after 39 laps. The remaining distance was scheduled for the following Sunday, November 20.

Turner led the restart, but his Oldsmobile departed with engine problems about 80 miles into the event. June Cleveland of Augusta, GA, who had never won a stock car race of any kind,

picked up the lead in the 85th lap and was in front on lap 110 when officials red-flagged the event due to darkness.

Cleveland, driving D.G. Hall's Buick, was declared the winner and picked up a $1,500 check.

Neither Lakewood event carried points to the championship, and neither one has ever been logged in the 1949 or 1950 season wrap-ups and rundowns NASCAR often printed. They were listed in the 1950 NASCAR yearbook, but were not included in the race review for the 1949 season.

Curiously, Tim Flock and June Cleveland *received credit* for a win in NASCAR records, yet the cars they drove, Oldsmobile and Buick, *did not get credit* for a victory. The driver victories are reflected in today's NASCAR records, but the car wins are not. Apparently, they have to be considered as special events which carried no championship points.

Another note of interest came before the 1950 season officially began. On December 5, 1949, the Central

Lee Petty would have won the 1950 championship if he had not been stripped of 809 points at mid-year.

States Racing Association, a rival sanctioning body that dealt with midwestern short track races, announced it was going to sanction a proposed 500-mile stock car race at the new Darlington Raceway.

Peanut farmer Harold Brasington had attended the 1948 Indianapolis 500 and was thrilled at the spectacle. He figured a race of similar magnitude for stock cars would be ideal in the South. The only problem was that there was no facility capable of staging a 500-miler.

Brasington decided he would build such a race track. Completion was scheduled for the summer of 1950.

NASCAR President Bill France was a little leery of a 500-mile race for stock cars. He feared that if the Strictly Stock automobiles broke down before the 500 miles were completed, it would be a black eye on the sport. Compared to other forms of racing, stock car racing could become a laughing stock.

The "official" 1950 season got underway at Daytona on February 5, 1950. Harold Kite, driving in his first Grand National race, won in a Lincoln. It was the first of 19 Grand National races for the season and kicked off what might be the most electrifying battle for the championship in the history of NASCAR.

Technically - due to the first scheduling of 'same day' Grand National races in different parts of the country - the lead changed hands in the point race no less than 10 times in the 19 races. Seven different drivers were atop the point standings during the 1950 season.

Defending champ Red Byron had the point lead after Charlotte's April 3rd race, having finished second and fourth in the first two starts. The crafty red-head appeared poised to make another run for the championship.

But before mid-season, Byron was stripped of all his

points for competing in a non-NASCAR sanctioned event. Penalties were stiff in the infant years for driving in so-called 'outlaw' events, and Byron was the first notable driver in 1950 to be handed a reprimand.

Lee Petty was another driver bitten by NASCAR's iron hand. During a three-week lull in the Grand National tour in July, Petty wandered outside the NASCAR sanctioned boundaries and paid dearly for it. Through eight races the Randleman, NC Plymouth driver had accumulated 809 points, which was good enough for third place in the standings. He was only 24.5 points out of first place in the wide open scramble for the lead. After NASCAR took all his points away, he had to start at zero in late July.

Another interesting announcement came in July. Sam Nunis declared that the first 500-mile stock car race would take place at Lakewood Speedway before Labor Day. Nunis' promotion would be open to both American and foreign automobiles. They would battle for 500 laps on Lakewood's dangerous and dusty oval.

So, by mid-summer, both the CSRA and Sam Nunis were talking about staging America's first 500-mile race for stock cars.

Interest and media hype were soaring. Although France was skeptical of a 500-miler, he was forced to play his hand. He met with Brasington at the nearly completed Darlington International Raceway and was informed that CSRA was having difficulty getting drivers to send in their entries. France then called Mason Benner, president of CSRA, and informed him that his Southern based drivers would most certainly fill the 75-car starting field. France and Benner worked out a deal whereby Darlington Raceway's Southern 500 would be Co-sanctioned by CSRA and NASCAR.

France felt it was necessary to take a step in some direction - the prospect of a 500-miler at Lakewood was scary. Once France and Benner signed the dotted line, Nunis decided to abandon ideas of

Pace Lap for 1950 Southern 500.

Bill Rexford

Wally Campbell was fastest qualifier at Southern 500 but started in 60th position. He finished 52nd.

holding a Lakewood 500. It was another victory for NASCAR.

The Southern 500 was the race of the year. It drew immediate national attention to a place called Darlington. The purse of $25,500 was the highest ever paid for a stock car event. Since points paralleled dollars, the winner would be assured a high finish in the point standings at year end. A bunch of dollars and a bunch of prestige were riding on the race. On Labor Day, 75 cars went to the post, and some 25,000 spectators were on hand.

Curtis Turner, who had led the point standings for five consecutive weeks, entered the Southern 500 as the point leader. He qualified for the pole with a speed of 82.034 mph. Seventy-five cars had earned starting positions in 15 days of time trials.

Turner crashed in the 275th lap, leaving him with a 60th place finish and a broken nose but no points. Johnny Mantz of Long Beach, CA, won the race by nine laps over Fireball Roberts. Mantz leaped to fifth place in the point standings.

Bill Rexford, who finished fourth, took the point lead by a 104-point margin over Roberts. Turner dropped to third. Red Byron, who wound up third in the 500, was back up to fourth place.

Later in the season, Byron once again ran an independently sanctioned affair and once again NASCAR took all his points away. He finished the year with zero points, twice having been penalized by NASCAR.

Roberts, who missed seven of the first 10 races in the 1950 season, took the point lead at Langhorne, the race following Darlington. He retained his lead the following week at North Wilkesboro despite falling out with engine problems.

Then, with three races to go, Rexford took the lead with a sixth place finish at Vernon, NY. Roberts had not entered. After the 17th of 19 races, Roberts was

Harold Brasington (left), President of the new Darlington Raceway, and Bob Colvin, who successfully promoted the first Southern 500.

back on top by a slim margin, having finished sixth at Martinsville. But later that same afternoon in a Grand National at Winchester, IN, Rexford finished third and retook the point lead.

In the final event of the year at Hillsboro, NC, both drivers had a shot at the title. Rexford departed early, leaving the door open to Roberts. Needing only a fifth place finish to sew up the 1950 championship, Roberts opted against driving conservatively - he charged to the checkered. Then on lap 126 of the scheduled 200 lapper, the engine in Roberts' Oldsmobile blew up, dropping him to 21st in the final rundown. He would earn no points, and Rexford was declared the 1950 Grand National champion.

Lee Petty wound up third in the final standings, having won at Hillsboro. His point total for the year was 1,590. Had he not been stripped of the 809 points in July, his total would have been 2,399, some 440 more than champion Rexford.

Byron earned a total of 1,630 points in only four 1950 starts, which would have been good for fourth place in the final tally. But the free-spirited veteran raced wherever and whenever he wanted to. No exclusive sanction for him. His name did not appear at all in the 1950 NASCAR Grand National point standings.

Overall, it was a very good year for Bill France and NASCAR. Racing was as wild and wooly as the untamed frontier, and every race was a showdown at high noon. In the 19 Grand Nationals, an incredible 14 different drivers reached the cherished confines of victory lane.

The 1950 Grand National season was real firewagon racing - filled with magic moments and magical men.

Race No. 1

Harold Kite Wins Daytona In First Grand National Start

DAYTONA BEACH, FL (Feb. 5) -- Harold Kite of East Point, GA, a former Army tank driver who began racing on the short tacks after World War II, drove past Red Byron in the 25th lap and went on to score a convincing victory in the

Bob Flock leads the pack out of the South turn at Daytona.

Grand National Race No. 1
48 Laps at Beach & Road Course
Daytona Beach, FL
200 Miles on 4.17-mile Beach & Road Course
February 5, 1950

Fin	St	No.	Driver	Team / Car	Laps	Money	Status
1	3	21	Harold Kite	Rogers Auto Sv. '49 Lincoln	48	$1,500	Running
2		22	Red Byron	Parks Novelty '50 Olds 88	48	1,000	Running
3	14	59	Lloyd Moore	Julian Buesink '49 Lincoln	48	600	Running
4	8	88	Al Gross	Hans Winter '50 Olds 88	48	550	Running
5	2	35	J. Van Landingham	Van Landingham '50 Buick	48	450	Running
6	4	90	Tim Flock	Daytona Motors '48 Cadillac	48	350	Running
7	21	7	Bob Flock	Bob Flock Garage '49 Olds 88	47	250	Running
8	26	4	Otis Martin	Raymond Lewis '49 Plymouth	47	175	Running
9	9	70	Buck Baker	Baker '49 Ford	47	175	Running
10	15	47	Fonty Flock	Ed Lawrence '47 Buick	46	150	Running
11	10	41	Curtis Turner	Paul Roberts '49 Lincoln	46	50	
12	17	10	Jim Rathmann	Rathmann '49 Lincoln	46	50	
13	22	80	Roscoe Thompson	Charles Venable '49 Lincoln	45	50	
14		5	Cotton Owens	Owens '49 Plymouth	45	50	
15	25	55	June Cleveland	D.G. Hall '48 Buick	45	50	Wheel
16	28	42	Lee Petty	Petty Special '49 Plymouth	45	50	
17	30	89	Al Keller	W.O. Taylor '49 Ford	44	50	
18	11	9	Frank Luptow	Luptow '49 Lincoln	43	50	
19		61	Will Albright	Albright '46 Pontiac	43	50	
20	23	18	Jack White	Brooks Motors '49 Lincoln	41	50	
21	6	32	Alton Haddock	J.L. McDonald '49 Lincoln	41	25	
22	29	56	Joe Jernigan	Lambert's Auto '49 Ford	41	25	
23	24	72	Lee Schmidt	LeRoy Schmidt '47 Buick	40	25	
24	18	37	Russ Lee	Chester Alford '49 Hudson	38	25	
25	27	48	Larry Shurter	Shurter '49 Ford	37	25	
26	5	91	Tommy Thompson	San Juan Mtrs. '49 Chrysler	34	25	
27	12	25	Jack Smith	Bishop Brothers '50 Olds 88	31	25	
28	16	12	Billy Carden	Bishop Brothers '49 Olds 88	30	25	
29	20	60	Bill Rexford	Julian Buesink '49 Olds 88	26	25	
30	19	50	Gober Sosebee	Ted Chester '49 Olds 88	21	25	
31		17	Bob Apperson	Apperson '47 Ford	14	25	
32		6	Marshall Teague	Paul Cox '49 Lincoln	10	25	
33		11	Fireball Roberts	Jim Davis '48 Hudson	8	25	
34		2	Bill Blair	Sam Rice '49 Cadillac	7	25	
35	1	3	Joe Littlejohn	Littlejohn '50 Olds 88	7	25	
36		24	Dick Clothier	Clothier '47 Pontiac	5	25	
37	7	44	Frank Mundy	Daytona Mtr Co '49 Cadillac	5	25	
38		77	Slick Smith	Davis Brothers '47 Hudson	4	25	
39	13	66	H. Buchanan	Buchanan '47 Nash	3	25	
40	31	67	Joe Harrison	Harrison '49 Ford	3	25	
41		94	Louise Smith	Smith Auto Parts '49 Ford	0	--	Crash

Time of Race: 2 hours, 26 minutes, 30 seconds
Average Speed: 89.894 mph
Pole Winner: Joe Littlejohn - 98.84 mph
Lap Leaders: Harold Kite 1-14, Red Byron 15-24, Kite 25-48.
Cautions: None   Margin of Victory: 53 seconds   Attendance: 9,500

200-mile Grand National lid-lifter of the 1950 season.

Kite, competing in his first Grand National event, pushed his Lincoln around the sandy course at a record 89.894 mph and beat runner-up Byron to the finish line by 53 seconds. Third place went to Lloyd Moore, Al Gross was fourth and J.C. Van Landingham, ending a lengthy retirement, finished fifth.

A crowd estimated at 9,500 watched Kite take the lead at the outset from pole sitter Joe Littlejohn. Kite, a Captain in the National Guard, held the top spot until Byron passed him on the 15th lap. The defending NAS-CAR champ relinquished the lead to Kite in the 24th lap when he made a pit stop. Several laps later Byron was forced to make another pit stop to repair gear shift problems. He finally returned to the fray, running seventh.

Kite went uncontested for the second half of the 48-lap affair on the 4.167-mile course, but Byron provided plenty of action as he worked his way up through the pack. He nipped Moore for second place with a final lap pass.

Forty-one cars started the event and 21 were still running at the finish despite the fact that conditions on the beach were less than ideal. Bob Flock turned in one of the most spirited efforts on the cloudy, breezy day. He finished seventh despite the the fact that the left front wheel of his Olds wobbled around every turn.

Race No. 2

Tim Flock Nabs Charlotte; Red Byron in Point Lead

CHARLOTTE, NC (Apr. 2) - Tim Flock, wheeling the same Lincoln that carried Harold Kite to victory at Daytona, drove around Red Byron in the 48th lap and stormed to victory in the 150-mile Grand National race at Charlotte Speedway. It was Flock's first win on the NASCAR major league tour.

Bob Flock finished second, a half lap behind his younger brother. Clyde Minter wound up third, Byron came in fourth and Bill Snowden was fifth.

Byron's fourth place effort, coupled with his runner-up finish at Daytona, enabled him to move to the top of the Grand National point standings, 2.5 points ahead of Tim Flock.

A crowd of 13,000 was on hand to watch Bob Flock lead the opening laps in his Oldsmobile. Pole sitter Byron then charged past and led for 42 laps on the three-quarter mile dirt track. Tim surged past Byron in the 48th lap and led the rest of the way. Lash LaRue, Western movie star, greeted Flock in victory lane.

"This is my biggest win," said the happy Flock. "To win a Grand National race is a dream come true."

June Cleveland was running in the top five when he flipped his Buick in the 85th lap. The roof was pancaked, and Cleveland was transported to a Charlotte hospital with cuts. He was reported not to be seriously injured. His crash occurred in the exact spot where Virginia driver Jesse Elmo "Hank" Stanley was killed a few weeks earlier in a Modified Sportsman race.

Curtis Turner, Lee Petty, Buck Baker, Fonty Flock and Bill Blair -- all rated as pre-race threats -- failed to finish the 200-lap grind.

Grand National Race No. 2
200 Laps at Charlotte Speedway
Charlotte, NC
150 Miles on .75-mile Dirt Track
April 2, 1950

Fin	St	No.	Driver	Team / Car	Laps	Money	Status
1	5	21	Tim Flock	Edmunds Motors '49 Lincoln	200	$1,500	Running
2	2	7	Bob Flock	Frank Christian '49 Olds 88	200	750	Running
3	12	19	Clyde Minter	Bridge St. Motors '50 Mercury	197	500	Running
4	1	22	Red Byron	Parks Novelty '50 Olds 88	196	300	Running
5	14		Bill Snowden	'49 Buick	194	200	Running
6	18	49	Glenn Dunnaway	'49 Plymouth	191	175	Running
7	16		Jack White	Moyer Co. '49 Mercury	190	150	
8	25	10	Fred Johnson	'49 Ford	189	125	
9	17	92	Herb Thomas	'47 Ford	172	100	
10	24		Huey Dunn	'49 Olds 88	172	75	
11	6		Frank Mundy	'49 Olds 88	170	50	
12	21	17	Bob Apperson	Apperson '49 Ford	168	50	
13	8	20	Bill Rexford	Julian Buesink '50 Olds 88	152	50	
14	15	14	Lloyd Moore	Julian Buesink '49 Lincoln	131	50	
15	9	41	Curtis Turner	Eanes Motor Co. '50 Olds 88	106	50	
16	10	30	Cotton Owens	'50 Ford	86	---	
17	7	55	June Cleveland	D.G. Hall '48 Buick	85	---	Crash
18	20	42	Lee Petty	Petty Special '49 Plymouth	84	---	
19	3	2	Bill Blair	Sam Rice '49 Cadillac	60	---	
20	22	6	Bill Harrison	'49 Lincoln	38	---	
21	13	47	Fonty Flock	Ed Lawrence '47 Buick	30	---	
22	4	87	Buck Baker	Baker '50 Ford	27	---	
23	19	79	Jim Paschal	'49 Ford	26	---	
24	11	5	Ray Erickson	Ed Hastings '48 Mercury	23	---	
25	23	28	Buddy Helms	Helms '47 Hudson	0	---	

Time of Race:
Average Speed:
Pole Winner: Red Byron - 67.839 mph
Lap Leaders: Bob Flock 1-5, Red Byron 6-47, Tim Flock 48-200.
Cautions: 1   Margin of Victory: Half lap   Attendance: 13,000

June Cleveland's Buick lies upside down after 85th lap crash at Charlotte. Cleveland was not seriously injured.

*Bob Flock #7 leads Red Byron, Buck Baker and Bill Blair down front chute at Charlotte Speedway
in early laps of 150-mile Grand National event. Tim Flock went on to score his first big league win.*

Race No. 3

Curtis Turner Prevails in 150-mile Langhorne Thriller

LANGHORNE, PA   (Apr. 16) -- Curtis Turner prevailed in an intense struggle at the Langhorne Speedway and won the 150-miler on the one-mile dirt track. His second career Grand National win came at an average speed of 69.399 mph.

The lead changed hands seven times as five drivers waged a furious duel. Tim Flock led the opening two laps from the pole position. Bill Blair pushed his Cadillac past Flock in the third lap and led until Flock assumed command again on lap eight. Flock led for 35 laps while 23 year-old rookie Bill Rexford moved into second. The two toured the circular oval in bumper-to-bumper fashion.

Rexford sneaked past Flock in the 43rd lap and paced the action for 18 laps. Rexford's Olds began sputtering, which allowed Turner to take the lead on lap 61. Ray Erickson moved into the spotlight when he gunned his Mercury past Turner in the 84th lap. He was bidding for his first Grand National triumph when a rock pierced his radiator, forcing him behind the wall after 114 laps. Turner took the lead at that point and led the rest of the way. Lloyd Moore, Jimmy Florian, Tim Flock and Lee Petty rounded out the top five.

Flock was running third when a wheel came off his Lincoln and bounced into the path of hardluck Blair, who struck   the errant wheel. The steering column in Blair's Caddy snapped, came up through the driver's compartment and hit the driver. The High Point, NC, star spent one night in the hospital.

Grand National Race No. 3
150 Laps at Langhorne Speedway
Langhorne, PA
150 Miles on 1-mile Dirt Track
April 16, 1950

Fin	St	No.	Driver	Team / Car	Laps	Money	Status
1		41	Curtis Turner	Eanes Motor Co. '50 Olds 88	150	$1,500	Running
2		59	Lloyd Moore	Julian Buesink '49 Lincoln	149	1,000	Running
3		27	Jimmy Florian	Euclid Motor Co. '50 Ford	144	700	Running
4	1	21	Tim Flock	Edmunds Motors '49 Lincoln	139	500	Spindle
5		42	Lee Petty	Petty Special '49 Plymouth	139	300	Rear End
6		90	Frank Mundy	Red Star Garage '49 Lincoln	135	200	Heating
7		66	Roscoe Hough	Hough '50 Ford	133	175	Running
8		293	Bob Dickson	'49 Lincoln	132	150	Running
9		8	Dick Linder	Packer '48 Pontiac	132	125	Heating
10		89	P. Cunningham	'49 Ford	130	100	Heating
11		11	Bob Apperson	Apperson '49 Olds 88	128	75	Heating
12		4	Baldy Wilson	'50 Ford	127	75	Running
13		56	Joe Jernigan	Lambert's Auto '49 Ford	125	75	Heating
14		55	Russell Bennett	'49 Kaiser	123	50	Engine
15		51	Fireball Roberts	'50 Ford	121	50	Heating
16	2	9	Len Brown	'49 Olds 88	119	100	Hose
17	4	25	Ken Wagner	Moyer Co. '49 Lincoln	119	50	Engine
18		N-5	Ray Erickson	Ed Hastings '48 Mercury	114	50	Heating
19		2	Bill Blair	Sam Rice '49 Cadillac	112	50	Steering
20	3	47	Paul Parks	'49 Cadillac	95	50	Engine
21		94	Louise Smith	Smith Auto Parts '47 Ford	84	25	Engine
22		80	Bill Rexford	Julian Buesink '50 Olds 88	84	25	Engine
23		92	Herb Thomas	Thomas '47 Ford	71	25	Engine
24		24	Lyle Scott	'49 Lincoln	65	25	Crash
25		18	Jack White	'49 Mercury	62	25	Engine
26		10	Fred Johnson	'48 Ford	55	---	Heating
27		73	Al Tibbetts	'49 Hudson	48	---	Hose
28		7	Charles Muscatel	'47 Mercury	26	---	Heating

Time of Race: 2 hours, 9 minutes, 40.98 seconds
Average Speed: 69.399 mph
Pole Winner: Tim Flock -
Fastest Qualifier: Paul Parks 77.067 mph
Lap Leaders: Tim Flock 1-2, Bill Blair 3-7, T. Flock 8-42, Bill Rexford 43-60,
   Curtis Turner 61-83, Ray Erickson 84-114, Turner 115-150

Cautions:	Margin of Victory: 1-lap plus	Attendance: 16,000

Turner won $1,500 for his efforts as only six cars finished after 28 started. Point leader Red Byron did

Curtis Turner's Oldsmobile at speed down the front chute at Langhorne Speedway. The Roanoke, VA speedster won for the second time in a row at the 1-mile dirt track.

not enter the race. Tim Flock took over the point lead on the strength of his fourth place finish.

Turner's John Eanes-owned Oldsmobile was equipped with Dunlop tires. Dunlop had plenty of space on Turner's car -- placing it's name on the hood and side doors.

Erickson's appearance was his last start of the year. A short time later, he lost an arm in a hot-rod crash. Also following the race, the FBI began investigating some "characters" who were trying to introduce racketeering and gambling into stock car racing.

Race No. 4

Turner Stomps Field at Martinsville

MARTINSVILLE, VA (May 21) - Curtis Turner bagged his second straight Grand National win with a decisive triumph at Martinsville Speedway.

The Roanoke, VA "Blond Bomber" dashed ahead of Buck Baker in the 11th lap and led the rest of the way to win the 150-lap, 75 mile feature at the half-mile oval.

Jim Paschal finished second in a four year-old Ford, Lee Petty was third and Glenn Dunnaway came in fourth.

Clyde Minter picked up fifth spot. Turner's Oldsmobile outdistanced the field by two full laps. He moved to up to only 2.5 points behind leader Tim Flock, who fell victim to rear end problems after 97

Grand National Race No. 4
150 Laps at Martinsville Speedway
Martinsville, VA
75 Miles on Half-mile Dirt Track
May 21, 1950

Fin	St	No.	Driver	Team / Car	Laps	Money	Status
1		41	Curtis Turner	Eanes Motor Co '50 Olds 88	150	$1,000	Running
2		79	Jim Paschal	'47 Ford	148	750	Running
3		42	Lee Petty	Petty Special '49 Plymouth	144	500	Running
4		49	Glenn Dunnaway	'49 Plymouth	144	300	Running
5		19	Clyde Minter	'50 Mercury	143	200	Running
6		31	Bill Long	'49 Lincoln	141	175	Running
7		91	Donald Thomas	Thomas '47 Ford	141	150	Running
8	1	87	Buck Baker	Police Special '50 Ford	139	125	Running
9		60	Bill Rexford	Julian Buesink '50 Olds 88	138	100	Running
10		59	Lloyd Moore	Police Special '50 Ford	137	75	Running
11		2	Bill Blair	Sam Rice '50 Mercury	135	50	Running
12		7	Bob Collins	'50 Pontiac	133	50	Wheel
13		212	Frank Boylan	'50 Ford	132	50	Running
14		92	Herb Thomas	Thomas '49 Ford	131	50	Spindle
15		98	Lyle Scott	'49 Lincoln	130	50	Running
16		293	Bob Dickson	'49 Lincoln	129	---	Running
17		14	Bill Greever	'49 Mercury	128	---	Running
18		94	Al Cross	'50 Olds 88	125	---	Running
19		72	Macon Powers	'46 Plymouth	125	---	Running
20		90	Tim Flock	Red Star Garage '49 Lincoln	97	---	Rear End
21		25	Bob Smith	'49 Ford	88	---	Engine
22		18	Jack White	'49 Mercury	65	---	Engine
23		21	Ruel Smith	'50 Pontiac	47	---	Wheel
24		28	Buddy Helms	Helms '47 Hudson	36	---	Engine
25		11	Bob Apperson	Apperson '49 Olds 88	14	---	Engine

Time of Race:
Average Speed
Pole Winner: Buck Baker: 54.216 mph
Lap Leaders: Buck Baker 1-10, Curtis Turner 11-150
Cautions: Margin of Victory: 2 3/4 laps   Attendance: 9,500

laps. Buck Baker started on the pole at 54.216 mph in a Ford Police Special. He faded to eighth at the finish. Herb Thomas was running among the leaders in his Ford when a spindle broke in the final laps. He got credit for 14th in the field of 25.

Race No. 5

Rexford Romps at Canfield; Moore Takes Point Lead

Lee Petty's brand new Plymouth #42 leans into Martinsville turn just ahead of Herb Thomas #92.

CANFIELD, OH (MAY 30) -- Bill Rexford of Conewango Valley, NY stalked Curtis Turner for over half the race, then took command to win the "Poor Man's 500", a 100-miler at Canfield Speedway.

Rexford took the lead in the 121st lap and went on to beat runner-up G l e n n Dunnaway by two laps. Lloyd Moore finished third and took the lead in the Grand National point standings by 36.5 points over Tim Flock, who finshed ninth. Lee Petty crossed the finish line in fourth place and Bill Blair took fifth.

The event was staged on the same day as the Indianapolis 500 -- hence the title "Poor Man's 500". The promoters did pay some lap money, with $5 going to the leader of each lap from the 101 through the 200. Rexford's earn-

Bill Rexford takes checkered flag at Canfield Motor Speedway. It was the first Grand National win for the 23 year-old youngster.

ings came to $1,400 with the lap money.

Turner led the first 120 laps before his engine went sour. He departed after 133 laps and wound up 19th.

A crowd of 11,000 showed up on Memorial Day and watched Al Gross, former stunt car driver for the Jimmy Lynch Thrill Show, flip his Olds in the ninth lap. Gross suffered a broken back and was taken to thehospital for an extended stay.

Frank Canale posted the second fastest qualifying time but overheating problems forced him to the sidelines after 74 laps.

Joe Merola was on hand with a new radically

Grand National Race No. 5
200 Laps at Canfield Motor Speedway
Canfield, OH
"Poor Man's 500"
100 Miles on Half-mile Dirt Track
May 30, 1950

Fin	St	No.	Driver	Team / Car	Laps	Money	Status
1		60	Bill Rexford	Julian Buesink '50 Olds 88	200	$1,400	Running
2		49	Glenn Dunnaway	'49 Plymouth	198	750	Running
3		59	Lloyd Moore	Julian Buesink '50 Ford V-8	198	500	Running
4		42	Lee Petty	Lee Petty '49 Plymouth	195	400	Running
5		22	Bill Blair	'50 Mercury	195	300	Running
6	1	27	Jimmy Florian	Euclid Motors Ford V-8	193	200	
7		48	Dick Burns	Mercury	190	150	
8		89	Bobby Courtwright	Ford	189	125	
9		90	Tim Flock	Red Star Garage '49 Lincoln	189	100	
10		293	Bob Dickson	Lincoln	187	75	
11		11	Art Gill	Ford	182	50	
12		9	Len Brown	Olds 88	171	50	
13		8	Dick Linder	La Belle Motors '49 Kaiser	161	50	
14		23	Mike Klapak	Ford 6	158	50	
15		18	Chuck Mahoney	Brooks Motors Mercury	151	50	
16		5	Bob Wilson	Nash	150	---	Crash
17		80	Hugh Darragh	Ford	142	---	
18		30	Elmer Wilson	Lincoln	137	---	Rear End
19	3	41	Curtis Turner	Eanes Motor Co. '50 Olds 88	133	100	Engine
20		100	Ace Shearer	Ford V-8	129	---	
21		32	Al Weaver	Ford V-8	119	---	
22		28	Lew Fattman	Chevrolet	105	---	
23		15	Milford Schall	Ford V-8	104	---	
24	2	1	Frank Canale	Olds 88	74	---	Heating
25		55	Carl Wilkerson	Dodge	72	---	
26		21	Frank Boylan	Ford V-8	64	---	
27		2	Bob Greer	Olds 88	56	---	
28		99	Al Gross	Olds 88	9	---	Crash
29			Joe Merola	'48 Tucker Torpedo	0	---	

Time of Race:
Average Speed:
Pole Winner: Jimmy Florian
Lap Leaders: Curtis Turner 1-120, Bill Rexford 121-200
Cautions: Margin of Victory: 2 laps plus   Attendance: 11,000

designed 1948 Tucker Torpedo, one of the most controversial and advanced automobiles ever to hit the market. The car conked out before Merola was able to complete a lap.

Race No. 6

Bill Blair Ends Famine With Victory at Vernon

VERNON, NY (June 18) -- Bill Blair of High Point, NC, finally avoided the bad luck gremlin, took the lead in the 25th lap and led the remaining distance to score his first Grand National win at the Vernon Fairgrounds.

A crowd of 15,000 showed up for the one year anniversary of NASCAR Grand National stock car racing.

Blair's Mercury was comfortably ahead of Lloyd Moore at the finish of the 100-miler. Moore extended his point lead to 216.5 points over Tim Flock, who did not enter. Chuck Mahoney was third at the stripe, while Dick Burns came in fourth and Lee Petty fifth.

Mahoney started on the pole and led the first 18 laps.

He was in the lead when his Mercury hit a loose wheel rolling on the track, blew a tire and bent an axle. His pit crew did an excellent job of repairing the damage, and even more incredible was his drive back into third place.

Bill Rexford finished sixth and moved into the top ten in points.

Ann Chester became the fourth female driver to race in the Grand National ranks. Her Plymouth fell victim to early problems and she finished 22nd in the 23 car field.

Bill Blair grabbed first win at Vernon.

Grand National Race No. 6
200 Laps at Vernon Fairgrounds
Vernon, NY
100 Miles on Half-mile Dirt Track
June 18, 1950

Fin	St	No.	Driver	Team / Car	Laps	Money	Status
1		2	Bill Blair	'50 Mercury	200	$1,000	Running
2		59	Lloyd Moore	Julian Buesink '50 Ford		750	Running
3	1	77	Chuck Mahoney	'50 Mercury		500	Running
4		18	Dick Burns	'50 Mercury		400	Running
5		42	Lee Petty	Petty Special '49 Plymouth		300	Running
6		60	Bill Rexford	Julian Buesink '49 Olds		200	
7		9	Art Lamey	'49 Plymouth		150	
8		27	Jimmy Florian	Euclid Motors '50 Ford		125	
9		25	Dick Linder	Don Rogala '50 Olds		100	
10		24	Dick Clothier	'50 Plymouth		75	
11		81	Pappy Hough	'50 Plymouth		50	
12		11	Art Gill	'47 Ford		50	
13		54	Ken Warmington	'49 Ford		50	
14		88	Harry Sents	'47 Ford		50	
15		13	Bill Bonner	'49 Dodge		50	
16		80	Hugh Darragh	'49 Ford		---	
17		66	Gene Austin	'50 Olds		---	
18		89	Neil Cole	'49 Ford		---	
19		35	Art Hammond	'47 Packard		---	
20		91	Herb Thomas	Thomas '50 Plymouth		---	
21		49	Glenn Dunnaway	'49 Plymouth		---	
22		72	Ann Chester	'47 Plymouth		---	
23		58	Harland Holmes	'49 Ford		---	

Time of Race:
Average Speed:
Pole Winner: Chuck Mahoney
Lap Leaders: Chuck Mahoney 1-18, Lloyd Moore 19-24, Bill Blair 25-200
Cautions: Margin of Victory: Attendance: 15,000

Race No. 7

Shirtless Florian Flawless in Ford

DAYTON, OH (June 25) -- Jimmy Florian muscled his Ford past Curtis Turner with 32 laps remaining and won the 100-mile event at Dayton Speedway. It was the first win in Grand National competition for the Ford nameplate.

The lead changed hands six times among four different drivers with Florian holding the upper hand on two occasions for a total of 40 laps.

Along with ushering in Ford's first win, Florian established another "first" on the muggy, sultry afternoon. He pulled into victory lane and climbed out wearing nothing but his white pants. The 27 year-old Cleveland mechanic said he decided not to wear a shirt due to the hot weather and since there was no NASCAR rule requiring him to do so. "It was awfully hot and I knew I'd be more comfortable without a shirt," said Florian. "I've done it several times before, but not in the Grand Nationals."

Dick Linder started on the pole and led on two occasions for 35 laps. He eventually finished second as

Jimmy Florian poses beside his Ford after winning Dayton 100-miler. Florian was not wearing a shirt on the hot and muggy afternoon.

Grand National Race No. 7
200 Laps at Dayton Speedway
Dayton, OH
100 Miles on Half-mile Dirt Track
June 25, 1950

Fin	St	No.	Driver	Team / Car	Laps	Money	Status
1		27	Jimmy Florian	Euclid Motors '50 Ford	200	$1,000	Running
2		25	Dick Linder	Don Rogala '50 Olds		750	Running
3			Buck Barr	'50 Ford		500	Running
4		41	Curtis Turner	Eanes Motor Co. '50 Olds 88		400	Running
5		9	Art Lamey	'49 Plymouth		300	Running
6		12	Herschel Buchanan	Buchanan '48 Nash		200	Running
7			Duane Carter	'46 Ford		150	
8		42	Lee Petty	Lee Petty Special '49 Plymouth		125	
9		77	Chuck Mahoney	Brooks Motors '50 Mercury		100	
10		8	Bill Rexford	Julian Buesink '50 Mercury		75	
11		60	George Hartley	Julian Buesink '50 Olds		50	
12		24	Dick Clothier	'49 Plymouth		50	
13			Ralph Dyer	'48 Nash		50	
14			F.L. Denney	'50 Ford		50	
15			Mike Klapak	'48 Nash		50	
16		2	Bill Blair	'50 Mercury		---	
17			Herb Craig	'47 Nash		---	
18			Nix Beard	'47 Ford		---	
19			Ralph Lyden	'49 Hudson		---	
20			Bob Scott	'46 Ford		---	
21			Gayle Warren	'49 Olds		---	
22			Ann Slaasted	'49 Lincoln		---	
23		59	Lloyd Moore	Julian Buesink '50 Ford		---	
24			Bill McGee	'50 Nash		---	
25		37	Frank Mundy	'50 Nash		---	

Time of Race: 1 hour, 34 minutes, 42.31 seconds
Average Speed: 63.351 mph
Pole Winner: Dick Linder - 66.543 mph
Lap Leaders: Dick Linder 1-5, Curtis Turner 6-78, Linder 79-108, Gayle Warren 109-118, Jimmy Florian 119-126, Turner 127-168, Florian 169-200

Cautions: Margin of Victory: Attendance: 12,000

Buck Barr came in third. Turner wound up fourth and Art Lamey was fifth.

Lloyd Moore finished 23rd in the field of 25 and failed to earn any championship points, but he still held a 202.5 point lead over Lee Petty who finished eighth. Florian jumped to third in the standings, 171.5 points out of first place.

Frank Mundy drove a Nash Ambassador, but fell out early with mechanical problems. Herschel Buchanan drove another Nash to a sixth place finish.

Race No. 8

Turner Flag-to-Flag Winner at Rochester

ROCHESTER, NY (July 2) -- Curtis Turner blitzed the field and cruised to an easy win in the 100-mile Grand National event at the Monroe County Fairgrounds. It was his fourth career win.

Turner, starting his Olds on the pole, jumped out to an early lead and led the entire 200 laps on the half-mile dirt track. He wound up three laps in front of runner-up Bill Blair, who nosed out Lee Petty in a stretch duel. Jimmy Florian was fourth and Bill Rexford fifth.

Turner averaged 50.614 mph as three caution flags broke the action for seven total laps. Following the race, Turner and Petty engaged in some "extra curricular activity". Each was fined $100 by NASCAR for fighting at the inspection station.

Dick Burns was badly shaken when his Mercury left the track and struck a light pole in the 133rd lap.

The event was the first Grand National race in which a father-son duo competed together. Roscoe "Pappy" Hough and his son Lee finished 18th and 25th.

Curtis Turner.

Turner's victory pushed him atop the point standings by a mere two points over Lloyd Moore.

Petty stood third in points, just 24.5 points out of first place, but he was stripped of all 809 points when NASCAR officials discovered he competed in a non-sanctioned race a week later at Concord, NC.

Grand National Race No. 8
200 Laps at Monroe Co. Fairgrounds
Rochester, NY
100 Miles on Half-mile Dirt Track
July 2, 1950

Fin	St	No.	Driver	Team / Car	Laps	Money	Status
1	1	41	Curtis Turner	Eanes Motor Co. '50 Olds	200	$1,000	Running
2		2	Bill Blair	Sam Rice '50 Mercury	197	750	Running
3		42	Lee Petty	Lee Petty '50 Plymouth	197	500	Running
4		27	Jimmy Florian	Euclid Motor Co. '50 Ford	192	400	Running
5		80	Bill Rexford	Julian Buesink '50 Olds 88	192	300	Running
6		24	Dick Clothier	Clothier '49 Plymouth	189	200	Running
7		59	Lloyd Moore	Julian Buesink '50 Lincoln	185	150	Running
8		98	Lyle Scott	'49 Lincoln	185	125	Running
9			Dick Jerrett	'49 Olds 88	184	100	Running
10		25	Dick Linder	Don Rogala '50 Olds 88	182	75	Running
11			Don White	'50 Ford	182	50	Running
12		293	Bob Dickson	'49 Lincoln	179	50	Running
13		11	Art Gill	'46 Ford	178	50	Running
14			Gayle Warren	'49 Olds 88	177	50	Running
15		58	Harland Holmes	'49 Ford	177	50	Running
16		54	Ken Warmington	'49 Ford	177	---	Running
17		77	Chuck Mahoney	Brooks Motors '50 Mercury	173	---	Running
18		66	Roscoe Hough	Hough '50 Ford	163	---	Wheel
19	′		Curt Foss	'49 Ford	158	---	Heating
20			Harry Sents	'48 Ford	145	---	Heating
21		92	Herb Thomas	Thomas '50 Plymouth	145	---	Hub
22		18	Dick Bruns	'49 Mercury	133	---	Crash
23			Irv Leitch	'50 Plymouth	113	---	Wheel
24			Ed Hamanard	'47 Packard	68	---	Crash
25		6	Lee Hough	Hough '50 Ford	60	---	Heating

Time of Race: 1 hour, 58 minutes, 32.58 seconds
Average Speed: 50.614 mph
Pole Winner: Curtis Turner - 54.794 mph
Lap Leaders: Curtis Turner 1-200
Cautions: 3 for 7 laps   Margin of Victory: 3 laps-plus   Attendance: 7,000
** Curtis Turner and Lee Petty each fined $100 for fighting at Inspection Station

Race No. 9

Turner Terrorizes Field at Charlotte

CHARLOTTE, NC (July 23) -- Curtis Turner jumped into the lead in the opening lap and never looked back as he streaked to victory in the 150-mile Grand National race at Charlotte Speedway.

Grand National Race No. 9
200 Laps at Charlotte Speedway
Charlotte, NC
150 Miles on .75-mile Dirt Track
July 23, 1950

Fin	St	No.	Driver	Team / Car	Laps	Money	Status
1	1	41	Curtis Turner	Eanes Motor Co. '50 Olds 88	200	$1,500	Running
2		77	Chuck Mahoney	Brooks Motors '50 Mercury		750	Running
3		92	Herb Thomas	Thomas '50 Plymouth		500	Running
4			Jimmie Lewallen	'50 Mercury		400	Running
5		18	Dick Burns	'50 Olds 88		300	Running
6		60	George Hartley	Julian Buesink '50 Ford		200	
7		9	Donald Thomas	Thomas '47 Ford		150	
8			Frank Mundy	'50 Olds 88		125	
9		90	Tim Flock	Red Star Garage '49 Lincoln		100	
10		37	Bill Snowden	Nash Motor Co. '50 Nash		75	
11		42	Lee Petty	Lee Petty Special '49 Plymouth		50	Wheel
12		49	Glenn Dunnaway	'49 Plymouth		50	Wheel
13		11	Bob Apperrson	Apperson '49 Olds 88		50	
14		87	Buck Baker	'50 Chevrolet		50	
15			Paul Smith	'48 Ford		50	
16		2	Bill Blair	Sam Rice '49 Cadillac		---	Spindle
17			Bill Joslin	'49 Ford		---	
18		24	Dick Clothier	'50 Pontiac		---	
19		80	Bill Rexford	Julian Buesink '50 Olds 88	125	---	Engine
20		79	Jim Paschal	'49 Ford		---	
21		59	Lloyd Moore	Julian Buesink '50 Olds 88		---	Engine
22		25	Dick Linder	Don Rogala '50 Olds 88		---	
23		19	Clyde Minter	'50 Mercury		---	
24			Lyle Scott	'49 Lincoln		---	
25		28	Buddy Helms	Helms '47 Hudson		---	
26			Gayle Warren	'49 Olds 88		---	

Time of Race:
Average Speed:
Pole Winner: Curtis Turner
Lap Leaders: Curtis Turner 1-200
Cautions: Margin of Victory: Attendance: 11,000

The muscular driver out of Roanoke, VA led from start to finish -- the second race in a row that Turner has led every lap. The triumph kept Turner in the Grand National point lead as Lloyd Moore dropped to 21st in the 26 car field.

Chuck Mahoney finished in second place, with Herb Thomas, Jimmie Lewallen and Dick Burns rounding out the top five.

Bill Blair and Bill Rexford pressured Turner in the early going, but Blair departed with a broken spindle and engine failure put Rexford out of action.

Lee Petty and Glenn Dunnaway were running in the top five when both Plymouth drivers lost wheels. They finished 11th and 12th respectively in the final rundown.

On the same day, Jim Roper, winner of the first Grand National race at Charlotte on June 19, 1949, won a 20 lap Strictly Stock outlaw feature at Pratt, Kansas on a 1.6-mile paved oval, averaging 67.659 mph.

Bill Blair #2 and Gayle Warren dive into a turn at Charlotte Speedway.

Race No. 10

21 Year-Old Fireball Wins Hillsboro

HILLSBORO, NC (Aug. 13) -- Glenn "Fireball" Roberts of Daytona Beach, FL, shoved his Sam Rice-owned Oldsmobile around Pee Wee Martin in the 58th lap and led the rest of the way to win the 100-mile Grand National event at Occoneechee Speedway.

It was the first win for the 21 year-old lead-foot, and it came in only his third Grand National start.

Curtis Turner started second on the grid and led the first 45 laps. Combined with the two previous races which he led from start-to-finish, he led

Sterling Long climbs out of his wrecked Hudson after Hillsboro mishap.

445 consecutive laps in Grand National competition. His quest for a third straight triumph was ended when a flat tire sent him to the pits after 45 laps. He lost two laps in the process, but came charging back to take second place. He was riding on the same lap with Roberts at the end.

Dick Linder, who started on the pole, finished in third place. Bill Rexford took fourth place and Clyde Minter was fifth. Lloyd Moore, who entered the race in second place in the point standings behind Turner, flipped his Mercury three times in time trials. He suffered a neck injury and was transported to Duke Memorial Hospital for treatment.

Sterling Long rolled his Hudson in a series of flips in the early going but climbed out unhurt.

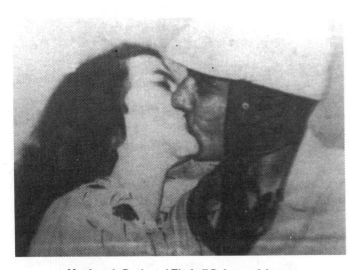

Newlyweds Doris and Fireball Roberts celebrate first Grand National victory in Hillsboro victory lane.

Grand National Race No. 10
100 Laps at Occoneechee Speedway
Hillsboro, NC
100 Miles on 1-mile Dirt Track
August 13, 1950

Fin	St	No.	Driver	Team / Car	Laps	Money	Status
1	15	71	Fireball Roberts	Sam Rice '49 Olds	100	$1,125	Running
2	2	41	Curtis Turner	Eanes Motor Co. '50 Olds	100	750	Running
3	1	25	Dick Linder	Don Rogala '50 Olds 88		500	Running
4		80	Bill Rexford	Julian Buesink '50 Olds 88		400	Running
5		19	Clyde Minter	'50 Mercury		300	Running
6			Gene Austin	'50 Olds		200	
7		42	Lee Petty	Lee Petty Special '49 Plymouth		150	
8		92	Herb Thomas	Thomas '50 Plymouth		125	
9		77	Chuck Mahoney	Brooks Motors '50 Mercury		100	
10		90	Johnny Mantz	Red Star Garage '49 Lincoln		75	
11		60	George Hartley	Julian Buesink '50 Ford		50	
12		47	Pee Wee Martin	Ed Lawrence '47 Buick		50	
13		37	Bill Snowden	Nash Motor Co. '50 Nash		50	
14			Lyle Scott	'49 Lincoln		50	
15			Don White	'49 Ford		50	
16			Pap White	'50 Mercury		---	
17		6	Marshall Teague	Paul Cox '49 Lincoln		---	
18			Bill Joslin	'49 Ford		---	
19		27	Jimmy Florian	Euclid Motor Co. '50 Ford		---	
20			Gayle Warren	'49 Olds		---	
21		0	Jimmie Lewallen	Sam Rice '50 Olds 88		---	
22		18	Dick Burns	'50 Olds 88		---	
23		10	Ray Duhigg	'50 Plymouth		---	
24		49	Glenn Dunnaway	'49 Olds 88		---	
25		11	Bob Apperson	Apperson '49 Olds		---	
26		31	Sterling Long	Gate City Trk Stop '49 Hudson		---	Crash
27		2	Bill Blair	'49 Olds 88		---	

Time of Race:
Average Speed:
Pole Winner: Dick Linder -
Lap Leaders: Curtis Turner 1-45, Pee Wee Martin 46-57, Fireball Roberts 58-100.
Cautions: 1   Margin of Victory: Attendance: 8,800

Race No. 11

Linder Takes Crash-Shortened Event at Dayton

DAYTON, OH (Aug. 20) -- Dick Linder, sharp-featured youngster out of Pittsburgh, PA, grabbed his first Grand National win in the scheduled 200 lapper at Dayton Speedway.

The race was shortened from 200 laps to 195 when the Lincoln of Johnny Mantz plowed through the guard rail and Joe Merola drove into the wreckage and debris. Merola was taken to St. Elizabeth Hospital with multiple cuts and bruises. Mantz was unhurt.

Red Harvey, a last minute substitute driver, responded brilliantly and finished second to Linder's Oldsmobile. Herb Thomas finished third, Lee Petty was fourth and Art Lamey came in fifth.

Lloyd Moore, recovered from his Hillsboro mishap, finished eighth.

Curtis Turner led the opening 48 laps from the pole but fell out with mechanical problems. A crowd of 12,000 was in attendance.

Race No. 12

Linder Spins - Then Wins at Hamburg

HAMBURG, NY (Aug. 27) -- Dick Linder recovered from an early spin, stormed back and won the 100-mile Grand National race at the Hamburg Fairgrounds. It was Linder's second straight win.

Linder's Olds edged hard-charging Fireball Roberts by 20 yards to pocket the $1,500 first prize. Curtis Turner, who led the first 74 laps, blew a tire and lost four laps in the pits getting a replacement. The crowd of 8,363 cheered wildly as he came back strong, making up three laps to finish third . Lloyd Moore came in

Grand National Race No. 11
200 Laps at Dayton Speedway
Dayton, OH
100 Miles on Half-mile Dirt Track
August 20, 1950

Fin	St	No.	Dr	Team / Car	Laps	Money	Status
1	2	25	Dick Linder	Don Rogala '50 Olds 88	195	$1,000	Running
2			Red Harvey	'49 Olds 88		750	Running
3		92	Herb Thomas	Thomas '50 Plymouth		500	Running
4		42	Lee Petty	Lee Petty Special '49 Plymouth		400	Running
5			Art Lamey	'49 Plymouth		300	Running
6			Paul Parks	'49 Cadillac		200	
7			Jack Kabat			150	
8		59	Lloyd Moore	Julian Buesink '50 Ford		125	
9		12	Joe Nagle	Nagle '50 Mercury		100	
10			Paul Smith	'48 Ford		75	
11			Tommy Thompson			50	Crash
12		90	Johnny Mantz	Red Star Garage '49 Lincoln		50	Crash
13			Carl Renner			50	
14		80	Bill Rexford	Julian Buesink '50 Olds 88		50	
15			George Jackson			50	
16			Jack Russell			---	
17			Jim Wesley			---	
18		18	Dick Burns	'50 Olds 88		---	
19		94	Louise Smith	Leslie Motor Co. '50 Nash		---	
20		60	George Hartley	Julian Buesink '50 Ford		---	
21			Joe Merola			---	Crash
22		27	Jimmy Florian	Euclid Motor Co. '50 Ford		---	
23	1	41	Curtis Turner	Eanes Motor Co. '50 Olds 88		---	
24		10	Ray Duhigg	'50 Plymouth		---	
25		23	Mike Klapak	'49 Ford		---	
26		78	Bud Moore	'50 Olds 88		---	
27		77	Chuck Mahoney	Brooks Motors '50 Mercury		---	
28			Gayle Warren	'49 Olds 88		---	

** Race shortened from 200 laps to 195 laps due to wreck
Time of Race: No Time Recorded
Average Speed: None Recorded
Pole Winner: Curtis Turner
Lap Leaders: Curtis Turner 1-48, Dick Linder 49-169, Red Harvey 170, Linder 171-195
Cautions: Margin of Victory: Attendance: 12,000

fourth and Jack White, winner of the inaugural at this half-mile track in 1949, was fifth.

Three female drivers entered the race and two of them, Ann Chester and Louise Smith, crashed hard. Neither was hurt. Sara Christian finished 14th in her first 1950 start.

Ken Warmington flipped his Ford three times without injury.

Linder took the lead from Turner in the 75th lap but spun out on lap 153. That gave the lead to Roberts, but it took Linder only 10 laps to pass the field. Once he got the lead, he kept Roberts in check.

Linder averaged 50.747 mph for the 100 miles. He had won the pole in qualifying at a speed of 53.113 mph.

Grand National Race No. 12
200 Laps at Hamburg Fairgrounds
Hamburg, NY
100 Miles on Half-mile Dirt Track
August 27, 1950

Fin	St	No.	Dr	Team / Car	Laps	Money	Status
1	1	25	Dick Linder	Don Rogala '50 Olds 88	200	$1,500	Running
2	3	11	Fireball Roberts	Sam Rice '49 Olds 88	200	750	Running
3	2	41	Curtis Turner	Eanes Motor Co. '50 Olds 88	199	500	Running
4		59	Lloyd Moore	Julian Buesink '50 Lincoln		400	Running
5			Jack White	Moyer Co. '50 Mercury		300	Running
6		80	Bill Rexford	Julian Buesink '50 Olds 88		200	
7			Frank Mundy	'50 Olds 88		150	
8		93	Ted Chamberlain	Chamberlain '50 Plymouth		125	
9		66	Roscoe Hough	Hough '50 Ford		100	
10			Bill Blair	'50 Mercury		75	
11			Frankie Schneider			50	
12			J. Borden			50	
13			Dick Jerrett	'49 Olds 88		50	
14		71	Sara Christian	Frank Christian '50 Ford		50	
15		58	Harland Holmes	'49 Ford		50	
16		77	Chuck Mahoney	Brooks Motors '50 Mercury		---	
17			F. Weichman			---	
18			Red Ryder	'49 Olds 88		---	
19			Lyle Scott	'49 Lincoln		---	
20			Morris Lamb			---	
21		72	Ann Chester	'47 Plymouth	92	---	Crash
22		94	Louise Smith	Leslie Motor Co. '50 Nash		---	Crash
23		54	Ken Warmington	'49 Ford		---	Crash
24		9	Art Lamey	'49 Plymouth		---	
25			Gayle Warren	'49 Olds 88		---	
26		27	Jimmy Florian	Euclid Motor Co. '50 Ford		---	
27		42	Lee Petty	Lee Petty Special '49 Plymouth		---	
28		6	Lee Hough	Hough '50 Ford		---	
29		60	George Hartley	Julian Buesink '50 Ford		---	
30		18	Dick Burns	'49 Mercury		---	
31		293	Bob Dickson	'49 Lincoln		---	
32		15	Paul Parks	'50 Plymouth		---	
33			Hugh Darragh	'49 Ford		---	

* Drivers listed in positions 21-33 are not necessarily in correct finish order. They all finished somewhere between 21st and 33rd.
Time of Race: 1 hour, 58 minutes, 14 seconds
Average Speed: 50.747 mph
Pole Winner: Dick Linder - 53.113 mph
Lap Leaders: Curtis Turner 1-74, Dick Linder 75-153, Fireball Roberts 154-162, Linder 163-200
Cautions: 1   Margin of Victory: 20 yards   Attendance: 8,363

Race No. 13

Madman Mantz Masters Darlington's 500-miler

DARLINGTON, SC (Sept 4) -- The Grand National circuit was just a little over a year old, but with its incredible popularity, the series needed a major event which would attract the attention of the entire country.

A 500-mile sojourn would do the trick, but there was not a facility groomed well enough to accommodate 500 miles of punishment from upwards of 70 automobiles.

Lakewood Speedway in Atlanta had planned on staging the first 500-miler for stock cars, and promoter Sam Nunis had already printed entry blanks. But Harold Brasington was building Darlington International Raceway, a giant 1.25-mile banked and paved track. This was the obvious choice for an event with a 500-mile dimension.

Most of the regular drivers on the NASCAR circuit had never driven a race on a paved track, but Johnny Mantz, the "Madman" out of Long Beach, CA, had extensive experience in AAA Indy cars. He was a late entrant as the driver in a 1950 Plymouth owned by Bill France and Alvin Hawkins, a NASCAR starter and flagman. Mechanic Hubert Westmoreland became the third co-owner and finely tuned the car, which had been used to run business errands, for the Darlington race.

Mantz had run only the Hillsboro and Dayton NASCAR events driving the Red Star Garage Lincoln usually manned by Tim Flock.

Mantz knew the race would overtax traditional tires and suggested the use of hard compound truck tires which were not unlike the tires used in Indianapolis competition.

Every driver found his own groove in inaugural Southern 500.

Grand National Race No. 13
400 Laps at Darlington Raceway
Darlington, SC
"Southern 500"
500 Miles on 1.25-mile Paved Track
September 4, 1950

Fin	St	No.	Driver	Team / Car	Laps	Money	Status
1	43	98	Johnny Mantz	Westmoreland/France '50 Ply	400	$10,510	Running
2	67	82	Fireball Roberts	Sam Rice '50 Olds	391	3,500	Running
3	7	22	Red Byron	Parks Novelty '50 Cadillac	390	2,000	Running
4	23	59	Bill Rexford	Julian Buesink '50 Olds	385	1,500	Running
5	15	77	Chuck Mahoney	Brooks Motors '50 Mercury	381	1,000	Running
6	35	42	Lee Petty	Petty Special '50 Plymouth	380	800	Running
7	38	71	Cotton Owens	'50 Plymouth	380	930	Running
8	64	2	Bill Blair	Sam Rice '49 Cadillac	375	600	Running
9	44	52	Hershel McGriff	City of Roses '50 Olds	374	500	Running
10	26	61	George Hartley	Julian Buesink '50 Olds	371	450	Running
11	16	9	Tim Flock	Buddy Elliott '50 Olds	370	400	Running
12	57	44	Johnny Grubb	'50 Plymouth	368	350	Running
13	62	26	Dick Linder	Don Rogala '50 Olds	367	300	Running
14	68	89	John DuBoise	'50 Ford	367	250	Running
15	72	72	Weldon Adams	Adams '49 Plymouth	367	225	Running
16	32	99	Barney Smith	'50 Olds	366	275	Running
17	3	51	Gober Sosebee	Cherokee Garage '50 Olds	364	290	Running
18	52	39	Elmer Wilson	'49 Plymouth	360	100	Running
19	21	4	Joe Eubanks	Bud Moore/Eubanks '50 Merc	359	---	Running
20	19	43	Shorty York	'50 Buick	358	---	Running
21	51	64	Walt Crawford	'50 Buick	358	---	Running
22	33		Murrace Walker	'50 Olds	358	---	Running
23	48		Gene Comstock	'50 Olds	355	---	
24	27	17	Jack White	'50 Ford	354	---	
25	71		Byron Beatty	'50 Ford	351		
26	53		Bill Widenhouse	'49 Plymouth	350	---	
27	4	7	Bob Flock	Bob Flock Garage '50 Olds	348	---	Running
28	10	47	Fonty Flock	'50 Olds	346	---	
29	13	19	Jack Smith	R & W Auto Service '50 Olds	345	---	Crash
30	30	34	Pee Wee Martin	Eanes Motor Co. '50 Olds	344	100	
31	5		Lee Morgan	'49 Olds	342	---	
32	8		Hub McBride	'50 Mercury	341		
33	11		Slick Smith	'50 Olds	340	---	
34	12	45	Ted Chamberlain	'50 Plymouth	358	---	Running
35	6		Virgil Livengood	'50 Olds	338	---	Running
36	9		Billy Carden	'50 Ford	338	---	Running
37	14	37	Bill Snowden	'50 Nash	338	---	Running
38	22	21	Harold Kite	Edmunds Motors '49 Lincoln	334	---	
39	25	49	Glenn Dunnaway	'50 Lincoln	333	---	
40	2	25	Jimmy Thompson	Leland Colvin '50 Lincoln	332	125	
41	65	27	Jimmy Florian	'50 Olds	331	---	Spindle
42	20		Bob Smith	'50 Olds	331	---	Running
43	24	0	Jimmie Lewallen	Sam Rice '50 Olds	330	---	
44	75		Jesse James Taylor	'50 Mercury	329	---	
45	29		Bub King	'50 Mercury	329	---	
46	36	24	Gene Darragh	'50 Hudson	323	---	
47	39		Roy Bentley	'50 Studebaker	319	---	
48	42		J.E. Hardie	'50 Studebaker	317	---	
49	34		Jerry Kemp	'50 Lincoln	315	---	
50	46	36	Bill Osborne	'50 Mercury	311	100	
51	37		Carson Dyer	'50 Lincoln	310	---	
52	60	33	Wally Campbell	Wally Marks '50 Olds	309	100	
53	40	79	Jim Paschal	Julian Buesink '50 Ford	307	---	
54	45	18	Charles Tidwell	'49 Olds	300	100	
55	41		Ruel Smith	'50 Pontiac	289	---	
56	47		Al Keller	'50 Olds	284	---	
57	50		Dick Soper	'50 Kaiser	282	---	
58	54		Pete Keller	'50 Studebaker	281	---	
59	56		P.E. Godfrey	'49 Lincoln	278	---	
60	1	41	Curtis Turner	Eanes Motor Co. '50 Olds	275	320	Crash
61	49		Bob Apperson	'49 Olds	249	---	
62	55		Tommy Thompson	'50 Hudson	238	---	
63	61	6	Marshall Teague	Paul Cox '50 Lincoln	230	---	
64	70	14	Tex Keene	'50 Plymouth	229	---	Crash
65	31		Clyde Minter	'50 Lincoln	219	100	
66	74		Rollin Smith	'50 Hudson	208	---	
67	17	86	Bill Henson	'49 Olds	200	100	
68	50	48	Gayle Warren	'49 Olds	188	---	
69	28	87	Buck Baker	Darlington Raceway '49 Olds	176	---	Crash
70	58	46	Ken Wagner	Moyer Co '49 Lincoln	155	100	

Fin	St	No.	Driver	Team / Car	Laps	Money	Status
71	18	62	Lloyd Moore	Julian Buesink '50 Lincoln	112	100	
72	73	48	Alton Haddock	'50 Ford	98	100	
73	69		Jack Yardley	'50 Ford	89	---	
74	66		Jack Carr	'50 Mercury	52	---	
75	63		Roscoe Thompson	'49 Olds	24	---	

Southern 500 Starting Grid

1-Curtis Turner - Olds 82.034 mph	2-Jimmy Thompson-Lincoln 79.454 mph	3-Gober Sosebee-Olds 80.461 mph
4-Bob Flock-Olds 81.484 mph	5-Lee Morgan-Olds 78.869 mph	6-Virgil Livengood-Olds 77.449 mph
7-Red Byron-Cadillac 80.789 mph	8-Hub McBride-Mercury 78.740 mph	9-Billy Carden-Ford 77.792 mph
10-Fonty Flock-Olds 80.035 mph	11-Slick Smith-Olds 77.821 mph	12-Ted Chamberlain-Plym 76.569 mph
13-Jack Smith-Olds 79.024 mph	14-Bill Snowden-Nash 75.960 mph	15-Chuck Mahoney-Mercury ??.??? mph
16-Tim Flock-Olds 80.750 mph	17-Bill Henson-Olds 78.905 mph	18-Lloyd Moore-Lincoln 79.440 mph
19-Shorty York-Buick 77.991 mph	20-Bob Smith-Olds 78.202 mph	21-Joe Eubanks-Mercury 77.866 mph
22-Harold Kite-Lincoln 77.316 mph	23-Bill Rexford-Olds 77.792 mph	24-Jimmie Lewallen-Olds 77.684 mph
25-Glenn Dunnaway-Lincoln 76.906 mph	26-George Hartley-Olds 76.970 mph	27-Jack White-Ford 76.960 mph
28-Buck Baker-Olds 74.301 mph	29-Bub King-Mercury 76.382 mph	30-Pee Wee Martin-Olds 81.165 mph
31-Clyde Minter-Lincoln 79.690 mph	32-Barney Smith-Olds 79.279 mph	33-Murrace Walker-Olds 79.957 mph
34-Jerry Kemp-Lincoln 78.170 mph	35-Lee Petty-Plymouth 78.781 mph	36-Gene Darragh-Hudson 78.330 mph
37-Carson Dyer-Lincoln 77.023 mph	38-Cotton Owens-Plymouth 77.361 mph	39-Roy Bentley-Studebaker 76.050 mph
40-Jim Paschal-Ford 75.092 mph	41-Ruel Smith-Pontiac 77.067 mph	42-J.E. Hardie-Studebaker 75.579 mph
43-Johnny Mantz-Plymouth 73.460 mph	44-Hershel McGriff-Olds 80.581 mph	45-Charles Tidwell-Olds 77.728 mph
46-Bill Osborne-Mercury 78.618 mph	47-Al Keller-Olds 78.477 mph	48-Gene Comstock-Olds 77.441 mph
49-Bob Apperson-Olds 78.145 mph	50-Dick Soper-Kaiser 75.829 mph	51-Walt Crawford-Buick 76.568 mph
52-Elmer Wilson-Plymouth 77.291 mph	53-Bill Widenhouse-Plymouth 74.637 mph	54-Pete Keller-Studebaker 75.976 mph
55-Tom Thompson-Hudson 77.234 mph	56-P.E. Godfrey-Lincoln 75.465 mph	57-Johnny Grubb-Plymouth 77.097 mph
58-Ken Wagner-Lincoln 80.305 mph	59-Gayle Warren-Olds 81.425 mph	60-Wally Campbell-Olds 82.400 mph
61-Marshall Teague-Lincoln 80.126 mph	62-Dick Linder-Olds 79.790 mph	63-Roscoe Thompson-Olds 80.108 mph
64-Bill Blair-Cadillac 79.852 mph	65-Jimmy Florian-Olds 79.762 mph	66-Jack Carr-Mercury 80.072 mph
67-Fireball Roberts-Olds 78.917 mph	68-John DuBoise-Ford 79.289 mph	69-Jack Yardley-Ford 79.214 mph
70-Tex Keene-Plymouth 78.165 mph	71-Byron Beatty-Ford 79.220 mph	72-Weldon Adams-Plymouth 79.018 mph
73-Alton Haddock-Ford 78.590 mph	74-Rollin Smith-Hudson 78.094 mph	75-Jesse James Taylor-Merc No Time

Time of Race: 6 hrs, 38 minutes, 40.26 seconds
Average Speed: 75.250 mph
Pole Winner: Curtis Turner - 82.034 mph
Fastest Qualifier: Wally Campbell - 82.400 mph
Lap Leaders: Gober Sosebee 1-4, Curtis Turner 5-26, Cotton Owens 27-49, Johnny Mantz 50-400.
Cautions: 2 for 13 Laps
Margin of Victory: 9-plus Laps
Attendance: 25,000

*   Johnny Mantz was the slowest qualifier in 75-car field with speed of 73.460 mph, nearly 2 mph slower than he averaged for the full 500 miles.

** Dorothy Shull of West Columbia, SC was the only woman attempting to qualify for the Southern 500, but on the 15th and last day of time trials, she spun her Olds three times in 2nd turn and did not make the field.

*** Herb Thomas, Bill Bennett, Louis Hawkins and Pap White qualified for the race but withdrew.

The NASCAR boys did not know it, but they were in trouble. Red Byron, driving a Parks Novelty 1950 Cadillac, ran 24 tires right off the rims while attempting to negotiate the high speed turns of Darlington.   In spite of this, Byron finished third overall.

Johnny Mantz romped to a lopsided victory while watching most of his rivals retreat to the pits countless times for replacement of blown tires. His black fast-back Plymouth took the lead in the 50th lap and led the rest of the way, finishing nine laps ahead of Fireball Roberts.

Johnny Mantz won Southern 500.

Including lap money, Mantz' winnings came to $10,510 of the $25,000 purse. Ironically, his qualifying speed of 73.460 mph was the absolute slowest in the entire field, but he managed to average 75.250 for the full 500 miles.

Red Byron, who had originally been flagged in second place, officially wound up third. Bill Rexford finished fourth and took a 104 point lead over Roberts in the race for the Grand National point championship. Chuck Mahoney finished fifth.

Curtis Turner started on the pole, but Gober Sosebee went down in the record books as having led the first four laps in superspeedway history. Turner got by Sosebee in the fifth lap and led for 22 laps before

Curtis Turner nurses a cut lip after Southern 500 crash.

Cotton Owens passed him. Mantz got by Owens on lap 50 and set sail.

Jimmy Florian provided the most excitement,

Joe Eubanks #4 leads the pack down the back chute at Darlington Raceway.

charging to second place after starting 65th. A broken spindle ended his bid for an upset triumph on the 331st lap. Turner flipped his Olds in the 275th lap and wound up 60th in the 75 car field. Wally Campbell registered the fastest time in the "Speed Trials" with a speed of 82.400 mph, but he started 60th on the grid. He wound up 52nd after suffering engine problems.

Originally the event was sanctioned by the Central States Racing Association. However, the CSRA had difficulty in getting entrants.

Bill France, who at first had a "hands off" policy regarding Darlington, realized the prospects of an immediate success, and he gladly stepped in to help the CSRA. Officially, the two organizations co-sponsored the event. NASCAR points were distributed, but the CSRA pay-off structure was used.   It took 15 days of qualifying to determine the 75-car field.

Dorothy Shull of W. Columbia, SC attempted to become the only female driver to compete in the race. However, in qualifying on the 15th and final day, she spun her Olds three times in the second turn and failed in her quest.

Race No. 14

Fonty Bags Langhorne 200; Roberts Leads Standings

LANGHORNE, PA (Sept 17) -- Fonty Flock of Decatur, GA scored his first Grand National win in the 200-mile contest at Langhorne Speedway as Fireball Roberts took the lead in the point standings.

Flock ran down Bill Blair in the 138th lap and led the remaining 63 laps to take the $1,500 top prize. Blair finished second and Roberts third. Roberts took a 46 point lead over Rexford who finished eighth. Lee Petty came in fourth with Neil Cole was fifth.

Wally Campbell started on the pole but lost the lead in the first lap to Curtis Turner, who led the first 31 laps. Flock took the lead in the 32nd lap and waged a tight duel with Blair for the rest of the race. Turner eventually left the race with mechanical problems.

John Schelesky was seriously injured when his Mercury crashed through the fence and tumbled 20 feet below into a tunnel entrance. He was immediately sent to Mercer Hospital in Trenton for emergency treatment.

Flock covered the 200 miles at an average speed of 72.801 mph in the event billed as "The Race You May Wait Eight More Years To See".

Buck Baker #87 starts near the rear at Langhorne. Baker came from 38th starting spot to finish 7th in 200 miler.

Race No. 15

Sales Sails Past Smith, Wins N. Wilkesboro

N. Wilkesboro, NC (Sept. 24.) -- Leon Sales of Winston-Salem, NC, grabbed the lead with eight laps to go and won the 125 mile Grand National race at North Wilkesboro Speedway. It was Sales' first ever Grand National start.

Jack Smith, a driver out of the Modified ranks, seemingly had the race well in hand, having led from the 138th lap when he passed Red Byron for the lead. But Smith's fate was sealed when his Plymouth's engine began to sputter al-

Herb Thomas #92 steers under Dick Burns at North Wilkesboro.

lowing Sales to breeze across the finish line first.

Sales had landed the Hubert Westmoreland tuned Plymouth that had carried Johnny Mantz to victory in the Southern 500 at Darlington.

Smith held on to finish second. Ewell Weddle was a

John Schelesky's Mercury left the 4th turn at Langhorne and landed on an access road leading to the infield.

Grand National Race No. 14
200 Laps at Langhorne Speedway
Langhorne, PA
200 Miles on 1-mile Dirt Track
September 17, 1950

Fin	St	No.	Driver	Team / Car	Laps	Money	Status
1		47	Fonty Flock	'50 Olds 88	200	$1,500	Running
2		2	Bill Blair	Sam Rice '49 Olds 88	200	1,000	Running
3	4	82	Fireball Roberts	Sam Rice '50 Olds 88		700	Running
4		42	Lee Petty	Lee Petty '49 Plymouth		400	Running
5			Neil Cole	'49 Ford		300	Running
6		88	P. Cunningham	'49 Cadillac	200		
7	38	87	Buck Baker	Darlington Raceway '50 Olds	175		
8		60	Bill Rexford	Julian Buesink '50 Olds 88	150		
9		44	Johnny Grubb	'50 Plymouth	125		
10		46	Ken Wagner	Moyer Co. '49 Lincoln	100		
11		61	George Hartley	Julian Buesink '50 Olds 88	75		
12		16	Paul Parks	'50 Plymouth	75		
13		92	Herb Thomas	Thomas '50 Plymouth	75		
14		65	Tommy Coates	'49 Olds 88	50		Crash
15			Elmer Wilson	'50 Olds 88	50		
16		59	Lloyd Moore	Julian Buesink '50 Lincoln	50		
17			Fred Daganaar	'49 Ford	50		
18		70	Lewis Hawkins	'50 Plymouth	50		
19	2	9	Tim Flock	Buddy Elliott '50 Olds 88	100		
20			Russell Bennett	La Belle Motor Co. '50 Kaiser	50		
21	1	18	Wally Campbell	Wally Marks '50 Olds 88	75		
22		12	John Schelesky	Joe Nagle '50 Mercury	25		Crash
23			Bob Read		25		Heating
24	3	41	Curtis Turner	Eanes Motor Co '50 Olds 88	25		
25			Len Brown	'49 Olds 88	25		
26			Charles Tidwell	'49 Olds 88	---		
27		20	Ray Duhigg	'50 Plymouth	---		
28		66	Roscoe Hough	Hough '50 Ford	---		
29			Bob Moore	'49 Olds 88	---		
30		25	Dick Linder	Don Rogala '50 Olds 88	---		
31		77	Chuck Mahoney	Brooks Motors '50 Mercury	---		
32		44	Frank Mundy	'50 Olds 88	---		
33		53	George Masker	'50 Kaiser	---		
34		48	Edward Adams	'46 Ford	---		
35		89	Al Keller	'50 Ford	---		
36		293	Bob Dickson	'49 Ford	---		
37		26	Buster Williamson	'49 Lincoln	---		
38	5	4	Don Cecchini	'59 Nash	---		
39		50	Buck McCardell	'49 Lincoln	---		
40			Mike Klapak	'50 Ford	---		
41		52	Bob Burkhart	'48 Kaiser	---		
42		78	Richard Cummings	'49 Lincoln	---		
43			Richard Hallock		---		
44		23	Ken Marriott	'49 lincoln	---		
45		8	Roland Stone	'50 Ford	---		
46		6	Bill Harrison	'49 Mercury	---		
47		97	John Meekins	'49 Mercury	---		
48			Dick Burns	'50 Mercury	---		

Time of Race: 2 hours, 44 minutes, 49.95 seconds
Average Speed: 72.801 mph
Pole Winner: Wally Campbell - 77.104 mph
Fastest Qualifier: Tim Flock - 78.329 mph
Lap Leaders: Curtis Turner 1-31, Fonty Flock 32-100, Bill Blair 101-137, F. Flock 138-200.
Cautions: Margin of Victory: 1/2 mile   Attendance: 20,000

Grand National Race No. 15
200 Laps at N. Wilkesboro Speedway
North Wilkesboro, NC
125 Miles on .625-mile Dirt Track
September 24, 1950

Fin	St	No.	Driver	Team / Car	Laps	Money	Status
1	11	98	Leon Sales	Westmoreland '50 Plymouth	200	$1,000	Running
2	13		Jack Smith	'50 Plymouth		750	Running
3		78	Ewell Weddle	'49 Lincoln		500	Running
4	5	92	Herb Thomas	Thomas Racing '50 Plymouth		400	Running
5	14	44	Gayle Warren	'50 Plymouth		300	Running
6	16	52	Weldon Adams	Adams '50 Plymouth		200	
7	15		Jimmy Thompson	'50 Plymouth		150	
8	6		Jerry Wimbish	'50 Olds 88		125	
9	7	7	Bob Flock	Bob Flock Garage '50 Olds 88		100	
10		94	Herbert Burns	'49 Lincoln		75	
11		2	Bill Blair	'50 Olds 88		50	
12		21	Harold Kite	'50 Mercury		50	
13	8		Billy Carden	'50 Olds 88		50	
14	9	87	Buck Baker	'50 Olds 88		50	
15	10	38	Clyde Minter	B.F. Goodrich '47 Buick		50	Wheel
16	1	82	Fireball Roberts	Sam Rice '49 Olds 88		50	Engine
17		15	Paul Parks	'50 Plymouth		---	
18	3	47	Fonty Flock	'50 Olds 88		---	Engine
19	2	22	Red Byron	Parks Novelty '50 Cadillac		---	Spindle
20	17	37	Slick Smith	'50 Nash		---	Crash
21			Dick Shubruk	'49 Lincoln		---	
22	4	41	Curtis Turner	Eanes Motor Co. '50 Olds 88		---	
23		58	Jim Cook	Walter Motor Co. '50 Mercury		---	Engine
24	12	75	Tim Flock	'50 Olds 88		---	
25			Jack Carr	'50 Olds 88		---	
26	18	14	Tex Keene	'50 Plymouth		---	

Time of Race:
Average Speed:
Pole Winner: Fireball Roberts - 73.266 mph
Lap Leaders: Red Byron 1-3, Fonty Flock 4-107, Byron 108-137, Jack Smith 138-192, Leon Sales 183-200.
Cautions: Margin of Victory: Attendance: 7,000

stretch of 103 laps, both ran into problems and failed to finish.

Point leader Fireball Roberts finished 16th and only picked 2.5 points on Bill Rexford in the point race. Rexford was not entered.

Peter Shaw, a 12 year-old boy from N. Wilkesboro, suffered a broken leg in a freak mishap during the race. A wheel came off Clyde Minter's Buick. While trying to avoid the errant wheel, Slick Smith's Oldsmobile struck young Shaw.

surprise third place finisher, and Herb Thomas came in fourth. Gayle Warren came from 14th to nab fifth place.

The lead changed hands five times among four different drivers as a crowd of 7,000 sat on the edge of their seats. Sales, who started 11th, never was a real threat until the final laps.

Early leaders Red Byron, who led on two occasions for a total of 33 laps, and Fonty Flock, who led for a

Race No. 16

Rexford Takes Point Lead As Linder Wins

VERNON, NY (Oct. 1) --   Dick Linder drove his Oldsmobile to his third win of the year in the 100-mile Vernon Fairgrounds Grand National event while

Bill Rexford took the point lead on the strength of a sixth place finish.

Oddly, Fireball Roberts, who had held a 148.5 point lead in the chase for the 1950 championship, did not enter the race. Rexford emerged from the Vernon race with a 31.5 point lead over Roberts.

Linder took the lead in the 72nd lap when Herb Thomas flew off the track after losing a wheel off his Plymouth. Thomas was uninjured but his Plymouth was badly

Dick Linder

damaged.

Linder had to use all of this talents, however, to hold off Ted Swaimm who finished only five car lengths behind. Lloyd Moore was third, followed by Tim Flock and Jack Reynolds, who came back from an early wreck.

Linder started on the pole and led the first 30 laps as a crowd of 9,200 looked on. Thomas led for 41 laps before his mishap allowed Linder to retake the lead.

Ann Bunselmeyer became the fifth female driver to race in the Grand National division. The New York driver wheeled a Packard, finishing 18th in the field of 29.

Bill Burton and Felix Wilkes were eliminated in separate wrecks on the half-mile dirt track.

Grand National Race No. 16
200 Laps at Vernon Fairgrounds
Vernon, NY
100 Miles on Half-Mile Dirt Track
October 1, 1950

Fip	St	No.	Driver	Team / Car	Laps	Money	Status
1	1	25	Dick Linder	Don Rogala '50 Olds 88	200	$1,000	Running
2		38	Ted Swain	Westmoreland '50 Plymouth	200	750	Running
3		59	Lloyd Moore	Julian Buesink '50 Mercury	198	500	Running
4		9	Tim Flock	Buddy Elliott '50 Olds 88	198	400	Running
5			Jack Reynolds	'50 Plymouth		300	Running
6		60	Bill Rexford	Julian Buesink '50 Olds 88		200	Running
7		42	Lee Petty	Bardahl '49 Plymouth		150	Running
8			Jimmy Thompson	'50 Plymouth		125	Running
9		77	Chuch Mahoney	Brooks Motors '50 Mercury		100	Engine
10			Dick Jerrett	'49 Olds		75	Running
11		92	Herb Thomas	Thomas '50 Plymouth		50	Crash
12			Robert Sprague			50	
13			Frank Keller			50	Crash
14			Jim Delaney			50	
15		15	Paul Parks	'50 Plymouth		50	
16			J. Borden			---	
17		93	Ted Chamberlain	Chamberlain '50 Plymouth		---	
18			Ann Bunselmyer	'49 Packard		---	
19			Bill Burton			---	Crash
20			Paul Smith			---	
21			Speedy Thompson	'50 Plymouth		---	
22			Frank Mundy	'50 Nash		---	
23			Paul Pettit	Ford		---	
24			John DuBois	Ford		---	
25			Augie Walackas	Chevrolet		---	
26			Dick Eagan	Ford		---	
27			Jack White	Ford		---	
28			George Bagnell	Mercury		---	
29			Felix Wilkes	Hudson		---	Crash

Time of Race:
Average Speed:
Pole Winner: Dick Linder -
Lap Leaders: Dick Linder 1-30, Herb Thomas 31-71, Linder 72-200.
Cautions: Margin of Victory: 5 car lengths   Attendance: 9,200

Grand National Race No. 17
200 Laps at Martinsville Speedway
Martinsville, VA
100 Miles on Half-mile Dirt Track
October 15, 1950

Fin	St	No.	Driver	Team / Car	Lap	Money	Status
1	19	92	Herb Thomas	Thomas '50 Plymouth	200	$1,000	Running
2		42	Lee Petty	Bardahl '49 Plymouth	199	750	Running
3		87	Buck Baker	Baker '40 Olds 88	198	500	Running
4	1	7	Fonty Flock	Bob Flock Garage '50 Olds 88	197	400	Running
5		52	Weldon Adams	'50 Plymouth	193	300	Running
6	5	11	Fireball Roberts	Sam Rice '49 Olds 88	192	200	Running
7		8	Jack Holloway	'50 Mercury	192	150	
8		25	Jimmy Thompson	Leland Colvin '50 Plymouth	190	125	
9		30	Jim Paschal	Chaney Motors '50 Henry J	188	100	
10		93	Ted Chamberlain	Chamberlain '50 Plymouth	183	75	
11		44	Johnny Grubb	'50 Olds 88	162	50	
12	2	9	Tim Flock	Buddy Elliott '50 Olds 88	162	50	Wheel
13		78	Ewell Weddle	'49 Lincoln	158	50	
14		38	Clyde Minter	B.F. Goodrich '47 Buick	106	50	
15		17	John Manning	'49 Ford	95	50	
16		2	Bill Blair	Sam Rice '50 Olds 88	69	---	
17	3	41	Curtis Turner	Eanes Motor Co. '50 Olds 88	66	---	Engine
18			Gayle Warren	'50 Plymouth	64	---	
19			Runt Harris	'49 Olds 88	41	---	
20		37	Slick Smith	Nash Motor Co. '50 Nash	31	---	Heating
21		98	Leon Sales	Sou 500 Winner '50 Plymouth	27	---	Crash

Time of Race:
Average Speed:
Pole Winner: Fonty Flock - 54.761
Lap Leaders: Fonty Flock 1-9, Curtis Turner 10-65, Herb Thomas 66-200
Cautions: Margin of Victory: 1-lap plus   Attendance: 6,700

Race No. 17

Thomas Laps Field in Martinsville Win

MARTINSVILLE, VA (OCT. 15) -- Herb Thomas snared his first Grand National win in the 100-mile event at Martinsville Speedway.

Thomas drove his Plymouth past Curtis Turner in the

Leon Sales crashed Hubert Westmoreland's Plymouth at Martinsville. This is the same car driven by Johnny Mantz at Darlington.

166th lap of the 200 lap feature, and led the rest of the way. Lee Petty finished second, a lap behind Thomas. Buck Baker, Fonty Flock and Weldon Adams filled out the top five.

Fireball Roberts finished sixth, while Bill Rexford finished third in a same day race at Winchester, IN. The result was that Rexford held a 110.5 point lead with only two races remaining on the 1950 schedule.

Fonty Flock won the pole at 54.761 mph in his Olds and he proceeded to lead the first nine laps. Turner hustled into the lead on lap 10 and was leading the race on lap 65 when he pulled into the pits with engine problems. He got credit for 17th in the final rundown.

An audience of 6,700 watched Thomas come from 19th starting spot to claim his first win.

Race No. 18

Moore's Mercury Wins at Winchester

WINCHESTER, IN (Oct. 15) -- Lloyd Moore of Frewsburg, NY, drove his Julian Buesink-owned Mercury to victory in the 100-mile Grand National

event on the haunted banks of the famous Funk's Speedway in Winchester, IN. It was his first big league stock car racing win.

Moore, who led the final 51 laps, became the 18th different driver to post a victory in the 26 Grand National races staged over the past 17 months.

Bucky Sager finished second after leading for 145 laps, and Bill Rexford was third. Chuck James came in fourth and Ray Duhigg fifth. Rexford padded his standings lead to 110.5 points over Fireball Roberts, who finished sixth in a same day event at Martinsville, VA.

Only 13 cars entered the race as most of the touring pros went to

Lloyd Moore won at Winchester.

Lee Petty #42 leads Jim Paschal #30 and Tim Flock at Martinsville.

Martinsville.

Dick Linder won the pole and led the opening three laps. Sager forged past on lap four and led until lap 149 when Moore went into the lead for good.

Buck Barr was taken out in a mid-race crash. He escaped injury.

Race No. 19

Fireball Blows; Loses Title as Petty Grabs Win

HILLSBORO, NC (Oct. 29) -- Lee Petty won the 200-mile Grand National finale at Occoneechee Speedway as Bill Rexford was declared NASCAR driving champion. The 23 year-old Rexford drove Oldsmobiles from the Julian Buesink shops in Findlay Park, NY to the title.

Petty took the lead from Fonty Flock in the 133rd lap and was leading when darkness forced officials to call a halt to the race after 175 laps had been completed.

Buck Baker wound up second, with Weldon Adams third, Tim Flock fourth, and Bill Blair fifth.

Fireball Roberts had an opportunity to take the title with a fifth place finish after Rexford had succumbed to engine problems early in the race. Instead of employing a conservative effort in order to take the championship, Roberts opted to charge hard all day. His reasoning was that the race paid $1,500 to win and the championship was worth $1,000.

Roberts started second and chased pole winner Fonty Flock for the first 71 laps. Rexford departed early and wound up 26th in the field of 29. Roberts was aware of his options in the early going.

Flock and Roberts put on a dynamic show for the 11,000 spectators. Roberts grabbed first in a daring move in the 72nd lap, then lost the advantage to Flock

Grand National Race No. 18
200 Laps at Funk's Speedway
Winchester, IN
100 Miles on Half-mile Oiled Dirt Track
October 15, 1950

Fin	St	No.	Driver	Team / Car	Laps	Money	Status
1		59	Lloyd Moore	Julian Buesink '50 Mercury	200	$1,000	Running
2		101	Bucky Sager	'49 Plymouth		750	Running
3		60	Bill Rexford	Julian Buesink '49 Ford		500	Running
4			Chuck James	'46 Ford		400	Running
5		10	Ray Duhigg	'50 Plymouth		300	Running
6			Carl Renner	Olds		200	Running
7		27	Jimmy Florian	Euclid Ford Co. '50 Ford		150	
8			Chuck Garrett	Chevrolet		125	
9			Bud Boone	Ford		100	
10			Buck Barr			75	Crash
11		39	Elmer Wilson	'49 Plymouth		50	
12			Leo Caldwell	Olds		50	Wheel
13	1	25	Dick Linder	Don Rogala '50 Olds		50	

Time of Race: 1 hour, 33 minutes, 56 seconds
Average Speed 63.875 mph
Pole Winner: Dick Linder - 68.834 mph
Lap Leaders: Dick Linder 1-3, Bucky Sager 4-149, Lloyd Moore 150-200
Cautions: Margin of Victory: Attendance: 5,000

*Lee Petty and the Plymouth he drove to victory
at Occoneechee Speedway.*

Grand National Race No. 19
200 Laps at Occoneechee Speedway
Hillsboro, NC
200 Miles on 1-mile Dirt Track
October 29, 1950

Fin	St	No.	Driver	Team / Car	Laps	Money	Status
1	15	42	Lee Petty	Petty Special '49 Plymouth	175	$1,500	Running
2	5	87	Buck Baker	Baker '50 Olds 88		1,000	Running
3	18	72	Weldon Adams	'50 Plymouth		500	Running
4	9	98	Tim Flock	Westmoreland '50 Plymouth		400	Running
5	6	41.5	Bill Blair	'50 Olds 88		300	Running
6	13	44	Gayle Warren	'50 Plymouth		200	
7	20	10	Ray Duhigg	'49 Plymouth		150	
8	12	99	Jim Delaney	'50 Plymouth		125	
9	10	18	Herbert Burns	'49 Lincoln		100	
10	14	8	Jack Holloway	'50 Mercury		75	
11	19	61	George Hartley	Julian Buesink '50 Mercury		50	
12	7	47	Johnny Grubb	'50 Olds 88		50	
13	4	21	Tommy Melvin	'50 Olds 88		50	
14	21	78	Ewell Weddle	'49 Lincoln		50	
15	24	93	Ted Chamberlain	Chamberlain '50 Plymouth		50	
16	16	26	Slick Smith	'50 Plymouth		---	
17	8	59	Lloyd Moore	Julian Buesink '50 Olds 88		---	
18	11	92	Herb Thomas	Thomas '50 Plymouth		---	
19	25	94	Louise Smith	Leslie Motor Co. '50 Nash		---	
20	1	7	Fonty Flock	Bob Flock Garage '50 Olds 88	132	---	Mount
21	2	11	Fireball Roberts	Sam Rice '49 Olds 88	126	75	Engine
22	22	3	Jimmy Ayers	'50 Plymouth		---	Crash
23	23	25	C.L. Grant	'49 Lincoln		---	
24	17	53	Jack Reynolds	'50 Plymouth		---	
25	3	38	Clyde Minter	B.F. Goodrich '47 Buick		---	
26	29	62	Bill Rexford	Julian Buesink '50 Olds 88		---	Engine
27	27	101	Bucky Sager	'50 Plymouth		---	
28	26	2	Jim Paschal	Westmoreland '50 Olds 88		---	
29	28	41	Curtis Turner	Eanes Motor Co. '50 Olds 88	1	---	Engine

* Race halted after 175 laps due to darkness
Time of Race:
Average Speed:
Pole Winner: Fonty Flock - 85.898 mph
Lap Leaders: Fonty Flock 1-71, Fireball Roberts 71-77, F. Flock 78, Roberts 79-80,
    F. Flock 81-132, Lee Petty 133-175
Cautions: 1   Margin of Victory: Attendance: 11,000

on lap 78. But on the next lap Roberts was back on top. Flock took command again on lap 81 and stretched his lead little by little.

In the 126th lap, the engine in Roberts' Olds gave up the ghost and the young Daytona Beach charger limped to the pit area. He was saddled with a 21st place finish. Neither he nor Rexford earned any points. But Rexford had his victory by 110.5 points.

The lead changed hands five times among three drivers. Petty led the final 43 laps.

The caution flag was displayed only once when Jimmy Ayers rolled his Plymouth three times in the first turn.

Louise Smith left the track during qualifying and landed upside down in a clump of trees. She was unhurt in the mishap.

Fonty Flock #7, leading the Hillsboro event, is hemmed in behind Ewell Weddle #78 and Clyde Minter #38.

1950 NASCAR Season
Final Point Standings Grand National Division

Rank	Driver	Points	Starts	Wins	Top 5	Top 10	Winnings
1	Bill Rexford	1,959.00	17	1	5	11	$6,175.00
2	Fireball Roberts	1,848.50	9	1	4	5	6,955.00
3	Lee Petty	1,590.00	17	1	9	13	7,695.00
4	Lloyd Moore	1,398.00	16	1	7	10	5,580.00
5	Curtis Turner	1,375.50	16	4	7	7	6,935.00
6	Johnny Mantz	1,282.00	3	1	1	2	10,835.00
7	Chuck Mahoney	1,217.50	11	0	3	6	2,760.00
8	Dick Linder	1,121.00	13	3	5	8	5,570.00
9	Jimmy Florian	801.00	10	1	3	6	2,695.00
10	Bill Blair	766.00	16	1	5	7	4,320.00
11	Herb Thomas	590.50	13	1	4	6	2,945.00
12	Buck Baker	531.50	9	0	2	5	2,195.00
13	Cotton Owens	500.00	3	0	0	1	1,100.00
14	Fonty Flock	458.50	7	1	2	3	2,170.00
15	Weldon Adams	440.00	4	0	2	3	1,305.00
16	Tim Flock	437.50	12	1	4	7	4,080.00
17	Clyde Minter	427.00	8	0	3	3	1,280.00
18	Dick Burns	341.50	8	0	2	3	930.00
19	Art Lamey	320.00	4	0	2	3	830.00
20	Bob Flock	314.00	4	0	1	3	1,180.00
21	George Hartley	298.00	8	0	0	2	875.00
22	Gayle Warren	287.00	10	0	1	2	550.00
23	Frank Mundy	275.50	8	0	0	3	550.00
24	Jim Paschal	220.50	6	0	1	2	850.00
25	Jack White	211.50	7	0	1	3	525.00
26	Roscoe "Pappy" Hough	207.50	5	0	0	2	325.00
27	Ray Duhigg	202.50	5	0	1	2	450.00
28	Leon Sales	200.00	2	1	1	1	1,000.00
	Jimmy Thompson	200.00	4	0	0	3	525.00
30	Harold Kite	187.00	3	1	1	1	1,550.00
31	Neil Cole	183.50	2	0	1	1	300.00
32	Buck Barr	180.00	2	0	1	2	575.00
	Red Harvey	180.00	1	0	1	1	750.00
	Ted Swaim	180.00	1	0	1	1	750.00
	Jack Smith	180.00	3	0	1	1	775.00
	Bucky Sager	180.00	2	0	1	1	750.00
37	Pepper Cunningham	177.50	2	0	0	2	300.00
38	Ewell Weddle	173.50	3	0	1	1	600.00
39	Donald Thomas	164.00	2	0	0	2	300.00
40	Bill Snowden	163.00	4	0	1	2	325.00
41	Chuck James	140.00	1	0	1	1	400.00
	Jimmie Lewallen	140.00	3	0	1	1	400.00
43	Dick Clothier	133.50	5	0	0	2	350.00
44	Paul Parks	124.50	6	0	0	1	375.00
45	Al Gross	124.00	2	0	1	1	550.00
46	Jack Reynolds	120.00	2	0	1	1	300.00
47	Jim Delaney	114.00	2	0	0	1	175.00
48	Carl Renner	108.00	2	0	0	1	250.00
49	Jack Holloway	107.50	2	0	0	2	225.00
50	Robert Dickson	105.00	6	0	0	2	275.00
	J.C. Van Landingham	105.00	1	0	1	1	450.00

The 1951 Season
Expanding into New Frontiers

Volume one of a four volume series . . . The Beginning 1949 - 1958

1951

One of the major factors in the immediate success of NASCAR's Grand National division was the fact that the Southeast finally had a sport which it could call its own. For decades the Southeast had been starving for a place in the arena of big time sports. There was no major league baseball team to support. Nor was there a professional football franchise. No Southern city had a pro basketball team.

Even the sport of auto racing rarely made stops below the Mason-Dixon line. The American Automobile Association, which sanctioned Indianapolis-type open wheel racing from 1902-1955, scheduled few championship meets in the South except for an occasional show at Atlanta's Lakewood Speedway.

When Bill France orchestrated the Grand National circuit, the Southern sports enthusiast who had labored long and hard with a lack of identity, welcomed stock car racing with open arms.

In 1949 and 1950, the Grand National tour made 27 stops at 14 different tracks in eight states. The farthest West NASCAR ventured was a 100-miler in Winchester, Indiana.

France felt he needed to expose his rambunctious

stock jockeys to the West coast -- and he was able to secure six events in the far West in 1951.

In addition to NASCAR's stretching well beyond its home base in Daytona Beach, France felt he needed a nationally known figure to be in the Grand National fold. He found a savior of sorts in Bill Holland, winner of the 1949 Indianapolis 500.

Holland was one of AAA's flashiest speed artists. In 1947, as a rookie at the "Brickyard", Holland was asked by car owner Lou Moore to drive the second car in his team which was headed by the idolized Mauri Rose. Moore needed the second vehicle in case Rose's car failed to make the distance. If that happened, Rose could perhaps take over the driving chores in the second car.

Bill Holland did not know the rules. He had the 500 virtually tucked away when Moore ordered him to back off via the pit board which read "E-ZY". Holland followed Moore's instructions and slackened his pace in the waning laps as running-mate Rose closed the gap dramatically.

Holland, thinking Moore's message meant he had a full lap on the field, waved as Rose motored into first

Bill Holland, 1949 Indianapolis 500 winner. Bill France put Holland in several early season Grand National events.

place with nine laps to go. When the checkered flag fell, Holland cruised over to victory lane only to find Rose was already there, sharing the accolades with car owner Moore.

Holland was livid. He could not believe that Moore had beguiled him in the world's most important auto race. And he exercised little restraint in his post race comments. The racing fraternity rallied behind the Miami newcomer.

In 1948, Rose again won the Indianapolis 500 with Holland second as the Moore team registered another one-two finish; this time the outcome was untarnished by questionable tactics. The following year, 1949, Holland finally captured the greatest spectacle in racing by winning the Indianapolis 500.

He finished second the following year in a rain-shortened 500. Bill Holland's name was widely recognized from coast to coast.

During the winter of 1950-1951, Holland was requested by promoters of a short track in Opa Locka, Florida, to drive in a three-lap Lion's Club event to raise funds for various Club charity projects. Holland graciously accepted without charging an appearance fee.

He drove in the three-lap event on the small dirt oval, and the fund raising campaign was considered a success. When the AAA Contest Board got wind of Holland's deed, they promptly suspended him for the entire 1951 season. In fact, it was not until 1954 that Holland was reinstated by the AAA in what was the most outrageous reprimand ever levied against an American auto racer.

Enter Big Bill France. He befriended the fallen AAA star and said he would help arrange a ride if Holland would join NASCAR. Not having anywhere else to race, Holland accepted France's offer.

France put Holland in the driver's seat of the 1950 Plymouth that had won the inaugural Southern 500 -- an automobile originally owned by France and Alvin Hawkins, and prepared by Hubert Westmoreland.

Holland drove in seven Grand National races, enjoyed one top five finish and earned a total of $535. The car was crashed heavily in a turn-over at Charlotte. Despite the lack of success, France and NASCAR got plenty of mileage from Holland's mere presence in the starting field.

By early summer of 1951, the Junior Chamber of Commerce of Detroit was preparing to celebrate the 250th anniversary for the Motor City. Located within

the city limits was the old Michigan State Fairgrounds and located within the fairgrounds there just happened to be a one-mile dirt race track. What better event for the Motor City celebration than a race between automobiles primarily built in the Detroit area?

Again Big Bill France came to the rescue. He convinced the leaders of the celebration that a stock car race featuring Detroit autos would be an ideal supplement for the gala festival. They agreed.

Bill France took his Southern based sport out to the far west.

A 250-lap contest, one lap for each of the 250 years, was slated for August 12th. France campaigned dilligently for each of the automobile manufacturers, who previously had had only a passing interest in stock car racing, to place at least one make of their car in the race.

At post time, a field of 59 cars had qualified, and no less than 15 different makes of cars, were on the starting grid. A crowd of 16,352 jammed the Fairgrounds to watch the event.

High level representatives from virtually every manufacturer were on hand. The event was an unabashed slugfest with Tommy Thompson, manning a huge Chrysler, out-dueling Curtis Turner in an epic finish.

Stock car racing, NASCAR style, was a big hit in the Motor City. An editorial which appeared in Illustrated Speedway News, read: "The stock car picture (has never) been brighter. NASCAR has outgrown its expansive plans and has set the pace the entire country followed. The gigantic Detroit 250-mile race served as the impetus that cracked the Maginot line of defense thrown up by the motor industry against the sport. They know we're here."

NASCAR threw the green flag on another racing division in 1951 -- the Short Track circuit. With the demand for NASCAR late model events, France opted to start another circuit for Grand National-type cars on tracks shorter than a half-mile in length.

Eleven Short Track events were staged in 1951 and Roscoe "Pappy" Hough was crowned champion.

Sanctioning NASCAR suspended and/or fined a number of drivers during the 1951 Grand National campaign, most notably, Marshall Teague. Teague, the original NASCAR treasurer, had opened the door for auto manufacturers to support individual racing teams when he sold stock car racing and himself to the

Fonty Flock won eight races and 12 pole positions during the 1951 NASCAR Grand National season. There was no such thing as public relations representatives to keep the media informed of a team's accomplishments. So Flock's Frank Christian-owned team put many of the track records on the side of the car. Just behind the number 14 are some of the records Flock set in 1951 -- at Lakewood, Langhorne, Occoneechee, Martinsville, Phoenix and Charlotte.

Hudson Motor Co. Hudson then backed the FABULOUS Hudson team owned by Teague. This set the stage for future financial and technical support.

Teague, whose ambitions had always included Indianapolis, lost all points he had earned at mid-season for competing in a AAA stock car race. Other drivers who were suspended, fined and stripped of points were Curtis Turner, Jack Smith, Bob Flock, Billy Carden, Ed Samples, Jerry Wimbish, and, for the second time in as many years, 1949 champ Red Byron.

For the season, Herb Thomas won seven races, including the second annual Southern 500. He was the Grand National champion by 146.2 points over eight-race winner Fonty Flock.

NASCAR gained many strides in 1951 and even had to battle near-sighted politicians who were lobbying the Congress to ban all auto racing. In North Carolina, California and New Jersey, bills were proposed to "prohibit and curtail all forms of auto racing".

Enter Big Bill France. He addressed the threat and was a factor in the Congressional bill never getting to the floor.

Wherever there is a stock car race, fans will gather in great numbers. In only its third year the Grand National Series was attracting capacity and overflow crowds indicated by this photo of the field lining up for the start at Columbus, Georgia on June 10, 1951.

Race No. 1

Teague Takes Daytona in Hudson Hornet

DAYTONA BEACH, FL (FEB 11) -- Marshall Teague, 29-year old hometown favorite whipped a field spiced with entrants from all over the country in what was termed a popular upset triumph in the 160-mile Grand National race on the sandy shores of the 4.1 mile Beach and Road Course.

Teague wheeled his *Fabulous* Hudson Hornet around Tim Flock's Lincoln with 12 laps remaining and held on to win by one minute, 14 seconds. Flock, who led the first 27 laps, was foiled when his pit crew had trouble gassing up his car on a routine pit stop. He was unable to make up the big deficit and settled for second place.

Fonty Flock's Olds took third place. Bill Blair and Buck Baker grabbed fourth and fifth places, both in Oldsmobiles.

Les Snow of Bloomington, IN was the first non-southern driver across the finish line and he wound up sixth.

The Daytona SpeedWeek finale held considerable interest since the contest drew a stellar field with many makes of automobiles forming a 54-car field. Bill Holland, winner of the 1949 Indianapolis 500, entered a Nash Ambassador, but a broken cam put him out early, leaving him with a 47th place finish. Johnny Mantz, winner of the first Southern 500 at Darlington, drove an industry supported Nash and wound up ninth. Bill Snowden finished 10th in a Ford Police Special.

Holland was able to compete in the NASCAR race only because he was suspended from the American Au-

Marshall Teague and his winning Hudson Hornet.

tomobile Association's Contest Board, which governs Indy car racing. Holland participated in a three lap Lion's Club charity race on November 15, 1950 at Opa Locka Speedway in Miami.

Teague said he had one close call in the 160 mile, flat out event. That came midway in the race when a

Grand National Race No. 1
39 Laps at Beach & Road Course
Daytona Beach, FL
160 Miles on 4.1-mile Beach & Road Course
February 11, 1951

Fin	St	No.	Driver	Team / Car	Laps	Money	Status
1	6	6	Marshall Teague	Teaguemobile '51 Hudson	39	$1,500	Running
2	1	91	Tim Flock	Esquire Motors '50 Lincoln		1,000	Running
3	3	14	Fonty Flock	Red Devil '50 Olds 88		600	Running
4	14	41.5	Bill Blair	'49 Olds 88		550	Running
5	7	87	Buck Baker	Griffin Motors '50 Olds 88		450	Running
6	9	55	Les Snow	Snow '49 Lincoln		350	
7	22	41	Curtis Turner	Nash Motors '51 Nash Ambassador		250	
8	30	16	Bill Snowden	Police Special '50 Ford		200	
9	16	98	Johnny Mantz	Don Willis Motors '51 Nash Amb		175	
10	8	59	Lloyd Moore	Julian Buesink '51 Lincoln		150	
11	12	1	Red Byron	Wally Marks '50 Olds 88		50	
12	21	83	Tommy Thompson	San Juan Motors '47 Chrysler		50	
13	13	61	Bill Rexford	Julian Buesink '50 Olds 88		50	
14		68	Barney Smith	Smith '50 Plymouth		50	
15	15	60	Don Eggert	Julian Buesink '49 Ford		50	
16	27	92	Herb Thomas	Thomas '50 Plymouth		50	
17	19	25	Speedy Thompson	'50 Olds 88		50	
18		77	Dick Linder	John Marcum '51 Studebaker		50	
19	28	144X	Len Fanelli	'50 Plymouth		50	
20	32	86	Eddie Sheeler	'51 Hudson		50	
21		138	Clyde Minter	B.F. Goodrich '47 Buick		25	
22	34	72	Weldon Adams	Harold Mays '50 Plymouth		25	
23	20	3	Rocky DiNatale	'50 Olds		25	
24		8	Billy Carden	Wheatley Motors '49 Lincoln		25	
25	33	101	Bucky Sager	'49 Plymouth		25	
26	39	13	Elmer Wilson	'50 Mercury		25	
27	26	33	Fred Thompson	'51 Mercury		25	
28		188	Don Oldenberg	'50 Packard		25	
29	38	2-B	Jack Smith	'50 Plymouth		25	
30	41	94	Buck Clardy	Louise Smith '50 Nash Ambassador		25	
31	40	42	Lee Petty	Lee Petty Special '49 Plymouth		25	
32	44	81-A	Pappy Hough	'50 Ford		25	
33		110	Jim Fieblekorn	'49 Mercury		25	
34	11	31	Carson Dyer	'50 Olds 88		25	
35		139	Ray Thompson	'51 Kaiser		25	
36	31	94-A	Joe Rogers	'50 Olds 88		25	
37	41	73	Ed Rooney	'47 Ford		25	
38	17	32	Alton Haddock	'51 Lincoln		25	
39	5	81	Ben Lalomia	'50 Olds 88		25	
40	35	34	Tip R. Key	'51 Kaiser		25	
41	29	25-A	Jimmy Thompson	'50 Lincoln		---	
42		23	Mike Klapak	Perry Smith '51 Studebaker		---	
43	43	46	Gordon Harvey	'51 Henry J		---	
44	4	9	Ed Samples	'49 Lincoln		---	
45		85	Fireball Roberts	'50 Plymouth		---	
46	25	56	Joe Jernigan	Lambert's Auto Service '49 Ford		---	
47		28	Bill Holland	'51 Nash Ambassador		---	
48	36	67	Earl Coleman	'50 Pontiac		---	
49	37	111	Herschel Buchanan	Buchanan '48 Nash		---	
50	18	70	Dawson Lechlider	'50 Olds 88		---	
51	23	57	Felix Wilkes	Fleming/Bavan '49 Hudson		---	
52	2	50	Gober Sosebee	Cherokee Garage '50 Olds 88		---	
53	10	88	Frank Luptow	Rocket '50 Olds 88		---	
54	24	18	Eddie Anderson	Nash of Blue Island '51 Nash Amb		---	

Time of Race: 1 hour, 56 minutes, 32 seconds
Average Speed: 82.328 mph
Pole Winner: Tim Flock - 102.20 mph
Lap Leaders: Tim Flock, 1-27, Marshall Teague 28-39
Cautions: None   Margin of Victory: 1 minute, 14 seconds   Attandance: 14,000

Bill Rexford leads Bill Blair and Weldon Adams out of the South turn and onto the beach at Daytona.

photographer darted onto the racing surface to take a picture. He stumbled into the path of Teague, who said he had to "veer quick to miss him."

Race No. 2

Turner's Nash Nips Petty at Charlotte

Curtis Turner's Nash storms through Charlotte turn.

CHARLOTTE, NC (Apr. 1) -- Curtis Turner held off

Bill Holland trashed the Hubert Westmoreland Plymouth at Charlotte.

a late gallop by Lee Petty and won the 112.5-mile Grand National race at Charlotte Speedway. It was his sixth career win, but the first in NASCAR for Nash.

In wheeling the new factory-backed Nash, Turner passed Fonty Flock in the 47th lap and was in front for the balance of the race. Petty clawed his way closer to Turner every lap in the closing stages, but fell one second short at the finish line. Marshall Teague wound up third. Herb Thomas was fourth and sprint car driver Frank Luptow came in fifth.

Fonty Flock led the first 46 laps in his Oldsmobile. After losing the lead to Turner, Fonty struggled to maintain the pace and eventually retired with overheating problems after 97 laps. He wound up 20th in the 39-car field.

Bill Holland, defrocked Indianapolis 500 champion, was running in eighth place with 10 laps to go, but flipped his Plymouth thoroughly demolishing the car. The Miami driver suffered only a cut hand in the wicked crash. A few weeks earlier Holland crash-landed Bill France's single engine plane on Cumberland Island, GA. He was uninjured in that mishap.

Lloyd Dennis tossed his Henry J on its roof in the 39th lap, but he escaped injury.

Turner averaged 70.545 mph in giving Nash its first Grand National win.

A crowd of 10,000 jammed the three-quarter-mile dirt track and watched Turner average 70,545 mph.

Defending Grand National champion Bill Rexford started 12th but fell to 21st in the final order when his Mercury fell victim to mechanical problems.

Tim Flock, Ed Samples, Lloyd Moore and Frank Mundy also failed to go the distance.

Race No. 3

Muddy Mobile Event to Tim Flock

MOBILE, AL (Apr.8) -- Tim Flock guided his Oldsmobile over a rough terrain and came home first in the 112.5-mile Grand National race at Lakeview Estates Speedway. It was his second career Grand National victory.

The event was promoted by driver Fonty Flock, who finished second to his little brother on the muddy oval. Herb Thomas came from 18th starting position to nail down third place. Bill Osborne was fourth and Donald Thomas came in fifth.

The race had been postponed from March 18 by rain and more thunder showers prevented time trials from taking place. The drivers drew straws to determine their starting positions.

Nash driver Eddie Anderson lost two left front wheels in the car-killing contest. Finally Anderson

Grand National Race No. 2
150 Laps at Charlotte Speedway
Charlotte, NC
112.5 miles on .75-mile Dirt Track
April 1, 1951

Fin	St	No.	Driver	Team / Car	Laps	Money	Status
1	7	41	Curtis Turner	Nash Motors '51 Nash Amb.	150	$1,000	Running
2	21	42	Lee Petty	Lee Petty Spl '49 Plymouth	150	700	Running
3	4	6	Marshall Teague	Teaguemobile '51 Hudson	148	450	Running
4	10	92	Herb Thomas	Thomas '50 Plymouth	145	350	Running
5	8	88	Frank Luptow	Rocket '50 Olds 88	143	200	Running
6	20	72	Weldon Adams	Harold Mays '50 Plymouth	142	150	
7	26	77	Ewell Weddle	'49 Lincoln	142	125	
8	11	11	Fireball Roberts	Sam Rice '50 Olds 88	139	100	
9	19	19	Joe Merola	'51 Olds 88	137	75	
10	33	10	Jim Fieblekorn	'49 Mercury	136	50	
11	25	0	Jimmie Lewallen	'49 Lincoln	135	25	
12	22	26	Bill Harrison	'49 Plymouth	133	25	
13	36	97	Buddy Helms	Helms '46 Hudson	132	25	
14	9	98	Bill Holland	Westmoreland '50 Plymouth	131	25	Crash
15	12	89	John DuBois	'51 Plymouth	127	25	
16	27	28	Slick Smith	'51 Plymouth	123	25	
17	31	5	Ray Erickson	Ed Hastings '49 Mercury	120	25	
18	3	41.5	Bill Blair	'50 Olds	117	25	
19	28	55	Bub King	'49 Ford	98	25	
20	1	14	Fonty Flock	Red Devil '50 Olds 88	97	25	Heating
21	12	8	Bill Rexford	'49 Mercury	96	25	
22	30	64	Ken Klutz	'47 Ford	95	25	
23	32	79	Ray Pruitt	'50 Dodge	93	25	
24	24	70	Leo Schneider	'51 Kaiser	64	25	
25	23	38	Clyde Minter	'50 Chevrolet	59	25	
26	29	15	James Ward	'50 Packard	55	25	
27	16	12	Guy "Crash" Waller	'50 Plymouth	52	25	
28	18	60	Dean Sprague	Julian Buesink '50 Mercury	46	25	
29	34	39	John Barker	Chaney Motors /51 Henry J	40	25	
30	15	25	Speedy Thompson	Leland Colvin '50 Plymouth	39	25	
31	17	80	Jim Paschal	Julian Buesink '50 Olds 88	39	10	
32	35	J-6	Lloyd Dennis	'51 Henry J	39	10	Crash
33	2	91	Tim Flock	Black Phantom '51 Olds 88	33	10	
34	6	23	Frank Mundy	Perry Smith '51 Studebaker	33	10	
35	14	59	Lloyd Moore	Buesink /Police Spec '49 Ford	22	10	
36		57	Felix Wilkes	Fleming/Bavan '49 Hudson	18	10	
37	5	9	Ed Samples	'49 Lincoln	15	10	
38		18	Eddie Anderson	Nash of Blue Island '51 Nash	8	10	
39		110	Earl Moss	'50 Ford	3	10	

Time of Race: 1 hour, 35 minutes, 41 seconds
 Average Speed: 70.545 mph
 Pole Winner: Fonty Flock - 68.337 mph
 Lap Leaders: Fonty Flock 1-46, Curtis Turner 47-150
 Cautions: Margin of Victory: 1 second   Attendance: 10,000

Grand National Race No. 3
150 Laps at Lakeview Speedway
Mobile, AL
112.5 Miles on .75-mile Dirt Track
April 8, 1951

Fin	St	No.	Driver	Team / Car	Laps	Money	Status
1	2	91	Tim Flock	Black Phantom '51 Olds 88	150	$1,000	Running
2	4	14	Fonty Flock	Red Devil '50 Olds 88	150	700	Running
3	19	92	Herb Thomas	Thomas '50 Plymouth		450	Running
4	16	9	Bill Osborne	'50 Olds 88		350	Running
5	21	93	Donald Thomas	Thomas '50 Plymouth		200	Running
6	6	19	Lamar Crabtree	'49 Ford		150	
7	15	42	Lee Petty	Lee Petty Special '50 Plymouth		125	
8	20	7	Bob Flock	'51 Plymouth		100	
9	7	8	Sonny Black	'48 Ford		75	
10	24	3	Jimmy Ayers	'50 Plymouth		50	
11	17	88	Frank Luptow	Rocket '50 Olds 88		25	
12	3	0	James Ellis	'50 Mercury		25	
13	13	23	Bill Rexford	Perry Smith '51 Studebaker		25	
14	14	30	Doug Wimpy	Chaney Motors '51 Henry J		25	
15	10	10	Willard Brooks	'49 Ford		25	
16	5	47	Ruel Smith	'51 Henry J		25	
17	9	41	Curtis Turner	'51 Nash Ambassador		25	GAs Tank
18	12	1	O.A. Dean	'40 Ford		25	
19	22	11	Fireball Roberts	Sam Rice '50 Olds 88		25	
20	23	80	Gene Tapia	'48 Ford		25	
21	18	72	Weldon Adams	Harold Mays '50 Plymouth		25	
22	8	45	Eddie Anderson	Nash of Blue Island '51 Nash		25	Front end
23	1	31	Red Harrelson	'47 Ford		25	
24	11	77	Bud Erb	'49 Plymouth		25	

Time of Race: 2 hours, 14 minutes, 18 seconds
 Average Speed: 50.260 mph
 Pole Winner: No time trials due to muddy track conditions. Red Harrelson drew pole.
 Lap Leaders: Tim Flock 1-2, Fonty Flock 3-4, T. Flock 5-150
 Cautions: Margin of Victory: Half-lap   Attendance: 9,500

busted the front end assembly on the rutted surface and was forced to retire. The inclement weather was blamed for the deplorable track conditions. One news reporter covering the race said in his article, "... the cars were in bad need of periscopes to see above the holes in the track."

Flock averaged 50.260 mph for the 150 laps on the .75-mile dirt track.

Race No. 4

Teague Leads All The Way at Gardena

GARDENA, CA   (Apr. 8)   -- Marshall Teague drove his Hudson Hornet into the lead at the drop of the green flag and never looked back as he won the 100-mile Grand National race at Carrell Speedway.

Teague maintained his point lead by winning as most of the other regulars were in Mobile, AL for a same-day Grand National race.

Johnny Mantz, with relief help from Slick Smith, finished second in a Nash. George Seeger was third, Fred Steinbroner fourth and Erick Erickson fifth.

Andy Pierce started on the pole but lost sight of Teague quickly. Danny Weinberg and Pierce were both eliminated in an early wreck. Weinberg's Hudson broke a wheel and flipped after tagging the rear of Pierce's Buick. Freddie Lee then smashed into Pierce, went airborne and landed on top of the Pierce Buick. This three-car mess completely blocked the race track. Dick Rathmann, running with a full head of steam, barely missed the wreckage. Rathmann was able to continue and finished seventh.

Frank Mundy hitched a ride out West with Teague, hoping to pick up a car to drive in the race. When no California car owner would let the 'stranger' borrow a car, Mundy improvised. Mundy had come 3,000 miles

| Grand National Race No. 4 200 Laps at Carrell Speedway Gardena, CA 100 Miles on Half-mile Dirt Track April 8, 1951 |

Fin	St	No.	Driver	Team / Car	Laps	Money	Status
1	2	6	Marshall Teague	Teaguemobile '51 Hudson	200	$1,000	Running
2	6	98	Johnny Mantz*	Mantz '51 Nash Ambassador		700	Running
3	8	2	George Seeger	Bill Cramer '49 Plymouth		450	Running
4	10	16	Fred Steinbroner	Bob Carpenter '48 Ford		350	Running
5	13	1	Erick Erickson	Advance Electric '48 Pontiac		200	Running
6	3	9	Dick Meyer	Grant Sniffen '50 Mercury		150	
7	5	12	Dick Rathmann	Warren Fraser '50 Ford		125	
8	12	39	Danny Letner	Bert Letner '50 Plymouth		100	
9	15		Leo Belethaupt	'48 Ford		75	
10	11	22	Lloyd Dane	Dane '49 Ford		50	
11	17		Frank Mundy	U-Drive-It Rental '50 Chevy		25	Running
12	19	17	Al Jacobs	Jacobs '50 Ford		25	
13	16		Dudley Froy	'49 Plymouth		25	
14	18	19	Les Bomar	V-Gap Spark Plug '49 Pontiac		25	
15	20	3	Stan Noble	'51 Mercury		25	
16	14	7	Chuck Meekins	Speedway Auto Parts '49 Plymouth		25	
17	9	69	Freddie Lee	Cliff Caldwell '48 Ford		25	Crash
18	1	54	Andy Pierce	Upshaw's Garage '48 Buick		25	Crash
19	4	4	Danny Weinberg	Coast Grain '48 Hudson		25	Crash
20	7	88	Woody Brown	Joe Mangini '50 Olds		25	

Time of Race: 1 hour, 38 minutes, 17 seconds
Average Speed: 61.047 mph
Pole Winner: Andy Pierce - 62.959 mph
Lap Leaders: Marshall Teague 1-200
Cautions: 1   Margin of Victory: Attendance: 9,000
* Relieved by Slick Smith

to drive in this race, so he went down to a local rental car agency and rented a '50 Chevrolet. Filing his entry, he qualified 17th and finished 11th. He waited until well past dark to return the car, "so that the attendants would not notice the 'bald' tires," said Mundy.

Race No. 5

Fonty Declared Winner of at   Hillsboro

HILLSBORO, NC (Apr. 15) -- Fonty Flock moved into the Grand National point lead with his flag-to-flag victory in the scheduled 150 miler at Occoneechee Speedway.

A crowd of 11,247 braved threatening weather that eventually curtailed the race after 95 laps had been completed. Frank Mundy finished second, Bill Blair was third, Tim Flock fourth and Neil Cole fifth.

Fonty assumed command in the point

Marshall Teague's #6 Hudson Hornet led all 200 laps at Gardena.

Fonty Flock won at Hillsboro, NC.

standings by 26 points over Marshall Teague who was idle. Teague remained out West in preparation for a 150-miler at Phoenix, AZ. Fonty started on the pole in his Oldsmobile and led all 95 laps. A rain storm hit the one-mile oval, turning it into a quagmire, forcing race director Bill France to call the race off.

Ray Erickson, who lost an arm in a hot-rod crash in early 1950, made his return to Grand National racing. He qualified eighth fastest, but departed in the opening laps when his Mercury developed engine problems.

Race No. 6

Teague Wins Third of Year at Phoenix

PHOENIX, AZ (Apr. 22) -- Marshall Teague took the lead from Fonty Flock in the 81st lap and held his Hudson Hornet in front the rest of the way to win the 150-mile Grand National race at the Phoenix State Fairgrounds. The victory moved Teague back on top in the point standings.

Erick Erickson wound up second with Tim Flock third. Fonty Flock was fourth, and Dick Meyer crossed the finish line in fifth spot.

Fonty Flock led the first 14 laps after starting on the pole. Teague took the lead on lap 15 and was pacing the field when he hooked bumpers with Al King in the 72nd lap. King's car flipped over. Teague stopped on

Grand National Race No. 5
150 Laps at Occoneechee Speedway
Hillsboro, NC
150 Miles on 1-mile Dirt Track
April 15, 1951

Fin	St	No.	Driver	Team / Car	Laps	Money	Status
1	1	14	Fonty Flock	Red Devil '50 Olds 88	95	$1,250	Running
2	7	23	Frank Mundy	Perry Smith '51 Studebaker	95	800	Running
3	2	41.5	Bill Blair	'50 Olds 88		600	Running
4	3	91	Tim Flock	Black Phantom '51 Olds 88		500	Running
5	5	52	Neil Cole	'50 Olds 88		300	Running
6	17	110	Earl Moss	Police Special '50 Ford		200	
7	9	92	Herb Thomas	Thomas '50 Plymouth		150	
8	13	71	Jim Paschal	'49 Olds 88		125	
9	20	42	Lee Petty	Lee Petty Special '49 Plymouth		100	
10	15	55	Glenn Dunnaway	'50 Plymouth		100	
11	18	2	Ewell Weddle	'50 Ford		25	
12	22	60	Bill Joslin	'49 Lincoln		25	
13	29	72	Weldon Adams	Harold Mays '50 Plymouth		25	
14	4	11	Fireball Roberts	Sam Rice '50 Olds 88		25	Wheel
15	31	66	Red Ryder	'49 Ford		25	
16	26	144	Johnny Grubb	'50 Plymouth		25	
17	33	37	Coleman Lawrence	Mitchell Motor Co. '50 Ford		25	
18	24	10	Jim Fieblekorn	'49 Mercury		25	
19	19	50	Bill Rexford	Julian Buesink '50 Mercury		25	Wheels
20	12	59	Lloyd Moore	Buesink Police Spl. '49 Ford		25	Heating
21	14	4	Joe Jernigan	Lambert Auto Service '49 Ford		25	
22	30	19	Bill Schade	'51 Olds 88		25	
23	28	90	Shorty York	'50 Plymouth		25	
24	27	26	Jimmy Thompson	Leland Colvin '50 Plymouth		25	
25	10	1	Walt Sprague	Police Special '49 Ford		25	Heating
26	6	62	P. Cunningham	'51 Hudson Hornet		25	Wheel
27	21	41	Curtis Turner	'51 Nash Ambassador		25	Heating
28	23	45	Eddie Anderson	Nash of Blue Island '51 Nash Amb		25	Heating
29	25	15	Ben Dickson	'50 Lincoln		25	
30	11	9	Frank Luptow	Rocket '50 Olds 88	18	25	Wheel
31	16	98	Bill Holland	Westmoreland '50 Plymouth	13	10	Valve
32	8	5	Ray Erickson	Ed Hastings '49 Mercury	20		
33	32	79	Ray Pruitt	'50 Dodge	10		

** Race shortened from 150 laps to 95 due to rain
Time of Race: 1 hour, 10 minutes, 20 seconds
Average Speed: 80.889 mph
Pole Winner: Fonty Flock - 88.287 mph
Lap Leaders: Fonty Flock 1-95
Cautions: 1 for 7 lap   Margin of Victory: 3/4-lap   Attendance: 11,247

Grand National Race No. 6
150 Laps at State Fairgrounds
Phoenix, AZ
150 Miles on 1-mile Dirt Track
April 22, 1951

Fin	St	No.	Driver	Team / Car	Laps	Money	Status
1		6	Marshall Teague	Teaguemobile '51 Hudson	150	$1,275	Running
2		1	Erick Erickson	Advance Electric '48 Pontiac	150	800	Running
3		91	Tim Flock	Black Phantom '51 Olds 88		600	Running
4	1	14	Fonty Flock	Red Devil '50 Olds 88		500	Running
5		9	Dick Meyer	Grant Sniffen '50 Mercury		300	Running
6	11	4	Danny Weinberg	Coast Grain '51 Hudson		200	
7			Ed Camrud	'49 Mercury		150	
8		18	Bill Holland	'51 Hudson		125	
9		12	George Seeger	Warren Fraser '50 Ford		100	
10		2	Bill Stammer	Charles Roscoe '49 Plymouth		100	
11		16	Fred Steinbroner	Bob Carpenter '48 Ford		25	
12		22	Lloyd Dane	'49 Ford		25	
13		28	Dudley Froy	'49 Plymouth		25	
14		19	Hal Cole	'51 Plymouth		25	
15		75	Buck Flatcher	'51 Mercury		25	
16		72	Bill Strickler	J & M Garage '48 Hudson		25	
17	12	69	Freddie Lee	Cliff Caldwell '48 Ford		25	Running
18			Frank Oviado			25	
19		65	Pat Wade	'47 Frazer		25	
20		99	Al King	'49 Ford	71	25	Crash
21		33	Lou Figaro	Jack Gaynor '51 Hudson		25	
22		92	Herb Thomas	Sanford Motors '50 Plymouth		25	
23		41.5	Bill Blair	'50 Olds 88		25	
24		77	Ernie Dietzman	'48 Hudson		25	
25		42	Lee Petty	Lee Petty Special '50 Plymouth		25	
26		3	Stan Noble	'51 Mercury		25	
27		120	Dick Rathmann	'51 Hudson		25	
28		98	Johnny Mantz	Mantz '51 Nash Ambassador		25	
29		10	Chuck Meekins	Smith & Jones '50 Ford	2	25	Crash
30			Bill Cheesbourg	'49 Lincoln		25	Crash

Time of Race: 2 hours, 21 minutes, 16 seconds
Average Speed: 60.153 mph
Pole Winner: Fonty Flock - 70.936 mph
Lap Leaders: Fonty Flock 1-54, Tim Flock 55-92, Marshall Teague 93-
  Erick Erickson   - 126, Teague 127-150
Cautions: Margin of Victory: 1/4 mile   Attendance: 12,000
* Drivers listed in positions 11-30 are not necessarily in correct finishing order

Marshall and Mitzi Teague celebrate in victory lane.

the track, dismounted and checked on the condition of King who was all right.   Teague then strapped himself back into his Hornet,   ran down Flock nine laps later and scampered to victory.

Allen Heath flipped his Plymouth in time trials. He was taken to the hospital with three broken ribs, a punctured lung and head injuries.   The car was repaired and Chuck Meekins drove it in the race, only to flip in the second lap at the exact point where Heath had his mishap a day earlier. Meekins wound up beside Heath in the same semi-private hospital room.

Teague won the race at an average speed of 60.153 mph.

Race No. 7

Fonty Flock Wins Race, Takes Point Lead

N. WILKESBORO, NC (Apr. 29) -- Fonty Flock regained the lead in the see-saw point battle with an impressive victory in the 93.75-mile Grand National race at North Wilkesboro Speedway.

Flock led the entire 150 laps as mechanical gremlins seemed to strike anyone running in second place. Fireball Roberts, Curtis Turner and Herb Thomas were all eliminated while attempting to chase down Flock while

Grand National Race No. 7
150 Laps at N. Wilkesboro Speedway
North Wilkesboro, NC
93.75 Miles on .625-mile Dirt Track
April 29, 1951

Fin	St	No.	Driver	Team / Car	Laps	Money	Status
1	1	14	Fonty Flock	Red Devil '50 Olds 88	150	$1,000	Running
2	5	91	Tim Flock	Black Phantom -51 Olds 88		700	Running
3	17	42	Lee Petty	Petty Special '49 Plymouth		450	Running
4	10	98	Bill Holland	Westmoreland '50 Plymouth		350	Running
5	13	93	Donald Thomas	Thomas '50 Plymouth		200	Running
6	29	59	Lloyd Moore	Julian Buesink '49 Ford		150	
7	20	60	Jimmie Lewallen	Julian Buesink '49 Ford		125	
8	15	155	Glenn Dunnaway	'50 Plymouth		100	
9	34	5	Dale Williams*	Ed Hastings '49 Mercury		75	
10	32	83	Jimmy Ayers	'50 Plymouth		50	
11	19	10	Jim Fieblekorn	'49 Mercury		25	
12	37	69	Dawson Lechlider	'50 Olds 88		25	
13	12	92	Herb Thomas	Thomas '50 Plymouth		25	Crash
14	22	50	Bill Rexford	'50 Mercury		25	
15	28	4	Ed Massey	'50 Plymouth		25	
16	27	19	Bill Schade	'51 Olds 88		25	
17	38	87	Jack Holloway	'50 Plymouth		25	
18	33	26	Leland Colvin	Colvin '50 Plymouth		25	
19	24	74	Paul Stanley	'49 Olds 88		25	
20	36	37	Coleman Lawrence	Lawrence '50 Ford		25	
21	30	55	Bub King	'50 Plymouth		25	Crash
22	14	90	Shorty York	'50 Plymouth		25	Crash
23	6	62	P. Cunningham	'51 Hudson Hornet		2.5	
24	9	41.5	Bill Blair	'50 Olds 88		25	Engine
25	25	39	John Barker	Chaney Motors '51 Henry J		25	
26	21	16	Bill Snowden	Snowden '48 Ford		25	
27	7	41	Curtis Turner	Eanes Motor Co. '50 Olds 88	65	25	Wheel
28	2	23	Frank Mundy	Perry Smith '51 Studebaker		25	Shocks
29	16	110	Earl Moss	'50 Ford		25	
30	26	78	Claude Joyce	'49 Lincoln		25	
31	23	72	Weldon Adams	Harold Mays '50 Plymouth		10	
32	11	25	Dick Linder	'50 Olds 88		10	
33	35	J-6	Bob Walters	'51 Henry J		10	
34	18	2	Ewell Weddle	'51 Hudson Hornet		10	
35	31	71	Ben Dixon	'49 Lincoln		10	
36	4	33	Lou Figaro	'47 Hudson		10	
37	8	38	Clyde Minter	B.F. Goodrich Tires '47 Buick		10	
38	3	11	Fireball Roberts	Sam Rice '50 Olds 88	3	10	Fuel Line

Time of Race: No time recorded
Average Speed: None recorded
Pole Winner: Fonty Flock - 31.17 seconds, 72.184 mph
Lap Leaders: Fonty Flock 1-150
Cautions: Margin of Victory: Attendance: 7,500
* Relieved by Lou Figaro

holding second place.

Marshall Teague, leader in the standings entering the race, did not start. Tim Flock wound up second in the event   and took over second in the driver standings. Lee Petty came in third, with Bill Holland fourth and Donald Thomas fifth.

Lou Figaro had a rough afternoon, crashing his Hudson early in the race. He then relieved Dale Williams and collided with Herb Thomas near

Lou Figaro, driving in relief of Dale Williams, motors toward the finish line with the hood up.

Bub King #55 and Shorty York #90 crash in North Wilkesboro event.

A crowd of 7,500 was on hand in cloudy weather to watch the race. No official time was recorded due to the many accidents.

the end of the race. Figaro continued to drive Williams' Mercury with the hood up and crawled to a ninth place finish.

Race No. 8

Turner Drops Nash; Wins Martinsville in Olds

MARTINSVILLE, VA (May 6) -- Curtis Turner ditched his heating-plagued Nash Ambassador, hopped into his reliable Oldsmobile and won the 100-mile Grand National race at Martinsville Speedway. It was the seventh career win for the Roanoke, VA speedster.

There were seven lead changes on the sunny afternoon with Marshall Teague leading on three occasions before his Hudson struck a rut in the track surface and flipped. The car was demolished, but Teague escaped injury. Turner took the lead in the 126th lap and led the rest of the way.

Frank Mundy finished second in a Studebaker and Tim Flock was third. Tim's efforts put him on top of

NASCAR President Bill France comforts Bob Flock after Martinsville crash. Flock was not seriously injured.

the point standings by a seven point margin over brother Fonty, who finished fifth behind fourth place finisher Herb Thomas.

Earl Moss and Bob Flock were treated at a local hospital following their separate crashes. Jim Fieblekorn and Bill Joslin were also knocked out in wrecks.

Flock's Plymouth crashed late in the race. The Atlanta driver was lifted from his battered car and placed on the

Tim and Fonty Flock lead as the green flag waves at Martinsville.

ground. NASCAR President Bill France attended to Flock until rescue personnel arrived. Flock was not seriously injured.

In a non-sanctioned race staged on the same day at Atlanta's Lakewood Speedway, the top five finishers were all former NASCAR regulars, who had all been fined in the past by NASCAR. Red Byron, Gober Sosebee, Jack Smith, Ed Samples and Weldon Adams were the top finishers in Lakewood's outlaw event.

Grand National Race No. 8
200 Laps at Martinsville Speedway
Martinsville, VA
100 Miles on Half-mile Dirt Track
May 6, 1951

Fin	St	No.	Driver	Team / Car	Laps	Money	Status
1	7	41	Curtis Turner	John Eanes '50 Olds 88	200	$1,000	Running
2	6	23	Frank Mundy	Perry Smith '51 Studebaker		700	Running
3	1	91	Tim Flock	Black Phantom '51 Olds 88		450	Running
4	28	92	Herb Thomas	Thomas '50 Plymouth		350	Running
5	2	14	Fonty Flock	Red Devil '50 Olds 88		200	Spindle
6	15	42	Lee Petty	Petty Special '49 Plymouth		150	
7	24	1	Walt Sprague	'49 Ford		125	
8	8	2	Bill Blair	'50 Olds 88		100	
9	31	26	Leland Colvin	Colvin '50 Plymouth		75	
10	21	7	Bob Flock	'51 Plymouth	187	50	Crash
11	30	90	Jack Holloway	'50 Plymouth		25	
12	32	39	John Barker	Chaney Motors '51 Henry J		25	
13	23	53	Clyde Minter	'50 Ford		25	
14	14	55	Bub King	'50 Plymouth		25	
15	22	155	Glenn Dunnaway	'50 Plymouth		25	
16	35	5	Bill Rexford	'49 Mercury		25	
17	33	37	Coleman Lawrence	Lawrence '50 Ford		25	
18	20	74	Paul Stanley	'49 Olds 88		25	
19	3	62	P. Cunningham	'51 Hudson Hornet		25	
20	10	33	Lou Figaro	'47 Hudson		25	
21	19	59	Lloyd Moore	Julian Buesink '49 Ford		25	
22	34	J-6	Bob WAlters	'51 Henry J		25	
23	4	6	Marshall Teague	Teaguemobile '51 Hudson	125	25	Crash
24	27	12	Erick Erickson	Packer '47 Pontiac		25	
25	18	38	Bill Lawrence	B.F. Goodrich Tires '47 Buick		25	
26	17	69	Dawson Lechlider	'50 Olds 88		25	
27	16	110	Earl Moss	'50 Ford	110	25	Crash
28	25	50	Bill Joslin	'49 Mercury	108	25	Crash
29	26	8	Bill Holluck	Wheatley Motors '49 Mercury		25	
30	12	98	Bill Holland	Westmoreland '50 Plymouth		25	
31	13	60	Jim Paschal	Julian Buesink '50 Ford		10	
32	5	11	Fireball Roberts	Sam Rice '50 Olds 88		10	
33	11	10	Jim Fieblekorn	'49 Mercury	56	10	Crash
34	9	2	Ewell Weddle	'48 Ford		10	
35	23	93	Donald Thomas	Thomas '50 Plymouth		10	

Time of Race:
  Average Speed:
  Pole Winner: Tim Flock 55.062 mph
  Lap Leaders: Tim Flock 1-2, Marshall Teague 3-10, T. Flock 11-18, Fonty Flock 19-44,
       Teague 45-90, Curtis Turner 91-96, Teague 97-125, Turner 126-200.
  Cautions: Margin of Victory: Attendance: 9,000

Race No. 9

Teague Wins at Canfield by Three laps

CANFIELD, OH (May 30) -- Marshall Teague hustled to his fourth Grand National win of the year by taking top honors in the second annual "Poor Man's 500" at the Canfield Fairgrounds.

Teague drove his Hudson Hornet across the finish line three full laps ahead of Tim Flock, who finished second and held onto the point lead. Fonty Flock wound up third, Herb Thomas was fourth and

Marshall Teague grabbed his 4th win of the season at Canfield, OH.

Lee Petty fifth.

Bill Rexford, defending Grand National champion who won this event a year ago, started on the pole. He lost control of his Olds in the 115th lap while running in the top 10. The car catapulted over the guard rail and landed in a ditch. Rexford complained of minor chest injuries. Mike Klapak flipped his Nash with two laps to go, but still covered enough ground to earn eighth place money.

A crowd of 17,000, the largest ever to see a Grand National event on a half-mile track, watched Teague average 49.308 mph as the race was slowed several times because of wrecks.

Race No. 10

Flock Wins, Teague Hurt at Columbus

COLUMBUS, GA (June 10) -- Tim Flock, 27 year-old speedster out of Atlanta, steered his Olds clear of a 96th lap wreck and came home first in the 100-mile Grand National event at Columbus Speedway.

Flock bagged his third Grand National win as Gober Sosebee, recently reinstated by NASCAR after competing in several "outlaw" races, finished second in a Cadillac after starting on the pole. It was the first time a Cadillac had started on the pole in a NASCAR event.

Herb Thomas, who ranked fourth in the point standings, finished third. Jim Paschal came in fourth and Lee Petty was fifth.

Promoter Fonty Flock was taken out of the race when he hit Fireball Roberts and Frank Mundy on the front

---

Grand National Race No. 9
200 Laps at Canfield Fairgrounds
Canfield, OH
"Poor Man's 500"
100 Miles on Half-mile Dirt Track
May 30, 1951

Fin	St	No.	Driver	Team / Car	Laps	Money	Status
1		6	Marshall Teague	Teaguemobile '51 Hudson	200	$1,000	Running
2		91	Tim Flock	Black Phantom '51 Olds 88	197	700	Running
3		14	Fonty Flock	Red Devil '50 Olds 88		450	Running
4		92	Herb Thomas	Thomas '50 Plymouth		350	Running
5		42	Lee Petty	Petty Special '49 Plymouth		200	Running
6		7	Bob Flock	'51 Plymouth		150	
7		23	Frank Mundy	Perry Smith '51 Studebaker		125	
8		77	Mike Klapak	John Marcum '51 Nash		100	Crash
9		120	Dick Rathmann	Walt Chapman '51 Hudson		75	
10		60	Don Eggert	Julian Buesink '50 Ford		50	Crash
11			Nook Walters	'50 Mercury		25	
12		10	Jim Fieblekorn	'49 Mercury		25	
13			Bill Cheesbourg	'49 Lincoln		25	
14			Owen Jones	'49 Ford		25	
15			Jim Romine	'51 Henry J		25	
16		26	Jim Delaney	Leland Colvin '48 Ford		25	
17			Walt Hartman	'50 Plymouth		25	
18		33	Lou Figaro	Jack Gaynor '47 Hudson		25	
19			Ray Erickson	'50 Olds		25	
20			Ed Lenz	'47 Ford		25	
21	1		Bill Rexford	'51 Olds 88	115	25	Crash
22			Mike Little	'51 Chrysler		25	
23			Leo Caldwell	'50 Plymouth		25	
24			Bob Matson	'51 Studebaker		25	
25			Jimmy Longo	'51 Hudson Hornet		25	
26		25	Dick Linder	'50 Olds 88		25	
27			Dick Stone	'50 Ford		25	
28			Jack Goodwin	'51 Studebaker		25	
29		12	Erick Erickson	Packer '47 Pontiac		25	
30			Jimmy Florian	'50 Olds		25	
31			Mike Ernest	'50 Olds		10	
32		62	P. Cunningham	'51 Hudson Hornet		10	
33			Bob Greer	'50 Plymouth		10	
34			Jack Fleming	'50 Ford		10	
35	1		Walt Sprague	'49 Ford		10	
36			Bob Jeffries	'51 Ford		10	
37			Bob Shaw	'51 Kaiser		10	
38		59	Lloyd Moore	Julian Buesink '49 Olds		10	

Time of Race: 2 hours, 1 minute, 41 seconds
Average Speed: 49.308 mph
Pole Winner: Bill Rexford - 54.233 mph
Lap Leaders: - - - - - - - - - Marshall Teague -200
Cautions: Margin of Victory: 3 plus laps under caution   Attendance: 17,000

Grand National Race No. 10
200 Laps at Columbus Speedway
Columbus, GA
100 Miles on Half-mile Dirt Track
June 10, 1951

Fin	St	No.	Driver	Team / Car	Laps	Money	Status
1	2	91	Tim Flock	Black Phantom '51 Olds 88	200	$1,000	Running
2	1	51	Gober Sosebee	West Peach Mtrs '50 Cadillac		700	Running
3		92	Herb Thomas	Sanford Motors '50 Plymouth		450	Running
4		60	Jim Paschal	Buesink Police Spl '50 Ford		350	Running
5		42	Lee Petty	Petty Special '49 Plymouth		200	Running
6	4	22	Red Byron	Dantone Racing Stable '51 Ford		150	
7		93	Donald Thomas	Thomas '50 Plymouth		125	
8		23	Frank Mundy	Perry Smith '51 Studebaker		100	
9		83	Jimmy Ayers	'50 Plymouth		75	
10		4	Ed Massey	'50 Plymouth		50	
11			Carson Dyer	'51 Ford		25	
12		28	Slick Smith	'51 Plymouth		25	
13			Gayle Warren	Blevins Motor Co. '51 Studebaker		25	
14			Weldon Adams	Harold Mays '50 Plymouth		25	
15		2	Bill Blair	'50 Olds 88		25	
16		26	Leland Colvin	Colvin '50 Plymouth		25	
17			C.H. Dingler	'49 Plymouth		25	
18			Bud Erb	'50 Mercury		25	
19			Pug Blalock	'50 Mercury		25	
20		50	Bill Joslin	'50 Mercury		25	
21			Johnny Barker	'51 Studebaker		25	
22			Walt Hartman	'51 Plymouth		25	
23		72	Wade Fields	Harold Mays '50 Plymouth		25	
24	23	11	Fireball Roberts	Sam Rice '50 Olds 88	96	25	Crash
25	6	14	Fonty Flock	Red Devil '50 Olds 88	96	25	Crash
26			Lou Figaro	'51 Olds 88		25	
27			Tommy Wells	'51 Henry J	81	25	Crash
28		87	Buck Baker	Baker '50 Plymouth		25	
29		7	Bob Flock	Bob Chester '50 Lincoln		25	
30			Leo Sigmon	'51 Henry J		25	
31	3	6	Marshall Teague	Teaguemobile '51 Hudson	11	10	Injury

Time of Race:
Average Speed:
Pole Winner: Gober Sosebee - 57.766 mph
Lap Leaders: - - - - - - - - - - Tim Flock -200
Cautions: 4   Margin of Victory: Attendance: 9,500

Cars lining up on front chute just before Grand National race at Columbus, GA.

got back around on lap 178. Paschal slipped to sixth place after a late pit stop.

A crowd of 7,750 was on hand for the race, which was threatened by heavily overcast skies.

chute on lap 96. Mundy continued while Roberts and Flock were out of action for the remainder of the afternoon.

Marshall Teague suffered an injured hand when a rock came through the windshield of his Hudson on the 11th lap. Tommy Wells was rushed to the hospital with injuries when he flipped his Henry J in a turn on lap 81.

Race No. 11

Mundy's Studebaker Stout at Columbia

COLUMBIA, SC (June 16) -- Frank Mundy drove Perry Smith's Studebaker to a popular triumph in the 100-mile Grand National race at Columbia Speedway. It was the first win for Mundy and Studebaker in Grand National competition.

Bill Blair finished second in a Plymouth, one lap behind Mundy in the first Grand National event staged under the lights. Marshall Teague finished third, Herb Thomas came in fourth and Buck Baker was fifth.

Mundy, who started on the pole, broke out on top early and led the first 144 laps. Jim Paschal's Ford assumed command on lap 145 and held first place until Mundy

Frank Mundy

Grand National Race No. 11
200 Laps at Columbia Speedway
Columbia, SC
100 Miles on Half-mile Dirt Track
June 16, 1951

Fin	St	No.	Driver	Team / Car	Laps	Money	Status
1	1	23	Frank Mundy	Perry Smith '51 Studebaker	200	$1,000	Running
2		98	Bill Blair	Westmoreland '50 Plymouth	199	700	Running
3	8	6	Marshall Teague	Teaguemobile '51 Hudson		450	Running
4		92	Herb Thomas	Thomas '50 Plymouth		350	Running
5		87	Buck Baker	Baker '50 Plymouth		200	Running
6		60	Jim Paschal	Julian Buesink '50 Ford		150	Running
7	4	91	Tim Flock	Black Phantom '50 Olds		125	Running
8	5	16	Bil Snowden	Snowden '50 Ford		100	Running
9	9	72	Weldon Adams	Harold Mays '50 Plymouth		75	Running
10			Jim Harris	'50 Plymouth		50	Running
11		50	Bill Joslin	'50 Mercury		25	
12	12	14	Fonty Flock	Red Devil '50 Olds		25	
13			Bob Flock	'50 Plymouth		25	
14	6		Lou Figaro	'51 Olds		25	
15		22	Gober Sosebee	West Peach Mtrs. '50 Cadillac		25	
16			Paul Pettit	'50 Plymouth		25	
17			Charles Gilman	'51 Hudson Hornet		25	
18	11		Jack McClure	'51 Henry J		25	
19			Jimmy Ingram	'51 Henry J		25	
20		42	Lee Petty	Petty Special '50 Plymouth		25	
21		4	Ed Massey	'50 Plymouth		25	
22	7	10	Ted Swaim	Julian Buesink '51 Ford		25	Crash
23			Tommy Wells	'51 Henry J		25	
24			Walt Hartman	'50 Plymouth		25	
25			C.H. Dingler	'50 Plymouth		25	
26		93	Donald Thomas	Thomas '50 Plymouth		25	
27		J-6	Bob Walters	'51 Henry J		25	
28		55	June Cleveland	D.G. Hall '48 Buick		25	Crash
29			Leo Sigmon	'51 Henry J		25	
30		83	Red Byron	Dantone Racing Stable '51 Ford		25	Crash
31	3	120	Dick Rathmann	Walt Chapman '51 Hudson Hornet		10	
32			Johnny Barker	'51 Studebaker		10	
33	2	82	Joe Eubanks	Oates Motor Co. '50 Olds		10	
34	10	26	Leland Colvin	Colvin '50 Plymouth		10	

Time of Race: 1 hour, 58 minutes, 23 seconds
Average Speed: 50.683 mph
Pole Winner: Frank Mundy - 57.563 mph
Fastest Qualifier: Fonty Flock - 57.989 mph
Lap Leaders: Frank Mundy 1-144, Jim Paschal 145-177, Mundy 178-200
Cautions: Margin of Victory 1-;plus lap   Attendance: 7,750

Race No. 12

Turner Outlasts Rookies to Win at Dayton

DAYTON, OH (JUNE 24) -- Curtis Turner motored past Tim Flock in the 24th lap and outlasted a pair of newcomers to post the victory in the 100-miler at Dayton Speedway. It was Turner's eighth Grand National

Car owner John Eanes congratulates
Curtis Turner after Dayton victory.

win, the most on the major league stock car racing circuit.

Dick Rathmann prevailed in a bone-jarring battle for runner-up honors over Tim and Fonty Flock, who took third and fourth spots. Fifth place went to Lloyd Moore.

Tim stretched his point lead to 315 over his brother, Fonty. Herb Thomas and Lee Petty, both high in the point race, fell victim to problems and did not finish in

Herb Thomas leads pack of cars on Dayton's high banks.

the top 10.

Red Harvey, driving an Oldsmobile, was battling for second place when he broke a hub late in the going. He still wound up in 10th place.

Another rookie, Walt Sprague, was in the hunt, but a broken wheel put him out in the last five miles. He had to settle for seventh place in the final rundown.

A crowd of 10,000 was on hand for the event on the half-mile track.

Grand National Race No. 12
200 Laps at Dayton Speedway
Dayton, OH
100 Miles on Half-mile Paved Track
June 24, 1951

Fin	St	No.	Driver	Team / Car	Laps	Money	Status
1		41	Curtis Turner	Eames Motor Co. '51 Olds	200	$1,000	Running
2	2	120	Dick Rathmann	Walt Chapman '51 Hudson	200	700	Running
3	1	91	Tim Flock	Black Phantom '51 Olds		450	Running
4	4	14	Fonty Flock	Red Devil '51 Olds		350	Running
5		59	Lloyd Moore	Julian Buesink '51 Ford		200	Running
6		6	Marshall Teague	Teaguemobile '51 Hudson		150	Running
7		1	Walt Sprague	'51 Olds		125	Wheel
8			Bub King	'51 Plymouth		100	
9		60	Don Eggert	Julian Buesink '50 Ford		75	
10			Red Harvey	'50 Olds		50	Hub
11		72	Wade Fields	'50 Ford		25	
12		42	Lee Petty	Petty Special '50 Plymouth		25	
13			Gene Comstock	'50 Olds		25	
14		54	Don Bailey	'50 Olds		25	
15			V.E. Miller			25	
16			Bob Green	'50 Olds		25	
17		10	Jim Fieblekorn	'51 Mercury		25	
18			Jack White	'50 Ford		25	
19			Dick Stone	'50 Ford		25	
20		27	Jimmy Florian	Euclid Motor Co. '50 Ford		25	
21	2	33	Wally Campbell	Wally Marks '50 Olds		25	
22	5	21	Lou Figaro	Jack Gaynor '51 Hudson Hornet		25	
23		23	Frank Mundy	Perry Smith '51 Studebaker		25	
24		92	Herb Thomas	Thomas '50 Plymouth		25	
25			Ray Duhigg	'51 Plymouth		25	
26			Mike Klapak	'51 Nash Ambassador		25	
27		17	Bob Greer	'51 Plymouth		25	
28		22	Oda Greene	'51 Hudson Hornet		25	
29		135	Bill Majot	Jim White '50 Chevrolet		25	

Time of Race:
Average Speed:
Pole Winner: Tim Flock - 70.838 mph
Lap Leaders: Tim Flock 1-23, Curtis Turner 24-200
Cautions: Margin of Victory: 3/4 lap   Attendance: 10,000
* 37 cars started. Drivers listed above in positions 21-29 are not necessarily in correct finish order.

Race No. 13

Figaro All the Way For First Win

GARDENA, CA (June 30) -- Lou Figaro, a little squirt from Los Angeles, proved he had the heaviest foot and grabbed his first Grand National win in the 100-miler at Carrell Speedway.

Figaro drove his Jack Gaynor Hudson into the lead from the pole position and had the power to stay in front for the entire 200 laps on the half-mile dirt track. Chuck Meekins finished second, 100 yards behind Figaro. Lloyd Dane wound up third, Freddie Lee was fourth and Fred Steinbroner came in fifth.

Allen Heath provided the thrills in the early going. The

Lou Figaro won Gardena event.

"Seattle Screwball" started 13th in a Ford and quickly moved to the front, waving at each rival as he passed. Engine problems interrupted Heath's quest for his first Grand National win.

George Seeger, starting second, made only two laps before he crashed his Studebaker.

Grand National Race No. 13
200 Laps at Carrell Speedway
Gardena, CA
100 Miles on Half-mile Dirt Track
June 30, 1951

Fin	St	No.	Driver	Team / Car	Laps	Money	Status
1	1	33	Lou Figaro	Jack Gaynor '51 Hudson	200	$1,000	Running
2	9	7	Chuck Meekins	Speedway Auto Sales '49 Ply	200	700	Running
3	8	22	Lloyd Dane	Dane '51 Ford		450	Running
4	12	11	Freddie Lee	Advance Electric '48 Pontiac		450	Running
5	22	16	Fred Steinbroner	Bob Carpenter '50 Ford		200	Running
6	3	1	Erick Erickson	Advance Electric '51 Pontiac		150	
7	14		Hal Cole	'50 Mercury		125	
8	7	98	Freddie Farmer	Johnny Mantz '51 Nash Amb.		100	
9	16	18	Bill Stammer	Charles Roscoe '49 Plymouth		75	
10	18	27	Jim Byrd	El Paso Special '49 Buick		50	
11	11		Hershel McGriff	'51 Olds		25	
12	17	72	Bill Stickler	J & M Garage '48 Hudson		25	
13	5	9	Dick Meyer	Grant Sniffen '50 Mercury		25	
14	4	6	Ray Chase	Oster-Barry '51 Hudson		25	
15	10	69	Bob Carpenter	Carpenter '48 Ford		25	
16	19	19	Les Bomar	V-Gap Spark Plug '49 Plymouth		25	
17	13	10	Allen Heath	Smith & Jones '49 Ford		25	Engine
18	6	12	Danny Weinberg	Warren Fraser '50 Ford		25	
19	21	3	Stan Noble	Noble '51 Henry J		25	
20	15	17	Al Jacobs	'50 Ford		25	
21	20		Jess Anderson	Dodge		25	
22	2	2jr.	George Seeger	Tony Sampo '51 Studebaker	2	25	Crash

Time of Race:
Average Speed:
Pole Winner: Lou Figaro - 76.988 mph
Lap Leaders: Lou Figaro 1-200
Cautions: 1   Margin of Victory: 100 yards   Attendance: 12,000

Race No. 14

Teague Grand
At Grand Rapids

GRAND RAPIDS, MI (July 1) -- Marshall Teague scampered into the lead in the 23rd lap and finished first in the 100-miler at Grand River Speedrome in Grand Rapids, MI. It was the fifth win of the season for the Daytona Beach Hudson driver

Dick Rathmann followed Teague across the finish line to take second place. Fonty Flock came in third and pole sitter Tim Flock fourth, who held on to a 295 point lead in the standings. Fifth place went to Lloyd Moore.

Tim led the first 22 laps with Fonty in hot pursuit. Teague muscled his Hudson pat the Flock brothers in one swoop in the 23rd lap. He led the rest of the way despite pitting twice.

Bob Greeg flipped his Plymouth early, halting the race for 15 minutes. No official time was kept due to the red flag.

Teague's triumph enabled him to move to within 392.5 points of leader Tim Flock. Herb Thomas was a distant fourth in the standings, 847 points behind the leader.

Grand National Race No. 14
200 Laps at Grand River Speedrome
Grand Rapids, MI
100 Miles on Half-mile Dirt Track
July 1, 1951

Fin	St	No.	Driver	Team / Car	Laps	Money	Status
1	3	6	Marshall Teague	Teaguemobile '51 Hudson	200	$1,000	Running
2		120	Dick Rathmann	Walt Chapman '51 Hudson		700	Running
3	2	14	Fonty Flock	Red Devil '50 Olds 88		450	Running
4	1	91	Tim Flock	Black Phantom '51 Olds 88		350	Running
5		59	Lloyd Moore	Julian Buesink '51 Ford		200	Running
6	6	42	Lee Petty	Petty Special '50 Plymouth		150	
7	4	23	Frank Mundy	Perry Smith '51 Studebaker		125	
8		27	Jimmy Florian	Euclid Motor Co. '50 Ford		100	
9			Quinton Daniels			75	
10	5	T-3	Tommy Lane	'51 Buick Roadmaster		50	
11		92	Herb Thomas	Thomas '51 Plymouth		25	
12		93	Donald Thomas	Thomas '50 Plymouth		25	
13		25	Dick Linder	Don Rogala '50 Olds 88		25	
14		33	Wally Campbell	Wally Marks '50 Olds 88		25	
15			Don Bailey	'50 Olds 88		25	
16		10	Jim Fieblekorn	'50 Mercury		25	
17			Bub King	'51 Plymouth		25	
18			Ray Duhigg	'50 Plymouth		25	
19		72	Wade Fields	Harold Mays '51 Plymouth		25	
20			Gene Comstock	'50 Olds 88		25	
21		60	Don Eggert	Julian Buesink '50 Ford		25	
22			Bob Greer	Plymouth		25	Crash

* Positions 11-22 are not necessarily in the correct final order. Number of starters unknown.
Time of Race: None Recorded
Average Speed: None Recorded
Pole Winner: Tim Flock - 84.3 mph
Lap Leaders: Tim Flock 1-22, Marshall Teague 23 -200
Cautions: Margin of Victory: Attendance: 7,653

Race No. 15

Fonty Breezes, Bags
Bainbridge Bucks

BAINBRIDGE, OH (July 8) -- Fonty Flock breezed uncontested to win the 100-mile Grand National event on the one-mile dirt track at the Bainbridge Fairgrounds.

Dick Rathmann challenged Flock early but had to settle for runner-up. Frank Mundy wound up in third place, Jimmy Florian was fourth and Oda Greene came in fifth.

Flock's win was his fourth in Grand National competition. He started on the pole for the seventh time in his career.

In a peculiar series of relief assignments, Marshall Teague took over for Herb Thomas on the 41st lap and brought his Plymouth home 12th. Thomas, who became fatigued when he called for Teague's help, later hopped into Norm McCarthy's Plymouth, finishing eighth. NASCAR's point system enabled relief drivers to pick up extra points, pro-rated on the percentage of laps they actually drove.

Point leader Tim Flock fell out early and failed to earn any points. Fonty cut the spread between himself and younger brother Tim to 95.5 points.

Flock averaged 65.753 mph for his flag-to-flag victory.

Spectators mill around Ralph Liguori's wrecked Ford which cleared the guard rail at Heidelberg Raceway and landed in a ditch.

Grand National Race No. 15
100 Laps at Bainbridge Fairgrounds
Bainbridge, OH
100 Miles on 1-mile Dirt Track
July 8, 1951

Fin	St	No.	Driver	Team / Car	Laps	Money	Status
1	1	14	Fonty Flock	Red Devil '50 Olds 88	100	$1,000	Running
2		120	Dick Rathmann	Walt Chapman '51 Hudson		700	Running
3		23	Frank Mundy	Perry Smith '51 Studebaker		450	Running
4		27	Jimmy Florian	Euclid Motor Co. '51 Ford		350	
5		22	Oda Greene	'51 Hudson Hornet		200	Running
6		42	Lee Petty	Petty Special '50 Plymouth		150	
7		10	Jim Fieblekorn	'51 Mercury		125	
8			Norm McCarthy *	'51 Plymouth		100	
9			Lyle Scott	'50 Lincoln		75	
10			Jim Romine	'50 Ford		50	
11		59	Lloyd Moore	Julian Buesink '50 Ford		25	
12		92	Herb Thomas **	Thomas '51 Plymouth		25	
13			Ray Duhigg	'50 Plymouth		25	
14			Quinton Daniels			25	
15			Dick Bailey	'50 Ford		25	
16			Dick Stone	'51 Ford		25	
17			Joe Carver			25	
18			Jerry Carver			25	
19		25	Dick Linder	Don Rogala '50 Olds 88		25	
20		91	Tim Flock	Black Phantom '51 Olds 88		25	
21			Bub King	'51 Plymouth		25	
22			Dan Daniels	Don Rogala '50 Olds 88		25	
23		54	Don Dailey	'50 Olds 88		25	
24			Don Eggert	Julian Buesink '50 Ford		25	
25		33	Wally Campbell	Wally Marks '50 Olds 88		25	
26			Mike Klapak			25	
27			Bob Moore	'50 Olds 88		25	
28			Jack Kabat			25	
29		72	Wade Fields	Harold Mays '50 Plymouth		25	
30			Gene Comstock	'50 Olds 88		25	
31		6	Marshall Teague	Teaguemobile '51 Hudson	41	10	
32			Bob Greer	'50 Olds 88		10	
33			Elmer Wilson	'48 Buick		10	
34			Bill Majot	Jim White '50 Chevrolet		10	

* Relieved by Herb Thomas
** Relieved by Marshall Teague
Time of Race: 1 hour, 31 minutes, 15 seconds
Average Speed: 65.753 mph
Pole Winner: Fonty Flock -
Lap Leaders: Fonty Flock 1-100
Cautions: Margin of Victory: Attendance:
Note: Drivers listed in positions 21-34 are not necessarily in correct finish order

Race No. 16

Thomas Takes Crash-marred Event at Heidelberg

HEIDELBERG, PA (July 15) -- Herb Thomas of Olivia, NC snared his first Grand National win of the year by taking first place in the 100-mile grind at Heidelberg Speedway.

Thomas avoided the spills and mechanical ills that beset 24 drivers in the starting field of 42, and moved into contention for the national driving title. Tim and Fonty Flock, leading in the point standings, both fell out early in a 21st lap crash and earned no points. Thomas retained his fourth spot in the standings, 590.5 points behind Tim Flock.

Jim Fieblekorn finished 2nd at Heidelberg for his best Grand National effort.

Thomas, who borrowed an Olds from Hubert Westmoreland for this event, drove around Fonty Flock in the 22nd lap and led the rest of the way. The Flock brothers, Wally Campbell, Dick Linder and Ralph Liguori all crashed heavily in the 21st lap. The scoring stand was destroyed, and Campbell was rushed to Allegheny Hospital with deep cuts on his arm and face. Fonty suffered a cut over his eye. Debris flew into the grandstands, injuring spectator John Fairman of Pitts-

Wally Campbell was hurt in Heidelberg crash

burgh. Liguori's Ford flew over the guard rail and landed in a ditch.

Jim Fieblekorn's Mercury was a surprise second place finisher. Augie Walackas wound up third, Bud Farrell was fourth and Tom Jerris fifth, as non-headliners grabbed four of the top five positions.

Race No. 17

Fonty Wins Weaverville; Regains Point Lead

WEAVERVILLE, NC   (July 29) -- Fonty Flock of Decatur, GA drove his Red Devil Oldsmobile to victory in the 100-mile Grand National race at Asheville-Weaverville Speedway, taking the lead in the point standings.

Tim Flock, leader in the standings for much of the season, continued his sour luck and finished 11th. Fonty left Weaverville with a 88.5 point lead in the standings that determine the champion.

Gober Sosebee finished second to Fonty in the 200 lapper. Herb Thomas came in third, Frank Mundy was fourth and Speedy Thompson fifth.

Grand National Race No. 16
200 Laps at Heidelberg Speedway
Heidelberg, PA
100 Miles on Half-mile Dirt Track
July 15, 1951

Fin	St	No.	Driver	Team / Car	Laps	Money	Status
1		2	Herb Thomas	Westmoreland '51 Olds 88	200	$1,000	Running
2		10	Jim Fieblekorn	'51 Mercury	199	700	Running
3			Augie Walackas	'51 Mercury		450	Running
4			Bud Farrell	'51 Plymouth		350	Running
5			Tom Jerris	'51 Buick		200	Running
6			Jack Flynn			150	
7			Bob Deitrich			125	
8			Dick Moffitt			100	
9			Harry Scott			75	
10			Charles Gilman	'51 Hudson Hornet		50	
11			Jerry Carver			25	
12			Nelson Applegate			25	
13			Ted Chamberlain	'50 Plymouth		25	
14			Whitey Worton			25	
15			Jack White			25	
16			Charles Kleber			25	
17			Gus Linder			25	
18		19	Joe Merola	'51 Olds 88		25	
19		59	Lloyd Moore	Julian Buesink '51 Ford		25	
20		121	John McGinley	Walt Chapman '51 Hudson Hornet		25	
21		42	Lee Petty	Lee Petty Special '51 Plymouth		25	
22			Quinton Daniels			25	
23			Art Knoll			25	
24			Jim Romine	'50 Ford		25	
25		102	Ray Duhigg	'50 Plymouth		25	
26			Dan Daniels	Don Rogala '50 Olds 88		25	
27			Tommy Lane			25	
28			Bub King	'51 Plymouth		25	
29			Sam Thompson		52	25	Crash
30		23	Frank Mundy	Perry Smith '51 Studebaker		25	
31		120	Dick Rathmann	Walt Chapman '51 Hudson		10	
32			Norm McCarthy	'51 Plymouth		10	
33		81	Roscoe Hough	'50 Ford		10	
34			Paul Pettit			10	
35			Nick Garin			10	
36	1	14	Fonty Flock	Red Devil '50 Olds 88	21	10	Crash
37		91	Tim Flock	Black Phantom '51 Olds 88	21	10	Crash
38	3	33	Wally Campbell	Wally Marks '50 Olds 88	21	10	Crash
39	2	25	Dick Linder	Don Rogala '50 Olds 88	21	10	Crash
40		00	Ralph Liguori	'50 Ford	20	10	Crash
41			Dick Bailey			---	
42			Mike Klapak			---	

Time of Race: Not recorded due to 6-car crash
Average Speed: None
Pole Winner: Fonty Flock - 61.983 mph
Lap Leaders: Fonty Flock 1-21, Herb Thomas 22-200
Cautions: Margin of Victory: 1-plus Lap   Attendance: 9,500
* Drivers listed 21-42 are not necessarily in correct finish positions

Grand National Race No. 17
200 Laps at Asheville-Weaverville Speedway
Weaverville, NC
100 Miles on Half-mile Dirt Track
July 29, 1951

Fin	St	No.	Driver	Team / Car	Laps	Money	Status
1	1	14	Fonty Flock	Red Devil '51 Olds 88	200	$1,000	Running
2		51	Gober Sosebee	Cherokee Garage '50 Olds 88		700	Running
3		92	Herb Thomas	Thomas '50 Plymouth		450	Running
4		23	Frank Mundy	Perry Smith '51 Studebaker		350	Running
5			Speedy Thompson	'51 Studebaker		200	Running
6			Bub King	'51 Plymouth		150	
7		217	Bill Miller	'51 Ford		125	
8			Billy Myers	'51 Ford		100	
9		16	Bill Snowden	Snowden '51 Olds 88		75	
10		7	Bob Flock	Gray Ghost '51 Olds 88		50	
11		91	Tim Flock	Black Phantom '51 Olds 88		25	
12			Barney Smith	'50 Plymouth		25	
13		98	Jack Smith	Westmoreland '50 Plymouth		25	
14		133	Bobby Booth	'50 Olds 88		25	
15		60	Jim Paschal	Julian Buesink '50 Ford		25	
16			Bobby Myers	'49 Ford		25	
17		80	Sonny Black	'50 Plymouth		25	
18		72	Weldon Adams	Harold Mays '50 Plymouth		25	
19		82	Joe Eubanks	Oates Motor Co. '50 Olds 88		25	
20		2	Ewell Weddle	'50 Ford		25	
21			Leon Harrell	'50 Ford		25	
22			Paul Austin	'50 Ford		25	
23		4	Gayle Warren	Blevins Motor Co. '51 Studebaker		25	
24			Charles Moore	'49 Kaiser		25	
25		42	Lee Petty	Lee Petty Special '51 Plymouth		25	
26			Billy Carden	'50 Olds 88		25	
27			Wade Fields	Harold Mays '50 Plymouth		25	
28		10	Jim Fieblekorn	'51 Mercury		25	
29		6	Marshall Teague	Teaguemobile '51 Hudson		25	
30		59	Lloyd Moore	Julian Buesink '50 Ford		25	

Time of Race:
 Average Speed:
 Pole Winner: Billy Carden - 64.608 mph (Qualified Fonty Flock's Car)
 Lap Leaders: - - - - - - - - - Fonty Flock -200
 Cautions: Margin of Victory: Attendance: 8,500
* Drivers listed in positions 25-30 are not necessarily in correct finish position

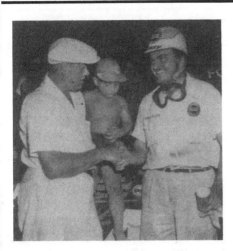

Fonty Flock receives congratulations from car owner Frank Christian after Asheville-Weaverville triumph.

A crowd of 8,500 braved threatening weather to watch the 30-car field dice it out at what has been described as the "world's first drive-in speedway". Billy Carden qualified Flock's car on the pole with a speed of 64.608.

Flock took the controls for the race.

Grand National Race No. 18
200 Laps at Monroe County Fairgrounds
Rochester, NY
100 Miles on Half-mile Dirt Track
July 31, 1951

Fin	St	No.	Driver	Team / Car	Laps	Money	Status
1		42	Lee Petty	Petty Special '51 Plymouth	200	$1,000	Running
2			Charles Gattalia	'51 Ford		700	Running
3			Ronnie Kohler	'51 Plymouth		450	Running
4		54	Don Bailey	'51 Studebaker		350	Running
5		81	Roscoe Hough	'51 Ford		200	Running
6			Bill Rexford	'51 Olds 88		150	
7			Chuck Stimus			125	
8		93	Ted Chamberlain	Chamberlain '50 Plymouth		100	
9			Ernie Yorton			75	
10		25	Dick Linder	Don Rogala '50 Olds 88		50	
11		1	Walt Sprague	'50 Ford		25	
12			Quinton Daniels			25	
13			James Shields			25	
14	1	14	Fonty Flock	Red Devil '50 Olds 88	101	25	Sway Bar
15		92	Herb Thomas	Thomas '51 Plymouth		25	
16		59	Lloyd Moore	Julian Buesink '51 Ford		25	
17		10	Jim Fieblekorn	'51 Mercury		25	
18			Dick Moffitt			25	
19			Fran Jeschke			25	
20			Jack Flynn			25	
21			Ed Benedict			25	
22			Fred Faber			25	
23		23	Frank Mundy	Perry Smith '51 Studebaker		25	
24		21	Jim Delaney	Bob Oseicki '51 Mercury	200	--	Disqualify

* Jim Delaney finished 2nd, but was disqualified for having an illegal cam shaft

Time of Race:
Average Speed
Pole Winner: Fonty Flock
Lap Leaders: Fonty Flock 1-101, Lee Petty 102-200
Cautions: Margin of Victory: Attendance:

Race No. 18

Flock Breaks Down; Petty Grabs Rochester Race

ROCHESTER, NY (July 31) -- Lee Petty worked his way into victory lane for the first time in the '51 season by coming out on top in the 100-miler at the Monroe County Fairgrounds.

The Randleman, NC Plymouth ace took the lead in the 102nd lap when leader Fonty Flock went behind the wall with a broken sway bar. Flock had won the pole position for the ninth time in his career and led the first 101 laps.

Jim Delaney crossed the finish line in second place, but his Bob Osiecki-prepared Mercury was disqualified for being equipped with a non-stock cam shaft. Charles Gattalia was elevated to runner-up honors. Ronnie Kohler was credited with third, Don Bailey was fourth, and Pappy Hough took fifth.

Jim Delaney finished 2nd at Rochester, but was disqualified.

Fonty held onto the point lead as Tim Flock did not enter.

Top threats Herb Thomas, Frank Mundy and Lloyd Moore ran into an assortment of problems and did not finish.

Race No. 19

Flock Ups Point Lead With Altamont Victory

ALTAMONT, NY (Aug 1) -- Fonty Flock rebounded and renewed his quest for the Grand National championship by winning the 100-miler at Altamont Speedway for his fifth win of the year.

The Decatur, GA veteran pushed his point lead to 293.5 points over Tim Flock, who has cut back his racing efforts due to a string of tough luck.

Herb Thomas finished second and remained third in the point standings, 558 points behind the leader. Lee Petty finished third, Perry Smith, driving his own Studebaker, finished fourth and Jerry Morese came in fifth.

The 100-mile victory was the fifth of the season and the sixth in Flock's Grand National career.

Lloyd Moore, who has been mired in a strong of sour

luck, wound up last after mechanical problems side-lined his Ford.

Grand National Race No. 19
200 Laps at Altamont Speedway
Altamont, NY
100 Miles on Half-mile Dirt Track
August 1, 1951

Fin	St	No.	Driver	Team / Car	Laps	Money	Status
1		14	Fonty Flock	Red Devil '51 Olds	200	$1,000	Running
2		92	Herb Thomas	Thomas '51 Plymouth		700	Running
3		42	Lee Petty	Lee Petty Special '51 Plymouth		450	Running
4		23	Perry Smith	Perry Smith '51 Studebaker		350	Running
5		227	Jerry Morese	'51 Ford		200	Running
6		81	Roscoe Hough	Hough '51 Ford		150	
7			Dick Moffitt			125	
8			Wimpy Ervin			100	
9			Jim Little			75	
10		25	Dick Linder	Don Rogala '50 Olds		50	
11			Hully Bunn			25	
12			Ronnie Kohler	'50 Plymouth		25	
13		54	Don Bailey	'51 Ford		25	
14			Ed Benedict	'51 Hudson		25	
15			Tommy Elliott			25	
16			Victor Brenzelli			25	
17			Rod Therrian			25	
18		67	Jim Reed	Reed '51 Ford		25	
19			Quinton Daniels			25	
20		59	Lloyd Moore	Julian Buesink '51 Ford		25	

Time of Race:
Average Speed:
Pole Winner:
Lap Leaders: - - - - - - - - - Fonty Flock   -200
Cautions: Margin of Victory: Attendance:

Race No. 20

Thompson Survives Motor City Mayhem

DETROIT, MI (Aug.12) -- Tommy Thompson survived a motorized rubdown with Curtis Turner during an epic slugfest for the lead and beat out Joe Eubanks to win the Motor City 250 Grand National race at the Michigan State Fairgrounds.

The 250-miler on the flat one-mile dirt track in the metropolis of Detroit was one of the most anticipated events with representatives from every automobile manufacturer attending the spectacle.

Tommy Thompson.

Grand National Race No. 20
250 Laps at Michigan Fairgrounds
Detroit, MI
"Motor City 250"
250 Miles on 1-mile Dirt Track
August 12, 1951

Fin	St	No.	Driver	Team / Car	Laps	Money	Status
1	5	40	Tommy Thompson	Thompson '51 Chrysler	250	*$5,000	Running
2	13	82	Joe Eubanks	Phil Oates '50 Olds 88	250	2,000	Running
3	15	98	Johnny Mantz	Mantz '51 Nash Ambassador	244	1,000	Running
4	25	83	Red Byron	Dantone Racing Stbl '50 Ford	241	600	Running
5	38	43	Paul Newkirk	'51 Nash Amb.	241	500	Running
6	47	34	Jack Goodwin	'51 Plymouth	239	400	Running
7	22	59	Lloyd Moore	Julian Buesink '51 Olds 88	239	300	Running
8	20	50	Ewell Weddle	'50 Ford	236	200	Running
9	30	41	Curtis Turner	Eanes Motor Co. '51 Olds 88	233	100	Heating
10	45	1-X	Erick Erickson	Packer '51 Pontiac	233	100	Running
11	56	135	Bill Majot	Jim White '50 Chevrolet	233	50	Running
12	52	10	Jim Fieblekorn	'51 Mercury	233	50	Running
13	44	42	Lee Petty	Petty Special '51 Plymouth	233	50	Running
14	14	33	Lou Figaro	Jack Gaynor '51 Hudson	231	50	Running
15	32	142	Bob Myers	St. Mary's '51 Packard	230	50	
16	55	60	Jim Paschal	Julian Buesink '50 Ford	228	25	
17	2	91	Tim Flock	Black Phantom '51 Olds 88	228	125	
18	54	67	Bob Jeffries	'51 Lincoln	225	25	
19	43	120	John McGinley	Walt Chapman '51 Hudson	224	25	
20	8	7	Bob Flock	Gray Ghost '51 Olds 88	223	25	
21	35	151	Les Snow	Snow '50 Olds	222	25	
22	33	38	Iggy Katona	'51 Ford	222	25	
23	39	88	Del Pearson	'51 Olds 88	216	25	
24	41	85	Bob Prince	'50 Hudson	199	25	
25	34	2	Bobby Myers	'51 Hudson Hornet	199	25	
26	37	22	Oda Greene	'51 Hudson Hornet	173	25	
27	48	48	Johnny Barker	'51 Studebaker	173	25	
28	46	102	Ray Duhigg	'51 Olds 88	167	25	
29	53	65	Jack White	'50 Olds 88	158	25	
30	27	36	Danny Letner	Bert Letner '51 Hudson	153	25	Heating
31	51	140	Walt Flanders	"See Floyd Rice" Ford	145	10	
32	10	12	Billy Carden	'50 Olds 88	142	10	
33	1	6	Marshall Teague	Teaguemobile '51 Hudson	136	10	Heating
34	17	18	George Seeger	George Mtrs. '51 Studebaker	133	10	
35	4	14	Fonty Flock	Red Devil '51 Olds	130	10	Crash
36	12	75	Bob Greer	Connell Cadillac '50 Olds 88	126	---	Crash
37	49	44	Jack Smith	Dantone Racing Stbl '51 Ply	123	---	Crash
38	42	198	Billy Myers	Westmoreland '51 Plymouth	123	---	Crash
39	11	777	Tony Suligoy	'51 Packard	115	---	Crash
40	58	750	Al Miller	'51 Henry J	115	---	
41	29	1	Walt Sprague	'50 Olds 88	113	---	
42	3	51	Gober Sosebee	West Peach '50 Cadillac	104	---	Tie Rod
43	18	133	Bobby Booth	'50 Olds 88	103	---	
44	31	32	Tommy Melvin	'50 Olds 88	92	---	Crash
45	16	8	Bud Riley	'51 Hudson Hornet	89	---	Crash
46	23	28	Ray Chase	Oster-Barry '51 Hudson	89	---	Heating
47	24	41.5	Bill Blair	'50 Olds 88	88	---	
48	40	175	Bill Holland	Connell '51 Cadillac	80	---	Crash
49	57	30	Elmer Wilson	'50 Buick	80	---	
50	21	23	Frank Mundy	Perry Smith '51 Studebaker	80	---	Crash
51	50	9	Freddie Farmer	Tom's Grill '51 Nash Amb.	77	---	
52	9	90	Jim Rathmann	'50 Packard	76	---	
53	26	118	Edward Benedict	'51 Hudson Hornet	75	---	Heating
54	28	11	Hershel McGriff	Superior '51 Olds 88	73	---	Crash
55	59	21	Dick Rathmann	Walt Chapman '51 Hudson	31	---	Heating
56	36	70	Johnny Wohlfiel	'51 Nash Amb.	27	---	
57	6	92	Herb Thomas	Thomas '51 Hudson	26	---	Heating
58	7	31	Jesse J. Taylor	Jesse James '51 Hudson	14	---	Heating
59	19	188	Pat Flaherty	'51 Olds 88	13	---	

* Plus a 1951 Packard Convertible valued at $3,700
Time of Race: 4 hours, 20 minutes, 28 seconds
Average Speed: 57.588 mph
Pole Winner: Marshall Teague - 1:44.15 (2 Laps), 69.131 mph
Fastest Qualifier: Frank Mundy - 1:43:21, 69.760 mph
Lap Leaders: Marshall Teague 1, Fonty Flock 2-24, Tommy Thompson 25-26, F. Flock 27, Thompson 28, F. Flock 29, Thompson 30-63, F. Flock 64-95, Gober Sosebee 96-102, F. Flock 103-130, Curtis Turner 131-212, Thompson 213-215, Turner 216-225, Joe Eubanks 226-232, Thompson 233-250
Cautions: 5   Margin of Victory: 37 seconds   Attendance: 16,352

The moment of truth in the Motor City 250 -- Tommy Thompson forges ahead of a smoking Curtis Turner after their rubdown 25 laps from the finish. Thompson went on to score his first Grand National win. Turner limped a few more laps before retiring with overheating problems. He had suffered a broken radiator in the mishap.

Thompson of Louisville, KY, was not intimidated by the presence of the rough-house Turner and was up to the challenge of the nation's famed master of the powerslide. Thompson and Turner plowed hard into each other with 25 miles to go and both spun into the wooden retaining wall. Eubanks swept into the lead on lap 226 as Thompson and Turner scrambled to get back in the race. Thompson was able to resume his hot pace, but Turner's Oldsmobile suffered a cracked radiator that eventually put him out of action.

Thompson ran down Eubanks, who had no idea he was leading, with 18 laps remaining and sped under the checkered flag first to snare the $5,000 top prize. Eubanks, motoring along at a conservative pace, finished

second, 37 seconds behind the winner. Johnny Mantz came in third, six laps down. Red Byron was fourth, nine laps back and Paul Newkirk, driving in his first Grand National race, was fifth.

A crowd of 16,352 filled the covered grandstands and watched the lead change hands 14 times, a Grand National record. A total of 59 cars went to the post in the $12,500 event.

There were many accidents in the race, most involving several cars. Fonty Flock was leading when his Olds was pancaked in a 10-car smash-up on lap 130. Flock was not injured. Others involved included Jack Smith, Billy Myers and Bill Holland. Lee Petty flipped his Plymouth in a later wreck, but faithfully carried out

Lee Petty rolled his Plymouth at Detroit but still managed to finish 13th.

his assignment and finished 13th.

Marshall Teague started on the pole with a speed of 69.131 mph, but his Hudson overheated after 136 laps. He wound up 33rd.

Overheating problems also took Herb Thomas' new Hudson out after only 26 laps.

Fonty Flock held a narrow point lead over Tim Flock in the point standings.

With 15 makes of cars in the starting field, the race had drawn the attention of nearly everyone who owned an automobile. Chrysler Corporation won the day with Thompson's victory.

Five caution flags slowed the winner's speed to 57.588 mph.

Fonty fell to second, losing a 293.5 point lead in two weeks.

Del Pearson finished second, with Oda Greene, Lou Figaro and Herb Thomas completing the top five.

Jesse James Taylor, driving his second race of the year in his high-powered Hudson, took the lead in the second lap from Fonty Flock. The two engaged in a spine-tingling struggle. Fonty was back on top by the fifth lap and held the top spot for 128 laps, when his bid was ended by mechanical problems. Tim, who started fourth, moved into the lead on lap 134 and was never headed.

Flock averaged 50.847 mph as two cautions slowed the field.

Del Pearson finished 2nd at Toledo.

Jack Smith's Plymouth was heavily damaged in big 130th lap pile-up at Detroit.

Race No. 21

Tim's Slump
Ends at Toledo

TOLEDO, OH (Aug 19) -- Tim Flock ended his eight week slump by gunning his Olds to victory in the 100-mile Grand National race at Ft. Miami Speedway.

The win moved Flock back on top of the point standings as pole sitter Fonty Flock failed to finish.

Grand National Race No. 21
200 Laps at Ft. Miami Speedway
Toledo, OH
100 Miles on Half-mile Dirt Track
August 19, 1951

Fin	St	No.	Driver	Team / Car	Laps	Money	Status
1	4	91	Tim Flock	Black Phantom '51 Olds 88	200	$1,000	Running
2		88	Del Pearson	'51 Plymouth		700	Running
3		22	Oda Greene	'51 Hudson Hornet		450	Running
4		33	Lou Figaro	Jack Gaynor '51 Hudson Hornet		350	Running
5		92	Herb Thomas	Thomas '51 Plymouth		200	Running
6	8	40	Tommy Thompson	'Thompson '51 Chrysler		150	
7	2	31	Jesse James Taylor	Jess James '51 Hudson Hornet		125	
8		18	George Seeger	George's Motors '51 Studebaker		100	
9		27	Jimmy Florian	Euclid Motor Co. '50 Ford		75	
10		3	Jimmy Ayers	'50 Plymouth		50	
11			Don Eggert	'51 Plymouth		25	
12		10	Jim Fieblekorn	'51 Mercury		25	
13			Herb Gott	Plymouth		25	
14		54	Don Bailey	'50 Ford	151	25	Crash
15		120	John McGinley	Walt Chapman '51 Hudson		25	
16		66	Bud Riley	Northeast '52 Hudson Hornet	149	25	Crash
17			Dick Moffitt		142	25	Wheel
18	1	14	Fonty Flock	Red Devil '51 Olds	133	25	
19		188	O. Jones	'50 Ford		25	Crash
20		38	Iggy Katona	Jolly Cartage Co. '51 Olds		25	Crash
21		1	Walt Sprague	'51 Olds		25	
22		25	Dick Linder	Don Rogala '50 Olds		25	
23			Paul Parks			25	
24		59	Lloyd Moore	Julian Buesink '51 Ford		25	
25		121	Dick Rathmann	Walt Chapman '51 Hudson		25	
26			Bob James		55	25	Wheel
27		82	Joe Eubanks	Phil Oates '50 Olds		25	
28		102	Ray Duhigg	'51 Plymouth	46	25	Wheel
29		42	Lee Petty	Petty Special '51 Plymouth		25	
30			Norm McCarthy			25	
31		28	Ray Chase	Oster-Barry '51 Hudson	28	10	Wheel
32			Bob Moore	'51 Olds		10	
33		23	Frank Mundy	Perry Smith '51 Studebaker		10	

Time of Race: 1 hour, 58 minutes, 00 seconds
Average Speed: 50.847 mph
Pole Winner: Fonty Flock - 55.521 mph
Lap Leaders: Fonty Flock 1, Jesse James Taylor 2-4, F. Flock 5-133, Tim Flock 134-200.
Cautions: 2   Margin of Victory: Attendance:

Race No. 22

Morristown Falls To Tim Flock

MORRISTOWN, NJ (Aug 24) -- Tim Flock, who sat out two races in order to get his act back together, won his second straight since his return in the 100-miler at Morristown Speedway.

Flock took the lead from his brother, Fonty, in the

Grand National Race No. 22
200 Laps at Morristown Speedway
Morristown, NJ
100 Miles on Half-mile Dirt Track
August 24, 1951

Fin	St	No.	Driver	Team / Car	Laps	Money	Status
1	1	91	Tim Flock	Black Phantom '51 Olds 88	200	$1,000	Running
2		42	Lee Petty	Petty Special '51 Plymouth		700	Running
3			Ronnie Kohler	'51 Plymouth		450	Running
4			John DuBois	'50 Plymouth		350	Running
5		21	Jim Delaney	Bob Oseicki '50 Ford		200	Running
6		421	Jack Reynolds	Wiss Brothers '50 Plymouth		150	
7		22	Oda Greene	'51 Hudson Hornet		125	
8			Dick Eagan	'50 Plymouth		100	
9		77	Chuck Mahoney	'51 Henry J		75	
10			Augie Walackas	'51 Olds		50	
11		227	Jerry Morese	'51 Ford		25	
12			Tommy Elliott	'51 Henry J		25	
13			Paul Erwin	'51 Henry J		25	
14		54	Don Bailey	'51 Studebaker		25	
15			Charles Gattalia	'51 Ford		25	
16			Jim Hart	'51 Kaiser		25	
17			Lou Volk	'51 Henry J		25	
18			Jack Bellinato	'50 Mercury		25	
19			Paul Pettitt	'50 Plymouth		25	
20			Richard Hancock	'50 Mercury		25	
21		70	Bud Farrell	William Gundaker '51 Plymouth		25	
22		1	Bill Rexford	Julian Buesink '51 Olds		25	
23		23	Frank Mundy	Perry Smith '51 Studebaker		25	
24		66	Roscoe Hough	Hough '51 Ford		25	
25		52	Neil Cole			25	
26		82	Joe Eubanks	Phil Oates '51 Hudson Hornet		25	
27			Reino Tulonen	'51 Henry J		25	
28		59	Lloyd Moore	Julian Buesink '51 Ford		25	
29		92	Herb Thomas	Thomas '51 Plymouth		25	
30	2	14	Fonty Flock	Red Devil '51 Olds	94	25	Crash
31			Nick Nicolette			10	
32			Charles Dyer			10	
33		120	Dick Rathmann	Walt Chapman '51 Hudson Hornet		10	
34			Nelson Applegate			10	
35		33	Wally Campbell	Wally Marks '51 Olds		10	
36			Tommy Coates			10	
37			Frankie Schneider			10	
38			Harold Strapp			10	
39			Jim Metzler			10	
40			Bob Read			10	
41			Jack White			10	
42			Tommy Correnti			10	
43			Don Rudolph			10	
44			Len Brown			10	

Time of Race:
Average Speed;
Pole Winner: Tim Flock - 58.670 mph
Lap Leaders: Tim Flock 1-3, Fonty Flock 4-89, T. Flock 90-200
Cautions: Margin of Victory: Attendance: 7,000
Drivers listed in positions 21-44 are not necessarily in correct finish order

90th lap and stayed on top of the leaderboard the rest of the day. Lee Petty finished second, Ronnie Kohler was third, John DuBois fourth and Jim Delaney fifth.

Fonty Flock was holding down second place when his Oldsmobile flipped in the second turn. He was not hurt in the mishap. Herb Thomas, Frank Mundy and Bill Rexford were other top drivers who failed to finish.

Wally Campbell, who was seriously injured in a July 15th race at Heidelberg, PA, made his first start since the crash, but mechanical ills took him out of the fray.

Tim Flock scored 2nd win in row at Morristown.

In other developments, Walt Sprague, 25, of Wellsville, NY, who had given such a good account of himself in the June 24th 100-miler at Dayton, OH, was killed in a 50 lap Modified race at Rochester, NY on the same day.

Race No. 23

Bob Flock Grabs First Win in Two Years

GREENVILLE, SC (Aug 25) -- Bob Flock of Atlanta drove his Gray Ghost Oldsmobile to victory in the 100-miler at Greenville-Pickens Speedway. It was Flock's first Grand National triumph since the '49 season finale at North Wilkesboro.

Tim Flock finished second, Buck Baker wound up

Bob Flock and his 'Gray Ghost' Oldsmobile.

third, while Fonty Flock and Erick Erickson were fourth and fifth.

Tim Flock's runner-up effort enabled him to pad his point lead in the point standings race.

Bob Flock gave Oldsmobile its 13th victory in the last 21 Grand National events. It was also Olds' 20th short track victory in the 36 events staged on tracks under .75 mile.

Pole sitter Frank Mundy leads 82-car field at the start of 2nd annual Southern 500.

Grand National Race No. 23
200 Laps at Greenville-Pickens Speedway
Greenville, SC
100 Miles on Half-mile Dirt Track
August 25, 1951

Fin	St	No.	Driver	Team / Car	Laps	Money	Status
1		7	Bob Flock	Gray Ghost '51 Olds 88	200	$1,000	Running
2		91	Tim Flock	Black Phantom '51 Olds 88		700	Running
3		87	Buck Baker	Baker '51 Plymouth		450	Running
4		14	Fonty Flock	Red Devil '51 Olds 88		350	Running
5		1-X	Erick Erickson	Packer '51 Pontiac		200	Running
6		92	Herb Thomas	Thomas '51 Plymouth		150	
7		42	Lee Petty	Petty Special '51 Plymouth		125	
8		31	Jesse James Taylor	Jesse James '51 Hudson		100	
9		120	Dick Rathmann	Walt Chapman '51 Hudson		75	
10		17	Buddy Shuman	R.H. Yandell '51 Ford		50	
11		16	Bill Snowden	Snowden '51 Ford		25	
12		93	Donald Thomas	Thomas '51 Plymouth		25	
13		23	Frank Mundy	Perry Smith '51 Studebaker		25	
14		21	Jim Delaney	Bob Oseicki '51 Ford		25	
15		41	Curtis Turner	Eanes Motor Co. '51 Olds 88		25	

* Drivers listed in positions 6-15 are not necessarily in correct order. Number of starters is unknown

Time of Race:
Average Speed:
Pole Winner:
Lap Leaders: - - - - - - - - - - - Bob Flock   -200
Cautions: Margin of Victory: Attendance:

Race No. 24
Herb and Hudson
Fabulous at Darlington

DARLINGTON, SC (Sept 3) -- Herb Thomas hopped into his hefty Hudson Hornet, took the lead from Curtis Turner in the 95th lap and romped to an effortless triumph in the second annual Southern 500 at Darlington Raceway.

It was the third win for the former truck driver, and it vaulted him into the point lead by nearly 400 markers ahead of Tim Flock, who

Herb Thomas' Hudson won on Darlington's superspeedway.

finished in 11th place some 21 laps behind the winner.

Thomas started second on the grid and jumped past pole sitter Frank Mundy in the opening lap as the 82 cars scrambled for position. Hot-shot rookie Jesse James Taylor moved past Thomas in the sixth lap and led through lap 11 when Hershel McGriff assumed command for one lap.

By the 13th lap, Marshall Teague, who posted the fastest qualifying time of 87.636 mph but started back in 47th place, took the lead from McGriff. Teague

Herb Thomas passes Shorty York #90 en route to Darlington victory.

made the most astonishing charge in stock car racing history, passing 46 cars in just 12 laps. The Daytona Beach daredevil took the high-side, rim-riding around his rivals in daring fashion. Teague kept his Hudson out front until the 51st lap when he blew a tire. He was battling to get back into the top 10 with less than 30 laps remaining when he crashed with Red Byron's Ford. Teague got credit for 33rd position.

Mundy qualified his Studebaker on the pole with a speed of 84.173 mph, but a loss of oil pressure knocked him out after 12 laps and he finished last in the 82 car field. Turner was foiled by engine problems and wound up 33rd. Taylor's consistent run was good enough for second place. Buddy Shuman came home third, McGriff was fourth and Fireball Roberts fifth.

Grand National Race No. 24
400 Laps at Darlington Raceway
Darlington, SC
"Southern 500"
500 Miles on 1.25-mile Paved Track
September 3, 1951

Fin	St	No.	Driver	Team / Car	Laps	Money	Status
1	2	92	Herb Thomas	Teaguemobile '51 Hudson	400	$8,800	Running
2	3	31	Jesse J. Taylor	Jesse James '51 Hudson	399	2,800	Running
3	19	17	Buddy Shuman	R.H. Yandell '51 Ford 8	391	1,500	Running
4	5	77	Hershel McGriff	'51 Olds 88	390	1,210	Running
5	7	11	Fireball Roberts	Saverance Motors '51 Ford	387	910	Running
6	38	1	Harold Kite	Julian Buesink '51 Olds 88	384	800	Running
7	27	46	Leon Sales	Westmoreland '51 Olds 88	384	700	Running
8	4	14	Fonty Flock	Red Devil '51 Olds 88	383	600	Running
9	6	16	Bill Snowden	Snowden '51 Ford 8	383	500	Running
10	55	24	Pap White	Lee Petty '51 Plymouth	383	400	Running
11	45	91	Tim Flock	Black Phantom '51 Olds 88	379	350	Running
12	16	12	Slick Smith	Frank Christian '50 Olds 88	379	240	Running
13	52	34	Jack Goodwin	Bill Caltrider '51 Plymouth	378	300	Running
14	15	8	Billy Carden	W. Peachtree Motors '50 Cad	377	300	Running
15	24	42	Lee Petty	Petty Special '51 Plymouth	373	250	Running
16	51	51	Gober Sosebee	Cherokee Garage '51 Olds 88	373	250	Running
17	47	70	Bud Farrell	William Gundaker '50 Plym	373	200	Running
18	23	99	Billy Myers	Westmoreland '51 Plymouth	373	200	Running
19	80	64	Bill Widenhouse	'51 Plymouth	371	150	Running
20	39	18	George Seeger	Tony Sampo '51 Stude	371	150	Running
21	11	4	Gayle Warren	Blevin Motor Co. '51 Stude	370	100	Crash
22	30	95	Freddie Farmer	Tom's Grill '51 Nash Amb	370	100	Running
23	82	71	Cotton Owens	'51 Plymouth	370	100	Running
24	60	83	Ed Benedict	Ken Swihart '51 Hudson	370	100	Running
25	54	83	Red Byron	Dantone Racing Stbl '51 Ford	368	100	Crash
26	29	66	Bud Riley	Northwest Mtrs. '51 Hudson	368	50	Running
27	10	7	Bob Flock	Gray Ghost '51 Olds 88	368	50	
28	62	0	Jimmie Lewallen	'51 Plymouth	367	50	
29	63	61	Tommy Melvin	Clarence Burbank '51 Olds 88	367	50	
30	31	86	Earl Moss	J.B. Watkins '51 Studebaker	366	50	
31	25	50	Ewell Weddle	Wheatley Motors '50 Ford 8	365	50	
32	48	90	Shorty York	Russ Lou '51 Nash Amb	363	50	
33	47	6	Marshall Teague	Teaguemobile '51 Hudson	361	500	Crash
34	41	78	Johnny Yountz	Westmoreland '51 Plymouth	361	50	Crash
35	49	10	Ted Swaim	Hight-Raley Motors '50 Ford 8	360	50	
36	50	67	Jim Fieblekorn	'51 Lincoln	360	50	
37	21	37	Gene Comstock	'50 Olds 88	357	50	
38	65	74	Oliver Dial	Preston Jones '51 Chevrolet	355	50	
39	22	60	Jim Paschal	Wheatley Motors '50 Ford 8	353	50	
40	79	32	Reino Tulonen	'51 Henry J	353	50	
41	61	94	Ted Chamberlain	Del Pearson '51 Plymouth	340	50	
42	73	96	J.E. Hardie	'51 Ford	339	50	
43		93	Donald Thomas	Thomas '51 Plymouth	337	50	
44	75	9	Iggy Katona	'51 Chrysler	337	50	
45	70	20	Joe Merola	'51 Olds 88	335	50	
46	76	33	Dave Anderson	Bill Caltrider '51 Kaiser	335	50	
47	57	49	Bob Pronger	Griffin Motors '50 Olds 88	332	50	
48	17	57	Jack Smith	Wally Marks '51 Olds 88	323	50	
49	78	43	Billy Tibbett	'51 Dodge	318	50	
50	69	75	Jimmy Warden	Cain-Bowman '51 Hudson	314	50	
51	58	5	Gene Darragh	Bob Griffin '50 Olds 88	309	50	
52	53	27	Gwyn Staley	The Wilkes Boys '51 Ford 6	303	50	
53	72	21	Jim Delaney	Bob Oseicki '51 Ford	294	50	
54	33	15	Erick Erickson	Packer Pontiac '51 Pontiac	281	50	
55	68	2	Bill Blair	'51 Ford 6	275	50	
56	18	87	Buck Baker	Troy Motor Co. '51 Ford 6	275	50	
57	26	41	Curtis Turner	John Eanes '51 Olds 88	272	480	Engine
58	40	72	Wade Fields	Jane Hinnant '51 Plymouth	268	50	
49	15	22	Lloyd Dane	'51 Ford	263	50	
60	64	48	Johnny Barker	Leo Sigman '51 Studebaker	258	50	
61	77	44	Buck Baity	'50 Buick	248	---	
62	8	28	Ray Chase	'50 Olds 88	237	---	
63	18	25	Jimmy Thompson	Bowie Motor Co. '51 Ford 8	236	---	
64	67	3	Jimmy Ayers	'50 Plymouth	225	---	
65	9	38	Frank Gise	B.R. Waller '51 Studebaker	215	---	Wheel
66	32	97	Sandy Lynch	'51 Ford 6	215	---	
67	28	80	Bob Johnson	I.D. Stenstrom '51 Studebaker	214	---	
68	66	89	Herb Trimble	'51 Olds 88	198	---	
69	37	55	Bub King	'50 Plymouth	149	---	
70	74	40	Tommy Thompson	A.L. Miller '51 Nash Amb.	148	---	RF Hub

Attendants rush to Red Byron - Marshall Teague crash site late in Southern 500.

West coast star George Seeger drove the Tony Sampo Studebaker to a respectable 20th place finish. While driving back to California after the race, driver Seeger and owner Sampo became involved in an argument. They stopped in Phoenix at a gas station for refueling. When Seeger went into the rest room for personal reasons, Sampo got into the car and drove off, leaving his driver flat in Pheonix with no transportation home. It was not reported how or when Seeger finally made it the rest of the way .

A crowd of 40,000 congregated on the humid flats of Darlington and watched Thomas cover the 500 miles at an average speed of 76.906 mph. Four cautions for a total of 26 laps, interrupted the hot pace.

Johnny Yountz flipped Hubert Westmoreland's Plymouth late in Darlington's Southern 500.

Fin	St	No.	Driver	Team / Car	Laps	Money	Status
71	34	52	Bill Rexford	George Hartley '50 Olds 88	143	---	
72	81	58	Fred Moore	Walt Jarrod '51 Mercury	112	---	
73	46	26	Weldon Adams	Leland Colvin '51 Plymouth	104	---	
74	36	47	Murrace Walker	'51 Studebaker	104	---	
75	72	82	Joe Eubanks	Phil Oates '51 Olds 88	92	---	
76	35	98	Johnny Mantz	Mantz '51 Nash Amb.	88	---	Valve
77	56	39	Rudy Hires	'51 Ford 6	82	---	
78	59	35	Sonny Black	'51 Plymouth	73	---	
79	13	59	Lloyd Moore	Julian Buesink '51 Ford 8	61	---	
80	42	19	Lee Connell	'51 Pontiac	58	---	Crash
81	20	73	Bobby Booth	Stanley Moore '50 Olds 88	53	---	
82	1	23	Frank Mundy	Perry Smith '51 Studebaker	12	---	Oil Press.

Time of Race: 6 hours, 30 minutes, 5 seconds
Average Speed: 76.906 mph
Pole Winner: Frank Mundy - 84.173 mph
Fastest Qualifier: Marshall Teague - 87.636 mph
Lap Leaders: Herb Thomas 1-5, Jesse James Taylor 6-11, Hershel McGriff 12,
　　Marshall Teague 13-51, Curtis Turner 52-94, H. Thomas 95-400
Cautions: 4 for 26 Laps　　Margin of Victory: 1-plus Lap　　Attendance: 40,000

Race No. 25

Flock Wins Disputed Columbia 100-miler

COLUMBIA, SC (Sept. 7) -- Tim Flock was declared the winner in a disputed 100-mile Grand National Event at Columbia Speedway. It was the sixth win of his career.

Fireball Roberts appeared to have won the race. His Ed Saverance-owned Ford was flagged the winner with Tim's Oldsmobile in second place. Flock's Ted Chester-owned team asked for a scoring check, and after an inspection of score cards, NASCAR officials declared Flock the winner.

The decision did not set too well with Saverance, who said his car was the first to finish the 200 laps on the half-mile track. Saverance refused to accept second place money of $700.

Fireball Roberts thought he had won at Columbia, but officially got 2nd.

Jimmie Lewallen finished in third place, Bob Flock was fourth and Buck Baker fifth. Officially, Flock led the last 128 laps.

Frank Mundy qualified in third place and ran with the leaders until his Perry Smith team ran out of tires. He had to withdraw on lap 104.

Herb Thomas crashed his Hudson Hornet in the 97th lap. He was not hurt in the crash.

Grand National Race No. 25
200 Laps at Columbia Speedway
Columbia, SC
100 Miles on Half-mile Dirt Track
September 7, 1951

Fin	St	No.	Driver	Team / Car	Laps	Money	Status
1	1	91	Tim Flock	Black Phantom '51 Olds	200	$1,000	Running
2	4	11	Fireball Roberts	Ed Saverance '51 Ford	200	700	Running
3		0	Jimmie Lewallen	'51 Plymouth		450	Running
4	2	7	Bob Flock	Gray Ghost '51 Olds		350	Running
5		87	Buck Baker	Griffin Motors '51 Olds		200	Running
6		93	Donald Thomas	Thomas '51 Plymouth		150	
7	12	71	Cotton Owens	'51 Plymouth		125	
8	14	70	Bud Farrell	'50 Plymouth		100	
9	10	16	Bill Snowden	Snowden '51 Ford		75	
10	8	14	Fonty Flock	Red Devil '51 Olds 88		50	
11	16	68	Del Pearson	'50 Plymouth		25	
12	9	28	Ray Chase	'50 Olds		25	
13		83	Bill Miller	'51 Ford		25	
14			Johnny Thompson	'50 Olds		25	
15			Jesse White	'51 Studebaker		25	
16	6	26	Weldon Adams	Leland Colvin '50 Plymouth		25	
17	3	23	Frank Mundy	Perry Smith '51 Studegaker	104	25	No Tires
18		42	Lee Petty	Petty Special '51 Plymouth		25	
19		55	Marshall Weatherly	Blythe Motors '51 Nash		25	
20		92	Herb Thomas	Teaguemobile '51 Hudson	97	25	Crash
21	5	31	Jesse J. Taylor	Jesse James '51 Hudson		25	
22			Tommy Wells	'51 Henry J		25	
23	7	18	George Seeger	George's Mtrs '51 Studebaker		25	
24	11	15	Erick Erickson	Packer '51 Pontiac		25	
25	13	64	Bill Widenhouse	'51 Plymouth		25	
26	15	99	Leonard Tippett	Tippett '51 Hudson Hornet		25	
27		82	Joe Eubanks	Oates Motor Co. '50 Olds		25	
28			Jack McClure	'51 Henry J		25	
29		1	Harold Kite	Julian Buesink '51 Olds		25	

Time of Race:
Average Speed:
Pole Winner: Tim Flock - 58.843 mph
Lap Leaders: Bob Flock 1-72, Tim Flock 73-200.
Cautions: 2 for 25 laps   Margin of Victory: Half lap   Attendance: 5,000

Race No. 26

Thomas Steals One From From Jesse James

MACON, GA (Sept. 8) -- Herb Thomas drove his Hudson past a faltering Jesse James Taylor and galloped to victory in the 100-mile Grand National race at Central City Speedway. It was Thomas' fourth win in his career, and he padded his point lead to 478.7 points over Fonty Flock. Tim Flock, who finished last in the field of 22, fell to third, 561.7 points behind Thomas.

Gober Sosebee finished second in an Olds, two laps behind Thomas. Jim Paschal wound up third, Fonty Flock was fourth and Donald Thomas fifth.

Taylor, the young rookie out of Macon, fell out with a split radiator after leading most of the first half of the

Carrie Burns greets Herb Thomas in victory lane after Macon Grand National.

race. He was looking for his first Grand National win.

A crowd of 8,000 watched as Bob Flock led the opening 11 laps before Taylor set sail. Thomas, who led the final 94 laps, covered the 100 miles at an average speed of 53.222 mph. Johnny Thompson provided a thrill when he flipped his Olds twice in a turn. He climbed out unhurt.

Billy Carden qualified his Cadillac a strong fourth. However, the bulky automobile drifted back in the field and eventually finished eighth.

Jesse James Taylor -- so close yet so far from first win at Macon.

150-mile Grand National race at Langhorne Speedway. It was Langhorne's first NASCAR event of the '51 season. Two rain-outs and a crowded slate forced postponement until September.

Tim Flock was leading the race by almost a full lap when he had to pit for oil and gas with five laps to go . He dropped to fifth in

Tim Flock's crew services Oldsmobile during Langhorne 150 pit stop.

Grand National Race No. 26
200 Laps at Central City Speedway
Macon, GA
100 Miles on Half-mile Dirt Track
September 8, 1951

Fin	St	No.	Driver	Team / Car	Laps	Money	Status
1	6	92	Herb Thomas	Thomas '51 Plymouth	200	$1,000	Running
2		51	Gober Sosebee	Cherokee Garage '51 Olds 88	198	700	Running
3		60	Jim Paschal	Julian Buesink '50 Ford		450	Running
4	3	14	Fonty Flock	Red Devil '51 Olds 88		350	Running
5		93	Donald Thomas	Thomas '51 Plymouth		200	Running
6		71	Cotton Owens	'51 Plymouth		150	
7	9	38	Frank Gise	'51 Studebaker		125	
8	4	8	Billy Carden	'50 Cadillac		100	
9			Bill Miller	'51 Ford		75	
10	11		Augie Walackas	'50 Olds 88		50	
11	10	3	Jimmy Ayers	'51 Plymouth		25	
12			C H Dingler	'50 Plymouth		25	
13		82	Joe Eubanks	Phil Oates '50 Olds 88		25	
14	7		Roscoe Thompson	'50 Olds 88		25	Crash
15	5	31	Jesse James Taylor	Jesse James '51 Hudson	106	25	Heating
16		97	Sandy Lynch	'51 Plymouth		25	
17			Gene Tapia			25	
18	1	7	Bob Flock	Gray Ghost '51 Olds 88		25	
19		55	Marshall Weatherly	Blythe Motors '51 Nash		25	
20	8		Johnny Thompson	'50 Olds 88		25	Crash
21		42	Lee Petty	Petty Special '51 Plymouth		25	
22	2	91	Tim Flock	Black Phantom '51 Olds 88		25	

Time of Race: 1 hour, 52 minutes, 44 seconds
Average Speed: 53.222
Pole Winner: Bob Flock - 54.266 mph
Lap Leaders: Bob Flock 1-11, Jesse James Taylor 12-106, Herb Thomas 107-200
Cautions: Margin of Victory: 2-plus Laps   Attendance: 8,000

Race No. 27

Thomas Takes Langhorne as Tim Pits

LANGHORNE, PA (Sept. 15) -- Herb Thomas went into the lead five laps from the finish and won the

Grand National Race No. 27
150 Laps at Langhorne Speedway
Langhorne, PA
150 Miles on 1-Mile Dirt Track
September 15, 1951

Fin	St	No.	Driver	Team / Car	Laps	Money	Status
1	3	92	Herb Thomas	Teaguemobile '51 Hudson	150	$1,275	Running
2	1	14	Fonty Flock	Red Devil '51 Olds 88	150	800	Running
3		21	Dick Rathmann	Walt Chapman '51 Hudson		600	Running
4		120	John McGinley	Walt Chapman '51 Hudson		500	Running
5		91	Tim Flock	Black Phantom '51 Olds 88		300	Running
6		6	Marshall Teague	Teaguemobile '51 Hudson		200	Running
7		67	Jim Fieblekorn	'51 Lincoln		150	Running
8		66	Bud Riley	Northeast Motors '51 Hudson		125	Running
9		42	Lee Petty	Petty Special '51 Plymouth		100	Running
10		2	Bill Blair	'51 Ford		100	Running
11		9	Iggy Katona	'51 Chrysler		25	
12		70	Bud Farrell	William Gundaker '51 Plymouth		25	
13			Nelson Applegate	'51 Hudson Hornet		25	
14		421	Jack Reynolds	Wiss Brothers '51 Hudson		25	
15		31	Jesse James Taylor	Jesse James '51 Hudson Hornet		25	
16			George E. Clark	'50 Olds 88		25	
17		99	Leonard Tippett	Tippett '51 Hudson Hornet		25	
18		66	Roscoe Hough	Hough '51 Ford		25	
19			Bill Miller	'51 Studebaker		25	
20		55	Marshall Weatherly	Blythe Motors '51 Nash Amb		25	
21			Don Black			25	Crash
22			Dick Eagan	'50 Plymouth		25	
23			Charles Gattalia	'51 Ford		25	
24			Eddie Sheeler			25	
25			Sam Packard	'49 Ford		25	
26			Rusty Rushton	'50 Ford		25	
27			Jim Ross			25	
28			John DuBois	'50 Plymouth	84	25	Crash
29			Bill Remaly		80	25	Crash
30	5	7	Bob Flock	Gray Ghost '51 Olds 88		25	
31			Augie Walackas	'51 Olds		25	
32			Sam DiRusso			25	
33			Eddie Larue			25	
34			Reino Tulonen	'51 Henry J		25	
35			Frank Holzhauer			25	Crash
36			Dawson Lechlider		49	25	Crash

* Drivers listed in positions 21-36 are not necessarily in correct finish order. 53 cars started.
Time of Race: 2 hours, 6 minutes, 41 seconds
Average Speed: 71.043 mph
Pole Winner: Fonty Flock - 81.733 mph
Lap Leaders: Fonty Flock 1-130, Tim Flock 131-145, Herb Thomas 146-150
Cautions: Margin of Victory: 1/4 Lap   Attendance: 37,000

Jesse James Taylor leads pack of cars out of 4th turn at Langhorne.

the final run-down behind Fonty Flock, Dick Rathmann and John McGinley, who took positions two through four.

The race was marred by a number of spectacular crashes leaving two drivers injured, one critically. Fritz Holzhauer was rushed to Trenton's Mercer Hospital with critical head injuries. Don Black was seriously injured in an early crash and was transported to Mercer Hospital.

Dawson Lechlider flipped in the 49th lap, but he escaped injury. Bill Remaly emerged unhurt after he flipped six times in the 80th lap. John DuBois wrecked on lap 84 without injury. Automobile racing is not for the faint-hearted.

Fonty Flock won the pole for the 11th time in his career and proceeded to lead the first 130 laps. Tim Flock took the lead when Fonty pitted, and Thomas squeaked past in the final stages.

A huge crowd of 37,000 watched Thomas average 71.043 mph for his fifth Grand National win.

Grand National Race No. 28
200 Laps at Charlotte Speedway
Charlotte, NC
150 Miles on .75-mile Dirt Track
September 23, 1951

Fin	St	No.	Driver	Team / Car	Laps	Money	Status
1		92	Herb Thomas	Teaguemobile '51 Hudson	200	$1,000	Running
2		90	Shorty York	'50 Plymouth		700	Running
3		93	Donald Thomas	Thomas '50 Plymouth		450	Running
4		2	Bill Blair	'51 Ford 6		350	Running
5		0	Jimmie Lewallen	'51 Plymouth		200	Running
6		17	Buddy Shuman	R.H. Yandell '51 Ford 6		150	
7	1	8	Billy Carden	Sam Knox '50 Olds 88		125	
8		88	Del Pearson	'51 Plymouth		100	
9		60	Jim Paschal	Julian Buesink '50 Ford		75	
10		53	Clyde Minter	'50 Ford		50	
11		91	Tim Flock	Black Phantom '51 Olds 88	151	25	Axle
12			J.C. White	'51 Studebaker		25	
13		87	Buck Baker	Griffin Motors '50 Olds 88		25	
14		82	Joe Eubanks	Oates Motor Co. '50 Olds 88		25	
15		71	Cotton Owens	'51 Plymouth		25	Crash
16		7	Bob Flock	Gray Ghost '51 Olds 88		25	
17		217	Bill Miller	'51 Ford		25	Crash
18		22	Billy Myers	R.G. Shelton '51 Hudson Hornet		25	
19		41	Curtis Turner	Eanes Motor Co. '51 Olds 88		25	Sway Bar
20		55	Marshall Weatherly	Blythe Motors '51 Nash Amb.		25	
21		31	Jesse James Taylor	Jesse James '51 Hudson Hornet		25	
22			Otis Martin	'50 Buick		25	
23			Bill LaGrance	'48 Ford		25	
24		64	Bill Widenhouse	'51 Plymouth		25	
25		26	Weldon Adams	Leland Colvin '50 Plymouth		25	
26		23	Frank Mundy	Perry Smith '51 Studebaker		25	

Time of Race:
Average Speed:
Pole Winner: Billy Carden - 66.914 mph
Lap Leaders: Billy Carden 1-38, Herb Thomas 39-58, Bob Flock 59-95, H. Thomas 96-139, Carden 140-159, H. Thomas 160-200.
Cautions: Margin of Victory: Attendance: 6,800
A total of 30 cars started.

Race No. 28

Thomas Takes 3rd Straight; Miller in Violent Spill

Veteran driver Bill Miller suffered a broken arm in a terrible turnover at Charlotte

CHARLOTTE, NC (Sept. 23) -- Charlotte Speedway hosted its second thriller of the year as Herb Thomas won his third straight victory. He had to come from behind on three occasions during the 150-miler.

Shorty York finished in second place, his best effort ever in a NASCAR event. Donald Thomas finished third, Bill Blair was fourth and Jimmie Lewallen fifth.

Bill Miller suffered a broken

arm in one of the worst looking turn-overs ever seen in Grand National racing. Miller's Ford was reduced to scrap in the wreck.

Billy Carden won his 2nd pole position at Charlotte.

Pole sitter Billy Carden led the first 38 laps before yielding to Thomas. Thomas led through lap 58 when Bob Flock took command. Flock led for 37 laps before falling out of the racae.

In the second half of the 100-miler, Thomas and Carden battled hard with Thomas gaining the upper hand for good with 41 laps to go.

Carden eventually wound up seventh in the Sam Knox Oldsmobile.

Tim Flock was sidelined or lap 151 when an axle snapped on his Oldsmobile.

Bill Miller's Ford literally comes apart in spectacular crash at Charlotte.

Race No. 29

Flock Outclasses Dayton Field

DAYTON, OH (Sept. 23) -- Fonty Flock headed to the Midwest to compete in a same day Grand National event and easily won the 100-miler at Dayton Speedway. It was Flock's seventh career win and kept him in contention for the championship.

Flock, starting on the pole, led the entire 200 laps, finishing a lap ahead of runner-up Neil Cole. Lloyd Moore came in third, Lee Petty fourth and Bud Riley fifth.

The crowd of 15,000 hardly had time to sit down when John McGinley's Hudson blasted through the guard rail in the first few laps. McGinley was not hurt, but it took his Walt Chapman-led crew more than an hour to dislodge the guard rail fron the front of the car.

Frank Carlin rolled his car in the same spot later in the race. Jim Delaney turned over and bounced through the retaining barrier while running sixth.

Grand National Race No. 29
200 Laps at Dayton Speedway
Dayton, OH
100 Miles on Half-mile Paved Track
September 23, 1951

Fin	St	No.	Driver	Team / Car	Laps	Money	Status
1	1	14	Fonty Flock	Red Devil '51 Olds 88	200	$1,000	Running
2	9	52	Neil Cole	'50 Olds 88	199	700	Running
3	2	59	Lloyd Moore	Julian Buesink '51 Ford		450	Running
4	12	42	Lee Petty	Petty Special '51 Plymouth		350	Running
5	10	66	Bud Riley	Northeast Motors '51 Hudson		200	Running
6	19		Ronnie Koehler	'49 Plymouth		150	
7			Jimmy Florian	'50 Olds 88		125	
8	28	54	Don Bailey	'50 Olds 88		100	
9		89	Herb Trimble	'51 Olds 88		75	
10			Bill Braun			50	
11		56	Ed Benedict	'51 Hudson Hornet		25	
12		40	Tommy Thompson	Thompson '51 Chrysler		25	
13			Jim Mayes			25	
14			Jerry Groh			25	
15			Art Plas			25	
16		67	Jim Reed	'50 Ford		25	
17		9	Iggy Katona	'51 Chrysler		25	
18		21	Jim Delaney	Bob Oseicki '51 Ford		25	Crash
19			Quinton Daniels			25	
20		81	Pappy Hough	'51 Ford		25	
21			Tommy Stenger			25	
22		22	Oda Greene	'52 Hudson Hornet		25	
23			Harold Lucas			25	
24			Hank Russ			25	
25		121	Dick Rathmann	Walt Chapman '51 Hudson Hornet		25	
26			Charles Gattalia			25	
27			Bob White			25	
28		67	Jim Fieblekorn	'51 Lincoln		25	
29			Frank Carlin			25	Crash
30		120	John McGinley	Walt Chapman '51 Hudson Hornet		25	Crash
31		60	Don Eggert	'50 Plymouth		10	

Time of Race:
Average Speed:
Pole Winner: Fonty Flock
Lap Leaders: Fonty Flock 1-200
Cautions: 2   Margin of Victory: 1 Lap plus   Attendance: 15,000

Race No. 30

Flock's Olds Nabs Wilson Event

WILSON, NC (Sept. 30) -- Fonty Flock drove his Oldsmobile to his second straight victory in the 100-mile Grand National at Wilson Speedway. It was his eighth career win, tying him with Curtis Turner for the most wins in the new Stock Car racing division.

The victory marked the 13th of the season for chief mechanic Buckshot Morris, who has the unusual position of turning the wrenches for two different car owners. Morris handles the mechanical chores for all of the Flock brothers. Two of them drive for owner Ted Chester, and Fonty drives for Frank Christian.

Fonty Flock

Bob Flock finished in second place with Jimmie Lewallen third. Jim Paschal wheeled his Ford into fourth spot and and Bill Snowden took fifth.

Point leader Herb Thomas experienced mechanical problems with his Hudson and finished 14th in the field of 17 cars.

Jimmie Lewallen loses wheel at Hillsboro.

Grand National Race No. 30
200 Laps at Wilson County Speedway
Wilson, NC
100 Miles on Half-mile Dirt Track
September 30, 1952

Fin	St	No.	Driver	Team / Car	Laps	Money	Status
1	1	14	Fonty Flock	Red Devil '51 Olds 88	200	$1,000	Running
2		7	Bob Flock	Gray Ghost '51 Olds 88		700	Running
3		0	Jimmie Lewallen	'51 Plymouth		450	Running
4		60	Jim Paschal	Julian Buesink '50 Ford		350	Running
5		16	Bill Snowden	Snowden '51 Ford		200	Running
6		87	Buck Baker	Baker '51 Plymouth		150	
7			Cal Johnson	'51 Henry J		125	
8		99	Leonard Tippett	'51 Plymouth		100	
9			Bill Champion	'50 Chevrolet		75	
10		93	Donald Thomas	Thomas '51 Plymouth		50	
11		2	Bill Blair	'51 Ford		25	
12			Ray Rhrockmorton	'51 Henry J		25	
13			Oliver Dial	'50 Ford		25	
14		92	Herb Thomas	Teaguemobile '51 Hudson Hornet		25	
15			Maudis Brissette	'51 Henry J		25	
16			Jack Holloway	'50 Plymouth		25	
17		88	Del Pearson	Pearson '50 Plymouth		25	

Time of Race:
Average Speed:
Pole Winner: Fonty Flock -
Lap Leaders: - - - - - - - - - - Fonty Flock   -200
Cautions: Margin of Victory: Attendance:

Race No. 31

Herb Hot at Hillsboro; Wins Sixth of Year

HILLSBORO, NC (Oct. 7) -- Herb Thomas hustled past Fonty Flock in the 86th lap and sped to victory in the 150-mile Grand National event at Occoneechee Speedway. It was the sixth win of the year for the Olivia, NC driver.

Leonard Tippet's best effort in Grand National competition netted him second place as Hudson Hornets finished first and second.

Herb Thomas.

Joe Eubanks came in third, with Jim Paschal and Lee Petty rounding out the top five.

Fonty Flock led the first 85 laps, but his motor began to balk, and he departed three laps after losing the lead to Thomas. He wound up 15th in the 24-car field.

Thomas covered the 150 miles at a 72.454 mph clip and stretched his lead in the point standings.

Grand National Race No. 31
150 Laps at Occoneechee Speedway
Hillsboro, NC
150 Miles on 1-mile Dirt Track
October 7, 1951

Fin	St	No.	Driver	Team / Car	Laps	Money	Status
1	1	92	Herb Thomas	Teaguemobile '51 Hudson	150	$1,000	Running
2		99	Leonard Tippett	'51 Hudson Hornet	149	700	Running
3		82	Joe Eubanks	Phil Oates '50 Olds 88	148	450	Running
4		60	Jim Paschal	Julian Buesink '50 Ford	147	350	Running
5		42	Lee Petty	Petty Special '51 Plymouth	147	200	Running
6		93	Donald Thomas	Thomas '51 Plymouth	142	150	
7			Furman Lancaster	'50 Lincoln	140	125	
8			Alton Haddock	'50 Ford	136	100	
9		2	Bill Blair	'51 Ford 6	136	75	
10		37	Coleman Lawrence	Lawrence '50 Ford	130	50	
11			J.C. White	'51 Studebaker	128	25	
12		22	Billy Myers	R.G. Shelton '51 Hudson	113	25	Hub
13		24	Jimmie Lewallen	'51 Plymouth	111	25	Engine
14		88	Del Pearson	Pearson '51 Plymouth	94	25	
15	2	14	Fonty Flock	Red Devil '51 Olds 88	88	25	Engine
16			Bob Walters	'51 Plymouth	79	25	
17			Leon Sales	'51 Nash Amb.	68	25	
18			Roscoe Tompson	'51 Ford	64	25	
19		87	Buck Baker	Baker '50 Plymouth	63	25	
20			Jerry Wimbish	'50 Olds 88	51	25	
21		51	Gober Sosebee	Cherokee Garage '50 Olds 88	42	25	
22			Slick Smith	'51 Studebaker	27	25	
23			Clyde Minter	'50 Plymouth	22	25	
24			Curtis Hunt	'51 Hudson Hornet	15	25	

Time of Race: 2 hours, 4 minutes, 13 seconds
Average Speed: 72.454 mph
Pole Winner: Herb Thomas - 79.628 mph
Lap Leaders: Fonty Flock 1-85, Herb Thomas 86-200.
Cautions: Margin of Victory: 1 lap plus   Attendance: 12,000

Race No. 32

Thomas Crashes; Cole Wins at Thompson

THOMPSON, CT (Oct. 12) -- Herb Thomas crashed out of the lead in the 97th lap and opened the door for Neil Cole to win his first Grand National race in Thompson Speedway's 100-miler.

Thomas' Hudson started in 14th position, but roared through the pack and had taken the lead from Frank Mundy by the 14th lap. He was running away from the field when he wrecked on lap 97 after blowing a tire.

Neil Cole

Cole, of Oakland, NJ, battled with Jim Reed after Thomas' departure. He took the lead from Reed in the 56th lap and led the rest of the way.

Reed, who led for 58 laps, finished second, a lap behind. Dick Egan came in third, Billy Carden was fourth and Reino Tulonen fifth.

Thirty-eight cars started the race with 23 running at the finish.

Grand National Race No. 32
200 Laps at Thompson Speedway
Thompson, CT
100 Miles on Half-mile Paved Track
October 12, 1951

Fin	St	No.	Driver	Team / Car	Laps	Money	Status
1	1	52	Neil Cole	John Golabek '50 Olds 88	200	$1,000	Running
2	4	67	Jim Reed	'51 Ford	199	700	Running
3	11		Dick Eagan	'50 Plymouth		450	Running
4	16	8	Billy Carden	Sam Knox '50 Olds 88		350	Running
5	6	32	Reino Tulonen	'51 Henry J		200	Running
6	22	81	Pappy Hough	'51 Ford		150	
7	15	91	Tim Flock	Black Phantom '51 Olds 88		125	
8	8		Joe Sommers	'50 Ford		100	
9	21		Bill Cintia	'50 Ford		75	
10	34	21	Jim Delaney	Bob Oseicki '51 Plymouth		50	
11	28		Charles Gattalia	Colonial Motors '51 Studebaker		25	
12	18	54	Don Bailey	'51 Studebaker		25	
13	31		George Cavanna	'50 Olds 88		25	
14	12	4	Steve Dabb	'50 Ford		25	
15	36		Billy Tibbett	'50 Ford		25	
16	38	59	Lloyd Moore	Julian Buesink '51 Ford		25	
17	19		Joe Ross	'51 Ford		25	
18	31		Lyle Scott	'51 Chrysler		25	
19	7	55	Rusty Rushton	'50 Olds 88		25	Tires
20	24		Roy Forsythe	'50 Plymouth		25	
21	2	23	Frank Mundy	Perry Smith '51 Studebaker		25	
22	3		Jerry Russo			25	
23	5		Ray Hill	Kaiser		25	Brakes
24	9		Junior Pooler			25	
25	10		Sam Packard	'49 Ford		25	
26	14	92	Herb Thomas	Teaguemobile '51 Hudson	97	25	Crash
27	17	60	Julian Buesink	Julian Buesink '50 Ford		25	
28	20		Paul Pettit			25	
29	23		Ronnie Koehler			25	
30	25		Dave Humphrey			25	
31	26		Dave Reiley			10	
32	27		Tom Gifford			10	
33	29		Jim Miller			10	
34	30		Ray Jannelle			10	
35	32		Dick Richter			10	
36	33		Joe Skovron			10	Crash
37	35		Frank Tavers			10	
38	37		Wimpy Ervin			10	

* Drivers listed in positions 21-38 are not necessarily in correct finish order.

Time of Race:
Average Speed:
Pole Winner: Neil Cole - 30.37 seconds, 59.269 mph
Lap Leaders: Frank Mundy 1-13, Herb Thomas 14-97, Jim Reed 98-155, Neil Cole 156-200
Cautions: 1 for 3 laps   Margin of Victory: 1 lap plus   Attendance:

Grand National Race No. 33
200 Laps at Pine Grove Speedway
Shippenville, PA
100 Miles on Half-mile Dirt Track
October 14, 1951

Fin	St	No.	Driver	Team / Car	Laps	Money	Status
1		91	Tim Flock	Black Phantom '51 Olds 88	200	$1,000	Running
2		120	John McGinley	Walt Chapman '51 Hudson		700	Running
3		8	Billy Carden	Sam Knox '50 Olds 88		450	Running
4			Jimmy Florian	'50 Olds 88		350	Running
5		59	Lloyd Moore	Julian Buesink '51 Ford		200	Running
6			Hap Jones			150	
7		56	Ed Benedict	'51 Hudson Hornet		125	
8			Bob Dietrich			100	
9			Russ Hepler			75	
10			Dick Stone			50	
11			Bob Lilienthal			25	
12			Wimpy Ervin			25	
13			Charles Gattalia	Colonial Motors '51 Studebaker		25	
14		52	Bill Rexford	'50 Olds 88		25	
15		54	Don Bailey	'51 Studebaker		25	
16			Jerry Groh			25	
17			Joe Merola	'50 Olds 88		25	
18			Nook Walters	'51 Plymouth		25	
19			Quinton Daniels			25	
20			Irving Leitch			25	

Time of Race:
Average Speed:
Pole Winner:
Lap Leaders: - - - - - - - - - Tim Flock -200
Cautions: Margin of Victory: Attendance:

Race No. 33

Flock Outruns McGinley at Shippenville

SHIPPENVILLE, PA (Oct. 14) -- Tim Flock of Atlanta grabbed his seventh career Grand National victory in the 100-mile event at Pine Grove Speedway.

John McGinley.

Flock outran John McGinley to take the $1,000 top prize. Third place went to Billy Carden, who was back in the good graces of NASCAR officials after being suspended. Jimmy Florian finished fourth and Lloyd Moore was fifth.

McGinley, of Chicora, PA, teamed with car owner Walt Chapman and gave a good acount of himself in the 200-lapper.

Most of the names and faces making the 20-car field were not Grand National regulars. This was another day of "same-day" Grand Nationals, and most of the regulars were at Martinsville, VA.

Race No. 34

Sunday Drive for Mundy at Martinsville

MARTINSVILLE, VA (Oct. 14) -- Frank Mundy, driving Bob Flock's Gray Ghost Oldsmobile, inherited the lead when a drive shaft snapped in Leonard Tippett's Hudson, rolled to his second career Grand National triumph in the 100-miler at Martinsville Speedway.

Mundy, who started third, took the lead in the 87th lap and led the rest of the way. Tippett, gunning for his first win, had led 19 laps when his Hudson crept to a halt on the backstretch.

A crowd of 7,500 watched five different drivers lead the 200-lapper. Pole sitter Herb Thomas led the first 28 laps but whacked the wall and retired for the day.

Broken drive shaft foiled Leonard Tippett's bid at Martinsville.

Curtis Turner, trying to end a four-month winless skid, took the lead when Thomas dropped out and was pulling away from the field when a tie rod broke in his Olds on lap 44. Billy Myers then led for 23 laps before Tippett moved to the front. Lee Petty finished second with Myers taking third. Bill Snowden finished fourth; Jimmie Lewallen was fifth.

Grand National Race No. 34
200 Laps at Martinsville Speedway
Martinsville, VA
100 Miles on Half-mile Dirt Track
October 14, 1951

Fin	St	No.	Driver	Team / Car	Laps	Money	Status
1	3	7	Frank Mundy	Gray Ghost '51 Olds 88	200	$1,000	Running
2	12	42	Lee Petty	Petty Special '51 Plymouth		700	Running
3	4	22	Billy Myers	R.G. Shelton '51 Hudson		450	Running
4	2	16	Bill Snowden	Snowden '51 Ford		350	Running
5	15	0	Jimmie Lewallen	'51 Plymouth		200	Running
6	18		Pappy Hough	Hough '51 Ford		150	
7	20	37	Coleman Lawrence	Lawrence '50 Ford		125	
8	14	98	Leon Sales	Westmoreland '50 Plymouth		100	
9	16	88	Dell Pearson	Pearson '51 Plymouth		75	
10	19		Cal Johnson	'51 Henry J		50	
11	7	99	Leonard Tippett	'51 Hudson Hornet	86	25	Drive Shft
12	13	2	Bill Blair	'51 Ford		25	
13	17	93	Donald Thomas	Thomas '50 Plymouth		25	
14	6	41	Curtis Turner	Eanes Motor Co. '51 Olds 88	44	25	Tie Rod
15	8		Jim Reed	'50 Lincoln		25	
16	10		Otis Martin	'48 Buick		25	
17	5	52	Neil Cole	'50 Olds 88		25	
18	1	92	Herb Thomas	Teaguemobile '51 Hudson	23	25	Crash
19	11	60	Jim Paschal	Julian Buesink '50 Ford		25	
20	23		Coleman Grant	'51 Nash Ambassador		25	
21	21		Bob Walters	'51 Plymouth		25	
22	9		J.C. White	'51 Studebaker		25	
23	22		Jack Wade	'51 Olds 88		25	

Time of Race:
Average Speed:
Pole Winner: Herb Thomas - 56.109 mph
Lap Leaders: Herb Thomas 1-28, Curtis Turner 29-44, Billy Myers 45-67, Leonard Tippett 68-86, Frank Mundy 87-200.
Cautions: Margin of Victory: Attendance: 7,500

Race No. 35

Burke Boss in Oakland's 400 Lapper

OAKLAND, CA (Oct. 14) -- Marvin Burke, making his first Grand National start, took home the bacon in the 250-mile race at the Oakland Stadium. The wily veteran picked up a $1,875 winner's check.

Burke's Mercury outlasted a big field to win the $7,500 event. Bob Caswell finished second in a Plymouth and Woody Brown was third Sam Hawks wound up fourth and Dick Meyer came in fifth.

Marvin Panch, young driver from Gardena, CA, drove in his first Grand National race and finished sixth.

The event was staged by Johnny Mantz, winner of the first Southern 500 at Darlington. Mantz had been assigned West Coast zone supervisor by NASCAR two weeks earlier.

boro Speedway. It was Flock's eighth win of the year and moved him to within 322.2 points of leader Thomas.

Although Thomas wound up 21st in the field of 26, the day was not lost as the Olivia, NC driver got into his brother Donald's Plymouth and carried it to a 13th place finish. He received a percentage of points in the relief driving role and kept his advantage in the standings.

Lee Petty finished second to Flock and Joe Eubanks was third. Tim Flock came in fourth with Cotton Owens fifth.

Leonard Tippett was taken to the hospital with undetermined injuries when his Hudson broke an axle and flipped in a turn. Bill Walters and Joe Wade escaped unhurt after both flipped their cars in unrelated accidents.

A crowd of 7,800 watched as Flock won, averaging 67.791 mph.

Grand National Race No. 35
400 Laps at Oakland Stadium
Oakland, CA
150 Miles on .625-mile Paved Track
October 14, 1951

Fin	St	No.	Driver	Team / Car	Laps	Money	Status
1			Marvin Burke	Bob Phillippi '50 Mercury	400	$1,875	Running
2		84	Bob Caswell	Lou Mangini '50 Plymouth		1,250	Running
3		88	Woody Brown	Joe Mangini '50 Olds		900	Running
4		55	Stan Hawks	'50 Plymouth		600	Running
5		9	Dick Meyer	Grant Sniffen '50 Mercury		450	Running
6		56	Marvin Panch	Panch '50 Mercury		350	
7		33	Lou Figaro	Jack Gaynor '51 Hudson		200	
8		48	Bill Norton	Larry Bettinger '51 Mercury		150	
9		41	Johnny Soares	Harry Schilling '50 Mercury		125	
10			Walt Davis	'50 Plymouth		100	
11		14	Fonty Flock	Red Devil '51 Olds 88		75	
12		7	Fred Lee	Speedway Auto Sales '51 Hudson		50	
13		16	Fred Steinbroner	Bob Carpenter '50 Ford		25	
14		6	Bill Ledbetter	Ledbetter '50 Ford		25	
15		22	Lloyd Dane	Dane '51 Ford		25	
16		19	Les Borner	V-Gap Spark Plug '49 Pontiac		25	
17			Hal Cole	'51 Plymouth		25	
18		35	Fuzzy Anderson	Bert Letner '51 Hudson		25	
19		2	Danny Weinberg	Tony Sampo '51 Studebaker		25	
20		120	Dick Rathmann	Walt Chapman '51 Hudson Hornet		25	
21		66	Bud Riley	Northeast Motors '51 Hudson Hornet		25	
22		25	Erick Erickson	Erickson '51 Kaiser		25	
23		27	Jim Byrd	El Paso Special '49 Buick		25	
24			Cy Blalock	Blalock '51 Henry J		25	
25			Claude Wallington	'50 Plymouth		25	
26		3	Allen Heath	Heath '50 Plymouth		25	
27		39	Danny Letner	Bert Letner '51 Hudson Hornet		25	
28		95	Freddie Farmer	'51 Nash Ambassador		25	
29		31	Lloyd Porter	Stan Noble '51 Henry J		25	

* Drivers listed in positions 11-29 are not necessarily in correct finish order. Number of starters unknown.
Time of Race:
  Average Speed:
  Pole Winner:
  Lap Leaders: - - - - - - - - - Marvin Burke -200
  Cautions: Margin of Victory: Attendance:

Race No. 36

Flock Closes In
As Thomas Fails to Finish

N. WILKESBORO, NC (Oct. 21) -- Fonty Flock took the lead when Herb Thomas pitted with a radiator leak and went on to win the 125-miler at North Wilkes-

Grand National Race No. 36
200 Laps at N. Wilkesboro Speedway
North Wilkesboro, NC
125 Miles on .625-mile Dirt Track
October 21, 1951

Fin	St	No.	Driver	Team / Car	Laps	Money	Status
1	4	7	Fonty Flock	Gray Ghost '51 Olds 88	200	$1,000	Running
2	12	42	Lee Petty	Petty Special '51 Plymouth		700	Running
3	3	82	Joe Eubanks	Oates Motor Co. '50 Olds 88		450	Running
4	5	91	Tim Flock	Black Phantom '51 Olds 88		350	Running
5	25	71	Cotton Owens	'51 Studbaker		200	Running
6	8	16	Bill Snowden	Snowden '51 Ford		150	
7	14	0	Jimmie Lewallen			125	
8	11	17	Buddy Shuman	R.H. Yandell '51 Ford 6		100	
9	9		Jerry Wimbish	'51 Olds 88		75	
10	2		Bob Flock	'51 Hudson Hornet		50	
11	21	98	Leon Sales	Westmoreland '50 Plymouth		25	
12	23	88	Del Pearson	Pearson '51 Plymouth		25	
13	13	93	Donald Thomas	Thomas '50 Plymouth		25	Tie Rod
14	16	60	Jim Paschal	Julian Buesink '50 Ford		25	
15	17	64	Bill Widenhouse	'50 Plymouth		25	
16	24	37	Coleman Lawrence	Lawrence '50 Ford		25	
17	19		Glenn Dunnaway	'51 Nash Ambassador		25	
18	6	22	Billy Myers	R.G. Shelton '51 Hudson Hornet		25	
19	26		Jack Wade	'51 Olds 88		25	Crash
20	7	99	Leonard Tippett	Tippett '51 Hudson Hornet	124	25	Crash
21	1	92	Herb Thomas	Thomas '51 Hudson	82	25	Radiator
22	22	90	Shorty York	'50 Plymouth		25	
23	20		Bill Walters		72	25	Crash
24	10	2	Bill Blair	'51 Ford		25	
25	15	27	Gwyn Staley	The Wilkes Boys '50 Ford		25	
26	18		J.C. White	'51 Studebaker		25	

Time of Race: 1 hour, 50 minutes, 38 seconds
Average Speed: 67.791 mph
Pole Winner: Herb Thomas - 68.828 mph
Lap Leaders: Herb Thomas 1-82, Fonty Flock 83-200.
Cautions: Margin of Victory: Attendance: 7,800

Race No. 37

Weinberg Winner At Hanford

HANFORD, CA (Oct 28) -- Danny Weinberg drove his Studebaker to victory in the 100 mile Grand National race at Hanford Speedway.

Marvin Panch finished second in a Mercury in his second Grand National start. Third place went to Bill Norton, Lloyd Dane was fourth and Woody Brown fifth.

It was only the fifth start in the Grand National career of Weinberg, a young driver out of Downey, CA. He won $1,000 for his efforts.

Grand National Race No. 37
200 Laps at Hanford Motor Speedway
Hanford, CA
100 Miles on Half-mile Dirt Track
October 28, 1951

Fin	St	No.	Driver	Team / Car	Laps	Money	Status
1		2	Danny Weinberg	Tony Sampo '51 Studebaker	200	$1,000	Running
2		56	Marvin Panch	'50 Mercury		700	Running
3		48	Bill Norton	Lary Bettinger '50 Mercury		450	Running
4		22	Lloyd Dane	Dane '51 Ford		350	Running
5		88	Woody Brown	Joe Mangini '50 Olds 88		200	Running
6			Claude Wallington	'50 Plymouth		150	
7	33	7	Fred Lee	Speedway Auto Sales '49 Plym		125	
8		10	Fred Russell	Smith & Jones '50 Ford		100	
9			Cy Blalock	Blalock '51 Henry J		75	
10		16	Fred Steinbroner	Bob Carpenter '50 Ford		50	
11		98	George Seeger	Johnny Mantz '51 Nash		25	
12		17	Al Jacobs	'50 Ford		25	
13		33	Lou Figaro	Jack Gaynor '51 Hudson Hornet		25	
14		6	Ray Chase	Oster-Barry '51 Hudson Hornet		25	
15		18	Bill Stammer	Charles Roscoe '49 Plymouth		25	
16		25	Erick Erickson	Erickson '51 Kaiser		25	
17		27	Jim Byrd	El Paso Special '49 Buick		25	
18		19	Les Bomar	V-Gap Spark Plug '49 Pontiac		25	
19		9	Dick Meyer	Grant Sniffen '50 Mercury		25	
20		84	Bob Caswell	Lou Mangini '50 Plymouth		25	
21		55	Sam Hawks	'50 Plymouth		25	
22		66	Bud Riley	'51 Hudson Hornet		25	
23		11	Chuck Meekins	Speedway Auto Sales '51 Plymouth		25	
24		14	Fonty Flock	Red Devil '51 Olds 88		25	
25		39	Danny Letner	Bert Letner '51 Hudson		25	
26		6	Bill Ledbetter	Ledbetter '50 Ford		25	
27		35	Fuzzy Anderson	Bert Letner '51 Hudson		25	
28		92	Herb Thomas	Teaguemobile '51 Hudson		25	
29		31	Lloyd Porter	Stan Noble '51 Henry J		25	
30		3	Allen Heath	Heath '50 Plymouth		25	
31			John Soares	'50 Oldsmobile		25	
32		54	Andy Pierce	Upshaw's Garage '50 Olds		25	
33							
34							

* Drivers listed in positions 11-34 are not necessarily in correct finish order.
Time of Race:
Average Speed:
Pole Winner:
Lap Leaders: - - - - - - - - - Danny Weinberg -200
Cautions: Margin of Victory: Attendance:

The event did not have a bearing on the race for the championship since none of the point leaders were entered.

Grand National Race No. 38
200 Laps at Speedway Park
Jacksonville, FL
100 Miles on Half-mile Dirt Track
November 4, 1951

Fin	St	No.	Driver	Team / Car	Laps	Money	Status
1	1	6	Herb Thomas	Teaguemobile '51 Hudson	200	$1,000	Running
2	10	44	Jack Smith	'51 Hudson Hornet		700	Running
3	4	14	Fonty Flock	Red Devil '51 Olds 88		450	Running
4	6	16	Bill Snowden	Snowden '51 Ford		350	Running
5	2	23	Frank Mundy	Perry Smith '51 Studebaker		200	Running
6			Tommy Moon	'51 Henry J		150	
7		42	Lee Petty	Petty Special '51 Plymouth		125	
8		0	Jimmie Lewallen	'51 Plymouth		100	
9		17	Buddy Shuman	R.H. Yandell '51 Plymouth		75	
10		8	Billy Carden	Sam Knox '50 Olds 88		50	
11		4	Eddie Anderson	'51 Nash Ambassador		25	
12		31	Jesse James Taylor	Jesse James '51 Hudson Hornet		25	
13		91	Tim Flock	Black Phantom '51 Olds 88		25	
14		87	Buck Baker	'51 Plymouth		25	
15	6	99	Leonard Tippett	'51 Hudson Hornet		25	
16	8	59	Lloyd Moore	Julian Buesink '51 Ford		25	
17		22	Billy Myers	R.G. Shelton '51 Hudson Hornet		25	
18		60	Jim Paschal	Julian Buesink '50 Ford		25	
19			Joe Eubanks	Phil Oates '51 Hudson Hornet	25		
20			Bill Blair	'51 Olds 88		25	
21	5		Donald Thomas			25	
22			Jimmy Florian	Euclid Motor Co. '51 Ford		25	

* Drivers listed in positions 11-22 are not necessarily in correct finish order
Time of Race: 1 hour, 52 minutes, 20 seconds
Average Speed: 53.412 mph
Pole Winner: Herb Thomas - 64.818 mph
Lap Leaders: - - - - - - - - - Herb Thomas -200
Cautions: Margin of Victory: Attendance:

Race No. 38

Thomas Wins at JAX in Teague's Hornet

JACKSONVILLE, FL (Nov. 4) -- Herb Thomas took the wheel of Marshall Teague's Hudson Hornet and streaked to victory in the Speedway Park 100-miler.

Thomas, bidding to become the '51 NASCAR Grand National Champion, had been suffering mechanical problems in his own car. Teague, recognized as the leader of Hudson racing operations, provided a fresh car for Thomas to drive down the stretch.

Jack Smith came from 10th starting position to finish second. Fonty Flock was third, Bill Snowden came in fourth and Frank Mundy was fifth.

Herb Thomas #6 and Frank Mundy #23 on the front row for the start of 100-miler at Jacksonville.

Thomas won the race at an average speed of 53.412 mph under overcast skies. He boosted his point lead to 362.2 points over Fonty Flock.

lost the baby and wound up in the hospital, too.

Pete Page tossed his Olds into a series of turn-overs in the first turn and was knocked unconscious. He was reported in fair condition at Grady Memorial Hospital.

Race No. 39

Taylor Badly Injured As Tim Flock Wins

ATLANTA, GA (Nov. 11) -- Tim Flock took a ride in Ted Chester's Hudson Hornet and zoomed to victory in the 100-mile Grand National event at Lakewood Speedway.

A crowd of 26,000 watched Flock take the lead from Bob Flock in the 14th lap and led the rest of the way on the one-mile oval. Bob came second, Jack Smith was third, Frank Mundy fourth and Gober Sosebee fifth. Outstanding young driver Jesse James Taylor suffered serious head injuries when his Hudson flipped in the first turn. The roof caved in on the Macon, GA driver, and it took rescue workers some 15 minutes to get him out of the car. He was listed in serious condition at Crawford Memorial Hospital. His wife, who was expecting,

Cars on pace lap at Atlanta's Lakewood Speedway.

Rescue workers tend to Jesse James Taylor after bad Lakewood crash.

Grand National Race No. 40
200 Laps at Carrell Speedway
Gardena, CA
100 Miles on Half-mile Dirt Track
November 11, 1951

Fin	St	No.	Driver	Taam / Car	Laps	Money	Status
1	10	48	Bill Norton	Larry Bettinger '51 Mercury	200	$1,000	Running
2	3	9	Dick Meyer	Grant Sniffen '50 Mercury		700	Running
3	20	25	Erick Erickson	Erickson '51 Kaiser		450	Running
4	4	33	Lou Figaro	Jack Gaynor '51 Hudson Hornet		350	Running
5	2	2	Danny Weinberg	Tony Sampo '51 Studebaker		200	Running
6	7	6	Bill Ledbetter	Ledbetter '50 Ford		150	
7	22	77	Burt Jackson			125	
8	8	98	Johnny Mantz	Mantz '51 Nash Ambassador		100	
9	9	39	Danny Letner	Bert Letner '51 Hudson Hornet		75	
10	29		Walt Davis			50	
11	1	14	Fonty Flock	Red Devil '51 Olds 88		25	
12	5	99	Ben Gregory	Coz Cancilla '50 Olds		25	
13	6	35	Fuzzy Anderson	Bert Letner '51 Hudson		25	
14	11	76	Don McLeish			25	
15	12	27	George Seeger	George Hicks '51 Hudson		25	
16	13	56	Marvin Panch	'50 Mercury		25	
17	14	66	Bud Riley	'51 Hudson Hornet		25	
18	15	10	Tommy Melvin	Smith & Jones '50 Ford		25	Crash
19	16	84	Bob Caswell	Lou Mangini '50 Plymouth		25	Crash
20	17	95	Freddie Farmer	'51 Nash Ambassador		25	
21	18	12	Bill Stammer	Stammer '51 Plymouth		25	
22	19	7	Fred Lee	Speedway Auto Sales '49 Plymouth		25	
23	21	54	Andy Pierce	Harley J Briggs '49 Plymouth		25	
24	23	97	Jack Gaynor	Gaynor '51 Hudson Hornet		25	LF Wheel
25	24	3	Allen Heath	Heath '50 Plymouth		25	Heating
26	25	55	Sam Hawks	'50 Plymouth		25	
27	26	11	Chuck Meekins	Speedway Auto Sales '51 Plymouth		25	
28	27	31	Lloyd Porter	Stan Noble '51 Henry J		25	
29	28	16	Fred Steinbroner	Bob Carpenter '50 Ford		25	
30		22	Lloyd Dane	Dane '51 Ford		25	
31		17	John Soares	'50 Olds		25	

* Drivers listed in positions 11-31 are not necessarily in correct finish order
Time of Race:
  Average Speed:
  Pole Winner: Fonty Flock
  Lap Leaders: Fonty Flock 1-71, Dick Meyer 72-104, Johnny Mantz 105-108, Meyer 109-157, Mantz 158-181, Bill Norton 182-200
  Cautions: Margin of Victory: Attendance: 6,100

Grand National Race No. 39
100 Laps at Lakewood Speedway
Atlanta, GA
100 Miles on 1-mile Dirt Track
November 11, 1951

Fin	St	No.	Driver	Team / Car	Laps	Money	Status
1	4	91	Tim Flock	Ted Chester '51 Hudson	100	$1,000	Running
2	3	7	Bob Flock	Gray Ghost '51 Olds 88		700	Running
3	5	44X	Jack Smith	'51 Hudson Hornet		450	Running
4	1	23	Frank Mundy	Perry Smith '51 Studebaker		350	Running
5	8	51	Gober Sosebee	Cherrokee Garage '51 Olds 88		200	Running
6			Ed Samples	'50 Olds 88		150	
7		59	Lloyd Moore	Julian Buesink '51 Ford		125	
8		17	Buddy Shuman	R.H. Yandell '51 Ford		100	
9			Red Duvall	'51 Packard		75	
10			Don Oldenberg	'50 Packard		50	
11		24	Jimmie Lewallen	J.O. Goode '51 Plymouth		25	
12		42	Lee Petty	Petty Special '51 Plymouth		25	
13			Neil Roberts	'51 Olds 88		25	
14			Glenn Dunnaway	'50 Plymouth		25	
15		16	Bill Snowden	Snowden '51 Ford		25	
16		8	Billy Carden	Frank Christian '50 Olds 88		25	
17		27	Jimmy Florian	Euclid Ford Co. '51 Ford		25	
18			Dan Rush	'50 Plymouth		25	
19	2	6	Herb Thomas	Teaguemobile '51 Hudson Hornet		25	Spindle
20		25	Dick Linder	Don Rogala '50 Olds 88		25	
21			Cal Fisher	Ford		25	
22		31	Jesse James Taylor	Jesse James '51 Hudson Hornet		25	Crash
23		99	Leonard Tippett	Tippett '51 Hudson Hornet		25	Crash
24			Roscoe Thompson	'51 Studebaker		25	
25		2	Bill Blair	'51 Olds 88		25	
26			Pete Page	Olds		25	Crash
27	31	55	Jim Paschal	Wheatley Motors '50 Cadillac		25	
28		87	Buck Baker	'51 Ford		25	
29			Bob Reuther	Olds		25	
30		93	Donald Thomas	Ford		25	
31		30	Tommy Moon	Chaney Motors '51 Henry J		25	

Time of Race: 1 hour, 40 minutes, 4 seconds
  Average Speed: 59.960 mph
  Pole Winner: Frank Mundy - 74.013 mph
  Lap Leaders: Frank Mundy 1, Bob Flock 2-13, Tim Flock 14-100
  Cautions: Margin of Victory: Attendance: 26,000

Race No. 40

Mantz Falters, Norton Wins at Carrell Speedway

GARDENA, CA (Nov. 11) -- Bill Norton got past Johnny Mantz with 19 laps remaining and held on to win the 100-mile Grand National event at Carrell Speedway.

Dick Meyer finished in second place, followed   by Erick Erickson, Lou Figaro, and Danny Weinberg.

Fonty Flock, Mantz and Meyer diced for the lead until Norton made his late race kick. Flock led for the first 71 laps from the pole, but his Oldsmobile broke down. Meyer and Mantz swapped the lead four times in the next 55 miles. Mantz, who led for 18 laps, faded near the end and got credit for an eighth place finish.

Fonty Flock became a stock car racing promoter on TV in California.

Tommy Melvin rolled his Ford mideway in the race. He was not hurt in the mishap.

Title contender Fonty Flock went on a number of live television programs in th e Southern California area, promoting the up-coming event. On one show, the producers said he "stole the show" from featured guest Gussie Moran, a famous tennis star.

checked into a hospital. A doctor determined that he had broken several ribs in the spill. Eight days later, following a further check-up, it was revealed that Flock had broken his neck. He was expected to miss the entire 1952 season.

Race No. 41

Mundy Wins Mobile; Thomas Champ

MOBILE AL (Nov. 25) - Frank Mundy led the entire way to win the 112.5-mile Grand National race at the Lakeview Estates Speedway. Herb Thomas was crowned NASCAR champion for the 1951 even though he finished next-to-last in the 22- car field.

Thomas started the race in Leonard Tippett's Hudson, but departed after 40 laps with rear end failure. He still beat Flonty Flock, who finished fourth, by 146.2 points in the national standings.

Tim Flock wound up second to Mundy. Red Duvall finished third, Fonty was fourth and Don Oldenberg fifth.

The victory proved to be the last for car owner Smith, who was killed December 8 when his private single engine aircraft crashed near Greensburg, IN. Smith was flying an invalid 83 year-old woman, her nurse and a control tower operator from Columbia, SC to Chicago when it went down in a wooded area. All four occupants were killed.

Bob Flock flipped his Olds in the early going. He was treated at trackside and left the speedway before the race ended. He drove himself to Pensacola, FL where he

Grand National Race No. 41
150 Laps at Lakeview Speedway
Mobile, AL
112.5 Miles on .75-mile Dirt Track
November 25, 1951

Fin	St	No.	Driver	Team / Car	Laps	Money	Status
1	1	23	Frank Mundy	Perry Smith '51 Studebaker	150	$1,000	Running
2		91	Tim Flock	Ted Chester '51 Hudson		700	Running
3		87	Red Duvall	Hammond Motors '51 Packard		450	Running
4		14	Fonty Flock	Augusta Speed Shop '51 Olds		350	Running
5		142	Don Oldenberg	Hammond Motors '51 Packard		200	Running
6		20	Buddy Shuman	Nat. Speed Sport News '51 Ford		150	
7		51	Gober Sosebee	Cherokee Garage '51 Olds		125	
8		9	Ed Samples	Samples Express '50 Olds		100	
9		24	Jimmie Lewallen	J O Goode '51 Plymouth		75	
10		80	Sonny Black	Mobile's Own '51 Plymouth		50	
11			Lucky Mays			25	
12		83	Bill Miller	'51 Ford		25	
13			Bud Erb			25	
14			Hank Lee			25	
15			Ted Tedrow			25	
16		42	Lee Petty	Lee Petty Special '51 Plymouth		25	
17			Gene Tapia			25	
18			Louis Luther			25	
19		12	Billy Carden	'50 Olds		25	
20		7	Bob Flock	Gray Ghost '51 Olds		25	Crash
21		99	Herb Thomas	Tippett '51 Hudson Hornet	40	25	Rear End
22		44	Jack Smith	'51 Hudson Hornet	34	25	Suspnsn

Time of Race:
Average Speed:
Pole Winner: Frank Mundy 61.113 mph
Lap Leaders: Frank Mundy 1-150
Cautions: Margin of Victory: Attendance:

Frank Mundy and car owner Perry Smith -- winners at Mobile.

1951 NASCAR Season
Final Point Standings Grand National Division

Rank	Driver	Points	Starts	Wins	Top 5	Top 10	Winnings
1	Herb Thomas	4,208.45	34	7	16	19	$21,050
2	Fonty Flock	4,062.25	33	8	20	22	15,535
3	Tim Flock	3,722.50	33	7	20	21	15,155
4	Lee Petty	2,392.25	31	1	11	19	7,340
5	Frank Mundy	1,963.50	24	3	8	11	7,095
6	Buddy Shuman	1,368.75	7	0	1	6	2,755
7	Jesse James Taylor	1,214.00	10	0	1	3	3,700
8	Dick Rathmann	1,040.00	13	0	4	7	3,480
9	Bill Snowden	1,009.25	12	0	3	9	2,365
10	Joe Eubanks	1,005.50	12	0	3	3	3,350
11	Lloyd Moore	996.50	21	0	4	7	2,335
12	Fireball Roberts	930.00	9	0	2	3	2,110
13	Jimmie Lewallen	874.25	12	0	4	8	2180
14	Bob Flock	869.00	16	1	4	9	3,680
15	Jim Paschal	858.50	16	0	4	7	2,360
16	Bill Blair	840.00	17	0	4	7	2,735
17	Gober Sosebee	784.00	10	0	4	5	2,953
18	Erick Erickson	723.50	13	0	3	6	2,285
19	Tommy Thompson	755.00	5	1	1	2	5,435
20	Donald Thomas	743.50	18	0	4	7	1,645
21	Johnny Mantz	725.00	7	0	2	4	2,025
22	Lou Figaro	684.20	13	1	3	4	2,135
23	Buck Baker	644.50	11	0	4	5	1,650
24	Dick Meyer	626.50	6	0	3	4	1,650
25	Harold Kite	625.00	2	0	0	1	800
26	Billy Carden	809.75	7	0	2	5	1,460
27	Jimmy Florian	462.50	8	0	2	5	1,100
28	Jim Fiebelkorn	455.00	15	0	1	4	1,355
29	Ronnie Kohler	432.00	5	0	2	3	1,100
30	Danny Weinberg	423.50	6	1	2	3	1,470
31	Roscoe Hough	423.00	9	0	1	4	760
32	Woody Brown	421.00	3	0	0	2	1,125
33	Neil Cole	382.00	5	1	3	3	2,050
34	Paul Newkirk	375.00	1	0	1	1	500
35	John McGinley	372.50	6	0	2	2	1.300
36	Marvin Panch	371.50	3	0	1	2	1,075
37	Oda Greene	366.50	5	0	2	3	825
38	Jack Goodwin	362.50	3	0	0	1	725
39	Jack Smith	360.50	7	0	2	2	1,275
40	Bob Caswell	350.00	3	0	1	1	1,325
41	Lloyd Dane	323.50	7	0	2	3	975
42	Cotton Owens	312.50	2	0	0	1	225
43	Fred Steinbroner	306.50	7	0	2	3	700
44	Ewell Weddle	293.50	7	0	0	2	435
45	George Seeger	278.00	9	0	1	3	910
46	Sam Hawks	262.50	3	0	1	1	650
47	Don Bailey	239.50	9	0	1	2	625
48	Bud Farrell	227.50	5	0	1	2	700
49	Harvey "Bud" Riley	262.50	8	0	1	2	475
50	Freddie Lee	224.00	5	0	1	1	450

The 1952 Season
Sparring with AAA
and Two-way Radios

Volume one of a four volume series . . . . The Beginning 1949 - 1958

1952

For fifty years the American Automobile Association had ruled motorsports in America. National champions had been declared since 1902. The AAA had the Indianapolis 500 safely tucked away and had sanctioned a variety of divisions from Championship Cars (Indy), Sprints, Midgets, Stocks and Big Cars. The AAA flag stretched to all corners of the country.

Virtually every other "fly-by-night" sanctioning body with the exception of IMCA (International Motor Contest Association) had survived only a few seasons before they succumbed to promotional failures.

In 1952, NASCAR was preparing for its fifth season of operation. Unlike most organizations which preceded it, Bill France's outfit had cultivated a progressive series from a loose-knit gang of moonshiners out for a 'legal' weekend joy ride. They were playing host to packed grandstands, and NASCAR had become the fastest growing racing organization in the country.

In 1948, one division -- the Modifieds -- operated under NASCAR.

Tim Flock won the 1952 Grand National championship "on his head".

A year later the Grand Nationals came aboard, and its impact was comparatively earth-shattering. By 1951, the Short Track circuit had been added, and, for 1952, another new division was in the works.

NASCAR had announced that it was going to conduct a series of "Speedway" division events. The vehicles eligible for the new classification were Indianapolis-type

cars equipped with stock power plants. France sensed the economically minded division would attract Southerners who wanted a taste of the mystique that drew 250,000 spectators to Indianapolis. Midwesterners who had been driven off the AAA championship trail because of rising costs would also be interested. The Speedway division's first event was a time trial session through Daytona Beach's measured mile during Speed-Week.

Buck Baker, established pilot in the Modified ranks and who would become the Grand National champion on two occasions, pierced the measured mile at 132.94, 142.29 and 140.41 mph in successive runs over a three-day period. For having the quickest time on the final day, Baker picked up a $1,000 top prize.

It was not until May 10th at Darlington Raceway that the first race was staged for the Speedway cars. Baker, driving a Cadillac powered open-wheeler, took the lead in the 144th lap of the 200 lapper and beat runner-up Bill Miller by five miles.

Seven events were held in May and June at established facilities like Martinsville, Atlanta's Lakewood Speedway, Charlotte and Langhorne. With the exception of Darlington, which attracted 21 cars, the starting fields were short of expectations. By July, promoters were concerned about signing up for the Speedway cars since a nation-wide steel strike was making it impossible for car owners to find the metal to build machinery. NASCAR issued a statement in July: "Due to an unusually warm summer coupled with the paralyzing nation-wide steel strike, many promoters have postponed dates until conditions take a turn for the better."

Although the steel strike was resolved in August, the Speedway division failed to attract any new race dates. Baker was crowned champion based on the seven events that were held.

The Speedway division never actually got off the ground. The AAA, recognizing their open-wheel rival was terminally ill, delivered a verbal stab at NASCAR racing in general. Arthur Harrington, Chairman of the AAA Contest Board, said in a prepared statement: "The Contest Board is bitterly opposed to what it calls 'junk cars' and believes the fad for such hippodroming is dying out."

Furthermore, the July 4th opening of the new Southland Speedway in Raleigh, NC -- a one-mile banked paved superspeedway -- had opted to go with a AAA national championship event for the inaugural instead of the NASCAR Grand Nationals. It was the first time the AAA had sponsored a championship affair in North Carolina since

Fireball Roberts in one of the NASCAR Speedway cars.

1926, when it directed a show at the old Charlotte Board track.

To counter the AAA's invasion, NASCAR quickly tossed a 200-mile Modified-Sportsman race at Darlington into the holiday schedule. The AAA Raleigh show drew 25,000 to watch Troy Ruttman win by two laps over Jack McGrath; and some 12,000 witnessed Curtis Turner tame a 56-car field in Darlington's race where driver Rex Stansell was killed in a late race mishap.

The AAA claimed victory on the battlefront with NASCAR.

NASCAR issued a statement shortly after July 4th that said, "The Raleigh event failed to live up to its advance billing", citing the fact that the average speed of 89.109 mph was much lower than AAA expected.

Behind the battle lines, progress was marching merrily on. Drivers and car owners began experimenting with two-way radios. The first known use of a two-way radio in a NASCAR event was on February 9, 1952, in the 125-mile Modified-Sportsman race at Daytona's Beach and Road Course. Driver Al Stevens of Odenton, MD, who operated a radio dispatched wrecking service, figured out a way he could turn his trade into an advantage on the enormous 4.1-mile race course. Stevens stationed two automobiles, each equipped with

Tony Bonadies was wired for sound in NASCAR Speedway event at Darlington.

a two-way radio, on the course, one at the North end of Daytona's beachfront facility, and the other at the South end. Another two-way radio was in the pits with car owner Cotton Bennett. Each radio operator could communicate with Stevens as he drove the race.

Stevens, driving a '37 Ford Sportsman car, finished third in his class and 27th overall in the 97-car field. He said the radio hook-up assisted him tremendsouly in averting spin-outs and pile-ups in the turns where cars often bogged down in the sand.

In the first Speedway division race at Darlington, Red Crise entered a Kurtis Kraft car powered by a Chrysler Firepower engine, with Tom Bonadies as driver. Crise hand-crafted a two-way radio of his own. He brought an army-type 'walkie-talkie' and strapped it to Bonadies old leather-strapped Cromwell helmet. This must have been very uncomfortable for the driver since walkie-talkie's of this vintage were massive pieces of machinery with heavy batteries. In the race, the Bronx, NY driver could talk to Crise in the pits by pressing the talk button. Although there was a great deal of static, and the noise from the open-wheelers reached epic decibels, Crise termed his experiment a success. Bonadies departed shortly after the half-way point with a blown head gasket and probably a terrific headache. He finished 18th in the field of 21 cars.

One of the high-water marks on the 1952 season was the acquisition of a number of major companies, who put several thousand dollars into race purses and the year-end point fund. Among these were Pure Oil Co., who added contingency monies into each race during Daytona's SpeedWeek festival and distributed some 7,856 gallons of fuel to the competitors free of charge.

Champion Spark Plugs tossed some $5,000 into the championship point funds for the Grand Nationals ($1,500), Sportsman, Modified and Short Track Divisions ($1,000 each), and the Speedway Class ($500).

Wynn's and Miracle Power, companies specializing in automobile related products, put additional dollars into the NASCAR point funds.

Chasing after the extra dollars were Herb Thomas and Tim Flock, who were locked in a tremendous battle for the Grand National championship. As the season wound down, Thomas and Flock were separated by less than 200 points. By merely starting the season finale at West Palm Beach on November 30th, Flock bagged his first Grand National title. He did it in spectacular fashion. On lap 164, Flock's Hudson whacked the retaining wall and flipped over, skidding down the front stretch on its roof. Uninjured, Flock happily said, "I bet I'm the only guy who ever won a championship while on his head."

Thomas won the race and fell short by 106 points in the standings.

Despite a growing number of accessory companies giving extra money to drivers, car owners, promoters and the sanctioning body, the drivers were not necessarily compelled to advise promoters of their intentions to race at his track. NASCAR pleaded with the drivers to cooperate in this matter, but few responded.

NASCAR Vice-President Ed Otto and Secretary Bill Tuthill.

take NASCAR until 1953 to figure out a way to solve this dilemma.

Finally we learned something about sportsmanship in 1952 from an ex-motorcycle racer who was trying his hand at Modifieds. Joe Weatherly, who would eventually become one of the most beloved Grand National champions, was one of the top short track throttle stompers in 1952, having won 49 times in 83 starts when the final statistics were tallied. His record included one stretch of eleven consecutive wins.

In a 25-lap Modified race at Richmond Speedway in August, Weatherly was riding leader Sam DiRusso's bumper in the final stretch duel. In the final lap, Weatherly's front bumper hooked DiRusso's mount, spinning him around in the turn and dropping him to third in the final order. Weatherly went on to win.

One short track race scheduled in July at Akron, OH, was cancelled by the promoter since *not one driver* had returned an entry blank. After the embarrassing cancellation, Ed Otto, a promoter of many talents, included a footnote on one of his entry blanks. It read: "Don't be a dope. You want racing, but you leave the promoter high and dry on publicity. Fill out and return. Ed Otto."

The NASCAR Public Relations Department expressed the need for drivers to inform promoters well in advance with several notices in the NASCAR newsletter. For the most part, everyone ignored it. It would

Immediately after the race had ended, Weatherly told race officials that he was overly aggressive in his victory jaunt and felt DiRusso was more deserving of taking home first place money. Weatherly instructed NASCAR officials to usher DiRusso into the victory lane. DiRusso was paid for first place, and Weatherly happily accepted third place money.

The 1,200 or so fans who were on hand at Richmond gave Weatherly a standing ovation.

The Hudsons of Dick Rathmann #120 and Tim Flock #91 collectively won 13 races in the 1952 NASCAR Grand National Season.

Race No. 1

Tim Flock Tops in 1952 Season Opener at Palm Beach

WEST PALM BEACH, FL (Jan. 20) - Tim Flock started up front and finished in front to win the 1952 Grand National season opener at Palm Beach Speedway driving the Ted Chester Hudson Hornet. It was Flock's ninth career win on NASCAR's premier stock car racing circuit.

Jack Smith #44 rounds the turn at start of West Palm Beach, FL Grand National race.

Lee Petty finished in second place, Fonty Flock was third, Yankee Frankie Schneider came in fourth with Buddy Shuman fifth.

Pancho Alvarez miraculously escaped injury when his Oldsmobile bounded high in the air and came down

Tim Flock receives congratulations after winning at Palm Beach Speedway.

Grand National Race No. 1
200 Laps at Palm Beach Speedway
West Palm Beach, FL
100 Miles on Half-mile Dirt Track
January 20, 1952

Fin	St	No.	Driver	Team / Car	Laps	Money	Status
1	1	91	Tim Flock	Ted Chester '51 Hudson	200	$1,025	Running
2	10	42	Lee Petty	Petty Special '51 Plymouth		700	Running
3	8	14	Fonty Flock	Frank Christian '51 Olds 88		450	Running
4	3	88	Frankie Schneider	Clark-Warwick '51 Olds 88		360	Running
5	6	17	Buddy Shuman	Shuman '51 Ford		210	Running
6	11	7	Frank Mundy	Gray Ghost '51 Olds 88		125	
7	14	787	Jim Millard	Ed Huegele '50 Mercury		100	
8	16	86	Bill Davis	Joe Mangini '51 Chevrolet		75	
9	4	9	Ed Samples	Claude Alexander '51 Olds 88		60	
10		36	Al Funderburk	Boyce Gillette '51 Plymouth		50	
11		3	Allan Clarke	'50 Chevrolet		25	
12		81	Pappy Hough	Hough '51 Ford		25	
13	20	15	Harvey Henderson	Henderson '50 Ford		25	
14	19	4jr.	Leo Caldwell	Bud Berry '50 Mercury		25	
15	15	182	Leo Richard	'51 Mercury		25	
16	13	23	Al Keller	'51 Studebaker		25	
17	7	2	Bill Blair	George Hutchens '51 Ford		25	
18	17	1	Dick Eagan	Eagan '51 Plymouth		25	Crash
19		888	Iggy Katona	Jolley Cartage Co. '51 Olds 88		25	
20	2	44	Jack Smith	Teaguemobile '51 Hudson	150	25	Crash
21		18	Jimmy Florian	Jimmy Florian '51 Olds 88		25	
22	21	82	Tom Gifford	'51 Studebaker		25	
23	18	47	Jim Reed	Reed '51 Lincoln		25	
24	9	94	Pancho Alvarez	'51 Olds 88		25	Crash
25	12	77	Chuck Mahoney	Ken Swihart '51 Hudson		25	
26	5	22	Leon Sales	R.G. Shelton '51 Hudson		25	
27		118	Johnny Thompson	Hans Winters '50 Olds 88		25	

Time of Race: No Time Recorded
Average Speed: None
Pole Winner: Tim Flock - 64.794 mph
Lap Leaders: - - - - - - - - - - Tim Flock　-200
Cautions: 2　　　　Margin of Victory:　　　Attendance: 6,000

squarely on its roof, flattening the entire car. Alvarez crawled from beneath the rubbish much to the delight of the 6,000 spectators.

Jack Smith, who started second in his Hudson, demolished his new mount in a solo wreck at the 150 lap mark.

There was no official time recorded due to the two red flags for the Alvarez and Smith wrecks.

Pancho Alvarez' Olds was flattened after Palm Beach bash.

Grand National Race No. 2
49 Laps at Beach & Road Course
Daytona Beach, FL
200 Miles on 4.1-mile Beach & Road Course
February 10, 1952

Fin	St	No.	Driver	Team / Car	Laps	Money	Status
1	11	6	Marshall Teague	Teaguemobile '52 Hudson	37	$1,500	Running
2	4	92	Herb Thomas	Teaguemobile '52 Hudson	37	1,000	Running
3	1	99	Pat Kirkwood	San Juan Motors '51 Chrysler	37	600	Running
4	6	14	Fonty Flock	Frank Christian '51 Olds 88		550	Running
5	7	51	Gober Sosebee	Cherokee Garage '51 Olds 88		450	Running
6	14	2	Bill Blair	George Hutchens '52 Olds 88		260	Running
7	3	40	Tommy Thompson	Thompson '51 Chrysler		250	Running
8	32	57	Tommy Moon	C.D. Wilson '51 Hudson Hornet		175	Running
9	31	42	Lee Petty	Petty Special '50 Lincoln		175	Running
10	2	59	Lloyd Moore	Julian Buesink '52 Chrysler		150	Running
11	35	88	Frankie Schneider	Clark-Warwick '50 Olds 88		50	
12	18	75	Larry Shurter	Shurter '50 Olds 88		50	
13	15	199	Leonard Tippett	Tippett '51 Hudson Hornet		50	
14	34	72	Donald Thomas	T.D. Meeks '50 Ford		50	
15	27	107	Bruce Atchley	Atchley '51 Hudson Hornet		50	
16		24	Jimmie Lewallen	J.O. Goode '51 Plymouth		50	
17	16	97	Dick Meyer	'50 Lincoln		50	
18		94-A	E.C. Ramsey	Louise Smith '50 Nash		50	
19		23	Al Keller	'51 Studebaker		50	
20	45	154	Leo Caldwell	Bud Berry '50 Mercury		50	
21		89	Ray Janehl	'51 Chrysler		25	
22	42	54	Paul Pettit	Pettit '51 Olds 88		25	
23	22	30	Ray Duhigg	'50 Olds 88		25	
24	30	142	Don Oldenberg	Hank Salat '51 Packard		25	
25	26	281	Roscoe Thompson	Ted Chester '51 Olds 88		25	
26	9	44	P. Cunningham	Teaguemobile '51 Hudson		25	
27	8	9	Ed Samples	Claude Alexander '51 Olds 88		25	
28	20	87	Buck Baker	Griffin Motors '50 Olds 88		25	
29	22	82	Joe Eubanks	Phil Oates '50 Olds 88		25	
30		16	Bill Snowden	Snowden '51 Cadillac		25	
31		77	Jack Smith	Harold Mays '51 Chrysler		25	
32	37	32	Tom Lechlider	Lechlider '50 Olds 88		25	
33	33	111	Jack Goodwin	'51 Lincoln		25	
34	12	39	Jim Mayes	Lloyd Schoenheit '51 Chrysler		25	
35	24	187	Red Duvall	'50 Packard		25	
36		100	Bob Apperson	Apperson '51 Chrysler		25	
37	5	250	Buck McCardell	H.R. Robertson '52 Chrysler		25	Wheel
38	10	90	A.D. Yates	Yates '52 Chrysler		25	Wheel
39	36	17	Buddy Shuman	Shuman '51 Ford		25	
40		3	Jimmy Ayers	Ayers '51 Studebaker		25	
41	21	41	Curtis Turner	John Eanes '52 Olds 88		---	Stuck
42		18	Jimmy Florian	Florian '51 Olds 88		---	
43	40	282	Tom Gifford	'51 Studebaker		---	
44	39	83	Bill Miller	Dantone Racing Stable '51 Ford		---	Transmsn
45	29	96	J.E. Hardie	Hardie '52 Studebaker		---	Oil Prs
46	19	103	George Gallup	Gallup '50 Olds 88		---	
47	13	4	Mike Klapak	Teaguemobile '51 Hudson		---	Rear End
48		12	Billy Carden	Bishop Bros. '51 Hudson		---	Clutch
49	43	66	George Fleming	Elmer Pooler '51 Hudson		---	
50	47	181	Mooney Williamson	Tom Lucas '51 Hudson		---	Con Rod
51	25	105	Joie Ray**	Grady Quinn '52 Henry J		---	Crash
52	44	11	Fireball Roberts	Saverance Motors '51 Ford		---	Rear End
53		47	Jim Reed	Reed '51 Lincoln		---	
54	28	188	Johnny Thompson	Hans Winters '50 Olds 88		---	Trnsmsn
55		91	Tim Flock	Ted Chester '51 Hudson Hornet		---	Con Rod
56		7	Gordon Bishop	Gray Ghost '51 Olds 88		---	
57	17	22	Leon Sales	R.G. Shelton '51 Hudson Hornet		---	Crash
58	38	52	Joe Gulde, Jr.	Hudson Guide Motors '51 Hudson		---	
59	46	34	L.C. Rigsby	'49 Plymouth		---	
60	41	120	Dick Rathmann	Walt Chapman '51 Hudson Hornet		---	Fuel Pmp
61		19	Smokey Purser	'50 Olds 88		---	Crash

* Race shortened from 49 to 37 laps due to onrushing tide.

Time of Race: 1 hour, 46 minutes, 19 seconds
 Average Speed 85.612 mph
 Pole Winner: Pat Kirkwood - 110.97 mph
 Lap Leaders: Herb Thomas 1, Marshall Teague 2-37
 Cautions: None
 Margin of Victory: 1 minute, 21 seconds   Attendance: 20,000

Race No. 2

Teaguemobiles Run 1-2 at Daytona

DAYTONA BEACH, FL (Feb. 10) - Marshall Teague outraced running-mate Herb Thomas and sped past an onrushing tide to win the 151.7-mile race at the 4.1-mile Daytona Beach and Road course. It was the second win in a row for Teague at his hometown track. He averaged 85.162 mph.

Teague was not permitted to compete in the NASCAR sanctioned event until he paid a $574.50 fine. He had driven in the Pan American race in Mexico in November 1951, a contest which was strictly off-limits to those drivers holding NASCAR license. Teague drove despite the warning and had to pay the fine to get back in the good graces of NASCAR.

Leon Sales' Hudson Hornet goes over North turn bank in Daytona Beach Grand National.

The scheduled 200 mile race was cut short due to an incoming tide. The event had to be held up for some time to allow the unexpectedly large crowd of 20,000 to find parking spaces along the beach. Once the race got underway, it was evident that the entire 48 laps could not be completed. The timing of racing between high tides is critical at Daytona Beach.

Teague beat Thomas by one minute and 21 seconds to take the $1,500 top prize. Both drivers were in identical Hudsons owned and prepared by Teague. Pat Kirkwood, who started on the pole, finished third. Fonty Flock came in fourth and Gober Sosebee was fifth.

The decision to cut the race came when the leaders were completing their 27th lap. Bill France notified the respective pit crews, who in turn, sent messages to their drivers via pitboard. Teague, having been signalled the race would be stopped at 37 laps, slackened his pace and rode the entire way without a pit stop. His fuel tank went dry as he took the checkered flag.

Tommy Thompson took an eventful route into seventh place. The Louisville, KY driver lost control of his Chrysler a few yards before the finish line and struck starter Johnny Bruner, who prefers to flag the cars at trackside instead of an overhead protective platform. Bruner was knocked ten feet into the air, but his injuries were minor.

Carl D. "Smokey" Purser, a top pilot from the 1930's, attempted a comeback but flipped his Olds in the opening lap. Purser suffered a broken arm in the mishap.

Race No. 3

Teague and Thomas Again at Jax

JACKSONVILLE, FL (Mar. 6) - Marshall Teague and Herb Thomas finished first and second in the 100-mile Grand National race at Jacksonville's Speedway Park, giving the Twin T's their second straight sweep.

Marshall Teague grabbed his 2nd straight win at Jacksonville, FL.

Frankie Schneider wound up third as the first three finishers completed all 200 laps on the half-mile dirt track. It was Teague's seventh career Grand National win.Tim Flock finished fourth.

The most crowd pleasing run belonged to fifth place finisher Tommy Moon. The local driver flipped his Hudson in the first lap.But the car righted itself and Moon continued in the race. The slim crowd of 2,800 cheered their local favorite as he passed his rivals. It was the first top 5 finish of his career.

Point leader Fonty Flock wound up sixth in the race.

One caution flag in the 149th lap for Bill Miller's crash, slowed the action for four laps. Teague averaged 55.197 mph for the 100 mile dash.

Grand National Race No. 3
200 Laps at Speedway Park
Jacksonville, FL
100 Miles on Half-mile Dirt Track
March 6, 1952

Fin	St	No.	Driver	Team / Car	Laps	Money	Status
1	1	6	Marshall Teague	Teague '52 Hudson	200	$1,000	Running
2	3	4	Herb Thomas	Teague '52 Hudson	200	700	Running
3	7	88	Frankie Schneider	Clark-Warwick '51 Olds 88	200	450	Running
4	2	91	Tim Flock	Ted Chester '51 Hudson		350	Running
5	4	157	Tommy Moon	C.D. Wilson '51 Hudson		200	Running
6	29	14	Fonty Flock	Frank Christian'51 Olds 88		150	Running
7		72	Donald Thomas	T.D. Meeks '50 Ford		125	
8		47	Jim Reed	Reed '50 Lincoln		100	
9		1	Dick Eagan	Eagan '51 Plymouth		75	
10		78	Bob Moore	Moore '51 Olds 88		50	
11		12	Billy Carden	Bishop Bros. '51 Studebaker		25	
12		18	Jimmy Florian	Florian '51 Olds		25	
13	5	199	Leonard Tippett	Tippett '51 Hudson Hornet		25	
14			Bob Dugan	'49 Plymouth		25	
15		7	Gordon Bishop	Gray Ghost '51 Olds 88		25	
16		281	Roscoe Thompson	Thompson '50 Olds 88		25	
17		83	Bill Miller	Daytone Racing '51 Ford 6	149	25	Crash
18		118	Johnny Thompson	Hans Winters '51 Olds 88		25	
19			Charles Stark	'49 Plymouth		25	
20		75	Larry Shurter	Shurter '51 Olds 88		25	
21		3	Jimmy Ayers	Ayers '51 Studebaker		25	
22		42	Lee Petty	Petty Engineering '51 Plymouth		25	
23		60	Jim Paschal	Julian Buesink '51 Ford		25	
24	6	11	Fireball Roberts	Saverance Motors '51 Ford 6		25	
25		17	Buddy Shuman	Shuman '50 Olds 88		25	
26		107	Bruce Atchley	Atchley '51 Hudson Hornet		25	
27		9	Ed Samples	Claude Alexander '50 Olds 88		25	
28		51	Gober Sosebee	Cherokee Garage '51 Olds 88		25	
29			Allan Clarke	'49 Chevrolet		25	

Tlime of Race: 1 hour, 48 minutes, 42 seconds
 Average Speed: 55.197 mph
 Pole Winner: Marshall Teague - 29.95 seconds, 60.100 mph
 Lap Leaders: Marshall Teague 1-200.
 Cautions: 1 for 4 laps   Margin of victory: Attendance: 2,800

Race No. 4

Thomas' Hornet Stings Wilkesboro Field

N. WILKESBORO, NC (Mar 30) - Herb Thomas dominated the entire 125-mile Grand National race at North Wilkesboro Speedway, leading from start to finish in an effortless victory ride.

Fonty Flock gave chase to Thomas' powerful Hudson Hornet, but had to settle for second place in his Oldsmobile. Bill Blair came in third, Donald Thomas finished fourth and Dave Terrell was fifth.

There were eight Hornets in the field, but Thomas manned the only one that finished the 200-lap grind on the .625-mile

Herb Thomas won at N. Wilkesboro.

dirt track.

Frankie Schneider, who entered the race second in the NASCAR point standings, flipped his Oldsmobile on lap 40. The errant car bounded into the path of Perk Brown, who smashed into the wreckage. Both were eliminated from competition. Neither driver was hurt.

A crowd of 10,000 watched Thomas finish a lap ahead of the field, averaging 75.075 mph in the process.

Dick Rathmann won at Martinsville.

Grand National Race No. 4
200 Laps at N. Wilkesboro Speedway
North Wilkesboro, NC
125 Miles on .625-mile Dirt Track
March 30, 1952

Fin	St	No.	Driver	Team / Car	Laps	Money	Status
1	1	92	Herb Thomas	Thomas '52 Hudson	200	$1,000	Running
2		14	Fonty Flock	Frank Christian '51 Olds 88	199	700	Running
3		2	Bill Blair	George Hutchens '52 Olds 88		450	Running
4		72	Donald Thomas	T.D. Meeks '51 Ford		350	Running
5		126	Dave Terrell	Terrell '51 Plymouth		200	Running
6		52	Neil Cole	John Golabek '50 Plymouth		150	Running
7		17	Buddy Shuman	Shuman '51 Ford 6	175	125	Shocks
8		60	Jim Paschal	Julian Buesink '50 Ford	165	100	Battery
9		42	Lee Petty	Petty Engineering '51 Plym	142	75	Handling
10			Otis Martin	'49 Buick	137	50	Running
11		82	Joe Eubanks	Oates Motor Co. '50 Olds 88	122	25	Clutch
12		199	Leonard Tippett	Tippett '51 Hudson Hornet	108	25	Rear End
13			Shorty Gibbs	'51 Ford	76	25	Brakes
14		128	Charles Gattalia	Colonial Mtrs. '51 Studebaker	69	25	Heating
15	2	89	Buck Baker	B.A. Pless '52 Hudson	68	25	Radiator
16		6	Marshall Teague	Teague '52 Hudson	57	25	Withdrew
17			Bobby Courtwright	'50 Olds 88	47	25	Battery
18		88	Frankie Schneider	Rocket '51 Olds 88	40	25	Crash
19		22	Perk Brown	R.G. Shelton '51 Hudson	39	25	Crash
20		41	Curtis Turner	John Eanes '52 Hudson	35	25	Radiator
21		91	Tim Flock	Ted Chester '51 Hudson	26	25	Gasket
22		24	Jimmie Lewallen	J O Goode '51 Plymouth	26	25	Tie rod
23		120	Dick Rathmann	Walt Chapman '51 Hudson	20	25	Radiator
24			Harold Mays	Mays '51 Chrysler	1	25	Crash

Time of Race: 2 hours, 8 minutes
Average Speed: 58.597 mph
Pole Winner: Herb Thomas - 75.075 mph
Lap Leaders: Herb Thomas 1-200
Cautions: Margin of Victory: 1 lap plus   Attendance: 10,000

Race No. 5

Rathman Breaks Ice At Martinsville

MARTINSVILLE, VA (Apr. 6) - Dick Rathmann of Los Angeles steered his Walt Chapman Hudson Hornet into the lead 20 laps from the finish and held off Bill Blair to win the 100-mile Grand National race at Martinsville Speedway.

It was Rathman's first NASCAR win, coming in his 16th start.

Point leader Fonty Flock dislocated a shoulder when his Olds threw a wheel and flipped while running second on lap 138.

The lead changed hands seven times among five different drivers. Rathmann was running with the leaders throughout the event but never led until taking over first place on lap 181 of the 200-lapper.

Buck Baker started on the pole and led the chase for 20 laps. His bid ended when a hub broke on his Hudson. Tim Flock took over and led on three occasions, but a broken spindle put his Hudson out after 162 laps.

Bill Blair led for 18 laps, but had to settle for second, 5.0 seconds behind Rathmann. Third place went to Perk Brown, with Lee Petty and Bobby Courtwright filling out the top five.

Jimmie Lewallen was badly shaken when his Plymouth turned over in the 118th lap.

Flock's shoulder injury was believed to be serious enough to keep him out of action for a couple of weeks.

A crowd of 6,500 enjoyed the race. Rathmann averaged 42.862 mph after five cautions slowed the field.

Grand National Race No. 5
200 Laps at Martinsville Speedway
Martinsville, VA
100 Miles on Half-mile Dirt Track
April 6, 1952

Fin	St	No.	Driver	Team / Car	Laps	Money	Status
1	9	120	Dick Rathmann	Walt Chapman '51 Hudson	200	$1,000	Running
2	6	2	Bill Blair	George Hutchens '52 Olds 88	200	700	Running
3	10	22	Perk Brown	R.G. Shelton '51 Hudson	199	450	Running
4	11	42	Lee Petty	Petty Engineering '51 Plym	199	350	Running
5	20		Bobby Courtwright	'50 Olds 88	197	200	Running
6	19	52	Neil Cole	John Golabek '50 Plymouth	189	150	Running
7	21	38	Clyde Minter	'49 Buick	175	125	Rear End
8	2	92	Herb Thomas	Thomas '52 Hudson	174	100	Running
9	7	88	Frankie Schneider	Clark-Warwick '51 Olds 88	171	75	Spindle
10	14	60	Jim Paschal	Julian Buesink '51 Ford	169	50	Heating
11	3	91	Tim Flock	Ted Chester '51 Hudson	162	25	Spindle
12	4	41	Curtis Turner	John Eanes '51 Hudson	162	25	Wheel
13	18	17	Buddy Shuman	Shuman '51 Ford 6	150	25	Running
14	12	94	E.C. Ramsey	Louise Smith Special '51 Ford	142	25	Wheel
15	5	14	Fonty Flock	Frank Christian '51 Olds 88	138	25	Crash
16	17	24	Jimmie Lewallen	J.O. Goode '51 Plymouth	118	25	Crash
17	13	128	Charles Gattalia	Colonial Mtrs '51 Studebaker	94	25	Spindle
18	8	82	Joe Eubanks	Oates Motor Co. '50 Olds 88	74	25	Steering
19	15	72	Donald Thomas	T.D. Meeks '51 Ford	68	25	RF Hub
20	1	89	Buck Baker	B.A. Pless '52 Hudson Hornet	29	25	Hubs
21	22	126	Dave Terrell	Terrell '49 Plymouth	29	25	RR Hub
22	16		Shorty Gibbs	'51 Nash	11	25	Hd Gask

Time of Race: 2 hours, 19 minutes, 59 seconds
Average Speed: 42.862 mph
Pole Winner: Buck Baker - 54.945 mph
Lap Leaders: Buck Baker 1-29, Tim Flock 30-34, Curtis Turner 35-39, T. Flock 40-43,
    Turner 44-50, T. Flock 51-162, Bill Blair 163-180, Dick Rathmann 181-200.
Cautions: 5   Margin of Victory: 5 seconds   Attendance: 6,500

*Jimmie Lewallen's Plymouth lies upside down at
Martinsville Speedway. The Archdale, NC driver was shaken badly in the wreck.*

Race No. 6

Buck Baker Gets First Win at Columbia Speedway

COLUMBIA, SC (Apr. 12) - Buck Baker, veteran out of Charlotte, took the lead in the 181st lap and held off Lee Petty by 14 seconds to win the 100-mile Grand National race at Columbia Speedway. It was his first big time NASCAR victory.

Dick Rathmann finished in third place. Frankie Schneider, running second with only two laps to go, finished fourth when he had to pit for gas. Joe Eubanks came in fifth.

Petty took over the point lead as idle Fonty Flock was still nursing a dislocated shoulder. Gober Sosebee filled in for Flock in the Frank Christian Oldsmobile. He led for 39 laps before falling off the pace. He eventually finished 12th.

Buck Baker.

Dick Rathmann and Leonard Tippett were eliminated in crashes. E.C. Ramsey was forced to park his Ford when he plowed into a 1950 Mercury driven by a spectator who was insanely attempting to cross the track during the race. An infuriated Ramsey dismounted his mangled car, dashed over to the dazed and intoxicated spectator and proceeded to beat him to a pulp. The police arrived, calmed down Ramsey and carted the fan to the jailhouse.

Baker averaged 53.460 mph, giving both him and his car owner, B.A. Pless, their first Grand National win.

Race No. 7

Sosebee's Cadillac Breaks; Blair Wins at Lakewood

ATLANTA, GA (Apr. 24) - Gober Sosebee was seven laps from paydirt when a broken spindle put his Cadillac out of action, and Bill Blair slipped through to win the 100-miler at Lakewood Speedway. Sosebee, wheeling a Cadillac owned by Sam Knox, was trying to give the Cadillac nameplate its first Grand National win.

Grand National Race No. 6
200 Laps at Columbia Speedway
Columbia, SC
100 Miles on Half-mile Dirt Track
April 12, 1952

Fin	St	No.	Driver	Team / Car	Laps	Money	Status
1	1	89	Buck Baker	B.A. Pless '52 Hudson Hornet	200	$1,000	Running
2		42	Lee Petty	Petty Engineering '51 Plym	200	700	Running
3		120	Dick Rathmann	Walt Chapman '51 Hudson		450	Running
4		88	Frankie Schneider	Rocket '51 Olds 88		350	Running
5		82	Joe Eubanks	Phil Oates '50 Olds 88		200	Running
6		72	Donald Thomas	T.D. Meeks '51 Ford		150	Running
7		17	Bluddy Shuman	Shuman '51 Ford 6		125	Running
8		60	Jim Paschal	Julian Buesink '51 Ford		100	Running
9		77	Jack Smith	Harold Mays '51 Chrysler		75	Running
10		18	Jimmy Florian	Florian '51 Ford		50	Running
11			Bobby Courtwright	'50 Olds 88		25	Running
12		14	Gober Sosebee	Frank Christian '50 Olds 88		25	Running
13		128	Charles Gattalia	Colonial Mtrs '51 Studebaker		25	Running
14		22	Perk Brown	R.G. Shelton '51 Hudson	167	25	Spindle
15			Bill Widenhouse	'50 Plymouth	162	25	Crash
16		9	Ed Samples	Claude Alexander '51 Olds 88	161	25	Engine
17		92	Herb Thomas	Thomas '52 Hudson Hornet		25	Running
18	2	91	Tim Flock	Ted Chester '51 Hudson Hornet		25	Running
19		199	Leonard Tippett	Tippett '51 Hudson Hornet	100	25	Crash
20	22	94	E.C. Ramsey	Louise Smith Special '51 Ford	81	25	Crash*
21		11	Fireball Roberts	Saverance Motors '51 Ford 6	59	25	Rear End
22		6	Marshall Teague	Teague '51 Hudson	23	25	Heating

* E.C. Ramsey crashed into spectator who was driving a '50 Mercury across track during race
Time of Race: 1 hour, 52 minutes, 14 seconds
Average Speed: 53.460 mph
Pole Winner: Buck Baker
Lap Leaders: Buck Baker 1-62, Gober Sosebee 63-101, Dick Rathmann 102-180
  Baker 181-200.
Cautions: Margin of Victory: 14 seconds   Attendance: 6,600

*Bill Blair's white Oldsmobile rounds
turn at Lakewood Speedway.*

Blair drove his George Hutchens Olds to his second career Grand National win. Ed Samples finished second and Lee Petty third, both in the same lap with winner Blair. Buck Baker finished fourth, and Ed Benedict was a surprising fifth place finisher.

Roscoe Thompson of Atlanta, was tabbed by car owner Frank Christian to replace the injured Fonty Flock, and he responded brilliantly. Thompson led for 11 laps and was holding down the lead when a broken right rear hub put his Olds out of action after 71 laps.

At the last moment, Fonty Flock decided he would try to drive in the race. Already having turned his ride over to Thompson, Flock scrambled into a back-up Christian car and drove as long as he could, hoping to keep within sight of point leader Petty. He was able to go only a few laps before calling on Jack Smith to relieve him. Smith's Studebaker had fallen out after 30 laps.

Smith carried Flock's Olds into seventh place in the final order, worth 152 points. Flock earned 58 points; Smith got the other 94. The distribution of points was based on the percentage of laps each drove in the car.

Blair averaged 66.877 mph on the low-banked one-mile dirt track. A standing room only crowd of 29,000 jammed the Lakewood grounds.

Race No. 8

Thomas Trudges to Victory at Muddy Macon

MACON, GA (Apr. 27) - Heavy rains at the Central City Speedway forced a three-hour delay, but the Grand National touring pros raced as long as daylight permitted on the muddy half-mile clay oval.

When the event was flagged to a halt, 198 laps had been completed and Herb Thomas was declared the winner for the 10th time in his career. The event had been scheduled as a 300 lapper.

*Another trophy for
Herb Thomas.*

Torrential rains hit the speedway, but promoters Alf Knight and Ted Chester were determined to give the fans a race. After work was done on the track when the rain finally stopped falling, a vote was taken from the 28 drivers on hand whether to attempt to start the race or not. The vote was 15-13 in favor of racing.

Jack Smith, wheeling the Studebaker previously owned by the late Perry Smith, started on the pole and

Grand National Race No. 7
100 Laps at Lakewood Speedway
Atlanta, GA
100 Laps on 1-mile Dirt Track
April 20, 1952

Fin	St	No.	Driver	Team / Car	Laps	Money	Status
1	7	2	Bill Blair	George Hutchens '52 Olds 88	100	$1,000	Running
2	16	9	Ed Samples	Claude Alexander '51 Olds 88	100	700	Running
3	17	42	Lee Petty	Petty Engineering '51 Plym	100	450	Running
4	4	89	Buck Baker	B.A. Pless '52 Hudson Hornet	99	350	Running
5	12	118	Ed Benedict	Ken Swihart '52 Hudson	98	200	Running
6	11	128	Charles Gattalia	Colonial Mtrs. '51 Studebaker	97	150	Running
7	6	4	Fonty Flock *	Frank Christian '51 Olds 88	96	125	Running
8	2	92	Herb Thomas	Thomas '52 Hudson	95	100	Running
9	3	51	Gober Sosebee	Sam Knox '50 Cadillac	93	75	Spindle
10	18	18	Jimmy Florian	Florian '51 Ford	93	50	Running
11	14	16	Bill Snowden	Snowden '52 Hudson Hornet	90	40	Steering
12	19	94	E.C. Ramsey	Louise Smith Special '51 Ford	82	25	RR Hub
13	8	41	Curtis Turner	John Eanes '52 Hudson	74	40	Crash
14	5	14	Roscoe Thompson	Frank Christian '52 Olds 88	71	25	RR Hub
15	1	91	Tim Flock	Ted Chester '51 Hudson	61	25	Axle
16	13	120	Dick Rathmann	Walt Chapman '51 Hudson	60	40	RF Hub
17	15	60	Jim Paschal	Julian Buesink '51 Ford	53	40	Rear End
18	20	83	Bill Miller	Dantone Racing '51 Ford 6	41	25	Heating
19	21	23	Jack Smith	'51 Studebaker	30	25	Steering
20	23		Buck McCardell	'51 Nash	22	25	RR Hub
21	9	22	Perk Brown	R.G. Shelton '51 Hudson	16	40	Rear End
22	10	57	Tommy Moon	C.D. Wilson '52 Hudson	9	35	Heating
23	22	110	Charles Causey	Bob Osiecki '51 Kaiser	7	25	Clutch
24	24	77	Harold Mays	Mays '51 Chrysler	0	35	DNS

* Relieved by Jack Smith
Time of Race: 1 hour, 29 minutes, 43 seconds
Average Speed: 66.877 mph
Lap Leaders: Tim Flock 1-60, Roscoe Thompson 61-71, Gober Sosebee 72-93, Bill Blair: 94-100
Cautions: Margin of Victory: Attendance: 29,000

Jack Smith won pole at Macon in Studebaker.

led the first 186 laps. A broken wheel knocked him out of action with what amounted to 12 laps remaining.

Thomas won $1,270 from the $5,000 purse. Point leader Fonty Flock drove virtually one-handed into second place, only a few car lengths behind the winner. Ed Samples finished third, Buck Baker fourth and Gober Sosebee fifth.

Dick Rathmann and Roscoe Thompson, who started second and third, crashed in separate incidents. Five cars were taken out by overheating problems, having their radiators clogged with thick mud.

The event was finally flagged due to darkness. Thomas averaged 53.853 mph.

Race No. 9

Rathmann Romps In Langhorne Laugher

LANGHORNE, PA (May 4) - Dick Rathmann bolted past pole sitter Herb Thomas in the first lap and led all the way in winning the 150-miler at Langhorne Speedway.

From the very outset, Rathmann flexed his muscles and when the checkered flag fell, he was five full laps ahead of runner-up Tim Flock. Lee Petty was third, 10 laps behind. Jack Reynolds and Fonty Flock rounded out the top five.

Petty increased his point lead to 135 over Fonty Flock. Herb Thomas had been ranked second, but he

Grand National Race No. 8
300 Laps at Central City Speedway
Macon, GA
150 Miles on Half-mile Dirt Track
April 27, 1952

Fin	St	No.	Driver	Team / Car	Laps	Money	Status
1	4	92	Herb Thomas	Thomas '52 Hudson	198	$1,270	Running
2	17	14	Fonty Flock	Frank Christian '51 Olds 88	198	800	Running
3	25	9	Ed Samples	Claude Alexander '51 Olds 88	198	600	Running
4	15	89	Buck Baker	B.A. Pless '52 Hudson Hornet	197	500	Running
5	20	51	Gober Sosebee	Cherokee Garage '50 Olds 88	195	300	Running
6	23	60	Jim Paschal	Julian Buesink '51 Ford	195	200	Running
7	8	42	Lee Petty	Petty Engineering '51 Plym	194	160	Running
8	6	72	Donald Thomas	T.D. Meeks '51 Ford	194	135	Running
9	5	91	Tim Flock	Ted Chester '51 Hudson	192	110	Running
10	7	128	Charles Gattalia	Colonial Mtrs '51 Studebaker	192	110	Running
11	16	22	Perk Brown	R.G. Shelton '51 Hudson	192	25	Running
12	9		Barney Smith	'52 Plymouth	191	25	Running
13	21	18	Jimmy Florian	Florian '51 Ford	190	25	Running
14	18	12	Billy Carden	Bishop Bros. '51 Plymouth	186	25	Running
15	27	7	Frank Mundy	'51 Plymouth	186	25	Running
16	1	23	Jack Smith	'51 Studebaker	186	75	Wheel
17	24	82	Joe Eubanks	Phil Oates '51 Olds 88	184	35	Running
18	11	3	Jimmy Ayers	Ayers '51 Studebaker	179	35	Running
19	14	93	Ted Chamberlain	Chamberlain '49 Plymouth	174	35	Running
20	10		C.H. Dingler	'50 Plymouth	160	35	Running
21	26	24	Jimmie Lewallen	J O Goode '51 Plymouth	153	25	Running
22	22	2	Bill Blair	George Hutchens '52 Olds 88	109	25	Heating
23	12	94	E.C. Ramsey	Louise Smith Special '51 Ford	56	35	Heating
24	2	120	Dick Rathmann	Walt Chapman '51 Hudson	43	64	Crash
25	28		Joe Staton	'51 Nash	41	25	Heating
26	13		Louise Smith	'51 Olds 88	20	35	Heating
27	19		Hank Lee	'52 Olds 88	20	25	Carb
28	3	4	Roscoe Thompson	Frank Christian '51 Olds 88	12	55	Crash

Time of Race: 1 hour, 50 minutes, 18 seconds
Average Speed: 53.853 mph
Pole Winner: Jack Smith - 54.429 mph
Lap Leaders: Jack Smith 1-186, Herb Thomas 187-198.   Cautions:
Margin of Victory: Attendance:
* Race was called at 198 laps due to darkness

Grand National Race No. 9
150 Laps at Langhorne Speedway
Langhorne, PA
150 Miles on 1-mile Dirt Track
May 4, 1952

Fin	St	No.	Driver	Team / Car	Laps	Money	Status
1	2	120	Dick Rathmann	Walt Chapman '52 Hudson	150	$1,275	Running
2	5	91	Tim Flock	Ted Chester '51 Hudson	145	810	Running
3	17	42	Lee Petty	PettyEngineering '51 Plym	140	600	Running
4	22	421	Jack Reynolds	Wiss Bros. '50 Plymouth	140	500	Running
5	6	14	Fonty Flock	Frank Christian '51 Olds 88	139	310	Running
6	3	89	Buck Baker	B.A. Pless '52 Hudson Hornet	138	210	Running
7	32		Tom Dawson	'51 Lincoln	134	150	Running
8	24	126	Dave Terrell	Terrell '49 Plymouth	134	125	Running
9	19		Bud Farrell	'51 Plymouth	132	100	Running
10	8	2	Bill Blair	George Hutchens '51 Olds 88	132	110	Running
11	37	12	Jim Paschal	'51 Ford	131	25	Running
12	11		Neil Cole	'51 Hudson	131	25	Engine
13	21		Eddie Adams	'49 Plymouth	128	25	Running
14	28	34	Ted Chamberlain	'50 Plymouth	124	25	Running
15	31		Bill James	'51 Plymouth	117	25	Running
16	23		Don Price	'49 Ford	116	25	Running
17	14	128	Charles Gattalia	Colonial Mtrs '51 Studebaker	112	25	Engine
18	30		Red Tomlinson	'49 Ford	111	25	Engine
19	4	99	Pat Kirkwood	Kirkwood '51 Chrysler	108	25	Engine
20	33	22	Perk Brown	R.G. Shelton '52 Hudson	108	25	Engine
21	1	92	Herb Thomas	Thomas '52 Hudson	96	50	Engine
22	16		Hank Lee	'52 Olds 88	94	25	Rear End
23	9	72	Donald Thomas	T.D. Meeks '50 Ford	87	25	Wtr Pmp
24	25		Louise Smith	'51 Olds 88	84	25	Engine
25	27		Larry Mann	'51 Nash	78	25	Engine
26	36	75	Larry Shurter	Shurter '50 Olds 88	76	25	Engine
27	29	47	Jim Reed	'50 Olds 88	75	25	Engine
28	13	103	George Gallup	Gallup '50 Olds 88	58	25	Crash
29	26		John DuBois	'50 Ford	53	25	Radiator
30	35	7	Frank Mundy	Gray Ghost '51 Olds 88	50	25	Rear End
31	7		Paul Pettit	'51 Olds 88	34	10	Crash
32	12	118	Ed Benedict	Ken Swihart '51 Hudson	28	10	Engine
33	10		Buck McCardell	'52 Hudson Hornet	27	10	Engine
34	18		Russ Hepler	'50 Ford	27	---	Heating
35	20	94	Joe Staton	Louise Smith '51 Ford	21	---	Heating
36	34		Wimpy Ervin	'51 Henry J	11	---	Carb
37	15	41	Curtis Turner	John Eanes '52 Hudson	5	---	Engine

Time of Race: 2 hours, 13 minutes
Average Speed: 67.669 mph
Pole Winner: Herb Thomas - 76.045 mph
Lap Leaders: Dick Rathmann 1-150
Cautions: Margin of Victory: 5 laps plus   Attendance: 20,000

Jack Reynolds came from 22nd to finish 4th at Langhorne.

dropped a notch when a blown engine left him with a 21st place finish in the field of 37.

Pat Kirkwood had worked his way to second place behind leader Rathmann, but his engine blew after 111 laps. He wound up 19th. Neil Cole followed Kirkwood into second place but engine problems put him out in the closing stages.

Thirty-eight cars qualified but only 37 started. George Fleming had earned the 17th spot but was involved in a spectacular mishap in a morning practice run. Fleming's Hudson flipped six times. He was transported to Mercer Hospital in Trenton for undetermined back injuries.

Race No. 10

Darlington 100 Falls To Dick Rathmann

DARLINGTON, SC (May 10) - Dick Rathmann drove his Hudson into the lead with 19 laps to go and won the 100-mile Grand National race at Darlington Raceway.

The event was hurriedly tossed into the 1952 schedule as a support race for the new NASCAR Speedway Division, a class for Indy cars with stock motors which was making its debut. There was a shortage of Speedway cars, so Raceway officials quickly arranged for a Grand National race.

Tim Flock finished second, Fonty Flock was third, and Jimmie Lewallen fourth. Fifth place went to Joe Eubanks.

Point leader Lee Petty finished in seventh place, four laps off the pace.

The drivers drew for starting positions since time did not permit a full round of qualifying. Fireball Roberts drew the pole and led the first 15 laps. Buck Baker, going for his second win of the season, passed Roberts and led for 15 laps before being passed by Tim Flock. Baker and Flock engaged in a spirited duel for several laps when Rathmann joined the shoot-out.

Herb Thomas hustled up toward the front, making it a four car battle. Rathmann took the lead for keeps on lap 62.

Rathmann averaged 83.818 mph for the 100 miles.

Grand National Race No. 10
80 Laps at Darlington Raceway
Darlington, SC
100 Miles on 1.25-mile Paved Track
May 10, 1952

Fin	St	No.	Driver	Team / Car	Laps	Money	Status
1	4	120	Dick Rathmann	Walt Chapman '51 Hudson	80	$1,000	Running
2	3	91	Tim Flock	Ted Chester '51 Hudson	80	700	Running
3	2	14	Fonty Flock	Frank Christian '51 Olds 88	78	450	Running
4	9	2	Jimmie Lewallen	George Hutchens '52 Olds 88	78	350	Running
5	6	82	Joe Eubanks	Phil Oates '52 Hudson	78	200	Running
6	24	72	Donald Thomas	T.D. Meeks '51 Ford	78	150	Running
7	13	42	Lee Petty	Petty Engineering '51 Plym	76	125	Running
8	1	11	Fireball Roberts	Saverance Motors '51 Ford	76	100	Running
9	8	41	Jim Paschal	John Eanes '52 Hudson	75	75	Running
10	12	7	Frank Mundy	Gray Ghost '50 Olds 88	75	50	Running
11	11	51	Gober Sosebee	Sosebee '51 Chrysler	74	25	Running
12	10	77	Weldon Adams	Harold Mays '51 Chrysler	74	25	Running
13	14	92	Herb Thomas	Thomas '52 Hudson	72	25	Running
14	19	96	J.E. Hardie	'52 Studebaker	69	25	Running
15	3	89	Buck Baker	B A Pless '52 Hudson	66	25	Radiator
16	15	128	Charles Gattalia	Colonial Mtrs '51 Studebaker	62	25	Heating
17	17	8	Jack Smith	Bishop Bros. '51 Studebaker	32	25	Heating
18	7	22	Perk Brown	R.G. Shelton '51 Hudson	30	25	Heating
19	18	21	Speedy Thompson	Bruce Root '51 Ford 6	26	25	Fuel Line
20	23	17	Bill Widenhouse	Buddy Shuman '51 Ford 6	19	25	Engine
21	16	9	Ed Samples	Claude Alexander '51 Olds 88	17	25	Handling
22	2	81	Roscoe Thompson	Thompson '51 Olds 88	13	25	Engine
23	21	99	Leonard Tippett	Tippett '51 Hudson Hornet	13	25	Engine
24	20	94	Joe Statton	'51 Nash Amb.	10	25	Tire

Time of Race: 1 hour, 11 minutes, 35 seconds
Average Speed: 83.818 mph
Pole Winner: No Time Trials - Drew for position
Lap Leaders: Fireball Roberts 1-15, Buck Baker 16-30, Tim Flock 31-35, Baker 36-42, Dick Rathmann 43, Baker 44-49, Herb Thomas 50-61, Rathmann 62-80.
Cautions: Margin of Victory: Attendance:

Race No. 11

Third Straight for Rathmann at Dayton

DAYTON, OH (May 18) - Dick Rathmann tied a record and won his third straight Grand National race in the 100-miler at Dayton Speedway.

Rathmann's Hudson beat runner-up Lloyd Moore's Ford by more than a lap. Tim Flock was third, Lee Petty fourth and Donald Thomas fifth. Petty extended his point lead to 159 over Fonty Flock, who finished 11th after starting on the pole.

Ted Chamberlain drove the final 120 laps with the steering nub alone. The steering wheel fell off, but the St. Petersburg veteran refused to quit. He managed to tour the half-mile paved track 164 times, which was good

Ted Chamberlain drove with steering nub.

enough for a 13th place finish.

Only one car failed to finish the race. Ed Benedict's Hudson broke a hub and stalled on the track after 94 laps.

Rathmann took the lead in the 48th lap and led the rest of the way.

Grand National Race No. 11
200 Laps at Dayton Speedway
Dayton, OH
100 Miles on Half-mile Paved Track
May 18, 1952

Fin	St	No.	Driver	Team / Car	Laps	Money	Status
1	3	120	Dick Rathmann	Walt Chapman '51 Hudson	200	$1,000	Running
2	7	59	Lloyd Moore	Julian Buesink '51 Ford	199	700	Running
3	2	91	Tim Flock	Ted Chester '51 Hudson	195	450	Running
4	11	42	Lee Petty	Petty Engineering '51 Plym	195	350	Running
5	12	72	Donald Thomas	T.D. Meeks '51 Ford	192	200	Running
6	6	92	Herb Thomas	Thomas '52 Hudson	189	150	Running
7	8	41	Jim Paschal	John Eanes '51 Hudson	186	125	Running
8	9	128	Charles Gattalia	Colonial Mtrs '51 Studebaker	184	100	Running
9	13	421	Jack Reynolds	Wiss Bros. '50 Plymouth	178	75	Running
10	4	22	Perk Brown	R.G. Shelton '51 Hudson	176	50	Running
11	1	14	Fonty Flock	Frank Christian '51 Olds 88	174	25	Running
12	5	8	Gene Comstock	'52 Hudson	169	25	Running
13	14	93	Ted Chamberlain	Chamberlain '50 Plymouth	164	25	Running
14	15	111	Robbie Robinson	'51 Hudson	162	25	Running
15	10	118	Ed Benedict	Ken Swihart '51 Hudson	94	25	RF Hub

Time of Race: 1 hour, 31 minutes, 54 seconds
Average Speed: 65.526 mph
Pole Winner: Fonty Flock - 71.884 mph
Lap Leaders: Tim Flock 1-47, Dick Rathmann 48-200.
Cautions: 1   Margin of Victory: 1 lap plus   Attendance: 8,000

Race No. 12

Thomas Nips Blair In Canfield Thriller

CANFIELD, OH (May 30) - Herb Thomas outran Bill Blair in a stretch duel and won the third annual "Poor Man's 500" at the Canfield Fairgrounds. It was the third win of the year for the Olivia, NC veteran.

Thomas' Hudson and Blair's Oldsmobile treated the crowd of 19,824 to a thrilling climax as the two throttle stompers crossed the finish line side-by-side. Thomas was ahead

Thomas won Canfield by 4 feet.

by a fender when the checkered flag fell.

Finishing third was Bob Moore, with Tim Flock fourth and Curtis Turner fifth.

Thomas' 11th career Grand National triumph ended Dick Rathmann's bid for four wins in a row.

Rathmann's potent Walt Chapman Hudson was not in the starting field. Rathmann was forced to take the wheel of a borrowed Ford. Although he won the pole position, the balding veteran drifted to an 11th place finish.

Point leader Lee Petty wound up 23rd in the field of 30 when engine problems sidelined his Plymouth after 70 laps. The Randleman, NC driver had his lead shaved to 77 points over Thomas.

The winner averaged 48.057 mph as four cautions slowed the pace. Jack Reynolds and George Hufford were eliminated in separate wrecks early in the contest. Neither driver was hurt.

Grand National Race No. 12
200 Laps at Canfield Fairgrounds
Canfield, OH
"Poor Man's 500"
100 Miles on Half-mile Dirt Track
May 30, 1952

Fin	St	No.	Driver	Team / Car	Laps	Money	Status
1	4	92	Herb Thomas	Thomas '52 Hudson	200	$1,000	Running
2	7	2	Bill Blair	George Hutchens '52 Olds 88	200	700	Running
3	10	78	Bob Moore	Moore '51 Olds 88	199	450	Running
4	2	91	Tim Flock	Ted Chester '51 Hudson	196	350	Running
5	9	41	Curtis Turner	John Eanes '51 Hudson	189	200	Running
6	8	82	Joe Eubanks	Phil Oates '51 Hudson	189	150	Running
7	17	44	Jimmie Lewallen	J.H. Petty '50 Plymouth	184	125	Running
8	15		Bill Rexford	'50 Ford	183	100	Running
9	27	93	Ted Chamberlain	Chamberlain '50 Plymouth	179	75	Running
10	30		Ernie Boost	'51 Plymouth	179	50	Running
11	1		Dick Rathmann	'50 Ford	174	25	Running
12	23		Paul Magee	'50 Plymouth	173	25	Running
13	25		Nook Walters	'50 Ford	171	25	Running
14	12		Neil Cole	'51 Hudson Hornet	169	25	Trnsmsn
15	18		Paul Pettit	'50 Olds 88	164	25	Running
16	13	72	Donald Thomas	T.D. Meeks '50 Ford	160	25	Running
17	3	14	Fonty Flock	Frank Christian '50 Olds 88	155	25	Engine
18	11	59	Lloyd Moore	Julian Buesink '50 Ford	151	25	Axle
19	14	118	Ed Benedict	Ken Swihart '51 Hudson	129	25	Hub
20	16	24	Ray Duhigg	J O Goode '50 Plymouth	119	25	Engine
21	29		Bob Shaw	'50 Ford	112	25	Crash
22	24	111	Robbie Robinson	'51 Hudson	94	25	Engine
23	6	42	Lee Petty	Petty Engineering '51 Plym	70	25	Engine
24	22		Mike Little	'50 Plymouth	62	25	Engine
25	26		Art Plas	'50 Plymouth	46	25	Engine
26	21		Bud Farrell	'50 Plymouth	41	25	Hub
27	20		Ralph Liguori	'50 Plymouth	38	25	Engine
28	28	421	Jack Reynolds	Wiss Bros. '50 Plymouth	35	25	Crash
29	19		George Hufford	'50 Plymouth	16	25	Crash
30	5	22	Perk Brown	R.G. Shelton '51 Hudson	15	25	Engine

Time of Race: 2 hours, 4 minutes, 51 seconds
Average Speed: 48.057 mph
Pole Winner: Dick Rathmann - 58.102 mph
Lap Leaders: - - - - - - - - - Herb Thomas   -200
Cautions: 4   Margin of Victory: 4 feet   Attendance: 19,824

Race No. 13

Sosebee's Chrysler Hums at Hayloft

AUGUSTA, FL (June 1) -- Gober Sosebee of Atlanta, pushed his Chrysler to the front of the pack and was declared the winner of the scheduled 100-miler at Hayloft Speedway when rains hit the half-mile dirt track after 154 laps.

Car owner Sam Knox (foreground) and Gober Sosebee formed winning team at Augusta.

It was the first Grand National win for Sosebee, and only the second in the 1952 season for a car other than Hudson.

Tommy Moon, who started on the pole, finished sec-ond in a Hudson. Third place went to David Ezell, June Cleveland was fourth, and Jerry Wimbish took fifth.

The triumph moved Sosebee, a non-regular on the circuit, into ninth place in the point standings.

Due to the many interruptions for rain showers, NASCAR scorers were unable to keep an official time of the race.

Race No. 14

Tim Wins at Toledo; Joins Hot Point Race

TOLEDO, OH (June 1) -- Tim Flock drove his Hudson into the lead in the 31st lap and led the rest of the way to win the 100-miler at Ft. Miami Speedway. It was his second win of the year and enabled him to join the wide open, four-man scramble in the Grand National point standings.

Dick Rathmann finished second to Flock. Lee Petty came in third and held a 127 point lead over Fonty Flock, who took second from Herb Thomas on the

Grand National Race No. 13
200 Laps at Hayloft Speedway
Augusta, GA
100 Miles on Half-mile Dirt Track
June 1, 1952

Fin	St	No.	Driver	Team / Car	Laps	Money	Status
1	2	51	Gober Sosebee	Sam Knox '52 Chrysler	154	$1,000	Running
2	1	57	Tommy Moon	C.D. Wilson '52 Hudson	154	700	Running
3	6		David Ezell	'52 Hudson Hornet	153	450	Running
4	5	172	June Cleveland	Carl Mays '51 Chrysler	150	350	Running
5	11		Jerry Wimbish	'50 Olds 88	150	300	Running
6	4	16	Bill Snowden	Snowden '51 Hudson	149	200	Running
7	8	77	Weldon Adams	'51 Plymouth	149	125	Running
8	10	126	Dave Terrell	Terrell '50 Plymouth	148	100	Running
9	14	72	Donald Thomas	T.D. Meeks '51 Nash	145	75	Running
10	7	9	Ed Samples	Claude Alexander '50 Olds 88	138	75	Rear End
11	12		Joe Deloach	'49 Ford	135	50	Running
12	9		Ray Harrelson	'50 Plymouth	63	50	Stalled
13	3		Cotton Owens	'50 Olds 88	57	50	Brnd Rod
14	13	94	Joe Staton	Smith Auto Parts '51 Ford	11	50	Heating

* Race shortened to 154 laps (77 miles) due to rain.
Time of Race: Not recorded
Average Speed: None
Pole Winner: Tommy Moon - 51.561 mph
Lap Leaders: --------- Gober Sosebee -154
Cautions: Margin of Victory: 22 seconds   Attendance:

Grand National Race No. 14
200 Laps at Ft. Miami Speedway
Toledo, OH
100 Miles on Half-mile Dirt Track
June 1, 1952

Fin	St	No	Driver	Team / Car	Laps	Money	Status
1	4	91	Tim Flock	Ted Chester '51 Hudson	200	$1,000	Running
2	2	120	Dick Rathmann	Walt Chapman '51 Hudson	200	700	Running
3	8	42	Lee Petty	Petty Engineering '51 Plym	194	450	Running
4	17	44	Ray Duhigg	J.H. Petty '51 Plymouth	193	350	Running
5	1	14	Fonty Flock	Frank Christian '50 Olds 88	175	200	Running
6	11	22	Perk Brown	R.G. Shelton '51 Hudson	172	150	Heating
7	5	82	Joe Eubanks	Phil Oates '51 Hudson	169	125	Plugs
8	14		Bud Farrell	'50 Plymouth	168	100	Running
9	12	421	Jack Reynolds	Wiss Bros. '50 Plymouth	164	75	Radiator
10	15		Ralph Liguori	'50 Plymouth	158	50	Tires
11	9	118	Bucky Sager	Ken Swihart '51 Hudson	151	25	Hub
12	6	78	Bob Moore	Moore '50 Olds 88	149	25	Oil Pres
13	19	93	Ted Chamberlain	Chamberlain '50 Plymouth	142	25	Radiator
14	10		Russ Hepler	'50 Ford	139	25	Tires
15	7	2	Bill Blair	George Hutchens '52 Olds 88	138	25	Engine
16	21	60	Bill Rexford	Julian Buesink '50 Ford	131	25	Running
17	24		Pete Toth	'50 Plymouth	125	25	Piston
18	18	8	Gene Comstock	Comstock '51 Hudson	121	25	Rod
19	23		Ernie Boost	'51 Plymouth	119	25	Wheel
20	13		Neil Cole	'50 Hudson	102	25	Heating
21	3	92	Herb Thomas	Thomas '51 Hudson	97	25	Oil
22	22		Dick Martin	'50 Olds 88	62	25	Hub
23	16	24	Jimmie Lewallen	Southern Mtr '50 Plymouth	41	25	Hub
24	20	111	Robbie Robinson	'51 Hudson	24	25	Piston

Time of Race: 2 hours, 7 minutes, 11 seconds
Average Speed: 47.175
Pole Winner: Fonty Flock - 57.034 mph
Lap Leaders: Fonty Flock 1-30, Tim Flock 31-200
Cautions: Margin of Victory: Attendance:

strength of his fifth place finish. Rookie Ray Duhigg wound up in fourth place.

Thomas started third in the field of 24, but lost the oil pressure in his Hudson after 97 laps.

Only seven cars were running at the finish, including Bill Rexford, the 1950 Grand National champion who wound up 16th, 69 laps behind winner Flock.

Race No. 15

Flock Takes Second in Row at Hillsboro

*Tim Flock hustled
to top honors at Hillsboro.*

HILLSBORO, NC (June 8) -- Tim Flock climbed to third place in the point standings with his second win in a row in the 100-miler at Occoneechee Speed- way. It was his 11th career Grand National triumph.

Fonty Flock and Dick Rathmann took second and third, completing all 100 laps around the gent- ly-banked one-mile dirt track. Bill Blair came in fourth and Jimmie Lewallen was fifth.

Point Leader Lee Petty finished sixth and maintained a 95-point lead over Fonty in the race for the champion- ship. Tim Flock pulled to within 186 points of leader Petty in the chase for the championship.

Herb Thomas started third in the 19 car field, but a right front hub broke on his Hudson, sending him to the pits. Buddy Shuman, driving the B.A. Pless Hud- son, fell victim to a broken axle in the 41st lap. Perk Brown left the race after just 18 laps with clutch failure. He wound up in last place.

A crowd of 12,500 watched Flock average 81.008 mph for the 100 miles.

Grand National Race No. 15
100 Laps at Occoneechee Speedway
Hillsboro, NC
100 Miles on 1-mile Dirt Track
June 8, 1952

Fin	St	No.	Driver	Team / Car	Laps	Money	Status
1	2	91	Tim Flock	Ted Chester '51 Hudson	100	$1,000	Running
2	1	14	Fonty Flock	Frank Christian'52 Olds 88	100	700	Running
3	4	120	Dick Rathmann	Walt Chapman '51 Hudson	100	450	Running
4	7	2	Bill Blair	George Hutchens '52 Olds 88	98	350	Running
5	12		Jimmie Lewallen	'52 Ford	97	200	Running
6	9	42	Lee Petty	Petty Engineering '51 Plym	97	150	Running
7	5	82	Joe Eubanks	Phil Oates '52 Hudson	96	125	Running
8	14	44	Ray Duhigg	J.H. Petty '51 Plymouth	96	100	Running
9	10		Clyde Minter	'52 Packard	96	75	Running
10	11	72	Donald Thomas	T.D. Meeks '51 Ford	95	50	Running
11	16	4	Otis Martin	'50 Ford	91	25	Running
12	15	19	Fred Dove	'49 Buick	87	25	Running
13	19		Coleman Lawrence	'52 Mercury	84	25	Running
14	17		Ernie Boost	'51 Plymouth	83	25	Running
15	13	107	Bruce Atchley	Atchley '51 Hudson	67	25	Brakes
16	3	92	Herb Thomas	Thomas '52 Hudson	58	25	Hub
17	6	89	Buddy Shuman	B.A. Pless '52 Hudson Hornet	41	25	Axle
18	16		Hank Carruthers	'52 Packard	18	25	Wheel
19	8	22	Perk Brown	R.G. Shelton '52 Hudson	18	25	Clutch

Time of Race: 1 hour, 14 minutes, 4 seconds
Average Speed: 81.008 mph
Pole Winner: Fonty Flock - 91.977 mph
Lap Leaders: - - - - - - - - - - Tim Flock   -100.
Cautions: Margin of Victory: Attendance: 12,500

Race No. 16

Thomas Trims Flock at Charlotte

*Herb Thomas won close decision over
Fonty Flock at Charlotte.*

CHARLOTTE, NC (June 15) -- Herb Thomas whizzed past Fonty Flock in the 32nd lap and went on to win the 112.5-mile Grand National race at Charlotte Speedway. It was the fourth win of the year for the Hudson pilot.   Second place went to Tim Flock. Bill Blair finished in third place, Lee Petty was fourth and Dick Rathmann nailed down fifth spot. Early leader Fonty Flock dropping off the pace in the late stages wound up 11th.

Petty extended his point lead to 151 ahead of Fonty Flock. Tim held onto third place, 170 out of first.

Gober Sosebee rolled his Chrysler three times in a solo crash with 20 laps to go. The Atlanta veteran was unhurt. Ray Duhigg wrecked his Plymouth several laps before the incident with no injury.

Thomas averaged 64.820 mph before a slim crowd of 3,500.

32nd place finish and 490 points out of first place.

Buddy Shuman and Herb Thomas finished second and third, giving the Hudson Hornets a 1-2-3 finish. Bill Blair round up fourth, and Pat Kirkwood was fifth.

Flock took the lead for good in the 112th lap and held his advantage over Shuman for the remainder of the event.

Grand National Race No. 16
150 Laps at Charlotte Speedway
Charlotte, NC
112.5 Miles on .75-mile Dirt Track
June 15, 1952

Fin	St	No.	Driver	Team / Car	Laps	Money	Status
1	2	92	Herb Thomas	Thomas '52 Hudson	150	$1,000	Running
2	3	91	Tim Flock	Ted Chester '51 Hudson	150	700	Running
3	6	2	Bill Blair	George Hutchens '52 Olds 88	149	450	Running
4	9	42	Lee Petty	Petty Engineering '51 Plym	146	350	Running
5	5	120	Dick Rathmann	Walt Chapman '51 Hudson	145	200	Running
6	15	66	Donald Thomas	Elmer Pooler '51 Plymouth	145	150	Running
7	7	82	Joe Eubanks	Phil Oates '52 Hudson	144	125	Running
8	4	89	Buddy Shuman	B.A. Pless '52 Hudson Hornet	142	100	Running
9	12	172	June Cleveland	Carl Mays '51 Chrysler	142	75	Running
10	16	19	Fred Dove	'49 Buick	140	50	Running
11	1	14	Fonty Flock	Frank Christian '51 Olds 88	133	25	Running
12	17	77	Weldon Adams	Harold Mays '51 Plymouth	133	25	Running
13	21		Coleman Lawrence	'52 Mercury	131	25	Running
14	10	51	Gober Sosebee	Sosebee '52 Chrysler	130	25	Crash
15	14	44	Ray Duhigg	J.H. Petty '51 Plymouth	113	25	Crash
16	19		Eddie Van Horn	'50 Ford	112	25	Running
17	13	41	Jimmie Lewallen	John Eanes. '50 Olds 88	73	25	Steering
18	11	22	Perk Brown	R.G. Shelton '52 Hudson	71	25	Rear End
19	23		Ralph Liguori	'50 Ford	50	25	Spindle
20	20	4	Otis Martin	'51 Ford	35	25	Head
21	24	52	Neil Cole	John Golabek '50 Plymouth	17	25	Cres inj.
22	22		"Bud" Harrelson	'50 Plymouth	10	25	Gasket
23	8		Jerry Wimbish	'51 Olds 88	7	25	Spindle
24	16	421	Jack Reynolds	Wiss Brothers '50 Plymouth	3	25	Tie Rod

Time of Race: 1 hour, 44 minutes, 8 seconds
Average Speed: 64.820 mph
Pole Winner: Fonty Flock - 70.038 mph
Lap Leaders: Fonty Flock 1-31, Herb Thomas 32-150.
Cautions: 3   Margin of Victory: Attendance: 3,500

Race No. 17

Tim Takes Point Lead With Detroit Win

DETROIT, MI   (JUNE 29) -- Tim Flock leaped into the point standings lead with a big win in the second annual Motor City 250 at the Michigan State Fairgrounds. Lee Petty was the big loser in the 250-miler on the one-mile dirt oval as a broken wheel knocked him out of the race after 100 laps, leaving him with a

Grand National Race No. 17
250 Laps at Michigan Fairgrounds
Detroit, MI
"Motor City 250"
250 Miles on 1-mile Dirt Track
June 29, 1952

Fin	St	No.	Driver	Team / Car	Laps	Money	Status
1	16	91	Tim Flock	Ted Chester '51 Hudson	250	*$5,050	Running
2	34	89	Buddy Shuman	B.A. Pless '52 Hudson	250	2,225	Running
3	17	92	Herb Thomas	Thomas '51 Hudson	249	1,000	Running
4	25	2	Bill Blair	George Hutchens '52 Olds 88	249	600	Running
5	37	99	Pat Kirkwood	San Juan Motors '51 Chrysler	246	500	Running
6	31	77	Dick Passwater	Frank Arford '52 Olds 88	243	400	Running
7	46	3	Hershel McGriff	Beryl Jackson '52 Olds 88	238	300	Running
8	26	73	Stuart Joyce	Joyce '52 DeSoto	229	200	Running
9	41	4	Otis Martin	Martin '51 Plymouth	226	100	Running
10	8	34	Ted Chamberlain	W.A. Caltrider, Inc. '51 Plym	226	100	Running
11	18	121	Frank Mundy	Walt Chapman '52 Hudson	225	50	Running
12	28	8	Gene Comstock	Comstock '52 Hudson	224	50	Running
13	25	22	Perk Brown	R.G. Shelton '51 Hudson	223	50	Running
14	33	98	Billy Myers	Joe Hawkins '51 Plymouth	220	50	Running
15	7	16	Charlie Hill	Curtis Turner '51 Ford	217	50	Running
16	21	55	Bub King	Carl Lay Motors '52 Hudson	216	50	Running
17	44	118	Bucky Sager	Ed Benedict '51 Hudson	216	50	Running
18	6	162	Fred Bethune	Bethune '52 DeSoto	209	50	Running
19	11	84	Red Duvall	Hank Salat '51 Packard	205	50	Steering
20	45	41	Jimmie Lewallen	R.G. Shelton '52 Hudson	203	50	Running
21	19	40	Tommy Thompson	Thompson '52 Hudson	190	25	Running
22	43	13	Dick Stacey	Jack Fisher '52 Chrysler	175	25	Running
23	5	11	Ray Chase	Dave Kennedy '51 Lincoln	173	25	Tie Rods
24	14	27	Bill Pruitt	James Barnes '52 Nash	169	25	Engine
25	15	82	Joe Eubanks	Phil Oates '52 Hudson	167	25	Axle
26	38	7	Bud Koehler	Walter Martinson '51 Nash	140	25	Heating
27	3	59	Lloyd Moore	Petty Eng '52 Chrysler	137	25	Wheel
28	12	26	John Scarfo	Detroit Kaiser Dlrs '51 Kaiser	135	25	Running
29	10	897	Norman Lynch	Lynch '52 Willys	130	25	Crash
30	36	1	Bill Holland	Robert McGrath '51 Hudson	123	25	Wheel
31	20	24	Ray Duhigg	J.O. Goode '51 Plymouth	120	25	Running
32	30	42	Lee Petty	Petty Eng. '52 Chrysler	100	75	Wheel
33	39	53	Jack Fisher	Fisher '52 Olds 88	95	25	
34	40	421	Jack Reynolds	Wiss Brothers '52 Plymouth	85	25	
35	47	54	Don Rudolph	Irvington Willys Co. '52 Willys	82	25	
36	46	174	Bill Rexford	Jim B. Copperheat '51 Nash	82	25	
37	32	74	Leon Meadows	Stuart Joyce '52 Plymouth	67	25	
38	1	120	Dick Rathmann	Walt Chapman '51 Hudson	64	175	Heating
39	4	6	Bob Pronger	Neilson Motors '52 Nash Amb.	49	25	
40	9	33	Ed Westveer	Dave Kennedy '52 Mercury	45	25	
41	45	25	Gibb Orr	J.E. Peters '51 Hudson Hornet	43	---	
42	23	65	Jim Fieblekorn	Ken Whitney '51 Ford	35	---	
43	27	43	Paul Newkirk	Newkirk '51 Nash Amb.	27	---	
44	22	20	Roger Attard	Attard '52 Hudson Hornet	25	---	
45	29	111	Robbie Robinson	Robinson '51 Hudson	20	---	
46	44	78	Bob Moore	Moore '52 Olds 88	16	---	
47	2	14	Fonty Flock	Frank Christian '52 Olds 88	10	---	Tie Rod

* Plus 1952 Nash Ambassador automobile
Time of Race: 4 hours, 10 minutes, 23 seconds
Average Speed: 59.908 mph
Pole Winner: Dick Rathmann - 70.23 mph
Fastest Qualifier: Herb Thomas - 71.400 mph
Lap Leaders: Dick Rathmann 1-44, Lee Petty 45-87, Tim Flock 88-110, Buddy Shuman 111, T. Flock 112-250.
Cautions: Margin of Victory   Attendance:

Dick Rathmann started on the pole and led the first 44 laps. He pitted at that point and departed 20 laps later with overheating problems. Petty led for a 43-lap stretch but was out of the hunt a short time later. After Petty's departure, Flock and Shuman had the race to themselves.

Flock won $5,050 plus a new Nash Ambassador. Shuman collected $2,225 for his runner-up effort.

Defending champion Tommy Thompson never got untracked and wound up 21st, sixty laps behind the winner.

Flock averaged 59.908 mph for his 12th career Grand National win.

Buddy Shuman won 100-miler at Niagara Falls.

laps when he struck the rolling Olds of Eddie Lenz. Lenz, driving in his first Grand National race, landed upside down with the roof caved in on the driver's compartment. Miraculously, the driver was unhurt.

Thomas' runner-up effort enabled him to move to within 42 points of Flock in the point race.

Shuman averaged 45.610 mph for his first Grand National career victory.

Tim Flock wings his way to victory in 2nd annual Motor City 250 at Detroit.

Race No. 18

Shuman Survives Niagara Falls Car-Killer

NIAGARA FALLS, ONT (July 1) -- Buddy Shuman of Charlotte drove his B.A. Pless Hudson to victory in the 100-mile Grand National event at Stamford Park Speedway in Niagara Falls, ONT. It was the first NASCAR Grand National to be staged outside the continental United States.

The 200-lapper on the half-mile dirt track was a car-killing contest as only three cars were running at race speed when the checkered flag fell. Herb Thomas wound up second and Ray Duhigg was third. Jack Reynolds got credit for fourth despite losing a wheel with 17 laps to go. Perk Brown limped home fifth.

Point leader Tim Flock wrecked his Hudson after 78

Grand National Race No. 18
200 Laps at Stamford Park
Niagara Falls, ONT
100 Miles on Half-mile Dirt Track
July 1, 1952

Fin	St	No.	Driver	Team / Car	Laps	Money	Status
1	8	89	Buddy Shuman	B.A. Pless '52 Hudson Hornet	200	$1,000	Running
2	1	92	Herb Thomas	Thomas '52 Hudson	198	700	Running
3	7	44	Ray Duhigg	J.H. Petty '51 Plymouth	193	450	Running
4	14	421	Jack Reynolds	Wiss Brothers '51 Plymouth	183	350	Wheel
5	13		Perk Brown	'50 Ford	176	200	Running
6	10	52	Neil Cole	John Golabek '50 Plymouth	168	150	Engine
7	16		Fonty Flock	'51 Henry J	163	125	Running
8	5	118	Bucky Sager	Ed Benedict '51 Hudson	154	100	Wheel
9	12	93	Ted Chamberlain	Chamberlain '50 Plymouth	134	75	In Pits
10	17		Albert Lemiurx	'50 Mercury Meteor	121	50	Running
11	11		Charles Barry	'51 Ford	87	25	Heating
12	3	120	Dick Rathmann	Walt Chapman '51 Hudson	78	25	Engine
13	2	91	Tim Flock	Ted Chester '51 Hudson	59	25	Crash
14	9	1	Eddie Lenz	'50 Olds 88	55	25	Crash
15	6	3	Hershel McGriff	Beryl Jackson '52 Olds 88	45	25	Engine
16	4	42	Lee Petty	Petty Engineering '51 Plym	40	25	Engine
17	15		Jack Hauher	'49 Ford	26	25	Engine

Time of Race: 2 hours, 11 minutes, 33 seconds
Average Speed: 45.610 mph
Pole Winner: Herb Thomas - 52.401 mph
Lap Leaders: - - - - - - - - - Buddy Shuman -200
Cautions: 3   Margin of Victory: 2 laps plus   Attendance:

Race No. 19

Flock Grabs 5th Win of Season at Shangri-La

OWEGO, NY (July 4) -- Tim Flock continued his hot streak and won the 100-mile Grand National race at Shangri-La Speedway. It was the fifth win of the year for Flock and his Ted Chester-owned Hudson Hornet team.

Herb Thomas finished in second place and stayed within a 50 point distance of Flock in the battle for the NASCAR championship.

Dick Rathmann came in third place with Bucky Sager fourth and Lee Petty fifth.

Flock averaged 56.603 mph in giving Hudson its 17th victory in the 19 Grand Nationals run in the 1952 season.

Six cars retired from the running after encountering tire trouble on the rough half-mile paved track. Several of the local competitors did not bring enough rubber with them and had to park their cars.

Grand National Race No. 20
200 Laps at Monroe Speedway
Monroe, MI
100 Miles on Half-mile Dirt Track
July 6, 1952

Fin	St	No.	Driver	Team / Car	Laps	Money	Status
1	1	91	Tim Flock	Ted Chester '51 Hudson	200	$1,000	Running
2	3	92	Herb Thomas	Thomas '52 Hudson	200	700	Running
3	7	42	Lee Petty	Petty Engineering '52 Plym	199	450	Running
4	4	14	Fonty Flock	Frank Christian '52 Olds	194	350	Running
5	9	44	Ray Duhigg	J H Petty '51 Plymouth	193	200	Running
6	11	84	Red Duvall	'51 Packard	189	150	Running
7	12	93	Ted Chamberlain	Chamberlain '50 Plymouth	185	125	Running
8	8		Iggy Katona	'51 Olds	180	100	Running
9	10	162	Fred Bethune	Bethune '52 DeSoto	168	75	Running
10	5	78	Bob Moore	Moore '51 Olds	160	50	Wheel
11	15	25	Gibb Orr	'51 Hudson	154	25	Wheel
12	2	89	Buddy Shuman	B A Pless '52 Hudson	146	25	Engine
13	6	118	Bucky Sager	Ed Benedict '52 Hudson	106	25	RF Hub
14	13	120	Dick Rathmann	Walt Chapman '52 Hudson	47	25	Clutch
15	14		Dick Martin	'50 Olds	10	25	RF Hub

Time of Race: 2 hours, 14 minutes, 50 seconds
Average Speed: 44.499 mph
Pole Winner: Tim Flock - 57.600 mph
Lap Leaders: - Tim Flock   -200.
Cautions: Margin of Victory: Attendance:

Grand National Race No. 19
200 Laps at Shangri-La Speedway
Owego, NY
100 Miles on Half-mile Paved Track
July 4, 1952

Fin	St	No.	Driver	Team / Car	Laps	Money	Status
1	1	91	Tim Flock	Ted Chester '51 Hudson	200	$1,000	Running
2	4	92	Herb Thomas	Thomas '52 Hudson	200	700	Running
3	3	120	Dick Rathmann	Walt Chapman '51 Hudson	199	450	Running
4	2	118	Bucky Sager	Ed Benedict '51 Hudson	199	350	Running
5	5	42	Lee Petty	Petty Engineering '50 Plym	198	200	Running
6	12	59	Lloyd Moore	Julian Buesink '51 Ford	197	150	Running
7	7	44	Ray Duhigg	J H Petty '51 Plymouth	196	125	Running
8	9	421	Jack Reynolds	Wiss Brothers '51 Plymouth	193	100	Running
9	6	52	Neil Cole	John Golebek '50 Plymouth	192	75	Running
10	20		Walt Carver	'51 Henry J	188	50	Running
11	10	93	Ted Chamberlain	Chamberlain '50 Plymouth	186	25	Running
12	14		Harold Morse	'50 Ford	186	25	Running
13	11		Bud Farrell	'51 Plymouth	181	25	Running
14	21		Charles Barry	'51 Plymouth	181	25	Running
15	17	43	Larry Mann	Green Hornet '51 Hudson	169	25	Running
16	23		Rod Turcott	'49 Ford	167	25	Tires
17	18		Dick Turcott	'49 Ford	163	25	Tires
18	8		Jim Reed	Reed Hudson	161	25	Running
19	26		Ken Rauch	'51 Henry J	133	25	Heating
20	16		Pete Vail	'50 Studebaker	92	25	Tires
21	19		Earl Zindahl	'51 Nash	88	25	Heating
22	15		Scott Gow	'50 Ford	46	25	Tires
23	13		Charles Weidler	'51 Hudson	33	25	Engine
24	22		Doug Congdon	'50 Olds	30	25	Tires
25	25		Geroge Hufford	'49 Plymouth	28	25	Engine
26	24		Joe Gillow	'49 Ford	20	25	Tires

Time of Race: 1 hour, 46 minutes
Average Speed: 56.603 mph
Pole Winner: Time Flock - 67.669 mph
Lap Leaders: - Tim Flock   -200.
Cautions: Margin of Victory: Attendance:

Race No. 20

Monroe Win Gives Flock 5 Wins in Last 7 Races

MONROE, MI (July 6) -- Tim Flock took his fifth win in the last seven races with an impressive drive in the 100-miler at Monroe Speedway. It was the sixth win of the season for the veteran Atlanta campaigner, and the 14th of his career.

Herb Thomas found himself finishing second for the third consecutive Grand National race. Lee Petty, trying to catch back up in the point race, came in third. Fonty Flock took fourth place and Ray Duhigg was fifth.

Flock, inching toward his first Grand National championship, upped his lead to 58 points over Thomas. Petty ranks third, 562 points behind Flock.

Buddy Shuman qualified second to Flock in the time trials, but engine failure put him out after 146 laps. He got credit for 12th place in the 15-car field.

Dick Rathmann suffered mechanical problems in qualifying and had to start 13th in the 15 car field. The clutch went out in his Hudson after just 47d laps, leaving him with 14th place in the final rundown. Bucky Sager qualified sixth, but a broken hub sent his Hudson out of the running after 106 laps.

Race No. 21

Petty Ends Famine with Morristown Victory

MORRISTOWN, NJ (JULY 11) -- Lee Petty ended a year-long winless skid with a popular triumph in the 100-mile Grand National race at Morristown Speedway. It was his first NASCAR win since July 31, 1951 at Rochester, NY.

Petty scampered past Tim Flock in the 125th lap and led the rest of the way. As he pushed his Plymouth past Flock's Hudson, he waved "bye-bye" to his rival and sped uncontested to the $1,000 top prize.

Flock finished second and Neil Cole third. Ralph Liguori ran a strong race to finish fourth, Ronnie Kohler came in fifth.

Lee Petty rolled to victory at Morristown, NJ.

Herb Thomas led the first 49 laps after winning the pole position. After losing the lead to Flock, he was forced into the wall by a slow car. Thomas lost a lap in the incident, but came on like gangbusters. He made up the lost lap and was closing in on the leader when a wheel bearing burned out after 124 laps.

As Thomas limped to the pit area, Petty zipped past Flock and set sail.

Local driver John DuBois ran with the leaders in the early going before being sidelined by a broken spindle after 150 laps.

Duke Keller flipped his Henry J in the fourth lap. The roof was mashed onto the steering wheel, but Keller was able to climb out unhurt. He beat and banged on the roof, raised it enough distance to get back in the car and drove for two more laps. A badly bent chassis forced him out after six laps.

Grand National Race No. 21
200 Laps at Morristown Speedway
Morristown, NJ
100 Miles on Half-mile Dirt Track
July 11, 1952

Fin	St	No.	Driver	Team / Car	Laps	Money	Status
1	3	42	Lee Petty	Petty Engineering '51 Plym	200	$1,000	Running
2	2	91	Tim Flock	Ted Chester '51 Hudson	200	700	Running
3	7	52	Neil Cole	John Golabek '50 Plymouth	196	450	Running
4	6		Ralph Liguori	'51 Hudson	196	350	Running
5	16		Ronnie Kohler	'50 Plymouth	192	200	Running
6	13		Pappy Hough	'52 Ford 6	189	150	Running
7	14		Nelson Applegate	'50 Dodge	188	125	Running
8	8	7	Jim Reed	Reed '50 Ford	188	100	Running
9	17	93	Ted Chamberlain	Chamberlain '51 Plymouth	185	75	Running
10	22		Ed Van Horn	'50 Ford	181	50	Running
11	19		Bobby Courtwright	'50 Olds	180	25	Running
12	4	22	Perk Brown	R G Shelton '51 Hudson	175	25	RF Hub
13	11		Jack Multrain	'50 Ford	173	25	Running
14	25		Bill Hammersley	'50 Ford	172	25	Running
15	29		Zeke DeRose	'50 Chevrolet	168	25	Running
16	20	126	Dave Terrell	Terrell '51 Plymouth	166	25	Running
17	18		Clyde Pittinger	'51 Olds	165	25	Running
18	30		Joe Kulser	'50 Plymouth	164	25	Running
19	21		Al Keller	'50 Ford	161	25	Ignition
20	24		Bill Barker	'50 Olds	150	25	Radiator
21	5		John DuBois	'51 Hudson	150	25	Spindle
22	10	44	Ray Duhigg	J H Petty '50 Plymouth	140	25	Spindle
23	15		Bud Farrell	'51 Plymouth	131	25	RR Hub
24	1	92	Herb Thoams	Thomas '51 Hudson	124	25	Bearings
25	9	421	Jack Reynolds	Wiss Brothers '51 Plymouth	113	25	RR Wheel
26	12	94	Joe Staton	Louise Smith '51 Ford	68	25	Heating
27	26		Francis Radaker	'50 Ford	64	25	A Frame
28	31		Pete Vail	'50 Studebaker	60	25	Axle
29	23		Thomas Gifford	'50 Studebaker	53	25	Wheel
30	30		Louise Smith	'51 Olds	14	25	Driver Ill
31	28		Duke Keller	'51 Henry J	6	25	Crash
32	32	43	Larry Mann	Green Hornet '51 Hudson	3	25	Radiator

Time of Race: 1 hour, 40 minutes, 34 seconds
Average Speed: 59.661 mph
Pole Winner: Herb Thomas - 60.996 mph
Lap Leaders: Herb Thomas 1-49, Tim Flock 50-124, Lee Petty 125-200.
Cautions: Margin of Victory: Attendance:

Race No. 22

Flock Edges Petty At Playland Park

SOUTH BEND, IN. (July 20) -- Tim Flock survived a scrape with Herb Thomas in the 42nd lap and went on to win the 100-mile Grand National race at Playland Park Speedway. It was Flock's seventh win of the year and moved him to a 250 point lead in the driver standings.

Lee Petty finished second. Herb Thomas, driving Bub King's car was third 11 lap down, and Herschel Buchanan was fourth. Fifth place went to Dick Passwater.

Thomas led the first 41 laps as Tim Flock gave chase in the early going. The two lead cars side-swiped each other, and Flock assumed command as Thomas went into a long slide. In an attempt to make up lost ground, Thomas flipped his Hudson in the 64th lap. He then hopped into King's car and drove it home third. He got a percentage of points for driving in relief.

Flock averaged 41.889 mph in the wreck-marred event. Only eight cars were running at the finish.

most of the local track regulars started up front, and the touring pros had to start at the rear.

George Gallup led the first 13 laps as the hot dogs worked their way into contention. Petty, who started 18th, grabbed the lead in the 14th lap and paced the action for 21 laps. Flock, who started 22nd in the field of 23, caught Petty after 30 laps and challenged for the lead. On lap 35, the two leaders locked horns and both cocked sideways in the turn. Flock and Petty broke loose from each other and maintained their one-two positions with Flock heading the way.

Flock was in command in the 176th lap when officials called off the race.

In an unusual decision, Gallup and Neil Cole tied for eighth place. A scoring mix-up caused Cole to be initially place out of the top 10. When officials checked the score cards, they discovered he had completed 170 laps, the same as Gallup. NASCAR decided to declare eighth place a deadlock between the two.

A crowd of 5,975 braved threatening weather to watch the race.

Grand National Race No. 22
200 Laps at Playland Park Speedway
South Bend, IN
100 Miles on Half-mile Dirt Track
July 20, 1952

Fin	St	No.	Driver	Team / Car	Laps	Money	Status
1	2	91	Tim Flock	Ted Chester '51 Hudson	200	$1,000	Running
2	11	42	Lee Petty	Petty Engineering '52 Chrysler	200	700	Running
3	5	55	Bub King *	T.H. King '52 Hudson Hornet	189	450	Running
4	10	4	Herschel Buchanan	Frank Christian '51 Olds 88	186	350	Running
5	7	77	Dick Passwater	Frank Arford '52 DeSoto	184	200	Running
6	13	8	Gene Comstock	Comstock '52 Hudson Hornet	174	150	Running
7	9		Glen Larson	'50 Ford	171	125	Running
8	15	94	Joe Staton	Louise Smith '50 Ford	170	100	Running
9	4	118	Bucky Sager	Ed Benedict '51 Hudsonn	165	75	Heating
10	8	84	Red Duvall	Hank Salat '51 Packard	144	50	Rear End
11	12		Jim Clark	'49 Ford	135	25	Rod Out
12	16		Paul Wensink	'52 Willys	127	25	Crash
13	18		Marion Leech	'51 Studebaker	117	25	RR Hub
14	17		Zane Howell	'50 Studebaker	109	25	Crash
15	6	14	Fonty Flock	Frank Christian '51 Olds 88	86	25	Axle
16	14	44	Ray Duhigg	J.H. Petty '51 Plymouth	70	25	Engine
17	3	40	Tommy Thompson	Thompson '52 Hudson Hornet	70	25	RF Wheel
18	1	92	Herb Thomas	Thomas '52 Hudson	64	25	Crash
19	19		Gene Darragh	'50 Ford	34	25	RR Wheel

* Herb Thomas relieved Bub King after 64th lap wreck
Time of Race: 2 hours, 23 minutes, 14 seconds
Average Speed: 41.889 mph
Pole Winner: Herb Thomas - 58.120 mph
Lap Leaders: Herb Thomas 1-41, Tim Flock 42-200.
Cautions: Margin of Victory: Attendance:

Race No. 23

Flock Still Hot; Wins Rain-Shortened Rochester Race

ROCHESTER, NY (AUG. 15) -- Tim Flock paddled his way to a victory in the rain-abbreviated Grand National race at the Monroe County Fairgrounds. It was the seventh win in the last ten starts for the title-bound Atlanta driver.

Herb Thomas was flagged in second place, falling 258 points behind Flock in the title chase. Dick Rathmann came in third, Lee Petty was fourth and Jim Reed fifth.

Due to the rains, no time trials were held. By chance,

Grand National Race NO. 23
200 Laps at Monroe Co. Fairgrounds
Rochester, NY
100 Miles on Half-mile Dirt Track
August 15, 1952

Fin	St	No.	Driver	Team / Car	Laps	Money	Status
1	22	91	Tim Flock	Ted Chester '52 Hudson	176	$1,000	Running
2	20	92	Herb Thomas	Thomas '52 Hudson	176	700	Running
3	21	120	Dick Rathmann	Walt Chapman '52 Hudson	174	450	Running
4	18	42	Lee Petty	Petty Engineering '52 Plym	174	350	Running
5	12	47	Jim Reed	'51 Ford	173	200	Running
6	16	24	Jimmie Lewallen	J O Goode '51 Plymouth	172	150	Running
7	14	44	Ray Duhigg	J.H. Petty '51 Plymouth	171	125	Running
8	2	103	George Gallup	Gallup '50 Olds	170	100	Running
*8	17		Neil Cole	'50 Plymouth	170	100	Running
10	7		Ralph Liguori	'50 Ford	167	50	Running
11	19	43	Larry Mann	Green Hornet '51 Hudson	167	25	Running
12	3		Dutch Hoag	'51 Ford	163	25	Running
13	11		Harold Wright	'50 Ford	162	25	Running
14	6		Fran Jischke	'50 Ford	158	25	Running
15	5		Stew Hayes	'50 Ford	156	25	Running
16	1		Pappy Hough	'51 Plymouth	155	25	Running
17	4		Bob Schwinaglo	'51 Plymouth	142	25	Tires
18	9		Herb Legg	'52 Chevrolet	133	25	Tires
19	8		Bill Brown	'50 Ford	111	25	Heating
20	13	59	Lloyd Moore	Julian Buesink '49 Ford	96	25	Heating
21	23		Larry Shurter	Shurter '50 Olds	62	25	Heating
22	15		Ronnie Kohler	'51 Plymouth	61	25	Heating
23	10	93	Ted Chamberlain	Chamberlain 49 Ford	41	25	Engine

* George Gallup and Neil Cole were each paid for 8th place. Scoring mix-up caused Neil Cole to be listed out of the top 11, and when score cards were tallied, it was discovered that he completed the same number of laps that Gallup did. Officials decided to declare both as 8th place finishers.
** Race shortened to 176 laps (88 miles) due to rain.
Time of Race: No time due to rain interruptions
Average Speed: None
Pole Winner: No time trials - inclement weather forced officials to draw for position.
Lap Leaders: George Gallup 1-13, Lee Petty 14-34, Tim Flock 35-176.
Cautions: Margin of Victory: Attendance: 5,975

Race No. 24

Bob Flock Makes Triumphant Return at Weaverville

Bob Flock

WEAVERVILLE, NC (Aug. 17) -- In November of 1951, Bob Flock suffered a broken neck and several fractured ribs in a mishap at Mobile, AL. It was feared the dynamic Atlanta racer might never compete in NASCAR's Grand National Division again.

But in Cinderella fashion, Flock roared to victory in his first start since his injury in the 100-miler at Asheville-Weaverville Speedway.

Flock outdistanced his brother Tim by two laps to claim his first Grand National win since October 16, 1949, when he won at North Wilkesboro.

Herb Thomas, Gene Comstock and Herschel Buchanan rounded out the top five.

NASCAR Commissioner E.G. "Cannonball" Baker made an announcement that any Grand National driver convicted of reckless driving on the highway will be regarded as breaking the NASCAR rule book. Baker said the Grand National division was in the public eye, and behavior off the track was expected to maintain a high level of dignity.

Race No. 25

Fonty Fantastic At Darlington

DARLINGTON, SC (Sept. 1) -- Fonty Flock wheeled his Oldsmobile into the lead in the 185th lap and led the rest of the way to win the third annual Southern 500 at Darlington Raceway. It was the first win of the year for the Decatur, GA veteran.

Fonty Flock waves to the crowd as he takes the checkered flag at Darlington.

After the checkered flag, Flock stopped his Frank Christian-owned mount on the front chute, climbed on the hood and led the huge throng of 32,400 persons in the singing of "Dixie", the South's national anthem. Flock drove the 400 laps around the 1.25-mile paved track wearing Bermuda shorts.

Young Johnny Patterson finished second, and Herb Thomas was third. Thomas' effort vaulted him into the point lead by 134 points over Tim Flock, who crashed his Hudson in the 321st lap. Tim then relieved Jack

---

Grand National Race No. 24
200 Laps at Asheville-Weaverville Speedway
Weaverville, NC
100 Miles on Half-mile Dirt Track
August 17, 1952

Fin	St	No.	Driver	Team / Car	Laps	Money	Status
1	6	7	Bob Flock	Ted Chester '51 Hudson	200	$1,000	Running
2	3	91	Tim Flock	Ted Chester '52 Hudson	198	700	Running
3	1	92	Herb Thomas	Thomas '52 Hudson	195	450	Running
4	10	8	Gene Comstock	Comstock '52 Hudson Hornet	192	350	Running
5	13	1	Herschel Buchanan	Buchanan '52 Nash Amb.	189	200	Running
6	14		Barney Smith	'51 Plymouth	187	150	Running
7	16	66	Donald Thomas	Elmer Pooler '51 Plymouth	185	125	Running
8	19	71	Coleman Lawrence	'50 Plymouth	178	100	Running
9	18	54	Weldon Adams	Harold Mays '51 Plymouth	176	75	Running
10	4	89	Buck Baker	B.A. Pless '52 Hudson Hornet	162	50	Running
11	17	94	E.C. Ramsey	Louise Smith '51 Ford	147	50	Running
12	9	14	Fonty Flock	Frank Christian '51 Olds 88	130	50	Tie Rod
13	8	172	June Cleveland	Carl Mays '51 Chrysler	128	50	Rear End
14	2	82	Joe Eubanks	Phil Oates '52 Hudson	115	50	Spindle
15	5	120	Dick Rathmann	Walt Chapman '51 Hudson	114	50	Spindle
16	11	58	Johnny Patterson	Lou Tanner '52 Hudson	76	50	Heating
17	15	107	Bruce Atchley	Atchley '51 Hudson Hornet	73	50	Engine
18	7	55	Bub King	Carl Lay Motors '52 Hudson	47	50	Spindle
19	12		Jerry Wimbish	'51 Olds	1	35	Spindle

Time of Race: 1 hour, 44 minutes, 44 seconds
Average Speed: 57.288 mph
Pole Winner: Herb Thomas - 64.888 mph
Lap Leaders: --------- Bob Flock -200
Cautions: Margin of Victory: 2 laps plus   Attendance:

Grand National Race No. 25
400 Laps at Darlington Raceway
Darlington, SC
"Southern 500"
500 Miles on 1.25-mile Paved Track
September 1, 1952

Fin	St	No.	Driver	Team / Car	Laps	Money	Status
1	1	14	Fonty Flock	Frank Christian '52 Olds 88	400	$9,430	Running
2	42	58	Johnny Patterson	Grady Akers '52 Hudson	399	3,000	Running
3	14	92	Herb Thomas	Thomas '52 Hudson	399	1,590	Running
4	33	55	Bub King	T.H. King '52 Hudson Hornet	398	1,230	Running
5	53	16	Banjo Matthews	Bill Snowden '52 Hudson	393	950	Running
6	8	42	Lee Petty	Petty Engineering '51 Plym	393	800	Running
7	2	82	Joe Eubanks	Phil Oates '52 Hudson	390	700	Running
8	3	1	Herschel Buchanan	Ponce Motors '52 Nash Amb.	390	600	Running
9	5	87	Buck Baker	Hal Wheatley '52 Lincoln	388	500	Running
10	50	24	Ray Duhigg	J O Goode '51 Plymouth	387	450	Running
11	16	9	Jack Smith *	Ted Chester '51 Hudson	387	420	Running
12	35	69	Rollin Smith	Smith '52 Hudson Hornet	385	350	Running
13	37	89	Jimmy Thompson	B.A. Pless '52 Hudson	383	300	Crash
14	47	51	Speedy Thompson	G. Sosebee '51 Ford	383	280	Running
15	48	59	Lloyd Moore	Julian Buesink '52 Ford	382	250	Running
16	38	53	Joe Weatherly	Junie Donlavey '52 Hudson	376	150	Running
17	43	98	Buddy Shuman	Joe Hawkins '51 Plymouth	376	100	Running
18	41	62	Keith Hamner	'52 Hudson Hornet	375	90	Running
19	31	25	Clyde Pittinger	S.J. Lorenzo '52 Olds 88	375	90	Running
20	10	99	Pat Kirkwood	San Juan Motors '51 Chrysler	373	90	Running
21	56	8	Gene Comstock	Fry Motors '52 Hudson	370	90	Running
22	57	39	W.E. Baker, Jr.	Baker '52 Olds 88	368	90	Running
23	59	28	Herb Fry	Fry '51 Hudson Hornet	366	95	Running
24	61	34	Iggy Katona	W.A. Caltrider, Inc. '51 Ply	365	75	Running
25	21	77	Dick Passwater	Frank Arford '52 Olds 88	364	105	Crash
26	23	83	Bill Miller	Dantone Race Stb '51 Ford	357	75	Running
27	11	85	Tony Bonadies	'51 Nash Rambler	350	325	Running
28	27	66	Donald Thomas	Elmer Pooler '51 Plymouth	345	60	Running
29	55	7	Bob Flock	Ted Chester '51 Hudson	338	60	Running
30	12	67	Irvin Blatt	Blatt '51 Mercury	337	60	Running
31	25	93	Ted Chamberlain	Call Me Squirt '50 Plymouth	337	60	Running
32	9	47	Al Fleming	L.W. Tickle '52 Willys	336	210	Running
33	36	91	Tim Flock *	Ted Chester '52 Hudson	321	50	Crash
34		94	E.C. Ramsey	Louise Smith '51 Ford	318	50	Crash
35	29	20	Dick Rathmann	Walt Chapman '52 Hudson	315	460	Crash
36	32	75	Al Conroy	Larry Shurter '52 Willys	308	150	Running
37	66	71	Coleman Lawrence	'50 Plymouth	297	50	Running
38	65	79	Charles Weidler	'51 Hudson Hornet	279	50	Running
39	45	31	Rudy Hires	'52 Hudson Hornet	267	50	Running
40	40	60	Ralph Liguori	'51 Hudson Hornet	256	50	Heating
41	24	3	Lamar Crabtree	Red Harrelson '51 Plymouth	254	---	Piston
42	28	30	Johnny Bridgers	Bridgers '52 Ford	244	---	Heating
43	44	57	Tommy Moon	C.D. Wilson '51 Hudson	240	---	Heating
44	17	2	Bill Blair	George Hutchens '52 Olds 88	223	---	Heating
45	51	17	June Cleveland	W.A. Smith '51 Plymouth	205	---	Running
46	34	52	Joe Guide, Jr	Sally Guide '51 Hudson	200	---	Running
47	58	61	Lewis Jones	Stan Parnell '51 Ford	193	---	Heating
48	6	22	Roy Hall	'52 DeSoto	182	---	Tires,Fuel
49	7	11	Fireball Roberts	Saverance Mtrs. '51 Ford	174	---	Engine
50	20	32	Jimmie Lewallen	R.G. Shelton '52 Hudson	168	20	Engine
51	30	74	Pete Kelley	'52 Hudson Hornet	162	---	Engine
52	46	6	Bobby Myers	George Hutchins '51 Ford	145	---	Engine
53	18	18	Bucky Sager	Red Harrelson '52 Hudson	142	---	LF Wheel
54	15	46	Bob Pronger	Griffin Motors '52 Olds 88	140	---	Engine
55	39	43	Larry Mann	Green Hornet '52 Hudson	139	---	Rear End
56	63	54	Weldon Adams	Fred Bridgers '51 Plymouth	125	---	Crash
57	52	26	Jimmy Ingram	'51 Nash Amb.	91	---	No Tires
58	60	27	Gwyn Staley	The Wilkes Boys '52 Ford	74	---	Heating
59	26	21	Johnny Gouveia	Gouveia '51 Plymouth	61	---	Heating
60	13	40	Tommy Thompson	Thompson '52 Hudson	37	200	Engine
61	49	41	Curtis Turner	John Eanes '52 Olds 88	35	---	Crash
62	54	5	Gene Darragh	Darragh '52 Hudson Hornet	32	---	Crash
63		15	Merritt Brown	'51 Studebaker	28	---	Engine
64	19	4	Slick Smith	Frank Christian '51 Olds 88	22	50	Engine
65	4	19	Clyde Minter	Paul Nunn '52 Packard	21	---	Fr. End
66	22	12	Jim Paschal	George Hutchens '52 Olds 88	18	---	Engine

* Jack Smith, starting in the No.9 Hudson, was relieved by Tim Flock
Time of Race: 6 hours, 42 minutes, 37 seconds
Average Speed: 74.512 mph

The front row for the 1952 Southern 500 -- Fonty Flock's Oldsmobile, Joe Eubanks' Hudson and the Nash of Herschel Buchanan. Flock won from the pole.

Smith, and took his car to 11th place

Bub King finished fourth in a fine drive, and Banjo Matthews came in fifth.

Fonty Flock, who started on the pole after qualifying at 88.55 mph, led the first 17 laps. Tommy Thompson moved to the top of the leader board in the 18th lap and was in front on lap 37 when he retired with an engine failure. Flock was back in the lead and led most of the way except for two brief periods when Dick Rathmann and Thomas led. In all, Flock led 321 laps en route to the $9,430 first prize.

The race was interrupted once by rain, and seven caution flags for a total of 40 laps. Flock averaged 74.512 mph, the slowest Southern 500 to date.

Joe Weatherly, top motorcycle rider, made his first Grand National start in a Junie Donlavey prepared Hudson. The Norfolk, VA driver started 38th and ran exceptionally strong, but finished 16th after having to make ten pit stops to cure overheating problems.

Joe Weatherly.

Pole Winner: Fonty Flock - 88.55 mph
Fastest Qualifier: Dick Rathmann - 89.950 mph
Lap Leaders: Fonty Flock 1-17, Tommy Thompson 18-37, F. Flock 38-104,
Dick Rathmann 105-139, F. Flock 140-180, Herb Thomas 181-184, F. Flock 185-400
Cautions: 7 for 40 laps
Margin of Victory: 1 lap plus
Attendance: 32,400

Race No. 26

Petty Wins Macon
in Final Laps

MACON, GA (Sept. 7) -- Herb Thomas suffered a heart-breaking defeat as Lee Petty came home first in the 300 lap Grand National event at Central City Speedway.

Thomas had taken the lead from Tim Flock on the 255th lap on the half-mile dirt track and appeared to be on his way to victory when the left rear tire on his Hudson blew on lap 294. The Olivia, NC driver elected not to pit and stayed on the track in a game effort to stay ahead of Petty.

Petty drove his Plymouth into the lead with five laps remaining and was 14 seconds ahead of Thomas when the checkered flag fell. Third place went to Flock, with Joe Eubanks fourth and Herschel Buchanan fifth.

Thomas took a 144-point lead over Flock in the driver standings.

Fonty Flock led the first 44 laps from the pole position, but a clogged fuel line put his Oldsmobile out of commission. Tim Flock took the lead at that point and led until lap 254 when the gas pedal on his Hudson worked its way loose. He spent two laps in the pit while his Ted Chester pit crew made repairs.

Dick Passwater of Indianapolis qualified second and was running in the top five when the right front wheel came off his Olds. The wheel bounced into the stands, injuring one spectator.

Stan Parnell had a long evening, blowing six tires and flipping his Olds twice. He finally had to quit after 159 laps.

Petty averaged 48.404 mph for his fifth career Grand National win.

Grand National Race No. 26
300 Laps at Central City Speedway
Macon, GA
150 Miles on Half-mile Dirt Track
September 7, 1952

Fin	St	No.	Driver	Team / Car	Laps	Money	Status
1	8	42	Lee Petty	Petty Engineerings '51 Plym	300	$1,260	Running
2	5	92	Herb Thomas	Thomas '52 Hudson	300	810	Running
3	3	91	Tim Flock	Ted Chester '52 Hudson	298	630	Running
4	24	82	Joe Eubanks	Phil Oates '52 Hudson	295	500	Running
5	15	1	Herschel Buchanan	Buchanan '52 Nash Amb.	289	300	Running
6	14	32	Jimmie Lewallen	R G Shelton '52 Hudson	285	210	Running
7	4		Carson Dyer *	'51 Hudson Hornet	283	170	Running
8	18	66	Donald Thomas	Elmer Pooler '51 Plymouth	281	125	Running
9	25	93	Ted Chamberlain	Chamberlain '50 Plymouth	269	100	Running
10	9		Barney Smith	'51 Plymouth	269	110	Running
11	11	55	Bub King	T.H. King. '51 Hudson	244	35	Running
12	2	77	Dick Passwater	Frank Arford '52 Olds 88	227	65	Spindle
13	6		Roscoe Thompson	'51 Studebaker	203	35	Engine
14	27		Olin Allen	'51 Olds 88	182	25	Running
15	16	16	Banjo Matthews	Bill Snowden '52 Hudson	170	25	Tie Rod
16	20		Stan Parnell	'50 Olds 88	159	50	Crash
17	17	116	Bill Snowden	Snowden '52 Hudson	145	25	RR Axle
18	26		Cotton Owens	'52 Ford	130	50	Crash
19	21	3	Lamar Crabtree	'50 Plymouth	95	25	Rear End
20	23	6	Jim Paschal	George Hutchens '51 Ford 6	93	25	Rear End
21	7	57	Tommy Moon	C.D. Wilson '52 Hudson	84	35	RR Axle
22	10	74	Pete Kelley	'52 Hudson Hornet	69	35	Tie Rod
23	12		Jerry Wimbish	'50 Olds 88	64	35	Engine
24	1	14	Fonty Flock	Frank Christian '51 Olds	44	75	Gas line
25	22	24	Ray Duhigg	J O Goode '51 Plymouth	39	50	Hub
26	13	172	June Cleveland	Carl Mays '51 Chrysler	30	35	Brakes
27	19	89	Buck Baker	B.A. Pless '52 Hudson Hornet	11	25	RR Axle

* Relieved by Fonty Flock
Time of Race: 3 hours, 5 minutes, 56 seconds
  Average Speed 48.404 mph
  Pole Winner: Fonty Flock - 59.113 mph
  Lap Leaders: Fonty Flock 1-44, Tim Flock 45-254, Herb Thomas 255-295,
    Lee Petty 296-300
  Cautions:
  Margin of Victory: 14.0 seconds (Herb Thomas, leading, blew tire in 294th lap. He stayed
    on the track, electing not to pit, and wound up 14 seconds behind Petty at the end of
    300 laps.
  Attendance:

Race No. 27

Petty Wins Langhorne;
Spill Fatal to Mann

LANGHORNE, PA (Sept. 14) -- Lee Petty of Randleman, NC, grabbed his second straight win in

*Larry Mann was killed in his 'Green Hornet' in
late stages of Langhorne 150.*

the 250-mile Grand National race at Langhorne Speedway, an event which was dipped in tragedy.

Larry Mann of Yonkers, NY, died from injuries when his Hudson Hornet overturned on lap 211. The rookie driver, who defied a long standing racing taboo by painting his car green, succumbed to massive head injuries at Nazareth Hospital.

Petty drove his Plymouth around Bill Blair with 41 laps remaining on the circular one-mile dirt track and stretched out a 3/4-lap margin by the end of the race.

Petty won $2,500.

Blair finished in second place, Herschel Buchanan was third, and Tim Flock fourth. Fifth place went to Dick Rathmann.

Herb Thomas won the pole but crashed on the 61st lap and lost the point lead. He now trails Tim Flock by 234 points.

There were several serious spills in addition to the fatal wreck of Mann, who became the first Grand National driver to die in a race. He was competing in his sixth outing. Nelson Applegate suffered a fractured skull when his Hudson crashed in the 125th lap. He was listed in serious condition at a nearby hospital.

After the race, NASCAR officials carefully inspected the first five cars. The five hour teardown did not reveal any illegalities.

Grand National Race No. 27
250 Laps at Langhorne Speedway
Langhorne, PA
250 Miles on 1-mile Dirt Track
September 14, 1952

Fin	St	No.	Driver	Team / Car	Laps	Money	Status
1	24	42	Lee Petty	Petty Engineering '51 Plym	250	$2,500	Running
2	10	2	Bill Blair	George Hutchens '52 Olds 88	250	1,250	Running
3	3	1	Herschel Buchanan	Buchanan '52 Nash Amb.	248	750	Running
4	12	91	Tim Flock	Ted Chester '52 Hudson	247	500	Running
5	8	120	Dick Rathmann	Walt Chapman '52 Hudson	246	450	Running
6	13	4	Slick Smith	Frank Christian '52 Olds 88	246	400	Running
7	23	52	Neil Cole	John Golabek '50 Plymouth	245	350	Running
8	2	24	Ray Duhigg	J O Goode '51 Plymouth	241	300	Running
9	6	421	Jack Reynolds	Wiss Bros. '50 Dodge	241	250	Running
10	29	167	Elton Hildreth	Hildreth Motors '50 Nash	237	200	Running
11	26		Iggy Katona	'51 Plymouth	236	150	Running
12	14	82	Joe Eubanks	Phil Oates '52 Hudson	235	125	Crash
13	5		Erwin Blatt	'51 Mercury	229	100	Running
14	18	60	Ralph Liguori	'52 Hudson Hornet	228	75	Running
15	31		Bud Farrell	'51 Plymouth	228	50	Running
16	27		Bill Barker	'51 Olds 88	226	50	Running
17	36		Walt Regan	'51 Hudson Hornet	225	50	Running
18	41		Bill Deakin	'51 Plymouth	225	50	Running
19	30		Pappy Hough	'51 Plymouth	221	50	Running
20	43	103	George Gallup	Gallup '50 Olds	213	50	Running
21	25		Jack Fisher	'52 Olds 88	212	35	Running
22	37	43	Larry Mann	Green Hornet '51 Hudson	211	35	Crash
23	32		Ed Van Horn	'50 Ford	208	35	Running
24	40		Wimpy Ervin	'52 Kaiser	206	35	Running
25	34	93	Ted Chamberlain	Chamberlain '50 Plymouth	204	35	Running
26	2	14	Fonty Flock	Frank Christian '52 Olds 88	204	35	Engine
27	28	96	Lucky Sawyer	'50 Ford	200	35	Running
28	33		Red Tomlinson	'51 Plymouth	200	35	Running
29	21		Ray Erickson	'52 Hudson Hornet	183	35	Engine
30	44	85	Tony Bonadies	'52 Olds 88	173	35	Running
31	38		Gene Darragh	'52 Hudson Hornet	171	35	Crash
32	19	118	Bucky Sager	Ed Benedict '51 Hudson	162	35	Running
33	20		Felix Wilkes	'51 Hudson Hornet	141	35	Crash
34	9		George Bush	'51 Olds 88	127	35	Running
35	15		Nelson Applegate	'51 Hudson Hornet	125	35	Crash
36	35		Chuck Garrett	'51 Olds 88	109	---	Crash
37	1	92	Herb Thomas	Thomas '52 Hudson	61	---	Crash
38	17	19	Fred Dove	'52 Packard	53	---	Heating
39	42	66	Donald Thomas	Elmer Pooler '51 Plymouth	43	---	Clutch
40	16		Charles Weidler	'50 Hudson	41	---	Heating
41	39		Lawrence Jacquelin	'51 Studebaker	34	---	Heating
42	22		Mike Magill	'52 Hudson Hornet	28	---	Spindle
43	11	41	Jimmie Lewallen	John Eanes '52 Olds 88	27	---	Rear End
44	7	87	Buck Baker	'51 Ford	26	---	Heating

Tim of Race: 3 hours, 27 minutes
Average Speed: 72.463 mph
Pole Winner: Herb Thomas - 85.287 mph
Lap Leaders: Fonty Flock 1-50, Tim Flock 51-59, Dick Rathmann 60-120, Bill Blair 121-209, Lee Petty 210-250
Cautions: Margin of Victory: 3/4-lap   Attendance: 20,000

Race No. 28

Rathmann Wins
Disputed Dayton Event

DAYTON, OH (Sept. 21) -- Dick Rathmann was declared the winner in a disputed 100-mile Grand National race at Dayton Speedway after Lee Petty had taken the checkered flag first.

In the final laps, Rathmann's Walt Chapman crew questioned the fact that Petty was headed for the $1,500 victory. Immediately after the conclusion of the 300-lap event, NASCAR officials studied the score cards. It was determined that Petty had been credited with one lap too many and Rathmann was given the first place check.

Petty got credit for second and Ray Duhigg was third. Lloyd Moore and Herb Thomas rounded out the top-five.

Point Leader Tim Flock finished sixth and held a 222-point cushion over Thomas.

Rathmann officially took the lead in the 264th lap when Fonty Flock's Oldsmobile dropped its gas tank. The Los Angeles Hudson driver led the rest of the way.

A crowd of 15,000 watched Rathmann beat Petty by 5.0 seconds, averaging 61.643 mph for the 150 miles.

Grand National Race No. 28
300 Laps at Dayton Speedway
Dayton, OH
150 Miles on Half-mile Paved Track
September 21, 1952

Fin	St	No.	Driver	Team / Car	Laps	Money	Status
1	3	120	Dick Rathmann *	Walt Chapman '51 Hudson	300	$1,500	Running
2	12	42	Lee Petty	Petty Engineering '51 Plym	300	1,000	Running
3	13	24	Ray Duhigg	J O Goode '50 Plymouth	297	700	Running
4	7	59	Lloyd Moore	Julian Buesink '51 Ford	295	600	Running
5	4	92	Herb Thomas	Thomas '52 Hudson	293	350	Running
6	2	91	Tim Flock	Ted Chester '52 Hudson	291	275	Running
7	16		Iggy Katona	'51 Plymouth	286	175	Running
8	15	77	Dick Passwater	Frank Arford '51 Olds 88	286	150	Running
9	14	18	Ed Benedict	Benedict '51 Hudson	284	100	Running
10	19		Hershal White	'50 Plymouth	283	75	Running
11	8	58	Johnny Patterson	Grady Akers '51 Hudson	280	50	Running
12	17		Nelson Stacy	'50 Ford	277	50	Running
13	22		Jack Harrison	'50 Ford	277	50	Running
14	25		Bobby Dugan	'49 Ford	275	50	Running
15	21		Mike Earnest	'50 Olds 88	168	50	Running
16	1	14	Fonty Flock	Frank Christian '51 Olds 88	263	25	Gas Tank
17	9		Charles Weidler	'50 Plymouth	259	25	Running
18	27		Tommy Thompson	'52 Buick	256	25	Running
19	23		Ray Atkinson	'49 Ford	255	25	Running
20	28		Don Kent	'49 Ford	255	25	Running
21	18	107	Bruce Atchley	Atchley '51 Hudson Hornet	155	25	Running
22	30		George Hufford	'50 Plymouth	148	25	Running
23	11	118	Bucky Sager	Ed Benedict '52 Hudson	145	25	Engine
24	26		Al Smith	'52 Nash	125	25	Wheels
25	6	55	Bub King	T.H. King '52 Hudson Hornet	109	25	Rod Out
26	24	167	Elton Hildreth	Hildreth Motors '51 Nash	94	25	A-Frame
27	20		Mel Cook	'50 Hudson	38	25	Heating
28	29		Buddy Cox	'49 Ford	29	25	Spindle
29	5	4	Slick Smith	Frank Christian '50 Olds 88	20	25	Engine
30	10	3	Ray Erickson	'51 Hudson Hornet	1	25	Clutch

* Lee Petty was flagged winner. After scoring re-check, it was discovered Dick Rathmann
    was actual winner
  Time of Race: 2 hours, 26 minutes
  Average Speed: 61.643 mph
  Pole Winner: Fonty Flock - 71.741 mph
  Lap Leaders: Fonty Flock 1-156, Lee Petty 157-158, Fonty Flock 159-263,
      Dick Rathmann 264-300.
  Cautions: Margin of Victory: 5.0 seconds   Attendance: 15,000

Point leader Tim Flock finished seventh and held a 174 point lead over Thomas with five races left on the 1952 Grand National slate.

Fireball Roberts made a rare Grand National appearance. He qualified his Ford in the 12th position, but wound up 16th when an axle snapped after 81 laps.

Grand National Race No. 29
200 Laps at Wilson County Speedway
Wilson, NC
100 Miles on Half-mile Dirt Track
September 28, 1952

Fin	St	No.	Driver	Team / Car	Laps	Money	Status
1	1	92	Herb Thomas	Thomas '52 Hudson	200	$1,000	Running
2	8	42	Lee Petty	Petty Engineering '51 Plym	199	700	Running
3	13	2	Bill Blair	George Hutchens '52 Olds 88	199	450	Running
4	11	12	Jim Paschal	Buckshot Morris '52 Olds 88	199	350	Running
5	9	120	Dick Rathmann	Walt Chapman '52 Hudson	198	200	Running
6	3	17	Buddy Shuman	Shuman '52 Hudson Hornet	196	150	Running
7	4	91	Tim Flock	Ted Chester '52 Hudson	192	125	Running
8	7	4	Slick Smith	Frank Christian '51 Olds 88	186	100	Running
9	2	32	Jimmie Lewallen	R.G. Shelton '52 Hudson	172	75	Running
10	22	71	Coleman Lawrence	'50 Plymouth	164	50	Running
11	19		Earl Moss	'51 Plymouth	162	25	Tie Rod
12	21	19	Fred Dove	'49 Buick	161	25	Spindle
13	17	167	Elton Hildreth	Hildreth Motors '51 Nash	151	25	Steering
14	15	24	Ray Duhigg	J O Goode '51 Plymouth	115	25	Rear End
15	6	118	Bucky Sager	Ed Benedict '51 Hudson	105	25	Head
16	12	11	Fireball Roberts	Ed Saverance '51 Ford 6	81	25	RR Axle
17	18	77	Weldon Adams	Harold Mays '51 Plymouth	51	25	Brakes
18	5	14	Fonty Flock	Frank Christian '52 Olds 88	34	25	Brakes
19	20		C.L. Grant	'51 Ford 6	28	25	RR Axle
20	16		Charles Weidler	'51 Hudson Hornet	27	25	Head
21	10	87	Buck Baker	'52 Ford	23	25	RR Axle
22	15	107	Bruce Atchley	Atchley '51 Hudson Hornet	12	25	Crash

  Time of Race: 2 hours, 49 minutes, 30 seconds
  Average Speed: 35.398 mph
  Pole Winner: Herb Thomas - 55.883 mph
  Lap Leaders: - - - - - - - - - Herb Thomas   -200
  Cautions: Margin of Victory: 1 lap plus   Attendance:

Race No. 29

Thomas Wins
Wilson at 35 MPH!

WILSON, NC (Sept. 28) -- Herb Thomas outran Lee Petty by a full lap and won the 100-mile Grand National race at Wilson Speedway. In his fifth win of the year, Thomas, starting on the pole, averaged a record low 35.398 mph on a rough battleground littered with the parts of suspension systems torn apart by the rutted surface. Several caution flags dropped for wrecks and crashes contributed to the low net speeds. Only ten cars in the field of 22 completed the race.

Bill Blair wound up third, Jim Paschal was fourth and Dick Rathmann fifth.

Race No. 30

Flock's Olds Bests
Hillsboro's Field

HILLSBORO, NC (Oct. 12) -- Fonty Flock zipped around Bill Blair in the seventh lap and was never headed as he scampered home first in the 150-mile Grand National race at the historic Occoneechee Speedway.

A crowd of 12,500 watched Flock average 73.489 mph for his 11th career Grand Ntional win. He collected $1,200 for his efforts.

Fonty Flock broadslides his Oldsmobile. He won the 150-miler at Hillsboro.

Donald Thomas' Hudson finished second with brother Herb at the wheel. Herb's own Hornet had broken a hub in the 23rd lap, so he drove Donald's car in relief to pick up as many championship points as possible Herb received 200 of the 240 points earned by the #9 car for finishing second.

Blair finished in third place with Tim Flock fourth and Lee Petty fifth. Tim's point lead over Thomas stood at 194.

Fonty made only one pit stop en route to his second win of the year. He brought his Oldsmobile into the pits on lap 110 so that his crew, headed by Red Vogt,

could put in a full load of fuel. This was accomplished in 45 seconds. Flock said the quick pit stop was a major factor in his victory.

Race No. 31

Broken Axle Foils Rathmann; Herb Thomas Wins

MARTINSVILLE, VA (Oct. 19) -- When Dick Rathmann fell out, Herb Thomas cruised into the lead 27 laps from the finish and went on to win the 100-mile Grand National race at Martinsville Speedway.

Rathmann had led for 102 laps and was a virtual shoo-in for the win, but a broken axle on his Hudson sent him to the showers. Thomas drove into the lead at

Grand National Race No. 30
150 Laps at Occoneechee Speedway
Hillsboro, NC
150 Miles on 1-mile Dirt Track
October 12, 1952

Fin	St	No.	Driver	Team / Car	Laps	Money	Status
1	4	14	Fonty Flock	Frank Christian '52 Olds 88	150	$1,200	Running
2	7	9	Donald Thomas *	Thomas '52 Hudson	150	700	Running
3	1	2	Bill Blair	George Hutchens '52 Olds 88	150	500	Running
4	5	91	Tim Flock	Ted Chester '52 Hudson	149	450	Running
5	9	42	Lee Petty	Petty Engineering '51 Plym	147	400	Running
6	11	55	Bub King	T.H. King '51 Hudson	143	325	Running
7	18	24	Ray Duhigg	J O Goode '51 Plymouth	140	250	Running
8	20	4	Slick Smith	Frank Christian '51 Olds 88	139	150	Running
9	29	19	Fred Dove	'49 Buick	139	125	Running
10	17		George Bush	'52 Olds 88	138	100	Running
11	13		Clyde Minter	'52 Packard	136	75	Running
12	19	93	Ted Chamberlain	Chamberlain '50 Plymouth	135	75	Running
13	24	167	Elton Hildreth	Hildreth Motors '51 Nash	133	75	Running
14	23		Ewell Weddle	'51 Plymouth	131	75	Running
15	22		Otis Martin	'50 Plymouth	131	75	Running
16	26	71	Coleman Lawrence	'50 Plymouth	125	50	Running
17	6	12	Jim Paschal	Buckshot Morris '52 Olds 88	117	50	Rear End
18	12	58	Johnny Patterson	Grady Akers '52 Hudson	105	50	Steering
19	25	96	Lucky Sawyer	'51 Plymouth	96	50	Radiator
20	2	32	Jimmie Lewallen	R G Shelton '52 Hudson	74	50	LR Hub
21	14		Joe Eubanks	'51 Ford	74	25	Heating
22	27		C.L. Grant	'51 Plymouth	68	25	RR Hub
23	8		Ted Swaim	'51 Plymouth	65	25	Fan Belt
24	10		Ralph Liguori	'51 Olds 88	51	25	Crash
25	16	107	Dick Rathmann	Bruce Atchley '51 Hudson	48	25	Mount
26	28		Albert Price	'50 Ford	37	25	Heating
27	3	92	Herb Thomas	Thomas '51 Hudson	23	25	RR Hub
28	16		Walt Reagan	'51 Hudson Hornet	13	25	RR Axle
29	21		Cotton Owens	'51 Ford 6	12	25	Gas Tank

* Relieved by Herb Thomas
Time of Race: 2 hours, 2 minutes, 28 seconds
Average Speed: 73.489 mph
Pole Winner: Bill Blair - 75.901 mph
Lap Leaders: Bill Blair 1-6, Fonty Flock 7-150.
Cautions: 2   Margin of Victory: Attendance: 12,500

Grand National Race No. 31
200 Laps at Martinsville Speedway
Martinsville, VA
100 Miles on Half-mile Dirt Track
October 19, 1952

Fin	St	No.	Driver	Team / Car	Laps	Money	Status
1	2	92	Herb Thomas	Thomas '52 Hudson	200	$1,000	Running
2	4	14	Fonty Flock	Frank Christian '52 Olds 88	200	700	Running
3	11	42	Lee Petty	Petty Engineering '52 Plym	199	450	Running
4	5	91	Tim Flock	Ted Chester '52 Hudson	195	350	Running
5	6	58	Johnny Patterson	Grady Akers '52 Hudson	194	200	Running
6	12	2	Bill Blair	George Hutchens '52 Olds 88	193	150	Running
7	22	44	Julian Petty	J H Petty '51 Plym	193	125	Running
8	14		Clyde Minter	'52 Packard	192	100	Running
9	16		Cotton Owens	'51 Ford 6	192	75	Running
10	8		Ralph Liguori	'52 Olds 88	191	50	Running
11	28	93	Ted Chamberlain	Chamberlain '50 Plymouth	188	25	Running
12	23		Ewell Weddle	'51 Plymouth	188	25	Running
13	10	12	Jim Paschal	Buckshot Morris '52 Olds 88	182	25	Running
14	29		C.L. Grant	'51 Plymouth	179	25	Running
15	26	71	Coleman Lawrence	'50 Plymouth	175	25	Running
16	7	120	Dick Rathmann	Walt Chapman '52 Hudson	173	25	RR Axle
17	21		Clyde Pittinger	'50 Plymouth	163	25	Running
18	13	9	Donald Thomas	Thomas '52 Hudson	155	25	W Pump
19	25	8	Gene Comstock	Comstock '52 Hudson Hornet	152	25	Crash
20	24	24	Bob Welborn	J.O. Goode '51 Plymouth	137	25	Steering
21	20	55	Bub King	T.H. King '52 Hudson Hornet	120	25	Running
22	1	22	Perk Brown	R.G. Shelton '52 Hudson	96	25	Springs
23	15	19	Fred Dove	'49 Buick	83	25	Heating
24	3	82	Joe Eubanks	Phil Oates '52 Hudson	80	25	Rear End
25	9	32	Jimmie Lewallen	R.G.Shelton '52 Hudson	78	25	RF Hub
26	18	167	Elton Hildreth	Hildreth Motors '51 Nash	74	25	Brakes
27	19	89	Buddy Shuman	B.A. Pless '52 Hudson Hornet	37	25	Crash
28	17	96	Lucky Sawyer	'51 Plymouth	37	25	Radiator
29	27		Jack Holloway	'50 Plymouth	12	25	Crash

Time of Race: 2 hours, 6 minutes, 10 seconds
Average Speed: 47.556 mph
Pole Winner: Perk Brown - 55.333 mph
Lap Leaders: Fonty Flock 1-3, Herb Thomas 4-7, F. Flock 8-12, H. Thomas 13-37,
    F. Flock 38-71, Dick Rathmann 72-173, H. Thomas 174-200.
Cautions: Margin of Victory: Attendance: 7,200

Nash pace car leads Martinsville field. Perk Brown and eventual winner Herb Thomas are on the front row.

standings leader Tim Flock.

It was Thomas' 15th career win and his seventh in the 1952 campaign.

Fonty Flock's Olds finished in second place, Donald Thomas was third, Tim Flock fourth and Dick Rathmann fifth.

Thomas started on the pole with a speed of 76.013 mph, but Fonty Flock led the opening eight laps from his outside front row starting position. Thomas dogged his rival for four miles before making the pass on lap nine. Once in the lead, Thomas kept his powder-blue Hudson in front. Thomas lapped all competitors except runner-up Flock and third place Donald Thomas.

Paul Richardson, Jim Paschal and Bub King were eliminated from the race by crashes. There were no drivers injured in any of the mishaps.

Thomas averaged 67.144 mph before an audience of 6,200.

that point and led the rest of the way.

Fonty Flock finished second, in the same lap with the winner. Lee Petty came in third, Tim Flock was fourth and Johnny Patterson fifth.

Thomas' victory enabled him to shave Tim Flock's point lead to 170.

Two drivers were injured in accidents at the half-mile dirt track. Gene Comstock, running six laps behind, rolled his Hudson twice in a turn after 152 laps. He was transported to the hospital with minor injuries.

Jack Holloway broke an ankle when an axle gave way on his Plymouth causing it to crash in the 12th lap.

Buddy Shuman flipped his Hudson, but he escaped unscathed.

Perk Brown, outstanding Modified driver who had been plagued with mechanical ills on the Grand National trail, started on the pole, but had to retire when the right rear spring broke on his Hudson.

Thomas averaged 47.556 mph before a crowd of 7,200.

Race No. 32

Herb Hustles to Wilkesboro Win

N. WILKESBORO, NC (Oct. 26) -- Herb Thomas took the lead in the ninth lap and led the rest of the way to win the 125-mile Grand national event at North Wilkesboro Speedway, pulling him to within 146 points of

Grand National Race No. 32
200 Laps at N. Wilkesboro Speedway
North Wilkesboro, NC
125 Miles on .625-mile Dirt Track
October 26, 1952

Fin	St	No.	Driver	Team / Car	Laps	Money	Status
1	1	9	Herb Thomas	Thomas '52 Hudson	200	$1,000	Running
2	2	14	Fonty Flock	Frank Christian '52 Olds 88	200	700	Running
3	6	92	Donald Thomas	Thomas '52 Hudson	200	450	Running
4	4	91	Tim Flock	Ted Chester '51 Hudson	199	350	Running
5	8	120	Dick Rathmann	Walt Chapman '52 Hudson	194	200	Running
6	15	44	Jimmie Lewallen	J.H. Petty '51 Plymouth	193	150	Running
7	3	22	Perk Brown	R G Shelton '52 Hudson	190	125	Running
8	20	19	Fred Dove	'52 Packard	188	100	Running
9	12	55	Bub King	T.H. King '51 Hudson Hornet	183	75	Crash
10	27	71	Coleman Lawrence	'50 Plymouth	172	50	Running
11	22		J.C. White	'50 Ford	164	25	Running
12	19	24	Bob Welborn	J O Goode '51 Plymouth	161	25	Spindle
13	14	42	Lee Petty	Petty Engineering '51 Plym	148	25	Spindle
14	17		Ewell Weddle	'51 Plymouth	146	25	Wheel
15	24		C.L. Grant	'51 Plymouth	146	25	Running
16	10	89	Buck Baker	B.A. Pless '51 Hudson Hornet	143	25	Spincle
17	18	167	Elton Hildreth	Hildreth Motors '51 Nash	126	25	LF Hub
18	13	12	Jim Paschal	Buckshot Morris '52 Olds 88	122	25	Crash
19	11	82	Joe Eubanks	Phil Oates. '52 Hudson	114	25	Steering
20	26	93	Ted Chamberlain	Chamberlain '50 Plymouth	88	25	Arm
21	23		George Bush	'52 Olds 88	67	25	Gears
22	7		Ralph Liguori	'52 Olds 88	66	25	Fuel Pmp
23	5	77	Dick Passwater	Frank Arford '52 Olds 88	62	25	Fuel Pmp
24	16		Charles Barry	'51 Plymouth	44	25	Wheel
25	21		Paul Richardson	'51 Olds 88	39	25	Crash
26	9	2	Bill Blair	George Hutchens '52 Olds 88	15	25	Spindle
27	25	94	Joe Staton	Louise Smith '51 Ford	10	25	Heating

Time of Race: 1 hour, 51 minutes, 52 seconds
Average Speed: 67.044 mph
Pole Winner: Herb Thomas - 76.013 mph
Lap Leaders: Fonty Flock 1-8, Herb Thomas 9-200
Cautions: 3 for 12 laps   Margin of Victory: Attendance: 6,200

Race No. 33

20 Year-old Donald Thomas Gets First Win at Lakewood

ATLANTA, GA (Nov. 16) -- Donald Thomas, who has spent his entire career in the shadow of his more famous brother, Herb, gained his first trip to victory lane in the 100-mile Grand National event at Lakewood Speedway.

Thomas, at age 20, became the youngest winner in NACAR Grand National history. Previously, 21 year-old Fireball Roberts held the distinction of being the youngest winner when he won at Hillsboro, NC in 1950.

The final twelve laps were driven by reliever Herb Thomas, whose Hudson was forced to the sidelines by a broken axle in the 86th lap.

Lee Petty wound up a close second to Donald Thomas. Joe Eubanks finished third, Tim Flock was fourth and Gober Sosebee claimed fifth place.

Donald Thomas became NASCAR's youngest Grand National winner at Lakewood Speedway.

Donald started on the pole with Herb on the outside. Herb got the jump at the green flag and led for 83 of the first 86 laps. He had stretched out a big lead when the axle broke as he exited the second turn.

Thomas dismounted quickly and flagged his brother to a halt at the crash site. Donald had been running second. Herb took control of Donald's car and managed to keep it in front of Lee Petty, who had been running third before the incident.

Tim Flock, whose crew consisted of car owner Ted Chester and chief mechanic B.B. Blackburn, yelled foul as Herb took on a relief driving assignment from the track rather than the pit area. Thomas stood to collect additional championship points for the relief driving role.

After leading the 87th and 88th laps under caution in Donald's car, Herb was blackflagged by NASCAR officials. He was ordered to the rear of the field as Petty took the lead on lap 89.

Despite the impromptu penalty, Thomas came charging back. He sped past Petty in the 94th lap and led the rest of the way.

In NASCAR records, Herb mistakenly received credit for posting the win. He finished 13th in the field of 24.

Donald Thomas' first Grand National win came at an average speed of 64.853 mph.

With one race to go, Tim Flock held a 194-point lead. The Atlanta Hudson driver merely has to start the finale at West Palm Beach to clinch his first NASCAR Grand National championship.

Grand National Race No. 33
100 Laps at Lakewood Speedway
Atlanta, GA
100 Miles on 1-mile Dirt Track
November 16, 1952

Fin	St	No.	Driver	Team / Car	Laps	Money	Status
1	1	9	Donald Thomas*	Thomas '52 Hudson	100	$1,080	Running
2	9	42	Lee Petty	Petty Engineering '51 Plym	100	700	Running
3	18	82	Joe Eubanks	Phil Oates '52 Hudson	100	450	Running
4	4	91	Tim Flock	Ted Chester '52 Hudson	99	385	Running
5	24	51	Gober Sosebee	Sosebee '52 Chrysler	98	200	Running
6	6	120	Jack Smih	Walt Chapman '52 Hudson	98	150	Running
7	22		George Bush	'52 Olds 88	96	120	Running
8	23		Ralph Liguori	'52 Olds 88	96	95	Running
9	20	8	Gene Comstock	Comstock '51 Hudson	94	70	Running
10	12	55	Bub King	T.H. King '51 Hudson Hornet	94	70	Running
11	21	93	Ted Chamberlain	Chamberlain '52 Plymouth	92	45	Running
12	7		Jimmie Lewallen	'51 Ford	88	45	Running
13	2	92	Herb Thomas	Thomas '52 Hudson	86	80	Axle
14	8	2	Dick Rathmann	George Hutchens '52 Olds 88	85	45	Running
15	17	22	Perk Brown	R.G. Shelton '52 Hudson	77	45	Piston
16	19	172	Buddy Shuman	Carl Mays '51 Plymouth	72	25	Gasket
17	13	19	Fred Dove	'52 Packard	68	40	Tie Rod
18	11	16	Fireball Roberts	Bill Snowden '52 Hudson	53	24	Spindle
19	3	14	Fonty Flock	Frank Christian '52 Olds 88	45	65	Drive Shf
20	5	81	Roscoe Thompson	'51 Studebaker	33	50	RR Hub
21	14	24	Bob Welborn	J O Goode '51 Plymouth	26	40	Brakes
22	10	12	Bill Blair	George Hutchens '52 Olds 88	22	25	Crash
23	15	63	Mike Magill	Blackbunt Svc. '51 Plymouth	22	25	Crash
24	16		Robert L. Weisemeyer	'51 Chrysler	9	25	Disqual.

* Herb Thomas relieved Donald Thomas in the No. 9 car in the 89th lap. NASCAR gave Herb credit for the victory in a reversal of original rundown. Under NASCAR rules Donald Thomas is the correct winner since he started the car that won the race.

Time of Race: 1 hour, 32 minutes, 31 seconds
Average Speed: 64.853 mph
Pole Winner: Donald Thomas - 72.874 mph
Lap Leaders: Herb Thomas 1-12, Fonty Flock 13-15, Herb Thomas 46-86, Donald Thomas 87-88, Lee Petty 89-93, Donald Thomas 94-100.
Cautions: 3   Margin of Victory: Attendance: 18,000

Race No. 34

Thomas Wins Finale; Tim Takes Title 'On His Head'

W. PALM BEACH, FL (Nov. 30) -- Tim Flock was declared 1952 Grand National Champion after flipping his Hudson at Palm Beach Speedway as Herb Thomas won the season ending 100-miler.

Flock crashed his car in the 164th lap and performed

Tim Flock won the 1952 NASCAR Grand National
championship despite turning his Hudson over
in season finale at West Palm Beach, FL.

Grand National Race No. 34
200 Laps at Palm Beach Speedway
West Palm Beach, FL
100 Miles on Half-mile Dirt Track
November 30, 1952

Fin	St	No.	Driver	Team / Car	Laps	Money	Status
1	1	92	Herb Thomas	Thomas '52 Hudson	200	$1,000	Running
2	4	14	Fonty Flock	Frank Christian '52 Olds 88	198	700	Running
3	3	22	Perk Brown	R.G. Shelton '52 Hudson	196	450	Running
4	8	42	Lee Petty	Petty Engineering '51 Plym	194	350	Running
5	12		Marion Edwards	'50 Dodge	183	200	Running
6	15		Rags Carter	'51 Plymouth	183	150	Running
7	10	13	Pop McGinnis	Irving Frye '51 Hudson Hornet	180	125	Running
8	5		Ralph Liguori	'52 Olds 88	174	100	Running
9	14	3	Alan Clarke	'50 Chevrolet	170	75	Crash
10	16		George Bush	'52 Olds 88	170	50	Crash
11	6	23	Al Keller	'50 Olds 88	167	25	Wheel
12	2	91	Tim Flock	Ted Chester '52 Hudson	164	25	Crash
13	18		Hank Tillman	'50 Ford	160	25	Running
14	11		Dub Livingston	'53 Dodge	152	25	Wheel
15	13		Oda Green	'52 Hudson Hornet	134	25	RF Hub
16	9	16	Banjo Matthews	Bill Snowden '52 Hudson	104	25	Heating
17	7		Jimmie Lewallen	'51 Ford 6	97	25	Gasket
18	19	9	Smokey Yunick	Thomas '52 Hudson	7	25	Ignition
19	17		Hank Pollard	'50 Ford	4	25	Radiator

Time of Race: 1 hour, 43 minutes, 26 seconds
Average Speed: 58.008 mph
Pole Winner: Herb Thomas - 63.716 mph
Lap Leaders: Herb Thomas 1-200.
Cautions: Margin of Victory: 2 laps plus   Attendance: 7,500

a series of violent rollovers in front of the stunned crowd of 7,500. He climbed out unhurt to a standing ovation. "I bet I'm the only driver who has won the championship on his head," Flock declared afterwards.

Flock sewed up the Grand National title by merely starting the race. He entered the event with a 194 point lead and finished 106 points in front of Thomas, who grabbed his eighth win of the year by a two-lap margin.

Fonty Flock finished second with Perk Brown, Lee Petty and Marion Edwards filling out the top five.

Thomas led the entire 200 laps after starting on the pole. Henry "Smokey" Yunick, Thomas' chief mechanic, started his first Grand National race in the same car Donald Thomas drove to victory in Atlanta. Yunick started 19th and finished 18th, falling victim to ignition failure after seven laps.

1952 NASCAR Season
Final Point Standings Grand National Division

Rank	Driver	Points	Starts	Wins	Top 5	Top 10	Winnings
1	Tim Flock	6,858.50	33	8	22	25	$22,890.00
2	Herb Thomas	6,752.50	32	8	19	22	18,965.00
3	Lee Petty	6,498.50	32	3	21	27	16,876.00
4	Fonty Flock	5,183.50	27	2	13	15	19,112.00
5	Dick Rathmann	3,952.50	27	5	14	14	11,248.00
6	Bill Blair	3,449.00	19	1	10	13	7,899.00
7	Joe Eubanks	3,090.50	19	0	4	9	3,630.00
8	Ray Duhigg	2,986.50	18	0	4	10	3,811.00
9	Donald Thomas	2,574.00	21	1	5	14	4,477.00
10	Buddy Shuman	2,483.00	14	1	3	7	4,587.00
11	Ted Chamberlain	2,208.00	17	0	0	6	1,277.00
12	Buck Baker	2,159.00	14	1	3	6	3,187.00
13	Perk Brown	2,151.50	19	0	3	6	2,187.00
14	Jimmie Lewallen	2,033.00	20	0	2	7	2,052.00
15	Bub King	1,993.00	10	0	2	5	2,737.00
16	Herschel Buchanan	1,868.00	5	0	4	5	2,468.00
17	Johnny Patterson	1,708.00	5	0	2	2	3,618.00
18	Jim Paschal	1,694.00	15	0	1	7	1,483.00
19	Neil Cole	1,618.00	10	0	1	7	1,793.00
20	Lloyd Moore	1,513.50	8	0	2	4	2,193.00
21	Gene Comstock	1,339.00	8	0	1	3	785.00
22	Banjo Matthews	1,240.00	3	0	1	1	1,000.00
23	Ralph Liguori	1,230.00	12	0	1	6	920.00
24	Jack Reynolds	1,177.50	10	0	2	6	1,450.00
25	Dick Passwater	1,148.00	6	0	1	3	945.00
26	Bucky Sager	1,119.50	10	0	1	3	710.00
27	Frankie Schneider	931.00	5	0	3	4	1,350.00
28	Otis Martin	873.50	5	0	0	2	275.00
29	Coleman Lawrence	846.00	8	0	0	3	375.00
30	Ed Samples	827.00	8	0	2	4	1,535.00
31	Fred Dove	780.00	8	0	0	3	390.00
32	Slick Smith	746.00	5	0	0	3	725.00
33	Iggy Katona	742.00	5	0	0	2	525.00
34	Jack Smith	729.00	8	0	0	2	820.00
35	Tommy Moon	726.00	6	0	2	3	1,145.00
36	Rollin Smith	700.00	1	0	0	0	350.00
37	Speedy Thompson	656.00	2	0	0	0	305.00
38	Jimmy Thompson	650.00	1	0	0	0	300.00
39	George Farrell	648.00	6	0	0	2	325.00
40	Weldon Adams	634.00	6	0	0	2	275.00
41	Clyde Minter	632.00	5	0	0	3	375.00
42	Elton Hildreth	614.00	6	0	0	1	375.00
43	Dave Terrell	612.00	5	0	1	3	475.00
44	Tommy Thompson	602.50	5	0	0	1	525.00
45	Bob Moore	579.50	5	0	1	3	575.00
46	Jim Reed	567.00	7	0	1	3	475.00
47	E.C. Ramsey	560.00	7	0	0	0	260.00
48	Jimmy Florian	551.00	6	0	0	2	175.00
49	Ed Benedict	526.00	5	0	1	2	360.00
50	Curtis Turner	505.00	6	0	1	1	265.00

The 1953 Season
'Pointless Finishes'
and A Hard Safety Lesson

Volume one of a four volume series . . . The Beginning 1949 - 1958

1953

As the NASCAR Grand National Circuit began reaching into new marketing areas of the continental United States, promoters hosting the headlining late model stock cars felt it was necessary to know well in advance which drivers would be participating in their races.

Quite understandably, the promoter's request was a reasonable one. How else could he promote his event?

The drivers, however, were reclusive and uncooperative. A free spirited laconic group, they never got into the habit of completing entry blanks to notify promoters of their intentions. If they showed up, they would race. If not, the promoter would know it by their absence. The fact is that except for the few well-financed teams, most of the drivers never knew whether they would have the money to make the next trip.

In an effort to address this situation, NASCAR instituted a new set of rules whereby no championship points would be distributed to those drivers who had not filed an entry blank with the promoter and the sanctioning body. From 1949-1952, points were awarded according to finish position regardless of whether an entry blank had been completed.

"The time has come when more attention must be paid to the filing of entry blanks," read a statement mailed to each of the 8,000-plus members in 1953. "Let the promoter know where you'll be. They have to know so they can advertise you and get the money to pay the purses."

A simple message in the mail failed to provoke a response from many of the series regulars. In the third

event of the 1953 Grand National season at Spring Lake, NC, no less than six drivers were not issued any points because they had failed to file an entry. Among those standing still in the point race were Bill Blair, Fred Dove, Ray Duhigg, Weldon Adams, Harold Nash and Coleman Lawrence.

Once more, NASCAR reiterated the importance of filing entries. "Drivers are required to post entries by a specified deadline," read a follow-up bulletin. "This new rule, clearly stated on each entry blank, will be enforced strictly at all NASCAR events in 1953."

Eventually, the drivers would learn to comply with the new standards.

As the Grand National circuit entered its fifth season, speeds were noticeably on the rise. The $202,507 tour was attracting more cars and more drivers, more publicity in daily newspapers -- and somewhat alarmingly, more parts failures in the area of spindles, hubs, axles and suspension systems.

The Hudson, Oldsmobile and Lincoln manufacturers began supplying "severe usage" kits on the race cars shipped to car owners -- many of whom had worked out individual arrangements with the factories. In announcing their approval for the sturdy "severe usage" kits,

*NASCAR's Big Three
Cannonball Baker, Bill France, Ed Otto.*

a NASCAR spokesman said, "Responding to the request from car owners across the nation for more durable equipment, these factories have come up with parts calculated to ease drivers through the most rugged conditions."

With NASCAR gladly accepting certain modifications "in the interest of safety", the sanctioning body began a campaign to make the cars and tracks safer for the competitors. They issued several bulletins, leaving car owners largely responsible to see that no short cuts were taken in the protection of the driver.

Frank Arford of Indianapolis, a driver and owner of two Grand National cars, became the second fatality within a year when he lost his life in a qualifying crash at Langhorne on June 20. Arford's Oldsmobile broke through the wooden retaining barrier on the front stretch, flipped and threw its driver out. The roof of the car was also flattened.

An investigation revealed that the seat brace had broken loose. The helpless driver slipped from under the belts and landed some thirty feet from his car.

Following the tragedy, NASCAR issued another bulletin to its members. "Grand National Circuit contestants are urged to install roll bars and to lock seats so they cannot break loose and slide forward," the statement read. "Those with divided (bucket) seats are urged to wire down the section on the driver's side to help eliminate strain on the safety belts."

Later that year, Fireball Roberts had a spill in a Modified race at Asheville-Weaverville Speedway in which his seat belt broke in a roll-over. Painfully bruised but otherwise unhurt, Fireball remarked, "I issue a warning to my fellow NASCAR drivers to check those seat belts. Mine had been rotted with battery acid (Modified cars usually had the batteries located inside the driver's compartment). I was lucky."

With the news of the Arford death and Fireball's outcry, most competitors forsook the short cuts in safety and inspected their protective gear.

In the late spring of 1953, the one-mile Raleigh Speedway, formerly Southland Speedway, joined the NASCAR fold. In its 1952 inaugural, the track operators had joined up with the AAA for an Indianapolis Car Championship contest.

During the early part of 1953, Bill France convinced the speedway directors that the Grand National circuit would be ideal for the neatly groomed facility. He assisted the promotion of a 300-mile race on May 30, directly opposite the Indianapolis 500.

Buddy Shuman in victory lane after tragic Modified -Sportsman race at Raleigh.

The Raleigh track was billed as a "one-mile *super fast track*", apparently a prelude to the more familiar superspeedway jargon we hear today. A press release isued by the Public Relations Department read, "North Carolina race fans will witness the biggest event in the history of speed activity in their state when Bill France presents a 300-mile Grand National Circuit race on Memorial Day, May 30, 1953."

In order to handcuff expenses -- and recalling that Johnny Mantz had blitzed the field in Darlington's first Southern 500 using a hard compound truck tire -- a special rule governed tire use in the Raleigh 300. "No special asphalt tread racing tire allowed," NASCAR insisted.

A crowd of 15,235 filled the grandstands to watch the field of 49 cars take the green flag at noon. Fonty Flock, who started 43rd after missing the time trials due to engine problems, roared through the pack, took the lead with 105 laps to go and beat Speedy Thompson by two laps. Flock became the first man to win two *super fast track* races. Top prize was $3,500.

The Raleigh Speedway board of directors was so impressed with NASCAR -- and Bill France in particular for actively promoting the affair -- that a 220-mile championship for Modified and Sportsman cars was scheduled for Saturday night, September 19th. With the field open to the sixty fastest qualifiers and some $15,000 in prize money up for grabs, the 'biggie' for the Weekend Warriors would be a show under the lights. It was the first superspeedway event staged at night.

As the command was given over the public address system to fire the engines, Bill Blevins, a 25 year old rookie out of Fayetteville, NC, had difficulty getting his Ford to crank. A utility truck pushed him out of the pits and onto the track.

Blevins' car started briefly but then the motor died out on the backstretch. Lacking experience, Blevins allowed his dark maroon colored car to stop in the high speed groove, apparently expecting to get another push before the start of the race.

No one in the NASCAR control tower nor anyone in the flag stand spotted Belvins' idle car on the backstretch.

The green flag was given to the field of 59 cars. As they whipped off the second turn, Blevins was a sitting duck. Thunder exploded as the crowd of 10,000

*Herb Thomas drove his Hudson Hornet to 12 victories in 37 starts in the 1953 NASCAR
Grand National season. He also won the championship for the second time.*

watched in horror. Blevins' car was pancaked by at least a dozen other onrushing race cars. No less than 15 automobiles were utterly destroyed. Hysterical race directors red flagged the remaining cars.

Rescue squads hurried to the crash site. There they found Blevins and Jesse Midkiff of Burlington, NC dead in their cars. Several other drivers were treated at local hospitals. It took an hour and 20 minutes to clear the wreckage.

Buddy Shuman of Charlotte won the tragic affair, which was tabbed "Black Saturday" by the print media.

Shuman won by a two-lap margin over Bill Widenhouse in the shortened 170-miler.

Shuman was quick to give credit to his pit crew. He made one pit stop in the race, and his crew put two new tires on and filled the fuel tank in one minute, 47 seconds. The "quick" pit work proved to be the margin of victory.

On the more positive side of the ledger, NASCAR and Langhorne Speedway combined to present the International Stock Car Grand Prix, a 200-mile event open to both foreign and domestic hard top automobiles. "This NASCAR sanctioned show is calculated to settle arguments galore about the merits of such imports as Mercedes and Jaguars on a circular track," said France in announcing the contest with promoters Irv Fried, Al Gerber and Red Crise.

A Jaguar driven by Lloyd Shaw won the pole position with a speed of 82.200 mph, but Dick Rathmann's Hudson Hornet romped to victory, leading all 200 laps. Grand National cars swept the first five places. A Jaguar and two Porsches finished in the top 10.

There were no Mercedes in the race, but there was a Volkswagen "Beetle" driven by home statesman Dick Hagey, who qualified at only 48 mph. The local driver managed to finish 19th in the field of 38, better than 70 miles behind Rathmann.

For the season, Herb Thomas set a record by winning twelve races and the Grand National title. He was also the leading money winner with $28,909.59 in purse and point money. The Hudson Hornets won 22 of the 37 races, including one stretch of 16 out of 20.

Race No. 1

Petty Team 1-2 At Palm Beach

W. PALM BEACH, FL (Feb. 1) -- Lee Petty wheeled his short wheelbased Dodge Diplomat into the lead in the 49th lap and led the rest of the way to capture the 100-mile test at Palm Beach Speedway. It was Petty's seventh career win on the Grand National trail.

Finishing second in a Petty Engineering Plymouth was Jimmie Lewallen, who was two laps behind the winner. Tim Flock was third, old-timer Herschel Buchanan came in fourth and the big surprise of the cool afternoon was the fifth place Lincoln driven by Don Oldenberg.

Dick Rathmann and Herb Thomas were the early leaders in the race, but both experienced mechanical problems, kicking the door open for Petty.

Bill France (right) joins Lee Petty (center) and Jimmie Lewallen in West Palm Beach victory lane. Petty and Lewallen ran 1-2 in Petty Engineering Dodges.

Rathmann started on the pole with a record qualifying effort of 65.028 mph and led the first three laps on the half-mile dirt oval. Thomas nudged past Rathmann and led from lap four through forty-eight when a universal joint snapped on his Hudson. The failure put the former Grand National champ out of action. Later, Thomas relieved his brother Donald and drove his car home ninth.

Al Keller flipped his Oldsmobile in the 79th lap. He escaped injury, but the car was demolished in the violent spill.

A crowd of 8,500 watched Petty average 60.220 mph in the 1953 NASCAR Grand National season opener.

Grand National Race No. 1
200 Laps at Palm Beach Speedway
West Palm Beach, FL
100 Miles on Half-mile Dirt Track
February 1, 1953

Fin	St	No.	Driver	Team / Car	Laps	Money	Status
1	7	42	Lee Petty	Petty Eng '53 Dodge	200	$1,000	Running
2	9	41	Jimmie Lewallen	Petty Eng '52 Plymouth	198	700	Running
3	4	91	Tim Flock	Ted Cehster '52 Hudson	197	450	Running
4	12	1	Herschel Buchanan	Buchanan '52 Nash Amb.	192	350	Running
5	10	86	Don Oldenberg	Bill House '53 Lincoln	186	200	Running
6	11	55	Bub King	T.H. King '52 Hudson	185	150	Running
7	22	60	Dub Livingston	Linvingston '53 Dodge	183	125	Crash
8	5	13	Pop McGinnis	Irving Fry '52 Hudson	182	100	Running
9	6	9	Donald Thomas *	Thomas '52 Hudson	181	75	Running
10	20	67	Sam DiRusso	DiRusso '52 Plymouth	180	50	Running
11	2	14	Fonty Flock	Frank Christian '52 Olds	174	25	Running
12	13	51	Gober Sosebee	Cherokee Garage '52 Chrys	172	25	Running
13	19	102	Marion Edwards	'50 Dodge	166	25	Running
14	16	167	Elton Hildreth	Hildreth Motors '51 Nash	159	25	Crash
15	21	57	Jack Culpepper	'49 Ford	119	25	Heating
16	14	T-2	Herb Tillman	'50 Olds	104	25	Heating
17	18		Jack Lawrence	'53 Dodge	101	25	RF Hub
18	17		Alan Clarke	'50 Chevrolet	76	25	Ignition
19	8	31	Al Keller	'50 Olds	73	25	Crash
20	15	37	Hank Ribet	Norm Johnson '50 Ford	68	25	Wheel
21	3	92	Herb Thomas	Thomas '53 Hudson	48	25	Univ Jnt
22	1	120	Dick Rathmann	Walt Chapman '53 Hudson	31	25	Coil
23	23	196	Lucky Sawyer	Sawyer '49 Ford	4	25	Ignition

* Relieved by Herb Thomas
Time of Race: 1 hour, 39 minutes, 38.02 seconds
Average Speed: 60.220 mph
Pole Winner: Dick Rathmann - 65.028 mph
Lap Leaders: Dick Rathmann 1-3, Herb Thomas 4-48, Lee Petty 49-200.
Cautions: Margin of Victory: 2 laps plus   Attendance: 8,500

Race No. 2

Blair Leads only Final Lap in Daytona Win

DAYTONA BEACH, FL (Feb. 15) -- Bill Blair of High Point, NC cashed in on the heartbreaking misfortune of Fonty Flock and stole the roses in the final lap of the 160-mile Grand National race at Daytona's Beach and Road Course on the shores of the Atlantic Ocean.

Flock, who had led since the opening lap, saw his Frank Christian-owned Oldsmobile run dry of fuel as he rode under the white flag. He was holding down a 65-second lead at the time. Teammate Slick Smith

Daytona winner Bill Blair is presented big trophy by Dianne Davis. Blair won the Grand National race on the final lap.

pushed the disabled car to the pits. However, by then Blair had swept first place honors by 26 seconds. Flock peeled out of the pits and finished second.

NASCAR rules permitted a car to be assisted *to* the pit area, but not to be pushed *from* the pits.

Third place went to Tommy Thompson who was one minute and nine seconds behind Blair's Oldsmobile. Herb Thomas was fourth, 21 seconds behind Thompson and fifth place went to Tim Flock, 20 seconds behind Thomas.

Pole winner Bob Pronger, the Chicago hot-head who blitzed the timing clocks at 115.77 mph, had a personal bet with front row starter Fonty Flock as to who would lead the first lap.

George Gallup leads pack of cars in South turn at Daytona.

Grand National Race No. 2
39 Laps at Beach & Road Course
Daytona Beach, FL
160 Miles on 4.1-mile Beach & Road Course
February 15, 1953

Fin	St	No.	Driver	Team / Car	Laps	Money	Status
1	6	2	Bill Blair	Blair '53 Olds Super 88	39	$1,500	Running
2	2	14	Fonty Flock	Frank Christian '53 Olds 8	39	1,000	Running
3	4	40	Tommy Thompson	Thompson '53 Lincoln	39	800	Running
4	3	92	Herb Thomas	Thomas '53 Hudson	39	600	Running
5	7	91	Tim Flock	Ted Chester '52 Hudson	39	500	Running
6	10	77	Dick Passwater	Frank Arford '52 Olds 88	38	400	Running
7	16	41	Curtis Turner	R.L. Bowling '53 Lincoln	38	300	Running
8	19	9	Donald Thomas	Thomas '52 Hudson	38	200	Running
9	13	38	Tom Cherry	Hot Rod Shop '53 Lincoln	38	180	Running
10	18	4	Slick Smith	Frank Christian '52 Olds 88	38	150	Running
11	17	51	Gober Sosebee	Cherokee Gar. '52 Chrysler	38	75	Running
12	9	120	Dick Rathmann	Walt Chapman '53 Hudson	37	75	Running
13	15	87	Buck Baker	Al Wheatley '53 Lincoln	37	75	Running
14	20	187	Red Duvall	Duane Duvall '53 Packard	37	75	Running
15	23	86	Don Oldenberg	Bill House '53 Hudson	37	75	Running
16	11	18	Bill Adams	Adams '53 Olds 88	36	50	Running
17	34	52	Joe Guide, Jr	Sally Guide '51 Hudson	36	50	Running
18	47	54	Obie Chupp	Wild Gene Horne '51 Hudson	36	50	Running
19	29	103	George Gallup	Gallup '50 Olds	36	50	Running
20	36	25	Cotton Priddy	Priddy '51 Olds	35	50	Running
21	27	55	Bub King	T.H. King '52 Hudson Hornet	35	25	Spin Out
22	40	33	Charlie Causey	'50 Olds	35	25	Running
23	44	8	Gene Comstock	Comstock '51 Hudson Hornet	35	25	Spin Out
24	37	7	Red Douglass	R.W. Douglass '53 Dodge	33	25	Running
25	57	291	Slow Poke Travis	'52 Ford	33	25	Running
26	56	67	Sam DiRusso	DiRusso '52 Plymouth	33	25	Running
27	30	13	Pop McGinnis	Irving Fry '52 Hudson Hornet	33	25	Running
28	51	96	Mason Bright	Bright '49 Plymouth	33	25	Running
29	28	71	Keith Hamner	Mason Darnell '52 Hudson	33	25	Running
30	46	1	Herschel Buchanan	Buchanan '52 Nash	33	25	Clutch
31	22	66	George Fleming	Joseph Braun '51 Hudson	33	25	Running
32	49	16	Johnny Roberts	J.F. Roberts '50 Ford	33	25	Running
33	25	30	Cotton Hodges	Jim Fowler '50 Olds	32	25	RF Hub
34	53	37	Hank Rivet	Norm Johnson '50 Ford	32	25	Running
35	24	15	Tommy Boger	Boger '52 Hudson	32	25	Spin Out
36	54	102	Marion Edwards	'50 Dodge	31	25	Running
37	55	90	Ted Lee	Lee '53 Hudson Wasp	30	25	Running
38	52	3	Hub McBride	'50 Nash	29	25	Running
39	50	196	Lucky Sawyer	Sawyer '49 Ford	23	25	Gas Line
40	45	T-2	Herb Tillman	'50 Olds	18	25	Gas Line
41	42	12	Jim Paschal	George Hutchens '49 Olds	17	---	Oil Press
42	14	98	Dan Walters	'50 Packard	15	---	Gasket
43	26	22	Perk Brown	R.G. Shelton '52 Hudson	14	---	Engine
44	35	186	Doug Wells	Gilbreath Motors '50 Olds	13	---	Heating
45	41	48	Red Farmer	Sikes Motors '51 Hudson	12	---	Heating
46	38	60	Dub Livingston	Livingston '53 Dodge	11	---	Tie Rod
47	48	79	Charles Weidler	Weidler '51 Hudson	9	---	Crash
48	33	19	Fred Dove	Sam Nunn '52 Packard	8	---	Bearing
49	12	82	Joe Eubanks	Phil Oates '52 Hudson	8	---	Gasket
50	8	58	Johnny Patterson	Lou Tanner '52 Hudson	6	---	Engine
51	1	46	Bob Pronger	Pronger '53 Olds 88	5	---	Crash
52	21	57	Tommy Moon	C.D. Wilson '52 Hudson	5	---	Engine
53	31	10	Wally Campbell	'53 Dodge	4	---	Engine
54	39	167	Elton Hildreth	Hildreth Motors '51 Nash	4	---	Heating
55	43	190	Buddy Shuman	J.R. Dunberry '52 Hudson	4	---	Clutch
56	32	93	Ted Chamberlain	Chamberlain '50 Plymouth	3	---	Clutch
57	5	78	Frank Arford	Arford '53 Olds 88	2	---	Gasket

Time of Race: 1 hour, 46 minutes, 51 seconds
Average Speed: 89.789 mph
Pole Winner: Bob Pronger - 115.77 mph
Lap Leaders: Fonty Flock 1-38, Bill Blair 39.
Cautions: None   Margin of Victory: 26 seconds   Attendance: 20,000

Flock and Pronger raced door-to-door as they came up the beach. As the daring duo reached the North turn, both drivers held their guns -- neither one willing to back off. Finally Fonty braked hard, allowing

Pronger to sail into the turn full bore. The errant Oldsmobile tumbled through the wooden guard rail, flipped down a sand dune, very nearly missing the bottom row of the grandstands, and landed on all fours on an access road.

Pronger continued, somewhat miraculously, and was running 16th in the field of 57 at the end of the first lap. He managed to go four more laps before retiring from the race.

Marshall Teague, winner of the last two Grand Nationals over the 4.1-mile course, was not eligible to compete since he had joined the rival AAA stock car circuit.

Blair averaged 89.789 mph for his third career win as a crowd of 20,000 sat in pleasant weather to watch the finale of the fourth annual SpeedWeek festival.

Lee Petty was forced to miss the race when a severe attack of internal hemorrhages felled the 39-year old veteran. He spent the better part of a week in Halifax Hospital and was released with strict orders from doctors to "get plenty of rest and quiet".

Race No. 3

Thomas Fabulous
At Spring Lake

SPRING LAKE, NC (Mar. 8) -- Herb Thomas blasted out of the starting blocks and authored a decisive triumph in the 100-miler on the neatly manicured Harnett Speedway. It was the 17th career victory for the Olivia, NC speedster, making him the winningest Grand National driver.

Thomas led the entire 200 laps around the half-mile

Grand National Race No. 3
200 Laps at Harnett Speedway
Spring Lake, NC
100 Miles on Half-mile Dirt Track
March 8, 1953

Fin	St	No.	Driver	Team / Car	Laps	Money	Status
1	1	92	Herb Thomas	Thomas '53 Hudson	200	$1,000	Running
2	3	120	Dick Rathmann	Walt Chapman '53 Hudson	197	700	Running
3		42	Lee Petty	Petty Engineering '53 Dodge		450	Running
4	7	78	Dick Passwater	Frank Arford '53 Olds		350	Running
5		1	Herschel Buchanan	Buchanan '53 Nash		200	Running
6	2	18	Mike Klapak	Bill Adams '53 Olds		150	
7		91	Tim Flock	Ted Chester '52 Hudson		125	
8		24	Ray Duhigg	J.O. Goode '52 Plymouth		100	
9		86	Don Oldenberg	Bill House '50 Packard		75	
10		71	Keith Hamner	Mason Darnell '52 Hudson		50	
11		55	Bub King	T.H. King '52 Hudson		25	
12		0	Ewell Weddle	Weddle '51 Plymouth		25	
13		167	Elton Hildreth	Hildreth '52 Nash		25	
14	4	14	Fonty Flock	Frank Christian '52 Olds		25	
15		37	Coleman Lawrence	Lawrence '50 Ford		25	
16		19	Fred Dove	Sam Nunn '50 Plymouth		25	
17		72	Donald Thomas	T.D. Meeks '50 Ford		25	
18			Jack Lawrence	'53 Dodge		25	
19			Harold Nash	'51 Olds		25	
20		43	Jimmie Lewallen	Dave Quate '53 Dodge		25	
21			Dub Livingston	'53 Dodge		25	
22			Harry Bennett	'52 Olds		25	
23	6	82	Joe Eubanks	Oates Motors '52 Hudson		25	
24			Lucky Sawyer	'49 Ford		25	
25			Johnny Roberts	'52 Ford		25	
26		23	Weldon Adams	'51 Studebaker		25	
27	8	2	Bill Blair	Blair '52 Olds		25	
28		58	Johnny Patterson	Lou Tanner '52 Olds		25	
29			Jim Lacy	'53 Dodge		25	
30	5	41	Curtis Turner	John Eanes '52 Olds		25	
31		25	Cotton Priddy	Priddy '51 Olds		25	
32		171	Wally Campbell	'53 Dodge		25	

Time of Race: 2 hours, 8 minutes, 8 seconds
Average Speed: 48.826 mph
Pole Winner: Herb Thomas - 51.918 mph
Lap Leaders: Herb Thomas 1-200.
Cautions: Margin of Victory: 3 laps plus   Attendance: 7,000

dirt track and finished three laps ahead of runner-up Dick Rathmann. Lee Petty, ignoring doctor's orders to

Herb Thomas pitches his Hudson into the first turn at Harnett Speedway en route to flag-to-flag victory.

"take it easy", finished third. Dick Passwater showed some short track savvy by earning fourth position, and Herschel Buchanan was fifth.

Thomas won the pole at 51.918 mph and covered the 100 miles at a 48.826 mph clip.

Although thirty-two cars started the race, there was only one mishap. Johnny Patterson spun in the first turn early in the race and his Olds tipped gently on its side. Infield spectators righted the machine, and the Huntington, WV youngster was on his way again. He wound up 28th.

A crowd of 7,000 watched the first Grand National race staged at the new facility.

Runner-up Dick Rathmann experienced tough luck on the way home after the race. He blew a clutch in his tow car while hauling the car to Strattonville, PA to have a crack in his race car's chassis repaired. After the repairs were made, Rathmann flipped both cars on the highway. He was not injured.

Race No. 4

Thomas Nips Rathmann In Stretch Duel at N. Wilkesboro

N. WILKESBORO, NC (Mar. 29) -- Herb Thomas cocked his Hudson in a four-wheel drift, throttled his way into the lead 18 laps from the finish and won the 125-mile Grand National event at North Wilkesboro Speedway

Finishing second was Dick Rathmann who had led for 60 laps before Thomas set sail. Fonty Flock finished third, Lee Petty was fourth and Jimmie Lewallen came in fifth.

A crowd of 7,500 braved bone-chilling winds in the Western Carolina foothills village to watch Thomas average 71.907 mph.

The lead changed hands six times among five drivers.Tim Flock led the first 100 laps, but was knocked out with engine problems while leading. Curtis Turner assumed command at lap 101, but he, too, ran into mechanical difficulties on lap 109 while leading.

Rathmann picked up the lead and led for 70 of thenext 72 laps. Thomas did not lead until he passed Rathmann in the final stretch.

Perk Brown wheeled down pit road for a routine pit stop after about 50 miles, but his R.G. Shelton pit crew was astonished to find the gas tank missing from thewhite Hudson. Brown had to park his car and he wound up 27th in the field of 34.

Grand National Race No. 4
200 Laps at N. Wilkesboro Speedway
North Wilkesboro, NC
125 Miles on .625-mile Dirt Track
March 29, 1953

Fin	St	No.	Driver	Team / Car	Laps	Money	Status
1	1	92	Herb Thomas	Thomas '53 Hudson	200	$1,000	Running
2	3	120	Dick Rathmann	Walt Chapman '53 Hudson	200	700	Running
3	4	14	Fonty Flock	Frank Christian '53 Olds 88		450	Running
4	12	42	Lee Petty	Petty Engineering '53 Dodge		350	Running
5	10	43	Jimmie Lewallen	Dave Quate '53 Dodge		200	Running
6	5	87	Buck Baker	Al Whealtey '53 Lincoln		150	Running
7	11	82	Joe Eubanks	Phil Oates '52 Hudson		125	Running
8	9	4	Slick Smith	Frank Christian '52 Olds 88		100	Running
9	19	78	Dick Passwater	Frank Arford '53 Olds 88		75	Running
10	15	55	Bub King	T.H. King '52 Hudson		50	Running
11	26	8	Gene Comstock	Comstock '52 Hudson		25	Running
12	30	60	Dub Livingston	'53 Dodge		25	Running
13	34	100	Otis Martin	'53 Mercury		25	Running
14	28	0	Ewell Weddle	Weddle '52 Plymouth		25	Running
15	32	96	Lucky Sawyer	'50 Ford		25	Running
16	21	86	Don Oldenberg	Bill House '52 Packard		25	Running
17	20	77	Frank Arford	Arford '52 Olds 88		25	Running
18	25	31	Steve McGrath	George Miller '52 Hudson		25	Running
19	33	71	Coleman Lawrence	Lawrence '52 Ford		25	Running
20	29	3	Clyde Minter	'52 Ford		25	Crash
21	31	19	Fred Dove	Sam Nunn '52 Plymouth		25	Running
22	8	41	Curtis Turner	John Eanes '53 Olds 88	109	25	Piston
23	2	91	Tim Flock	Ted Chester '53 Hudson	100	25	Bearings
24	14	58	Johnny Patterson	H.B. Ranier '52 Hudson		25	Running
25	23	2	Bill Blair	Blair '53 Olds 88		25	Crash
26	13	1	Herschel Buchanan	Buchanan '52 Nash		25	Spindle
27	6	22	Perk Brown	R.G. Shelton '52 Hudson		25	Gas Tank
28	24	13	Pop McGinnis	Irving Frye '52 Hudson		25	Clutch
29	15	167	Elton Hildreth	Hildreth Motors '51 Nash		25	Crash
30	22	44	Ray Duhigg	J.H. Petty '52 Plymouth		25	Gas Line
31	7	12	Buddy Shuman	Buckshot Morris '50 Olds		25	
32	17	171	Wally Campbell	'53 Dodge		25	RF Hub
33	18	72	Donald Thomas	T.D. Meeks '51 Ford		25	Crash
34	27	11	June Cleveland	Cleveland '52 Studebaker		25	Engine

Time of Race: 1 hour, 44 minutes, 18 seconds
Average Speed: 71.907 mph
Pole Winner: Herb Thomas - 78.424 mph
Lap Leaders: Tim Flock 1-100, Curtis Turner 101-109, Dick Rathmann 110-119,
      Fonty Flock 120-122, Rathmann 123-182, Herb Thomas 183-200.
Cautions: Margin of Victory: 1/3 lap   Attendance: 7,500

Race No. 5

Passwater, McGinnis Shine at Charlotte

CHARLOTTE, NC (Apr. 5) -- Indianapolis lad Dick Passwater, playing the role of an opportunist, drove his Oldsmobile into the lead three laps from the finish and scored an upset victory in the 112.5-mile race at Charlotte Speedway.

Passwater was the survivor in the thrill-packed contest which produced the most lead changes, 18 among six drivers, in NASCAR history.

Tim Flock, who led seven times for a total of 87 laps

*Left front wheel flies off Pop McGinnis' Hudson
in final lap at Charlotte.*

Grand National Race No. 5
150 Laps at Charlotte Speedway
Charlotte, NC
112.5 Miles on .75-mile Dirt Track
April 5, 1953

Fin	St	No.	Driver	Team / Car	Laps	Money	Status
1	9	78	Dick Passwater	Frank Arford '53 Olds 88	150	$1,000	Running
2		51	Gober Sosebee	Cherokee Garage '53 Olds 88	150	700	Running
3		1	Herschel Buchanan	Buchanan '52 Nash	150	450	Running
4	1	91	Tim Flock	Ted Chester '53 Hudson	150	350	Running
5	5	13	Pop McGinnis	Irving Frye '52 Hudson	149	200	LF Wheel
6		100	Otis Martin	'51 Mercury		150	Running
7		19	Fred Dove	Sam Nunn '52 Plymouth		125	Running
8		18	Mike Klapak	Bill Adams '53 Olds 88		100	Running
9		55	Bub King	T.H. King '52 Hudson Hornet		75	Running
10		3	Coleman Lawrence	Lawrence '51 Ford		50	Running
11		42	Lee Petty	Petty Engineering '53 Dodge		25	
12	3	92	Herb Thomas	Thomas '53 Hudson		25	Clutch
13	2	120	Dick Rathmann	Walt Chapman '53 Hudson		25	Wheel
14	4	87	Buck Baker	Griffin Motors '53 Olds 88		25	Wheel
15		31	Steve McGrath	George Miller '52 Hudson		25	Spindle
16		2	Bill Blair	Blair '53 Olds 88		25	
17		8	Gene Comstock	Comstock '51 Hudson Hornet		25	Crash
18		43	Jimmie Lewallen	Dave Quate '53 Dodge		25	
19		0	Ewell Weddle	Weddle Racing '52 Plymouth		25	
20		82	Joe Eubanks	Phil Oates '52 Hudson		25	
21		12	Jim Paschal	George Hutchens '52 Plymouth		25	
22		11	June Cleveland	Cleveland '52 Studebaker		25	
23		12	Buddy Shuman	Buckshot Morris '49 Olds		25	
24	6	41	Curtis Turner	John Eanes '53 Olds 88		25	Engine
25		14	Fonty Flock	Frank Christian '53 Olds 88		25	Oil Press
26		167	Elton Hildreth	Hildreth Motors '51 N;ash		25	RR Hub
27		4	Slick Smith	Frank Christian '52 Olds 88		25	Engine
28		72	Donald Thomas	T.D. Meeks '50 Ford		25	Mount

Time of Race:
Average Speed:
Pole Winner: Tim Flock - 71.108 mph
Lap Leaders: Tim Flock 1-60, Buck Baker 61-78, T.Flock 79-82, Dick Rathmann 83-85,
T. Flock 86-90, Rathmann 91-97, T. Flock 98-102, Rathmann 103-111, T. Flock 112,
Rathmann 113, T. Flock 114-120, Rathmann 121, T. Flock 122-126, Rathmann 127-130,
Herb Thomas 131-134, Pop McGinnis 135-147, Dick Passwaterr 148-150.
Cautions: Margin of Victory: 1/4 lap   Attendance: 8,500

n the 150-lapper, fell off the pace with 25 laps left
when his Hudson began to lose power. When Flock
dropped back with just 24 laps left, it produced a wide-
open scramble for first place.

Dick Rathmann charged to the front on lap 127, but
was able to hold on for only four laps before Herb
Thomas grabbed the lead. Thomas, bidding for his
third straight triumph, began pulling away, but clutch
failure put him out on lap 134.

Pop McGinnis, rookie driver out of Huntington, WV,
stormed to the front and was poised to give his Irving
Frye team its biggest win. McGinnis stayed on the
point for 13 laps, but he had to make a quick pit stop
three laps from home to take on fuel.

It was at that point that Passwater, driving an
Oldsmobile for Indiana sportsman Frank Arford, scooted into the lead for good. Passwater, driving in his
tenth Grand National race, finished a quarter lap ahead
of runner-up Gober Sosebee to win the $1,000 top
prize. Herschel Buchanan came in third and Tim Flock
limped home fourth.

McGinnis lost a wheel
while running third in the
final lap and did not finish. He still got credit for
fifth place in the final rundown. A crowd of 8,500
watched the countless lead
changes from their feet.

One accident resulted in
two spectator injuries.
McGinnis brushed Gene
Comstock just past the
half-way point, sending
Comstock's Hudson into
a series of side-over-side
flips. The car, spitting debris in all directions,
rolled up an incline and
through a fence. It came
to rest pinning spectators

Buck Baker #87 and Tim Flock #91 battle for the lead in early going at Charlotte.

Charles Barclay and William Couthers underneath. The car was quickly rolled off the two men, and they were taken to a hospital in Shelby, NC. Neither was believed to be seriously injured.

The victory moved Passwater into third place in the Grand National point standings. Thomas led Flock by 125 points with Passwater behind by 162 points.

Race No. 6

Flock Brothers Boycott Richmond; Petty Wins

RICHMOND, VA (Apr. 19) -- Lee Petty's Red Ram Dodge bounded over the rough terrain and rang the victory bell in the 100-mile race at the Atlantic Rural Fairgrounds. The sorry condition of the track and a misunderstanding was responsible for drivers Tim and Fonty Flock boycotting the 200-lapper.

During qualifications, which Buck Baker wound up winning at the laughable speed of 48.465 mph, the track surface was terribly choppy. The Flock brothers opted to wait to take their time trials, hoping conditions would improve. Officials closed qualifications before the two Georgia stars could get on the track. They were instructed to start the race from the rear of the 27-car field.

Both Flocks scoffed at the orders and loaded up their cars. They refused to compete.

Dick Rathmann finished second, Buck Baker was third and Dick Passwater was fourth. Fifth place went to Bill Blair.

Race No. 7

Rathmann Outduels Thomas for Macon Victory

MACON, GA (Apr. 26) -- Dick Rathmann of Los Angeles shot past Herb Thomas in the 166th lap and led the rest of the way to win the 100-mile Grand National race at Central City Speedway.

It was the first win of the 1953 season for the Hudson Hornet driver.

Dick Rathmann gets saddled in his Hudson before Macon race.

Thomas finished second and Jimmie Lewallen was third. Fonty Flock was fourth and Dick Passwater nabbed fifth spot. Tim Flock, back in the fold with brother Fonty after a one week boycott, finished sixth in a Hudson owned by co-promoter of the race, Ted Chester.

Lee Petty was taken out near the half-way point when his Dodge tumbled over the second turn. He was unhurt. Dub Livingston and Herschel Buchanan were also victims in a late race crash.

Grand National Race No. 6
200 Laps at Atlantic Rural Fairgrounds
Richmond, VA
100 Miles on Half-mile Dirt Track
April 19, 1953

Fin	St	No.	Driver	Team / Car	Laps	Money	Status
1		42	Lee Petty	Petty Engineering '53 Dodge	200	$1,000	Running
2		120	Dick Rathmann	Walt Chapman '52 Hudson		700	
3	1	87	Buck Baker	Griffin Motors '53 Olds 88		450	
4		78	Dick Passwater	Frank Arford '53 Olds 88		350	
5		2	Bill Blair	Blair '53 Olds 88		200	
6		44	Ray Duhigg	J. H. Petty '52 Plymouth		150	
7		9	Donald Thomas	Thomas '51 Hudson Hornet		125	
8		8	Gene Comstock	Comstock '51 Hudson Hornet		100	
9		19	Fred Dove	Sam Nunn '51 Plymouth		75	
10		92	Herb Thomas	Thomas '53 Hudson Hornet		50	
11			Virgil Livengood	'53 Olds		25	
12			Lou Johnson	'53 Dodge		25	
13			Al Kent	'51 Henry J		25	
14			Joe O'Dell	'50 Ford		25	
15		55	Bub King	'52 Olds		25	
16		46	Ralph Liguori	Al Wheatley '53 Lincoln		25	
16		4	Slick Smith	Frank Christian '51 Olds		25	
18		167	Elton Hildreth	Hildreth '51 Nash		25	
19			Buck Mason	'52 Dodge		25	
20		7	Jim Reed	Reed '51 Ford		25	
21		12	Jim Paschal	George Hutchens '53 Olds		25	
22		32	Jimmie Lewallen	R.G. Shelton '52 Hudson		25	
23			Jim Lacy	'53 Dodge		25	
24			Ollie Olson	'52 Hudson		25	
25		1	Herschel Buchanan	Buchanan '52 Nash		25	
26			Al Keller	'52 Hudson		25	
27		71	Coleman Lawrence	Lawrence '50 Ford		25	

Time of Race: 2 hours, 11 minutes, 46 seconds
Average Speed: 45.535 mph
Pole Winner: Buck Baker - 48.465 mph
Lap Leaders: - - - - - - - - - - Lee Petty   -200
Cautions: Margin of Victory: Attendance:
* Ralph Liguori and Slick Smith tied for 16th place

Rathmann averaged 56.417 mph before 7,000 spectators. Thomas led Passwater by 138 points in the driver standings.

Grand National Race No. 7
200 Laps at Central City Speedway
Macon, GA
100 Miles on Half-mile Dirt Track
April 26, 1953

Fin	St	No.	Driver	Team / Car	Laps	Money	Status
1		120	Dick Rathmann	Walt Chapman '52 Hudson	200	$1,000	Running
2		92	Herb Thomas	Thomas '53 Hudson		700	Running
3		43	Jimmie Lewallen	Dave Quate '53 Olds		450	Running
4		14	Fonty Flock	Frank Christian '53 Olds		350	Running
5		78	Dick Passwater	Frank Arford '53 Olds		200	Running
6		91	Tim Flock	Ted Chester '53 Hudson		150	
7		82	Joe Eubanks	Phil Oates '52 Hudson		125	
8		87	Buck Baker	Griffin Motors '53 Olds		100	
9		93	Ted Chamberlain	Chamberlain '51 Plymouth		75	
10			Virgil Livengood	'53 Olds		50	Crash
11		1	Herschel Buchanan	Buchanan '52 Nash		25	Crash
12			Ralph Liguori	'49 Olds		25	
13		72	Donald Thomas	Ted Meeks '50 Ford		25	
14		55	Bub King	T.A. King '52 Hudson		25	
15		60	Dub Livingston	'53 Dodge		25	
16		51	Gober Sosebee	Cherokee Garage '53 Olds		25	
17		19	Fred Dove	Sam Nunn '50 Plymouth		25	
18		71	Coleman Lawrence	Lawrence '50 Ford		25	
19		42	Lee Petty	Petty Engineering '53 Dodge		25	Crash
20		2	Bill Blair	Blair '52 Olds		25	
21		12	Jim Paschal	George Hutchens '52 Plymouth		25	
22			Gordon Bracken	'52 Plymouth		25	
23			Leonard Lawrence	'50 Ford		25	
24		4	Slick Smith	Frank Christian '51 Olds		25	

Time of Race: 1 hour, 46 minutes, 21 seconds
Average Speed: 56.417 mph
Pole Winner:
Lap Leaders: Fonty Flock 1-120, Herb Thomas 121-165, Dick Rathmann 166-200.
Cautions: Margin of Victory: Attendance: 7,000

Grand National Race No. 8
150 Laps at Langhorne Speedway
Langhorne, PA
150 Miles on 1-mile Dirt Track
May 3, 1953

Fin	St	No.	Driver	Team / Car	Laps	Money	Status
1	25	87	Buck Baker	Griffin Motors '53 Olds 88	150	$1,525	Running
2		42	Lee Petty	Petty Engineering '53 Dodge	150	1,000	Running
3		14	Fonty Flock	Frank Christian '53 Olds 88		800	Running
4		1	Herschel Buchanan	Buchanan '52 Nash Ambassador		600	Running
5	1	91	Tim Flock	Ted Chester '53 Hudson Hornet		500	Running
6		44	Ray Duhigg	J H Petty'52 Plymouth		400	Running
7		92	Herb Thomas	Thomas '53 Hudson Hornet		300	
8		18	Bill Adams	Adams '53 Olds 88		200	
9		46	Ralph Liguori	Liguori '53 Olds 88		180	
10		93	Ted Chamberlain	Chamberlain '51 Plymouth		150	
11			Ronnie Kohler	'50 Dodge		75	
12			Leon Lundy	'53 Ford		75	
13			Joe O'Dell	'49 Ford		75	
14			Jim Lacy	'53 Dodge		75	
15			Mike Magill	'53 Lincoln		75	
16			Dick Rathmann	'53 Plymouth		50	
17			Buck Mason	Joe Kersey '53 Dodge		50	
18		2	Bill Blair	Blair '53 Olds 88		50	
19		78	Dick Passwater	Frank Arford '53 Olds 88		50	
20			Don Price	'50 Ford		50	
21		100	Otis Martin	'53 Olds 88		25	
22		8	Gene Comstock	Comstock '53 Hudson Hornet		25	
23			Lou Johnson	'53 Dodge		25	
24		52	Neil Cole	John Golabek '50 Plymouth		25	
25			Larry Schultz	'53 Plymouth		25	
26		9	Donald Thomas	Thomas '51 Hudson Hornet		25	
27		31	Al Keller	'53 Olds 88		25	
28		32	Jimmie Lewallen	R.G. Shelton '51 Hudson Hornet		25	
29		43	Jim Paschal	'53 Olds 88		25	
30		79	Charles Weilder	'51 Hudson Hornet		25	
31		55	Bub King	T.H. King '52 Hudson Hornet		25	
32			Bill Hammersly	'51 Ford		25	
33			Gene Parry	'51 Nash Ambassador		25	
34		167	Elton Hildreth	Hildreth Motors '53 Nash Amb.		25	
35		4	Slick Smith	Frank Christian '51 Olds 88		25	

Time of Race: 2 hours, 3 minutes, 43.33 seconds
Average Speed: 72.743 mph
Pole Winner: No Time Trials. Tim Flock drew pole
Lap Leaders: Tim Flock 1-9, Herb Thomas 10-22, T. Flock 23-82, Buck Baker 83-110,
     Lee Petty 111-136, Baker 137-150.
Cautions: Margin of Victory: 51 seconds   Attendance: 15,000

Race No. 8

Langhorne 150
Falls to Baker

LANGHORNE, PA (May 3) -- Buck Baker, a former bus driver out of Charlotte, drove his Griffin Motors Oldsmobile into the lead with 14 laps remaining and won the 150-miler at Langhorne Speedway. It was the first win for Baker in the 1953 Grand National season and the second of his career.

Lee Petty, who had led for 26 laps in his Dodge before Baker's final spurt, wound up second, 51 seconds behind the winner. Fonty Flock took third spot, Herschel Buchanan was fourth and Tim Flock fifth.

Drivers were forced to draw their starting positions out of a hat when rains washed out Saturday's qualifying trials. Baker drew 25th place in the field of 35.

It took Baker only 83 laps to assume command. Tim Flock and Herb Thomas each led in the early going, with Flock falling back when his engine went sour.

Baker led for 28 laps shortly past the half way point. Petty took the lead when Baker pitted for fuel on lap 111. It took Baker 26 laps to run down Petty. He won $1,525 for his efforts.

Herb Thomas, who finished seventh, took a 253 point lead over Tim Flock in the NASCAR point

An aerial photo of the magnificent Langhorne Speedway. The circular 1-mile battleground was unlike any other in the country. It was considered one of the most dangerous tracks in America, yet it's victory lane was one of the most cherished pieces of real estate in all of auto racing.

Race No. 9

Baker Gets 2nd In Row at Columbia

COLUMBIA, SC (May 9) -- Buck Baker moved into fifth place in the NASCAR point standings with his second straight victory in the 100-mile race at Columbia Speedway.

Baker outdistanced Tim Flock to win the $1,000 pay check and moved to within 385 points of standings leader Herb Thomas, who finished eighth after starting on the pole.

Jimmie Lewallen finished in third place, Ray Duhigg was fourth and Lee Petty fifth.

Baker started third on the grid and spent the early laps chasing Thomas and Gober Sosebee. The man from Charlotte averaged 53.707 mph, good enough to win the event.

standings.

A crowd of 15,000 braved threatening weather conditions and watched Baker cover the 150 miles at an average speed of 72.743 mph.

Grand National Race No. 9
200 Laps at Columbia Speedway
Columbia, SC
100 Miles on Half-mile Dirt Track
May 9, 1953

Fin	St	No.	Driver	Team / Car	Laps	Money	Status
1	3	87	Buck Baker	Griffin Motros '53 Olds 88	200	$1,000	Running
2	12	91	Tim Flock	Ted Chester '53 Hudson		700	Running
3	6	32	Jimmie Lewallen	R.G. Shelton '51 Hudson		450	Running
4	5	44	Ray Duhigg	J.H. Petty '52 Plymouth		350	Running
5	7	42	Lee Petty	Petty Engineering '53 Dodge		200	Running
6	2	51	Gober Sosebee	Cherokee Garage '53 Olds 88		150	Running
7	13	2	Bill Blair	Blair '53 Olds 88		125	
8	1	92	Herb Thomas	Thomas '53 Hudson Hornet		100	
9	11		Phil Jennings	'51 Plymouth		75	
10	9	10	Ralph Dyer	'53 Nash Ambassador		50	
11	8	13	Pop McGinnis	Irving Frye '52 Hudson Hornet		25	
12	16	167	Elton Hildreth	Hildreth Motors '53 Nash Amb.		25	
13	15	4	Slick Smith	Frank Christian '51 Olds 88		25	
14	14	14	Fonty Flock	Frank Christian '53 Hudson Hornet		25	
15	10	1	Herschel Buchanan	Buchanan '53 Nash Ambassador		25	
16	4	120	Dick Rathmann	Walt Chapman '53 Hudson Hornet		25	

Time of Race: 1 hour, 51 minutes, 43 seconds
Average Speed: 53.707 mph
Pole Winner: Herb Thomas - 58.670 mph
Lap Leaders: - - - - - - - - - Buck Baker   -200.
Cautions: Margin of Vlictory: Attendance:

Race No. 10

Flock Ends Skid With Hickory Win

HICKORY, NC (May 16) -- Tim Flock ended a nine month skid and won the 100 mile Grand National race at Hickory Speedway. It was his 17th career big league win.

Joe Eubanks, who had sat out the 1953 season made his return and finished second to Flock. Third place went to Ray Duhigg. Dick Passwater came in fourth and

Tim Flock cracked the victory column for the first time in 1953 at Hickory.

Dick Rathmann finished fifth.

Herb Thomas spun and crashed into the fence, leaving him with a 20th place finish in the field of 27. His point lead was cut to 11 points over Flock.

Lee Petty, Fonty Flock and Buck Baker all finished out of the top ten and failed to gain any ground in the point race.

However when NASCAR officials checked the score cards, it was discovered that, on paper, Lee Petty had completed the 200 laps on the half-mile dirt track before Thomas did.

Petty was then declared the winner for the third time in the 1953 season. Thomas yelled foul, claiming Petty never passed him on the track. Most of the 9,000 spectators in attendance seemed to agree with Thomas. They went home thinking the Olivia, NC speedster had won the race.

Thomas got paid for second place. Dick Rathmann wound up third with Ray Duhigg and Ralph Liguori rounding out the top five.

Eubanks was holding down second place when a broken spindle put him out of action on lap 85. He wound up 25th in the field of 35.

Grand National Race No. 10
200 Laps at Hickory Speedway
Hickory, NC
100 Miles on Half-mile Dirt Track
May 16, 1953

Fin	St	No.	Driver	Team / Car	Laps	Money	Status
1		91	Tim Flock	Ted Chester '53 Hudson	200	$1,000	Running
2		82	Joe Eubanks	Phil Oates '52 Hudson		700	Running
3		44	Ray Duhigg	J.H. Petty '52 Plymouth		450	Running
4		78	Dick Passwater	Frank Arford '53 Olds 88		350	Running
5		120	Dick Rathmann	Walt Chapman '53 Hudson	200	200	Running
6		24	Bob Welborn	J.O. Goode '52 Plymouth		150	
7		100	Otis Martin	'53 Mercury		125	
8		1	Herschel Buchanan	Buchanan '51 Nash Amb.		100	
9		13	Pop McGinnis	Irving Frye '52 Hudson Hornet		75	
10		3	Clyde Minter	'51 Ford		50	
11		19	Fred Dove	Sam Nunn '50 Plymouth		25	
12		2	Bill Blair	Blair '52 Olds		25	
13		108	Arden Mounts	Mounts '52 Hudson		25	
14		8	Gene Comstock	Comstock '53 Hudson		25	
15		42	Lee Petty	Petty Engineering '53 Dodge		25	
16		71	Coleman Lawrence	Lawrence '50 Ford		25	
17			Russell Armentourt	'53 Dodge		25	
18		46	Ralph Liguori	Al Wheatley '53 Lincoln		25	
19		87	Buck Baker	Griffin Motors '53 Olds		25	
20		92	Herb Thomas	Thomas '53 Hudson		25	Crash
21		93	Ted Chamberlain	Chamberlain '50 Plymouth		25	
22			Ralph Dyer	'53 Nash		25	
23		167	Elton Hildreth	Hildreth Motors '51 Nash		25	
24		4	Slick Smith	Frank Christian '51 Olds		25	
25			Jim Paschal	'51 Ford		25	
26		14	Fonty Flock	Frank Christian '53 Olds 88	57	25	Steering
27		72	Donald Thomas	T.D. Meeks '50 Ford		25	

Time of Race:
Average Speed:
Pole Winner:
Lap Leaders: - - - - - - - - - Tim Flock   -200
Cautions: Margin of Victory: Attendance:

Race No. 11

Thomas Finishes First at Martinsville; Petty Declared Winner

MARTINSVILLE, VA (May 17) -- Herb Thomas zipped past Joe Eubanks in the 74th lap, led the rest of the way, and was flagged the winner of the 100-mile Grand National reace at Martinsville Speedway.

Grand National Race No. 11
200 Laps at Martinsville Speedway
Martinsville, VA
100 Miles on Half-mile Dirt Track
May 17, 1953

Fin	St	No.	Driver	Team / Car	Laps	Money	Status
1		42	Lee Petty	Petty Eng. '53 Dodge	200	$1,000	Running
2		92	Herb Thomas	Thomas '53 Hudson	200	700	Running
3		120	Dick Rathmann	Walt Chapman '53 Hudson		450	Running
4		44	Ray Duhigg	Julian Petty '52 Plymouth		350	Running
5		46	Ralph Liguori	Al Wheatley '53 Lincoln		200	Running
6		78	Dick Passwater	Frank Arford '53 Olds		150	Running
7		87	Buck Baker	Griffin Motors '53 Olds		125	Running
8		24	Bob Welborn	J.O. Goode '52 Plymouth		100	Running
9			Clyde Minter	'51 Ford		75	Running
10			Lyle Scott	'53 Dodge		50	Running
11			Ralph Dyer	'53 Nash		25	
12		93	Ted Chamberlain	Chamberlain '50 Plymouth		25	
13			Gifford Wood	'49 Ford		25	
14			Bub King	'50 Mercury		25	
15			Otis Martin	'49 Olds		25	
16			Bill O'Dell	'49 Ford		25	
17		37	Coleman Lawrence	Lawrence '50 Ford		25	Running
18		72	Donald Thomas	T.D. Meeks '50 Ford		25	
19		2	Bill Blair	Blair '52 Olds		25	
20		41	Curtis Turner	John Eanes '53 Olds		25	
21		58	Johnny Patterson	Grady Akers '52 Hudson		25	
22		1	Herschel Buchanan	Buchanan '52 Nash		25	
23		8	Gene Comstock	'53 Hudson		25	
24		19	Fred Dove	Sam Nunn '50 Plymouth	86	25	
25		82	Joe Eubanks	Phil Oates '52 Hudson	85	25	Spindle
26		13	Pop McGinnis	Irving Frye '52 Hudson		25	
27		28	Eddie Skinner	Frank Dodge '53 Olds		25	
28		32	Jimmie Lewallen	R.G. Shelton '52 Hudson		25	
29		14	Fonty Flock	Frank Christian '52 Olds		25	
30		21	Glen Wood	Wood Bros. '53 Lincoln		25	
31			J. L. Justice	'50 Ford		10	
32		91	Tim Flock	Ted Chester '53 Hudson	18	20	Springs
33		4	Slick Smith	Frank Christian '52 Olds		10	
34		43	Jim Paschal	Dave Quate '53 Dodge		10	
35		108	Arden Mounts	Mounts '52 Hudson		10	

Time of Race:
Average Speed:
Lap Leaders: Tim Flock 1-2, Joe Eubanks 3-73, Herb Thomas 74-200.
Cautions: Margin of Victory: Attendance: 9,000
* Herb Thomas took the lead on lap 74 and led the rest of the way. However, a check of scoring cards revealed that Petty had won. No change was issued on lap leaders.

Lee Petty won the 100-miler at Martinsville in his Dodge. That's son Richard peeking out from behind the wheel.

Grand National Race No. 12
200 Laps at Powell Motor Speedway
Columbus, OH
100 Miles on Half-mile Dirt Track
May 24, 1953

Fin	St	No.	Driver	Team / Car	Laps	Money	Status
1	2	92	Herb Thomas	Thomas '53 Hudson	200	$1,000	Running
2	4	120	Dick Rathmann	Walt Chapman '53 Hudson	200	700	Running
3	6	87	Buck Baker	Griffin Motors '53 Olds 88	198	450	Running
4	8	41	Curtis Turner	John Eanes '53 Olds 88	198	350	Running
5	20	13	Pop McGinnis	Irving Frye '53 Hudson	193	200	Running
6	14	10	Ralph Dyer	'53 Nash Amb	192	150	Running
7	11	118	Ed Benedict	Benedict '52 Hudson Hornet	189	125	Running
8	17	42	Lee Petty	Petty Engineering'53 Dodge	184	100	Running
9	12	8	Gene Comstock	Mounts '53 Hudson Hornet	183	75	Running
10	16	55	Bub King	T.H. King '52 Hudson Hornet	182	50	Running
11	26		Dick Linder	'52 Ford	176	25	Running
12	24	93	Ted Chamberlain	Chamberlain '51 Plymouth	174	25	Running
13	10	78	Dick Passwater	Frank Arford '53 Olds 88	159	25	Running
14	7	51	Gober Sosebee	Cherokee Garage '53 Olds 88	131	25	Running
15	1	14	Fonty Flock	Frank Christian '53 Olds 88	111	25	Running
16	21	167	Elton Hildreth	Hildreth Motors '53 Nash	98	25	Steering
17	27		Chet Williams	'51 Ford	97	25	Crash
18	25	108	Arden Mounts	Mounts '51 Hudson Hornet	88	25	Clutch
19	3	82	Joe Eubanks	Phil Oates '52 Hudson	84	25	Gasket
20	5	58	Johnny Patterson	Grady Akers '52 Hudson	74	25	Engine
21	15	4	Slick Smith	Frank Christian '52 Olds 88	59	25	Heating
22	9	91	Tim Flock	Ted Chester '53 Hudson	57	25	Bearing
23	18	44	Ray Duhigg	J.H. Petty '52 Plymouth	39	25	Spindle
24	19	1	Herschel Buchanan	Buchanan '52 Nash Amb.	38	25	Crash
25	23		Paul Parks	'53 Dodge	33	25	Heating
26	27	72	Donald Thomas	T.D. Meeks '50 Ford	32	25	Radiator
27	13		Virgil Livengood	'53 Olds	7	25	Engine

Time of Race: 1 hour, 46 minutes, 54 seconds
Average Speed: 56.127 mph
Pole Winner: Fonty Flock - 59.288 mph
Lap Leaders: - - - - - - - - - Herb Thomas   -200.
Cautions: Margin of Victory: Attendance: 7,500

Modified hot shot Glen Wood of Stuart, VA, made his first Grand National start and finished 30th in a Lincoln.

Oddly, even though Petty was declared the official winner, Thomas received credit for leading laps 74-200.

Race No. 12

Thomas on Top at Powell Motor Speedway

COLUMBUS, OH (May 24) -- Herb Thomas prevailed in a late race showdown with Dick Rathmann and won the 100-miler at Powell Motor Speedway. It was win number 19 for Thomas and his third of the 1953 season.

Rathmann chased Thomas in the late stages, but had to settle for second place. Buck Baker finished third, Curtis Turner fourth and Pop McGinnis fifth.

A crowd of 7,500 watched Thomas win the 200 lapper on the half-mile dirt track at an average speed of 56.127 mph. Fonty Flock earned the pole at 59.288 mph, but struggled and finished 15th, 89 laps behind winner Thomas.

Local driver Chet Williams crashed after 97 laps. His Ford was heavily damaged after an encounter with the guard rail.

IMCA veteran Herschel Buchanan stuffed his Nash into the wall after 38 laps. Neither Williams nor Buchanan was injured in the mishaps.

Race No. 13

Fonty From 43rd to 1st in Big Raleigh 300

RALEIGH, NC (May 30) -- Fonty Flock wheeled his Frank Christian Hudson Hornet into the lead in the 196th lap and streaked to victory in the inaugural Raleigh 300 at the Raleigh Speedway. It was the first event for the high-banked, one mile paved oval since a reorganization of management took place during the winter.

Flock started 43rd on the grid after missing qualifications due to engine problems. Starting on the inside of the 14th row in the three-abreast start, Flock carefully knifed his way through traffic in the early going. Once through the pack, Flock stretched his lead to two laps over Speedy Thompson's Olds at the finish. Time Flock finished third, Herb Thomas was fourth and

Cars on Pace Lap of Raleigh 300.

Dick Passwater fifth.

Slick Smith, Flock's running mate, started on the pole and led the first four laps. Fastest qualifier Bill Blair, who started third on the outside of the front row, passed Smith and led for 13 laps. Buck Baker, Thomas, Blair and Hershel McGriff traded the lead four times before Fonty took the lead for good.

The 300 lapper produced some scoring headaches as runner-up Thompson was originally listed in fourth place with Passwater seventh.

In addition to the scoring confusion, Tim Flock's riding companion, a monkey named Jocko Flocko, broke loose from his specially designed seat and scrambled around in the cockpit of Flock's Hudson. The defending Grand National champ had to make an extra pit stop late in the going and handed Jocko to a member of his

Curtis Turner's Olds at speed down front chute during Raleigh 300.

Grand National Race No. 13
300 Laps at Raleigh Speedway
Raleigh, NC
"Raleigh 300"
300 Miles on 1-mile Paved Track
May 30, 1953

Fin	St	No.	Driver	Team / Car	Laps	Money	Status
1	43	14	Fonty Flock	Frank Christian '53 Hudson	300	$3,500	Running
2	7	12	Speedy Thompson	Buckshot Morris '53 Olds 88	298	1,800	Running
3		91	Tim Flock	Ted Chester '53 Hudson	297	1,200	Running
4	5	92	Herb Thomas	Thomas '53 Hudson	296	1,000	Running
5		78	Dick Passwater	Frank Arford '53 Olds 88	296	800	Running
6		120	Dick Rathmann	Walt Chapman '53 Hudson	295	600	Running
7	1	4	Slick Smith	Frank Christian '51 Olds 88	295	500	Running
8		42	Lee Petty	Petty Engineering '53 Dodge	295	450	Running
9		44	Ray Duhigg	J.H. Petty '52 Plymouth	294	400	Running
10	2	82	Joe Eubanks	Phil Oates '52 Hudson	292	350	Running
11		43	Jim Paschal	Dave Quate '53 Dodge	292	300	Running
12		10	Ralph Dyer	'53 Nash Amb.	288	250	
13	4	87	Buck Baker	Griffin Motors '53 Olds 88	288	200	
14		41	Curtis Turner	John Eanes '53 Olds 88	283	150	
15		71	Otis Martin	'50 Ford	281	125	
16	8	9	Donald Thomas	Thomas '51 Hudson	280	100	
17		34	Andy Winfree	'51 Ford	277	100	
18		24	Bob Welborn	J.O. Goode '51 Plymouth	276	100	
19	6	5	Hershel McGriff	Earl Morley Mtrs. '53 Olds 88	274	100	Bearing
20		21	Glen Wood	Wood Brothers '53 Lincoln	274	100	
21		6	Cotton Owens	'51 Ford 6	274	50	
22		99	Stewart McDonald	Gowen's Auto '53 Plymouth	271	50	
23		23	Gayle Warren	'53 Studebaker	270	50	
24		15	Ted Lee	'51 Ford	264	50	
25		3	Coleman Lawrence	'50 Ford	263	50	
26		93	Ted Chamberlain	Chamberlain '51 Plymouth	256	50	
27		27	Earl Foushee	'51 Plymouth	256	50	
28		77	Frank Arford	Arford '52 Olds 88	253	50	
29		108	Arden Mounts	Comstock '51 Hudson	231	50	
30		40	Gordon Bracken	'53 Nash Rambler	221	50	
31		17	Roy Bentley	'51 Plymouth	220	25	
32		8	Gene Comstock	Mounts '52 Hudson	214	25	
33	3	2	Bill Blair	Blair '53 Olds 88	213	25	Crash
34		16	Johnny Ray	'53 Lincoln	202	25	
35		72	Earl Moss	T.D. Meeks '50 Ford	190	25	
36		46	Ralph Liguori	Liguori '53 Lincoln	190	25	
37		13	Pop McGinnis	Irving Frye '52 Hudson	187	25	
38		55	Bub King	T.H. King '52 Hudson Hornet	165	25	
39		11	Fireball Roberts	Ed Saverance '52 Ford 8	154	25	
40		60	Dub Livingston	'53 Dodge	115	25	
41		73	Elton Hildreth	Hildreth Motors '53 Nash	110	25	
42		1	Herschel Buchanan	Buchanan '53 Nash Amb.	93	25	
43		481	Johnny Zeke	'53 Dodge	84	25	Crash
44		101	Clyde Minter	'50 Mercury	81	25	
45		128	Russell Armentrout	'53 Dodge	60	25	
46		19	Fred Dove	Sam Nunn '51 Plymouth	45	25	
47	9	22	Jimmie Lewallen	'52 Olds 88	41	25	
48		58	Johnny Patterson	Grady Akers '52 Hudson	33	25	
49		74	J.L. Justice	'50 Ford	9	25	

Time of Race: 4 hours, 14 minutes, 51 seconds
Average Speed: 70.629 mph
Pole Winner: Slick Smith - 76.23 mph
Fastest Qualifier: Bill Blair - 76.620 mph
Lap Leaders: Slick Smith 1-4, Bill Blair 5-17, Buck Baker 18-56, Herb Thomas 57,
   Blair 58-94, Hershel McGriff 95-195, Fonty Flock 196-300.
Cautions: Margin of Victory: 2 laps plus   Attendance: 15,235

Ted Chester pit crew. It cost him second place money.

The fun-loving Fonty became the first driver to win two superspeedway events. He had won the 1952 Southern 500 at Darlington.

Fonty Flock charged through the pack early and broke into the top ten as early as the 20th lap. By the 100th lap, he had moved into third behind McGriff and

Thomas. McGriff led for 101 laps before Flock passed him for good. McGriff retired on lap 274 when a wheel bearing burned out in his Oldsmobile.

Flock averaged 70.629 mph before a crowd of 15,235. He won $3,500 from a total purse of $15,250.

Race No. 14

Petty Gets Fourth of Year at Shreveport

SHREVEPORT, LA (June 7) -- Lee Petty racked up his fourth win of the year by driving his Petty Enterprises Dodge to victory in the 100-miler at the Louisiana State Fairgrounds Speedway.

Dick Rathmann finished in second place, Herb Thomas in third and Tim Flock fourth. Fifth place went to Buck Baker.

Thomas continued to hold the point lead. He held a 296 point lead over Rathmann after the 14th race on the 1953 slate. Petty ranked third, 58 behind Rathmann.

Top contenders Hershel McGriff, Ray Duhigg and Dick Passwater all ran into an assortment of difficulty and failed to finish.

Petty averaged 53.199 mph for the 200 trips around the half-mile dirt track.

Race No. 15

Thomas' 20th Comes at Five Flags

PENSACOLA, FL (June 14) -- Herb Thomas notched his 20th career win with a victory in the rain-shortened Grand National event at Five Flags Speedway. It was the fourth win of the year for the Olivia, NC throttle-stomper.

The race had originally been scheduled for May 31 but eighteen inches of rain in a five-day period washed out the event.

Officials were forced to red flag the scheduled 200 lapper at 140 laps when the half-mile dirt track became too wet for the high-powered automobiles to safely negotiate.

Dick Rathmann was flagged in second place, Lee Petty was third, and Buck Baker fourth. Tim Flock nailed down fifth place.

Rathmann ran on Thomas' tail pipes in the early going and Flock pressured the leaders before a long pit stop dropped him well off the pace.

Thomas averaged 63.316 mph on the gray Florida afternoon.

Grand National Race No. 14
200 Laps at Louisiana Fairgrounds
Shreveport, LA
100 Miles on Half-mile Dirt Track
June 7, 1953

Fin	St	No.	Driver	Team / Car	Laps	Money	Status
1		42	Lee Petty	Petty Engineering '53 Dodge	200	$1,000	Running
2		120	Dick Rathmann	Walt Chapman '53 Hudson		700	Running
3	1	92	Herb Thomas	Thomas '53 Hudson		650	Running
4		91	Tim Flock	Ted Chester '52 Hudson		350	Running
5		87	Buck Baker	Griffin Motors '53 Olds 88		200	Running
6		1	Herschel Buchanan	Buchanan '51 Nash		150	
7		51	Gober Sosebee	Cherokee Garage '53 Olds 88		125	
8		10	Ralph Dyer	Nash		100	
9			Elbert Allen	Hudson Hornet		75	
10		4	Slick Smith	Frank Christian '51 Olds 88		50	
11		14	Fonty Flock	Frank Christian '53 Olds 88		25	
12			J.W. Gentry	Nash		25	
13			Roxy Dancy	Plymouth		25	
14		5	Hershel McGriff	Earl Morley Motors '53 Olds		25	
15			Bud Rinaldo	Olds		25	
16		44	Ray Duhigg	J.H. Petty '53 Plymouth		25	
17		78	Dick Passwater	Frank Arford '53 Olds 88		25	
18			Red Dowdy	Olds		25	
19		28	Eddie Skinner	Frank Dodge '53 Olds 88		25	

Time of Race: 1 hour, 46 minutes, 7 seconds
Average Speed: 53.199 mph
Pole Winner: Herb Thomas - 58.727 mph
Lap Leaders: - - - - - - - - - Lee Petty   -200.
Cautions: Margin of Victory: Attendance:

Grand National Race No. 15
200 Laps at Five Flags Speedway
Pensacola, FL
100 Miles on Half-mile Dirt Track
June 14, 1953

Fin	St	No.	Driver	Team / Car	Laps	Money	Status
1		92	Herb Thomas	Thomas '53 Hudson	140	$1,000	Running
2	1	120	Dick Rathmann	Walt Chapman '53 Hudson		900	Running
3		42	Lee Petty	Petty Enterprises '53 Dodge		450	Running
4		87	Buck Baker	Griffin Motors '53 Olds 88		350	Running
5		91	Tim Flock	Ted Chester '53 Hudson		200	Running
6		78	Dick Passwater	Frank Arford '53 Olds		150	
7		82	Joe Eubanks	Phil Oates '52 Hudson		125	
8		4	Slick Smith	Frank Christian '53 Olds		100	
9		51	Gober Sosebee	Cherokee Garage '53 Olds		75	
10			Fred Moore	'51 Hudson		50	
11			Lamar Crabtree	'53 Olds		25	
12		77	Frank Arford	Arford '53 Olds		25	
13			Elbert Allen	'52 Hudson		25	
14		33	Gordon Bracken	'53 Hudson		25	
15			Leonard Lawrence	'50 Ford		25	
16			Gene Tapia	'50 Plymouth		25	
17		43	Jim Paschal	Dave Quate '53 Dodge		25	
18			Gwyn Staley	'53 Olds		25	

* Race called at 140 laps due to rain
Time of Race: 1 hour, 6 minutes, 20 seconds
Average Speed: 63.316 mph
Lap Leaders: - - - - - - - - - Herb Thomas   -140.
Cautions: Margin of Victory: Attendance:

Race No. 16

Rathmann All the Way at Langhorne; Arford Killed

LANGHORNE, PA (June 21) -- For the second time in as many years, Dick Rathmann led a Grand National event at Langhorne Speedway from start to finish. This time he won the International 200, an event open to foreign cars.

Frank Arford of Indianapolis, car owner for top ranking Dick Passwater and a part-time driver, was killed while attempting to qualify. Popular Ray Duhigg crashed heavily in the race and suffered a broken neck.

Rathmann's Hudson Hornet wound up four full laps ahead of runner-up Lee Petty to bag the $2,500 winner's prize. Jim Paschal wound up third, nine laps behind. Herb Thomas and Bill Blair filled out the top five.

Dick Allwine finished sixth in a Jaguar, the highest finisher for the foreign makes. He was 16 laps behind Rathmann. A dozen foreign-made automobiles added the International flavor in the 38 car field. Lloyd Shaw won the pole in a Jaguar, but never led a lap and eventually finished 23rd.

Arford's death was expected to take Passwater off the circuit, unless he could land a ride elsewhere. Arford's Oldsmobile broke loose just before the main grandstand and walloped the wall. The car crashed through the fence and the seat brace broke, allowing the driver to slip out of the seat belt. He landed 30 feet from his car and died a short time later at Mercer Hospital in Trenton.

Sophomore driver Duhigg suffered his serious injuries when his Dodge turned over several times after hitting Jimmie Lewallen's Olds. Ironically, Duhigg was driving Dave Quate's Dodge, a car Lewallen had driven earlier in the year. Lawrence Shultz's Plymouth went through the retaining barrier and fell off a 20-foot cliff. The Highland Falls, NY driver escaped with minor injuries.

Lee Petty's Dodge ran strong at Langhorne Speedway.

Grand National Race No. 16
200 Laps at Langhorne Speedway
Langhorne, PA
200 Miles on 1-mile Dirt Track
June 21, 1953

Fin	St	No.	Driver	Team / Car	Laps	Money	Status
1	2	120	Dick Rathmann	Walt Chapman '53 Hudson	200	$2,500	Running
2	21	42	Lee Petty	Petty Engineering '53 Dodge	196	1,500	Running
3	37	80	Jim Paschal	George Hutchens '53 Dodge	191	900	Running
4	17	92	Herb Thomas	Thomas '53 Hudson	188	700	Running
5	34	2	Bill Blair	Blair '53 Olds 88	187	500	Running
6	4	15	Dick Allwine	'53 Jaguar	184	400	Running
7	3	91	Tim Flock	Ted Chester '53 Hudson	182	300	Running
8	12	10	Nick Fornoro	Porsche	181	200	Running
9	38	23	Willie Oswald	Porsche	174	150	Running
10	24	60	Bill Rexford	'52 Chevrolet	173	150	Running
11	9	4	Charlie Miller	'53 Jaguar		100	
12	5	8	Frankie Schneider	'53 Jaguar		100	
13	30	53	Ronnie Kohler	John Golabek '50 Plymouth		100	
14	7	82	Joe Eubanks	Phil Oates '52 Hudson		100	
15	31	5	Frank Price	'50 Plymouth		100	
16	13	213	Mike Magill	'53 Lincoln		50	
17	28	7	Geoffrey Dessault	Olds		50	
18	22	66	P. Cunningham	'52 Hudson Hornet		50	
19	32	18	Dick Hagey	Volkswagen		40	
20	36	41	Jimmie Lewallen	John Eanes '52 Olds 88		40	Crash
21	26	43	Ray Duhigg	Dave Quate '53 Dodge		40	Crash
22	8	16	Johnny Zeke	Jaguar		40	
23	1	22	Lloyd Shaw	'53 Jaguar		40	
24	14	46	Ralph Liguori	Al Wheatley '53 Lincoln		40	
25	23	33	Gordon Bracken	'52 Hudson Hornet		40	
26	27	34	Andy Winfree	'51 Plymouth		40	
27	16	1	Steve McGrath	Aston Martin		40	
28	25	99	Lawrence Schultz	Gowen's Auto '53 Plymouth		40	Crash
29	18	167	Elton Hildreth	Hildreth Motors '53 Nash Amb		40	
30	11	40	Tommy Thompson	Olds		40	
31	10	14	Fonty Flock	Frank Christian '53 Hudson		40	
32	20	192	Nick Nicolette	Olds		40	
33	29	131	Ray Sherman	Hudson		40	
34	33	31	Al Keller	George Miller '53 Hudson		40	
35	19	78	Slick Smith	Frank Arford '51 Olds 88		40	
36	6	87	Buck Baker	Griffin Motors '53 Olds 88		40	
37	15	E-40	Ken Marriott	Jaguar		40	
38	35	4	Leo Bergeron	Hudson		40	

Time of Race: 3 hours, 6 minutes, 14.18 seconds
Average Speed: 64.434 mph
Pole Winner: Lloyd Shaw - 82.200 mph
Lap Leaders: Dick Rathmann 1-200.

Cautions: 4	Margin of Victory: 4 laps plus	Attendance: 17,000

Race No. 17

Thomas Tough At Tri-City

HIGH POINT, NC (June 26) -- Herb Thomas took his fifth win of the year and firmly planted the "bridesmaid" tag on Dick Rathmann in the 100-mile race at Tri-City Speedway. It was the seventh time Rathmann had finished second in a Grand National race in the 1953 season.

Third place went to Joe Eubanks, Buck Baker was fourth and Lee Petty fifth. Thomas increased his point lead to 242 over Rathmann.

The 200-lapper on the half-mile dirt track was promoted by Mary Lee Blair, sister-in-law of driver Bill Blair, who finished 19th in the field of 23 after engine problems kayoed his Hudson.

Thomas averaged 58.186 mph for his 21st career Grand National win.

Pop McGinnis #13 rides the wall at Wilson Speedway.

Thompson, big winner in Modified circles, was leading and making a strong bid for his first Grand National win when his Oldsmobile blew a tire on lap 191. He made a pit stop and his pit crew could not get the tire off. Thompson returned to the track riding on one bare rim. He struggled the rest of the way and finished sixth.

Grand National Race No. 17
200 Laps at Tri-City Speedway
High Point, NC
100 Miles on Half-mile Dirt Track
June 26, 1953

Fin	St	No.	Driver	Team / Car	Laps	Money	Status
1	1	92	Herb Thomas	Thomas '53 Hudson	200	$1,000	Running
2		120	Dick Rathmann	Walt Chapman '53 Hudson		700	Running
3		82	Joe Eubanks	Phil Oates '52 Hudson		450	Running
4		87	Buck Baker	Griffin Motors '53 Olds 88		350	Running
5		42	Lee Petty	Petty Engineering '53 Dodge		200	Running
6		80	Jim Paschal	George Hutchens '53 Dodge		150	
7		78	Slick Smith	'52 Olds 88		125	
8		41	Jimmie Lewallen	John Eanes '53 Olds 88		100	
9			Buck Smith	'50 Plymouth		75	
10		34	Andy Winfree	'50 Plymouth		50	
11			Carl Burris	'53 Olds		25	
12		72	Donald Thomas	T.D. Meeks '50 Ford		25	
13		167	Elton Hildreth	Hildreth Motors '53 Nash		25	
14			Ermon Rush	'52 Ford		25	
15		46	Ralph Liguori	Liguori '50 Olds 88		25	
16			Charles Causey	'53 Olds 88		25	
17		33	Gordon Bracken	'53 Hudson Hornet		25	
18		19	Fred Dove	Sam Nunn '51 Plymouth		25	
19		2	Bill Blair	Blair '52 Hudson Hornet		25	
20		13	Pop McGinnis	Irving Frye '52 Hudson Hornet		25	
21		44	Bob Welborn	J.H. Petty '50 Plymouth		25	
22		91	Tim Flock	Ted Chester '53 Hudson Hornet		25	
23		14	Fonty Flock	Frank Christian '53 Hudson		25	

Time of Race: 1 hour, 43 minutes, 7 seconds
Average Speed: 58.186
Pole Winner: Herb Thomas - 66.152 mph
Lap Leaders: - - - - - - - - - Herb Thomas -200.
Cautions: Margin of Victory: Attendance:

Race No. 18

Flock Wins Wilson
In Final Laps

WILSON, NC (June 28) -- Fonty Flock steered his Hudson Hornet around Speedy Thompson with nine laps left and won the 100-mile Grand National event at Wilson Speedway. It was his 13th career win on the major league stock car tour.

Dick Rathmann finished second for the eighth time in the 1953 season. Herb Thomas came in third, Joe Eubanks was fourth and Buck Baker fifth.

Grand National Race No. 18
200 Laps at Wilson Speedway
Wilson, NC
100 Miles on Half-mile Dirt Track
June 28, 1953

Fin	St	No.	Driver	Team / Car	Laps	Money	Status
1		14	Fonty Flock	Frank Christian '53 Hudson	200	$1,000	Running
2		120	Dick Rathmann	Walt Chapman '53 Hudson		700	Running
3		92	Herb Thomas	Thomas '53 Hudson		450	Running
4		82	Joe Eubanks	Phil Oates '52 Hudson		350	Running
5		87	Buck Baker	Griffin Motors '53 Olds 88		200	Running
6		12	Speedy Thompson	Buckshot Morris '53 Olds 88		150	
7		91	Tim Flock	Ted Chester '53 Hudson		125	
8		19	Fred Dove	Sam Nunn '51 Plymouth		100	
9		42	Lee Petty	Petty Engineering '53 Dodge		75	
10		41	Jimmie Lewallen	John Eanes '52 Olds 88		50	
11		4	Slick Smith	Frank Christian '51 Olds 88		25	
12			Hildrey M. Thomas	'51 Olds 88		25	
13		34	Andy Winfree	'51 Plymouth		25	
14		2	Bill Blair	Blair '53 Olds 88		25	
15		8	Gene Comstock	Mounts '52 Hudson Hornet		25	
16		24	Bob Welborn	J.O. Goode '51 Plymouth		25	
17		108	Arden Mounts	Comstock '51 Hudson Hornet		25	
18		33	Fred Moore	Blackburn Auto '53 Hudson		25	
19			Buck Smith	'51 Plymouth		25	
20		167	Elton Hildreth	Hildreth Motors '53 Nash Amb.		25	
21		13	Pop McGinnis	Irving Frye '53 Hudson		25	Crash
22		9	Donald Thomas	Thomas '53 Hudson Hornet		25	

Time of Race: 1 hour, 51 minutes, 31 seconds
Average Speed: 53.803 mph
Lap Leaders: - - - - - - - - - Speedy Thompson -191, Fonty Flock 192-200.
Cautions: Margin of Victory: Attendance:

Pop McGinnis survived a wild ride early in the race. His Hudson struck the wooden guard rail and flipped onto its driver's side. McGinnis scrambled out unhurt. Flock averaged 53.803 mph. Thomas' point lead stood at 234 over Rathmann.

In a same day development, Ernie Derr won a stock car race under the International Motor Contest Association banner at Des Moines, Iowa, which was televised in part by NBC Sports. It was possibly the first time a stock car race had been aired on a nation wide basis. The event was telecast on July 3rd on NBC's Gillette Cavalcade of Sports program.

Race No. 19

Thomas Edges Rathmann at Rochester

ROCHESTER, NY (July 3) -- Herb Thomas gunned his Hudson past Tim Flock in the 25th lap and edged Dick Rathmann in a stirring duel to win the 100-mile race at the Monroe County Fairgrounds. It was the sixth win of the year for the 30 year-old driver.

Rathmann took second place for the third straight

event and his ninth this season. He was only ten car lengths behind Thomas when the checkered flag fell.

Lee Petty finished third, Flock was fourth and 1950 Grand National champ Bill Rexford, making a return to the big leagues, was fifth.

Flock led the first 24 laps after he drew the pole position in a pre-race selection.

Thomas averaged a record 56.939 mph as he increased his point lead to 242 over Rathmann.

Race No. 20

Petty Wins Spartanburg; Flock injured in Freak Mishap

SPARTANBURG, SC (July 4) -- Lee Petty drove his Dodge to victory in the 100-miler at the Piedmont Interstate Fairgrounds, an event which was marred by afternoon injuries suffered by Tim Flock.

Flock and another driver had arrived trackside early in the afternoon after an all-night trip from upstate New York. The two were taking a nap on the infield grass when they were run over by a Champion Spark Plug

Grand National Race No. 19
200 Laps at Monroe County Fairgrounds
Rochester, NY
100 Miles on Half-mile Dirt Track
July 3, 1953

Fin	St	No.	Driver	Team / Car	Laps	Money	Status
1		92	Herb Thomas	Thomas '53 Hudson	200	$1,000	Running
2		120	Dick Rathmann	Walt Chapman '53 Hudson	200	700	Running
3		42	Lee Petty	Petty Engineering '53 Dodge	200	450	Running
4	1	91	Tim Flock	Ted Chester '53 Hudson	199	350	Running
5		60	Bill Rexford	'53 Chevrolet		200	Running
6			Bobby Cameron	'51 Plymouth		150	
7			John Meggers	'53 Plymouth		125	
8			Jerry Earl	'49 Chevrolet		100	
9			Russ Truelove	'49 Ford		75	
10		167	Elton Hildreth	Hildreth Motors '52 Nash Amb		50	
11			John Ross	'49 Ford		25	
12			Ralph Sheeler	'49 Ford		25	
13			John Torresa	'49 Ford		25	
14			Leo Burgeron	'50 Meteor		25	
15			Elmer Musclow	'52 Hudson		25	
16			Jim Fox	'49 Ford		25	
17			Wimpy Sipple	'49 Ford		25	
18			Billy Rafter	'53 Plymouth		25	

Time of Race: 1 hour, 45 minutes, 22.46 seconds
Average Speed: 56.939 mph
Pole Winner: No Time Trials - Tim Flock drew pole
Lap Leaders: Tim Flock 1-24, Herb Thomas 25-200.

Cautions:	Margin of Victory: 10 car lengths	Attendance:

Grand National Race No. 20
200 Laps at Piedmont Interstate Fairgrounds
Spartanburg, SC
100 Miles on Half-mile Dirt Track
July 4, 1953

Fin	St	No.	Driver	Team / Car	Laps	Money	Status
1		42	Lee Petty	Petty Engineering '53 Dodge	200	$1,000	Running
2	1	87	Buck Baker	Griffin Motors '53 Olds 88		700	Running
3		92	Herb Thomas	Thomas '53 Hudson		450	Running
4		14	Fonty Flock	Frank Christian '53 Hudson		350	Running
5		58	Johnny Patterson	Grady Akers '52 Hudson Hornet		200	Running
6		82	Joe Eubanks	Phil Oates '52 Hudson		150	
7			Elbert Allen	'52 Hudson		125	
8		51	Gober Sosebee	Sosebee '53 Olds		100	
9		108	Arden Mounts	Comstock '53 Hudson		75	
10		120	Dick Rathmann	Walt Chapman '53 Hudson		50	
11			Otis Martin	'52 Ford		25	
12		8	Gene Comstock	Mounts '53 Hudson		25	
13		4	Slick Smith	Frank Christian '52 Olds		25	
14		19	Fred Dove	Sam Nunn '50 Plymouth		25	
15		80	Jim Paschal	George Hutchens '53 Dodge		25	
16		41	Curtis Turner	John Eanes '52 Olds		25	
17		46	Ralph Liguori	Al Wheatley '53 Lincoln		25	
18			Ralph Dutton	'53 Dodge		25	
19			Ermon Rush	'52 Ford		25	

Time of Race: 1 hour, 45 minutes, 23 seconds
Average Speed: 56.934 mph
Pole Winner: Buck Baker - 58.027 mph
Lap Leaders: - - - - - - - - - - Lee Petty   -200.

Cautions:	Margin of Victory:	Attendance:

Lee Petty and his Dodge Coronet which he drove to victory at Spartanburg.

Race No. 21

Rathmann Beats Thomas at Morristown

MORRISTOWN, NJ (July 10) -- Dick Rathmann emerged victorious after a race long struggle with Herb Thomas and won the 100-miler at Morristown Speedway. It was the third win of the year for the Los Angeles Hudson driver. He was presented with the Miracle Power Trophy from New York Yankee pitcher Jim McDonald.

The principle chargers swapped the lead six times with Rathmann bolting to the front for good on lap 101. Thomas wound up second, a lap and a half behind. Lee Petty grabbed third place, Jim Paschal was fourth and local star Ronnie Kohler fifth.

George Clark's Plymouth struck a rut in the track surface, broke and axle and flipped into the infield. The East Hartford, CT driver suffered a sprained back in the crash.

Thomas won the pole at 61.106 mph, but Rathmann averaged a much speedier 69.417 mph in the 200 lap race.

representative, who backed over the drivers in his passenger car. Flock sustained the most serious injuries when the car parked on his head. Doctors said he would be out of action for a few months.

Buck Baker finished second to Petty. Herb Thomas came in third, Fonty Flock was fourth and Johnny Patterson was fifth.

Petty averaged 56.934 mph for the 100 mile dash.

Grand National Race No. 21
200 Laps at Morristown Raceway
Morristown, NJ
100 Miles on Half-mile Dirt Track
July 10, 1953

Fin	St	No.	Driver	Team / Car	Laps	Money	Status
1	2	120	Dick Rathmann	Walt Chapman '53 Hudson	200	$1,000	Running
2	1	92	Herb Thomas	Thomas '53 Hudson	199	700	Running
3		42	Lee Petty	Petty Engineering '53 Dodge	198	450	Running
4		80	Jim Paschal	George Hutchens '53 Dodge		350	Running
5		53	Ronnie Kohler	John Golabek '50 Plymouth		200	Running
6			Eddie Riker	'49 Plymouth		150	
7		167	Elton Hildreth	Hildreth Motors '53 Nash		125	
8			Charlie Barry	'51 Plymouth		100	
9			John Meggers	'53 Plymouth		75	
10			Bill Cleveland	'50 Ford		50	
11			Neil McDonald	'51 Mercury		25	
12			Jack Smith	'50 Ford		25	
13			Buddy Krebs	'52 Hudson		25	Crash
14			Bobby Fritts	'51 Ford		25	
15			Charlie Hoff	'51 Henry J		25	
16			Phil DeMola	'50 Ford		25	
17			Ed DeWolff	'50 Ford		25	
18			Tony Polito	'49 Olds		25	
19			Ed Paskevich	'50 Ford		25	
20			Nick Nicolette	'50 Olds		25	
21			Ralph Sheeler	'50 Ford		25	
22			Don Stumpf	'50 Dodge		25	
23			George Clarke	'48 Plymouth		25	Crash

Time of Race: 1 hour, 26 minutes, 26 seconds
Average Speed: 69.417 mph
Pole Winner: Herb Thomas - 61.016 mph
Lap Leaders: Herb Thomas 1-3, Dick Rathmann 4-9, Thomas 10-17, Rathmann 18-24,
    Thomas 25-100, Rathmann 101-200.
Cautions: Margin of Victory: 1 lap plus   Attendance:

Race No. 22

Thomas Outlasts Baker for Lakewood Win

ATLANTA, GA (July 12) -- Herb Thomas gave the mighty Hudson Hornets their 13th win in 22 races by taking first place in the 100-miler at Lakewood Speedway.

The seventh win of the season had propelled the veteran Tarheel to a 284 point lead over Dick Rathmann, who once again finished second. Lee Petty was third in a Dodge, the only driver other than a Hudson pilot to finish in the top five.

Joe Eubanks took fourth place and Jerry Wimbish came in fifth.

Buck Baker started second on the grid and led the first 84 laps. As he moved closer to his third win of the year, his Oldsmobile encountered tire problems. Thomas took the lead on lap 85 and led the rest of the

vay in the 100-lap event. Baker eventually finished
event.

A crowd of 12,000 surrounded the track to watch
homas win at an average speed of 70.685 mph.

Grand National Race No. 22
100 Laps at Lakewood Speedway
Atlanta, GA
100 Miles on 1-mile Dirt Track
July 12, 1953

in	St	No.	Driver	Team / Car	Laps	Money	Status
1	1	92	Herb Thomas	Thomas '53 Hudson	100	$1,000	Running
2		120	Dick Rathmann	Walt Chapman '53 Hudson		700	Running
3		42	Lee Petty	Petty Engineering '53 Dodge		450	Running
4		82	Joe Eubanks	Phil Oates '52 Hudson		350	Running
5			Jerry Wimbish	'52 Hudson Hornet		200	Running
6		50	Gober Sosebee	Cherokee Garage '53 Olds		150	
7	2	87	Buck Baker	Griffin Motor Co. '53 Olds		125	
8			Neil Roberts	'53 Olds		100	
9			C.H. Dingler	'51 Studebaker		75	
10		33	Gordon Bracken	Blackburn Auto '53 Hudson		50	
11			Nero Steptoe	'50 Mercury		25	
12		14	Fonty Flock	'53 Hudson		25	
13		80	Jim Paschal	George Hutchens '53 Dodge		25	
14		41	Curtis Turner	Eanes Motor Co. '53 Olds		25	
15			Roscoe Thompson	'52 Olds		25	
16			Max King	'51 Studebaker		25	
17			Jimmy Ayers	'51 Ford		25	

Time of Race: 1 hour, 24 minutes, 53 seconds
Average Speed: 70.685 mph
Pole Winner: Herb Thomas - 72.756 mph
Lap Leaders: Buck Baker 1-84, Herb Thomas 85-100.
Cautions: Margin of Victory: Attendance: 12,000

Grand National Race No. 23
200 Laps at Rapid Valley Speedway
Rapid City, SD
100 Miles on Half-mile Dirt Track
July 22, 1953

in	St	No.	Driver	Team / Car	Laps	Money	Status
1	1	92	Herb Thomas	Thomas '53 Hudson	200	$1,000	Running
2		120	Dick Rathmann	Walt Chapman '53 Hudson		700	Running
3		14	Fonty Flock	Frank Christian '53 Hudson		450	Running
4		42	Lee Petty	Petty Engineering '53 Dodge		350	Running
5		87	Buck Baker	Griffin Motors '53 Olds 88		200	Running
6			Bill Harrison	'52 Hudson		150	
7			Eddie Skinner	'53 Olds		125	
8			Leo Ray	'51 Nash		100	
9			Dick Fellows	'50 Plymouth		75	
10			C.H. Dingler	'51 Studebaker		50	
11			Ray Springer	'50 Ford		25	
12			Mel Krueger	'49 Ford		25	
13			Ted Lee	'52 Hudson		25	
14			Bob Caswell	'49 Plymouth		25	
15			Johnny Beauchamp	'52 Hudson		25	

Time of Race: 1 hour, 44 minutes, 46 seconds
Average Speed: 57.270 mph
Pole Winner: Herb Thomas - 55.727 mph
Lap Leaders:--------- Herb Thomas   -200.
Cautions: Margin of Victory: Attendance:

Race No. 23

Thomas' Hudson
Rapid at Rapid Valley

RAPID CITY, SD (July 22) -- The Grand National
tour headed for the wild west in the hot summer, and
Herb Thomas lassoed the field in the 100-miler at
Rapid Valley Speedway. It was Thomas' eighth win of
the season.

For the 11th time this season, Dick Rathmann sped
home with runner-up honors. The point race stood at
Thomas leading Rathmann by 292 points.

Third place went to Fonty Flock with Lee Petty fourth
and Buck Baker fifth. Thomas' win gave the buzzing
Hornets their eighth win in the last nine events on the
Grand National slate.

Thomas started on the pole with a speed of 55.727
mph. The average speed for the race was 57.270 mph.

IMCS hot shot Johnny Beauchamp entered his first
NASCAR event and wound up dead last in the 15 car
field.

The half-mile Rapid Valley Speedway located in Rapid City, SD.

Race No. 24

Rathmann Nips Thomas
With Last Lap Pass

N. PLATTE, NE (July 26) -- Dick Rathmann
passed Herb Thomas in the final lap and won the 100-
mile Grand National event at the Lincoln City
Fairgrounds.

*Fonty Flock's Hudson busted through barrier
during Grand National event at North Platte, NE.*

It was only the second time in history that a Grand National event was settled by a last lap pass.

Rathmann edged Thomas by six feet to win the $1,000 top prize. Third place went to Lee Petty. Buck Baker finished fourth and Marvin Copple was fifth.

Fonty Flock plowed through the wooden guard rail on the steeply banked dirt track early in the race. He was not injured. Flock wound up 16th in the 18 car field

Rathmann averaged 54.380 mph for his ninth career victory.

Race No. 25

Thomas Dazzling At Davenport

DAVENPORT, IA (Aug. 2) -- The Grand National tour wrapped up its Western swing as Herb Thomas came home first in the Davenport 100-miler. It was the 25th career win for Thomas and the ninth this year.

Finishing second was Buck Baker, with Lee Petty third, Dick Rathmann fourth and Fonty Flock fifth.

Thomas had little trouble beating the slim 14 car field. The triumph enabled the Sanford, NC veteran to increase his lead in the Grand National standings to 332 points over Rathmann.

Thomas averaged 62.500 mph in the 200 lap event on the half-mile dirt track.

Grand National Race No. 24
200 Laps at Lincoln City Fairgrounds
North Platte, NE
100 Miles on Half-mile Dirt Track
July 26, 1953

Fin	St	No.	Driver	Team / Car	Laps	Money	Status
1		120	Dick Rathmann	Walt Chapman '53 Hudson	200	$1,000	Running
2	1	92	Herb Thomas	Thomas '53 Hudson	200	700	Running
3		42	Lee Petty	Petty Engineering '53 Dodge		450	Running
4		87	Buck Baker	Griffin Motors '53 Olds 88		350	Running
5			Marvin Copple	'49 Olds		200	Running
6			Bill Harrison	'52 Hudson		150	
7			Byron Clouse	'49 Hudson		125	
8			C.H. Dingler	'51 Studebaker		100	
9			Tubby Harrison	'49 Plymouth		75	
10			Sandy Slack	'51 Henry J		50	
11			Bill Mann	'49 Hudson		25	
12			Red Knuter	'49 Plymouth		25	
13			Eddie Skinner	'53 Olds		25	
14			Johnny Beauchamp	'53 Hudson		25	
15			Don Ostendorf	'53 Olds		25	
16		14	Fonty Flock	Frank Christian '53 Hudson		25	Crash
17			Mel Krueger	'49 Ford		25	
18			Ted Lee	'49 Ford		25	

Time of Race: 1 hour, 50 minutes, 20 seconds
Average Speed: 54.380 mph
Pole Winner: Herb Thomas - 54.397 mph
Lap Leaders: Thomas 1- , - - - - - - - Thomas -199, Rathmann 200
Cautions: Margin of Victory: 6 feet   Attendance:

Grand National Race No. 25
200 Laps at Davenport Speedway
Davenport, IA
100 Miles on Half-mile Dirt Track
August 2, 1953

Fin	St	No.	Driver	Team / Car	Laps	Money	Status
1		92	Herb Thomas	Thomas '53 Hudson	200	$1,000	Running
2	1	87	Buck Baker	Griffin Motors '53 Olds 88		700	Running
3		42	Lee Petty	Petty Engineering '53 Dodge		450	Running
4		120	Dick Rathmann	Walt Chapman '53 Hudson		350	Running
5		14	Fonty Flock	Frank Christian '53 Hudson		200	Running
6			Bill Harrison	'53 Hudson		150	
7			Mel Krueger	'49 Ford		125	
8			Johnny Beauchamp	'52 Hudson		100	
9			Tubby Harrison	'49 Plymouth		75	
10			Keith Lucas	'52 Studebaker		50	
11			Ernie Derr	'53 Olds		25	
12			Jerry Draper	'50 Ford		25	
13			Paul Newkirk	'51 Nash Rambler		25	
14			Red Unteidt	'53 Olds		25	

Time of Race: 1 hour, 36 minutes
Average Speed: 62.500 mph
Pole Winner: Buck Baker - 54.397 mph
Lap Leaders: - - - - - - - - - Herb Thomas -200.
Cautions: Margin of Victory: Attendance:

Race No. 26

Turner Ends Famine In Hillsboro Hundred

HILLSBORO, NC (Aug. 9) -- Forgotten Curtis Turner, a non-winner in Grand National competition for more than two years, hopped in Frank Christian's Oldsmobile and led all the way to win the 100 mile contest at Occoneechee Speedway.

A crowd of 4,000 showed up on the hot, dusty afternoon to watch the Roanoke, VA star rope his first Grand National win since June 24, 1951, when he won at Dayton, Ohio. Herb Thomas finished second with Lee Petty   third.

Curtis Turner won Hillsboro Hundred.

Fourth place went to Joe Eubanks and fifth to Bill Blair.

Dick Rathmann, second ranking driver in the point standings, crashed in the third lap and finished last in the 19 car field. Rathmann then relieved Slick Smith and brought his Olds home seventh.

Two caution flags held Turner's winning speed to 75.125 mph.

Race No. 27

Flock Wins Third of Year at Weaverville

WEAVERVILLE, NC (Aug. 16) -- Fonty Flock prepped for his title defense in the Southern 500 by topping the field in the 100-miler at Asheville-Weaverville Speedway. It was the third victory of the year for the Decatur, GA veteran.

Grand National Race No. 26
100 Laps at Occoneechee Speedway
Hillsboro, NC
100 Miles on 1-mile Dirt Track
August 9, 1953

Fin	St	No.	Driver	Team / Car	Laps	Money	Status
1	1	41	Curtis Turner	Frank Christian '53 Olds 88	100	$1,000	Running
2		92	Herb Thomas	Thomas '53 Hudson	100	700	Running
3		42	Lee Petty	Petty Engineering '53 Dodge	99	450	Running
4		82	Joe Eubanks	Phil Oates '52 Hudson		350	Running
5		2	Bill Blair	Blair '53 Olds 88		200	
6		80	Jim Paschal	George Hutchens '53 Dodge		150	
7		4	Slick Smith	Frank Christian '51 Olds 88		125	
8		167	Elton Hildreth	Hildreth Motors '53 Nash Amb		100	
9		22	Jimmie Lewallen	'53 Olds		75	
10			Jimmy Ayers	'51 Plymouth		50	
11			Fred Dove	'50 Ford		25	
12		14	Fonty Flock	Frank Christian '53 Hudson		25	Rear End
13			Johnny Meggers	'53 Plymouth		25	
14			Elbert Allen	'52 Hudson		25	
15			Virgil Stockton	'53 Hudson		25	
16		91	Tim Flock	Ted Chester '53 Hudson		25	
17			Buck Smith	'49 Plymouth		25	
18		87	Buck Baker	Griffin Motors '53 Olds		25	Crash
19		120	Dick Rathmann	Walt Chapman '53 Hudson	3	25	Crash

Time of Race: 1 hour, 19 minutes, 52 seconds
Average Speed: 75.125 mph
Pole Winner: Curtis Turner - 89.078 mph
Lap Leaders: Curtis Turner 1-100.
Cautions: 2   Margin of Victory: 1/2 lap   Attendance: 4,000

Grand National Race No. 27
200 Laps at Asheville-Weaverville Speedway
Weaverville, NC
100 Miles on Half-mile Dirt Track
August 16, 1953

Fin	St	No.	Driver	Team / Car	Laps	Money	Status
1		14	Fonty Flock	Frank Christian '53 Hudson	200	$1,000	Running
2		92	Herb Thomas	Thomas '53 Hudson		700	Running
3		2	Bill Blair	Blair '53 Olds 88		450	Running
4		87	Buck Baker	Griffin Motors '53 Olds 88		350	Running
5		22	Jimmie Lewallen	'52 Olds 88		200	Running
6		4	Slick Smith	Frank Christian '53 Olds		150	
7		42	Lee Petty	Petty Engineering '53 Dodge		125	
8		8	Gene Comstock	Arden Mounts '53 Hudson		100	
9		3	Jimmy Ayers	'52 Hudson		75	
10		91	Tim Flock	Ted Chester '53 Hudson		50	
11			Johnny Meggers	'53 Plymouth		25	
12			Wayne Niedecken	'53 Dodge		25	
13		80	Jim Paschal	George Hutchens '53 Dodge		25	
14		120	Dick Rathmann	Walt Chapman '53 Hudson		25	
15		72	Donald Thomas	T.D. Meeks '50 Ford		25	
16		167	Elton Hildreth	Hildreth '51 Nash		25	
17			Buck Smith	'49 Plymouth		25	
18	1	41	Curtis Turner	Frank Christian '51 Olds		25	Crash
19		18	Arden Mounts	Mounts '53 Hudson		25	

Time of Race: 1 hour, 36 minutes, 6 seconds
Average Speed: 62.434 mph
Pole Winner: Curtis Turner
Lap Leaders: - - - - - - - - - Fonty Flock   -200.
Cautions: Margin of Victory: Attendance:

Fonty Flock

Herb Thomas finished in second place. Third went to Bill Blair, fourth to Buck Baker and fifth to Jimmie Lewallen.

Curtis Turner started on the pole, but he wrecked his Oldsmobile early and wound up 18th in the field of 19 cars.

Buck Baker and Dick Rathmann were other top contenders who failed to finish.

Flock averaged 62.434 mph for his 14th career Grand National win.

Fonty Flock finished second, giving the powerful Hudson Hornets another 1-2 finish. Lee Petty, Dick Rathmann and Jim Paschal rounded out the top five.

Curtis Turner took his second straight pole position, but once again he was on the sidelines after a few laps. This time, he wound up 15th in the field of 19.

Thomas averaged 51.040 mph for his 26th career victory.

Herb Thomas

Grand National Race No. 28
200 Laps at Princess Anne Speedway
Norfolk, VA
100 Miles on Half-mile Dirt Track
August 23, 1953

Fin	St	No.	Driver	Team / Car	Laps	Money	Status
1		92	Herb Thomas	Thomas '53 Hudson	200	$1,000	Running
2		14	Fonty Flock	Frank Christian '53 Hudson		700	Running
3		42	Lee Petty	Petty Engineering '53 Dodge		450	Running
4		120	Dick Rathmann	Walt Chapman '53 Hudson		350	Running
5		80	Jim Paschal	George Hutchens '53 Dodge		200	Running
6		87	Buck Baker	Griffin Motors '53 Olds		150	
7			Andy Winfree	'52 Plymouth		125	
8			John Meggers	'53 Plymouth		100	
9			Ralph Rose	'51 Ford		75	
10		51	Gober Sosebee	Cherokee Garage '53 Olds		50	
11		167	Elton Hildreth	Hildreth '51 Nash		25	
12			Curtis Estes	'52 Hudson		25	
13			Ed Paskovitch	'52 Ford		25	
14			Snuffy Smith	'51 Nash		25	
15	1	41	Curtis Turner	Frank Christian '51 Olds		25	
16		24	Bob Welborn	J O Goode '52 Plymouth		25	
17			Dick Girvin	'52 Henry J		25	
18			Buck Smith	'52 Plymouth		25	
19			Fred Dove	'50 Plymouth		25	

Time of Race: 1 hour, 57 minutes, 33.20 seconds
Average Speed: 51.040 mph
Pole Winner: Curtis Turner - 54.200 mph
Lap Leaders: - - - - - - - - - Herb Thomas -200 .
Cautions: Margin of Victory: Attendance:

Race No. 28

Thomas Wins 7th in
Last 14 Starts at Norfolk

NORFOLK, VA (Aug. 23) -- Herb Thomas, batting 500 since June 14th, racked up another victory in the 100-mile Grand National event at Princess Anne Speedway. It was his tenth win of the year, the first time a driver had put double digits in the win column in one season.

Race No. 29

Fonty Beats Slim
Field at Hickory

HICKORY, NC (Aug. 29) -- Fonty Flock took the lead in the sixth lap and led the rest of the way to capture the Hickory 200 at Hickory Speedway for his fourth win of the season.

Only twelve cars started the 100-miler, an all time Grand National low.

Herb Thomas put in another strong run and finished second. It marked the ninth consecutive Grand National event in which Thomas finished either first or second.

Grand National Race No. 29
200 Laps at Hickory Speedway
Hickory, NC
100 Miles on Half-mile Dirt Track
August 29, 1953

Fin	St	No.	Driver	Team / Car	Laps	Money	Status
1	2	14	Fonty Flock	Frank Christian '53 Hudson	200	$1,000	Running
2	3	92	Herb Thomas	Thomas '53 Hudson		700	Running
3	6	82	Joe Eubanks	Phil Oates '52 Hudson		450	Running
4	5	42	Lee Petty	Petty Engineering '53 Dodge		350	Running
5	4	22	Jimmie Lewallen	'52 Plymouth		200	Running
6		4	Slick Smith	Frank Christian '51 Olds 88		150	
7	1	91	Tim Flock	Ted Chester '53 Hudson		125	
8		19	Fred Dove	Sam Nunn '51 Plymouth		100	
9			Ralph Rose			75	
10			Buck Baker	'50 Ford		50	
11			Ned Jarrett	Mellie Bernard '50 Ford		25	
12	8	120	Dick Rathmann	Walt Chapman '53 Hudson		25	

Time of Race:
Average Speed:
Pole Winner: Tim Flock - 79.362 mph
Lap Leaders: Tim Flock 1-5, Fonty Flock 6-200.
Cautions: Margin of Victory: Attendance:

Joe Eubanks came in third, Lee Petty was fourth and Jimmie Lewallen fifth.

For the second time in the last four races, hot-shot Dick Rathmann finished in last place.

Pole winner Tim Flock led the first five laps in his return since being run over by a non-competing automobile at Spartanburg in early July. Fonty blasted past in the sixth lap and was never headed.

Ned Jarrett, a farm boy with big league aspirations, started his first Grand National race and wound up in eleventh place.

Fireball Roberts #11 leads eventual winner Buck Baker down back chute at Darlington Raceway.

Race No. 30

Thomas Falters in Final Laps; Baker Takes Southern 500

DARLINGTON, SC (Sept. 7) -- Buck Baker drilled his speedy Oldsmobile past a laboring Herb Thomas with ten laps to go and cruised home first to win the fourth annual Southern 500 at Darlington International Raceway. The dramatic victory, in what turned out to be NASCAR's most competitive event in its history, vaulted the former bus driver into fourth place in the point standings.

The lead changed hands no less than 35 times, although among four drivers. Baker, Thomas, Fireball Roberts and Fonty Flock treated the throng of 37,000 screaming spectators to one of the best races ever in stock car racing history.

Thomas, who led for 124 laps, was holding a narrow cushion over Baker with only ten laps to go when the engine in his Hudson popped. He coasted to a halt on the back-stretch.

Baker raced into the lead as fellow Hornet driver Gene Comstock came to Thomas' aid and pushed him around the track for two laps. NASCAR officials

Gene Comstock #8 pushes Herb Thomas down the front stretch at Darlington Raceway in waning laps of Southern 500. Engine failure robbed Thomas of his 2nd Labor Day classic victory.

Grand National Race No. 30
364 Laps at Darlington Raceway
Darlington, SC
"Southern 500"
500 Miles on 1.375-mile Paved Track
September 7, 1953

Fin	St	No.	Driver	Team / Car	Laps	Money	Status
1	7	87	Buck Baker	Griffin Motors '53 Olds 88	364	$6,285	Running
2	1	14	Fonty Flock	Frank Christian '53 Hudson	361	3,040	Running
3	10	44	Curtis Turner	Frank Christian '53 Olds 88	359	1,500	Running
4	13	49	Dick Meyer	Meyer '53 Dodge	355	1,000	Running
5	4	92	Herb Thomas	Thomas '53 Hudson	354	1,550	Engine
6	16	80	Jim Paschal	George Hutchens '53 Dodge	354	800	Running
7	19	46	Speedy Thompson	Buckshot Morris '53 Olds 88	351	750	Running
8	5	29	Donald Thomas	'53 Hudson Hornet	350	700	Running
9	22	00	Dick Passwater	Passwater '53 Olds 88	350	630	Running
10	9	91	Tim Flock	Ted Chester '53 Hudson	349	520	Running
11	44	42	Lee Petty	Petty Engineering '53 Dodge	344	450	Running
12	24	67	Elton Hildreth	Hildreth Motors '53 Nash	343	400	Running
13	21	6	Jimmie Lewallen	'53 Olds 88	340	350	Running
14	8	89	Buddy Shuman	B.A.Pless '53 Hudson Hornet	338	345	Running
15	32	21	Neil Roberts	'53 Chrysler	335	300	Running
16	25	22	George Osborne	'53 Hudson Hornet	331	275	Running
17	29	7	Lloyd Hulette	Hulette '53 Buick	328	250	Running
18	30	8	Gene Comstock	Comstock '53 Hudson	324	225	Running
19	33	71	Fred Dove	'51 Ford 6	324	200	Running
20	50	18	Bobby Myers	'53 Olds 88	321	190	Running
21	55	55	Bub King	T.H. King '53 Packard	309	175	Running
22	34	60	Tyre Rakestraw	'53 Chevrolet	308	160	Running
23	47	51	Gober Sosebee	Cherokee Garage '52 Olds	301	150	Running
24	39	50	Bob Weatherly	'52 Plymouth	289	140	Running
25	37	97	Lacy Jackson	'52 Hudson Hornet	288	130	Crash
26	48	30	Johnny Bridges	'51 Ford	279	120	Running
27	40	10	Chet Williams	'51 Ford	277	110	Running
28	15	06	Marvin Panch	'53 Dodge	275	110	Heating
29	50		Elmer Cooper	'53 Nash Rambler	271	110	Running
30	22	08	Arden Mounts	Mounts '53 Hudson Hornet	262	110	Radiator
31	12	9	Jim Reed	'53 Hudson Hornet	260	110	Engine
32	38	99	Matt Gowen	Gowen's Auto '53 Plymouth	250	110	Running
33	45	2	Bill Blair	Blair '53 Olds 88	250	110	Radiator
34	20	23	Mike Magill	'53 Lincoln	244	110	Crash
35	54	25	Bill Norton	'52 Olds 88	241	110	Running
36	14	47	Otis Martin	'53 Plymouth	238	110	Running
37	28	73	Bill Widenhouse	'53 Nash Amb.	234	110	Running
38	26	75	Junior Johnson	'53 Olds Holiday	222	110	Crash
39	44	16	Weldon Adams	Adams Racing '51 Ford	217	110	Engine
40	35	74	J.L. Justice	'52 Ford	217	110	Heating
41	56		Bob Hunter	'53 Olds 88	210	105	Running
42	3	120	Dick Rathmann	Walt Chapman '53 Hudson	208	155	Hub
43	42	4	Slick Smith	Frank Christian '53 Olds 88	200	105	Gas Tank
44	31	77	Dick Allwine	Dick Curry '53 Chevrolet	198	105	Fuel Line
45	6	11	Fireball Roberts	Ed Saverance '53 Olds 88	198	340	A-Frame
46	19	13	Emory Lewis	Ernest Woods '53 Olds 88	195	105	Engine
47	53	19	Clyde Minter	'53 Mercury	190	105	Oil Press
48	49	45	Ben Dixon	'52 Hudson Hornet	187	105	Heating
49	57		Lonnie Bragg	'52 Olds 88	149	105	Engine
50	36	88	Laird Bruner	'53 Olds 88	142	105	Trans
51	58		Joe Guide jr	Sally Guide '52 Hudson	111	100	Oil Press
52	18	58	Johnny Patterson	Grady Akers '53 Hudson	98	120	Crash
53	51	48	Slim Rominger	'49 Lincoln	69	100	Fuel Pmp
54	11	45	Ralph Liguori	Al Wheatley '53 Lincoln	68	100	Crash
55	27	84	Gayle Warren	'53 Studebaker	57	100	Gas Line
56	2	82	Joe Eubanks	Phil Oates '52 Hudson	40	100	Spindle
57	43	33	Pop McGinnis	Irving Frye '52 Hudson	31	100	Engine
58	46		Merritt Brown	'53 Studebaker	20	100	Trans
59	52	79	Ned Jarrett	Jarrett '50 Olds 88	8	100	Oil Line

Time of Race: 5 hours, 23 minutes, 19 seconds
Average Speed: 92.881 mph
Pole Winner: Fonty Flock - 107.983 mph (6 lap qualifying run)
Lap Leaders: 35 lead changes among 4 different drivers. Buck Baker led 151 laps, Herb
    Thomas led 124 laps, Fonty Flock led 48 laps, Fireball Roberts led 41 laps. Baker took
    lead for final time with 10 laps to go.
Cautions: 4 for 17 laps
Margin of Victory: 3 plus laps
Attendance: 37,000
* Crew Chief on winning car was 21 year-old Boyce Hagler

Race teams had plenty of tires stacked up in Southern 500 pit area.

disallowed the distance Thomas traveled while on
Comstock's front bumper, and he fell heartbreakingly
into fifth place in the final rundown.

Fonty Flock wound up second, some three laps be
hind Baker. Curtis Turner finished third and Californi
driver, Dick Meyer, was fourth. Baker collected
$6,285 for his efforts.

Flock held the lead with 75 laps remaining when he
drove into the pits for two rear tires. His Frank
Christian pit crew had problems replacing the rubber.
It took one minute and 55 seconds to get Flock back
out on the track. He lost three laps in the pits, and tha
was his deficit when the checkered flag fell.

Dick Rathmann, mired in a slump during the champi
onship drive, started third but fell out on lap 155 with a
broken hub. His 42nd place finish in the field of 50
cars left him 722 points behind Thomas in the poin
standings. Lee Petty struggled to an 11th place finish
and found himself in third place in the standings, 140
points behind Rathmann.

There were several hair-raising crashes, per usual for
the biggest race of the year. Johnny Patterson put his
Hudson through the wall, taking 40 feet of guard rai
with him. On lap 244, Mike Magill plunged through
the gap in the retaining wall, crashing his Lincoln heav
ily into the parking lot. Magill suffered a broken leg
and rib in the mishap.

Junior Johnson and Lacy Jackson escaped injury in
separate crashes down the backstretch. Dick Passwater
made his first Grand National start since his former car
owner, Frank Arford, was killed at Langhorne in June
 The Indianapolis driver finished a respectable ninth i
the 500 mile grind.

Baker was quick to give credit to his 21 year-old crew
chief, Boyce Hagler, who finely tuned the Griffi
Motors Oldsmobile. The 34-year old Baker averaged
record 92.881 mph for the 500 miles.

Race No. 31

Thompson Breaks Ice With Macon Victory

Speedy Thompson drove Buckshot Morris' Oldsmobile to victory at Macon.

MACON, GA (Sept. 13) -- Speedy Thompson flashed past Lee Petty in the 177th lap and roared to his first Grand National win in the 100-miler at Central City Speedway. Thompson, who cut his teeth in the Modified cars, proved he could be capable of tackling the professional giants with his popular triumph.

Petty finished second and Gober Sosebee was third. Joe Eubanks finished fourth after starting on the pole. Tim Flock was fifth.

The lead changed hands seven times before Thompson showed his tail pipes to the field. Eubanks, Sosebee, Petty and Curtis Turner all took turns leading before Thompson flexed his muscles in the stretch run. Turner departed with engine problems after 132 laps.

C.H. Dingler blew a tire and crashed over the banking on lap 119.

Thompson averaged 55.172 mph and became the tenth different winner on the tour for the 1953 season.

Boyish Speedy Thompson proved he could run with the big boys at Macon, GA.

Grand National Race No. 31
200 Laps at Central City Speedway
Macon, GA
100 Miles on Half-mile Dirt Track
September 13, 1953

Fin	St	No.	Driver	Team / Car	Laps	Money	Status
1		12	Speedy Thompson	Buckshot Morris '53 Olds 88	200	$1,000	Running
2		42	Lee Petty	Petty Enterprises '53 Dodge		700	Running
3		51	Gober Sosebee	Cherokee Garage '53 Olds 88		450	Running
4	1	82	Joe Eubanks	Phil Oates '53 Hudson		350	Running
5		91	Tim Flock	Ted Chester '53 Hudson		200	Running
6		92	Herb Thomas	Thomas '53 Hudson		150	
7		87	Buck Baker	Griffin Motors '53 Olds		120	
8			Bob Walden	'50 Plymouth		100	
9		4	Slick Smith	Frank Christian '53 Olds		75	
10			Andy Winfree			50	
11		41	Curtis Turner	John Eanes '53 Olds	132	25	Engine
12							
13							
14							
15			C.H. Dingler		119	25	Crash
16		120	Dick Rathmann	Walt Chapman '53 Hudson		25	
17							
18							
19							
20							

Time of Race: 1 hour, 48 minutes, 45 seconds
Average Speed: 55.172 mph
Pole Winner: Joe Eubanks - 60.810 mph
Lap Leaders: Joe Eubanks 1-11, Gober Sosebee 12-59, Curtis Turner 60-108,
   Lee Petty 109-117, Turner 118-132, Sosebee 133-157, Petty 158-176,
   Speedy Thompson 177-200.
Cautions: Margin of Victory: Attendance:

Race No. 32

Langhorne Friendly Turf for Rathmann

Dick Rathmann lapped field at Langhorne.

LANGHORNE, PA (Sept. 20) -- Dick Rathmann ended a string of sour luck by taking a $2,500 victory in the 250-miler at Langhorne Speedway. It was his fifth win of the year but his first in nearly two months.

Rathmann finished better than a lap ahead of Herb Thomas in posting his third win at the *"Great Left Turn"* in his last five outings. Twice before, he had led all the way.

In this 250-miler, Rathmann led on two occasions for a total of 95 laps. Speedy Thompson came in third, with Jim Reed and Jim Paschal finishing fourth and fifth respectively.

Thomas virtually sewed up the 1953 Grand National title. His point lead stood at 874 over Rathmann with five races remaining.

Thomas led the first 22 laps from his pole position. Rathmann took the lead for the first time on lap 23, gave up first place to Thompson on lap 61, then scrambled back after a pit stop to run down Thomas with 57 laps remaining.

Four caution flags held Rathmann's average speed down to 67.046 mph. A crowd of 18,000 was on hand to see him bag his 10th career win.

Race No. 33

Thomas, Rathmann 1-2 at Bloomsburg

BLOOMSBURG, PA (Oct. 3) -- Herb Thomas and Dick Rathmann, leading drivers on the powerful Hudson Hornet team on the Grand National trail, finished first and second in the 100-miler at the Bloomsburg Fairgrounds.

It was the eleventh win of the season for Thomas and the twelfth time Rathmann had finished second. Third place went to Buck Baker. Elton Hildreth hit the top five for the first time with a fourth place finish and Bob Welborn was fifth.

Hildreth's fine run was one of the rare top five appearances for a Nash Ambassador. A total of 21 cars started the race.

Jim Paschal started on the pole in his Dodge, but fell out near the half way point. He wound up 16th.

Grand National Race No. 32
250 Laps at Langhorne Speedway
Langhorne, PA
250 Miles on 1-mile Dirt Track
September 20, 1953

Fin	St	No.	Driver	Team / Car	Laps	Money	Status
1		120	Dick Rathmann	Walt Chapman '53 Hudson	250	$2,500	Running
2	1	92	Herb Thomas	Thomas '53 Hudson	249	1,250	Running
3		12	Speedy Thompson	Buckshot Morris '53 Olds 88	248	750	Running
4		9	Jim Reed	'52 Hudson Hornet		500	Running
5		80	Jim Paschal	George Hutchens '53 Dodge		450	Running
6		42	Lee Petty	Petty Engineering '53 Dodge		400	
7		41	Curtis Turner	Frank Christian '53 Olds 88		350	
8		82	Joe Eubanks	Phil Oates '52 Hudson		300	
9		22	Jimmie Lewallen	'53 Olds 88		250	
10		18	Bobby Myers	'53 Olds 88		200	
11		87	Buck Baker	Griffin Motors '53 Olds 88		150	
12		51	Gober Sosebee	Cherokee Garage '53 Olds 88		125	
13		77	Dick Allwine	'53 Chevrolet		100	
14			Don Glass	'51 Nash		75	
15		53	Ronnie Kohler	John Golabek '50 Plymouth		50	
16		19	Fred Dove	'50 Ford		50	
17		55	Bub King	T.H. King '53 Olds 88		50	
18		06	Marvin Panch	'53 Dodge		50	
19		34	Andy Winfree	'51 Plymouth		50	
20			John McGorrien	'52 Dodge		50	
21			George Clark	'51 Plymouth		35	
22			Wimpy Ervin	'52 Dodge		35	
23			Ralph Sheeler	'49 Ford		35	
24			Lou Thomas	'52 Plymouth		35	
25			Bill O'Dell	'49 Ford		35	
26			John Dodd, Sr	'52 Willys		35	
27		167	Elton Hildreth	Hildreth Motors '53 Nash Amb.		35	
28			Eddie Riker	'49 Plymouth		35	
29		24	Bob Welborn	J O Goode '51 Plymouth		35	
30			Ed DeWolff	'50 Ford		35	
31		2	Bill Blair	Blair '53 Olds 88		35	
32		89	Buddy Shuman	B.A. Pless '53 Hudson Hornet		35	Crash
33			Bob Harris	'53 Dodge		35	
34			Mickey Rorer	'50 Ford		35	
35		14	Fonty Flock	Frank Christian '53 Hudson		35	
36		4	Slick Smith	Frank Christian '52 Hudson		---	
37			Bill Cleveland	'50 Ford		---	
38			Gene Darragh	'50 Ford		---	
39		91	Tim Flock	Ted Chester '53 Hudson		---	
40		99	Matt Gowen	Gowen Auto Parts '53 Plymouth		---	

Time of Race: 3 hours, 43 minutes, 43.52 seconds
Average Speed: 67.046 mph
Pole Winner: Herb Thomas -
Lap Leaders: Herb Thomas 1-22, Dick Rathmann 23-60, Speedy Thompson 61-109,
   H. Thomas 110-193, Rathmann 194-250.
Cautions: 4   Margin of Victory: 1 lap plus   Attendance: 18,000

Grand National Race No. 33
200 Laps at Bloomsburg Fairgrounds
Bloomsburg, PA
100 Miles on Half-mile Dirt Track
October 3, 1953

Fin	St	No.	Driver	Team / Car	Laps	Money	Status
1		92	Herb Thomas	Thomas '53 Hudson	200	$1,000	Running
2		120	Dick Rathmann	Walt Chapman '53 Hudson		700	Running
3		87	Buck Baker	Griffin Motors '53 Olds 88		450	Running
4		167	Elton Hildreth	Hildreth Motors '53 Nash Amb.		350	Running
5		24	Bob Welborn	J O Goode '51 Plymouth		200	Running
6		42	Lee Petty	Petty Engineering '53 Dodge		150	
7		93	Ted Chamberlain	Chamberlain '51 Plymouth		125	
8			Robert Walden	'50 Plymouth		100	
9			Wimpy Ervin	'50 Dodge		75	
10			Ed DeWolff	'49 Ford		50	
11			Mickey Rorer	'50 Ford		25	
12			Frank Katucka	'50 Ford		25	
13			Jim Baker	'51 Ford		25	
14			Frank Price	'52 Ford		25	
15		14	Fonty Flock	Frank Christian '53 Hudson		25	
16	1	80	Jim Paschal	George Hutchens '53 Dodge		25	
17			Ed Van Horn	'50 Ford		25	
18			Ernie Weidler	'52 Hudson		25	
19			Frank Kapack	'53 Dodge		25	
20			Ed Spencer	'52 Ford		25	
21			Vic Strassburg	'52 Mercury		25	

Time of Race:
Average Speed:
Pole Winner: Jim Paschal - 55.935 mph
Lap Leaders: - - - - - - - - - Herb Thomas -200.
Cautions: Margin of Victory: Attendance:

Herb Thomas and Fonty Flock on the front row for the 100-mile Wilson, NC Grand National race.

Speedway's 100 mile race. It was the 24th win in the last 22 months for the crafty speed artist.

Thomas won the pole at 56.962 mph and maintained his qualifying speed throughout the 200 lapper. He averaged 56.022 mph for the entire distance.

Speedy Thompson finished second and Fonty Flock was third. Lee Petty nailed down fourth place and Ralph Liguori's fine run netted him fifth place.

A crowd of 10,000 was on hand, many of whom climbed on roof tops outside the track to watch the event.

Joe Eubanks, third fastest qualifier, departed early and wound up 15th in the 17 car field.

Thomas' win gave the Hudson Hornets their 16th win in the past 20 Grand National events.

Race No. 34

Thomas Flag-to-Flag in Wilson Romp

WILSON, NC (Oct. 4) -- Herb Thomas nabbed his twelfth win of the year and locked up the 1953 Grand National championship in impressive style in Wilson

Grand National Race No. 34
200 Laps at Wilson Speedway
Wilson, NC
100 Miles on Half-mile Dirt Track
October 4, 1953

Fin	St	No.	Driver	Team / Car	Laps	Money	Status
1	1	92	Herb Thomas	Thomas '53 Hudson	200	$1,000	Running
2	8	12	Speedy Thompson	Buckshot Morris '53 Olds 88		700	Running
3	2	14	Fonty Flock	Frank Christian '53 Hudson		450	Running
4	7	42	Lee Petty	Petty Engineering '53 Dodge		350	Running
5		45	Ralph Liguori	'51 Plymouth		200	Running
6	5	120	Dick Rathmann	Walt Chapman '53 Hudson		150	
7	6	87	Buck Baker	Griffin Motors '53 Olds 88		125	
8	10	167	Elton Hildreth	Hildreth '53 Nash Amb.		100	
9		22	Jimmie Lewallen	R G Shelton '53 Olds 88		75	
10	4	51	Gober Sosebee	Cherokee Garage '53 Olds 88		50	
11		41	Curtis Turner	Frank Christian '53 Olds 88		25	
12		19	Fred Dove	'51 Ford		25	
13			Don Vershure	'53 Hudson Hornet		25	
14			Clyde Minter	'53 Mercury		25	
15	3	82	Joe Eubanks	Phil Oates '53 Hudson		25	
16			Parks Surrat	'50 Plymouth		25	
17			Ermon Rush	'51 Ford		25	

Time of Race: 1 hour, 47 minutes, 6 seconds
Average Speed: 56.022 mph
Pole Winner: Herb Thomas - 56.962 mph
Lap Leaders: Herb Thomas 1-200.
Cautions: Margin of Victory: Attendance: 10,000

Grand National Race No. 35
160 Laps at N. Wilkesboro Speedway
North Wilkesboro, NC
100 Miles on .625-mile Dirt Track
October 11, 1953

Fin	St	No.	Driver	Team / Car	Laps	Money	Status
1		12	Speedy Thompson	Buckshot Morris '53 Olds 88	160	$1,000	Running
2		14	Fonty Flock	Frank Christian '53 Hudson	158	700	Running
3		44	Ray Duhigg	J.H. Petty '52 Plymouth	156	450	Running
4		24	Bob Welborn	J.O. Goode '51 Plymouth	156	350	Running
5		42	Lee Petty	Petty Engineering '53 Dodge	155	200	Running
6	1	87	Buck Baker	Griffin Motors '53 Olds 88	155	150	
7		2	Bill Blair	Blair '53 Olds 88	155	125	
8		82	Joe Eubanks	Phil Oates '52 Hudson	154	100	
9		22	Jimmie Lewallen	R G Shelton '53 Olds 88	153	75	
10		55	Bub King	T.H. King '53 Olds 88	153	50	
11		58	Johnny Patterson	Grady Akers '53 Hudson	153	25	
12		93	Donald Thomas	Thomas '53 Hudson	153	25	
13		91	Tim Flock	Ted Chester '53 Hudson	152	25	
14		51	Gober Sosebee	Cherokee Garage '53 Olds	151	25	
15		92	Herb Thomas	Thomas '53 Hudson	151	25	
16		45	Ralph Liguori	'51 Plymouth	149	25	
17		08	Arden Mounts	Mounts '51 Hudson Hornet	143	25	
18			Bob Walden	'50 Plymouth	143	25	
19			Parks Surrat	'51 Plymouth	141	25	
20		93	Ted Chamberlain	Chamberlain '50 Plymouth	139	25	
21			Clyde Minter	'50 Mercury	136	25	
22		41	Curtis Turner	Frank Christian '53 Olds 88	131	25	
23		80	Jim Paschal	George Hutchens '53 Dodge	125	25	
24		120	Dick Rathmann	Walt Chapman '53 Hudson	124	25	
25		19	Fred Dove	'50 Ford	110	25	
26			Slim Rominger	'50 Olds	84	25	
27			Don Vershure	'53 Hudson Hornet	53	25	
28		167	Elton Hildreth	Hildreth Motors '53 Nash	41	25	
29			Bud Jones	'50 Plymouth	36	25	
30			Pete Stewart	'51 Ford	20	25	
31			Ralph Dutton	'53 Dodge		25	

Time of Race: 1 hour, 24 minutes, 16 seconds
Average Speed: 71.202 mph
Pole Winner: Buck Baker - 28.74 seconds, 78.288 mph
Lap Leaders: Curtis Turner 1-6, Buck Baker 7, Turner 8, Baker 9-10, Turner 11=17, Baker 18-69, Fonty Flock 70-88, Baker 89-103, F.Flock 104-105, Turner 106-109, Baker 110-119, F.Flock 120-135, Speedy Thompson 136-160.
Cautions: 3 for 16 laps   Margin of Victory: 2 laps plus   Attendance: 2,000

Race No. 35

Small Wilkesboro Crowd Sees Thompson Win Big

N. WILKESBORO, NC (Oct. 11) -- Speedy Thompson of Monroe, NC hammered his Oldsmobile past Fonty Flock 25 laps from the finish and won the 100 miler at North Wilkesboro Speedway. It was the second victory of the season for Thompson since joining the Buckshot Morris Oldsmobile team.

Flock finished in second place. The call of the day went to Ray Duhigg, who finished third in a Plymouth owned by Julian Petty. It was Duhigg's first start since suffering a broken neck at Langhorne on June 21st.

Bob Welborn finished fourth and Lee Petty was fifth.

The lead changed hands 13 times in the 160 lapper on the .625-mile track. A small turnout of only 2,000 watched the electrifying run, which saw the lead change hands five times in the first eleven laps. Thompson was in front only once, but it was the most important 25 final laps.

New Grand National Champion Herb Thomas went out after 151 laps and wound up 15th in the 31 car field. Other top contenders Jim Paschal, Curtis Turner and Dick Rathmann also encountered mechanical problems and did not finish.

Thompson averaged 71.202 mph as three caution flags showed the field for 16 laps.

Race No. 36

Baker Breaks; Paschal Posts First Win

MARTINSVILLE, VA (Oct. 18) -- Jim Paschal of High Point, NC, always a strong contender but never a winner, broke through with a popular victory in the 100-mile Grand National race at Martinsville Speedway. it took him 60 races to find his first big NASCAR win.

Paschal's Big Bear Dodge stomped past a stricken Buck Baker in the 128th lap and led the rest of the way. Lee Petty finished second, Bill Blair was third, and Fonty Flock fourth. Carl Burris, a familiar face in the Modified and Sportsman ranks, finished fifth in an outstanding run.

Baker grabbed the lead at the outset and led the first 127 laps. A burned wheel bearing on his Olds put him out and opened the door for Paschal.

Herb Thomas finished last in the 26 car field, falling victim to fuel pump problems.

Dick Rathmann was not on hand, having split with car owner Walt Chapman. Russ Hepler was tabbed to replace Rathmann, but the new team opted to drive in a 150 lapper at New Castle, PA's independent show, which he won.

A crowd of 8,500 was on hand to watch Paschal win at an average speed of 56.013 mph.

Jim Paschal guides his George Hutchens-owned Dodge around the Martinsville Speedway. Paschal scored his first Grand National win in the 100-miler.

Grand National Race No. 36
200 Laps at Martinsville Speedway
Martinsville, VA
100 Miles on Half-mile Dirt Track
October 18, 1953

Fin	St	No.	Driver	Team / Car	Laps	Money	Status
1		80	Jim Paschal	George Hutchens '53 Dodge	200	$1,000	Running
2	5	42	Lee Petty	Petty Engineering '53 Dodge	200	700	Running
3	9	2	Bill Blair	Blair '53 Olds 88	199	450	Running
4	1	14	Fonty Flock	Frank Christian '53 Hudson	199	350	Running
5			Carl Burris	'51 Plymouth	194	200	Running
6	7	13	Emory Lewis	Ernest Woods '53 Olds 88	192	150	Running
7		24	Bob Welborn	J.O. Goode '51 Plymouth	185	125	Running
8			Clyde Minter	'50 Mercury	185	100	Running
9			Bill Morgan	'51 Ford	184	75	Running
10			Bob Walden	'50 Plymouth	183	50	Running
11			Bill O'Dell	'49 Ford	182	25	
12		22	Jimmie Lewallen	R G Shelton '53 Olds 88	176	25	
13			Bob Sampson	'53 Dodge	172	25	
14		58	Johnny Patterson	Grady Akers '53 Hudson	170	25	
15		19	Fred Dove	'51 Ford	169	25	
16			Bud Harless	'51 Ford	168	25	
17			George Osborne	'53 Hudson Hornet	146	25	
18			Gifford Wood	'52 Plymouth	136	25	
19			Parks Surrat	'51 Plymouth	130	25	
20	2	87	Buck Baker	Griffin Motors '53 Olds 88	127	25	Bearing
21		08	Arden Mounts	Comstock '51 Hudson Hornet	68	25	
22		167	Elton Hildreth	Hildreth Motors '53 Nash	66	25	Heating
23	3	82	Joe Eubanks	Phil Oates '52 Hudson	55	25	Engine
24	4	44	Curtis Turner	Frank Christian '53 Olds 88	46	25	Engine
25			Ralph Dutton	'53 Dodge	46	25	
26	6	92	Herb Thomas	Thomas '53 Hudson	28	25	Fuel Pmp

Time of Race: 1 hour, 47 minutes, 7 seconds
Average Speed: 56.013 mph
Pole Winner: Fonty Flock - 58.958 mph
Lap Leaders: Buck Baker 1-127, Jim Paschal 128-300.
Cautions: Margin of Victory: Attendance: 8,500

Herb Thomas #92 leads Fonty Flock at Lakewood Speedway.

Lou Faver flipped his Kaiser in the 12th lap. He was not hurt.

Don Versure did a nasty turnover in the first turn on lap 33, also without injury.

A crowd of 9,000 watched Baker average 63.180 mph for his fifth career victory.

Race No. 37

Baker Wins Season Finale at Atlanta

ATLANTA, GA (Nov. 1) -- Buck Baker put the lid on the 1953 NASCAR season with a come from behind victory at Lakewood Fairgrounds Speedway. It was his fourth win of the year.

Baker shoved his Griffin Motors Oldsmobile around Herb Thomas in the 79th lap and led the final 22 laps on the one-mile flat dirt track. Fonty Flock finished second. Lee Petty spun off the fourth turn in the final lap in a desperate bid to overtake Flock. He still managed to finish third.

Jim Paschal and Jimmie Lewallen were fourth and fifth respectively.

Thomas wound up 14th in the field of 26 and won the Grand National title by 646 points over Petty.

Rathmann, who missed the final two races, wound up third in the driver standings.

Grand National Race No. 37
100 Laps at Lakewood Speedway
Atlanta, GA
100 Miles on 1-mile Dirt Track
November 1, 1953

Fin	St	No.	Driver	Team / Car	Laps	Money	Status
1		87	Buck Baker	Griffin Motors '53 Olds 88	100	$1,000	Running
2		14	Fonty Flock	Frank Christian '53 Hudson		700	Running
3		42	Lee Petty	Petty Engineering '53 Dodge		450	Running
4		80	Jim Paschal	George Hutchens '53 Dodge		350	Running
5		22	Jimmie Lewallen	R G Shelton '53 Olds 88		200	Running
6		58	Johnny Patterson	Grady Akers '53 Hudson		150	
7		13	Pop McGinnis	Irving Frye '52 Hudson		125	
8		82	Joe Eubanks	Phil Oates '52 Hudson		100	
9		24	Bob Welborn	J.O. Goode '51 Plymouth		75	
10		0	Ewell Weddle	Weddle '50 Plymouth		50	
11		51	Gober Sosebee	Cherokee Garage '53 Olds 88		25	
12			C.H. Dingler	'50 Plymouth		25	
13			Edsel Massey	'51 Studebaker		25	
14		92	Herb Thomas	Thomas '53 Hudson Hornet		25	
15			Ralph Dutton	'53 Dodge		25	
16		41	Curtis Turner	Frank Christian '53 Olds 88		25	Heating
17			Chick Housley	'53 Olds 88		25	
18			Tommy Thompson	'53 Olds 88		25	
19		81	Roscoe Thompson	'51 Studebaker		25	Rear End
20	1	91	Tim Flock	Ted Chester '53 Hudson	50	25	Heating
21			Ray Erickson	'52 Hudson Hornet		25	
22		2	Bill Blair	Blair '53 Olds 88		25	
23			Don Vershure	'53 Hudson Hornet	33	25	Crash
24			Charlie Causey	'50 Olds 88		25	
25			Harold Nash	'52 Olds		25	Piston
26		110	Lou Faver	'51 Kaiser	12	25	Crash

Time of Race: 1 hour, 24 minutes, 58 seconds
Average Speed: 63.180 mph
Pole Winner: Tim Flock - 73.580 mph
Lap Leaders: Tim Flock 1, Fonty Flock 2-26, Herb Thomas 27-78, Buck Baker 79-100.
Cautions: Margin of Victory: Attendance: 9,000

1953 NASCAR Season
Final Point Standings Grand National Division

Rank	Driver	Points	Starts	Wins	Top 5	Top 10	Winnings
1	Herb Thomas	8,460	37	12	27	31	$28,909.58
2	Lee Petty	7,814	36	5	25	31	18,446.50
3	Dick Rathmann	7,362	36	5	22	25	20,269.35
4	Buck Baker	6,713	33	4	16	26	18,166.20
5	Fonty Flock	6,174	32	4	17	17	17,755.48
6	Tim Flock	5,011	25	1	11	18	8,281.86
7	Jim Paschal	4,211	21	1	6	9	5,570.75
8	Joe Eubanks	3,603	24	0	7	15	5,253.60
9	Jimmie Lewallen	3,508	22	0	7	13	4,221.80
10	Curtis Turner	3,373	19	1	3	5	4,371.45
11	Speedy Thompson	2,958	7	2	5	7	6,546.45
12	Slick Smith	2,670	23	0	0	10	2,301.45
13	Elton Hildreth	2,625	25	0	1	5	1,996.45
14	Gober Sosebee	2,525	17	0	2	9	2,721.45
15	Bill Blair	2,457	23	1	6	11	4,534.30
16	Fred Dove	1,997	20	0	0	4	1,239.30
17	Bub King	1,624	14	0	0	5	1,035.30
18	Gene Comstock	1,519	13	0	0	3	989.30
19	Donald Thomas	1,408	17	0	0	4	1,764.30
20	Ralph Liguori	1,336	12	0	2	3	1,097.60
21	Pop McGinnis	1,113	13	0	2	5	975.00
22	Otis Martin	1,068	8	0	0	2	610.00
23	Andy Winfree	954	5	0	0	3	300.00
24	Bob Welborn	761	9	0	2	6	1,160.00
25	Johnny Patterson	753	11	0	1	2	645.00
26	Ted Chamberlain	738	9	0	0	3	500.00
	Neil Roberts	738	2	0	0	1	400.00
28	Buddy Shuman	713	4	0	0	0	395.00
29	Arden Mounts	644	10	0	0	1	395.00
	Bobby Myers	644	2	0	0	1	390.00
31	Clyde Minter	636	8	0	0	3	430.00
32	George Osborne	612	2	0	0	0	300.00
33	Jim Reed	590	3	0	1	1	635.00
34	Gordon Bracken	538	6	0	0	1	215.00
35	Don Oldenberg	527	4	0	1	2	375.00
36	C.H. Dingler	520	4	0	0	3	250.00
37	Elbert Allen	488	4	0	0	2	250.00
38	Mike Magill	486	3	0	0	0	235.00
	Lloyd Hulette	486	1	0	0	0	250.00
40	Bill Harrison	480	3	0	0	3	450.00
41	Tommy Thompson	463	3	0	1	1	865.00
42	Coleman Lawrence	446	8	0	0	1	250.00
43	Dub Livingston	435	6	0	0	1	225.00
44	Buck Smith	400	5	0	0	1	175.00
45	Jimmy Ayers	384	3	0	0	2	150.00
46	Bob Walden	356	4	0	0	3	275.00
47	Eddie Skinner	352	4	0	0	1	200.00
48	Bill Adams	346	2	0	0	1	250.00
49	Mel Kreuger	336	3	0	0	1	175.00
50	Johnny Beauchamp	328	3	0	0	1	150.00

The 1954 Season
Driver Defections and
a new thing called Television

Volume one of a four volume series . . . . . .   The Beginning 1949 - 1958

1954

Tim Flock, the youngest member of the famous Flock brothers, was one of NASCAR's most dazzling speed artists. Winner of the 1952 Grand National Championship, the slender Atlanta driver played the sport with abandon, delight and a touch of class.

For the 1954 season, Flock had paired up with car owner Ernest Woods. After the 1953 campaign, Ted Chester, who owned the Hudson Tim drove to the title, disbanded his operation. Flock and Woods struck a deal to seek the championship in Oldsmobiles.

At Daytona's SpeedWeek in February, Flock started the year off with a bang, winning the 160-mile Grand National by one minute and 28 seconds over runner-up Lee Petty. But an impromptu post race inspection revealed an alleged minor violation in the carburetor of the Flock-Woods Oldsmobile.

Two time Grand National Champ Tim Flock, flanked by Bill France and Cannonball Baker.

The car was disqualified and Flock was placed at the rear of the 62-car rundown, earning no points and losing the $1,700 first place check. It was the second time in 24 months that Flock had been stripped from an apparent Daytona victory. He had been disqualified after winning the 1952 Modified-Sportsman race because his car was equipped with wooden roll bars.

NASCAR President Bill France said disqualifying Flock "was one of the toughest decisions I have ever had to make", but he added that strict enforcement of the rules was necessary for the continued advancement of the sport.

Flock was so incensed that he vowed to quit racing. He stepped out of the Ernest Woods ride, retreated to Atlanta and opened a Pure filling station.

Flock's walkout seemed to set a trend for the early part of the 1954 season. Brother Fonty quit NASCAR in March to join the SAFE (Society of Autosports and Fellowship Education) stock car tour, giving up one of the most cherished rides on the tour, the Frank Christian Oldsmobile team.

In June, Al Keller, who won two races early in the year including a 100-mile road race at Linden, NJ in a Jaguar, announced he was moving over to the AAA Indy Car circuit to pursue a career in open wheel Championship cars.

Toward the end of the year, Hershel McGriff, who took the Christian ride when Fonty Flock jumped ship, said that he would retire at season's end to devote full time to the lucrative logging business in his native Oregon.

Fonty was miffed following a Grand National event at Atlanta's Lakewood Speedway on March 21st. In the 100-miler, Flock, Dick Rathmann, Herb Thomas, and Buck Baker treated the foot-stomping crowd of 20,000 to perhaps the most exicitng race stock car fans had ever witnessed.

Pat Purcell, NASCAR's Executive Manager, remarked afterwards, "Those four boys ran the best damn race I've ever seen. One hundred nerve racking miles (and they) were looking one another in the eye."

Flock suffered a flat tire in the late stages which put him off the pace. Thomas nipped Baker by a single car length, with third place Rathmann hot on the tail-pipes of Baker.

Immediately after the completion of the electrifying event, NASCAR penalized Thomas a full lap for improperly rejoining the race after a pit stop. For a few minutes, Baker was elevated to victory circle.

After the official rundown had been announced, it was pointed out that Baker had committed the same violation as Thomas. NASCAR docked Baker a lap and also penalized Rathmann for improperly making a fuel stop. That put Gober Sosebee in first with Flock second.

Finally, NASCAR waived all the penalties and declared the finish official the way they crossed the finish line. Fonty quit NASCAR's premier series two weeks later.

Keller, originally out of Buffalo, had raced with NASCAR off and on since 1948. He captured his first Grand National race at Savannah, GA on March 28th. A versatile driver, Keller was assigned to drive a Jaguar entered by bandleader Paul Whiteman in NASCAR's maiden voyage into road racing.

Johnny Patterson and Reds Kagle wearing the new fangled GenTex helmet.

A make-do 2-mile track, utilizing the runways of the Linden, NJ Airport, was the scene of NASCAR's plunge into the "sophisticated" world of road racing. To add international flavor, the event was open to foreign sports cars.

Keller took the lead from Herb Thomas with 54 miles to go and sprinted away to take the checkered flag. From victory lane, Keller said he was quitting NASCAR to join AAA and get a crack at the Indianapolis 500.

Keller would start five Indianapolis classics, with a fifth place finish in 1961 his best effort. On November 19th of that year, he was burned to death when his flaming car went over the fence in Phoenix.

Despite the defections of three of its current stars, NASCAR claimed its Grand National circuit contained a flair that, most assuredly, would endure for decades. It also found its way into a fascinating electronic toy called 'television'.

Al Keller won two races, then quit the NASCAR tour.

A half-hour TV program entitled *Wire Wheels* made its debut on WABD-TV in New York City with the entire first show devoted to Daytona's SpeedWeek activities.

Out west, racer Mel Larson was producing a weekly program called *Desert Dust*, which aired on KYTL-TV in Phoenix. Another program, *Autorama*, hit the airways on WICC-TV in Bridgeport, CT.

It was graphic testimony that NASCAR's heroism was growing under the spellbound gaze of thousands.

With NASCAR's prescribed profile coming into focus on a national level, a wide range of companies began to manufacture specialized racing equipment. Pure Oil Co., which became affiliated with NASCAR in 1952, introduced a special racing tire for stock cars featuring an all-nylon cord. Each tire sold for $37.90, including tax and delivery.

It was the first time any company had bothered to manufacture a tire for stock car racing. Previously, over-the-counter rubber was all that was available for the stock car jockeys.

A short time later, General Textile Mills produced a new racing helmet to replace the old leather strapped Cromwell headpiece, which had seen no major improvements since the late '30's.

The GenTex 70 helmet was a "radical departure from the older type helmets," said a press release from the company. "Its military type head sling is designed to cushion shock and lessen the danger of concussion". Price tag was $35.

Advancement continued. In July, flameproof coveralls were made available to the racing fraternity by Treesdale Laboratories of Pittsburgh. Their *Permaproof Fyre Safe Fisher Fabric* coveralls were sold for only $9.25. By the autumn, most of NASCAR's regulars had been outfitted in the baggy coveralls.

With NASCAR gaining so much widespread national exposure, Bill France jumped full bore into an area which had been virtually monopolized by the AAA for a half century. France announced the beginning of the NASCAR Auto Association, an auto club which provided - for a fee - travel information, hotel, restaurant and garage service to its members.

France said the NAA "will accept as affiliates only the better hotels and motels, and those recommended will have to maintain a high standard that will assure the motoring public of the finest in accommodations". France, always a whiz at slogans, came up with another good one: *It pays to stop with friends - and your friends are wherever you see the sign of NASCAR.*

With a base of 11,000 members, the NASCAR Auto

Association was considered a viable threat to AAA.

The problem was the same old thorn -- uncooperative drivers and owners. It irritated NAA affiliates to have vacancies while race cars on trailers were parked in the Mom and Pop Motel across the street.

The NAA lasted a little over three years.

Scheduled for an August 22 opening, the Memphis-Arkansas Speedway, *"The largest stock car racing facility in the country"*, was built at LeHi, AR, a massive mile and one-half dirt track. Construction delays forced postponement until October 10th. Buck Baker won the Mid-South 250 at an average speed of 89.013 mph.

Lee Petty won the 1954 championship via consistency, while twelve-time winner Herb Thomas finished second, 283 points behind. Petty won seven races and was *running at the finish* 32 times in 34 starts.

Also in 1954, Louis Jerome "Red" Vogt, mechanic par excellence, was the first man to receive a lifetime NASCAR membership. It was a fitting honor for the man who named NASCAR.

Al Keller takes the George Miller Hudson high in the turn at West Palm Beach. Keller led the 100-miler for 45 laps before a blown head gasket forced him out of the race.

Race No. 1

Grand National Race No. 1
200 Laps at Palm Beach Speedway
West Palm Beach, FL
100 Miles on Half-mile Dirt Track
February 7, 1954

Fin	St	No.	Driver	Team / Car	Laps	Money	Status
1	3	92	Herb Thomas	Thomas '53 Hudson	200	$1,600	Running
2		87	Buck Baker	Griffin Motors '53 Olds 88	198	1,050	Running
3		42	Lee Petty	Petty Engineering '54 Dodge	198	750	Running
4		80	Jim Paschal	George Hutchens '54 Dodge	196	350	Running
5		24	Ray Duhigg	J.O. Goode '50 Plymouth	190	300	Running
6		6	Ralph Liguori	Liguori '54 Dodge	189	250	Running
7		86	Don Oldenberg	Oldenberg '54 Mercury	188	200	Running
8		126	Dave Terrell	Terrell '54 Dodge	186	150	Running
9		82	Joe Eubanks	Phil Oates '51 Hudson	185	100	Running
10		181	Tommy Elliott	Millard Wright '52 Plymouth	185	100	Running
11		43	Bob Welborn	Petty Engineering '53 Dodge	183	25	Steering
12		14	Fonty Flock	Frank Christian '53 Hudson	177	25	Running
13		10	Mel Krueger	'53 Hudson Hornet	174	25	Running
14		47	Bill Irvin	'51 Plymouth	170	25	Running
15	R-D		Alan Clarke	'50 Dodge	166	25	Heating
16		96	Mason Bright	'53 Dodge	165	25	Running
17		21	Laird Bruner	Garmen Arnica '53 Olds 88	164	25	Wheel
18		77	Cotton Hodges	'50 Olds	164	25	Running
19		33	Pop McGinnis	Irving Frye '52 Hudson Hornet	157	25	Running
20		107	Johnny Roberts	'50 Ford	138	25	Running
21		101	Bucky Sager	'53 Studebaker	98	---	Generator
22		28	Eddie Skinner	Frank Dodge '53 Olds	86	---	Fuel Pmp
23	1	3	Dick Rathmann	John Ditz '54 Hudson	68	---	Gasket
24	2	23	Al Keller	George Miller '54 Hudson	52	---	Gasket
25		187	Red Duvall	Hank Salat '53 Packard	49	---	Radiator
26		97	Jim Jones	'52 Olds	7	---	Shocks

Time of Race: 1 hour, 41 minutes, 46 seconds
Average Speed: 58.958 mph
Pole Winner: Dick Rathmann - 66.371 mph
Lap Leaders: Dick Rathmann 1-3, Al Keller 4-49, Rathmann 50-67, Herb Thomas 68-70, Buck Baker 71-149, Thomas 150-200.
Cautions: 1 for 2 laps   Margin of Victory: 2 laps plus   Attendance: 4,500

Herb Thomas Outduels Buck Baker at Palm Beach

WEST PALM BEACH, FL (Feb. 7) -- Herb Thomas, driving a 1953 Hudson Hornet, took the lead with 54 laps remaining and went on to score a two-lap victory over Buck Baker in the 1954 season opener at Palm Beach Speedway. It was Thomas' 29th career win on NASCAR's major league stock car tour, and he collected $1,600 of a $5,300 purse. This contest was one of the highest paying 100-milers in NASCAR history.

Baker, who led for 79 laps, wound up second in an Oldsmobile. Third place went to Lee Petty, Jim Paschal was fourth, and Ray Duhigg survived a crash with five laps to go to salvage fifth place.

Dick Rathmann started on the pole and led the first three laps. Al Keller, driving a new Hudson owned by George Smith, passed Rathmann on lap four and led through the 49th lap, when Rathmann went back in front. Rathmann was leading when his Hudson went behind pit wall with a blown head gasket. The same fate had put Keller out 16 laps earlier.

With Rathmann and Keller sidelined, Thomas and Baker picked up the battle for first place, and NASCAR's most prolific winner prevailed in the end.

A crowd of 4,500 watched the race under sunny 76 degree weather. Thomas average 58.958 mph for the 100 miles.

It was the 29th career Grand National win for the former saw mill operator out of Olivia, NC.

Race No. 2

Petty Daytona Winner; Flock Quits After Disqualification

DAYTONA BEACH, FL (Feb.21) -- Lee Petty of Randleman, NC was declared the winner of the 160-mile Grand National race in Daytona's SpeedWeek finale after the apparent winner, Tim Flock, was disqualified for a minor rules infraction.

It marked the second time in three years that Flock has been disqualified from a Daytona victory. He also lost the 1952 Modified-Sportsman win on a technicality. In a teardown after Flock had finished first in the race, the carburetor in Flock's Ernest Woods-owned Oldsmobile was found to have been polished, and the butterfly shaft was soldered. NASCAR President Bill France said it was a difficult decision for him to disqualify Flock, but he added that rules must be obeyed by everyone, including the sport's top names. Any car found not complying with the rule book must be disqualified.

The decision infuriated Flock to the point that he quit the Grand National circuit.

Flock had beaten Petty's Chrysler by one minute, 28 seconds for an average speed of 90.400 mph. Petty's official time was clocked at 89.108 mph. Buck Baker drove his Olds into second place, 9.0 seconds behind Petty. Baker, hampered with failing brakes, slammed his car into the sandy corners in a full broadside in order to negotiate the turns.

Lee Petty kicks the sand in the North turn en route to Daytona triumph.

Wild riding Curtis Turner finished third, Dick Rathmann was fourth and Bill Blair fifth.

The famous Beach and Road Course at Daytona. The 1954 race was supposed to have been the final one on the beachfront facility.

Grand National Race No. 2
39 Laps at Beach & Road Course
Daytona Beach, FL
160 Miles on 4.1-Mile Beach & Road Course
February 21, 1954

Fin	St	No.	Driver	Team / Car	Laps	Money	Status
1	1	42	Lee Petty	Petty Eng. '54 Chrysler	39	$1,700	Running
2	10	87	Buck Baker	Griffin Motors '53 Olds	39	1,325	Running
3	13	14	Curtis Turner	Frank Christian '54 Olds	39	900	Running
4	8	3	Dick Rathmann	John Ditz '54 Hudson	38	625	Running
5	26	2	Bill Blair	Blair '54 Olds	38	475	Running
6	23	122	Jack Smith	Smith '54 Olds	38	425	Running
7	6	13	Emory Lewis	Ernest Woods '53 Olds	38	300	Running
8	14	25	Fireball Roberts	Leland Colvin '53 Olds	38	200	Running
9	17	51	Gober Sosebee	Cherokee Garage '54 Olds	38	150	Running
10	37	77	Stan Kross	'54 Hudson	38	125	Running
11	25	35	Don White	White '54 Olds	38	90	Running
12	9	98	Hershel McGriff	Beryl Jackson '54 Olds	37	80	Running
13	2	48	Otis Martin	'54 Chrysler	37	70	Running
14	27	118	Byron King	'54 Buick	37	60	Running
15	7	16	Jack Conley	'53 Lincoln	37	50	Rear End
16	20	7A	Jim Reed	Reed '54 Olds	37	40	Running
17	12	9	Ed Samples	Claude Alexander '54 Olds	36	40	Running
18	31	82	Joe Eubanks	Phil Oates '51 Hudson	36	40	Running
19	39	61	Jimmie Lewallen	'53 Olds	36	40	Running
20	47	12	Speedy Thompson	Buckshot Morris '53 Olds	36	40	Running
21	46	23	Al Keller	George Miller '54 Hudson	36	25	Running
22	35	21	Laird Bruner	Garmen Amica '53 Olds	36	25	Running
23	36	86	Don Oldenberg	Oldenberg '54 Mercury	36	25	Running
24	28	101	Bucky Sager	'53 Studebaker	35	25	Running
25		52	Joe Guide, Jr	Sally Guide '51 Hudson	35	25	Running
26	24	41	Dick Garlington	Frank Christian '51 Olds	35	25	Running
27	38	80	Jim Paschal	George Hutchens '64 Dodge	35	25	Running
28		33	Pop McGinnis	Irving Frye '52 Hudson	35	25	Running
29	43	30	Nero Steptoe	'52 Olds	35	25	Running
30	48	7	Mike Brown	'53 Packard	35	25	Running
31	32	44A	Bob Welborn	Petty Engineering '53 Dodge	35	25	Running
32	42	126	Dave Terrell	Terrell '54 Dodge	35	25	Running
33	29	96	Mason Bright	'53 Olds	35	25	Running
34	41	34	Virgil Livengood	'54 Nash	35	25	Running
35	30	50	Elbert Allen	'53 Olds	34	25	Running
36	50	155	Mel Krueger	'53 Hudson	34	25	Running
37	49	15	Jimmy Florian	'52 Hudson	34	25	Running
38	44	1	Elton Hildreth	Hildreth Motors '53 Nash	34	25	Out / gas
39	45	28	Eddie Skinner	Frank Dodge '53 Dodge	33	25	Running
40	51	47	Harvey Eakin	Eakin '53 Nash	33	25	Running
41	40	10	Bob Sampson	'53 Dodge	32	---	Heating
42	54	141	Billy Rafter	'49 Plymouth	32	---	Running
43	55	10A	Hap Jones	'54 Nash	31	---	Running
44	53	47A	Bill Irvin	'51 Plymouth	28	---	Running
45	21	28	William Kearney	'51 Plymouth	28	---	Clutch
46		44	Harold Nash	'52 Olds	27	---	Running
47	15	17	Jim Romine	'53 Hudson	25	---	Engine
48	57	107	Johnny Roberts	'50 Ford	22	---	H Gasket
49		58	Johnny Patterson	H B Ranier '52 Olds	22	---	Running
50	56	144	Art Binkley	'51 Ford	21	---	Running
51	33	6	Ralph Liguori	Liguori '54 Dodge	21	---	Stalled
52	58	166	Ernest Palmer	'53 Willys	20	---	Running
53	18	53	Bill Cornwall	'54 Olds	18	---	Running
54	22	16	Ted Rambo	Bob Cancro '54 Lincoln	16	---	Running
55	34	22	George Osborne	'53 Hudson	16	---	Gas Line
56	3	40	Tommy Thompson	San Juan Motors '54 Chrysler	15	---	Crash
57	11	99	Fonty Flock	'54 Buick	13	---	Clutch
58	16	39	Bill Barker	'54 Olds	12	---	Heating
59	5	92	Herb Thomas	Thomas '54 Hudson	10	---	Gas Line
60	19	4	Slick Smith	Frank Christian '54 Olds	5	---	Engine
61	52	37	Victor Geisler	'51 Ford	2	---	Not Expl.
62	4	88	Tim Flock	Ernest Woods '54 Olds	39	---	Disq

Time of Race: 1 hour, 47 minutes, 40 seconds
Average Speed: 89.108 mph
Pole Winner: Lee Petty 123.41 mph
Lap Leaders: Herb Thomas 1-2, Lee Petty 3-39.
Cautions: None
Margin of Victory: 9.0 seconds
Attendance: 27,000.

A record crowd of 27,000 was on hand for what was predicted to be the final event staged at the historic Beach and Road Course. Plans for the new Daytona Beach Motor Speedway, as it was named in its planning stages, was to have been completed by the 1955 winter SpeedWeek.

Race No. 3

Sunday Ride for Thomas at Jacksonville

JACKSONVILLE, FL (Mar. 7) -- Herb Thomas of Olivia, NC walked off with his second win of the year in the 100-mile Grand National race at Jacksonville's Speedway Park. It was the 30th triumph for Thomas, putting him 13 ahead of his nearest challenger, Tim Flock, who quit the NASCAR circuit two weeks earlier.

Grand National Race No. 3
200 Laps at Speedway Park
Jacksonville, FL
100 Miles on Half-mile Dirt Track
March 7, 1954

Fin	St	No.	Driver	Team / Car	Laps	Money	Status
1	2	92	Herb Thomas	Thomas '53 Hudson	200	$1,000	Running
2	5	14	Fonty Flock	Frank Christian '53 Hudson	198	650	Running
3	21	42	Lee Petty	Petty Engineering '54 Dodge	197	450	Running
4	8	82	Joe Eubanks	Phil Oates '51 Hudson	197	350	Running
5	3	87	Buck Baker	Griffin Motors '53 Olds 88	194	300	Running
6	9	86	Don Oldenberg	Oldenberg '54 Mercury	194	250	Running
7	6	23	Al Keller	George Miller '54 Hudson	191	200	Running
8	22	181	Tommy Elliott	Millard Wright '51 Plymouth	182	150	Running
9	20	6	Ralph Liguori	Liguori '54 Dodge	179	100	Running
10	14	4	Tommy Moon	'54 Hudson	179	100	Running
11	23	147	Bill Irvin	'51 Plymouth	177	25	Running
12	13	78	Elbert Allen	'53 Olds	173	25	Running
13	1	44	Curtis Turner	Elmer Brooks '52 Olds	162	25	
14	24	114	Parks Surrat	R. Spearman '51 Plymouth	158	25	
15	18	28	Eddie Skinner	Frank Dodge '53 Olds	153	25	
16	4	51	Gober Sosebee	Cherokee Garage '54 Olds	150	25	
17	10	58	Johnny Patterson	H.B. Ranier '53 Hudson	126	25	
18	17	1	Elton Hildreth	Hildreth Motors '54 Nash	111	25	
19	12	43	Bob Welborn	Dave Quate '53 Dodge	76	25	
20	16	101	Bucky Sager	'53 Studebaker	57	25	
21	19	126	Dave Terrell	Terrell '54 Dodge	54	---	
22	15	21	Laird Bruner	Garmen Amica '53 Olds	20	---	Crash
23	7	3	Dick Rathmann	John Ditz '54 Hudson	13	---	Engine
24	11	80	Jim Paschal	George Hutchens '54 Dodge	5	---	

Time of Race: 1 hour, 46 minutes, 16 seconds
Average Speed: 56.461 mph
Pole Winner: Curtis Turner - 63.581 mph
Lap Leaders: Herb Thomas 1-31, Fonty Flock 32-46, Lee Petty 47-74, Thomas 75-200.
Cautions: Margin of Victory: 2 laps plus   Attendance: 10,000

Thomas took the lead in the opening lap from pole sitter Curtis Turner and led all but 43 laps of the half-mile clay oval. Fonty Flock, who led for 15 laps, wound up second, two laps behind the fleet Thomas. Lee Petty, who was in front for 28 laps, wound up third and held on to his Grand National point lead. Fourth place went to Joe Eubanks, and Buck Baker was fifth.

A jam-packed audience of 10,000 was on hand in warm, sunny weather to watch Thomas complete the 200 laps at an average speed of 56.461 mph.

Turner, who never got untracked, eventually finished 13th. Dick Rathmann, Gober Sosebee and Jim Paschal, all early threats, failed to finish.

Curtis Turner and Herb Thomas share the front row on pace lap at Jacksonville.

Race No. 4

Three-car Blanket Finish At Lakewood - But Who Won?

ATLANTA, GA (Mar. 21) -- Herb Thomas, who nosed out Buck Baker and Dick Rathmann in a three-car blanket finish, watched as NASCAR officials dropped him to fourth place. He then rejoiced when NASCAR put him back on top of the final rundown following one of the most peculiar incidents in Grand National history.

A crowd of 20,000 was on its collective feet and cheered Thomas' single car length win over Baker and Rathmann in the 100-mile contest on Atlanta's Lakewood Speedway. After the race, supervisor Johnny Bruner penalized Thomas one full lap for not falling in at the rear of the field after making a yellow flag pit stop. Bruner's decision placed Baker on top.

A few hours after the decision had been handed down, it was brought to the attention of the NASCAR brass that Baker, too, had pitted and not fallen in at the rear. NASCAR then penalized Baker one lap. Third place finisher Rathmann was not elevated to the winner's pedestal; he was docked a lap because his crew allegedly put fuel in his gas tank when the car was still partially on the racing surface. Fifth place finisher Fonty Flock was also dropped a lap when his crew wiped some mud off his windshield. Well now! This

Grand National Race No. 4
100 Laps at Lakewood Speedway
Atlanta, GA
100 Miles on 1-mile Dirt Track
March 21, 1954

Fin	St	No.	Driver	Team / Car	Laps	Money	Status
1	1	92	Herb Thomas	Thomas '53 Hudson	100	$1,000	Running
2		87	Buck Baker	Griffin Motors '53 Olds 88	100	650	Running
3		3	Dick Rathmann	John Ditz '54 Hudson Hornet	100	450	Running
4		51	Gober Sosebee	Cherokee Garage '54 Olds	99	350	Running
5		99	Fonty Flock	'53 Hudson Hornet	99	300	Running
6		42	Lee Petty	Petty Engineering '54 Dodge	99	250	Running
7		14	Curtis Turner	Frank Christian '54 Olds	99	200	Running
8		82	Joe Eubanks	Phil Oates '51 Hudson	98	150	Running
9		144	C.H. Dingler	'52 Hudson Hornet	96	100	Running
10		2	Bill Blair	Blair '52 Hudson Hornet	96	100	Running
11		61	Jimmie Lewallen	'53 Olds	95	25	
12		21	Laird Bruner	Garmen Amica '53 Olds	95	25	
13		6	Ralph Liguori	Liguori '54 Dodge	94	25	
14		78	Jerry Wimbish	'53 Olds	92	25	
15		112	Floyd Curtis	'51 Hudson	91	25	
16		X	Jim Clarke	'53 Olds	90	25	
17		126	Dave Terrell	Terrell '54 Dodge	89	25	
18		86	Don Oldenberg	Oldenberg '54 Mercury	89	25	
19		80	Jim Paschal	George Hutchens '54 Dodge	88	25	
20		48	Otis Martin	'54 Chrysler	87	25	
21		43	Bill Irvin	Dave Quate '53 Dodge	86	---	
22		25	Fireball Roberts	Leland Colvin '53 Olds	85	---	
23		17	Joe H. Martin	'51 Ford	85	---	
24		122	Jack Smith	Smith '54 Olds	69	---	
25		23	Al Keller	George Miller '54 Hudson	49	---	
26		77	Stan Kross	'54 Hudson	---	---	Crash
27		9	Bill Harrison	'52 Hudson Hornet	---	---	Crash
28		44	Harold Nash	'52 Olds	---	---	
29		28	Eddie Skinner	Frank Dodge '53 Olds	---	---	
30		1	Elton Hildreth	Hildreth Motors '53 Nash	---	---	
31		88	Bob Flock	Ernest Woods '54 Olds	---	---	
32		26	Ted Rambo	Bob Cancro '53 Lincoln	---	---	
33		13	Emory Lewis	Ernest Woods '53 Olds	---	---	
34		41	Dick Garlington	Frank Christian '51 Olds	11	---	Crash

Time of Race: 1 hour, 39 minutes, 11 seconds
Average Speed: 60.494 mph
Pole Winner: Herb Thomas - 75.514 mph
Lap Leaders: - - - - - - - - - - - - - - - Herb Thomas   -100.
Caution Flags: 2   Margin of Victory: 1 car length   Attendance: 20,000
* Herb Thomas was flagged winner, then penalized one lap. Buck Baker was awarded victory, then he, too, was docked a lap. Victory was given back to Thomas with all top three finishers completing 100 laps.

would make Gober Sosebee, the fourth place finisher, the winner. The screaming and hollering was furious.

NASCAR officials held an impromptu conference. They made the only decision reasonable men could have made - cancel all the penalties. The race stood as the cars finished the race. Thomas, the winner, with Baker, Rathmann, Sosebee and Flock, second through fifth.

Richard Garlington flipped his Olds four times in the 11th lap and was taken to Crawford-Long Hospital unconscious. Stan Kross and Bill Harrison walked away from a violent crash at the mid-point of the race.

Bob Flock took over the Ernest Woods Olds which hs brother Tim had vacated, but he fell out early and wound up 31st in the field of 34.

Baker, driving the No. 87 Oldsmobile, took the point lead by an eleven point margin over Lee Petty, who finished sixth.

Donald Thomas ran a strong 4th at Savannah, GA in the John Ditz-owned Hudson.

Race No. 5

Keller Cuts Field at Oglethorpe; Gets First Win

SAVANNAH, GA (Mar. 28) -- Al Keller of Buffalo wheeled his George Miller Hudson to his first career Grand National victory in the 100-mile event at Oglethorpe Speedway Park. It was the first time NASCAR's premier stock car racing series had made a stop at the half-mile dirt track on the outskirts of Savannah.

Buck Baker finished second to retain his Grand National point lead. Gober Sosebee came in third and Donald Thomas, getting his first assignment in the highly regarded #3 John Ditz Hudson, finished a respectable fourth. Dick Rathmann, regular chauffer for the #3, was in California for a same-day NASCAR event. Fifth place went to Joe Eubanks.

Herb Thomas started on the pole and had fourth place locked up until he broke a right rear hub with three laps go to. The incident knocked him down to tenth in the final order.

Fonty Flock ran with the leaders until transmission problems during a routine pit stop 30 laps from home knocked him out of action. After the race, Flock would announce that he was quitting the NASCAR circuit to join the SAFE (Society of Autosport and Fellowship Education) tour. Flock admitted he was peeved at NASCAR during a recent race at Atlanta when he was penalized for having mud wiped off his windshield. His brother Tim retired from racing after

Grand National Race No. 5
200 Laps at Oglethorpe Speedway Savannah, GA
100 Miles on Half-mile Dirt Track
March 28, 1954

Fin	St	No.	Driver	Team / Car	Laps	Money	Status
1	3	23	Al Keller	George Miller '54 Hudson	200	$1,000	Running
2		87	Buck Baker	Griffin Motors '53 Olds 88	198	650	Running
3	8	51	Gober Sosebee	Cherokee Garage '54 Olds	194	450	Running
4	2	3	Donald Thomas	John Ditz '54 Hudson	189	350	Running
5	5	82	Joe Eubanks	Phil Oates '51 Hudson	188	300	Running
6		6	Ralph Liguori	Liguori '54 Dodge	184	250	Running
7		80	Jim Paschal	George Hutchens '54 Dodge	181	200	Runing
8		181	Tommy Elliott	Millard Wright '52 Plymouth	179	150	Running
9	4	28	Eddie Skinner	Eagle Club Casino '53 Olds	176	100	Running
10	1	92	Herb Thomas	Thomas '53 Hudson	175	100	RR Hub
11		14	Fonty Flock	Frank Christian '53 Hudson	170	25	Trans.
12	10	88	Bob Flock	Ernest Woods '54 Olds	167	25	Running
13	6	13	Emory Lewis	Ernest Woods '53 Olds	139	25	Clutch
14		16	Ted Rambo	Bob Cancro '54 Lincoln	137	25	RF Hub
15		126	Dave Terrell	Terrell '54 Dodge	137	25	Running
16		93	Ted Chamberlain	Chamberlain '51 Plymouth	114	25	RR Hub
17		43	Bill Irvin	Dave Quate '53 Dodge	109	25	Rear End
18		24	Jimmie Lewallen	J.O. Goode '50 Plymouth	36	25	Bearing
19	12	122	Jack Smith	Smith '54 Olds	34	25	Heating
20		44	Bob Welborn	Petty Engineering '51 Plym	26	25	Radiator
21		162	Artie Mitchell	'51 Olds	9	---	Flagged

Time of Race: 1 hour, 40 minutes, 18 seconds
Average Speed: 59.820 mph
Pole Winner: Herb Thomas - 63.202 mph
Lap Leaders:- - - - - - - - - Al Keller -200.
Cautions: Margin of Victory: 2 laps plus   Attendance:

NASCAR disqualified his car after an apparent Daytona victory.

Lee Petty, second in the Grand National point standings, took his Dodge out west for a same day race.

Bill Weiman lost a wheel and flipped his Olds in the 20th lap, but he was not seriously injured.

Rathmann averaged 50.692 mph to become the first "last to first" winner in NASCAR Grand National History.

Marvin Panch broadslides his Dodge at Oakland. The half-mile track had a layer of dirt spread just inside the high banked paved turns.

Race No. 6

Last to First - Rathmann Spectacular at Oakland

OAKLAND, CA (Mar. 28) -- Dick Rathmann, having to start at the rear of the field, charged through the pack and won the 125-mile event at the Oakland Speedway. It was the 11th career win for Rathmann, but the first on his native west coast.

Rathmann and his Erick Erickson team did not arrive at the half-mile dirt track until qualifications had ended. He was forced to start in scratch position in the 26 car field. He snaked his way through the traffic as Hershel McGriff and Marvin Panch led the early stages. Rathmann knifed his Hudson Hornet into the lead in the 43rd lap and led the rest of the way.

Panch finished second, one lap behind. Third place went to John Soares, Clyde Palmer was fourth and Lloyd Dane fifth. McGriff wound up 20th after a tie rod snapped on his Oldsmobile.

Panch thrilled the crowd of 8,500 with his electrifying broadsliding off the corners.

Grand National Race No. 6
250 Laps at Oakland Speedway
Oakland, CA
125 Miles on Half-mile Paved & Dirt Track
March 28, 1954

Fin	St	No.	Driver	Team / Car	Laps	Money	Status
1	26	3	Dick Rathmann	Erick Erickson '52 Hudson	250	$1,000	Running
2	5	98	Marvin Panch	Beryl Jackson '54 Dodge	249	650	Running
3	3	4	John Soares	Charles Vance '54 Dodge	247	450	Running
4	11	1	Clyde Palmer	'51 Mercury	238	350	Running
5	9	18	Lloyd Dane	Dane '50 Olds	234	300	Running
6	2	42	Lee Petty	Petty Engineering '54 Dodge	232	250	Running
7	10	8	Sam Hawks	'53 Dodge	230	200	Running
8	19	24	Bob Havenmann	'54 Ford 6	228	150	Running
9	18	7	Jim Heath	'54 Ford 6	226	100	Running
10	20	90	Jim Cook	'50 Ford	226	100	Running
11	4	12	Ben Gregory	'53 Olds	222	25	Tie Rod
12	8	99	Joe Valente	Valente '50 Olds	220	25	Tie Rod
13	23	51	Rick Henderson	'51 Chevrolet	217	25	Running
14	12	84	Bob Caswell	Lou Mangini '52 Plymouth	210	25	Running
15	17	15	Cliff Roberts	'50 Plymouth	194	25	Running
16	16	33	Bill Stammer	'53 Pontiac	190	25	Running
17	24	44	H.R. Kahl	'52 Plymouth	174	25	Running
18	25	11	Dick Carter	'51 Dodge	171	25	Running
19	14	48	Paul Phipps	'51 Mercury	167	25	Running
20	1	9	Hershel McGriff	'54 Olds	129	25	Tie Rod
21	7	21	Bill Amick	Carmen Amica '54 Olds	124	---	Tie Rod
22	21	23	Richard Brown	'52 Olds	118	---	Tie Rod
23	23	21x	Bill Williams	'50 Plymouth	113	---	Running
24	13	88	Woody Brown	Joe Mangini '50 Olds	52	---	Tie Rod
25	6	38	Art Watts	'53 Dodge	52	---	Tie Rod
26	15	14	Bill Weiman	'51 Olds	20	---	Crash

Time of Race: 2 hours, 27 minutes, 57 seconds
Average Speed: 50.692 mph
Pole Winner: Hershel McGriff - 55.624 mph
Lap Leaders: - - - - - - - - - Dick Rathmann 143-250.
Cautions: Margin of Victory: 1 lap plus   Attendance: 8,500

Bill Weiman flipped his Oldsmobile in 20th lap at Oakland after losing a right rear tire.

Race No. 7

Rathmann Scores on Three Wheels at N.Wilkesboro

N. WILKESBORO, NC (Apr. 4) -- Dick Rathmann scored his second straight victory despite popping a tire with two laps remaining in the 100-miler at North Wilkesboro Speedway. It was the 12th career win for Rathmann, but the first for car owner John Ditz.

Rather than pitting to get new rubber on his Hudson, Rathmann continued to drive the final two laps on the rim. He took the checkered flag just 20 seconds in front of charging runner-up Herb Thomas. Joe Eubanks finished third, Curtis Turner was fourth and Lee Petty fifth. Petty's top five finish coupled with Buck Baker's 15th place effort, put Petty on top of the point standings by 38 points.

Gober Sosebee, the 'Wild Injun' out of Atlanta, led the first 94 laps from the pole position. Rathmann passed Sosebee for first place in the 95th lap, but could only hold on to the lead for two laps. Sosebee went back in front until Rathmann muscled his way into the lead for good on lap 115.

Sosebee was running second when a spindle broke on his Oldsmobile and put him out after 152 laps.

Gober Sosebee's Oldsmobile limps down front chute at North Wilkesboro with a broken spindle.

A crowd of 5,500 braved a chilling blast of arctic air under cloudy skies to watch Rathmann average 68.545 mph for the 160 lap event.

Grand National Race No. 7
160 Laps at N. Wilkesboro Speedway
North Wilkesboro, NC
100 Miles on .625-mile Dirt Track
April 4, 1954

Fin	St	No.	Driver	Team / Car	Laps	Money	Status
1		3	Dick Rathmann	John Ditz '54 Hudson	160	$1,000	Running
2		92	Herb Thomas	Thomas '54 Hudson	160	650	Running
3		82	Joe Eubanks	Phil Oates '51 Hudson	160	450	Running
4		14	Curtis Turner	Frank Christian '52 Olds 88	158	350	Running
5		42	Lee Petty	PettyEngineering '54 Dodge	156	300	Running
6		6	Ralph Liguori	Liguori '54 Dodge	156	250	Running
7		23	Al Keller	George Miller '54 Hudson	155	200	Running
8		34	Andy Winfree	'50 Plymouth	155	150	Running
9		80	Jim Paschal	George Hutchens '54 Dodge	155	100	Running
10		24	Jimmie Lewallen	J.O. Goode '50 Plymouth	154	100	Running
11		44	Bob Welborn	Petty Engineering '51 Plym	154	25	Running
12	1	51	Gober Sosebee	Cherokee Garage '54 Olds	152	25	Spindle
13		71	Fred Dove	Dove '54 Chevrolet	149	25	Running
14		43	Bill Irvin	Dave Quate '53 Dodge	149	25	Running
15		87	Buck Baker	Griffin Motors '53 Olds 88	142	25	Running
16		28	Eddie Skinner	Frank Dodge '53 Olds	139	25	Running
17		58	Bud Harless	H.B. Ranier '53 Hudson	129	25	Crash
18		75	Ralph Dutton	'53 Dodge	70	25	Wheel
19		1	Elton Hildreth	Hildreth Motors '53 Nash	58	25	Hose
20		16	Ted Rambo	Bob Cancro '54 Lincoln	46	25	Crash
21		108	Arden Mounts	Mounts '51 Hudson	44	25	Wheel
22		126	Dave Terrell	Terrell '54 Dodge	31	---	Bearing
23		77	Stan Kross	'54 Hudson	26	---	Piston
24		100	Blackie Pitt	Gary Drake '50 Plymouth	12	---	Wheel

Time of Race: 1 hour, 27 minutes, 32 seconds
Average Speed: 68.545 mph
Pole Winner: Gober Sosebee - 78.698 mph
Lap Leaders: Gober Sosebee 1-94, Dick Rathmann 95-96, Sosebee 97-114,
    Rathmann 115-160.
Cautions: Margin of Victory: 20 seconds   Attendance: 5,500

Race No. 8

Thomas Brothers 1-2 In Hillsboro Thriller

HILLSBORO, NC (Apr. 18) -- Herb Thomas ducked under his brother Donald in the 66th lap and held on to win by a single car length in the 100 mile Grand National event at Orange Speedway. It was the fourth win of the year for the Olivia, NC throttle stomper and his second victory of 1954 by a car length margin.

Buck Baker finished in third place, Dick Rathmann

Gober Sosebee and Buck Baker on the front row at Hillsboro.

was fourth and Curtis Turner fifth. Lee Petty finished sixth and clung to a narrow 14-point lead over Baker in the Grand National point standings.

Baker led the first 12 laps in his Oldsmobile. Donald Thomas, bidding for his second career win, pushed his Hudson into the lead in the 13th lap and built up a slight margin in the next 50 go-rounds.

Herb had moved into second place by the mid-point in the 100 lapper. On lap 65, Emory Lewis flipped his Oldsmobile directly in front of leader Donald Thomas. Donald took quick evasive action and steered around the rolling Lewis. Herb, riding several car lengths behind the mishap, was able to digest the situation. He nosed his Hudson to the bottom of the track and passed his brother in the process.

The two Thomas brothers ran bumper-to-bumper for the remainder of the race.

There was another brother act in the race. Bud Harless, Police Chief in Gilbert WV, and his brother Marshall finished 15th and 20th respectively.

Herb Thomas averaged 77.386 mph for his 32nd career Grand National victory.

Herb and Donald Thomas share in the victory celebration at Orange Speedway. The talented brothers finished 1-2.

Grand National Race No. 8
100 Laps at Orange Speedway
Hillsboro, NC
100 Miles on 1-mile Dirt Track
April 18, 1954

Fin	St	No.	Driver	Team / Car	Laps	Money	Status9
1	4	92	Herb Thomas	Thomas '54 Hudson	100	$1,000	Running
2		31	Donald Thomas	John Ditz '53 Hudson Hornet	100	650	Running
3	1	88	Buck Baker	Ernest Woods '54 Olds	100	450	Running
4	5	3	Dick Rathmann	John Ditz '54 Hudson	100	350	Running
5		14	Curtis Turner	Frank Christian '54 Olds	99	300	Running
6		42	Lee Petty	PettyEngineering '54 Dodge	98	250	Running
7	3	82	Joe Eubanks	Phil Oates '51 Hudson	97	200	Running
8		16	Ted Rambo	Bob Cancro '54 Lincoln	97	150	Running
9		21	Laird Bruner	Garmen Amica '53 Olds	96	100	Running
10		24	Ray Duhigg	J.O. Goode '50 Plymouth	95	100	Running
11		6	Ralph Liguori	Liguori '54 Dodge	94	25	Running
12		143	Andy Winfree	'50 Plymouth	92	25	Running
13		108	Arden Mounts	Mounts '51 Hudson Hornet	91	25	Running
14		100	Blackie Pitt	Gary Drake '49 Plymouth	90	25	Running
15		8	Bud Harless	H.B. Ranier '53 Hudson	90	25	Running
16		47	Harvey Eakin	Eakin '53 Nash	89	25	Running
17		28	Eddie Skinner	Frank Dodge '53 Olds	88	25	Running
18		78	Elbert Allen	'53 Olds	86	25	Running
19		1	Elton Hildreth	Hildreth Motors '53 Nash	86	25	Running
20		10	Marshall Harless	'49 Ford	82	25	Running
21		22	Perk Brown	R.G. Shelton '51 Hudson	77	25	Running
22		71	Fred Dove	Dove '54 Chevrolet	64	---	Heating
23		13	Emory Lewis	Ernest Woods '53 Olds	61	---	Crash
24		87	Jim Paschal	Griffin Motors '53 Olds	37	---	Oil Pan
25		61	Jimmie Lewallen	'53 Olds	31	---	Spring
26	2	51	Gober Sosebee	Cherokee Garage '54 Olds	21	---	Piston
27		43	Bob Welborn	Dave Quate '53 Dodge	17	---	Gasket
28		126	Dave Terrell	Terrell '54 Dodge	8	---	Hub

Time of Race: 1 hour, 17 minutes, 32 seconds
Average Speed: 77.386 mph
Pole Winner: Buck Baker - 86.767 mph
Lap Leaders: Buck Baker 1-12, Donald Thomas 13-65, Herb Thomas 66-100.
Cautions: 1   Margin of Victory: 1 car length   Attendance: 5,700

Race No. 9

Sosebee Wins Disputed Macon Affair

MACON, GA (Apr. 25) -- Gober Sosebee of Atlanta was declared the winner of the 100-mile Grand National race at Central City Speedway following a scoring dispute.

Dick Rathmann's Hudson was flagged in first place in the 200 lap contest on the half-mile dirt track. Sosebee crossed the finish line six seconds behind Rathmann, but the former moonshining pioneer claimed he was nearly a lap ahead of Rathmann at the time.

Gober Sosebee won at Macon.

NASCAR officials studied the score cards overnight. On Monday morning the word from the Daytona Beach headquarters was that Sosebee had won his second career Grand National race.

Rathmann got credit for finishing second. Jim Paschal was third, a lap behind the leaders. Al Keller finished fourth and Curtis Turner was fifth.

Lee Petty wound up ninth and led the standings by just eight points over Buck Baker, who finished eighth.

Sosebee averged 55.410 mph in his Oldsmobile. He had taken the lead from Keller with 32 laps remaining and led the rest of the way. The lead changed hands six times among four different drivers.

Twenty-two cars started the 100 miler and 19 were on the track at the end.

The disputed finish was the third time in nine 1954 races that NASCAR officials have dealt with controversial overtones.

Matt Gowan's Plymouth was badly crunched in Langhorne turnover.

ten races of the 1954 NASCAR Grand National season.

Thomas was a lap ahead of the field when the checkered flag fell. Al Keller finished a strong second, Dick Rathmann was third and Joe Eubanks was fourth.

Grand National Race No. 9
200 Laps at Central City Speedway
Macon, GA
100 Miles on Half-mile Dirt Track
April 25, 1954

Fin	St	No.	Driver	Team / Car	Laps	Money	Status
1	7	51	Gober Sosebee	Cherokee Garage '54 Olds	200	$1,000	Running
2	1	3	Dick Rathmann	John Ditz '54 Hudson	200	650	Running
3	3	87	Jim Paschal	Griffin Motors '53 Olds	199	450	Running
4	6	23	Al Keller	George Miller '54 Hudson	199	350	Running
5	8	14	Curtis Turner	Frank Christian '53 Olds	199	300	Running
6	4	31	Donald Thomas	John Ditz '53 Hudson	197	250	Running
7	20	44	Bob Welborn	PettyEngineering '51 Plym	197	200	Running
8	2	88	Buck Baker	Ernest Woods '54 Olds	195	150	Running
9	12	42	Lee Petty	PettyEngineering '54 Dodge	195	100	Running
10	9	6	Ralph Liguori	Liguori '54 Dodge	193	100	Running
11	5	82	Joe Eubanks	Phil Oates '51 Hudson	192	25	Running
12	13	141	Bill Blair	John Eanes '53 Hudson	191	25	Running
13	14	98	Jim Clarke	'53 Olds	189	25	Running
14	19	52	Walt Flinchum	'49 Plymouth	185	25	Running
15	18	144	C.H. Dingler	'53 Hudson	179	25	Running
16	15	78	Elbert Allen	'53 Olds	179	25	Running
17	16	28	Eddie Skinner	Frank Dodge '53 Olds	176	25	Running
18	10	92	Herb Thomas	Thomas '54 Hudson	145	25	Clutch
19	22	304	Wallace Simpson	'53 Olds	143	25	Running
20	21	100	Blackie Pitt	Gary Drake '49 Plymouth	102	25	Running
21	17	77	Stan Kross	'54 Hudson	56	---	Spindle
22	11	122	Jack Smith	Smith '54 Olds	34	---	Piston

Time of Race: 1 hour, 48 minutes, 17 seconds
Average Speed: 55.410 mph
Pole Winner: Dick Rathmann - 57.859 mph
Lap Leaders: Dick Rathmann 1-4, Buck Baker 5-32, Gober Sosebee 33-58, Al Keller 59-100, Rathmann 101-115, Keller 116-168, Sosebee 169-200.
Cautions: Margin of Victory: Attendance:

Race No. 10

Herb Thomas Still Batting .500; Wins Langhorne

LANGHORNE, PA (May 2) -- Herb Thomas, leading a Hudson Hornet sweep, finished first in the 150-miler at Langhorne and scored his fifth win in the first

Grand National Race No. 10
150 Laps at Langhorne Speedway
Langhorne, PA
150 Miles on 1-mile Dirt Track
May 2, 1954

Fin	St	No.	Driver	Team / Car	Laps	Money	Status
1	2	92	Herb Thomas	Thomas '54 Hudson	150	$1,685	Running
2		23	Al Keller	George Miller '54 Hudson	149	810	Running
3		3	Dick Rathmann	John Ditz '54 Hudson	149	610	Running
4		82	Joe Eubanks	Phil Oates '51 Hudson	133	510	Running
5		45	Paul Pettitt	Pettitt '53 Hudson Hornet	132	325	Running
6	3	87	Buck Baker	Griffin Motors '53 Olds	132	225	Running
7		43	Whitey Brainard	'49 Ford	130	150	Running
8		100	Blackie Pitt	Gary Drake '49 Plymouth	130	125	Running
9	1	42	Lee Petty	San Juan Motors '54 Chrysler	121	380	Running
10		84	Gary Mathieson	'50 Ford	114	100	Running
11		177	Bobby Courtwright	'50 Ford	107	25	Running
12		21	Laird Bruner	Garmen Amica '53 Olds	102	25	Running
13		13	Wimpy Ervin	'51 Henry J	100	25	Heating
14		98	Jim Clarke	'53 Olds	81	25	Running
15		2	Bill Blair	Blair '53 Hudson Hornet	68	25	Gasket
16		1	Elton Hildreth	Hildreth '54 Nash	65	25	Piston
17		99	Matt Gowen	Gowen's Auto '53 Plymouth	53	25	Crash
18		120	Russ Hepler	Walt Chapman '53 Hudson	43	25	Bearings
19		106	Bill Chevalier	'51 Ford	33	25	Head
20		47	Harvey Eakin	Eakin '53 Nash	30	25	Gasket
21		64	Jack Harrison	'54 Olds	19	25	Heating
22		77	Stan Kross	'54 Hudson	15	25	Bearings
23		51	Gober Sosebee	Cherokee Garage '54 Olds	14	25	Clutch
24		126	Dave Terrell	Terrell '54 Dodge	10	25	Bearings
25		28	Eddie Skinner	Frank Dodge '53 Olds	0	25	DNS

Time of Race: 2 hours, 0 minutes, 11.18 seconds
Average Speed: 74.883 mph
Pole Winner: Lee Petty - 87.217 mph
Lap Leaders: Lee Petty 1-75, Herb Thomas 76-150.
Cautions: 1   Margin of Victory: 1 lap plus   Attendance: 19,000

Packed grandstand and crowded infield occupants watch the start of 150-miler at Langhorne Speedway.

Fifth place went to Paul Pettitt. Hudson Hornets swept the first five places.

Buck Baker finished sixth and took the point lead from Lee Petty, who wound up ninth. Baker left Langhorne with a 28 point lead in the standings.

Petty led the first 75 laps, but overheating problems on his Chrysler knocked him 29 laps off the pace. Thomas took the lead for good in the 76th lap when Petty went to the pits.

Dick Rathmann, who was pressuring Thomas in the late stages, fell from contention when he had to make an unscheduled pit stop to replace a flat tire. The pit stop took 76 seconds and dropped him a lap behind Thomas.

Matt Gowen tossed his Plymouth in a series of flips near the one-third mark in the race. The car was heavily damaged, but Gowen was unhurt.

A crowd of 19,000 watched Thomas average 74.883 mph for his second win on the one-mile circular track.

Race No. 11

Rathmann Wrecks; Baker First at Wilson

WILSON, NC (May 9) -- Buck Baker took the lead when a blown tire sent leader Dick Rathmann into the wall with 30 laps remaining and went on to score his first win of the year in the 100-mile Grand National race at Wilson Speedway. It was Baker's first win of the season and the sixth of his career.

Al Keller finished second for the second straight race. Third place went to a surprising Ralph Liguori, who brought his Dodge from 13th starting position to crowd the front runners. Lee Petty finished fourth and pole sitter Jim Paschal was fifth.

Baker was able to stretch his point lead to 54 points over Petty.

Baker and Herb Thomas dueled for the lead through the first half of the race. Rathmann took over on lap 106 and was pulling away when his mishap occurred. He was credited with 13th in the final rundown.

A broken spindle put Thomas' Smokey Yunick-prepared Hudson out of action.

Baker, who started fifth, averaged 52.279 mph on the half-mile dirt track.

Buck Baker got first '53 victory at Wilson.

Grand National Race No. 11
200 Laps at Wilson Speedway
Wilson, NC
100 Miles on Half-mile Dirt Track
May 9, 1954

Fin	St	No.	Driver	Team / Car	Laps	Money	Status
1	5	88	Buck Baker	Ernest Woods '54 Olds	200	$1,000	Running
2	2	23	Al Keller	George Miller '54 Hudson	199	650	Running
3	13	6	Ralph Liguori	Liguori '53 Dodge	199	450	Running
4	8	42	Lee Petty	Petty Eng '54 Dodge	197	350	Running
5	1	87	Jim Paschal	Griffin Motors '53 Olds	196	300	Running
6	9	2	Bill Blair	Blair '53 Hudson Hornet	196	250	Running
7	12	12	Joe Weatherly	Buckshot Morris '53 Olds	196	200	Running
8	11	13	Emory Lewis	Ernest Woods '53 Olds	184	150	Running
9	15	19	Clyde Minter	Ken Pace '49 Mercury	178	100	Running
10	3	92	Herb Thomas	Thomas '54 Hudson	178	100	Spindle
11	7	98	Jim Clarke	'53 Olds	175	25	Running
12	14	126	Dave Terrell	Terrell '54 Dodge	174	25	Running
13	4	3	Dick Rathmann	John Ditz '54 Hudson	170	25	Crash
14	10	31	Donald Thomas	John Ditz '53 Hudson	130	25	Rear End
15	6	82	Joe Eubanks	Phil Oates '51 Hudson	65	25	Spindle
16	16	100	Blackie Pitt	Gary Drake '49 Plymouth	23	25	Spindle

Time of Race: 1 hour, 54 minutes, 46 seconds
Average Speed: 52.279 mph
Pole Winner: Jim Paschal - 55.469 mph
Lap Leaders: Buck Baker 1-13, Herb Thomas 14-31, Baker 32-105, Dick Rathmann 106-170, Baker 171-200.
Cautions: Margin of Victory: 1 lap plus   Attendance:

Race No. 12

Paschal Leads All But 7 Laps in Martinsville Triumph

MARTINSVILLE, VA (May 16) -- Jim Paschal drove his Griffin Motors Oldsmobile around Bill Blair in the eighth lap and led the rest of the way to win the 100-mile Grand National race at Martinsville Speedway. It was Paschal's second big league win -- both of them coming on the half-mile dirt track operated by Clay Earles.

Lee Petty finished second and left Martinsville with a 74 point lead over Buck Baker, who crashed with Elton Hildreth in the 132nd lap. Curtis Turner finished third, Al Keller was fourth and Laird Bruner fifth.

Baker accepted the role as driver of the Ernest Woods team and let Paschal drive his own mount. The Woods team encountered a double whammy as both Baker and Joel Million wrecked their cars. Million smashed his Olds in the 22nd lap.

A crowd of 8,500 was on hand despite a damp afternoon in the Virginia mountains. Rain forced officials to conduct a "draw" for starting positions. Ralph Li-

guori drew the pole but never lead the race. The Dodge driver departed after 158 laps with a broken spindle.

Blair led the opening seven laps, but wound up 17th when a spindle knocked his Hudson out of the race.

Paschal averaged 46.153 mph for his first win in the 1954 campaign.

Race No. 13

Rain Shortened Sharon Event Won by Petty

SHARON, PA (May 23) -- Lee Petty took the lead in the 101st lap and was in front when rain terminated the 100-mile Grand National race at Sharon Speedway after 160 of the scheduled 200 laps had been completed. It was Petty's second win of the year.

The triumph moved Petty to an 82 point lead over Buck Baker, who finished second. Dick Rathmann came in third, Joe Eubanks was fourth and Laird Bruner fifth.

Herb Thomas, who has been mired in a recent slump, lost control of his Hudson and plowed through the fence in the 142nd lap. He escaped injury.

Glenn Laughlin of Akron, OH wrecked his Oldsmo-

Grand National Race No. 12
200 Laps at Martinsville Speedway
Martinsville, VA
100 Laps on Half-mile Dirt Track
May 16, 1954

Fin	St	No.	Driver	Team / Car	Laps	Money	Status
1		87	Jim Paschal	Griffin Motors '53 Olds 88	200	$1,000	Running
2		42	Lee Petty	Petty Eng '54 Chrysler	199	650	Running
3		21	Curtis Turner	Garmen Amica '53 Olds 88	198	450	Running
4		23	Al Keller	George Miller '54 Hudson	195	350	Running
5		28	Laird Bruner	Frank Dodge '53 Olds 88	187	300	Running
6		126	Dave Terrell	Terrell '54 Dodge	187	250	Running
7		19	Clyde Minter	Ken Pace '50 Mercury	185	200	Running
8		71	Fred Dove	Dove '54 Chevrolet	185	150	Running
9		92	Herb Thomas	Thomas '54 Hudson	179	100	Running
10		100	Blackie Pitt	Gary Drake '50 Plymouth	176	100	Running
11		3	Dick Rathmann	John Ditz '54 Hudson	174	25	Running
12		30	Perk Brown	'50 Mercury	172	25	Running
13		82	Joe Eubanks	Phil Oates '51 Hudson	171	25	Running
14		108	Arden Mounts	Mounts '52 Hudson Hornet	171	25	Running
15		51	Gober Sosebee	Cherokee Garage '54 Olds 88	166	25	Drv.Shft
16	1	6	Ralph Liguori	Liguori '54 Dodge	158	25	Spindle
17	2	2	Bill Blair	Blair '53 Hudson Hornet	133	25	Spindle
18		88	Buck Baker	Ernest Woods '54 Olds	132	25	Crash
19		1	Elton Hildreth	Hildreth Motors '53 Nash	128	25	Crash
20		31	Donald Thomas	John Ditz '53 Hudson	90	25	Timing
21		52	Walt Flinchum	'50 Plymouth	84	---	Rear End
22		45	Paul Pettitt	Pettitt '52 Hudson Hornet	34	---	Trans.
23		111	Bill O'Dell	'49 Ford	27	---	Heating
24		13	Joel Million	Ernest Woods '53 Olds	22	---	Crash

Time of Race: 2 hour, 10 minutes, .04 seconds
Average Speed: 46.153 mph
Pole Winner: No Time Trials. Ralph Liguori drew No. 1 Starting Position
Lap Leaders: Bill Blair 1-7, Jim Paschal 8-200.
Cautions: 3   Margin of Victory: 1 lap plus   Attendance: 8,500

Grand National Race No. 13
200 Laps at Sharon Speedway
Sharon, PA
100 Miles on Half-mile Dirt Track
May 23, 1954

Fin	St	No.	Driver	Team / Car	Laps	Money	Status
1		42	Lee Petty	Petty Eng '54 Chrysler	160	$1,000	Running
2		87	Buck Baker	Griffin Motors '53 Olds	159	650	Running
3	1	3	Dick Rathmann	John Ditz '54 Hudson	157	450	Running
4		82	Joe Eubanks	Phil Oates '51 Hudson	154	350	Running
5		21	Laird Bruner	Garmen Amica '53 Olds	153	300	Running
6		2	Bill Blair	Blair '53 Hudson Hornet	152	250	Running
7		35	Chuck Garrett	'54 Nash	149	200	Running
8		126	Dave Terrell	Terrell '54 Dodge	145	150	Running
9		93	Ted Chamberlain	Chamberlain '50 Plymouth	142	100	Running
10		92	Herb Thomas	Thomas '53 Hudson	142	100	Crash
11		88	Al Metz	'51 Plymouth	131	25	Running
12		147	Bill Irvin	'51 Plymouth	127	25	Running
13		343	Roland LaRue	'49 Hudson	118	25	Running
14		37	Mike Brown	'51 Packard	114	25	Heating
15		12	John McGinley	Walt Chapman '53 Hudson	109	25	Rear End
16		100	Blackie Pitt	Gary Drake '50 Plymouth	105	25	Engine
17		2-D	Al Bollinger	'49 Ford	103	25	Running
18		79	Jim Ewing	'52 Studebaker	100	25	Spindle
19		120	Russ Hepler	Walt Chapman '53 Hudson	99	25	Steering
20		13	Jim Paschal	Ernest Woods '53 Olds	82	25	Heating
21		29	Glenn Laughlin	'51 Dodge	54	---	Crash
22		137	Dick Stone	'53 Olds	12	---	Radiator

Time of Race: No Time Recorded
Average Speed: None
Pole Winner: Dick Rathmann - 62.090 mph
Lap Leaders: Dick Rathmann 1-46, Buck Baker 47-100, Lee Petty 101-160.
Cautions: Margin of Victory: 1 lap plus   Attendance: 4,000

ile in the 54th lap and was taken to a local hospital for overnight observation.

A crowd of 4,000 was in attendance despite the poor weather. Because of the frequent rain interruptions, no official average speed was recorded.

Rathmann started on the pole and led the first 46 laps. Baker passed Rathmann on lap 47 and led for 54 laps before Petty drove into the lead for good.

Race No. 14

Quick Pit Work Nets Victory For Thomas in Raleigh 250

RALEIGH, NC (May 20) -- Herb Thomas and his Smokey Yunick Hudson team used lightening quick pit stops and motored to a two-lap victory in the second annual 'Raleigh 250' at the half-million dollar Raleigh Speedway. It was Thomas' sixth win of the season and his second superspeedway victory in his career.

There were no caution flags during the 250 lapper on the banked one-mile paved track, which put a premium on pit stop activity. Thomas made two stops en route to the $2,250 pay-off, taking a total of one minute, 49 seconds getting fuel and tires. Runner-up Dick Rathmann's John Ditz squad serviced the #3 Hudson twice, but took three minutes, 45 seconds. Hershel McGriff, who was signed by Frank Christian to take the wheel of his Oldsmobile the rest of the year, came in third. Lee Petty was fourth and Jimmie Lewallen fifth.

Herb Thomas won superspeedway event at Raleigh Speedway.

Smokey Yunick, Herb Thomas' crew chief.

Buck Baker was running on the Rathmann's tail pipe when the engine of his Olds expired with eleven laps remaining. Baker dropped to ninth in the final rundown. It also put him 182 points behind leader Petty in the point standings.

There were seven lead changes among four different drivers as the crowd of 10,500 enjoyed the speed show. Thomas led on three occasions for a total of 204 laps. Rathmann was in front twice for 34 laps, Curtis Turner led once for 10 laps and Baker led once

Grand National Race No. 14
200 Laps at Raleigh Speedway
Raleigh, NC
"Raleigh 250"
250 Miles on 1-mile Paved Track
May 29, 1954

Fin	St	No.	Driver	Team / Car	Laps	Money	Status
1	1	92	Herb Thomas	Thomas '54 Hudson	250	$2,250	Running
2		3	Dick Rathmann	John Ditz '54 Hudson	248	1,175	Running
3		14	Hershel McGriff	Frank Christian '54 Olds	246	800	Running
4		42	Lee Petty	Petty Eng '54 Dodge	244	700	Running
5		80	Jimmie Lewallen	George Hutchens '54 Mercury	241	600	Running
6	16	23	Al Keller	George Miller '54 Hudson	240	525	Running
7		24	Ray Duhigg	J.O. Goode '50 Plymouth	236	450	Running
8		1	Elton Hildreth	Hildreth Motors '51 Nash	235	350	Running
9	2	88	Buck Baker	Ernest Woods '54 Olds	233	250	Engine
10		2	Bill Blair	Blair '54 Hudson	231	200	Running
11		6	Ralph Liguori	Liguori '54 Dodge	230	150	Running
12		61	Slick Smith	'54 Hudson	225	150	Running
13		11	Eddie Riker	'50 Olds	223	100	Running
14		120	Russ Hepler	Walt Chapman '53 Hudson	221	100	Running
15		4	Charlie Cregar	'51' Plymouth	221	100	Running
16		126	Dave Terrell	Terrell '54 Dodge	219	100	Running
17		100	Blackie Pitt	Gary Drake '50 Plymouth	218	100	Running
18		93	Ted Chamberlain	Chamberlain '50 Plymouth	212	100	Running
19		52	Walt Flinchum	'49 Plymouth	195	100	Running
20		25	Fireball Roberts	Leland Colvin '53 Olds	181	100	RFHub
21		13	Joel Million	Ernest Woods '53 Olds	179	50	Running
22	35	44	Curtis Turner	Elmer Brooks '52 Olds	160	50	Drv Shft
23		21	Laird Bruner	Garmen Amica '53 Olds	135	50	Bearing
24		71	Fred Dove	Dove '54 Chevrolet	132	50	Spindle
25		28	Eddie Skinner	Frank Dodge '54 Olds	104	50	Ignition
26		108	Arden Mounts	Comstock '51 Hudson Hornet	90	50	Crash
27		12	Speedy Thompson	Buckshot Morris '53 Olds	86	50	Engine
28		87	Jim Paschal	Griffin Motors '53 Olds	72	50	Brakes
29		31	Donald Thomas	John Ditz '53 Hudson	66	50	Bearings
30		98	Jim Clarke	'53 Olds	62	50	Heating
31		97	Clarence Burch	'54 Willys	58	50	Rear End
32		48	Cliff Wood	'50 Hudson	51	50	Brakes
33		82	Joe Eubanks	Phil Oates '51 Hudson	23	50	Piston
34		103	Clyde Minter	'51 Mercury	15	50	Gasket
35		47	Harvey Eakin	Eakin '53 Nash	5	50	Bearing

Time of Race: 3 hours, 22 minutes, 57 seconds
Average Speed: 73.909 mph
Pole Winner: Herb Thomas - 76.660 mph (2 lap average)
Lap Leaders: Buck Baker 1-2, Herb Thomas 3-112, Curtis Turner 113-122, Dick Rathmann 123-125, H. Thomas 126-167, Rathmann 168-198, H. Thomas 199-250.
Cautions: None   Margin of Victory: 2 laps plus   Attendance: 10,500

Herb Thomas wings his way down Raleigh backstretch.

for 2 laps.

Turner, driving an Oldsmobile owned by Elmer Brooks, started last in the 35-car field, but charged through the pack only to be sidelined by a broken drive shaft after 160 laps.

Thomas' 34th career win came at an average of 73.909 mph.

Race No. 15

Baker Wins Charlotte After Blowing Engine

CHARLOTTE, NC (May 30) -- In spite of blowing his engine coming off the fourth turn in the last lap of the race, Buck Baker drove the Griffin Motors Oldsmobile to victory in the 100 miler at Charlotte Speedway for his second Grand National win of the year. Smoke began to belch from beneath his Olds as he whipped into the home stretch to take the checkered. He managed to beat Lee Petty to the finish line by one second.

Petty, finishing second, managed to keep his lead in the point standings. Joe Eubanks finished third and Russ Hepler, driving Walt Chapman's Hudson, which

has been off the tour for most of the season, finished fourth. Bill Blair nailed down fifth spot.

Baker took the lead from pole sitter Al Keller in the 68th lap and led the remaining 66 laps in the 133-lap race. Keller's Hudson encountered tire problems and struggled to a 16th place finish in the field of 25 cars.

A crowd of 4,000 had to sit through two caution flags, one for 19 laps while water trucks tackled the heavy dust conditions.

Grand National Race No. 15
133 Laps at Charlotte Speedway
Charlotte, NC
100 Miles on .75-mile Dirt Track
May 30, 1954

Fin	St	No.	Driver	Team / Car	Laps	Money	Status
1	2	87	Buck Baker	Griffin Motors '53 Olds 88	133	$1,000	Running
2		42	Lee Petty	Petty Eng '54 Chrysler	133	650	Running
3		82	Joe Eubanks	Phil Oates '51 Hudson	132	450	Running
4		120	Russ Hepler	Walt Chapman '53 Hudson	128	350	Running
5		2	Bill Blair	Blair '53 Hudson Hornet	126	300	Running
6		98	Jim Clarke	'53 Olds	124	250	Running
7		71	Fred Dove	Dove '54 Chevrolet	124	200	Running
8		8	Pop McGinnis	Frank Christian '53 Hudson	123	150	Running
9		126	Dave Terrell	Terrell '54 Dodge	123	100	Running
10		14	Hershel McGriff	Frank Christian '54 Olds	121	100	Engine
11		1	Elton Hildreth	Hildreth Motors '51 Nash	120	25	Running
12		52	Walt Flinchum	John Golabek '51 Plymouth	118	25	Running
13		108	Dick Rathmann	Comstock '53 Hudson	115	25	Running
14		93	Slick Smith	Ted Chamberlain '50 Plym	114	25	Running
15		103	Billy Minter	'51 Mercury	108	25	Running
16	1	23	Al Keller	George Miller '54 Hudson	96	25	Running
17		55	Frank Stutts	'52 Flord	82	25	Heating
18		92	Herb Thomas	Thomas '54 Hudson	75	25	Rear End
19		19	Clyde Minter	Ken Pace '51 Mercury	67	25	Crash
20		3	Arden Mounts	John Ditz '54 Hudson	40	25	Axle
21		51	Gober Sosebee	Cherokee Garage '54 Olds	40	---	Clutch
22		28	Laird Bruner	Frank Dodge '53 Olds	39	---	Coil
23		80	Jimmie Lewallen	George Hutchens '51 Plym	37	---	Vapor Lk
24		11	Eddie Riker	'50 Plymouth	1	---	Radiator
25		6	Ralph Liguori	Liguori '54 Dodge	0	---	Crash

Time of Race: 2 hours, 10 seconds
Average Speed: 49.805 mph
Pole Winner: Al Keller - 68.947 mph
Lap Leaders: Buck Baker 1-42, Al Keller 43-67, Baker 68-133.
Cautions: 2 for 26 laps   Margin of Victory: 1.0 seconds   Attendance: 4,000

Grand National Race No. 16
500 Laps at Carrell Speedway
Gardena, CA
250 Miles on Half-mile Dirt Track
May 30, 1954

Fin	St	No.	Driver	Team / Car	Laps	Money	Status
1	17	4	John Soares	Charles Vance '54 Dodge	496	$1,500	Running
2	4	33	Lloyd Dane	Jim Dane '53 Hudson Hornet	495	800	Running
3	1	39	Danny Letner	Joe Bearscheck '52 Hudson	490	600	Running
4	2	12	Ben Gregory	Coz Cancilla '53 Olds	486	400	Running
5	8	73	George Seeger	Carl Dane '54 Ford	486	350	Running
6	21	66	Erick Erickson	Walt Smith '50 Olds	477	250	Running
7	6	89	Bill West	'51 Hudson	476	200	Running
8	20	16	Tony Nelson	'49 Ford	475	200	Running
9	10	99	Joe Valente	Valente '50 Olds	468	150	Running
10	7	65	Bill Babe	'52 Olds	466	150	Running
11	14	24	Bob Havenmann	'54 Ford	466	125	Running
12	23	52	Eddie Pagan	Pagan '50 Plymouth	459	100	Running
13	16	35	Bill Smith	'51 Hudson	455	100	Running
14	28	82	Bob Turell	'53 Ford	450	100	Running
15	30	45	Bill Galearisi	Galearisi '50 Ford	445	100	Running
16	29	40	Tom Drake	'50 Ford	444	50	Running
17	9	30	Bill Stammer	'53 Pontiac	441	50	Running
18	5	88	Woody Brown	Joe Mangini '50 Olds	428	50	Running
19	24	15	Cliff Roberts	'50 Plymouth	422	25	Running
20	15	6	John Kieper	Kieper '54 Ford	420	25	Running
21	22	80	Arley Scranton	Western Auto Salv '50 Ford	413	25	Running
22	32	93	Bob Rose	'52 Henry J	393	25	Crash
23	19	17	Jerry Keyes	'54 Dodge	338	25	Tie Rod
24	27	41	Ernie Young	Walt Palozi '50 Plymouth	337	25	RF Hub
25	31	90	Ted Lee	'50 Ford	328	25	Fuel Pmp
26	11	50	Jim Cook	'50 Olds	299	---	Rear End
27	3	91	Sam Lamm	Fred Bince '53 Dodge	200	---	Steering
28	12	5	Chuck Meekins	'52 Olds	191	---	Wheel
29	18	48	Allen Heath	McCullock '54 Kaiser	52	---	Fuel Pmp
30	26	44	H.R. Kahl	'52 Plymouth	51	---	Crash
31	25	32	Pat Freeman	'53 Hudson Jet	20	---	Radiator
32	13	28	Bud Diamond	'52 Hudson	11	---	Wheel

* Final Race for Carrell Speedway. Track was torn down on June 1, 1954. This event started cars three abreast.
** Race was scheduled for 500 laps. Due to scoring mix-up, the lead car ran only 496 laps. Error was not discovered until the following day.
Time of Race: 4 hours, 38 minutes, 27 seconds
Average Speed: 53.438 mph
Pole Winner: Danny Letner - 62.849 mph
Lap Leaders: Danny Letner 1-105, Lloyd Dane 106-285, John Soares 286-496.
Cautions: Margin of Victory: 1 lap plus   Attendance: 12,000

Race No. 16

Soares Wins Final Event At Carrell Speedway

GARDENA, CA (May 30) -- John Soares took the lead from Lloyd Dane in the 286th lap and led the rest of the way to win the 500-lap, 250 mile Grand National race at Carrell Speedway. The winner actually covered only 496 laps as individual car scorers had difficulty keeping up with everything for 500 laps on the half-mile dirt track. The event was the swan song for the famous Carrell Speedway, which was slated to be torn down two days later.

Soares started 17th on the grid, but wheeled his Charles Vance Dodge into the winner's circle after Dane and Danny Letner headed the first 285 laps.

A crowd of 12,000 saw only one accident. Bob Rose flipped his Henry J on lap 293 without injury.

The race, run on Memorial Day the same afternoon as the Indianapolis 500, was dubbed the "Poor Man's 500". The 32-car field started three abreast, Indianapolis style.

Soares averaged 53.438 mph as the race lasted over four and a half hours.

Allen Heath, the "Seattle Screwball", drove a Kaiser Manhattan in the race, but fell out early with fuel pump failure and wound up 29th.

Dane finished second, one lap behind the winner. Letner, Ben Gregory and George Seeger rounded out the top five.

### Grand National Race No. 17 200 Laps on Columbia Speedway Columbia, SC 100 Miles on Half-mile Dirt Track June 6, 1954						
Fin	St	No.	Driver	Team / Car	Laps	Money	Status

Fin	St	No.	Driver	Team / Car	Laps	Money	Status
1	10	44	Curtis Turner	Elmer Brooks '52 Olds	200	$1,000	Running
2	3	14	Hershel McGriff	Frank Christian '54 Olds	198	650	Running
3	5	3	Dick Rathmann	John Ditz '54 Hudson	197	450	Running
4	8	12	Speedy Thompson	Buckshot Morris '53 Olds	197	350	Running
5	4	42	Lee Petty	Petty Eng '54 Chrysler	195	300	Running
6	2	92	Herb Thomas	Thomas '54 Hudson	193	250	Crash
7	6	82	Joe Eubanks	Phil Oates '51 Hudson	190	200	Crash
8	1	88	Buck Baker	Ernest Woods '54 Olds	185	150	Running
9		6	Ralph Liguori	Liguori '54 Dodge	183	100	Running
10		19	Clyde Minter	Ken Pace '51 Mercury	174	100	Running
11		100	Blackie Pitt	Gary Drake '49 Plymouth	165	25	Radiator
12		114	Parks Surratt	R. Spearman '51 Plymouth	165	25	Running
13	9	25	Fireball Roberts	Leland Colvin '53 Olds	164	25	Spindle
14	7	28	Eddie Skinner	Frank Dodge '53 Olds	159	25	Running
15	11	126	Dave Terrell	Terrell '54 Dodge	154	25	Wheel
16		21	Laird Bruner	Garmen Amica '53 Olds	151	25	Fuel Tnk
17		71	Fred Dove	Dove '54 Chevrolet	131	25	Rear End
18		51	Gober Sosebee	Cherokee Garage '54 Olds	23	25	Heating

Time of Race: 1 hour, 45 minutes, 47 seconds
Average Speed: 56.719 mph
Pole Winner: Buck Baker - 62.240 mph
Lap Leaders: - - - - - - - - - Curtis Turner -200.
Cautions: Margin of Victory: 2 laps plus   Attendance

Race No. 17

Turner Wins for Car Owner Brooks at Columbia

COLUMBIA, SC (June 6) -- Curtis Turner of Roanoke, VA scampered home first to win the 100-mile Grand National race at Columbia Speedway. It was Turner's 10th career victory on the NASCAR big league trail, but only his second in the last three years.

Turner gave Elmer Brooks, his car owner, his first Grand National triumph. The 30 year-old veteran had begun the season in Frank Christian Oldsmobiles and switched to Brooks at Raleigh a week earlier.

Finishing second, two laps behind Turner was Hershel McGriff, who had landed the Christian mount for the remainder of the 1954 season. Dick Rathmann finished third, Speedy Thompson was fourth and Lee Petty fifth.

Herb Thomas and Joe Eubanks crashed in the final laps and wound up sixth and seventh respectively. Pole winner Buck Baker came in eighth and fell 198 points behind Petty in the Grand National point standings.

Turner became the ninth different winner in the 17 events staged in the 1954 campaign.

Race No. 18

Keller's Jaguar Triumphs in NASCAR's First Road Race

LINDEN, NJ (June 13) -- Al Keller drove Paul Whiteman's Jaguar around Herb Thomas in the 23rd lap and led the rest of the way to win the International 100 on the runways of the Linden Airport. It was the first road race in NASCAR Grand National history.

Joe Eubanks finished second in a Hudson. Buck Baker was third in an Oldsmobile after starting on the

Al Keller, in the #4 Jaguar, en route to victory at Linden Airport, NASCAR's first road race.

pole. Bob Grossman came in fourth and Harry LaVois was fifth, both driving Jaguars.

In a field of 43 automobiles, 21 were foreign cars, the second time NASCAR has permitted the use of anything other than American made family sedans.

Baker led the first ten laps on the twisting, two-mile track. Thomas led for two laps before Baker jumped back in front. Thomas regained the lead in the 14th lap and led for nine laps before Keller's lightweight Jag forged to the lead.

After the race, Keller announced he was quitting the NASCAR tour to join the AAA Championship trail and, ultimately, to get a shot at the Indianapolis 500. He was the third former Grand National winner to quit the NASCAR stock car tour in 1954. Tim and Fonty Flock defected in the early months.

Keller started seventh and won $1,000 for his efforts. He averaged 77.569 mph as four caution flags broke the action.

Grand National Race No. 18
50 Laps at Linden Airport
Linden, NJ
100 Miles on 2-mile Paved Road Course
June 13, 1954

Fin	St	No.	Driver	Team / Car	Laps	Money	Status
1	7	4	Al Keller	Paul Whiteman Jaguar	50	$1,000	Running
2		82	Joe Eubanks	Phil Oates '51 Hudson	50	650	Running
3	1	88	Buck Baker	Ernest Woods '54 Olds 88	49	500	Running
4		32	Bob Grossman	Jaguar	49	400	Running
5		7-A	Harry LaVois	Jaguar	49	275	Running
6		2	Bill Claren	Jaguar	49	275	Running
7		92	Herb Thomas	Thomas '54 Hudson	49	200	Running
8		3	Dick Rathmann	John Ditz '54 Hudson	49	150	Running
9		21	Laird Bruner	Garmen Amica '53 Olds	48	130	Running
10		42	Lee Petty	Petty Eng '54 Dodge	48	120	Running
11		11	Eddie Riker	'49 Olds	48	110	Running
12		121	Earl Beer	Autsin Healy	46	100	
13		27	Phillips Bell	Jaguar	45	75	
14		9	Tom Rivers	MG	45	175	
15		211	Jack Clarke	'50 Plymouth	45	40	
16		201	J. Kilgore	Porsche	45	130	
17		13	Joel Million	Ernest Woods '53 Olds	44	25	
18		1	George Clarke	'51 Hudson	44	25	
19		204	Fred Cole	MG	44	100	
20		17	Tex Brooke	'51 Hudson	43	25	
21		83	Joe Bossard	'50 Plymouth	43	25	
22		93	Ted Chamberlain	Chamberlain '50 Plymouth	42	25	
23		14	Jack Smith	Smith '50 Plymouth	41	25	
24		74	Peck Peckham	'54 Hudson	41	25	
25		40	Arnold Ladd	MG	41	45	
26		12	Ray Laughlin	Jaguar	40	---	
27		126	Dave Terrell	Terrell '54 Dodge	40	---	
28		14	Jack Spearman	Jaguar	39	---	
29		20	Don Johnson	'51 Henry J	39	---	
30		8	Hershel McGriff	Jaguar	37	---	Crash
31		150	Dick Hallock	'53 Hudson	37	---	
32		81	Bill Barker	'50 Ford	36	---	
33		30	G. McBride	MG	35	30	
34		35	Vince Gray	Jaguar	34	---	
35		206	Bill Chevalier	'50 Ford	33	---	Wheel
36		113	Wimpy Ervin	'51 Henry J	32	---	
37		6	Dick Keene	Jaguar	31	---	
38		202	B. Fisher	Jaguar	29	---	
39		15	J. Christopher	Jaguar	23	---	
40		7	Jim Reed	Reed '54 Ford	13		Tie Rod
41		69	J. Farnell	Morgan	10	25	
42		10	F. Ballentine	MG	9	25	
43		33	M.R. Peterson	Jaguar	6	---	

Time of Race: 1 hour, 17 minutes, 21 seconds
Average Speed: 77.569 mph
Pole Winner: Buck Baker - 80.536 mph
Lap Leaders: Buck Baker 1-10, Herb Thomas 11-12, Baker 13, Thomas 14-22, Al Keller 23-50.
Cautions: 4   Margin of Victory: Attendance:

Grand National Race No. 19
200 Laps at Hickory Speedway
Hickory, NC
100 Miles on Half-mile Dirt Track
June 19, 1954

Fin	St	No.	Driver	Team / Car	Laps	Money	Status
1	1	92	Herb Thomas	Thomas '54 Hudson	200	$1,000	Running
2		42	Lee Petty	Petty Eng '54 Chrysler	200	650	Running
3		88	Buck Baker	Ernest Woods '54 Olds	198	450	Running
4		3	Dick Rathmann	John Ditz '54 Hudson	198	350	Running
5		23	Junior Johnson	George Miller '54 Hudson	194	300	Running
6		82	Joe Eubanks	Phil Oates '51 Hudson	193	250	Running
7		14	Hershel McGriff	Frank Christian '51 Olds	192	200	Running
8		6	Ralph Liguori	Liguori '54 Dodge	192	150	Running
9		12	Speedy Thompson	Buckshot Morris '53 Olds	190	100	Running
10		80	Jimmie Lewallen	George Hutchens '50 Plym	184	100	Running
11		100	Blackie Pitt	Gary Drake '54 Olds	184	25	Running
12		19	Clyde Minter	Ken Pace '51 Mercury	180	25	Running
13		48	Ken Reeder	'53 Dodge	179	25	Running
14		71	Fred Dove	Dove '49 Hudson	168	25	Running
15		114	Parks Surrat	R. Spearman '50 Plymouth	167	25	Running
16		711	Walt Flinchum	'51 Plymouth	166	25	Running
17		21	Laird Bruner	Garmen Amica '53 Olds	160	25	Running
18		17	Jed Jarrett	M. Bernard '53 Studebaker	159	25	Running
19		126	Dave Terrell	Terrell '54 Dodge	141	25	Spindle
20		24	Ray Duhigg	J.O. Goode '50 Plymouth	127	25	Heating
21		90	Jim Paschal	'53 Dodge	116	---	Heating
22		28	Bill Blair	Frank Dodge '53 Olds	93	---	Heating
23		29	Dink Widenhouse	'53 Olds	79	---	Handling
24		11	Pete Stewart	'51 Studebaker	77	---	Hub

Time of Race: 1 hour, 12 minutes, 24 seconds
Average Speed: 82.872 mph
Pole Winner: Herb Thomas 81.669 mph
Lap Leaders: Herb Thomas 1-200.
Cautions: Margin of Victory: Attendance: 4,000

Race No. 19

Herb's Hornet Hot At Hickory

HICKORY, NC (June 19) -- Herb Thomas steered his Hudson Hornet into the lead in the opening lap and sped to victory in the 100-mile Grand National event at Hickory Speedway. It was the seventh win of the season for the Olivia, NC veteran driver.

Point leader Lee Petty finished second and maintained a 166-point lead in the standings over Buck Baker,

who finished third. Fourth place went to Dick Rathmann and Junior Johnson finished fifth. Johnson got
his first driving assignment in the George Miller Hudson previously driven by Al Keller, who defected to the
AAA circuit.

Thomas won the pole and led the entire 200 laps
around the half-mile dirt oval.

Track regular Ned Jarrett drove a Studebaker and
wound up finishing 18th in the field of 24. Jarrett was
41 laps behind winner Thomas.

A crowd of 4,000 watched Thomas average 82.872
mph for his 35th career Grand National triumph.

Race No. 20

Petty's Chrysler Tames Big Field at Rochester

ROCHESTER, NY (June 25) -- Lee Petty wheeled
his Chrysler around Herb Thomas in the 141st lap and
led the rest of the way to win the 100-mile Grand National contest at the Monroe County Fairgrounds. It
was Petty's third win of the year and the 14th of his career.

Thomas, who started on the pole for the 30th time in
his six year career on NASCAR's big league stock car
tour, finished second. Dick Rathmann came in third,
Buck Baker was fourth and Hershel McGriff fifth.

Petty upped his point lead to 198 over Baker in the
chase for the NASCAR driving title.

Thirty-two cars started the 200 lapper on the half-mile
dirt track and 24 were running at the finish. There was
only one crash -- a solo mishap when Wally Branston
flipped his Oldsmobile in the 52nd lap. He was not
hurt.

Petty averaged 52.455 mph before a crowd of 6,300.

Grand National Race No. 20
200 Laps at Monroe County Fairgrounds
Rochester, NY
100 Miles on Half-mile Dirt Track
June 25, 1954

Fin	St	No.	Driver	Team / Car	Laps	Money	Status
1		42	Lee Petty	Petty Eng '54 Chrysler	200	$1,000	Running
2	1	92	Herb Thomas	Thomas '54 Hudson	200	650	Running
3		3	Dick Rathmann	John Ditz '54 Hudson	199	450	Running
4		87	Buck Baker	Griffin Motors '53 Olds 88	198	350	Running
5		14	Hershel McGriff	Frank Christian '54 Olds	198	300	Running
6		212	John McGinley	'51 Hudson	196	250	Running
7		23	Ralph Liguori	George Miller '54 Hudson	194	200	Running
8		80	Jimmie Lewallen	George Hutchens '54 Mercury	185	150	Running
9		126	Dave Terrell	Terrell '54 Dodge	182	100	Running
10		82	Joe Eubanks	Phil Oates '51 Hudson	181	100	Running
11		211	Jack Clarke	'49 Plymouth	180	25	Running
12		4	Ken Fisher	'54 Hudson	179	25	Running
13		34	Don Welch	'51 Henry J	175	25	Running
14		93	Ted Chamberlain	Chamberlain '50 Plymouth	173	25	Running
15		18	Elmer Musclow	'49 Ford	171	25	Running
16		25	Billy Vee	'50 Plymouth	168	25	Running
17		22	Bob Schwingle	'49 Ford	165	25	Running
18		100	Blackie Pitt	Gary Drake '54 Olds	164	25	Running
19		21	Laird Bruner	Garmen Amica '54 Olds	162	25	Running
20		120	Russ Hepler	Walt Chapman '53 Hudson	160	25	Running
21		55	Hank Chaffee	'49 Dodge	157	---	Running
22		100	Jim Luke	'49 Olds	154	---	Ignition
23		142	Ash Tharrett	'49 Ford	153	---	Running
24		44	Bill Blair	Elmer Brooks '52 Olds	150	---	Axle
25		69	Walter Milczarski	'53 Dodge	142	---	Running
26		75	Sonny Walters	'49 Buick	134	---	Running
27		7	Jim Reed	Reed '52 Hudson	80	---	Wheel
28		114	Wally Branston	'53 Olds	52	---	Crash
29		63	Ronnie Hayes	'49 Hudson	43	---	Heating
30		17	Charles McDuffie	Jim Reed '51 Ford	41	---	Trans
31		214	Bob Haden	'52 Hudson	23	---	Tire
32		711	Fran Dischke	'49 Packard	22	---	Fuel Pmp

Time of Race: 1 hour, 54 minutes, 23 seconds
Average Speed: 52.455 mph
Pole Winner: Herb Thomas - 60.422 mph
Lap Leaders: Herb Thomas 1-140, Lee Petty 141-200.
Cautions: Margin of Victory: Attendance: 6,300

Race No. 21

Thomas Wins Williams Grove Before Wall-to-Wall Crowd Of 21,600

MECHANICSBURG, PA (June 27) -- Herb Thomas drove his Smokey Yunick Hudson around Dick
Rathmann in the 62nd lap and led the rest of the way to
win the 100-miler at Williams Grove Speedway. The
200 lap event attracted a crowd of 21,600 race fans,
one of the largest audiences ever to witness an auto
racing event at this half-mile shrine.

Rathmann, who started on the pole, finished second
only four car lengths behind winner Thomas, who
gained admittance to victory circle for the eighth time in
the 1954 Grand National season.

Third place went to Hershel McGriff as Joe Eubanks
finished fourth and Jimmie Lewallen fifth.

Ralph Liguori, privateer on the Grand National trail,
was assigned to drive the potent George Miller Hudson. The Bronx, NY driver was running third in the
lead lap when he crashed through the fence with five
laps to go. He wound up eighth in the final rundown.

A field of 41 cars took the green flag and 27 were

running at the finish. Under NASCAR procedure, only the top 20 finishers earned a trip to the pay window which meant over half the field failed to earn any prize money. Jack Clarke drove his Plymouth 176 laps, good enough for 21st place, but did not earn a dime for his efforts.

Thomas and Rathmann swapped the lead six times in the early going and the two Hudson pilots were never more than a few car lengths apart throughout the race. The average speed for the thriller was 51.085 mph.

Race No. 22

Thomas Outruns Lewallen To Win Spartanburg 100

SPARTANBURG, SC (July 3) -- Herb Thomas took his second straight win and the 37th of his career in a 100-miler at the Piedmont Interstate Fairgrounds.

Jimmie Lewallen, journeyman driver out of Archdale, NC, took the wheel of Joe Blair's Mercury and finished second, one lap behind Thomas' victorious Hudson. Lee Petty came in third, Buck Baker was fourth and Joe Eubanks fifth.

Hershel McGriff of Bridal Veil, OR, who came East to drive the highly regarded Frank Christian Oldsmobile when Fonty Flock defected to the SAFE circuit, started on the pole but experienced tire problems and faded to 10th.

Jimmie Lewallen finished 2nd at Spartanburg Fairgrounds.

Twenty-one cars started the 100-miler and only six failed to see the checkered flag. Top contenders who were on the sidelines early included Speedy Thompson, Ray Duhigg, Slick Smith and Bill Blair

Thomas averaged 59.181 mph on the half-mile dirt track.

Spartanburg winner Herb Thomas endorsing Purolator Oil Filters.

Grand National Race No. 21
200 Laps at Williams Grove Speedway
Mechanicsburg, PA
100 Miles on Half-mile Dirt Track
June 17, 1954

Fin	St	No.	Driver	Team / Car	Laps	Money	Status
1		92	Herb Thomas	Thomas '54 Hudson	200	$1,000	Running
2	1	3	Dick Rathmann	John Ditz '54 Hudson	200	650	Running
3		14	Hershel McGriff	Frank Christian '54 Olds 88	199	450	Running
4		82	Joe Eubanks	Phil Oates '51 Hudson	199	350	Running
5		80	Jimmie Lewallen	George Hutchens '54 Mercury	197	300	Running
6		87	Buck Baker	Griffin Motors '53 Olds 88	197	250	Running
7	15	42	Lee Petty	Petty Engineering '54 Dodge	196	200	Running
8		23	Ralph Liguori	George Miller '54 Hudson	195	150	Crash
9		1	Elton Hildreth	Hildreth '51 Nash	193	100	Running
10		100	Blackie Pitt	Gary Drake '54 Olds	193	100	Running
11		121	Dean Pelton	'51 Studebaker	193	25	Running
12		7	Jim Reed	Reed '51 Hudson Hornet	192	25	Crash
13		43	Whitey Brainard	'49 Ford	187	25	Running
14		21	Laird Bruner	Garmen Amica '53 Olds	185	25	Running
15		44	Bill Blair	Elmer Brooks '52 Olds	184	25	Running
16		11	Ed Riker	'51 Olds	183	25	Running
17		126	Dave Terrell	Terrell '54 Dodge	181	25	Running
18		81	Bill Barker	'50 Plymouth	181	25	Running
19		111	Bill O'Dell	'49 Ford	180	25	Running
20		74	Peck Peckham	'51 Hudson	188	25	Running
21		2	Jack Clarke	'49 Plymouth	176	---	Running
22		119	Ray Duhigg	'49 Ford	175	---	Running
23		30	Hilly Rife	'54 Dodge	174	---	Running
24		34	Gene Holcomb	'54 Nash Rambler	172	---	Running
25		93	Ted Chamberlain	Chamberlain '50 Plymouth	170	---	Running
26		6	Dick Kable	Ralph Liguori '54 Dodge	168	---	Oil Press
27		150	Dick Hallett	'50 Lincoln	167	---	Running
28		41	Ken Fisher	'54 Hudson	161	---	Running
29		71	Ed Paskovitch	'50 Ford	153	---	Running
30		40	Frank Hanellburg	'53 Hudson	147	---	Running
31		17	Charles McDuffie	Jim Reed '51 Ford	109	---	Fuel Line
32		47	Harvey Eakin	Eakin '53 Nash	97	---	Bearing
33		212	John McGinley	'53 Hudson	94	---	Crash
34		48	Shelly Colby	'53 Dodge	82	---	Brakes
35		148	Charles Hansen	'53 Olds	78	---	Wheel
36		172	John Dodd, Sr	'52 Willys	62	---	Brakes
37		69	Volney Schulze	'50 Ford	46	---	Heating
38		58	Pete Moxley	'54 Nash Rambler	40	---	Piston
39		120	Russ Hepler	Walt Chapman '53 Hudson	40	---	Spindle
40		4	Charlie Cregar	'54 Chrysler	24	---	Wheel
41		171	Dizzy Dean	'51 Hudson	1	---	Wheel

Time of Race: 1 hour, 57 minutes, 27 seconds
Average Speed: 51.085 mph
Dick Rathmann - 54.945 mph
Lap Leaders: Dick Rathmann 1-5, Herb Thomas 6-10, Rathmann 11-15, Thomas 16-21, Rathmann 22-61, Thomas 62-200.
Cautions: Margin of Victory: 4 car lengths   Attendance: 21,600

Grand National Race No. 22
200 Laps at Piedmont Interstate Fairgrounds
Spartanburg, SC
100 Miles on Half-mile Dirt Track
July 3, 1954

Fin St	No.	Driver	Team / Car	Laps	Money	Status
1	92	Herb Thomas	Thomas '54 Hudson	200	$1,000	Running
2	5	Jimmie Lewallen	Joe Blair '54 Mercury	199	650	Running
3	42	Lee Petty	Petty Eng '54 Chrysler	199	450	Running
4	88	Buck Baker	Ernest Woods '54 Olds 88	196	350	Running
5	82	Joe Eubanks	Phil Oates '52 Hudson	194	300	Running
6	13	Jim Paschal	Ernest Woods '53 Olds	194	250	Running
7	3	Dick Rathmann	John Ditz '54 Hudson	194	200	Running
8	19	Clyde Minter	Ken Pace '51 Mercury	193	150	Running
9	108	Arden Mounts	Mounts '51 Hudson	192	100	Running
10	1	14	Hershel McGriff	Frank Christian '54 Olds	189	100	Running
11	28	Eddie Skinner	Frank Dodge '53 Olds	187	25	Running
12	100	Blackie Pitt	Gary Drake '53 Olds	185	25	Running
13	126	Dave Terrell	Terrell '54 Dodge	182	25	Running
14	2	Bill Blair	Blair '53 Hudson	173	25	Clutch
15	114	Parks Surratt	R. Spearman '51 Plymouth	159	25	Running
16	71	Fred Dove	Dove '49 Hudson	143	25	Running
17	21	Laird Bruner	Garmen Amica '53 Olds	84	25	Spindle
18	91-B	Virgil Stockton	'52 Hudson Hornet	48	25	Spindle
19	44	Slick Smith	Elmer Brooks '52 Olds	38	25	Radiator
20	87	Ray Duhigg	Griffin Motors '53 Olds	17	25	Axle
21	12	Speedy Thompson	Buckshot Morris '53 Olds	6	---	Fuel Pmp

Time of Race: 1 hour, 41 minutes, 23 seconds
Average Speed: 59.181 mph
Pole Winner: Hershel McGriff - 58.120 mph
Lap Leaders: - - - - - - - - - - Herb Thomas   -200.
Cautions: Margin of Victory: 1 lap plus   Attendance:

Grand National Race No. 23
200 Laps at Asheville-Weaverville Speedway
100 Miles on Half-mile Dirt Track
July 4, 1954

Fin St	No.	Driver	Team / Car	Laps	Money	Status
1	1	92	Herb Thomas	Thomas '54 Hudson	200	$1,000	Running
2	5	Jimmie Lewallen	Joe Blair '54 Mercury	199	650	Running
3	3	Dick Rathmann	John Ditz '54 Hudson	199	450	Running
4	100	Lee Petty	Gary Drake '54 Olds	196	350	Running
5	51	Gober Sosebee	Cherokee Garage '54 Olds	193	300	Running
6	82	Joe Eubanks	Phil Oates '52 Hudson	188	250	Running
7	21	Laird Bruner	Garmen Amica '53 Olds	188	200	Running
8	126	Dave Terrell	Terrell '54 Dodge	186	150	Running
9	49	Walt Flinchum	'51 Plymouth	183	100	Running
10	13	Jim Paschal	Ernest Woods '53 Olds	183	100	Running
11	108	Arden Mounts	Mounts '51 Hudson	180	25	Running
12	4-X	Fred Starr	'54 Hudson	163	25	Running
13	14	Hershel McGriff	Frank Christian '52 Olds	161	25	Spindle
14	88	Buck Baker	Ernest Woods '54 Olds	137	25	Bearings
15	71	Fred Dove	Dove '49 Hudson	137	25	
16	19	Clyde Minter	Ken Pace '51 Mercury	135	25	Heating
17	28	Blackie Pitt	Frank Dodge '53 Olds	119	25	Piston
18	12	Speedy Thompson	Buckshot Morris '53 Olds	97	25	Distrib
19	91-B	Virgil Stockton	'52 Hudson	66	25	Wheel
20	87	Ray Duhigg	Griffin Motors '53 Olds	63	25	Spindle
21	10	Dick Grice	'54 Lincoln	52	---	Rear End

Time of Race: 1 hour, 37 minutes, 51 seconds
Average Speed: 61.318 mph
Pole Winner: Herb Thomas ' 67.771 mph
Lap Leaders: - - - - - - - - - - Herb Thomas   -200.
Cautions: Margin of Victory: 1 lap plus   Attendance:

Race No. 23

Thomas Bags Third in Row At Weaverville

WEAVERVILLE, NC (July 4) -- Herb Thomas tied a record by winning his third straight Grand National race at the neatly contoured Asheville-Weaverville Speedway.

Thomas finished a lap ahead of runner-up Jimmie Lewallen in the 100-miler on the half-mile dirt track. Dick Rathmann finished third, Lee Petty was fourth in Blackie Pitts regular ride, and Gober Sosebee finished fifth.

Petty's Chrysler had broken down in a practice session so he was forced to look for a ride elsewhere to protect his point lead. Gary Drake, owner of the Oldsmobile driven by rookie Pitt, let Petty drive the car in the race. Pitt moved over to Frank Dodge's Olds usually driven by Eddie Skinner and wound up 17th in the field of 21.

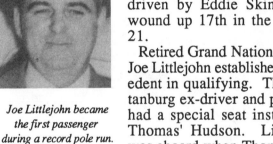

Joe Littlejohn became the first passenger during a record pole run.

Retired Grand National driver Joe Littlejohn established a precedent in qualifying. The Spartanburg ex-driver and promoter had a special seat installed in Thomas' Hudson. Littlejohn was aboard when Thomas set a qualifying track record of 67.771 mph. It marked the first time in recorded history that a Grand National car had a passenger during a record run.

During the race Thomas averaged 61.318 mph for his 38th career win.

Race No. 24

Rathmann Halts Thomas Streak at Willow Springs

WILLOW SPRINGS, IL (July 10) -- Dick Rathmann ended Herb Thomas' three race win streak by taking first place in the 100-mile Grand National event at Santa Fe Speedway. It was Rathmann's third win of the season.

Thomas' bid for a record fourth win in a row fell short by three-quarters of a lap as he finished second. Hershel McGriff came in third with Lee Petty and Buck

Dick Rathmann

Baker rounding out the top five.

Baker led the first 46 laps before Rathmann took the lead for good.   A crowd of 6,208 showed up for NASCAR's first venture into the Chicago area.

Virgil Stockton was involved in the only wreck of the day. His Hudson slipped sideways and cracked the retaining wall in the 171st lap. He was not injured.

Rathmann averaged 72.216 mph for his 13th career Grand National victory.

Grand National Race No. 24
200 Laps at Santa Fe Speedway
Willow Springs, IL
100 Miles on Half-mile Dirt Track
July 10, 1954

Fin	St	No.	Driver	Team / Car	Laps	Money	Status
1	5	3	Dick Rathmann	John Ditz '54 Hudson	200	$1,000	Running
2	3	92	Herb Thomas	Thomas '54 Hudson	200	650	Running
3	4	14	Hershel McGriff	Frank Christian '51 Olds 88	200	450	Running
4	6	42	Lee Petty	Petty Eng '54 Chrysler	199	350	Running
5	1	88	Buck Baker	Ernest Woods '54 Olds 88	197	300	Running
6	14	7	Jim Reed	Reed '52 Hudson Hornet	196	250	Running
7	10	82	Joe Eubanks	Phil Oates '51 Hudson	196	200	Running
8	7	21	Laird Bruner	Garmen Amica '53 Olds	195	150	Running
9	15	24	Ray Duhigg	J.O. Goode '50 Plymouth	195	100	Running
10	22	48	Bill Moore	'50 Plymouth	183	100	Running
11	2	12	Jim Paschal	Buckshot Morris '53 Olds	180	25	Running
12	16	11	Al Ruyle	'52 Mercury	178	25	Running
13	18	126	Dave Terrell	Terrell '54 Dodge	175	25	Running
14	12	91-B	Virgil Stockton	'52 Hudson	171	25	Crash
15	11	57	Art Doogan	'49 Ford	165	25	Running
16	20	M-22	Frank Ropp	'49 Ford	163	25	Running
17	23	25	Sam Pearson	'49 Ford	150	25	Running
18	21	1	Red Wright	'51 Ford	132	25	Clutch
19	19	50	Danny Curley	'51 Ford	125	25	Heating
20	8	100	Blackie Pitt	Gary Drake '54 Olds	113	25	Hub
21	13	V-2	Legs Whitcomb	'50 Ford	97	---	Bearings
22	9	15	Bill Brown	'54 Buick	41	---	Trans
23	17	69	Bay Darnell	'50 Ford	18	---	Heating

Time of Race: 1 hour, 23 minutes, 5 seconds
Average Speed: 72.216 mph
Pole Winner: Buck Baker - 75.662 mph
Lap Leaders: Buck Baker 1-46, Dick Rathmann 47-200.
Cautions: Margin of Victory: 3/4 lap   Attendance: 6,208

Race No. 25

Petty Pads Point Lead
With Grand Rapids Win

GRAND RAPIDS, MI (July 11) -- Lee Petty drove his Chrysler to victory in the 100-mile Grand National race at the Grand River Speedrome. It was the fourth win of the season for the NASCAR point leader. Petty's lead over Buck Baker stood at 286 points.

*Lee Petty won
at Grand Rapids, MI.*

Baker wound up second in the same lap with Petty at the finish of the 200-lapper. Dick Rathmann took third, Ray Duhigg was fourth and Jim Reed got credit for fifth place wtih relief driver Herb Thomas at the helm.

Blackie Pitt, highly touted rookie driver, crashed in the last few laps and wound up seventh. Pitt crashed through the fence and wound up in a drainage ditch. Pitt was unhurt.

Virgil Stockton wrecked for the second time in as many races, yet finished in 10th place. It was the first time the Melvindale, MI driver had cracked the top 10 in a Grand National race.

Thomas started on the pole and led the opening two laps, but a broken tie-rod put his Hudson on the sidelines after 49 laps. He relieved two other drivers before climbing into Reed's car.

Baker led for 117 laps before Petty took the lead for keeps in the 119th lap

Petty averaged 52.090 mph for his 15th career win.

Grand National Race No. 25
200 Laps at Grand River Speedrome
Grand Rapids, MI
100 Miles on Half-mile Dirt Track
July 11, 1954

Fin	St	No.	Driver	Team / Car	Laps	Money	Status
1	7	42	Lee Petty	Petty Eng '54 Chrysler	200	$1,000	Running
2		88	Buck Baker	Ernest Woods '54 Olds 88	200	650	Running
3		3	Dick Rathmann	Pure '54 Hudson	196	450	Running
4		24	Ray Duhigg	J.O. Goode '51 Plymouth	193	350	Running
5		7	Jim Reed*	Reed '54 Hudson	192	300	Running
6		126	Dave Terrell	Terrell '54 Dodge	186	250	Running
7		100	Blackie Pitt	Gary Drake '54 Olds	185	200	Crash
8		52	Walt Flinchum	'51 Plymouth	183	150	Running
9		82	Joe Eubanks	Oates Motor Co. '52 Hudson	180	100	Running
10		91-B	Virgil Stockton	'52 Hudson	178	100	Crash
11		4	Clare Lawicki	'49 Ford	175	25	Running
12		12	Chuck Neale	'51 Plymouth	170	25	Running
13		2	Jack Cummiford	'52 Olds	170	25	Running
14		00	Bud Bennett	'53 Olds	167	25	Running
15		31	Hank Russ	'54 Ford	165	25	Running
16		883	Andy Biddle	'51 Ford	142	25	Running
17		241	Dick Jennette	'50 Ford	115	25	Running
18		13	Jim Paschal	Ernest Woods '53 Olds 88	96	25	Tie Rod
19		49	Richard Brownlee	'51 Plymouth	74	25	King Pin
20		9	Donald Thomas	Smokey Yunick '53 Hudson	68	25	Engine
21		14	Hershel McGriff	Frank Christian '52 Olds 88	61	---	Fuel Line
22	1	92	Herb Thomas	Smokey Yunick '54 Hudson	49	---	Tie Rod
23		21	Laird Bruner	Garmen Amica '53 Olds	48	---	Carb
24		1	Erv Atkinson	'49 Hudson	35	---	Wheel
25		36	Andy Bruni	'50 Ford	34	---	Piston

* Herb Thomas relieved Jim Reed in Car #7 and drove it a 5th place finish.
Time of Race: 1 hour, 55 minutes, 11 seconds
Average Speed: 52.090 mph
Pole Winner: Herb Thomas - 59.055 mph
Lap Leaders: Herb Thomas 1-2, Buck Baker 3-119, Lee Petty 120-200.
Cautions: Margin of Victory: Attendance: 4,000

Race No. 26

Rathmann 'Tires' Out; Baker Wins at Morristown

MORRISTOWN, NJ (July 30) -- A blown tire on Dick Rathmann's Hudson less than 11 miles from the finish opened the door for Buck Baker to win the 100-miler at Morristown Speedway. It was Baker's third win of the season.

Herb Thomas finished second, a lap off the pace. Hershel McGriff, Rathmann and Jimmie Lewallen completed the top five. Point leader Lee Petty wound up sixth.

Rathmann had taken the lead from pole sitter Baker in the 78th lap and was cruising uncontested for his fourth win of the year. But just 21 laps from the finish, a tire blew out, forcing the Los Angeles driver to the pits. He lost four laps getting a replacement.

Fred Starr, newcomer out of Brooklyn, flipped his Hudson in the sixth lap. Johnny Zeke tried to take evasive action, but dumped his Dodge in the same spot. Three laps later, Ed Paskevich rolled his Plymouth. None of the drivers were hurt.

A crowd of 5,000 was on hand to watch Baker average 58.968 mph for his eighth career Grand National triumph.

Grand National Race No. 26
200 Laps at Morristown Speedway
Morristown, NJ
100 Miles on Half-mile Dirt Track
July 30, 1954

Fin	St	No.	Driver	Team / Car	Laps	Money	Status
1	1	88	Buck Baker	Ernest Woods '54 Olds 88	200	$1,000	Running
2		92	Herb Thomas	Thomas '54 Hudson	199	650	Running
3		14	Hershel McGriff	Frank Christian '53 Olds 88	199	450	Running
4		3	Dick Rathmann	John Ditz '54 Hudson	196	350	Running
5		5	Jimmie Lewallen	Joe Blair '54 Mercury	195	300	Running
6		42	Lee Petty	Petty Eng '54 Chrysler	195	250	Running
7		4	Ken Fisher	'54 Hudson	193	200	Running
8		48	Charlie Hansen	'51 Hudson	191	150	Running
9		126	Dave Terrell	Terrell '54 Dodge	188	100	Running
10		181	Ronnie Kohler	Millard Wright '52 Plymouth	184	100	Running
11		100	Blackie Pitt	Gary Drake '54 Olds 88	181	25	Running
12		780	Dick Sanford	'50 Dodge	180	25	Running
13		101	George Clark	'52 Hudson Hornet	179	25	Running
14		2	Bill Blair	Blair '53 Hudson Hornet	174	25	RF Drum
15		104	Ed Van Horn	'50 Ford	172	25	Running
16		71	Gene Roberts	'50 Ford	168	25	Running
17		141	Jack Smith	'50 Ford	165	25	Running
18		70	Ken Kiser	'50 Dodge	164	25	Running
19		83	Joe Bossard	'50 Ford	163	25	Running
20		177	George Cole	'50 Ford	159	25	Running
21		20	Nick Spano	'51 Henry J	147	10	Heating
22		323	George Norvath	'50 Ford	143	10	Running
23		81	Bill Barker	'50 Plymouth	135	10	Spindle
24		74	Peck Peckham	'51 Hudson	125	10	Axle
25		148	Pete Moxley	'53 Olds 88	109	10	King Pin
26		12	Ed DeWolff	'50 Ford	92	10	Spindle
27		69	Bill Cleveland	'50 Ford	74	10	Heating
28		13	Jim Paschal	Ernest Woods '53 Olds 88	71	10	Axle
29		111	Art Faber	'50 Plymouth	61	10	Wheel
30		82	Joe Eubanks	Phil Oates '51 Hudson	17	10	Radiator
31		17	Tex Brooks	'50 Hudson	14	10	Hub
32		1	Elton Hildreth	Hildreth Motors '51 Nash	10	10	Crash
33		28	Ed Paskovich	'50 Plymouth	9	10	Crash
34		481	John Zeke	'54 Dodge	6	10	Crash
35		4-X	Fred Starr	'54 Hudson	6	10	Crash

Time of Race: 1 hour, 41 minutes, 45 seconds
Average Speed: 58.968 mph
Pole Winner: Buck Baker - 66.666 mph
Lap Leaders: Buck Baker 1-77, Dick Rathmann 78-178, Baker 179-200.
Cautions: Margin of Victory: 1 lap plus   Attendance: 5,000

Grand National Race No. 27
300 Laps at Oakland Stadium
Oakland, CA
150 Miles on Half-mile Paved & Dirt Track
August 1, 1954

Fin	St	No.	Driver	Team / Car	Laps	Money	Status
1		3	Danny Letner	'52 Hudson Hornet	300	$1,000	Running
2	1	98	Marvin Panch	Beryl Jackson '54 Dodge	300	650	Running
3		68	Allen Adkins	Gus Davis '54 Dodge	299	450	Running
4		6	Ben Gregory	Coz Cancilla '54 Olds 88	299	350	Running
5		33	Lloyd Dane	Dane '53 Hudson Hornet	298	300	Running
6		2	Jim Graham	'54 Olds 88	291	250	Running
7		35	Bill Smith	'51 Hudson Hornet	290	200	Running
8		65	Chuck Meekins	'52 Olds 88	290	150	Running
9		1	Clyde Palmer	'51 Mercury	288	100	Running
10		10	Charles Pemberton	'53 Dodge	288	100	Running
11		38	Art Watts	'54 Hudson	284	25	Running
12		16	Tony Nelson	'51 Hudson Hornet	284	25	Running
13		88	Woody Brown	Joe Mangini '50 Olds	276	25	Running
14		50	Jim Cook	'50 Olds	276	25	Running
15		26	Ed Normi	'52 Plymouth	274	25	Running
16		28	Bud Diamond	'52 Hudson Hornet	266	25	
17		12	Eli Vukovich	'53 Olds 88	262	25	Running
18		52	Marian Pagan *	'52 Plymouth	261	25	Running
19		59	Al Neves	'53 Ford	245	25	Running
20		15	Sam Hawks	'50 Plymouth	244	25	
21		099	Dick Zimmerman	'54 Mercury	229	---	
22		41	Ernie Young	'51 Plymouth	224	---	
23		4	John Soares	Charles Vance '54 Dodge	222	---	
24		82	Bill Bade	'53 Ford	222	---	
25		31	Red Ortwein	'51 Hudson Hornet	194	---	
26		89	Bill West	'52 Hudson Hornet	187	---	
27		22	George Seeger	'54 Ford	183	---	
28		99	Joe Valente	Valente '50 Olds	145	---	
29		51	Rick Henderson	'51 Chevrolet	193	---	
30		60	Howard Phillippi	'51 Hudson Hornet	65	---	
31		11	Dick Carter	'52 Plymouth	51	---	
32		84	Bob Caswell	Lou Mangini '52 Plymouth	297	---	Disqual

Time of Race: 2 hours, 49 minutes, 40 seconds
Average Speed: 53.045 mph
Pole Winner: Marvin Panch - 55.248 mph
Lap Leaders: - - - - - - - - - Marvin Panch 244-249, Danny Letner 250-280, Panch 281-287, Letner 288-293, Panch 294, Letner 295-300.
Cautions: Margin of Victory: 2 car lengths   Attendance: 7,500
* Relieved by Eddie Pagan

Race No. 27

Letner Edges Panch in Oakland 150

OAKLAND, CA (Aug. 1) -- Danny Letner drove his Hudson to a narrow victory over Dodge-driving

Marvin Panch in the 150-mile Grand National event at Oakland Stadium.

Letner passed Panch with six laps to go to win the $1,000 top prize. Panch finished two car lengths behind in second place. Bob Caswell's Plymouth was flagged in third place but was disqualified for having an illegal cam shaft.

Allen Adkins was awarded third place as Ben Gregory finished fourth and Lloyd Dane fifth.

Marian "Mopsy" Pagan, wife of well-known racer Eddie Pagan, drove a Plymouth and finished 18th, completing 261 laps. Eddie relieved his wife on the 57th lap and drove the rest of the way. Eli Vukovich, brother of famed AAA driver and two-time Indianapolis 500 winner Bill Vukovich, finished 17th in an Oldsmobile. It was his first effort in the Grand National ranks.

Letner averaged 53.045 mph for his first Grand National victory.

Race No. 28

Petty Pushes Closer to Title with Charlotte Win

CHARLOTTE, NC (Aug. 13) -- Lee Petty drove his Chrysler to an easy victory in the 100-miler at the Southern States Fairgrounds. Petty increased his point lead to 278 over Buck Baker, who started on the pole and wound up fifth.

Dick Rathmann came across the stripe in second place, two laps behind the winner. Bob Welborn was third and Dink Widenhouse fourth in his second Grand National start.

Herb Thomas ran with the leaders early on, but had steering problems in the 111th lap. Jim Paschal and Jimmie Lewallen were other top threats who failed to finish.

Perk Brown, top Modified driver, made his return to Grand National racing, but steering failure put his Hudson out after 97 laps.

Gober Sosebee was running just behind the leaders when he crashed his Oldsmobile late in the race. Sosebee still got credit for 10th place based on the 158 laps he completed.

Petty averaged 51.362 mph for his 16th career win.

Perk Brown made Grand National comeback, but did not finish.

Grand National Race No. 28
200 Laps at Southern States Fairgrounds
Charlotte, NC
100 Miles on Half-mile Dirt Track
August 13, 1954

Fin	St	No.	Driver	Team / Car	Laps	Money	Status
1		42	Lee Petty	Petty Eng '54 Chrysler	200	$1,000	Running
2		3	Dick Rathmann	John Ditz '54 Hudson	198	650	Running
3		87	Bob Welborn	Griffin Motors '53 Olds 88	196	450	Running
4		B-29	Dink Widenhouse	Widenhouse '53 Olds 88	196	350	Running
5	1	88	Buck Baker	Ernest Woods '54 Olds 88	192	300	Running
6		100	Blackie Pitt	Gary Drake '54 Olds 88	192	250	Running
7		82	Joe Eubanks	Phil Oates '51 Hudson	191	200	Running
8		2	Bill Blair	Blair '54 Hudson	186	150	Running
9		6	Cotton Owens	'53 Olds 88	183	100	Running
10		51	Gober Sosebee	Cherokee Garage '54 Olds 88	158	100	Crash
11		126	Dave Terrell	Terrell '54 Dodge	157	25	Radiator
12		28	Laird Bruner	Frank Dodge '53 Olds 88'	144	25	Heating
13		90	Sam Smith	'53 Dodge	137	25	Crash
14		92	Herb Thomas	Thomas '54 Hudson	111	25	Steering
15		14	Hershel McGriff	Frank Christian '51 Olds	111	25	Fuel Tank
16		22	Perk Brown	R.G. Shelton '51 Hudson	97	25	Steering
17		55	Frank Stutts	'52 Ford	94	25	Crash
18		5	Jimmie Lewallen	Joe Blair '54 Mercury	80	25	Gasket
19		11	George Parrish	'53 Studebaker	76	25	Axle
20		13	Jim Paschal	Ernest Woods '53 Olds 88	54	25	Bearing
21		19	Clyde Minter	Ken Pace '49 Mercury	28	---	Cont Arm
22		10	Bill Blackwell	'49 Plymouth	4	---	Flagged

Time of Race: 1 hour, 56 minutes, 49 seconds
Average Speed: 51.362 mph
Pole Winner: Buck Baker - 57.270 mph
Lap Leaders: - - - - - - - - - Lee Petty   -200.
Cautions: Margin of Victory: 2 laps plus   Attendance:

Race No. 29

McGriff Breaks Ice with Big Bay Meadows Win

SAN MATEO, CA (Aug. 22) -- Hershel McGriff of Bridal Veil, OR grabbed his first Grand National victory by coming home first in the 250-miler at Bay Meadows Speedway. The win came in his 24th start.

McGriff, wheeling the Frank Christian Oldsmobile, outdistanced Bill Amick to nail down the $2,425 first prize. Dick Rathmann finished third, Allen Adkins was fourth and Lee Petty fifth.

Buck Baker struggled to a 17th place finish in a Cadillac, some 19 laps behind the

Hershel McGriff

Erick Erickson's terrific charge was interrupted by mechanical ills.

winner. He fell to 518 points behind Petty in the Grand National point standings.

Erick Erickson started dead last in the 41 car field, but thrilled the crowd of 10,000 by storming into the top five by the half-way point. The Buick driver was hampered with recurring mechanical problems and wound up 22nd in the final order.

McGriff, winner of the first Mexical Road Race in 1950, averaged 64.710 mph for the 250 miles.

Race No. 30

Petty Cops Corbin Century; Sixth Win of Year

CORBIN, KY (Aug. 29) -- Lee Petty moved another step closer to his first Grand National championship by taking the 100-miler at Corbin Speedway. It was Petty's sixth win of the year and upped his point lead to 534 over Buck Baker.

Hershel McGriff finished in second place and Baker was third. Herb Thomas crossed the line in fourth place and Donald Thomas was fifth.

Ray Duhigg, on the comeback trail since suffering a broken neck at Langhorne in 1953, was saddled in the Ernest Woods Oldsmobile, but transmission failure put him out after only two laps.

Jim Paschal put Woods' other Olds on the pole, but he was sidelined by a blown head gasket after 28 laps.

Petty averaged 63.080 mph for his 17th career win.

Grand National Race No. 29
250 Laps at Bay Meadows Speedway
San Mateo, CA
250 Miles on 1-mile Dirt Track
August 22, 1954

Fin	St	No.	Driver	Team / Car	Laps	Money	Status
1	1	14	Hershel McGriff	Frank Christian '54 Olds 88	250	$2,425	Running
2		28	Bill Amick	Frank Dodge '53 Olds 88	250	1,500	Running
3		12	Dick Rathmann	'53 Olds 88	249	900	Running
4		68	Allen Adkins	Gus Davis '54 Dodge	249	700	Running
5		42	Lee Petty	Petty Eng '54 Chrysler	247	500	Running
6		92	Herb Thomas	Thomas '54 Hudson	247	400	Running
7		3	Danny Letner	Joe Bearscheck '52 Hudson	245	300	Running
8		33	Lloyd Dane	Dane '53 Hudson Hornet	244	200	Running
9		84	Bob Caswell	Lou Mangini '52 Plymouth	244	200	Running
10		98	Marvin Panch	Beryl Jackson '54 Dodge	244	200	Running
11		2	Jim Graham	'54 Olds 88	239	150	Running
12		65	Chuck Meekins	'52 Olds	238	150	Running
13		10	Charles Pemberton	'53 Dodge	237	100	Running
14		16	Tony Nelson	'53 Hudson Hornet	236	100	Running
15		88	Woody Brown	Joe Mangini '50 Olds	235	100	Running
16		99	Joe Valente	Valente '50 Olds	233	100	Running
17		87	Buck Baker	'54 Cadillac	231	100	Running
18		6	Ben Gregory	Coz Cancilla '54 Olds 88	228	50	Running
19		97	Sam Lamm	Fred Bince '53 Dodge	226	50	Running
20		89	Bill West	'51 Hudson Hornet	225	50	Running
21		52	Eddie Pagan	Pagan '52 Plymouth	223	40	Running
22	41	25	Erick Erickson	Erickson '54 Buick	215	40	Running
23		100	Blackie Pitt	Gary Drake '54 Olds 88	214	40	Running
24		33-X	Bob Deehan	'53 Dodge	213	40	Running
25		7	Jim Heath	'54 Ford	210	40	Rear End
26		1	Al Neves	'51 Mercury	210	40	Running
27		15	Sam Hawks	'50 Plymouth	203	40	Running
28		73	Art Watts	'54 Hudson	200	40	Gasket
29		51	Rick Henderson	'51 Ford	199	40	Running
30		60	Howard Phillippi	'51 Hudson Hornet	199	40	Running
31		50	Jim Cook	'50 Olds	184	40	Running
32		41	Ernie Young	'51 Plymouth	178	40	Running
33		90	Ted Lee	'50 Ford	164	40	Running
34		4	John Soares	Charles Vance '54 Dodge	160	40	Crash
35		11	Dick Carter	'51 Hudson Hornet	154	40	Wheel
36		77	Bill Bade	'52 Plymouth	144	40	Running
37		31	Red Ortwein	'51 Hudson Hornet	144	40	Heating
38		099	Dick Zimmerman	'54 Mercury	121	40	Engine
39		35	Bill Smith	'51 Hudson Hornet	83	40	Piston
40		19	George Rogge	'50 Olds	64	40	Crash
41		8	Ed Normi	'53 Dodge	39	40	Engine

Time of Race: 3 hours, 50 minutes, 48 seconds
Average Speed: 64.710 mph
Pole Winner: Hershel McGriff - 75.566 mph
Lap Leaders: - - - - - - - - - Hershel McGriff -250.
Cautions: Margin of Victory: Attendance: 10,000

Grand National Race No. 30
200 Laps at Corbin Speedway
Corbin, KY
100 Miles on Half-mile Dirt Track
August 29, 1954

Fin	St	No.	Driver	Team / Car	Laps	Money	Status
1		42	Lee Petty	Petty Eng '54 Chrysler	200	$1,000	Running
2		14	Hershel McGriff	Frank Christian '52 Olds 88	200	650	Running
3		87	Buck Baker	Griffin Motors '53 Olds 88	198	450	Running
4		92	Herb Thomas	Thomas '54 Hudson	195	350	Running
5		9	Donald Thomas	Thomas '53 Hudson	191	300	Running
6		100	Blackie Pitt	Gary Drake '54 Olds 88	189	250	Running
7		82	Joe Eubanks	Phil Oates '52 Hudson	189	200	Running
8		4	John Soares	Charles Vance '54 Dodge	186	150	Running
9		15	Marvin Panch	'50 Plymouth	186	100	Running
10		112	Floyd Curtis	'51 Hudson Hornet	179	100	Running
11		53	John W. Smith	'49 Plymouth	174	25	Running
12		21	Laird Bruner	Garmen Amica '53 Olds 88	169	25	Running
13		8	Dick Rathmann	Frank Christian '51 Hudson	148	25	Rear End
14		54	Dick Vermillion	'52 Buick	139	25	Fuel Tank
15		2	Kenneth Taylor	'51 Ford	137	25	Running
16		6	Ralph Liguori	Liguori '54 Dodge	115	25	Suspsn
17		51	Gober Sosebee	Cherokee Garage '54 Olds 88	43	25	Engine
18		10	Bub King	'54 Lincoln	34	25	Shocks
19	1	88	Jim Paschal	Ernest Woods '54 Olds 88	28	25	Gasket
20		90	Jimmie Lewallen	'53 Dodge	12	25	Fuel Pmp
21		13	Ray Duhigg	Ernest Woods '53 Olds 88	2	---	Trans

Time of Race: 1 hour, 35 minutes, 7 seconds
Aveaage Speed: 63.080 mph
Pole Winner: Jim Paschal - 65.789 mph
Lap Leaders: - - - - - - - - - Lee Petty -200.
Cautions: Margin of Victory: Attendance:

Herb Thomas flashes under the checkered flag at Darlington. The Hudson driver became the first man to win two Southern 500 classics.

Race No. 31

Thomas Chases Down Turner; Captures Southern 500

DARLINGTON, SC (Sept. 6) -- Herb Thomas pushed his Hudson Hornet into the lead just twenty laps from the finish and outsped Curtis Turner to win the fifth annual Southern 500 at Darlington Raceway. It was Thomas' eleventh win of the season.

The Olivia, NC farmer became the first driver to win three superspeedway events on NASCAR's Grand National circuit. He won this event in 1951 and was victorious on Raleigh's one-mile paved track in May.

Thomas struggled past Turner with 27 miles to go and crossed the finish line 26 seconds ahead of his rival to win the $6,830 first prize. Turner pocketed $6,245 for his runner-up efforts, boosted largely by lap money. The wild lumberman out of Roanoke, VA led for 266 laps.

Finishing third was Marvin Panch, with Johnny Patterson fourth and Jim Paschal fifth.

Point leader Lee Petty wound up 38th in the final order. The Chrysler driver departed after 50 laps with coil problems. He took the wheel of Panch's Dodge and ushered it home third.

Buck Baker, Petty's closest adversary in the NASCAR point chase entering the race, wound up 44th after blowing an engine in his Oldsmobile on lap 66. Baker relieved Laird Bruner and wound up 23rd but fell to third place in the standings. Petty left Darlington with a 354 point lead over Herb Thomas.

The lead changed hands twelve times among six different drivers. Turner, who started 17th, scrambled up through the pack and took the lead for the first time on lap 44. He was pacing the field in Elmer Brooks' entry for most of the afternoon before Thomas' stretch run.

Other leaders included Baker, who led the first 34 laps from the pole position, Bill Amick, Pop McGinnis and Ken Fisher who was driving in relief of Charlie Cregar.

Thomas covered the 500 miles in five hours, 16 minutes and 1 second for an average speed of 95.026 mph. Two cautions for a total of four laps slowed the action. A crowd of 28,000 was on hand for the event.

Grand National Race No. 31
364 Laps at Darlington Raceway
Darlington, SC
500 Miles on 1.375-mile Paved Track
September 6, 1954

Fin	St	No.	Driver	Team / Car	Laps	Money	Status
1	23	92	Herb Thomas	Thomas '54 Hudson	364	$6,830	Running
2	17	44	Curtis Turner	Elmer Brooks '52 Olds 88	364	6,245	Running
3	24	98	Marvin Panch	Beryl Jackson '54 Dodge	362	2,155	Running
4	27	58	Johnny Patterson	H.B. Ranier '54 Mercury	360	1,165	Running
5	34	88	Jim Paschal	Ernest Woods '54 Olds 88	357	975	Running
6	7	40	John Soares	Charles Vance '54 Dodge	348	855	Running
7	2	25	Fireball Roberts	Leland Colvin '53 Olds 88	343	730	Running
8	25	7	Gwyn Staley	Paul Whiteman '54 Cadillac	342	670	Running
9	40	13	Joel Million	Ernest Woods '53 Olds 88	339	600	Running
10	38	12	Speedy Thompson	'54 Buick	337	550	Running
11	21	18	Arden Mounts	Comstock '54 Hudson	335	500	Running
12	41	53	Elmo Langley	'54 Olds 88	335	450	Running
13	9	8	Gene Comstock	Comstock '52 Hudson	334	400	Running
14	4	28	Eddie Skinner	Frank Dodge '53 Olds 88	332	350	Running
15	14	82	Joe Eubanks	Phil Oates '51 Hudson	330	325	Running
16	50	1	Elton Hildreth	Hildreth Motors '53 Nash	327	300	Running
17	28	17	Bill Widenhouse	Bob Widenhouse '54 Mercury	326	275	Running
18	31	47	Harvey Eakin	Eakin '53 Nash	321	250	Running
19	6	97	Bill Amick	Frank Christian '54 Olds 88	317	225	Running
20	11	64	Charlie Cregar	'51 Plymouth	313	280	Running
21	19	32	Art Watts	'54 Hudson	312	175	Running
22	12	11	George Parrish	'53 Studebaker	299	160	Running
23	29	21	Laird Bruner	Garmen Amica '54 Olds 88	294	150	Rear End
24	35	27	Jim Gillette	'52 Plymouth	293	140	Running
25	42	48	Otis Martin	'54 Chrysler	290	130	Running
26	32	85	Walt Harvey	'50 Ford	284	120	Running
27	37	16	Buck Mason	'51 Plymouth	283	110	Running
28	30	70	Charles Brinkley	'51 Hudson Hornet	268	100	Engine
29	43	20	Van Van Wey	Van Wey '54 Ford	260	120	Crash
30	15	6	Ralph Liguori	Liguori '54 Dodge	253	120	Running
31	10	93	Ted Chamberlain	Chamberlain '53 Dhrysler	252	75	Running
32	48	55	Frank Stutz	'50 Ford	250	75	Running
33	5	26	Dave Terrell	Terrell '54 Dodge	231	75	Rear End
34	16	83	Cotton Owens	'51 Hudson	228	75	Engine
35	22	33	Pop McGinnis	Irving Frye '53 Hudson	221	115	Fuel Pmp
36	44	71	Dean Pelton	'50 Ford	216	75	Gasket
37	47	15	Joe Sheppard	'54 Ford	215	75	Running
38	13	42	Lee Petty	Petty Eng '54 Chrysler	173	75	Coil
39	39	23	Erick Erickson	'54 Buick	131	75	Rear End
40	8	4	Ken Fisher	'54 Hudson	118	75	Radiator
41	18	5	Jimmie Lewallen	Joe Blair '54 Mercury	110	75	Crash
42	20	29	Dink Widenhouse	Widenhouse '53 Olds 88	101	75	Vapor Lk
43	26	10	Blackie Pitt	Gary Drake '54 Olds 88	98	75	Piston
44	1	87	Buck Baker	Griffin Motors '54 Olds 88	66	465	Engine
45	3	14	Hershel McGriff	Frank Christian '54 Olds 88	37	95	Engine
46	49	20	John McGinley	Walt Chapman '53 Hudson	36	75	Bearing
47	46	43	Danny Letner	'51 Hudson Hornet	26	75	Engine
48	33	90	Bob Welborn	'53 Dodge	14	75	Piston
49	45	79	Hassell Reid	'49 Plymouth	11	75	Piston
50	36	75	Jimmy Thompson	'52 Olds 88	4	75	Fuel Tank

Time of Race: 5 hours, 16 minutes, 1 second
Average Speed: 95.026 mph
Pole Winner: Buck Baker - 108.261 mph (4 lap average)
Lap Leaders: Buck Baker 1-34, Bill Amick 35-43, Curtis Turner 44-129,
   Charlie Cregar 130-137, Pop McGinnis 138-141, Turner 142-190,
   Herb Thomas 191-203, Turner 204-297, Thomas 298-301, Turner 302-307,
   Thomas 308-313, Turner 314-344, Thomas 345-364.
Cautions: 2 for 4 laps.   Margin of Victory: 26 seconds   Attendance: 28,000

Race No. 32

McGriff Masters Macon;
Baker Booted, Flock Back

MACON, GA (Sept. 12) -- Hershel McGriff took the lead from Tim Flock with 20 laps to go and went on to win his second Grand National race of the year at Central City Speedway.

Buck Baker finished second, only two seconds behind McGriff's Olds, but was disqualified in a technical inspection following the race. Flock, who was elevated to second place, was ironically driving a back-up Olds owned by Baker It was Flock's first NASCAR start since February, when he "retired" in disgust after being disqualified from a Daytona victory.

Lee Petty wound up in third place, Joe Eubanks was fourth and Ralph Liguori fifth.

Baker started on the pole, but Flock was credited with earning the pole with Baker's disqualification. Flock led the first 180 laps, but faded in the late stages, finishing 25 seconds behind McGriff.

Charlie Mincey got a ride in the Elmer Brooks Oldsmobile that Curtis Turner had driven at Darlington. The local Modified hot-shot was running in the top five when he ran out of gas with 16 laps remaining. He officially got credit for ninth place in the field of 21 cars. Mincey flipped the car in the opening laps, but it landed on all four wheels and he kept racing.

A crash in the 19th lap took Herb Thomas out of action for the afternoon. He then relieved Bill Blair and brought his Hudson home eighth.

McGriff averaged 50.256 mph before 8,000 fans.

Grand National Race No. 32
200 Laps at Central City Speedway
Macon, GA
100 Miles on Half-mile Dirt Track
September 12, 1954

Fin	St	No.	Driver	Team / Car	Laps	Money	Status
1		14	Hershel McGriff	Frank Christian '51 Olds 88	200	$1,000	Running
2	1	89	Tim Flock	Buck Baker '53 Olds 88	200	650	Running
3		42	Lee Petty	Petty Eng '54 Chrysler	200	450	Running
4		82	Joe Eubanks	Phil Oates '51 Hudson	199	350	Running
5		6	Ralph Liguori	Liguori '54 Dodge	197	300	Running
6		90	Bob Welborn	'53 Dodge	189	250	Running
7		88	Jim Paschal	Ernest Woods '54 Olds 88	189	200	Running
8		2	Bill Blair*	Blair '53 Hudson Hornet	188	150	Running
9		44	Charlie Mincey	Elmer Brooks '52 Olds 88	184	100	Fuel
10		23	Erick Erickson	Erickson '54 Buick	183	100	Crash
11		85	Bill Tuten	'50 Ford	179	25	Running
12		15	Buster Whaley	'50 Plymouth	171	25	Running
13		5	Jimmie Lewallen	Joe Blair '54 Mercury	144	25	Running
14		100	Blackie Pitts	Gary Drake '54 Olds 88	142	25	Hub
15		25	Bill Widenhouse	Widenhouse '53 Olds 88	136	25	Fuel Line
16		51	Gober Sosebee	Cherokee Garage '54 Olds 88	136	25	Trans
17		13	Joel Million	Ernest Woods '53 Olds 88	127	25	Spindle
18		4-W	John Soares	Charles Vance '54 Dodge	85	25	Crash
19		97	Bill Amick	Frank Christian '54 Olds 88	58	25	Piston
20		92	Herb Thomas	Thomas '54 Hudson	19	25	Crash
21		87	Buck Baker	Griffin Motors '53 Olds 88	200	---	Disqual.

*Relieved by Herb Thomas
Time of Race: 1 hour, 58 minutes, 45 seconds
Average Speed: 50.526 mph
Pole Winner: Tim Flock - 56.907 mph (Buck Baker had won pole at 58.006 mph, but lost
   credit for pole when he was disqualiied.
Lap Leaders: Tim Flock 1-180, Hershel McGriff 181-200.
Cautions: Margin of Victory: 25 seconds   Attendance: 8,000

Race No. 33

Second in Row for McGriff at Charlotte

Car owner Frank Christian and winner Hershel McGriff in Charlotte victory lane.

CHARLOTTE, NC (Sept. 24) -- Hershel McGriff of Bridal Veil, OR, drove Frank Christian's Oldsmobile to his second straight Grand National win at the Southern States Fairgrounds.

McGriff finished better than a lap ahead of runner-up Lee Petty in the 100-mile chase on the half-mile dirt track. Buck Baker wound up third, with Dick Rathmann fourth. Fifth place went to Joe Eubanks.

Tim Flock, making his second start since February, finished ninth, once again driving an Oldsmobile from the Baker stable.

Herb Thomas finished sixth and fell 402 points behind Petty in the NASCAR standings.

McGriff ranks sixth in the Grand National standings despite missing the first half of the season. He acquired the Frank Christian ride at mid-season.

The winner averaged 53.167 mph in the accident-free race.

Grand National Race No. 33
200 Laps at Southern States Fairgrounds
Charlotte, NC
100 Miles on Half-mile Dirt Track
September 24, 1954

Fin	St	No.	Driver	Team / Car	Laps	Money	Status
1	1	14	Hershel McGriff	Frank Christian '54 Olds 88	200	$1,000	Running
2		42	Lee Petty	PettyEng '54 Chrysler	199	650	Running
3		87	Buck Baker	Griffin Motros '54 Olds 88	199	450	Running
4		3	Dick Rathmann	John Ditz '54 Hudson	196	350	Running
5		82	Joe Eubanks	Phil Oates '51 Hudson	195	300	Running
6		92	Herb Thomas	Thomas '54 Hudson	191	250	Running
7		B-29	Dink Widenhouse	Widenhouse '53 Olds 88	190	200	Running
8		5	Jimmie Lewallen	Joe Blair '54 Mercury	189	150	Running
9		89	Tim Flock	Buck Baker '53 Olds 88	189	100	Running
10		19	;Clyde Minter	Ken Pace '50 Mercury	187	100	Running
11		25	Bill Widenhouse	Bob Widenhouse '53 Olds 88	184	25	Running
12		4-W	John Soares	Charles Vance '54 Dodge	172	25	Running
13		49	Charlie Cregar	'54 Olds	171	25	Running
14		78	Hassell Reid	'50 Plymouth	168	25	Running
15		148	Al Watkins	'52 Plymouth	159	25	Running
16		100	Blackie Pitt	Gary Drake '54 Olds 88	154	25	Gas Line
17		33	Jimmy Ayers	'54 Dodge	151	25	Running
18		71	Billy Minter	'49 Hudson	121	25	Steering
19		48	Chuck Hanson	'51 Hudson	118	25	Steering
20		126	Dave Terrell	Terrell '54 Dodge	104	25	Radiator
21		97	Bill Amick	Frank Christian '54 Olds 88	90	---	Springs
22		98	Marvin Panch	Beryl Jackson '53 Olds 88	73	---	Piston
23		88	Jim Paschal	Ernest Woods '54 Olds 88	60	---	Fuel Pmp
24		52	Andy Winfree	'51 Plymouth	54	---	Brakes
25		77	Fred Dove	'51 Hudson Hornet	12	---	Tie Rod

Time of Race: 1 hour, 52 minutes, 51 seconds
Average Speed: 53.167 mph
Pole Winner: Hershel McGriff - 54.054 mph
Lap Leaders: - - - - - - - - - Hershel McGriff   -200.
Cautions: Margin of Victory: 1 lap plus   Attendance:

Race No. 34

Spill-filled Langhorne Marathon to Thomas

LANGHORNE, PA (Sept. 26) -- Herb Thomas set a track record and notched his 40th career Grand national win in the 250-miler at Langhorne Speedway. The Olivia, NC throttle-stomper averaged 71.186 mph in the wreck-marred race. The caution flag was out six times due to crashes.

Thomas took the lead from Buck Baker with 99 laps to go and outran Lee Petty to bag the $2,450 top prize. Hershel McGriff wound up third, Baker fell to fourth and Erick Erickson finished fifth.

The race was only four laps old when a massive 10-car crash occurred on the one-mile circle track. Eight cars were wiped out in the melee. No drivers were seriously injured.

In the 166th lap, Harvey Eakins crashed his Nash through the guard rail and plunged 30 feet below into a tunnel passage. It took rescue workers several minutes to extract Eakins from the wreckage. He was taken to Mercer Hospital in Trenton with back injuries.

Junior Johnson received plaudits from the throng of 22,000 with his 'never-say-die' attitude. Driving a Cadillac entered by famous band leader Paul Whiteman, Johnson pitted early in the race with rear end problems. The pit crew did a magnificent job in

Grand National Race No. 34
250 Laps at Langhorne Speedway
Langhorne, PA
250 Miles on 1-mile Dirt Track
September 26, 1954

Fin	St	No.	Driver	Team / Car	Laps	Money	Status
1	1	92	Herb Thomas	Thomas '54 Hudson	250	$2,450	Running
2	2	42	Lee Petty	Petty Eng. '54 Chrysler	250	1,150	Running
3	6	14	Hershel McGriff	Frank Christian '54 Olds 88	250	850	Running
4	3	87	Buck Baker	Griffin Motors '54 Olds 88	245	625	Running
5	20	23	Erick Erickson	Erickson '54 Buick	245	600	Running
6		5	Jimmie Lewallen	Joe Blair '54 Mercury	244	500	Running
7	13	3	Dick Rathmann	John Ditz '54 Hudson	244	300	Running
8	7	44	Tim Flock	Elmer Brooks '54 Olds 88	243	250	Running
9		6	John Dodd, Sr	'54 Dodge	240	300	Running
10		82	Joe Eubanks	Phil Oates '51 Hudson	237	175	Running
11		88	Jim Paschal	Ernest Woods '54 Olds 88	235	150	Running
12		4	Ken Fisher	'54 Hudson	228	100	Running
13		98	Marvin Panch	Beryl Jackson '53 Olds 88	225	100	Running
14		13	Joel Million	Ernest Woods '53 Olds 88	225	100	Running
15		7	Junior Johnson	Paul Whiteman '54 Cadillac	222	200	Running
16		28	Eddie Skinner	Frank Dodge '53 Olds 88	221	75	Running
17		121	Reds Kagle	'51 Studebaker	220	175	Running
18		10	Van Van Wey	Van Wey '54 Ford	220	75	Running
19		93	Ted Chamberlain	Chamberlain '54 Chrysler	213	75	Running
20		71	Dean Pelton	'50 Ford	211	55	Running
21		X-4	Bill Lone	'50 Plymouth	209	150	Running
22		111	Bill O'Dell	'49 Ford	208	50	Running
23		X-18	Charles Bluett	'50 Plymouth	207	50	Running
24		129	Junie Lancaster	'50 Plymouth	202	50	Running
25		491	Dick Ross	'51 Studebaker	201	50	Running
26		25	Bill Widenhouse	Bob Widenhouse '53 Olds 88	200	50	Running
27		101	Dan Danello	'52 Hudson Hornet	199	50	Running
28		38	E.J. Turner	'53 Hudson Hornet	199	50	Running
29		X-2	John Ford	'53 Packard	198	50	Running
30		34	Gene Holcomb	'54 Nash	197	50	Running
31		178	John Lindsay	'50 Plymouth	197	50	Running
32		79	Leon Lundy	Lundy '51 Plymouth	192	50	Running
33		181	Ronnie Kohler	Millard Wright '50 Plymouth	184	50	Running
34		150	Dick Hallock	'50 Lincoln	184	150	Running
35		X-7	Jim Reed	Reed '51 Hudson Hornet	180	50	Running
36		100	Blackie Pitt	Gary Drake '54 Olds 88	172	50	Steering
37		47	Harvey Eakin	Eakin '53 Nash	166	50	Crash
38		2	Bill Blair	Blair '53 Hudson Hornet	163	50	Engine
39		69	Bill Cleveland	'50 Ford	150	50	Heating
40		91	Laird Bruner	'53 Olds 88	135	50	Drv Shft
41		49	Charlie Cregar	'54 Olds 88	128	---	Crash
42		171	Chris Miller	'51 Hudson Hornet	126	---	Crash
43		L-28	Ed Paskovitch	'50 Plymouth	98	---	Stalled
44		126	Dave Terrell	Terrell '54 Dodge	96	---	Rear End
45		18	Arden Mounts	Comstock '54 Hudson	84	---	Engine
46		48	Charles Hanson	'51 Hudson Hornet	75	---	Bearings
47		6	Ralph Liguori	Liguori '54 Dodge	52	---	Engine
48		19	Joe Bell	'50 Hudson	48	---	Rear End
49		641	Bob Kennedy	'50 Plymouth	46	---	Hub
50	5	97	Bill Amick	Frank Christian '54 Olds 88	45	---	Crash
51		177	Bill Morgan	'51 Hudson Hornet	44	---	Crash
52		40	John Soares	Charles Vance '54 Dodge	31	---	Engine
53		104	Ed Van Horne	'50 Ford	25	---	Heating
54		X-5	Dom Persicketti	'49 Olds	25	---	Crash
55		64	Al Neal, Sr	'51 Studebaker	13	---	Crash
56		1	Elton Hildreth	Hildreth Motors '54 Nash	7	---	Crash
57		52	Kenneth Bridge	Mark Handley '52 Hudson	5	---	Crash
58		96	Ray Elston	'52 Hudson Hornet	5	---	Crash
59		53	Elmo Langley	'53 Olds	5	---	Crash
60		90	Bob Welborn	'53 Dodge	4	---	Crash
61			Bill Tanner	Mel Gould '53 Dodge	4	---	Crash
62		481	Jack Lacey	'53 Dodge	3	---	Crash
63		L-2	Ed DeWolff	'50 Ford	3	---	Crash
64		11	P. Cunningham	'54 Hudson	0	---	DNS

Time of Race: 3 hours, 30 minutes, 42.89 seconds
Average Speed: 71.186 mph
Pole Winner: Herb Thomas - 89.418 mph
Lap Leaders: Herb Thomas 1-11, Buck Baker 12-26, Thomas 27-44, Lee Petty 45-69,
    Baker 70-96, Hershel McGriff 97-114, Thomas 115-149, Baker 150-151, Thomas 152-250.
Cautions: 6 for 25 laps.   Margin of Victory:
Attendance: 22,000

Herb Thomas' Hudson takes checkered flag at Langhorne.

replacing the rear end, and sent Johnson back onto the track 28 laps behind. The Ronda, NC newcomer wound up 15th in the field of 64, just 28 laps behind winner Thomas.

The lead changed hands eight times among four drivers. Only the first four finishers led in the 250-lapper.

Race No. 35
Baker Outlasts Petty in Memphis-Arkansas Inaugural

LEHI, AR (Oct. 10) -- Buck Baker drove his Griffin Motors Oldsmobile into the lead with only 17 laps remaining and won the Mid-South 250 at the new Memphis-Arkansas Speedway.

The huge 1.5-mile high banked dirt oval made its debut as the largest stock car racing track in the country, and Lee Petty had the field covered from the start. The Randleman, NC Chrysler driver jumped into the lead in the opening lap and led the first 150 laps. A broken axle forced a long unscheduled pit stop. Baker raced into the lead and led the final 17 laps to cash in on the $2,750 first prize.

Dick Rathmann wound up second, five laps behind. Petty completed 161 laps before departing and still got credit for third place. Herb Thomas and Herschel Buchanan rounded out the top five.

The 167-lap affair was overtaxing on several drivers. Lou Figaro got out of his Hudson in the late stages and had to be hospitalized with heat exhaustion. Johnny

Grand National Race No. 35
167 Laps at Memphis-Arkansas Speedway
LeHi, AR
"Mid-South 250"
250 Miles on 1.5-mile Dirt Track
October 10, 1954

Fin	St	No.	Driver	Team / Car	Laps	Money	Status
1		87	Buck Baker	Griffin Motors '54 Olds 88	167	$2,750	Running
2		3	Dick Rathmann	John Ditz '54 Hudson	162	1,150	Running
3	2	42	Lee Petty	Petty Engineering '54 Chrys	161	850	Axle
4		92	Herb Thomas	Thomas '54 Hudson	161	700	Running
5		4	Herschel Buchanan	'54 Hudson	160	500	Running
6		114	Slick Smith	Frank Christian '52 Olds 88	160	400	Running
7		98	Marvin Panch	Beryl Jackson '54 Olds	158	400	Running
8		189	Lou Figaro	'54 Hudson	154	300	Running
9		14	Hershel McGriff	Frank Christian '54 Olds 88	154	300	Running
10		44	Gober Sosebee	Elmer Brooks '52 Olds 88	153	300	Running
11		23	Jimmie Lewallen	George Miller '53 Hudson	153	200	Running
12		10	Van Van Wey	Van Wey '54 Ford	149	300	Running
13		27	Erick Erickson	Erickson '54 Buick	147	300	Piston
14		85	Charles Hardiman	'54 Hudson	146	200	Running
15		6	Ralph Liguori	Liguori '54 Dodge	146	300	Running
16		08	Frank Smith	'54 Ford	144	100	Running
17		100	Blackie Pitt	Gary Drake '54 Olds 88	138	100	Running
18		86	Don Oldenberg	Oldenberg '54 Mercury	138	200	Running
19		68	John Erickson	'53 Dodge	137	100	Vapor Lk
20		202	Bo Fields	'54 Plymouth	137	200	Rrunning
21		148	Charles Hanson	'53 Olds 88	135	50	Running
22		71	Tim Flock	Atlanta Muffler '54 Hudson	129	50	Running
23		90	Charles Merrill	'53 Hudson	129	50	Running
24		93	Ted Chamberlain	'51 Hudson Hornet	129	50	Running
25		15	Ed Massey	'50 Plymouth	127	50	Running
26		52	Joe Guide, Jr.	Sally Guide '52 Hudson	125	50	Running
27		25	Bill Widenhouse	Bob Widenhouse '54 Olds 88	120	50	Running
28		485	Robert Slensby	'50 Plymouth	117	50	Running
29		47	Jim McLain	'50 Ford 6	112	50	Running
30		291	C.H. Dingler	'51 Hudson Hornet	108	50	Running
31		188	Hooker Hood	Hood '54 Olds 88	102	50	Running
32		82	Joe Eubanks	Phil Oates '51 Hudson	99	50	Fuel Line
33		51	Lloyd Chick	'53 Olds 88	94	50	Running
34		13	Joel Million	Ernest Woods '53 Olds 88	92	50	Rear End
35		76	Leland Sowell	'52 Chrysler	84	50	Crash
36		58	Johnny Patterson	H.B. Ranier '54 Mercury	74	50	Fuel Pmp
37		33	Jimmy Ayers	'54 Dodge	68	50	Gasket
38		599	Bud Chaddock	'53 Hudson Hornet	66	50	Spindle
39		91	Laird Bruner	'53 Olds 88	62	50	Trans
40		18	Arden Mounts	Mounts '54 Hudson	61	50	Gasket
41		133	Bud Harless	'53 Hudson Hornet	55	---	Vapor Lk
42		100	Charles Brinkley	'51 Hudson Hornet	51	---	Vapor Lk
43		176	Dutch Munsinger	'53 Dodge	46	---	Trans
44		5	Ray Duhigg	Joe Blair '54 Mercury	43	---	Steering
45		280	Roscoe Rand	'53 Lincoln	33	100	Tie Rod
46		7	Jim Reed	Reed '53 Hudson Hornet	31	---	Gasket
47		88	Jim Paschal	Ernest Woods '54 Olds 88	27	---	Piston
48		X-2	Dave Terrell	Bob Colvin '54 Packard	18	100	Engine
49		317	Lucky Walters	'54 Hudson Jet	18	---	A-Frame
50		49	Harold Lutz	'53 Olds 88	11	50	Piston
51	1	17	Junior Johnson	Paul Whiteman '54 Cadillac	10	50	Piston
52		112	Richard Jones	'52 Chrysler	1	---	Crash

Time of Race: 2 hours, 48 minutes, 51 seconds
Average Speed: 89.013 mph
Pole Winner: Junior Johnson (Time not available)
Fastest Qualifier: Harold Lutz - 92.767 mph
Lap Leaders: Lee Petty 1-150, Buck Baker 151-167.
Cautions: Margin of Victory: 5 laps plus   Attendance: 12,000

Hudson sponsored by the Atlanta Muffler Service, was overcome by fumes from a leaky muffler. He required oxygen after a 22nd place finish in the race.

Leland Sowell underwent immediate surgery for internal injuries after a grinding crash in the 84th lap.

Junior Johnson won the pole for Paul Whiteman's Cadillac team in the opening round of qualifying. Harold Lutz posted the quickest time trial of the weekend with a 92.767 mph lap. Ironically, Johnson fell out on lap 10 and Lutz on lap 11, both victims of blown engines.

Baker averaged 89.013 mph for his ninth career Grand National win. A crowd of 12,000 was on hand.

Buck Baker won the first superspeedway event held on a dirt track.

Lee Petty led first 150 laps at Memphis-Arkansas Speedway, but broke an axle late and didn't finish.

Race No. 36

Petty Clinches Championship With Martinsville Triumph

Patterson brought Figaro's mount home eighth in the field of 52.

Blackie Pitt also needed medical attention after the two hour and 48 minute race. Tim Flock, driving a

MARTINSVILLE, VA. (Oct. 17) -- Lee Petty locked up his first Grand National driving title with a victory in the scheduled 100-miler at Martinsville Speedway.

The race was curtailed by 35 laps when darkness descended on the picturesque half-mile dirt oval. It was the second time Petty had won a darkness-shortened Grand National event.

Hershel McGriff finished in second place, in the same lap with Petty and in a position to challenge for his fourth win of the year. Third place went to Buck Baker, Dick Rathmann took fourth and Jim Reed was fifth with relief help from Herb Thomas.

Grand National Race No. 36
200 Laps at Martinsville Speedway
Martinsville, VA
100 Miles on Half-mile Dirt Track
October 17, 1954

Fin	St	No.	Driver	Team / Car	Laps	Money	Status
1	1	42	Lee Petty	Petty Eng '54 Chrysler	165	$1,000	Running
2		14	Hershel McGriff	Frank Christian '54 Olds 88	165	650	Running
3		87	Buck Baker	Griffin Motors '54 Olds 88	163	450	Running
4		3	Dick Rathmann	John Ditz '54 Hudson	163	350	Running
5		7	Jim Reed	Reed '52 Hudson Hornet	162	300	Running
6		88	Jim Paschal	Ernest Woods '53 Olds 88	161	250	Running
7		86	Dlon Oldenberg	Oldenberg '54 Mercury	161	200	Running
8		48	John Dodd, Jr.	'51 Hudson Hornet	161	150	Running
9		187	Lou Figaro	'54 Hudson	161	100	Running
10		2	Bill Blair	Blair '53 Hudson Hornet	160	100	Running
11		61	Bob Welborn	'53 Olds 88	160	25	Running
12		19	Clyde Minter	Ken Pace '50 Mercury	160	25	Running
13		82	Joe Eubanks	Phil Oates '51 Hudson	158	25	Running
14		8	Bud Harless	H.B. Ranier '53 Hudson	157	25	Running
15		28	Eddie Skinner	Frank Dodge '53 Olds 88	157	25	Running
16		92	Herb Thomas	Thomas '54 Hudson	156	25	Running
17		18	Arden Mounts	Comstock '53 Hudson Hornet	154	25	Running
18		5	Jimmie Lewallen	Joe Blair '54 Mercury	152	25	Crash
19		98	Marvin Panch	Beryl Jackson '53 Olds 88	152	25	Running
20		248	Giff Woods	'49 Hudson	152	25	Running
21		X-2	Carl Burris	Bob Colvin '53 Packard	150	---	Running
22		93	Ted Chamberlain	Chamberlain '50 Plymouth	149	---	Running
23		51	Gober Sosebee	Cherokee Garage '52 Olds 88	148	---	Radiator
24		V-2	Jim Gillette	'52 Plymouth	148	---	Running
25		111	Bill O'Dell	'49 Ford	141	---	Running
26		481	Jim Cooper	'49 Ford	141	---	Heating
27		491	Dick Ross	'51 Studebaker	140	---	Crash
28		71	Ken Pace	'49 Hudson	138	---	Running
29		77	Fred Dove	'51 Hudson Hornet	127	---	Running
30		13	Joel Million	Ernest Woods '53 Olds 88	126	---	Running
31		80	Ray Duhigg	George Hutchens '50 Plym	122	---	Heating
32		126	Dave Terrell	Terrell '54 Dodge	113	---	Gas Line
33		17	Junior Johnson	Paul Whiteman Cadillac	109	---	Heating
34		148	Chuck Hanson	'53 Olds 88	97	---	Axle
35		6	Ralph Liguori	Liguori '54 Dodge	84	---	Susp
36		78	Hassell Reid	'50 Plymouth	83	---	Spindle
37		11	George Parrish	'53 Studebaker	65	---	Spindle
38		103	Billy Minter	'54 Chevrolet	63	---	Crash
39		100	Blackie Pitt	Gary Drake '53 Olds 88	50	---	Spindle
40		B-29	Dink Widenhouse	Widenhouse '53 Olds 88	34	---	Crash
41		163	Glen Wood	'50 Olds	33	---	Crash
42		182	Cotton Owens	'51 Hudson	32	---	Clutch
43		25	Bill Widenhouse	Bob Widenhouse '53 Olds	21	---	Piston
44		52	Walt Flinchum	'51 Plymouth	9	---	Trans

Time of Race: 1 hour, 51 minutes, 7 seconds
Average Speed: 44.547 mph
Pole Winner: Lee Petty - 53.191 mph
Lap Leaders: Lee Petty 1-13, Hershel McGriff 14-20, Petty 21-70, McGriff 71, Petty 71-165.
Cautions: 3   Margin of Victory: Attendance: 8,500
* Race called at 165 laps due to darkness

Three caution flags broke the action. The most serious altercation occurred in the 34th lap when Dink Widenhouse and Glen Wood flipped their cars simultaneously in the third turn. Bill O'Dell, Dave Terrell and Billy Minter were also involved. No drivers were injured.

Some 44 cars started the event, which produced some tight traffic jams from start to finish. Twenty-six cars finished the race.

Petty and McGriff swapped the lead five times as the crowd of 8,500 were on their feet much of the afternoon.

Petty averaged 44.547 mph for the 165 lap event.

Gwyn Staley's Cadillac in pits before North Wilkesboro race.

Race No. 37

Figaro Fatality Mars McGriff Win at N. Wilkesboro

N. WILKESBORO, NC (Oct. 24) -- Hershel McGriff was declared the winner of the death-marred 1954 Grand National season finale at North Wilkesboro Speedway. Lou Figaro, from Inglewood, CA, succumbed from injuries after his Hudson flipped three laps from the finish. The roof caved in on the diminutive driver and he never regained consciousness.

Figaro was rushed to Wilkes General Hospital where he died late Monday of massive head injuries. The 37 year-old driver was the second competitor to lose his life during the running of a Grand National event. Larry Mann was killed in a race at Langhorne in 1952. Frank Arford died at the wheel in 1953 at Langhorne during qualifying. Figaro was a 17-year veteran of AAA, IMCA and NASCAR competition.

McGriff took the lead from Dick Rathmann in the

85th lap and led the rest of the way to bag his fourth win of the year.

Buck Baker was flagged in second place, Herb Thomas, Slick Smith and Rathmann rounded out the top five. Champion Lee Petty failed to finish, falling victim to a broken hub after only 12 laps.

It was the second time Petty had accumulated the most points over a complete season. In 1950, he was stripped of 809 points for driving in a non-sanctioned event, which cost him the title. Counting point money, the seasonal winnings for the 40 year-old veteran came to $21,101.35. Thomas was the leading money winner with $29,974.05 in earnings.

Grand National Race No. 37
160 Laps at N. Wilkesboro Speedway
North Wilkesboro, NC
100 Miles on .625-mile Dirt Track
October 24, 1954

Fin	St	No.	Driver	Team / Car	Laps	Money	Status
1	1	14	Hershel McGriff	Frank Christian '54 Olds 88	157	$1,000	Running
2		87	Buck Baker	Griffin Motors '54 Olds 88	157	650	Running
3	5	92	Herb Thomas	Thomas '54 Hudson	157	450	Running
4		143	Slick Smith	Frank Christian '51 Olds 88	156	350	Running
5	2	3	Dick Rathmann	John Ditz '54 Hudson	156	300	Running
6		98	Marvin Panch	Beryl Jackson '54 Olds 88	154	250	Running
7		6	Ralph Liguori	Liguori '54 Dodge	153	200	Running
8		2	Bill Blair	Blair '53 Hudson Hornet	151	150	Running
9		19	Clyde Minter	Ken Pace '50 Mercury	151	100	Running
10		82	Joe Eubanks	Phil Oates '51 Hudson	150	100	Running
11		18	Arden Mounts	Comstock '54 Hudson	150	25	Running
12		88	Jim Paschal	Ernest Woods '54 Olds 88	149	25	Running
13		187	Lou Figaro *	'54 Hudson	146	25	Crash
14		188	Hooker Hood	Hood '54 Olds 88	146	25	Running
15		1	Elton Hildreth	Hildreth Motors '53 Nash	145	25	Running
16		13	Joel Million	Ernest Woods '53 Olds 88	144	25	Running
17		9	Donald Thomas	Thomas '53 Hudson	144	25	Running
18		126	Dave Terrell	Terrell '54 Dodge	144	25	Running
19		103	Billy Minter	'54 Chevrolet	120	25	Running
20		71	Ken Pace	'49 Hudson	120	25	Running
21		61	Ned Jarrett	'53 Olds	114	---	Spindle
22		5	Jimmie Lewallen	Joe Blair '54 Mercury	90	---	Tie Rod
23		182	Cotton Owens	'51 Hudson Hornet	87	---	Piston
24		77	Fred Dove	'51 Hudson Hornet	56	---	Gas Tank
25		33	Jim Frey	'52 Hudson Hornet	52	---	Engine
26		8	Bud Harless	'53 Hudson Hornet	51	---	Gasket
27		51	Gober Sosebee	Cherokee Garage '54 Olds 88	42	---	Radiator
28		100	Blackie Pitt	Gary Drake '54 Olds 88	37	---	Gas Tank
29		28	Eddie Skinner	Frank Dodge '53 Olds 88	33	---	Piston
30		B-29	Dink Widenhouse	Widenhouse '53 Olds 88	20	---	Spindle
31		7	Gwyn Staley	Paul Whiteman '54 Cadillac	15	---	Vapor Lk
32	3	42	Lee Petty	Petty Eng.'54 Chrysler	12	---	Hub

* Race called at 157 laps, 3 short of scheduled distance due to Lou Figaro's wreck.
   Figaro died the following day of a skull fracture and brain damage when the roof of
   his car caved in during a roll-over

Time of Race: 1 hour, 30 minutes, 20 seconds
Average Speed: 65.175 mph
Pole Winner: Hershel McGriff - 77.612 mph
Lap Leaders: Dick Rathmann 1-82, Hershel McGriff 83, Rathmann 84, McGriff 85-157.
Cautions: 4   Margin of Victory: Attendance: 8,500

1954 NASCAR Season
Final Point Standings Grand National Division

Rank	Driver	Points	Starts	Wins	Top 5	Top 10	Winnings
1	Lee Petty	8,649	34	7	24	32	$21,101.35
2	Herb Thomas	8,366	34	12	19	27	29,974.05
3	Buck Baker	6,893	34	4	23	28	19,367.87
4	Dick Rathmann	6,760	32	3	23	26	15,938.84
5	Joe Eubanks	5,467	32	0	9	23	8,558.46
6	Hershel McGriff	5,137	24	4	13	17	12,999.23
7	Jim Paschal	3,903	27	1	5	11	5,450.70
8	Jimmie Lewallen	3,233	22	0	5	10	4,668.37
9	Curtis Turner	2,994	10	1	7	8	10,119.84
10	Ralph Liguori	2,905	23	0	2	12	3,494.84
11	Blackie Pitt	2,661	26	0	0	5	1,924.11
12	Dave Terrell	2,645	30	0	0	8	2,224.84
13	Bill Blair	2,362	19	0	2	10	2,649.84
14	Laird Bruner	2,243	23	0	2	6	2,079.84
15	Gober Sosebee	2,114	18	1	4	7	3,149.84
16	John Soares	2,072	8	1	2	4	3,261.56
17	Marvin Panch	1,935	10	0	3	7	4,746.56
18	Eddie Skinner	1,794	15	0	0	1	1,016.56
19	Joel Million	1,779	9	0	0	1	1,091.56
20	Elton Hildreth	1,710	13	0	0	2	1,151.56
21	Arden Mounts	1,705	12	0	0	1	875.00
22	Fireball Roberts	1,648	5	0	0	2	1,080.00
23	Speedy Thompson	1,480	7	0	1	3	1,165.00
24	Johnny Patterson	1,417	4	0	1	1	1,240.00
25	Erick Erickson	1,337	6	0	1	3	1,365.00
26	Ray Duhigg	1,245	12	0	2	5	1,375.00
27	Slick Smith	1,122	6	0	1	2	950.00
28	Clyde Minter	1,116	12	0	0	6	900.00
29	Gwyn Staley	1,088	2	0	0	1	670.00
30	Lloyd Dane	984	4	0	3	4	1,600.00
31	Donald Thomas	980	8	0	3	4	1,675.00
32	Ted Chamberlain	920	10	0	0	1	475.00
33	Danny Letner	915	4	1	2	3	1,975.00
34	Elmo Langley	864	2	0	0	0	450.00
35	Tim Flock	860	5	0	1	3	1,050.00
36	Fred Dove	832	12	0	0	2	525.00
37	Bill Widenhouse	805	6	0	0	0	425.00
38	Gene Comstock	780	1	0	0	0	400.00
39	Walt Flinchum	756	5	0	0	2	425.00
40	Charlie Cregar	716	5	0	0	0	405.00
41	Bill Amick	700	4	0	0	0	250.00
42	Harvey Eakin	698	7	0	0	0	425.00
43	Lou Figaro	690	3	0	0	2	425.00
44	Ken Fisher	668	5	0	0	1	400.00
45	Jim Reed	631	9	0	2	3	965.00
46	Russ Hepler	624	6	0	1	1	525.00
	Allen Adkins	624	2	0	2	2	1,150.00
48	Van Van Wey	602	3	0	0	0	495.00
49	Tony Nelson	568	3	0	0	1	325.00
50	Johnny Dodd, Jr.	552	1	0	0	1	150.00

The 1955 Season
Racing Under Fire
and Mega-buck Cars

Volume one of a four volume series . . . . . . The Beginning 1949 - 1958

1955

On March 20, 1955, AAA driver Larry Crockett was killed in a hideous crash at Langhorne Speedway. Six weeks later on May 1, Mike Nazaruk was burned to death in a flaming crash at the same track.

In the 1955 Indianapolis 500, Bill Vukovich, seeking a third straight 500-mile victory, died when his car gyrated endlessly outside the speedway's backstretch and finally landed upside down in a fiery heap.

Crashes were plentiful on the AAA tour in 1955.

Other AAA drivers fatally injured in 1955 alone while at the wheel were Jack McGrath, Jerry Hoyt and Manuel Ayulo. The 1955 racing season was frequently punctuated by the cold breath of tragedy.

At about 6:00 pm on June 1, 1955, the unthinkable occurred during the 39th running of the 24 Hours of

LeMans road race. In the 34th lap, a Mercedes manned by Pierre Levegh, a wealthy, relatively inexperienced 'once a year racer', clipped the wheels of an Austin Healy driven by Lance Macklin. Levegh's car skidded into a protective barrier near the entrance to pit lane.

The car richocheted across the race course, catapulted over a six foot dirt wall, bounced over a picket fence and exploded in a clap of thunder as it landed where the crowd was thickest.

The car disintegrated. Flaming sections tumbled through the densely populated area. The rear end sailed skyward and landed in another group of spectators near an underpass. The front axle with parts of the chassis, scythed through the crowd.

Screams of pain and terror arose as fragments of the car fell earthward. Smoke and flame spread over a wide area.

For 300 feet along the track, pieces of clothing and parts of bodies were scattered. One grotesque, headless corpse hung from a telegraph pole for hours - beyond help - beyond hope.

It was easily the darkest hour in auto racing history.

"82 Perish In Fiery (LeMans) Crash", read the headline in National Speed Sport News. The death toll would eventually rise to well over 100.

Negative ramifications shot through the veins of auto racing world wide. In some nations, all forms of vehicle racing were banned. The very well-being of auto racing in the United States was threatened.

Senator Richard Neuberger, a Democrat from Oregon, called for a ban of all auto racing in America in a speech before the United States Senate on July 12, 1955.

In a plea to President Dwight D. Eisenhower, Neuberger said, *"Mr. President, I think the time has come to forbid automobile racing and similar carnage in the*

United States. I doubt if there is as much blood shed in Spanish bull rings as today is occurring on automobile race tracks in this country. Now even women racing drivers are getting killed in fiery and dreadful wrecks....

"We allow children to visit race tracks where men and women are constantly in the peril of being maimed or killed. If automobile racing is necessary to perfect motor vehicles as proponents of racing ridiculously claim, then I suppose we next will hear that we must run stallions off cliffs to improve horse flesh.

"I believe the time has come for the United States to be a civilized nation and to stop carnage on racetracks (which) are purposely staged for the profit and for the delight of thousands of screeching spectators."

Although utterly senseless, Neuberger's speech made headlines. Headlines which had the racing fraternity shivering.

Less than a month later, on August 3, 1955, Andrew J. Sordoni, president of the American Automobile Association, which had sanctioned Indy car racing for 54 years, delivered a verbal bombshell that brought a stunned racing world to its knees: *"Upon completion of the schedule of events already undertaken for the year 1955, the AAA will disassociate itself from all types of automobile racing in the United States."*

The AAA withdrawal stirred responses and opinions from everyone:

Bernard Kahn (Sports Editor, Daytona Beach News-Journal): *"AAA withdrawing leaves NASCAR practically alone in the driver's seat in the stock car field ... Racing's future is not jeopardized by the AAA decision. The stage is now set for a blood transfusion in automobile racing. It may come from energetic Bill France, NASCAR President ... Automobile racing is here to stay like sex, the atom bomb and ice cream."*

Russ Catlin (former AAA Press Chief): *"There will be a period of reconstruction that should be very interesting. Out of it a strong man will emerge. As long as such men as Tony Hulman ... and Bill France -- men with a true love for the sport -- are around, racing need worry little about its future."*

Editorial (New York Daily News, August 5, 1955): *"The AAA is well advised, we think. In the old days, these races contributed a lot to the improvement of the*

breed. Those days are long gone. Auto races in these times attract a lot of people who morbidly expect to see somebody killed or injured - and often do. Why should the AAA cater to that morbidity any longer?"

Andy Granatelli (Chicago Auto Racing, Inc.): *"You don't abandon a sport because of accidents. You take steps to make it safer. Withdrawal of the AAA from racing could improve, rather than hinder, the sport."*

In Sordoni's August 3rd announcement, he added that automobile racing no longer was an asset to the development of the highway passenger car, a claim that provoked a sharp response from NASCAR's France. *"Automobile racing (has) for a long time (contributed) and still is contributing much to the automotive industry,"* declared France. *"Racing has been the experimental area and the proving ground for the major improvements which have been made in automobiles.*

"The tire industry today is spending thousands of dollars in experiments with racing automobiles to develop tires which will meet the safety standards required on today's super highways," he added.

With the anti-racing pellets flying, NASCAR further stressed its contributions to the general motoring public. *"As for safety, NASCAR has taken the lead in this field for the past several years,"* declared France. *"Two years ago, NASCAR officials were concerned about automobile doors flying open during an accident. We required extra reinforced door fasteners on all cars. As a direct result from this experience, the automobile manufacturers have improved and strengthened their door locks for 1956."*

Although a bleak future was being sketched by the hands of fate, no ashes fell over NASCAR. France issued a statement regarding the sanctioning body he founded eight years earlier. *"NASCAR represents hundreds of speedway operators, thousands of contestants and millions of fans from coast to coast. NASCAR has become the world's largest racing organization. We plan to continue expanding and to function as it is.*

NASCAR President Bill France and car owner Carl Kiekhaefer.

"NASCAR's reputation has been built on a solid foundation and is continuing to improve safety and sportsmanship on the speedways of America," continued France. *"We will continue to enlarge its program for all types of stock car racing, supervision of speed and automotive tests."*

Evidently the automotive manufacturers felt the NASCAR Grand National circuit was a viable place to test their cars, too. And it was an excellent marketing area.

Chevrolet and Ford entered stock car racing with mega-buck financing to selected NASCAR teams. A few executives in Detroit and Dearborn noticed that sales would often parallel the performance of a particular brand of car. They reasoned that if their brand of automobile won more races, sales would be greater. It was worth trying, anyway.

Chevrolet stepped into NASCAR racing, then jumped full bore into a nation-wide advertising campaign with an accent on high speed performance. The vigorous campaign began with the erection of some 16,000 billboards - all of which noted NASCAR. Additionally, 7,500 daily newspapers carried national ads. Chevrolet hit the network television market with commercials centered around performance on the NASCAR circuit.

Barney Clark, director of the Chevrolet racing program, said, *"This is the sort of concentration that is pretty overwhelming when you add it up."*

Chevrolet won only two races on the Grand National circuit in 1955, but the biggie, Darlington's Southern 500, was one of them. Chevrolet was quite proud of Herb Thomas' achievement on Labor Day. Chevrolet Motor Division arranged to have the winning car hauled to the Texas State Fair in Dallas, one of the largest outdoor fairs in the country. Apparently, this was the first "show car" ever.

Chevrolet and Ford invested large sums of money into NASCAR Grand National racing. The sanctioning body, car owners and drivers were the immediate beneficiaries.

Chrysler, on the other hand, was the main beneficiary of Carl Kiekhaefer's entrance into stock car racing. Kiekhaefer, a man of peculiar character who had made millions with his Mercury Outboard firm, happened to choose Chryslers as his race cars. He had one primary function -- to sell his outboard boat motors.

Along the way, he could acquire a little additional knowledge about reciprocating engines which could be applied to his Mercury Outboards.

Kiekhaefer won most of the races he entered. And

Chrysler Corporation just loved it. Sales of their new Chrysler 300 soared, and they didn't have to invest a dime into racing.

Kiekhaefer's plunge into stock car racing was rather sudden. So sudden that he did not have a driver when he hauled his car to Daytona Beach for SpeedWeek 1955. The first choice was apparently Hershel McGriff, the Oregonian who had had such a fine season in 1954. But McGriff had announced that he was headed back to Oregon, forsaking racing for the lumber

Carl Kiekhaefer brought big bucks, huge car haulers and a touch of class to the NASCAR circuit.

business from whence he came.

Bill France had recommended McGriff, but McGriff stuck to his guns. Had he accepted the Kiekhaefer ride and not taken a 15-year detour from auto racing, there is no telling what NASCAR's record book might look like today.

Kiekhaefer eventually teamed with Tim Flock, who had quit NASCAR a year earlier and was itching to get back in full time.

Flock became an instant sensation. He won eighteen pole positions and eighteen Grand National races - both judged at the time to be unbeatable. He bagged the championship and pocketed $37,779.60 in prize and point money.

Kiekhaefer was hell-bent on winning. He entered cars in 40 Grand National races and won 22 of them. His cars finished first and second in four races. Eleven times his main man, driver Tim Flock, led every lap in an event.

About the only major event he did not win was Darlington's Southern 500. The best he could do there was third.

There was one other *"superspeedway"* on the 1955 slate - a 300 miler on October 9th at the huge Memphis-Arkansas Speedway. It was the largest track on the NASCAR tour at 1.5 miles. Kiekhaefer made

Tim Flock won 18 races and the 1955 Grand National championship.

The Kiekhaefer Chrysler that Tim Flock drove to the 1955 Championship

ure his Mercury Outboard insignia was on the winning car whether he owned it or not.

Kiekhaefer entered four Chryslers in the 300-miler. All three Flock brothers -- Tim, Fonty and Bob -- were saddled in his "Big White Cars", along with AAA star Norm Nelson. He also sponsored virtually every other front runner. Speedy Thompson, Buck Baker and Banks Simpson carried Mr. K's logo. And Thompson won. Tim and Bob finished fourth and fifth.

Although Tim Flock dominated the Grand National tour, he did not assume command in the point race until the 33rd event had been completed. Lee Petty, who also drove a Chrysler, led the points for 31 of the first 32 races, mostly with consistently high finishes.

Chrysler had a double dose of good with both Kiekhaefer and Petty campaigning in their 300s. In late spring, Chrysler released a national two-page advertise-ment to magazines. Petty was pictured with his wife and two children, Richard and Maurice, standing beside a Chrysler. It marked the first time Richard Petty had been in a national advertisement, more than three years before he drove his first race car.

In July of 1955, Lee Petty became the first driver to have a fan club established for his supporters. Morris Metcalfe, a race-crazed fan who would eventually be NASCAR's Scoring Director, organized the Lee Petty Fan Club. There were no membership dues. The only requirement to join was a keen interest in NASCAR and Lee Petty, and that the member drive a Chrysler. Hundreds joined up.

The 1955 season got off to a rocky start. During the threatened ban of all auto racing in this country, NASCAR grew stronger. It had passed the most difficult test of all.

Race No. 1

Petty's Chrysler Hot at Cool High Point; Grabs '55 Opener

HIGH POINT, NC (Nov. 7, 1954) -- Lee Petty of Randleman, NC drove his Chrysler around early leader Dick Rathmann in the seventh lap and breezed to victory in the 100-mile Grand National lid-lifter for the 1955 season at Tri-City Speedway.

It was Petty's 19th career victory, and he became the first competitor to win at least one race in each of NASCAR's first

Lee Petty won '55 season opener.

seven seasons.

Buck Baker was flagged in second place, a half-lap behind Petty. Third place went to Herb Thomas, Gober Sosebee was fourth and Jimmie Lewallen fifth.

Cold wintery weather conditions kept the attendance figure down to 2,000 as Oscar and Vernon Ellington made their debut as promoters in the NASCAR ranks.

Twenty-one cars started the 200-lapper on the new half-mile dirt track and a dozen were running at the finish. Ken Pace of Martinsville, VA flipped his Hudson in the 153rd lap. His injuries were considered minor.

Rathmann ran with the leaders until clutch failure put his Hudson out after 110 laps. He wound up 13th in the final rundown.

Race No. 2

Thomas Noses Out Choquette In Wild Palm Beach Event

W. PALM BEACH, FL (Feb. 6) -- Herb Thomas finally prevailed in the hard fought 100-mile Grand national race at Palm Beach Speedway today.

Thomas pushed his Hudson across the finish line three car lengths ahead of Lake Worth, FL Modified driver Jack Choquette. The lead changed hands eleven times between Thomas and Buck Baker who eventually finished third. But it was Choquette, a local star

Grand National Race No. 1
200 Laps at Tri-City Speedway
High Point, NC
100 Miles on Half-mile Dirt Track
November 7, 1954

Fin	St	No.	Driver	Team / Car	Laps	Money	Status
1	3	42	Lee Petty	Petty Engineering '54 Chrysler	200	$1,000	Running
2	5	14	Buck Baker	Frank Christian '54 Olds 88	200	650	Running
3	1	92	Herb Thomas	Thomas '54 Hudson	199	450	Running
4	4	51	Gober Sosebee	Cherokee Garage '54 Olds 88	196	350	Running
5	12	5	Jimmie Lewallen	Joe Blair '54 Mercury	196	300	Running
6	13	B-29	Dink Widenhouse	Wideshouse '53 Olds 88	192	250	Running
7	11	111	Blackie Pitt	Gary Drake '54 Olds 88	189	200	Running
8	8	8	Bud Harless	Edgar Clay '53 Hudson	187	150	Running
9	15	19	Clyde Minter	Ken Pace '50 Mercury	178	100	Running
10	10	9	Donald Thomas	Thomas '53 Hudson	170	100	Running
11	20	71	Ken Pace	'49 Hudson	151	25	Crash
12	21	11	George Parrish	W.H. Pontress '53 Studebaker	112	25	Wheel
13	2	13	Dick Rathmann	John Ditz '54 Hudson	110	25	Clutch
14	7	1	Elton Hildreth	Hildreth Motors '53 Nash	102	25	Trans
15	9	82	Joe Eubanks	Phil Oates '52 Hudson	93	25	Running
16	17	48	John Dodd, Jr	Dodd '51 Hudson Hornet	68	25	Trans
17	6	7	Junior Johnson	Paul Whiteman '54 Cadillac	51	25	Bearing
18	14	18	Bill Blair	Comstock '54 Hudson	43	25	Crash
19	16	77	Fred Dove	'51 Hudson Hornet	40	25	Running
20	18	52	Bob Welborn	'51 Plymouth	10	25	Radiator
21	19	80	Jim Paschal	George Hutchens '51 Plym	7	---	Rear End

Time of Race: 1 hour, 35 minutes, 25 seconds
Average Speed: 62.882 mph
Pole Winner: Herb Thomas 71.942 mph
Lap Leaders: Dick Rathmann 1-6, Lee Petty 7-200.
Cautions: Margin of Victory: 1/2 lap   Attendance: 2,000

Grand National Race No. 2
200 Laps at Palm Beach Speedway
West Palm Beach, FL
100 Miles on Half-mile Dirt Track
February 6, 1955

Fin	St	No.	Driver	Team / Car	Laps	Money	Status
1	2	92	Herb Thomas	Thomas '54 Hudson	200	$1,000	Running
2	6	23	Jack Choquette	George Miller '54 Hudson	200	650	Running
3	3	87	Buck Baker	Griffin Motors '54 Olds 88	200	450	Running
4	1	3	Dick Rathmann	John Ditz '54 Hudson	200	350	Running
5	5	42	Lee Petty	Petty Engineering '54 Chrysler	196	300	Running
6	9	59	Blackie Pitt	Brownie Pitt '54 Olds 88	194	250	Running
7	14	18	Arden Mounts	Mounts '54 Hudson	191	200	Running
8	10	188	Dutch Hoag	'53 Olds 88	189	150	Running
9	7	51	Lloyd Chick	'54 Buick	189	100	Running
10	12	9	Bill Harrison	'53 Olds 88	188	100	Running
11	13	2	Marion Edwards	'51 Plymouth	180	25	Running
12	16	F-8	Allan Clarke	'54 Buick	179	25	Running
13	18	28	Eddie Skinner	Frank Dodge '53 Olds 88	165	25	Oil Line
14	4	55	Junior Johnson	B & L Motors '55 Olds 88	124	25	Steering
15	11	6	Ralph Liguori	Liguori '54 Hudson	57	25	Rear End
16	15	4	Ken Fisher	Fisher '54 Chrysler	9	25	Carb

Time of Race: 1 hour, 47 minutes, 7 seconds
Average Speed: 56.013 mph
Pole Winner: Dick Rathmann - 65.454 mph
Lap Leaders: Herb Thomas 1 - , Buck Baker - , Thomas - , Baker - , Thomas -
    Baker - , Thomas - , Baker - , Thomas - , Baker - , Thomas -200.
Cautions: Margin of Victory: 3 car lengths   Attendance: 3,000

Local star Jack Choquette finished a close second at West Palm Beach.

driving his first Grand National race, who provided the fireworks as he charged into contention in the closing stages. Tabbed to drive the George Miller Hudson, Choquette scooted past Baker with two laps to go, only to fall short at the finish line as Thomas won his 41st career race.

Dick Rathmann, who started on the pole, finished fourth. Lee Petty was fifth.

A crowd of 3,000 was on hand to watch Thomas average 56.013 mph on the half-mile dirt track. Only sixteen cars went to the starting post. Hooker Hood and Bill Lamont were unable to start due to practice crashes.

Race No. 3

Late Pit Stop Foils Rathmann; Petty Wins Second of Year

JACKSONVILLE, FL (Feb. 13) -- Lee Petty grabbed his second win in three starts by shoving his Chrysler across the finish line first to win the 100-miler at Speedway Park.

Rathmann, who had led on four occasions for 30 laps, appeared headed for his first win of the season until he pitted for fuel while leading with ten laps to go. Petty hustled into the lead and led the rest of the way.

Rathmann, Herb Thomas, Buck Baker and Junior Johnson rounded out the top five.

Petty and Thomas were deadlocked for the point lead as the tour headed for the annual Daytona SpeedWeek festival.

Petty led four times for a total of 168 laps as the lead changed hands eight times among three drivers.

Local driver, Woody Richmond,

Herb Thomas took one of his final rides in a Hudson at Jacksonville.

lost a wheel in the early going putting his Hudson out of action. He then relieved Lloyd Chick and departed with a broken tie rod ten miles later.

Prevailing cold weather kept the crowd down to 3,000, but the sparse crowd was treated to a spine-tingling affair. Petty averaged 69.031 mph, a speed that was nearly six mph faster than Rathmann's pole winning effort of 63.514 mph.

Grand National Race No. 3
200 Laps at Speedway Park
Jacksonville, FL
100 Miles on Half-mile Dirt Track
February 13, 1955

Fin	St	No.	Driver	Team / Car	Laps	Money	Status
1	2	42	Lee Petty	Petty Engineering '54 Chys	200	$1,000	Running
2	1	3	Dick Rathmann	John Ditz '54 Hudson	200	650	Running
3	4	92	Herb Thomas	Thomas '54 Hudson	200	450	Running
4	6	87	Buck Baker	Griffin Motors '54 Olds 88	194	350	Running
5	9	55	Junior Johnson	B & L Motors '55 Olds	191	300	Running
6	5	5	Jimmie Lewallen	Joe Blair '54 Mercury	188	250	Running
7	8	59	Blackie Pitt	Brownie Pitt '54 Hudson 88	187	200	Running
8	15	18	Arden Mounts	Mounts '54 Hudson	186	150	Running
9	19	6	Ralph Liguori	Liguori '54 Hudson	183	100	Clutch
10	17	39	Dave Terrell	Terrell '55 Plymouth	174	100	Running
11	18	11	Bo Fields	'53 Plymouth	154	25	Running
12	11	28	Eddie Skinner	Frank Dodge '53 Olds 88	141	25	Running
13	10	23	Jack Choquette	George Miller '54 Hudson	111	25	Cylinder
14	7	9	Bill Harrison	'53 Olds 88	91	25	Trans
15	13	8	Bud Harless	Edgar Clay '53 Hudson	79	25	Oil Press
16	12	15	Lloyd Chick	'54 Buick	56	25	Tie Rod
17	16	4	Ken Fisher	Fisher '54 Chrysler	54	25	Carb
18	14	80	Woody Richmond	'53 Hudson Hornet	33	25	Spindle
19	3	51	Gober Sosebee	Cherokee Garage '54 Olds 88	9	25	Carb

Time of Race: 1 hour, 26 minutes, 55 seconds
Average Speed: 69.031 mph
Pole Winner: Dick Rathmann - 63.514 mph
Lap Leaders: Dick Rathmann 1-4, Lee Petty 5-35, Rathmann 36-43, Herb Thomas 44-45,
Petty 46-120, Rathmann 121-125, Petty 126-177, Rathmann 178-190, Petty 191-200.
Cautions: Margin of Victory   Attendance: 3,000

Race No. 4

Fireball Disqualified; Flock Declared Daytona Winner

DAYTONA BEACH, FL (Feb. 27) -- Tim Flock of Atlanta, twice disqualified from victories at the Daytona Beach Road Course, got a measure of revenge in the 160-mile Grand National event when first finishing Fireball Roberts was disqualified.

Roberts, wheeling the Fish Carburetor Buick, led the entire way to apparently give car owner Bob Fish his first Grand National win. NASCAR Commissioner

Fireball Roberts in the Fish Carburetor Buick #M-1, leads Dick Joslin into the North turn at Daytona.
Roberts finished first in the 160-miler, but was disqualified following a post race inspection.

E.G. "Cannonball" Baker stripped Roberts of the win nearly 24 hours after the race had been completed.

Baker claimed that mechanic Red Vogt had altered the push rods 16/1000 of an inch. He declared Flock the official winner.

Flock, who had quit racing a year earlier after he was disqualified on a technicality, had gotten the assignment in a new Chrysler owned by Carl Kiekhaefer of Fond Du Lac, WI, who entered the racing game to advertise his Mercury Outboard Motors.

Curtis Turner broadslides his Oldsmobile through
South turn during Daytona Beach 160.

Flock's victory was worth $2,350 of the $9,775 purse. Lee Petty finished second, 9.0 seconds behind the winner and took sole possession of the point lead. Ray Duhigg wound up in third place, Curtis Turner was fourth and Fonty Flock fifth.

Fonty was driving in his first Grand National race in eleven months. He quit NASCAR in March of 1954 and joined the SAFE stock car tour. NASCAR President Bill France required that Flock post a $1,000 "good faith" bond in order to be reinstated.

Tim Flock joined car owner Carl
Kiekhaefer and won their first start
at Daytona.

After the race, third place finisher Ray Duhigg quit the NASCAR circuit to run independent races in the midwest. He was killed at Salem, IN on October 9, 1955, when his car blew a tire and flipped outside the speedway.

Grand National Race No. 4
39 Laps on Beach & Road Course
Daytona Beach, FL
160 Miles on 4.1-mile Beach & Road Course
February 27, 1955

Fin	St	No.	Driver	Team / Car	Laps	Money	Status
1	1	300	Tim Flock	Carl Kiekhaefer '55 Chrysler	39	$2,350	Running
2	2	42	Lee Petty	Petty Eng. '55 Chrysler	39	1,600	Running
3	11	24	Ray Duhigg	J.O. Goode '55 Buick Century	39	1,000	Running
4	12	99	Curtis Turner	Parks Cigarette '55 Olds	39	800	Running
5	14	14	Flonty Flock	Frank Christian '55 Olds	39	625	Running
6	9	82	Joe Eubanks	Oates Motor Co. '55 Olds	39	525	Running
7	5	47	Dick Joslin	Van Landingham '55 Buick	38	425	Running
8	10	63	Bill Tanner	Al Liberty '55 Buick	38	325	Running
9	22	87	Buck Baker	Griffin Motors '54 Olds 88	38	200	Running
10	43	185	Jack Radtke	'55 Chevrolet	38	150	Running
11	18	110	Bud Kutina	'55 Olds	38	140	Running
12	27	23	Jack Choquette	George Miller '54 Hudson	38	125	Running
13	3	88	Dick Rathmann	Ernest Woods '55 Olds	38	100	Running
14	21	37	Marvin Copple	'55 Olds	37	85	Running
15	41	241	Axel Anderson	'55 Mercury	37	75	Running
16	40	140	Mack Hanbury	Caplan Motors '53 Hudson	37	50	Running
17	16	331	Willard Hoit	'55 Chevrolet	37	50	Running
18	15	13	Bob Dawson	William P. Webb '55 Dodge	37	50	Running
19	24	237	Jim Wilson	'55 Dodge	37	50	Running
20	46	16	Ray Chaike	'54 Dodge	37	50	Running
21	29	166	Bud Palmer	W.E. Campbell '55 Dodge	36	35	Running
22	25	39	Jim McLain	Maurice Thompson '55 Olds	36	35	Running
23	34	147	Harvey Eakin	Eakin '55 Nash	35	35	Running
24	37	460	Gene Simpson	Brooks Bros '55 Plymouth	35	35	Running
25	47	8	Bud Harless	Edgar Clay '53 Hudson	35	35	Running
26	7	78	Jim Paschal	Ernest Woods '55 Olds	35	35	Fuel Pmp
27	35	26	Russ Truelove	Truelove '55 Ford	35	35	Running
28	42	599	Floyd Chaddock	'53 Hudson Hornet	35	35	Running
29	36	9	Dave Terrell	Terrell '55 Plymouth	35	35	Running
30	32	18	Arden Mounts	Mounts '54 Hudson	34	35	Running
31	44	1	Bo Fields	Carl S. Wesson '53 Plymouth	33	25	Running
32	39	75	Ed Paskovich	'53 Dodge	33	25	Running
33	31	28	Eddie Skinner	Frank Dodge '53 Olds 88	32	25	Running
34	11	238	Jack Farris	Max Schwimer '55 Olds	30	25	Running
35	6	55	Junior Johnson	B & L Motors '55 Olds	25	25	Clutch
36	17	92	Herb Thomas	Walt Chapman '55 Packard	22	---	Engine
37	30	69	Volney Schulze	'54 Dodge	22	---	Heating
38	28	33	Gene Comstock	Comstock '53 Hudson	19	---	Vapor Lk
39	33	41	Ralph Shaffer	'55 Olds	16	---	Heating
40	20	59	Jimmie Lewallen	Brownie Pitt '54 Olds 88	14	---	Trans
41	8	188	Hooker Hood	Hood '54 Olds 88	14	---	Trans
42	26	349	Charlie Cregar	James Gess '54 Olds 88	10	---	Trans
43	23	56	Tommy Ringstaff	J.B. Cunningham '55 Packard	7	---	Valve
44	45	65	Bill Blair	Ken Whitney '55 Ford	6	---	Trans
45	13	51	Gober Sosebee	C.D. Farnell '55 Olds	4	---	Piston
46	38	48	Louis Headley	'55 Chevrolet	3	---	Ignition
47	19	4	Ken Fisher	Fisher '55 Chrysler	2	---	Carb
48	4	M-1	Fireball Roberts	Fish Carburetor '55 Buick	39	---	Disqual.

Time of Race: 1 hour, 44 minutes, 17 seconds
Average Speed: 91.999 mph
Pole Winner: Tim Flock - 130.293 mph
Lap Leaders: Tim Flock 1-39.
Cautions: None   Margin of Victory 9.0 seconds   Attendance: 27,000

Chrysler New Yorker wound up four full laps ahead of runner-up Don White, former IMCA champion making his second NASCAR start.

Dick Rathmann, leader of the first 64 laps after winning his third pole of the young 1955 season, fell to third in the final order, six laps behind the fleet Petty. Herb Thomas came in fourth and Eddie Skinner notched his best career finish by taking fifth.

Petty's third win of the season moved him into a solid 234 point lead, but it was White who captured the hearts of the 3,750 spectators. The slightly built Keokuk, IA driver was forced to overcome a four lap pit stop midway in the race. After rejoining the fray, White was as quick or quicker than eventual winner Petty.

Eighteen cars started the race and a dozen were running at the finish. Glenn Blackwell entered a Dodge, but he was not allowed to start when NASCAR officials determined the car did not meet safety standards.

Grand National Race No. 5
200 Laps at Oglethorpe Speedway
Savannah, GA
100 Miles on Half-mile Dirt Track
March 6, 1955

Fin	St	No.	Driver	Team / Car	Laps	Money	Status
1	6	42	Lee Petty	Petty Eng. '54 Chrysler	200	$1,000	Running
2	4	1	Don White	'55 Olds	196	650	Running
3	1	3	Dick Rathmann	John Ditz '54 Hudson	194	450	Running
4	8	92	Herb Thomas	Thomas '54 Hudson	192	350	Running
5	11	28	Eddie Skinner	Frank Dodge '53 Olds 88	185	300	Running
6	14	9	Dave Terrell	Terrell '55 Plymouth	182	250	Running
7	12	140	Mack Hanbury	Caplan Motors '53 Hudson	182	200	Running
8	16	78	Jim Paschal	Ernest Woods '55 Olds	182	150	Running
9	15	8	Joel Million	Ernest Woods '55 Olds	181	100	Running
10	17	75	Ed Paskovich	'54 Dodge	170	100	Running
11	2	99	Curtis Turner	Parks Cigarette '55 Olds	167	25	Running
12	18	13	Bob Dawson	'55 Dodge	153	25	Running
13	9	23	Jack Choquette	George Miller '54 Hudson	120	25	Fuel Pmp
14	5	55	Junior Johnson	B & L Motors '55 Olds	95	25	Piston
15	3	59	Blackie Pitt	Brownie Pitt '54 Olds	72	25	Bearing
16	7	87	Buck Baker	Griffin Motors '54 Olds 88	46	25	V Joint
17	10	5	Jimmie Lewallen	Joe Blair '54 Mercury	20	25	Gas Line
18	13	51	Gober Sosebee	C.D. Farnell '55 Olds	8	25	Piston

Time of Race: 1 hour, 39 minutes, 45 seconds
Average Speed: 60.150 mph
Pole Winner: Dick Rathmann - 62.805 mph
Lap Leaders: Dick Rathmann 1-64, Lee Petty 65-200.
Cautions: Margin of Victory: 4 laps plus   Attendance: 3,750

Race No. 5

Petty 3-for-5 After Savannah Win

SAVANNAH, GA (Mar. 6) -- Lee Petty continued his hot pace by trouncing the field in the 100-mile Grand National Race at Oglethorpe Speedway. Petty's

Race No. 6

Fonty Wins Columbia; Scoring Stand Destroyed in Crash

COLUMBIA, SC (Mar. 26) -- Fonty Flock, back in the saddle of the Frank Christian team he quit a year earlier, scored his first Grand National win in 19

Fonty Flock gave Chevrolet its first Grand National win at Columbia, SC.

months in the 100-miler at Columbia Speedway.

Car owner Christian, who traded his familiar Oldsmobiles for a Chevrolet, got Flock back after Hershel McGriff retired at the conclusion of the 1954 season. It was the first time the Chevrolet nameplate had won a NASCAR Grand National race.

Don White took runner-up honors for the second straight race. Dick Rathmann finished third and Buck Baker fourth.

Tim Flock, who led the first 134 laps in the Kiekhaefer Chrysler, wound up fifth. Point leader Lee Petty finished sixth.

A spectacular four-car crack-up in the 132nd lap destroyed the scoring stand. Since the timing equipment was wiped out, there was no official speed recorded Gober Sosebee's Oldsmobile plowed through the scoring stand after tangling with Joel Million, Billy Myers and Jim McLain. No driver injuries were reported.

The victory was Flock's 16th in Grand National competition. A slim crowd of 2,900 was on hand.

Race No. 7

Paschal Paces Field At Hillsboro

HILLSBORO, NC (March 27) -- Steady Jim Paschal stormed past Tim Flock in the 49th lap and breezed to victory in the 100-mile event at Orange Speedway near the Occoneechee Farm Indian Reservation for his first win of the year.

The High Point, NC veteran, driving an Oldsmobile beat runner-up Buck Baker by a half lap to win the $1,000 top prize. Don White finished third, Joel Million was fourth and Fonty Flock fifth.

Four top executives of the Chevrolet division of General Motors were among the 8,000 in attendance to

Grand National Race No. 6
200 Laps at Columbia Speedway
Columbia, SC
100 Miles on Half-mile Dirt Track
March 26, 1955

Fin	St	No.	Driver	Team / Car	Laps	Money	Status
1		14	Fonty Flock	Frank Christian '55 Chevrolet	200	$1,000	Running
2		1	Don White	'55 Olds		650	Running
3		3	Dick Rathmann	Blue Crown '54 Hudson		450	Running
4		87	Buck Baker	Griffin Motors '54 Olds 88		350	Running
5	1	300	Tim Flock	Carl Kiekhaefer '55 Chrysler		300	Running
6		42	Lee Petty	Petty Eng.'54 Chrysler		250	Running
7		55	Junior Johnson	B & L Motors '55 Olds		200	Running
8		78	Jim Paschal	Helzafire '55 Olds		150	Running
9		6	Ralph Liguori	Wheatley Motors '54 Dodge		100	Running
10		92	Herb Thomas	Thomas '55 Chevrolet		100	Running
11	20	59	Blackie Pitt	Brownie Pitt '54 Olds 88		25	Running
12	12	B-29	Dink Widenhouse	Widenhouse '53 Olds 88		25	Running
13	13	82	Joe Eubanks	Oates Motor Co. '53 Hudson		25	Running
14	19	28	Eddie Skinner	Frank Dodge '53 Olds 88		25	Running
15	18	460	Gene Simpson	Brooks Bros '55 Plymouth		25	Running
16	10	140	Mack Hanbury	Caplan Motors '53 Hudson Hornet		25	Running
17	15	51	Gober Sosebee	C.D. Farnell '53 Olds 88		25	Crash
18	9	88	Joel Million	Ernest Woods '55 Olds		25	Crash
19	17		Billy Myers	'55 Plymouth		25	Crash
20	22		Jim McLain	'55 Olds		25	Crash
21	16		Glenn Blackman	'55 Dodge		---	Crash
22	11	5	Jimmie Lewallen	Joe Blair '54 Mercury		---	Tire

Time of Race: No Time Recorded
Average Speed: None
Pole Winner: Tim Flock -
Lap Leaders: Tim Flock 1-134, Fonty Flock 135-200.
Cautions: Margin of Victory: Attendance: 2,900

Grand National Race No. 7
100 Laps at Orange Speedway
Hillsboro, NC
100 Miles on 1-mile Dirt Track
March 27, 1955

Fin	St	No.	Driver	Team / Car	Laps	Money	Status
1	3	78	Jim Paschal	Ernest Woods '55 Olds	100	$1,000	Running
2	2	87	Buck Baker	Griffin Motors '54 Olds	100	650	Running
3	5	1	Don White	'55 Olds	100	450	Running
4	19	88	Joel Million	Ernest Woods '55 Olds	99	350	Running
5	4	14	Fonty Flock	Frank Christian '55 Chevrolet	99	300	Running
6		42	Lee Petty	Petty Eng. '55 Dodge	98	250	Running
7	15	6	Ralph Liguori	Wheatley Motors '54 Dodge	95	200	Running
8	13	140	Mack Hanbury	Caplan Motors '53 Hudson	94	150	Running
9	18	73	John Dodd, Jr.	Dodd '53 Hudson	93	100	Running
10	16	56	Tommy Ringstaff	J.B. Cunningham '55 Packard	92	100	Running
11	21	460	Gene Simpson	Brooks Bros '55 Plymouth	91	25	Running
12	6	55	Junior Johnson	B & L Motors '55 Olds	86	25	King Pin
13	8	9	Donald Thomas	Thomas '54 Hudson	80	25	Engine
14	10	98	Dick Rathmann	'53 Olds 88	76	25	Spindle
15	9	28	Eddie Skinner	Frank Dodge '53 Olds 88	67	25	Running
16	11	92	Herb Thomas	Thomas '55 Chevrolet	65	25	Wheel
17	1	300	Tim Flock	Carl Kiekhaefer '55 Chrysler	49	25	Spindle
18	7	59	Blackie Pitt	Brownie Pitt '54 Olds	48	25	Steering
19	20	80	John Capps	'50 Lincoln	17	25	Crash
20	12	5	Jimmie Lewallen	Joe Blair '54 Mercury	9	25	Fuel Pmp
21	17	19	Fred Dove	'50 Mercury	2	---	Engine

Time of Race: 1 hour, 12 minutes, 54 seconds
Average Speed: 82.304 mph
Pole Winner: Tim Flock - 91.696 mph
Lap Leaders: Tim Flock 1-48, Jim Paschal 49-100.
Cautions: 1   Margin of Victory: 1/2 lap   Attendance: 8,000

Jim Paschal

watch the 100-lapper on the cold, blustery afternoon. Generally, they were disappointed as only one Chevy finished among the top ten.

Herb Thomas, who has traded his trusty Hudson Hornet for a Chevrolet, departed after 65 laps when a wheel broke.

Lee Petty finished sixth and held a 186 point lead over Baker.

The 100-lapper on the gently banked one-mile dirt oval was interrupted only once by the caution flag. Newcomer John Capps flipped his Lincoln in the 21st lap. He was not hurt.

Paschal averaged 82.304 mph for his third career Grand National triumph.

Race No. 8

Baker Edges Rathmann in Closest Finish Ever

N. WILKESBORO, NC (Apr. 3) -- Buck Baker and Dick Rathmann were the principles in the closest finish in Grand National history at North Wilkesboro Speedway.

Baker, driving the Griffin Motors Oldsmobile, held off a fast closing Rathmann by a mere three feet at the stripe to gain his first win of the 1955 season. The Charlotte veteran led all 160 laps on the .625-mile oval, but was hard pressed by Hudson driving Rathmann in the late stages.

Curtis Turner finished in third place, four laps behind the leaders. Point leader Lee Petty came in fourth and Eddie Skinner nabbed fifth place.

Baker became the sixth different winner in the 1955 season. He averaged 73.126 mph for his tenth career

Buck Baker won at North Wilkesboro by 3 feet.

triumph.

Dink Widenhouse, young Concord, NC Oldsmobile driver, won the pole position with a speed of 77.72 mph, but he departed early with engine problems and wound up 19th in the 22 car field.

A crowd of 10,000 was on hand for the 100-mile thriller.

Grand National Race No. 8
160 Laps at N. Wilkesboro Speedway
North Wilkesboro, NC
100 Miles on .625-mile Dirt Track
April 3, 1955

Fin	St	No.	Driver	Team / Car	Laps	Money	Status
1	2	87	Buck Baker	Griffin Motors '54 Olds 88	160	$1,000	Running
2	8	3	Dick Rathmann	John Ditz '54 Hudson	160	650	Running
3	7	99	Curtis Turner	Parks Cigarette '55 Olds	156	450	Running
4	10	42	Lee Petty	Petty Eng. '55 Chrysler	155	350	Running
5	17	28	Eddie Skinner	Frank Dodge '53 Olds 88	154	300	Running
6	20	98	Dave Terrell	Terrell '53 Olds	152	250	Running
7	15	5	Jimmie Lewallen	Joe Blair '54 Mercury	151	200	Running
8	22	460	Gene Simpson	Brooks Bros '55 Plymouth	151	150	Running
9	9	88	Joel Million	Ernest Woods '55 Olds	144	100	Running
10	16	59	Blackie Pitt	Brownie Pitt '54 Olds 88	140	100	Running
11	14	58	Tommy Ringstaff	J.B. Cunningham '55 Packard	126	25	Axle
12	12	72	John Dodd, Sr	Dodd '53 Hudson Hornet	109	25	Spindle
13	13	300	Tim Flock	Carl Kiekhaefer '55 Chrysler	106	25	Coil
14	11	18	Herb Thomas	Arden Mounts '54 Hudson	105	25	Wheel
15	19	80	Jimmy Thompson	'53 Hudson Hornet	84	25	Frame
16	6	78	Jim Paschal	Ernest Woods '55 Olds	70	25	Vapor Lk
17	13	73	John Dodd, Jr	Dodd '53 Hudson Hornet	64	25	Gasket
18	4	55	Junior Johnson	B & L Motors '55 Olds	58	25	Bearing
19	1	B-29	Dink Widenhouse	Widenhouse '53 Olds 88	56	25	Engine
20	5	14	Fonty Flock	Frank Christian '55 Chevrolet	33	25	Axle
21	18	6	Ralph Liguori	Liguori '53 Dodge	16	---	Tire
22	21	57	Boyce Hildreth	Hildreth Motors '53 Hudson	5	---	Gasket

Time of Race: 1 hour, 22 minutes, 3 seconds
Average Speed: 73.126 mph
Pole Winner: Dink Widenhouse - 77.72 mph
Lap Leaders: Buck Baker 1-160.
Cautions: Margin of Victory: 3 feet   Attendance: 10,000

Race No. 9

Thomas Conks Out at End; Flock Wins Montgomery

MONTGOMERY, AL (Apr. 17) -- Tim Flock inherited the lead with 10 laps to go and coasted to victory in the 100-mile Grand National event at Montgomery Motor Speedway.

Herb Thomas, who had snatched first place from Flock on lap 175, had his Chevrolet in the lead when the engine blew with 10 laps left. Flock wheeled his Chrysler into the lead at that point and beat runner-up

Joel Million by four laps.

Fonty Flock came in third, with Curtis Turner and Thomas rounding out the top five.

Lee Petty finished sixth and maintained his point lead.

Baker, second in points, completed 157 laps, good enough for 12th place in the 15 car field.

Pole winner Jim Paschal led the opening laps in his Oldsmobile fielded by Ernest Woods. Flock, who started fifth, scooted past Paschal in the 10th lap and led until Thomas passed him with 25 laps to go.

Paschal made several unscheduled pit stops and wound up 10th, 16 laps behind.

Flock averaged 60.872 mph for his second win of the year.

Tim Flock's Chrysler led all the way at Langhorne.

wound up in second place at the time of the red flag. Junior Johnson was third, followed by Dick Rathmann and Herb Thomas.

Grand National Race No. 9
200 Laps at Montgomery Motor Speedway
Montgomery, AL
100 Miles on Half-mile Dirt Track
April 17, 1955

Fin	St	No.	Driver	Team / Car	Laps	Money	Status
1	5	300	Tim Flock	Carl Kiekhaefer '55 Chrysler	200	$1,000	Running
2	4	88	Joel Million	Ernest Woods '55 Olds	196	650	Running
3	3	14	Fonty Flock	Frank Christian '55 Chevrolet	196	450	Running
4	7	99	Curtis Turner	Parks Cigarette '55 Olds	192	350	Running
5	12	92	Herb Thomas	Thomas '55 Chevrolet	190	300	Piston
6	10	42	Lee Petty	Petty Eng. '54 Chrysler	190	250	Running
7	6	59	Blackie Pitt	Brownie Pitt '54 Olds	186	200	Running
8	8	5	Jimmie Lewallen	Joe Blair '54 Mercury	184	150	Coil
9	9	3	Dick Rathmann	John Ditz '54 Hudson	184	200	Running
10	1	78	Jim Paschal	Ernest Woods '55 Olds	184	100	Running
11	11	155	Henry Ford	Ford '54 Chrysler	171	25	Running
12	2	87	Buck Baker	Griffin Motors '54 Olds 88	157	25	Running
13	13	14	J.H. Petty	'53 Chrysler	0	25	
14	14		Jim Bossic		0	25	
15	15		Morris Hill		0	25	

Time of Race: 1 hour, 38 minutes, 34 seconds
  Average Speed: 60.872 mph
  Pole Winner: Jim Paschal - 64.29 mph
  Lap Leaders: Jim Paschal 1-9, Tim Flock 10-174, Herb Thomas 175-190, T. Flock 191-200.
  Cautions: Margin of Victory: 4 laps plus   Attendance:

Race No. 10

Flock All The Way in Rainy Langhorne

LANGHORNE, PA (Apr. 24) -- Tim Flock pushed his powerful Mercury Outboard Chrysler 300 into the lead at the outset and led all the way to win the 150-mile Grand National race at Langhorne Speedway.

Flock was in front when a rain storm curtailed the event after 124 laps had been completed. Buck Baker

Grand National Race No. 10
150 Laps at Langhorne Speedway
Langhorne, PA
150 Miles on 1-mile Dirt Track
April 24, 1955

Fin	St	No.	Driver	Team / Car	Laps	Money	Status
1	1	300	Tim Flock	Carl Kiekhaefer '55 Chrysler	124	$1,430	Running
2	5	87	Buck Baker	Griffin Motors '54 Olds 88	124	860	Running
3	13	55	Junioor Johnson	B & L Motors '55 Olds	124	600	Running
4	2	3	Dick Rathmann	John Ditz '54 Hudson	124	515	Running
5		92	Herb Thomas	Thomas '55 Buick	122	350	Running
6	8	88	Joel Million	Ernest Woods '55 Olds	122	210	Running
7	10	42	Lee Petty	Petty Eng. '55 Chrysler	122	150	Running
8	26	56	Jim Ord	Hank Salat '55 Packard	118	175	Running
9	18	460	Gene Simpson	Brooks Bros '55 Plymouth	117	150	Running
10	20	121	Harvey Henderson	'53 Hudson Hornet	112	150	Running
11	7	L-28	Carl Krueger	'55 Chevrolet	112	35	Running
12	23	156	Henry Ford	Ford '54 Chrysler	110	25	Running
13		348	Chuck Hansen	'53 Olds	109	25	Running
14		L-4	George Holcomb	'54 Dodge	106	25	Running
15		75	Ed Paskovich	'53 Dodge	105	25	Running
16	22	26	Russ Truelove	Truelove'55 Ford	104	75	Running
17		L-10	Tony DeStafano	'55 Plymouth	103	25	Gasket
18	24	5	Jimmie Lewallen	Joe Blair '54 Mercury	97	75	Bearing
19	19	59	Blackie Pitt	Brownie Pitt '54 Olds	95	25	Crash
20	15	98	Dave Terrell	Terrell '55 Olds	93	25	Springs
21	9	97-A	Bill Blair	J.M. Fitzgibbons '54 Olds	90	35	Radiator
22	4	14	Fonty Flock	Frank Christian '55 Chevrolet	70	85	Engine
23	16	4	Ken Fisher	Fisher '55 Chrysler	58	25	Axle
24	3	78	Jim Paschal	Ernest Woods '55 Olds	45	35	Vapor Lk
25	11	18	Archie Nepstad	'55 Buick	41	25	Crash
26	32	73	Jim Cramblitt	'53 Hudson Hornet	22	25	Beaaring
27	27	96	Les Young	Ray Elston '53 Hudson	21	25	Crash
28	28	1	Elton Hildreth	Hildreth Motors '54 Nash	18	75	Engine
29		7	Jim Reed	Reed '53 Hudson Hornet	12	25	Fuel Pmp
30	12	63	Bill Tanner	Al Liberty '55 Chevrolet	7	25	Rear End
31	14	71	John Dodd, Jr.	Dodd '55 Dodge	5	---	Crash
32	6	6	Pepper Cunningham	'55 Chrysler	3	---	Tire

Time of Race: 1 hour, 42 minutes, 4 seconds
  Average Speed: 72.893 mph
  Pole Winner: Tim Flock - 86.699 mph
  Lap Leaders: Tim Flock 1-124.
  Cautions: 3   Margin of Victory: 1 car length, under caution   Attendance: 23,000
* Race shortened to 124 laps due to rain

The event was marred by three spectacular crashes, one of which sent Leslie Young, driving under the name of Ray Elston, to the hospital with critical injuries. Young's Hudson Hornet went out of control in the 25th lap and rolled twice. He was taken to the hospital with a brain concussion.

Archie Nepstad's Buick crashed through the guard rail in the 43rd lap. He escaped injury. Blackie Pitt, NASCAR's top rookie in 1954, suffered serious head injuries when his Oldsmobile crashed in the 98th lap.

Flock scampered his way around the 'Horne at an average speed of 72.893 mph to grab his third win of the year. The triumph moved him up to fifth in the point standings. Point leader Lee Petty finished seventh.

Lou Headley, driving a # 43 Plymouth, flipped on his second qualifying lap and was unable to start. Headley was transported to the hospital with shoulder injuries.

Bob Welborn's Chevrolet at speed down Charlotte front stretch. He finished in fifth place.

Race No. 11

Baker Wins Charlotte; Herb Thomas Badly Hurt

CHARLOTTE, NC May 1) -- Buck Baker took the lead in the final 16 miles and won the 100-miler at Charlotte Speedway, an event in which Herb Thomas was seriously injured.

Thomas, who had won the pole position, crashed heavily in the 41st lap while running fourth. His Buick hooked a rut and flipped over several times. The two-time Grand National champion was thrown from his car and was rushed to Charlotte Memorial Hospital with a fractured leg, severe bruises, a concussion, a lacerated arm and shoulder injuries.

Thomas was expected to miss at least six months while recuperating.

Tim Flock finished second in the affair promoted by Bruton Smith. Third place went to Dave Terrell, who turned in a surprising effort in his Oldsmobile. Gober Sosebee was fourth and Bob Welborn finished fifth in Julian Petty's Chevrolet.

Jim Ord flipped his Packard in the 100th lap and had to take a trip to the hospital to have several stitches placed in his arm.

Flock led the first 112 laps in his Chrysler. Baker, who started 16th in his Buick, showed exceptional muscle as he slashed through the pack working his way into contention. He hugged Flock's rear bumper for nearly 15 laps before making the final decisive pass.

Baker averaged 52.630 mph in the 100-miler.

Herb Thomas' Buick begins it's dive at Charlotte Speedway. The 2-time Grand National champion suffered multiple injuries.

Grand National Race No. 11
133 Laps at Charlotte Speedway
Charlotte, NC
100 Miles on .75-mile Dirt Track
May 1, 1955

Fin	St	No.	Driver	Team / Car	Laps	Money	Status
1	16	89	Buck Baker	Baker '55 Buick	133	$1,000	Running
2	2	300	Tim Flock	Carl Kiekhaefer '55 Chrysler	133	650	Running
3	10	98	Dave Terrell	Terrell '55 Olds	131	450	Running
4	7	51	Gober Sosebee	C.D. Farnell '55 Olds	127	350	Fuel
5	11	44	Bob Welborn	J H Petty '55 Chevrolet	127	300	Running
6	17	71	John Dodd, Jr.	Dodd '55 Dodge	126	250	Running
7	18	6	Ralph Liguori	Liguori '54 Dodge	125	200	Running
8	21	121	Harvey Henderson	'53 Hudson Hornet	123	150	Running
9	13	28	Eddie Skinner	Frank Dodge '53 Olds	122	100	Running
10	25	4	Ken Fisher	Fisher '55 Chrysler	117	100	Running
11	23	460	Gene Simpson	Brooks Bros '55 Plymouth	109	75	Spin
12	5	B-29	Dink Widenhouse	Widenhouse '53 Olds 88	105	60	Running
13	14	56	Jim Ord	Hank Salat '55 Packard	99	50	Crash
14	20	18	Arden Mounts	Mounts '54 Hudson	89	50	Running
15	8	42	Lee Petty	Petty Eng. '55 Chrysler	85	50	Steering
16	22	11	George Parrish	W.H. Pontress '53 Studebaker	70	50	Injury
17	4	87	Speedy Thompson	Griffin Motors '54 Olds	57	50	Radiator
18	26	3	Dick Rathmann	John Ditz '54 Hudson	55	50	Carb
19	6	78	Jim Paschal	Ernest Woods '54 Olds 88	50	50	Cont Arm
20	3	55	Junior Johnson	B & L Motors '55 Olds	43	50	Gas Tank
21	1	92	Herb Thomas	Thomas '55 Buick	41	---	Crash
22	19	88	Joel Million	Ernest Woods '55 Olds	36	---	Disqual
23	9	14	Fonty Flock	Frank Christian '55 Chevrolet	27	---	Heating
24	12	8	Bud Harless	Edgar Clay '53 Hudson	23	---	Heating
25	15	97-A	Bill Blair	J.M. Fitzgibbons '54 Olds	15	---	Heating
26	24	0	Ed Cole	'54 Ford 6	3	---	Shocks

Time of Race: 1 hour, 53 minutes, 43 seconds
Average Speed: 52.630 mph
Pole Winner: Herb Thomas - 70.184 mph
Lap Leaders: Tim Flock 1-112, Buck Baker 113-133.
Cautions: 2 for 18 laps   Margin of Victory: Attendance: 6,000

Grand National Race No. 12
200 Laps at Hickory Speedway
Hickory, NC
100 Miles on Half-mile Dirt Track
May 7, 1955

Fin	St	No.	Driver	Team / Car	Laps	Money	Status
1	2	55	Junior Johnson	B & L Motors '55 Olds	200	$1,000	Running
2	1	300	Tim Flock	Carl Kiekhaefer '55 Chrysler	200	650	Running
3	5	78	Jim Paschal	Ernest Woods '55 Olds	200	450	Running
4	10	42	Lee Petty	Petty Eng.'55 Chrysler	198	350	Running
5	19	5	Jimmie Lewallen	Joe Blair '54 Mercury	196	300	Running
6	9	88	Joel Million	Ernest Woods '55 Olds	195	250	Running
7	21	B-29	Dink Widenhouse	Widenhouse '53 Olds 88	193	200	Running
8	4	28	Eddie Skinner	Frank Dodge '53 Olds 88	193	150	Running
9	7	14	Buddy Shuman	Frank Christian '55 Chevrolet	193	100	Running
10	12	98	Dave Terrell	Terrell '55 Olds	191	100	Crash
11	13	87	Buck Baker	Griffin Motors '54 Olds 88	191	75	Running
12	15	121	Harvey Henderson	'53 Hudson Wasp	189	60	Running
13	18	460	Gene Simpson	Brooks Bros '55 Plymouth	185	50	Running
14	11	63	Bill Tanner	Al Liberty '55 Chevrolet	182	50	Running
15	23	71	Fred Dove	'55 Olds	180	50	Running
16	20	0	Ed Cole	'54 Ford 6	173	50	Running
17	8	3	Dick Rathmann	John Ditz '54 Hudson	141	50	Tire
18	6	44	Bob Welborn	Welborn '55 Chevrolet	132	50	Gears
19	22	11	George Parrish	W.H. Pontress '53 Studebaker	95	40	Axle
20	19	303	Henry Ford	Ford '55 Chrys	85	50	Trans
21	3	2	Gwyn Staley	Westmoreland '55 Chevrolet	56	---	Heating
22	14	4	Ken Fisher	Fisher '55 Chrysler	50	---	Rear End
23	16	349	Charlie Cregar	Engler's '54 Olds 88	37	---	Rear End

Time of Race: 1 hour, 21 minutes, 36 seconds
Average Speed: 58.823 mph
Pole Winner: Tim Flock - 67.478 mph
Lap Leaders: Tim Flock 1-23, Gwyn Staley 24-56, Jim Paschal 57-64,
     Junior Johnson 65-158, Flock 159-171, Johnson 172-200.
Cautions: 6 for 32 laps   Margin of Victory: I car length (under caution)   Attendance: 4,500

Race No. 12

Hometown Favorite Junior Johnson Gets First GN Win

HICKORY, NC (May 7) -- Junior Johnson of Ronda, NC, overcame a pair of spin-outs and won the 100-mile Grand National race at Hickory Speedway.

The local star, who began his career on this same oval, drove past Tim Flock in the 172nd lap and led the rest of the way.

Flock held on to finish second, just ahead of third place finisher Jim Paschal. Lee Petty was fourth with Jimmie Lewallen fifth.

It was Johnson's first career big league stock car racing win.

Flock and Johnson started on the front row and battled furiously in the opening laps. Johnson's B & L Motors Oldsmobile hooked the rear of Flock's Chrysler, sending both into a spin on lap 23.

Gwyn Staley swept past both and took the lead on lap 24. Paschal got around Staley in the 57th lap and led

Charlie Cregar #349 and Lee Petty #42 zip around Henry Ford #303 at Hickory Speedway.

until lap 64 when Johnson took the lead for the first time.

The leadfoot driver with the enlarged belly held first place for 96 laps before spinning out in the second turn on lap 158. Flock took the lead, but could not hold off the determined Johnson in the final laps.

The race ended under the caution flag when Dave Terrell crashed with six laps to go. In all there were six yellow flags for a total of 32 laps.

A crowd of 4,500 watched Johnson cover the 200 laps on the half-mile track at a 58.823 mph clip.

Phoenix, AZ. It was his fourth win of the year and the 21st of his career.

Flock, second place finisher less than twelve hours earlier in a 100-miler at Hickory, NC, hopped aboard a private jet which belonged to his car owner, Carl Kiekhaefer, led all 100 laps and beat runner-up Marvin Panch by a lap and a half. Panch had obtained a week-end pass from the U.S. Army in order to compete.

Tim Flock won at Phoenix.

Third place went to Clyde Palmer, with pole sitter Bill Amick fourth and Allen Adkins fifth.

It was the third time in the 1955 season that Flock has led every lap in a Grand National race.

Flock averaged 71.485 mph.

Grand National Race No. 13
100 Laps at Fairgrounds Raceway
Phoenix, AZ
100 Miles on 1-mile Dirt Track
May 8, 1955

Fin	St	No.	Driver	Team / Car	Laps	Money	Status
1	2	301	Tim Flock	Carl Kiekhaefer '55 Chrysler	100	$1,000	Running
2	3	98	Marvin Panch	Panch '55 Mercury	99	650	Running
3	16	47	Clyde Palmer	'55 Mercury	98	450	Running
4	1	3	Bill Amick	'55 Dodge	97	350	Running
5	7	7	Allen Adkins	Gus Davis '54 Dodge	97	300	Running
6	12	5	Speedy Thompson	'53 Olds	96	250	Running
7	6	6	Ben Gregory	'54 Olds	96	200	Running
8	11	23	Ken Johns	'55 Chevrolet	96	150	Running
9	20	24	Bob Havenmann	'54 Dodge	95	100	Running
10	13	26	Ed Brown	'55 Chevrolet	93	100	Running
11	14	33	Lloyd Dane	'53 Hudson Hornet	91	25	Running
12	8	84	Danny Letner	'55 Plymouth	91	25	Running
13	21	28	Roy Clark	'53 Dodge	90	25	Running
14	23	44	Ronald Hornaday	'54 Ford	90	25	Running
15	19	78	Frank Douglas	'54 Chevrolet	89	25	Running
16	27	77	Owen Loggins	'54 Dodge	88	25	Running
17	22	76	Cliff Richmond	'55 Chevrolet	88	25	Running
18	25	18	Rick DeLewis	'54 Hudson	88	25	Running
19	24	41	Ernie Young	Walt Palozi '50 Plymouth	87	25	Running
20	18	2	John Soares	Gus Davis '55 Dodge	86	25	Running
21	26	53	Herb Crawford	'51 Studebaker	80	---	Running
22	17	99	Dick Zimmerman	Oscar Maples '54 Mercury	77	---	Throttle
23	29	278	Fifi Scott	'53 Hudson	74	---	Tire
24	10	65	Chuck Meekins	Jim Rush '55 Olds	45	---	Tie Rod
25	28	17	Rex DeLewis	'55 Ford	42	---	Crash
26	15	55	Mel Larson	Larson '55 Olds	40	---	Heating
27	9	39	Bill West	Jim Dane '53 Hudson Hornet	24	---	Conn Rod
28	5	14	Fonty Flock	Frank Christian '55 Chevrolet	16	---	Shocks
29	4	25	Erick Erickson	Erickson '54 Buick	15	---	Tie Rod

Time of Race: 1 hour, 23 minutes, 56 seconds
Average Speed: 71.485 mph
Pole Winner: Bil Amick - 75.519 mph
Lap Leaders: Tim Flock 1-100.
Cautions: Margin of Victory: 1 1/2 Laps   Attendance:

Race No. 13

With No Sleep, Weary Flock wins at Phoenix

PHOENIX, AZ (May 8) - Driving on very little sleep, Tim Flock piloted his Chrysler to a flag-to-flag triumph in the 100-miler at the Fairgrounds Raceway in

Race No. 14

Wild-riding Letner Tops At Tucson Rodeo Grounds

TUCSON, AZ (May 15) -- Danny Letner drove his Oldsmobile around Allen Adkins' fuel starved Dodge with just two laps to go and won the 100-mile Grand National event at the Tucson Rodeo Grounds.

Adkins, who had led twice for 72 laps, was holding a 3.0-second cushion over Letner when he had to dash to the pits for a couple of gallons of fuel less than a mile from the finish. He returned to the track a lap behind Letner, but still managed to finish second.

Lloyd Dane was third, Chuck Meekins finished fourth and Bill Amick fifth.

The lead changed hands seven times among five drivers and the crowd of 4,000 spectators were never sure of the outcome until the drop of the checkered flag. Ed Brown, who qualified second, led on two occasions for 44 laps, was running third when the right front wheel buckled under his Chevrolet, putting him out with eight laps remaining.

Marvin Panch had come from tenth starting spot to first in 55 laps. He was leading the race when a broken right rear wheel forced his Mercury behind pit wall. He wound up 16th in the 19-car field.

Letner, of Downey, CA, averaged 51.428 mph in his Oldsmobile for the 200 laps on the half-mile dirt track.

Grand National Race No. 14
200 Laps at Tucson Rodeo Grounds
Tucson, AZ
100 Miles on Half-mile Dirt Track
May 15, 1955

Fin	St	No.	Driver	Team / Car	Laps	Money	Status
1	3	6	Danny Letner	Coz Cancilla '54 Olds	200	$1,000	Running
2	6	7	Allen Adkins	Gus Davis '54 Dodge	199	650	Running
3	5	33	Lloyd Dane	Jim Dane '53 Hudson Hornet	198	450	Running
4	11	65	Chuck Meekins	Jim Rush '52 Olds	196	350	Running
5	1	3	Bill Amick	Gus Davis '55 Dodge	194	300	Running
6	15	24	Bob Havenmann	'54 Dodge	193	250	Running
7	2	26	Ed Brown	'55 Chevrolet	192	200	Wheel
8	13	55	Mel Larson	Larson '55 Olds	190	150	Running
9	8	54	Johnny Mock	'54 Olds	183	100	Running
10	16	53	Herb Crawford	'51 Studebaker	174	100	Running
11	14	76	Cliff Richmond	'55 Chevrolet	158	25	Running
12	12	99	Dick Zimmerman	'54 Mercury	145	25	Running
13	19	278	Fifi Scott	'50 Hudson	142	25	Running
14	17	41	Ernie Young	Walt Palozi '50 Plymouth	125	25	Heating
15	9	47	Roy Clark	'55 Mercury	103	25	Tie Rod
16	10	98	Marvin Panch	Panch '55 Mercury	70	25	Wheel
17	4	14	Jack Richardson	'55 Chevrolet	50	25	Axle
18	18	18	Rick DeLewis	'54 Hudson	34	25	Hub
19	7	77	Owen Loggins	'54 Dodge	30	25	A Frame

Time of Race: 1 hour, 56 minutes, 40 seconds
Average Speed: 51.428 mph
Pole Winner: Bill Amick - 56.179 mph
Lap Leaders: Bill Amick 1-28, Ed Brown 29-54, Marvin Panch 55-69, Brown 70-87,
     Allen Adkins 88-139, Danny Letner 140-171, Adkins 171-198, Letner 199-200.
Cautions: Margin of Victory: 1 lap plus   Attendance: 4,000

Race No. 15

Johnson Dazzling; But Flock Marches on at Martinsville

MARTINSVILLE, VA (May 15) -- Tim Flock grabbed win number five of the 1955 Grand National season by taking the 100-miler at Martinsville Speedway.

Lee Petty finished second, making it a one-two sweep for the mighty Chrysler. Third place went to Junior Johnson, who put on a dazzling show for the overflow crowd of 11,000.

Johnson, who qualified second, led the first 107 laps in his Oldsmobile. He had lapped everyone in the 27 car field except Flock when a tire blew out. He retreated to the pits where it took his B & L Motors pit crew four laps to change the tire. Johnson returned to the track running far down in the order, but he managed to make up two of the lost laps.

Fourth place went to Jimmie

Lewallen and Bob Welborn was fifth.

Pole sitter Jim Paschal was running second when overheating problems forced him to take his Olds to the pits for a lengthy stay. He eventually finished ninth, 14 laps behind the winner.

Flock's fourth win in the last four weeks came at an average speed of 52.554 mph.

Grand National Race No. 15
200 Laps at Martinsville Speedway
Martinsville, VA
100 Miles on Half-mile Dirt Track
May 15, 1955

Fin	St	No.	Driver	Team / Car	Laps	Money	Status
1	4	300	Tim Flock	Carl Kiekhaefer '55 Chrysler	200	$1,000	Running
2	7	42	Lee Petty	Petty Eng. '55 Chrysler	200	650	Running
3	2	55	Junior Johnson	B & L Motors '55 Olds	198	450	Running
4	8	88	Jimmie Lewallen	Ernest Woods '55 Olds	198	350	Running
5	14	44	Bob Welborn	Welborn '55 Chevrolet	194	300	Running
6	11	87	Buck Baker	Griffin Motors '54 Olds	192	250	Running
7	17	121	Harvey Henderson	'53 Hudson Hornet	192	200	Running
8	15	28	Eddie Skinner	Frank Dodge '53 Olds	189	150	Running
9	1	78	Jim Paschal	Ernest Woods '55 Olds	187	100	Running
10	16	71	Fred Dove	'55 Olds	183	100	Running
11	19	41	Arden Mounts	Mounts '54 Hudson	181	75	Running
12	27	27	John Gouveia	'55 Chevrolet	179	60	Running
13	22	73	Jim Cramblitt	'53 Hudson Hornet	178	50	Running
14	25	460	Gene Simpson	Brooks Bros '55 Plymouth	169	50	Running
15	26	0	Ed Cole	'54 Ford 6	167	50	Running
16	13	71-A	John Dodd, Jr.	Dodd '55 Dodge	151	50	Gasket
17	23	11	George Parrish	W.H. Pontress '53 Studebaker	123	50	Running
18	9	14	Speedy Thompson	Frank Christian '55 Chevrolet	109	50	Tie Rod
19	12	1-A	Carl Krueger	Krueger '55 Chrysler	107	50	Wheel
20	6	2	Gwyn Staley	Westmoreland '55 Chevrolet	102	50	Heating
21	20	19	Gordon Smith	'55 Chevrolet	95	---	Wheel
22	18	5	Perk Brown	Joe Blair '54 Mercury	93	---	Engine
23	5	301	Fonty Flock	Mercury Outboards '55 Chyrs	85	---	Brakes
24	10	97-A	Bill Blair	J.M. Fitzgibbons '54 Olds	45	---	Heating
25	21	4	Ken Fisher	Fisher '55 Chrysler	40	---	Carb
26	3	7	Jim Reed	Reed '55 Chevrolet	27	---	Heating
27	24	1	Ken Pace	'54 Chevrolet	9	---	Hub

Time of Race: 1 hour, 54 minutes, 10 seconds
Average Speed: 52.554 mph
Pole Winner: Jim Paschal - 58.823 mph
Lap Leaders: Junior Johnson 1-107, Tim Flock 108-200.
Cautions: 2   Margin of Victory: Attendance: 11,000

Tim Flock #300, Fonty Flock #301 and Buck Baker #87 in close formation at Martinsville.

Race No. 16

Flock Boys 1-2 at Richmond In Kiekhaefer Cars

RICHMOND, VA (May 22) -- Tim Flock posted his sixth win of the year as he came from 22nd starting position to nail down top honors in the 100-mile Grand National race at the Atlantic Rural Exposition Fairgrounds.

Torrential rains played havoc with the half-mile racing surface. Flock and most of the other favorites were forced to take a back seat when qualifications were rained out. The entire 28 car starting field was determined by a blind draw. Flock drew 22nd position. His brother, Fonty, started tenth in a twin Kiekhaefer Chrysler 300. Other leading contenders, Lee Petty and Junior Johnson drew 20th and 25th positions respectively.

Arden Mounts drew the pole. Jim Paschal, who started fourth, came from the second row to take the lead in the opening lap as the entire field slid at a snail's pace while scrambling for position on the muddy track.

Dick Rathmann got around Paschal on lap 59 and led until the 67th lap when Paschal broadslid his way back into the lead. Flock took the lead in the 78th lap and led the rest of the way.

Fonty Flock finished about a half-lap behind his brother. Lee Petty finished third, Paschal was fourth and Johnson fifth.

The surface was rutted and choppy in the late stages of the race. Clumps of mud clogged fuel lines and choked off radiators as only 13 cars were running at the finish.

Flock's average winning speed was 54.298 mph, and the victory moved him into third place in the point standings behind Petty and Buck Baker.

Grand National Race No. 16
200 Laps at Atlantic Rural Exposition Fairgrounds
Richmond, VA
100 Miles on Half-mile Dirt Track
May 22, 1955

Fin	St	No.	Driver	Team / Car	Laps	Money	Status
1	22	300	Tim Flock	Carl Kiekhaefer '55 Chrysler	200	$1,000	Running
2	10	301	Fonty Flock	Carl Kiekhaefer '55 Chrysler	200	650	Running
3	20	42	Lee Petty	Petty Eng. '55 Chrysler	200	450	Running
4	4	78	Jim Paschal	Ernest Woods '55 Olds	199	350	Running
5	25	55	Junior Johnson	B & L Motors '55 Olds	197	300	Running
6	19	44	Bob Welborn	Welborn '55 Chevrolet	192	150	Running
7	24	460	Gene Simpson	Brooks Bros '55 Plymouth	190	200	Running
8	12	53	Elmo Langley	'53 Olds	181	150	Running
9	8	69	Volney Schulze	'54 Dodge	179	100	Running
10	9	11	George Parrish	W.H. Pontress '53 Studebaker	176	100	Running
11	26	98	Dave Terrell	Terrell '55 Olds	172	75	Piston
12	11	43	Bill Brown	'55 Chevrolet	169	60	Running
13	5	54	Nace Mattingly	Mattingly '55 Ford	157	50	Running
14	23	900	Johnny Roberts	'55 Chevrolet	145	50	Heating
15	1	18	Arden Mounts	Mounts '54 Hudson	141	50	Running
16	7	28	Eddie Skinner	Frank Dodge '53 Olds 88	141	50	Bearing
17	21	89	Buck Baker	Baker '55 Buick	133	50	Wheel
18	27	121	Harvey Henderson	'53 Hudson Hornet	115	50	Spindle
19	14	303	Henry Ford	Ford '55 Chrysler	115	50	Rear End
20	3	140	Mack Hanbury	Caplan Motors '53 Hudson	111	50	Running
21	15	8	Billy Carden	Bishop Bros. '55 Buick	109	---	Heating
22	16	302	Carl Krueger	Krueger '55 Chrysler	99	---	Spindle
23	18	4	Ken Fisher	Fisher '55 Chrysler	95	---	Tie Rod
24	2	3	Dick Rathmann	John Ditz '55 Chrysler	66	---	Drv Shft
25	17	71	Fred Dove	'55 Olds	64	---	Piston
26	13	97-A	Sonny Hutchins	J.M. Fitzgibbons '54 Olds	15	---	Heating
27	28	444	Chick Dawson	'55 Studebaker	11	---	Fuel Line
28	6	88	Jimmie Lewallen	Ernest Woods '55 Olds	3	---	Mud

Time of Race: 1 hour, 50 minutes, 30 seconds
Average Sped: 54.298 mph
Pole Winner: No Time Trials
Lap Leaders: Jim Paschal 1-58, Dick Rathmann 59-66, Paschal 67-77, Tim Flock 78-200.
Cautions: Margin of Victory: Attendance:

Race No. 17

Rain-Shortened Raleigh Event to Johnson

RALEIGH, NC. (May 28) -- Junior Johnson stormed past pole winner Tim Flock in the 10th lap and went on to score his second win of the season in the 100-miler at the Raleigh State Fairgrounds.

Johnson, the hefty mountain kid, rim-rode the half-mile dirt track and lapped the field before the half-way point in the race. He had his Oldsmobile out front when a rain storm forced officials to red flag the race after 172 laps had been completed.

Fonty Flock finished in second place. Finishing third through fifth were Buck Baker, Lee Petty and Gwyn Staley.

Tim Flock's Chrysler departed after 15 laps when the

Junior Johnson (right) and Buck Baker, 1st and 3rd place finishers at Raleigh.

brakes failed. He wound up 25th in the 27 car field.

The race marked the return of Donald Thomas, younger brother of injured Herb Thomas. Donald finished 18th in a Hudson readied by Smokey Yunick.

Johnson won $1,350 for his 50.522 mph victory.

driver to complete the prescribed 200 lap distance. Fred Dove enjoyed his best career finish by taking third. Dick Rathmann came in fourth, with John Dodd, Jr. fifth.

A crowd of 6,500 watched a caution filled contest. In all, eight yellow flags interrupted the action. Gene Simpson, Mack Hanbury and Donald Thomas were taken out by wrecks.

Fonty and Tim Flock, driving team Kiekhaefer Chryslers, both fell victim to oil pressure problems within two laps of each other.

Petty averaged 50.583 mph for his 22nd career victory.

Grand National Race No. 17
200 Laps at State Fairgrounds
Raleigh, NC
100 Miles on Half-mile Dirt Track
May 28, 1955

Fin	St	No.	Driver	Team / Car	Laps	Money	Status
1	3	55	Junior Johnson	B & L Motors '55 Olds	172	$1,350	Running
2	6	301	Fonty Flock	Carl Kiekhaefer '55 Chrysler	171	875	Running
3	7	87	Buck Baker	Griffin Motors '54 Olds 88	171	550	Running
4	11	42	Lee Petty	Petty Eng. '55 Chrysler	170	400	Running
5	13	2	Gwyn Staley	Westmoreland '55 Chevrolet	167	315	Running
6	7	78	Jim Paschal	Ernest Woods '55 Olds	166	265	Running
7	8	171	John Dodd, Jr.	Dodd '55 Dodge	165	220	Running
8	15	8	Billy Carden	Bishop Bros. '55 Buick	165	165	Running
9	10	71	Fred Dove	'55 Olds	164	125	Running
10	17	28	Eddie Skinner	Frank Dodge '53 Olds 88	164	100	Running
11	9	97-A	Bill Blair	J.M. Fitzgibbons '54 Olds	163	90	Running
12	25	B-29	Dink Widenhouse	Widenhouse '53 Olds 88	163	75	Running
13	22	19	Gordon Smith	'55 Chevrolet	160	65	Running
14	21	18	Arden Mounts	Mounts '54 Hudson Hornet	160	65	Running
15	23	5	Richard Brownlee	Joe Blair '54 Mercury	154	65	Running
16	18	121	Harvey Henderson	'53 Hudson Hornet	151	65	Running
17	26	11	George Parrish	W.H. Pontress '53 Studebaker	142	50	Running
18	14	92	Donald Thomas	Thomas '54 Hudson	139	85	Running
19	2	44	Bob Welborn	Welborn '55 Chevrolet	118	175	Tie Rod
20	19	140	Mack Hanbury	Caplan '53 Hudson Hornet	101	50	Gasket
21	12	303	Henry Ford	Ford '55 Chrysler	98	40	Brakes
22	24	69	Volney Schulze	'54 Dodge	46	25	Trans
23	16	3	Dick Rathmann	John Ditz '55 Chrysler	36	25	Tie Rod
24	4	14	Speedy Thompson	Frank Christian '55 Chevrolet	25	75	Radiator
25	1	300	Tim Flock	Carl Kiekhaefer '55 Chrysler	15	125	Brakes
26	20	460	Gene Simpson	Brooks Bros '55 Plymouth	5	40	Axle
27	27	302	Lloyd Dane	Carl Kreuger '55 Chrysler	0	25	Engine

Time of Race: 1 hour, 42 minutes, 8 seconds
Average Speed: 50.522 mph
Pole Winner: Tim Flock - 58.612 mph
Lap Leaders: Tim Flock 1-9, Junior Johnson 10-172.
Cautions: 6 for 20 laps   Margin of Victory: 1 lap plus   Attendance:
* Race shortened to 172 laps due to rain

Race No. 18

Petty Wins Caution-filled Forsyth Feature

WINSTON-SALEM, NC (May 29) -- Lee Petty broke out of a mild slump by tooling his Chrysler to a half-lap victory in the 100-mile race at the Forsyth County Fairgrounds. It was Petty's fourth win of the 1955 Grand National season, but his first since March 7.

Jim Paschal finished in second place, the only other

Grand National Race No. 18
200 Laps at Forsyth County
Fairgrounds
Winston-Salem, NC
100 Miles on Half-mile Dirt Track
May 29, 1955

Fin	St	No.	Driver	Team / Car	Laps	Money	Status
1	9	42	Lee Petty	Petty Eng. '54 Chrysler	200	$1,000	Running
2	7	78	Jim Paschal	Ernest Woods '55 Olds	200	650	Running
3	15	71	Fred Dove	'55 Olds	197	450	Running
4	11	3	Dick Rathmann	John Ditz '55 Chrysler	193	350	Running
5	12	171	John Dodd, Jr.	Dodd '55 Dodge	190	300	Running
6	17	19	Gordon Smith	'55 Chevrolet	186	250	Running
7	5	44	Bob Welborn	Welborn '55 Chevrolet	186	200	Running
8	22	5	Perk Brown	Joe Blair '54 Mercury	182	150	Running
9	20	18	Arden Mounts	Mounts '54 Hudson	181	100	Running
10	13	28	Eddie Skinner	Frank Dodge '53 Olds 88	179	100	Running
11	16	69	Volney Schulze	'54 Dodge	178	75	Running
12	2	87	Buck Baker	Griffin Motors '54 Olds	173	60	Axle
13	11	11	George Parrish	W.H. Pontress '53 Studebaker	164	50	Running
14	3	2	Gwyn Staley	Westmoreland '55 Chevrolet	160	50	Rear End
15	8	92	Donald Thomas	Thomas '54 Hudson	142	50	Crash
16	23	140	Mack Hanbury	Caplan Motors '53 Hudson	135	50	Crash
17	19	121	Harvey Henderson	'53 Hudson Hornet	131	50	Oil Press
18	10	8	Billy Carden	Bishop Bros. '55 Buick	121	50	Piston
19	14	97-A	Bill Blair	J.H. Fitzgibbons '54 Olds	114	50	Gas Tank
20	6	300	Tim Flock	Carl Kiekhaefer '55 Chrysler	64	50	Oil Press
21	1	301	Fonty Flock	Carl Keikhaefer '55 Chrysler	62	---	Oil Press
22	4	55	Junior Johnson	B & L Motors '55 Olds	20	---	Rear End
23	18	460	Gene Simpson	Brooks Bros '55 Plymouth	10	--	Crash

Time of Race: 1 hour, 58 minutes, 37 seconds
Average Speed: 50.583 mph
Pole Winner: Fonty Flock - 56.710 mph
Lap Leaders: Fonty Flock 1-41, Buck Baker 42-167, Lee Petty 168-200.
Cautions: 8   Margin of Victory: 1/2 lap   Attendance: 6,500

Race No. 19

Johnson Passes Flock, Snares New Oxford 100

NEW OXFORD, PA (June 10) -- Junior Johnson motored past Tim Flock on lap 99 and led the rest of the way to win the 100-mile Grand National race at

Lincoln Speedway. It was Johnson's third win of the season, each of them coming after passing Flock in a decisive move.

Flock finished second, two laps behind. Buck Baker, Jim Reed and Nace Mattingly rounded out the top five.

Fonty Flock led the first 15 laps, getting the jump on pole sitter Johnson at the start. Tim Flock passed his brother on lap 16 and led for 83 laps before Johnson took the lead for good.

Point leader Lee Petty was running second in the late stages, but a broken control arm relegated his Chrysler to a 14th place finish. He still held a 314 point lead over Buck Baker in the standings. Tim Flock ranked third, 854 points out of first place.

Johnson averaged 65.371 mph. Thirty-one cars started the race and 19 were running at the finish.

Race No. 20

Flock Avoids Wreck; Laps Field at Rochester

ROCHESTER, NY (June 17) -- Tim Flock slithered past an opening lap wreck which sidelined point leader Lee Petty and led all the way to win the 100-mile Grand National race at the Monroe County Fairgrounds.

It was Flock's seventh victory on the 1955 Grand National traveling tour. The Atlanta Chrysler driver finished a lap ahead of runner-up Fonty Flock, who drove the final 150 laps without brakes. Both were driving Chryslers from the Kiekhaefer Mercury Outboard shops.

Bob Welborn finished third, Jimmie Lewallen was fourth and Harvey Henderson took fifth spot.

Buck Baker, driving his Griffin Motors Olds, started on the pole. However he got mixed up with Petty, coming hard from the outside front row, and never led the race. He finally exited at the half-way point when the engine blew.

Two caution flags for a total of eight laps held Flock's average speed down to 57.170 mph.

Grand National Race No. 19
200 Laps at Lincoln Speedway
New Oxford, PA
100 Miles on Half-mile Dirt Track
June 10, 1955

Fin	St	No.	Driver	Team / Car	Laps	Money	Status
1	1	55	Junior Johnson	B & L Motors '55 Olds	200	$1,000	Running
2	3	300	Tim Flock	Carl Kiekhaefer '55 Chrysler	198	650	Running
3	7	87	Buck Baker	Griffin Motors '54 Olds	197	450	Running
4	12	7	Jim Reed	Reed '55 Chevrolet	195	350	Running
5	15	54	Nace Mattingly	Mattingly '55 Ford	190	300	Running
6	14	73	John Dodd, Jr.	Dodd '53 Hudson Hornet	188	250	Running
7	17	58	Bill Bowman	'54 Nash	187	200	Running
8	8	2	Gwyn Staley	Westmoreland '55 Chevrolet	186	150	Running
9	25	302	Carl Krueger	Krueger '55 Chrysler	185	100	Running
10	20	900	Johnny Roberts	'55 Chevrolet	184	100	Running
11	19	72	John Dodd, Sr.	Dodd '53 Hudson Hornet	183	75	Running
12	22	17	Millard Wright	Wright '54 Olds	182	60	Running
13	11	110	Gene Simpson	'55 Buick	178	50	Running
14	4	42	Lee Petty	Petty Eng.'55 Chrysler	175	50	Cont Arm
15	18	19	Gordon Smith	'55 Chevrolet	174	50	Running
16	28	69	Volney Schulze	'54 Dodge	170	50	Running
17	16	28	Eddie Skinner	Frank Dodge '53 Olds 88	164	50	Running
18	27	30	Walt Regan	'54 Dodge	162	50	Running
19	26	41	Junie Gough	'54 Dodge	150	50	Running
20	13	27	Johnny Gouveia	'55 Chevrolet	149	50	Brakes
21	31	140	Mack Hanbury	Caplan Motors '53 Hudson	147	---	Running
22	23	348	Chuck Hansen	'54 Dodge	142	---	Hub
23	5	44	Bob Welborn	Welborn '55 Chevrolet	127	---	Steering
24	10	98	Dave Terrell	Terrell '55 Olds	94	---	Brakes
25	24	34	Gene Holcomb	'54 Nash	82	---	Engine
26	9	88	Jimmie Lewallen	Ernest Woods '55 Olds	77	---	Brakes
27	6	78	Jim Paschal	Ernest Woods '55 Olds	70	---	Brakes
28	2	301	Fonty Flock	Carl Kiekhaefer '55 Chrysler	63	---	Brakes
29	21	4	Ken Fisher	Fisher '55 Chrysler	28	---	Hub
30	30	121	Harvey Henderson	'53 Hudson Hornet	11	---	Spindle
31	29	75	Ed Paskovich	'54 Dodge	8	---	Engine

Time of Race: 1 hour, 31 minutes, 47 seconds
Average Speed: 65.371 mph
Pole Winner: Junior Johnson - 75.853 mph
Lap Leaders: Fonty Flock 1-15, Tim Flock 16-98, Junior Johnson 99-200.
Cautions: Margin of Victory: 2 laps plus   Attendance:

Grand National Race No. 20
200 Laps at Monroe County
Fairgrounds
Rochester, NY
100 Miles on Half-mile Dirt Track
June 17, 1955

Fin	St	No.	Driver	Team / Car	Laps	Money	Status
1	3	300	Tim Flock	Carl Kiekhaefer '55 Chrysler	200	$1,000	Running
2	4	301	Fonty Flock	Carl Kiekhaefer'55 Chrysler	199	650	Running
3	10	44	Bob Welborn	Welborn '55 Chevrolet	196	450	Running
4	8	88	Jimmie Lewallen	Ernest Woods '55 Olds	194	350	Running
5	15	121	Harvey Henderson	'53 Hudson Hornet	191	300	Running
6	11	73	John Dodd, Jr.	Dodd '53 Hudson Hornet	185	250	Rear End
7	17	28	Eddie Skinner	Frank Dodge '53 Olds	182	200	Running
8	18	8	Emory Mahon	'54 Chevrolet	182	150	Tire
9	21	77	Al Weber	Dave Everett '55 Ford	175	100	Running
10	13	40	Gene Simpson	Bud Harbaugh '55 Buick	175	100	Running
11	20	4	Bob Beck	Beck '55 Chevrolet	158	75	Running
12	6	55	Junior Johnson	B & L Motors '55 Olds	152	60	Clutch
13	7	7	Jim Reed	Reed '55 Chevrolet	137	50	Spindle
14	14	98	Dave Terrell	Terrell '55 Olds	124	50	Gas Line
15	9	78	Jim Paschal	Ernest Woods '55 Olds	116	50	Rod Brng
16	1	87	Buck Baker	Griffin Motors '55 Olds	100	50	Engine
17	5	96	Dutch Hoag	'55 Chevrolet	96	50	Wheel
18	19	97-A	Millard Wright	Wright '54 Olds	43	50	Gasket
19	12	54	Paul Pettitt	'55 Chevrolet	10	50	Fuel Pmp
20	2	42	Lee Petty	Petty Eng. '55 Chrysler	1	50	Tie Rod
21	16	19	Gordon Smith	'55 Chevrolet	1	---	Crash

Time of RAce: 1 hour, 44 minutes, 57 seconds
Average Speed: 57.170 mph
Pole Winner: Buck Baker - 61.141 mph
Lap Leaders: Tim Flock 1-200.
Cautions: 2 for 8 laps   Margin of Victory: 1 lap plus   Attendance: 6,000

Race No. 21

Johnson 3 out of 5 After Fonda Triumph

FONDA, NY (June 18) -- Junior Johnson zipped around Tim Flock in the 96th lap and scored a popular triumph in the 100-miler at Fonda Speedway.

It was Johnson's third Grand National win in the last five races on NASCAR's premier tour. Flock finished second, Lee Petty was third with Buck Baker and Bob Welborn rounding out the top five.

Pole sitter Flock led the first 95 laps as Johnson, who started in ninth place, worked his way to the front. Once in the lead, Johnson never looked back. He was a lap ahead of runner-up Flock and some nine

Junior Johnson took victory at Fonda, NY.

laps in front of third place Petty.

The caution flag was out only once for four laps when Al Weber tossed his Ford into a roll in the 28th lap. He was not hurt.

Fonty Flock, who put brother Tim's Chrysler on the pole in qualifications, started his own Chrysler in fourth spot. But engine problems put him out after 140 laps.

Johnson averaged 58.413 mph for his fourth career win.

Grand National Race No. 22
200 Laps at Airborne Speedway
Plattsburg, NY
100 Miles on Half-mile Dirt Track
June 19, 1955

Fin	St	No.	Driver	Team / Car	Laps	Money	Status
1	1	42	Lee Petty	Petty Eng. '55 Chrysler	200	$1,000	Running
2	3	87	Buck Baker	Griffin Motors '54 Olds	199	650	Running
3	2	2	Tim Flock	Westmoreland '55 Chevrolet	197	450	Running
4	5	44	Bob Welborn	Welborn '55 Chevrolet	194	350	Running
5	4	302	Carl Krueger	Krueger '55 Chrysler	190	300	Running
6	7	121	Harvey Henderson	'53 Hudson Hornet	187	250	Running
7	6	98	Dave Terrell	Terrell '55 Olds	182	200	Running
8	9	27	John McVitty	'55 Chevrolet	174	150	Running
9	10	28	Eddie Skinner	Frank Dodge '53 Olds 88	170	100	Running
10	8	348	Chuck Hansen	'55 Olds	157	100	Running
11	16	15	Fonty Flock	'53 Olds	109	75	Heating
12	12	4	Ted Pritcher	'54 Chrysler	38	60	Coil
13	14	11	George Combs	'53 Hudson Hornet	27	50	Wheel
14	15	7	Frank Powell	'53 Chrysler	23	50	Spindle
15	11	1	Chick Norris	'55 Olds	10	50	Gas Line
16	13	14	Julian Petty	'53 Chrysler	5	50	Fuel Pmp

Time of Race: 1 hour, 41 minutes, 34 seconds
Average Speed: 59.074 mph
Pole Winner: 55.744 mph
Lap Leaders: Lee Petty 1-25, Buck Baker 26-62, Petty 63-200.
Cautions: Margin of Victory: 1 lap plus   Attendance:

Grand National Race No. 21
200 Laps at Fonda Speedway
Fonda, NY
100 Miles on Half-mile Dirt Track
June 18, 1955

Fin	St	No.	Driver	Team / Car	Laps	Money	Status
1	9	55	Junior Johnson	B & L Motors '55 Olds	200	$1,000	Running
2	1	300	Tim Flock	Carl Kiekhaefer '55 Chrysler	199	650	Running
3	3	42	Lee Petty	Petty Eng. '55 Chrysler	191	450	Running
4	6	87	Buck Baker	Griffin Motors '54 Olds 88	188	350	Running
5	5	44	Bob Welborn	Welborn '55 Chevrolet	188	300	Running
6	11	98	Dave Terrell	Terrell '55 Olds	176	250	Running
7	15	121	Harvey Henderson	'53 Hudson Hornet	174	200	Running
8	17	27	John McVitty	'55 Chevrolet	169	150	Running
9	19	136	Dick Hallock	'53 Hudson Hornet	153	100	Running
10	12	26	Russ Truelove	Truelove '55 Ford	151	100	Rear End
11	4	301	Fonty Flock	Carl Kiekhaefer '55 Chrysler	139	75	Engine
12	2	7	Jim Reed	Reed '55 Chevrolet	130	60	Axle
13	7	88	Jimmie Lewallen	Ernest Woods '55 Olds	95	50	Rear End
14	14	40	Gene Simpson	Bud Harbaugh '55 Buick	91	50	Rear End
15	13	302	Carl Krueger	Krueger '55 Chrysler	88	50	Spindle
16	10	54	Paul Pettitt	'55 Chevrolet	40	50	Springs
17	18	77	Al Weber	Dave Everett '55 Ford 6	26	50	Crash
18	8	2	Gwyn Staley	Westmoreland '55 Chevrolet	15	50	Heating
19	16	28	Eddie Skinner	Frank Dodge '53 Olds 88	15	50	Brakes

Time of Race: 1 hour, 42 minutes, 43 seconds
Average Speed: 58.413 mph
Pole Winner: Fonty Flock * - 61.770 mph
Lap Leaders: Tim Flock 1-95, Junior Johnson 96-200.
Cautions: 1 for 4 laps   Margin of Victory: 1 lap plus   Attendance:
* Fonty Flock qualified car #300 on pole. Tim Flock drove it in the race.

Race No. 22

Petty Plucks Plattsburg 100 For Fifth '55 Win

PLATTSBURG, NY (June 19) -- Lee Petty topped off the Northern swing by taking the win in the 100-mile Grand National event at Airborne Speedway. It was his fifth victory of the year.

Buck Baker finished in second place, and Tim Flock was third. Flock was handling the controls of the Hubert Westmoreland Chevrolet normally driven by Gwyn Staley. His powerful Kiekhaefer Chrysler encountered mechanical problems in a practice session.

Bob Welborn finished fourth with Carl Krueger fifth. Petty led the first 25 laps after starting on the pole. Baker forged to the front for 37 laps before Petty got back into the lead for good.

Julian Petty, the winner's brother, finished last in the 16 car field when the fuel pump quit working on his Chrysler after just five laps.

Lee Petty averaged 59.074 mph, considerably faster than his pole winning effort of 55.744 mph, which was achieved on a soggy track surface.

Grand National Race No. 23
200 Laps at Southern States Fairgrounds
Charlotte, NC
100 Miles on Half-mile Dirt Track
June 24, 1955

Fin	St	No.	Driver	Team / Car	Laps	Money	Status
1	1	301	Tim Flock	Carl Kiekhaefer '55 Chrys	200	$1,000	Running
2	4	87	Buck Baker	Griffin Motors '54 Olds	198	650	Running
3	5	2	Gwyn Staley	Westmoreland '55 Chevrolet	198	450	Running
4	7	44	Bob Welborn	Welborn '55 Chevrolet	198	350	Running
5	3	55	Junior Johnson	B & L Motors '55 Olds	194	300	Running
6	10	B-29	Dink Widenhouse	Widenhouse '53 Olds	193	250	Running
7	2	78	Jim Paschal	Ernest Woods '55 Olds	187	200	Running
8	9	82	Joe Eubanks	Phil Oates '53 Hudson	185	150	Running
9	12	42	Lee Petty	Petty Engineering '54 Chrysler	185	100	Running
10	11	28	Eddie Skinner	Frank Dodge '53 Olds 88	177	100	Running
11	13	33	Al Watkins	'54 Dodge	174	75	Running
12	16	94	Ed Cole	'54 Ford	171	60	Running
13	8	98	Dave Terrell	Terrell '55 Olds	123	50	Rod Brng
14	20	121	Harvey Henderson	'53 Hudson Hornet	94	50	Engine
15	6	71	Speedy Thompson	'55 Olds	85	50	Shocks
16	19	19	Gordon Smith	'55 Chevrolet	77	50	Crash
17	14	5	Richard Brownlee	Joe Blair '54 Mercury	74	50	Crash
18	18	75	Max Berrier	'53 Plymouth	55	50	Axle
19	15	57	Boyce Hildreth	'53 Hudson Hornet	41	50	U Joint
20	17	11	George Parrish	W.H. Pontress '53 Studebaker	38	50	Oil Line

Time of Race: 1 hour, 56 minutes, 59 seconds
Average Speed: 51.289 mph
Pole Winner: Tim Flock - 57.915 mph
Lap Leaders: Tim Flock 1-200
Cautions: Margin of Victory: 2 laps plus 24 seconds   Attendance: 7,200

Race No. 23

Flock Leads All 200 Laps at Charlotte

CHARLOTTE, NC (June 24) -- Back in the saddle of the immaculate Kiekhaefer Mercury Outboard '55 Chrysler 300, Tim Flock

chalked up his eighth win of the season in the 100-mile Grand National race at the Southern States Fairgrounds.

Flock led all 200 laps around the half-mile dirt track, marking the fourth time in the current season the Atlanta Speedster had led from start to finish. Buck Baker wound up second, two laps and 24 seconds behind the winner. Gwyn Staley, Bob Welborn and Junior Johnson filled out the top five.

Lee Petty finished ninth and saw his point lead slashed to 154 over second place Baker. Flock, who missed the first three races of the year, ranks third, 550 behind Petty.

Richard Brownlee's Mercury slapped the wall in the 74th lap, and Gordon Smith wrecked his Chevrolet in a 79th lap crash. Neither driver was hurt.

Flock, who earned the pole for the 21st time in his career, averaged 51.289 mph.

Race No. 24

Flock Outruns Flock; Kiekhaefer Kars Run 1-2

SPARTANBURG, SC (July 6) -- Tim Flock, hitting stride in the hot summer months, bolted to his ninth win of the year by taking a flag-to-flag triumph in the 100-mile Grand national race at the Piedmont Interstate Fairgrounds.

Drivers for the Carl Kiekhaefer Chrysler team finished first and second in the 100 mile grind. Fonty Flock, in the same laps as the winner, took second place. Buck Baker was fourth in his Chrysler, two laps behind third place finisher Lee Petty. Cotton Owens took fifth place.

Wrecks claimed two contenders. Jimmie Lewallen, who started fourth in the Ernest Woods Oldsmobile, clobbered the wall in the ninth lap. He wound up last

The three Flock brothers beside two of the potent Kiekhaefer Chryslers. Tim and Fonty finished 1-2 at Spartanburg.

in the 27-car field.

Gwyn Staley, running in the top five, hit the wall after 103 laps and had to park his Chevrolet.

Flock averaged 49.106 mph after six caution flags broke the action.

Point leader Petty went to Memphis-Arkansas Speedway for a practice session a few days after the Spartanburg event. While practicing for the upcoming 250-miler at the 1.5-mile superspeedway, Petty's Chrysler crashed through the retaining barrier, left the speedway and landed in a lake. He tore down 90 feet of guard rail and uprooted 15 fence posts in the mishap. Petty was shaken but otherwise uninjured.

100-mile Grand National contest at Columbia Speedway. It was the second win of the season for Paschal.

Paschal nosed out runner-up Jimmie Lewallen by six car lengths to

Jim Paschal beams from Columbia Speedway victory lane.

post his fourth career Grand National win. Lewallen, who started on the pole for the first time in his career, gave car owner, Col. Ernest Woods, his first 1-2 finish in Grand National competition.

Tim Flock finished in third place, and Billy Carden was fourth. Fifth at the stripe was Buck Baker.

Banjo Matthews was headed for a top five finish, but the A-frame snapped in his Frank Christian Chevrolet with less than 10 laps to go. He got credit for sixth place in the final order.

Point leader Lee Petty started second, but wound up 13th when the engine popped in his Chrysler. Crashes took out Junior Johnson and Gordon Smith.

Paschal averaged 55.469 mph. Lewallen had taken the pole at 59.741 mph.

Grand National Race No. 24
200 Laps at Piedmont Interstate Fairgrounds
Spartanburg, SC
100 Miles on Half-mile Dirt Track
July 6, 1955

Fin	St	No.	Driver	Team / Car	Laps	Money	Status
1	1	300	Tim Flock	Carl Kiekhaefer '55 Chrysler	200	$1,100	Running
2	2	301	Fonty Flock	Carl Kiekhaefer '55 Chrysler	200	650	Running
3	6	42	Lee Petty	Petty Eng.'55 Chrysler	200	450	Running
4	7	303	Buck Baker	Henry Ford '55 Chrysler	198	350	Running
5	14	70	Cotton Owens	'55 Chevrolet	195	300	Running
6	13	14	Banjo Matthews	Frank Christian '55 Chevrolet	195	250	Running
7	21	9	Donald Thomas	Thomask '54 Hudson	193	200	Running
8	12	73	John Dodd, Jr.	Dodd '55 Olds	190	150	Running
9	17	82	Joe Eubanks	Oates Motor Co. '53 Hudson	190	100	Running
10	16	71	Bob Welborn	'55 Olds	170	100	Rear End
11	26	28	Eddie Skinner	Frank Dodge '53 Olds	166	75	Running
12	20	460	Gene Simpson	Brooks Bros '55 Plymouth	159	60	Running
13	8	92	Speedy Thompson	Thomas '55 Buick	145	50	Rear End
14	9	3	Dick Rathmann	John Ditz '55 Chrysler	132	50	Cont Arm
15	27	94	Ed Cole	Clarence DeZalia'54 Ford	129	50	Wheel
16	5	2	Gwyn Staley	Westmoreland'55 Chevrolet	103	50	Crash
17	24	19	Gordon Smith	'55 Chevrolet	91	50	Spindle
18	11	121	Harvey Henderson	'53 Hudson Hornet	79	50	Spindle
19	3	55	Junior Johnson	B & L Motors '55 Olds	78	50	Trans
20	10	78	Jim Paschal	Ernest Woods '55 Olds	77	50	Trans
21	15	04	Pee Wee Jones	Westmoreland '55 Chevrolet	61	---	Crash
22	18	8	Billy Carden	Bishop Bros. '55 Buick	44	---	Rear End
23	23	5	Richard Brownlee	Joe Blair '54 Mercury	43	---	Shocks
24	25	81	Jimmy Thompson	'53 Hudson Hornet	41	---	Spindle
25	22	18	Arden Mounts	Mounts '53 Hudson Hornet	16	---	A Frame
26	19	98	Dave Terrell	Terrell '53 Olds	14	---	Shocks
27	4	88	Jimmie Lewallen	Ernest Woods '55 Olds	0	---	Crash

Time of Race: 2 hours, 2 minutes, 11 seconds
  Average Speed: 49.106 mph
  Pole Winner: Tim Flock - 58.517 mph
  Lap Leaders: Tim Flock 1-200.
  Cautions: 6   Margin of Victory: Attendance:

Race No. 25

Paschal-Lewallen Finish 1-2 For Woods Team

COLUMBIA, SC (July 9) -- Jim Paschal drove the Ernest Woods Helzafire Oldsmobile to victory in the

Grand National Race No. 25
200 Laps at Columbia Speedway
Columbia, SC
100 Miles on Half-mile Dirt Track
July 9, 1955

Fin	St	No.	Driver	Team / Car	Laps	Money	Status
1	5	78	Jim Paschal	Ernest Woods '54 Olds	200	$1,000	Running
2	1	88	Jimmie Lewallen	Ernest Woods '55 Olds	200	700	Running
3	9	300	Tim Flock	Carl Kiekhaefer '55 Chrysler	200	475	Running
4	4	8	Billy Carden	Bishop Bros. '55 Buick	197	365	Running
5	10	303	Buck Baker	Henry Ford '55 Chrysler	195	310	Running
6	7	14	Banjo Matthews	Frank Christian '55 Chevrolet	191	250	A Frame
7	8	28	Eddie Skinner	Frank Dodge '53 Olds	184	200	Running
8	14	97-A	Blackie Pitt	J.H. Fitzgibbons '54 Olds	178	150	Running
9	12	460	Gene Simpson	Brooks Bros '55 Plymouth	175	100	Radiator
10	11	71	Bob Welborn	'55 Olds	172	100	Running
11	15	94	Ed Cole	Clarence Dezalin '54 Ford	167	75	Running
12	13	19	Gordon Smith	'55 Chevrolet	153	60	Crash
13	2	42	Lee Petty	Petty Eng.'55 Chrysler	142	50	Engine
14	3	55	Junior Johnson	B & L Motors '55 Olds	113	50	Crash
15	6	301	Fonty Flock	Carl Kiekhaefer '55 Chrysler	97	50	Axle
16	16	04	Gwyn Staley	Westmoreland '55 Chevrolet	55	50	Running

Time of Race: 1 hour, 48 minutes, 10 seconds
  Average Speed: 55.469 mph
  Pole Winner: Jimmie Lewallen 59.741 mph
  Lap Leaders: - - - - - - - - - Jim Paschal   -200.
  Cautions: Margin of Victory: 6 car lengths   Attendance:

Tim Flock rides under the checkered flag at Asheville-Weaverville Speedway.
It was the 10th win of the season for the Atlanta, GA veteran.

of topping Herb Thomas' single season win record of twelve in 1954 and 1955.

Flock finished a full lap ahead of his brother, Fonty, in the 100-miler. Jim Paschal finished third, Donald Thomas was fourth and Eddie Skinner fifth.

Lee Petty, who had been snakebit in recent events, went only three laps before his Chrysler suffered carburetor problems. He finished last in the 18-car field and saw his point lead dwindle to 26 points over Buck Baker, who finished ninth.

Outside pole winner Junior Johnson was running with the leaders, but his day came to an end after 66 laps when the right front wheel broke on his Oldsmobile. Jimmie Lewallen and Bob Welborn were two other favorites who failed to finish.

Flock averaged 62.739 mph for his 27th career Grand National win.

Race No. 26

Tim's Tenth Of Year Comes In Weaverville Cakewalk

WEAVERVILLE, NC (July 10) -- For the sixth time in the 1955 season, Tim Flock took the lead at the drop of the flag and led the entire distance to win a Grand National race. This time, Flock waved his magic wand at the Asheville-Weaverville Speedway. It was his 10th win of the season, making him virtually assured

Junior Johnson's Oldsmobile sags with broken wheel at Weaverville.

Grand National Race No. 26
200 Laps at Asheville-Weaverville Speedway
Weaverville, NC
100 Miles on Half-mile Dirt Track
July 10, 1955

Fin	St	No.	Driver	Team / Car	Laps	Money	Status
1	1	300	Tim Flock	Carl Kiekhaefer '55 Chrysler	200	$1,000	Running
2	16	301	Fonty Flock	Carl Kiekhaefer '55 Chrysler	199	700	Running
3	4	78	Jim Paschal	Ernest Woods '55 Olds	198	475	Running
4	8	9	Donald Thomas	Thomas '54 Hudson	189	365	Running
5	14	28	Eddie Skinner	Frank Dodge '53 Olds	180	310	Running
6	6	2	Gwyn Staley	Westmoreland '55 Chevrolet	174	250	Running
7	10	19	Gordon Smith	'55 Chevrolet	174	200	Running
8	12	18	Arden Mounts	Mounts '54 Hudson	171	150	Running
9	18	89	Buck Baker	Baker '55 Buick	162	100	Runing
10	3	88	Jimmie Lewallen	Ernest Woods '55 Olds	161	100	Axle
11	11	5	Richard Brownlee	Joe Blair '54 Mercury	157	75	Fuel
12	9	121	Harvey Henderson	'53 Hudson Hornet	150	60	Running
13	5	04	Pee Wee Jones	Westmoreland '55 Chevrolet	143	50	RR Hub
14	7	71	Bob Welborn	'55 Olds	122	50	Running
15	2	55	Junior Johnson	B & L Motors '55 Olds	66	50	RF Hub
16	13	8	Billy Carden	Bishop Bros '55 Buick	53	50	Rear End
17	17	97-A	Blackie Pitt	J.H. Fitzgibbons '54 Olds	39	50	Engine
18	15	42	Lee Petty	Petty Eng. '55 Chrysler	3	50	Carb.

Time of Race: 1 hour, 35 minutes, 38 seconds
Average Speed: 62.739 mph
Pole Winner: Tim Flock - 69.310 mph
Lap Leaders: Tim Flock 1-200.
Cautions: Margin of Victory: 1 lap plus   Attendance:

Race No. 27

Two Lap Deficit No Problem for Tim; Wins Morristown

MORRISTOWN, NJ (July 15) -- Tim Flock, the lanky Atlanta star, proved it is just as profitable to be lucky as it is to be good as he rode a wave of good fortune to win the 100-mile race at Morristown Speedway.

Flock led the first 150 laps, but made a pit stop to correct a badly worn right front tire and lost two and a half laps in the process. Junior Johnson picked up first place and led for 40 laps. The Atlanta flash, however, was charging hard to make up the deficit, but it appeared that he was too late. Then the lucky break -- misfortune struck the Johnson Olds as a tire blew with the checkered flag in sight. Tim flew by as Johnson headed for the pits. Johnson wound up fourth, four laps behind the winner.

Lee Petty finished second to Flock, two laps back.

Grand Natonal Race No. 27
200 Laps at Morristown Speedway
Morristown, NJ
100 Miles on Half-mile Dirt Track
July 15, 1955

Fin	St	No.	Driver	Team / Car	Laps	Money	Status
1	1	300	Tim Flock	Carl Kiekhaefer '55 Chrysler	200	$900	Running
2		42	Lee Petty	Petty Eng.'55 Chrysler	198	600	Running
3		98	Dave Terrell	Terrell '54 Olds	197	425	Running
4		55	Junior Johnson	B & L Motors'54 Olds	196	335	Running
5		7	Jim Reed	Reed '55 Chevrolet	195	290	Running
6		78	Jim Paschal	Ernest Woods '55 Olds	195	250	Running
7		1	Charles Dyer	'55 Chevrolet	192	200	Running
8	3	44	Bob Welborn	Welborn '55 Chevrolet	190	150	Running
9		27	John Gouveia	'55 Chevrolet	188	100	Running
10		178	Johnny Lindsey	'55 Chevrolet	187	100	Running
11		155	Bill Gross	'55 Chevrolet	186	75	Running
12		54	Lou Spears	'55 Ford	185	60	Running
13		81	Pappy Hough	'53 Olds	183	50	Running
14		198	Ted Pitcher	'54 Olds	181	50	Running
15		302	Carl Krueger	Krueger '55 Chrysler	174	50	Running
16		171	Elmo Langley	'55 Dodge	174	50	Spindle
17		28	Eddie Skinner	Frank Dodge '53 Olds	172	50	Running
18		48	Charles Hansen	'55 Olds	163	50	Running
19		40	Gene Simpson	'54 Buick	156	50	Hydraulic
20		97-A	Blackie Pitt	J.H. Fitzgibbons '54 Olds	154	50	Running
21		101	Charles D'Anello	'54 Hudson	123	25	Flagged
22		11	Homer Newland	'54 Dodge	120	25	Running
23		303	Buck Baker	Henry Ford '55 Chrysler	116	25	Oil Pres
24		73	John Dodd, Jr.	Dodd '53 Hudson Hornet	83	25	Running
25		43	George Gregory	'55 Chevrolet	82	25	Heating
26		301	Fonty Flock	Carl Kiekhaefer '55 Chrysler	72	---	Oil Press
27		3	Dick Rathmann	John Ditz '55 Chrysler	60	25	Connect.
28		88	Jimmie Lewallen	Ernest Woods '55 Olds	17	25	Spindle
29		24	Bob Gould	'55 Chevrolet	17	25	Crash
30		63	Bill Tanner	Al Liberty '55 Chevrolet	13	25	Crash

Time of Race: 1 hour, 43 minutes, 17 seconds
Average Speed: 58.092 mph
Pole Winner: Tim Flock - 63.649 mph
Lap Leaders: Tim Flock 1-150, Junior Johnson 151-190, T. Flock 191-200.
Cautions: 1   Marrgin of Victory: 2 laps plus   Attendance: 9,000

Terrell was third, with Johnson and Jim Reed rounding out the top five.

Buck Baker's Chrysler left the race after 116 laps with fluctuating oil pressure and wound up 23rd. In the process he fell 188 points behind Petty in the battle for the national driving championship.

A crowd of 9,000 jammed the grandstands to watch Flock average 58.092 mph on the half-mile dirt track.

Grand National Race No. 28
200 Laps at Altamont-Schnectady
Fairgrounds
Altamont, NY
100 Miles on Half-mile Dirt Track
July 29, 1955

Fin	St	No.	Driver	Team / Car	Laps	Money	Status
1	7	55	Junior Johnson	B & L Motors '55 Olds	177	$900	Running
2	5	78	Jim Paschal	Ernest Woods '55 Olds	176	600	Running
3	10	42	Lee Petty	Petty Eng.'55 Chrysler	172	525	Running
4	16	88	Jimmie Lewallen	Ernest Woods '55 Olds	170	335	Running
5	13	40	Gene Simpson	Bud Harbaugh '55 Buick	170	200	Running
6	22	97-A	Blackie Pitt	J.H. Fitzgibbons '55 Olds	164	250	Running
7	18	26	Russ Truelove	Truelove '55 Ford	164	200	Running
8	4	44	Bob Welborn	Welborn '55 Chevrolet	164	150	Running
9	14	1	Charles Dyer	'55 Chevrolet	164	100	Running
10	3	86	Don Oldenberg	Oldenberg '55 Buick Conv	164	150	Crash
11	1	301	Tim Flock	Carl Kiekhaefer '55 Chrysler	160	75	Running
12	21	178	John McGinley	'55 Chevrolet	157	60	Running
13	12	121	Harvey Henderson	'55 Hudson	154	50	Running
14	19	28	Eddie Skinner	Frank Dodge '53 Olds	154	50	Running
15	23	81	Pappy Hough	'53 Olds	149	50	Running
16	20	73	John Dodd, Jr.	Dodd '54 Olds	145	50	Running
17	6	98	Dave Terrell	Terrell '54 Olds	134	50	Engine
18	24	404	Herk Moak	'54 Ford	132	50	Running
19	15	3	Ken Goodermoat	'55 Chevrolet	118	50	Heating
20	25	27	John Gouveia	'55 Chevrolet	98	50	Oil Line
21	17	155	Bill Gross	'55 Chevrolet	79	---	Crash
22	11	900	Johnny Roberts	'55 Chevrolet	59	---	Engine
23	8	7	Jim Reed	Reed '55 Chevrolet	52	---	Crash
24	9	76	Dutch Munsinger	'55 Buick	49	---	Engine
25	2	303	Buck Baker	Henry Ford '55 Chrysler	8	---	Piston

Time of Race: No Time Recorded
Average Speed: None
Pole Winner: Tim Flock - 56.603 mph
Lap Leaders: Buck Baker 1-8, Junior Johnson 9-70, Jim Paschal 71-89, Johnson 90-177.
Cautions: Margin of Victory: 1 lap plus   Attendance: 5,936
* Wreck involving Don Oldenberg halted race after 177 laps of scheduled 200 lapper.
No official time recorded.

Race No. 28

Crash Halts Altamont 100; Johnson Declared Winner

ALTAMONT, NY (July 29) -- Junior Johnson was declared winner of the scheduled 100-miler at Altanont-Schnectady Fairgrounds Speedway when a single car crash forced officials to red flag the race after 177 laps.

Don Oldenberg, driving a '55 Buick convertible, crashed through the fence. Oldenberg was not injured, but the guard rail was irreparable. NASCAR officials judged the race track unsafe and declared Johnson the winner.

Jim Paschal was credited with second, followed by Lee Petty, Jimmie Lewallen and Gene Simpson.

The audience of 5,936 was disappointed in NASCAR's ruling, but in the wake of the terrible LeMans tragedy a month earlier when 82 people were killed by a runaway race car, the sanctioning body was unwilling to take any chances. The sport of auto racing was already under fire from politicians and the general public.

Buck Baker led the first eight laps but departed with a blown engine while leading. Johnson grabbed the lead for the first time on lap nine when Baker left. He paced the action for 62 laps before Paschal forged to the front. Johnson passed Paschal in the 90th lap and was in front when Oldenberg's crash occurred.

Grand National Race No. 29
200 Laps at New York State Fairgrounds
Syracuse, NY
100 Miles on 1-mile Dirt Track
July 30, 1955

Fin	St	No.	Driver	Team / Car	Laps	Money	Status
1	1	300	Tim Flock	Carl Kiekhaefer '55 Chrysler	100	$950	Running
2	4	88	Jimmie Lewallen	Ernest Woods '55 Olds	100	650	Running
3	6	42	Lee Petty	Petty Eng. '55 Chrysler	99	525	Running
4	8	44	Bob Welborn	Welborn '55 Chevrolet	98	385	Running
5	5	78	Jim Paschal	Ernest Woods '55 Olds	98	290	Running
6	11	40	Gene Simpson	Bud Harbaugh '55 Buick	97	300	Running
7	9	86	Don Oldenberg	Oldenberg '55 Buick	96	200	Running
8	7	76	Dutch Munsinger	'55 Buick	96	150	Running
9	2	55	Buck Baker	B & L Motors '55 Olds	93	100	Running
10	16	178	John Lindsay	'55 Chevrolet	93	100	Running
11	21	28	Eddie Skinner	Frank Dodge '53 Olds	93	75	Running
12	17	81	Pappy Hough	'53 Olds	90	60	Running
13	14	1	Charles Dyer	'55 Chevrolet	90	50	Running
14	12	26	Russ Truelove	Truelove '55 Ford	88	100	Running
15	15	24	Bob Gould	'55 Chevrolet	85	50	Running
16	22	97-A	Blackie Pitt	J.H. Fitzgibbons '55 Olds	79	50	Running
17	19	31	Dick Walter	'53 Plymouth	78	100	Running
18	20	303	Junior Johnson	Henry Ford '55 Chrysler	75	50	Engine
19	10	8	Emory Mahon	'55 Chevrolet	74	50	Running
20	18	27	John McVitty	'55 Chevrolet	40	50	Heating
21	13	121	Harvey Henderson	'53 Hudson Hornet	30	50	Oil Press
22	2	7	Jim Reed	Reed '55 Chevrolet	22	---	Heating

Time of Race: 1 hour, 18 minutes, 24.5 seconds
Average Speed: 76.522 mph
Pole Winner: Tim Flock - 78.311 mph
Lap Leaders: Tim Flock 1-100.
Cautions: None   Margin of Victory: Attendance: 6,000

Race No. 29

Flock Flashes to Victory On Syracuse Mile

SYRACUSE, NY (July 30) -- Record setting Tim Flock led from start to finish and won the 100-mile Grand National race at the New York State Fairgrounds. It was his record-tying 12th win of the season and seven of those have come by leading the entire distance. He also started on the pole.

Jimmie Lewallen finished in second place, with Lee Petty third. Bob Welborn was fourth and Jim Paschal fifth.

Flock averaged 76.522 mph as the race was uninterrupted by the yellow flag.

Buck Baker and Junior Johnson swapped seats for the 100-miler. Baker, in an effort to keep within reach of Petty in the point race, took the wheel of Johnsons' B & L Motors Oldsmobile and finished ninth. Baker's Chrysler suffered problems in a shakedown session. Johnson drove the car 75 laps before it fell out. He wound up 18th in the 22-car field. Don Oldenberg, driving a convertible, was seventh.

Race No. 30

Scoring Flap Mars Bay Meadows; Flock On Top

SAN MATEO, CA (July 31) -- Johnny Kieper apparently crossed the finish line first in the 250-miler at the Bay Meadows Race Track, but Tim Flock was officially declared the winner. A major scoring snafu marred the running of the West Coast Grand National event.

NASCAR officials knew the score cards were out of order before the mid-way point of the race, but they decided to go ahead and run the race. Attempts to correct the scoring problem during the running of the race were unsuccessful. Kieper was flagged in first place, but the results were immmediately announced as "unofficial".

Hours after the race, it was discovered that Kieper had run 251 laps on the one mile dirt track rather than the scheduled 250. However, it was also learned that Flock had actually covered 252 laps. Flock was declared the winner and collected the $2,050 first prize check.

Kieper was given second place, with Danny Letner,

Marvin Panch and Buck Baker third through fifth.

Flock, Baker and Lee Petty made the starting call after competing in a 100-miler the night before at Syracuse, NY. Kiekhaefer had planned all along to fly Flock out West to get more championship points. Baker and Petty were unable to make the long trip by automobile so Kiekhaefer, in the interest of fairness, allowed Baker and Petty to board the plane also. Petty finished sixth.

held his Helzafire Oldsmobile on the point for the remaining distance in the 100 miler at Southern States Fairgrounds. It was Paschal's third win of the season.

Only seven cars finished the event as the half-mile dirt track was badly rutted when the race ended. Paschal averaged only 48.806 mph.

Tim Flock won the pole for the 13th time in the 1955 season. He led the first 52 laps before making a lengthy pit stop.

Gwyn Staley finished second, two laps behind Paschal. Buck Baker, Bob Welborn and Flock were third through fifth.

Jimmie Lewallen crashed in the 85th lap when a tie rod snapped on his Oldsmobile. Junior Johnson called it quits after 131 laps when a wheel bearing burned out in his Olds.

Point leader Lee Petty wound up 10th after an axle broke on the rough track.

Grand National Race No. 30
250 Laps at Bay Meadows Race Track
San Mateo, CA
250 Miles on 1-mile Dirt Track
July 31, 1955

Fin	St	No.	Driver	Team / Car	Laps	Money	Status
1	1	300	Tim Flock	Carl Kiekhaefer '55 Chrysler	252	$2,050	Running
2	2	11	Johnny Kieper	Beryl Jackson '55 Olds	251	1,450	Running
3	3	6	Danny Letner	Cos Cancilla '54 Olds	249	700	Running
4	4	98	Marvin Panch	John Hernandez '55 Mercury	247	650	Running
5	29	89	Buck Baker	Baker '55 Buick	247	550	Running
6	6	42	Lee Petty	Petty Engineering '55 Dodge	246	450	Running
7	8	33	Bill West	Jim Dane '53 Hudson Hornet	243	350	Running
8	7	99	Lloyd Dane	Les Milfield '54 Mercury	242	250	Running
9	10	96	Ed Negre	Beryl Jackson '53 Olds	239	200	Stalled
10	12	12	Bill Stammer	Beach City '55 Chevrolet	238	250	Running
11	21	84	Ed Normi	Lou Mangini '52 Plymouth	237	250	Running
12	5	2	Allen Adkins	Charlie Vance '55 Dodge	233	150	Crash
13	9	47	Mickey McGreevey	Al Lingons '55 Mercury	232	150	Running
14	15	26	Ed Brown	Brown '55 Chevrolet	228	100	Running
15	17	15	Roger Hagerty	Curly Weida '55 Dodge	228	100	Running
16	16	65	Chuck Meekins	Jim Rush '52 Olds	226	100	Running
17	23	9	Cobb Pagan	'55 Chevrolet	225	100	Running
18	19	77	Owen Loggins	'54 Dodge	223	100	Running
19	20	24	Bob Havenmann	'54 Dodge	218	50	Running
20	13	95	Joe Roletto	'55 Buick	212	50	Running
21	30	63	Frank Parry	'50 Ford	205	50	Running
22	26	69	Chet Thompson	'52 Plymouth	199	40	Running
23	32	52	Dusty Fuller	'50 Hudson	197	40	Running
24	14	5	Dick Rathmann	Don Oliver '53 Olds	197	40	Conn Rd
25	28	90	Hal Prentice	'55 Ford	197	90	Running
26	27	20	Bill Williams	'55 Dodge	195	40	Running
27	33	4	Cliff Wright	'53 Hudson Hornet	178	40	Running
28	31	60	Eliso Bowie	'53 Cadillac	172	90	Running
29	18	3	Bill Amick	'55 Dodge	155	40	Crash
30	25	66	Carl Hamill	'54 Hudson Jet	144	40	Crash
31	11	34	Sherman Clark	Clark '55 Chevrolet	110	40	Tire
32	22	50	Jim Cook	'50 Olds	110	40	Conn Rd
33	24	39	Bob Stanclift	'51 Hudson	36	40	No Expl
34	34	7	Crash Carson	'55 Ford	8	40	Oil Press

Time of Race: 3 hours, 40 minutes, 30 seconds
 Average Speed: 68.571 mph
 Pole Winner: Fonty Flock * - 79.330 mph
 Lap Leaders: - - - - - - - - - Tim Flock   -252 .
 Cautions: Margin of Victory: 1 lap plus   Attendance:
 * Fonty Flock qualified car #300 on pole. Tim Flock drove it in the race.

Grand National Race No. 31
200 Laps at Southern States Fairgrounds
Charlotte, NC
100 Miles on Half-mile Dirt Track
August 5, 1955

Fin	St	No.	Driver	Team / Car	Laps	Money	Status
1	3	78	Jim Paschal	Ernest Woods '55 Olds	200	$1,100	Running
2	2	2	Gwyn Staley	Westmoreland '55 Chevrolet	198	700	Running
3	9	303	Buck Baker	'55 Chrysler	198	475	Running
4	6	44	Bob Welborn	Welborn '55 Chevrolet	195	365	Running
5	1	300	Tim Flock	Mercury Outboards '55 Chrys	192	310	Running
6	11	87	Buddy Shuman	Griffin Motors '54 Olds	186	250	Running
7	12	28	Eddie Skinner	Frank Dodge '53 Olds	183	200	Running
8	10	55	Junior Johnson	B & L Motors '55 Olds	131	150	Bearing
9	14	178	John Lindsay	'55 Chevrolet	123	100	Bearing
10	8	42	Lee Petty	PettyEng. '55 Chrysler	110	100	RR Axle
11	15	5	Richard Brownlee	Joe Blair '54 Mercury	105	75	Gas Line
12	5	88	Jimmie Lewallen	Ernest Woods '55 Olds	82	60	Tie Rod
13	4	8	Billy Carden	'55 Buick	71	50	Shocks
14	13	97-A	Blackie Pitt	'54 Olds	56	50	Tie Rod
15	7	B-29	Dink Widenhouse	Widenhouse '53 Olds	24	50	Piston

Time of Race: 2 hour, 2 minutes, 56 seconds
 Average Speed: 48.806 mph
 Pole Winner: Tim Flock - 57.859 mph
 Lap Leaders: Tim Flock 1-52, Jim Paschal 53-200.
 Cautions: Margin of Victory: 2 laps plus   Attendance: 5,600

Race No. 31

Paschal Wins on Choppy Charlotte Track; Only 7 Finish

CHARLOTTE, NC (Aug. 5) -- Jim Paschal of High Point, NC, breezed into the lead in the 53rd lap and

Race No. 32

Petty Edges Paschal in Winston-Salem 100

WINSTON-SALEM, NC (Aug. 7) -- Lee Petty, unveiling a new '55 Dodge he had specially prepared for Darlington's Southern 500, flashed past Jim Paschal in

*Arden Mounts walks away from his overturned
Hudson at Winston-Salem.*

Carden fourth and Eddie Skinner fifth.

Herb Thomas, seriously injured in the May 1 event at Charlotte, made his first start since the accident. The Olivia, NC two-time Grand National Champ started eighth, but a clutch failure put him out after 31 laps. He wound up 21st in the 22 car field.

Tim Flock started on the pole but fell to seventh in the final order due to a sputtering engine.

Arden Mounts lost control of his Hudson in the 70th lap and flipped over the inside guard rail. The car landed upside down. Dejectedly, Mounts walked back to the pit area.

Petty averaged 50.111 mph for his 24th career victory.

the late stages and nabbed his sixth win of the year in the 100-mile Grand National contest at the Forsyth County Fairgrounds.

Petty scampered across the finish line just 6.0 seconds in front of Paschal to pocket the $1,100 first prize. Buck Baker finished in third place, with Billy

Grand National Race No. 32
200 Laps at Forsyth County Fairgrounds
Winston-Salem, NC
100 Miles on Half-mile Dirt Track
August 7, 1955

Fin	St	No.	Driver	Team / Car	Laps	Money	Status
1	3	42	Lee Petty	Petty Eng. '55 Dodge	200	$1,100	Running
2	5	78	Jim Paschal	Ernest Woods '55 Olds	200	700	Running
3	4	89	Buck Baker	Baker '55 Buick	199	475	Running
4	9	8	Billy Carden	Bishop Bros. '55 Buick	198	365	Running
5	19	28	Eddie Skinner	Frank Dodge '55 Olds	189	310	Running
6	10	44	Bob Welborn	Welborn '55 Chevrolet	187	250	Running
7	1	301	Tim Flock	Carl Kiekhaefer '55 Chrysler	179	200	Running
8	17	58	Bill Bowman	'54 Nash	177	150	Running
9	11	04	Billy Myers	Westmoreland '55 Chevrolet	170	100	Running
10	13	8	Charles Hanson	'55 Olds	162	100	Running
11	16	178	John Lindsay	'55 Chevrolet	137	75	Spindle
12	18	97-A	Blackie Pitt	J.M. Fitzgibbons '54 Olds	136	60	Running
13	5	2	Gwyn Staley	Westmoreland '55 Chevrolet	117	50	Axle
14	15	19	Gordon Smith	'55 Chevrolet	116	50	Heating
15	21	5	Richard Brownlee	Joe Blair '54 Mercury	112	50	Running
16	2	300	Fonty Flock	Carl Kiekhaefer '55 Chrysler	93	50	Oil Press
17	12	98	Dave Terrell	Terrell '55 Olds	90	50	Coil
18	14	18	Arden Mounts	Mounts '54 Hudson	67	50	Crash
19	7	55	Junior Johnson	B & L Motors '55 Olds	53	50	Engine
20	20	94	Ed Cole	Clarence DeZalia '54 Ford 6	40	50	Radiator
21	8	92	Herb Thomas	Thomas '54 Hudson	31	---	Clutch
22	22	11	George Parrish	W.H. Pontress '53 Studebaker	26	---	RR Hub

Time of Race: 1 hour, 59 minutes, 44 seconds
  Average Speed: 50.111 mph
Pole Winner: tim Flock - 59.016
Lap Leaders: Tim Flock 1- , - - - - - - - - - Lee Petty - 200.

Cautions: Margin of Victory: 6 car lengths   Attendance:

Grand National Race No. 33
167 Laps at Memphis-Arkansas Speedway
LeHi, AR
"Mid-South 250"
250 Miles on 1.5-mile Dirt Track
August 14, 1955

Fin	St	No.	Driver	Team / Car	Laps	Money	Status
1	1	301	Fonty Flock	Carl Kiekhaefer '55 Chrysler	167	$2,950	Running
2	6	87	Speedy Thompson	Griffin Motors '54 Olds	167	1,675	Running
3	2	300	Tim Flock	Carl Kiekhaefer '55 Chrysler	165	1,175	Running
4	5	78	Jim Paschal	Ernest Woods '55 Olds	163	815	Running
5	3	89	Buck Baker	Baker '55 Buick	161	685	Running
6	7	44	Bob Welborn	Welborn '55 Chevrolet	160	525	Running
7	8	55	Junior Johnson	B & L Motors '55 Olds	155	350	Running
8	27	14	Slick Smith	Frank Christian '55 Chevrolet	155	275	Running
9	19	3	Jimmy Ayers	'55 Ford	153	300	Running
10	10	23	Ken Johns	'55 Chevrolet	153	150	Running
11	9	98	Dave Terrell	Terrell '55 Olds	152	125	Running
12	20	28	Eddie Skinner	Frank Dodge '53 Olds	150	100	Running
13	21	52	Joe Guide, Jr.	Sally Guide '53 Hudson	150	200	Running
14	12	92	Herb Thomas	Thomas '55 Chevrolet	149	100	Running
15	24	32	Ted Cannady	'53 Ford 6	145	100	Running
16	29	20	Banks Simpson	Waldron & Co. '55 Buick	141	75	Running
17	28	40	Gene Simpson	Bud Harbaugh '55 Buick	141	75	Running
18	17	33	Al Watkins	'54 Dodge	140	175	Running
19	11	42	Lee Petty	Petty Eng. '55 Dodge	135	175	U Joint
20	23	155	Roscoe Rand	'54 Chrysler	125	50	Running
21	14	88	Jimmie Lewallen	Ernest Woods '55 Olds	96	50	Gas Line
22	26	39	Jim McLain	'55 Olds	82	50	Running
23	16	188	Hooker Hood	Hood '54 Olds	65	50	Piston
24	18	51-X	Jack Hubbard	'55 Ford	56	50	Push Rod
25	13	71	Harold Kite	'55 Olds	23	50	Piston
26	22	90	Woody Wilson	'53 Hudson Hornet	18	50	Heating
27	4	8	Billy Carden	Bishop Bros. '55 Buick	11	50	Bearing
28	25	19	Gordon Smith	'55 Chevrolet	5	50	Engine
29	15	56	Gwyn Staley	'55 Cadillac	3	150	Bearing

Time of Race: 2 hours, 47 minutes, 12 seconds
  Average Speed: 89.892 mph
Pole Winner: Fonty Flock - 99.944 mph
Lap Leaders: Fonty Flock 1-17, Tim Flock 18-96, Fonty Flock 97-167.

Cautions: None   Margin of Victory: Attendance: 15,000

Race No. 33

Fonty Flock Rides To Victory In Mid-South 250

LeHI, AR (Aug.14) -- Fonty Flock gunned his Kiekhaefer Chrysler to an impressive victory in the twice rained-out Mid-South 250 at the new Memphis-Arkansas Speedway

It was the second win of the year for the Decatur, GA veteran, who juggles his racing schedule with his insurance company. It was also his third superspeedway triumph.

Flock took the lead in the 97th lap and outran Speedy Thompson's Oldsmobile to stake claim to the $2,950 first prize. Tim Flock finished third, two laps behind. Jim Paschal nabbed fourth place and Buck Baker took fifth.

Tim Flock had passed his brother in the 18th lap and stretched his advantage to a half lap when his Chrysler ran out of gas. The big white Chrysler crept to a halt on the backstretch. Good Samaritan Fonty came to his brother's aid and pushed him back to the pits.

Fonty's good deed nearly cost him the race. Thompson had been running over a lap down, and he was able to get back in the lead lap. There were no caution flags in the 167 lap event on the 1.5-mile high banked dirt track.

By finishing third, Tim Flock took the lead in the standings for the first time in the 1955 campaign. Previous leader Lee Petty fell out on lap 135 with a U-joint failure. Flock took a 122 point lead in the driver standings.

Junior Johnson offered the most serious challenge to the Flock brothers, passing Fonty for second place in the early going. But Johnson was overcome by carbon monoxide funes. Gwyn Staley, driving relief, took the Johnson Oldsmobile to a seventh place finish, 12 laps behind the leaders.

Flock averaged 89.892 mph before a crowd of 15,000.

Race No. 34

Thomas Back in Victory Lane With Raleigh Win

RALEIGH, NC (Aug. 20) -- Making his third start since recovering from multiple injuries suffered at Charlotte in May, Herb Thomas steered his Smokey Yunick Buick around Fonty Flock in the 76th lap and

went on to win the 100-mile race at Raleigh Speedway.

It was Thomas' second win of the year and the 42nd of his career as he prepped for the Southern 500 on Raleigh's one-mile paved track. The 100 miler was staged under the lights.

Tim Flock, Bob Welborn and Jimmie Lewallen finished second through fourth, all in the same lap as the winner. Gwyn Staley was fifth, one lap back.

The lead changed hands four times among three

Herb Thomas won at Raleigh in successful comeback.

Grand National Race No. 34
100 Laps at Raleigh Speedway
Raleigh, NC
100 Miles on 1- Mile Paved Track
August 20, 1955

Fin	St	No.	Driver	Team / Car	Laps	Money	Status
1	3	92	Herb Thomas	Thomas '55 Buick	100	$1,500	Running
2	1	300	Tim Flock	Carl Keikhaefer '55 Chrysler	100	1,000	Running
3	6	44	Bob Welborn	Welborn '55 Chevrolet	100	600	Running
4	10	88	Jimmie Lewallen	Ernest Woods '55 Olds	100	500	Running
5	8	2	Gwyn Staley	Westmoreland '55 Chevrolet	99	400	Running
6	9	89	Buck Baker	Baker '55 Buick`	99	300	Running
7	5	55	Junior Johnson	B & L Motors '55 Olds	99	200	Running
8	7	28	Eddie Skinner	Frank Dodge '53 Olds	99	150	Running
9	2	301	Fonty Flock	Carl Keikhaefer '55 Chrysler	99	100	Running
10	16	04	Jimmy Massey	Westmoreland '55 Chevrolet	98	100	Running
11	13	87	Speedy Thompson	Griffin Motors '54 Olds	98	100	Running
12	24	159	Lloyd Moore	Julian Buesink '55 Ford	97	75	Running
13	18	7	Jim Reed	'Reed '55 Chevrolet	97	75	Running
14	14	98	Dave Terrell	Terrell '55 Olds	96	75	Running
15	23	6	Ralph Liguori	Liguori '55 Buick	95	75	Running
16	12	20	Banks Simpson	Waldron & Co. '55 Buick	94	75	Running
17	11	82	Joe Eubanks	Phil Oates '55 Olds	94	75	Running
18	19	71	Billy Carden	'55 Oldsmobile	94	75	Running
19	20	24	Bobby Waddell	Jimmy Pardue '55 Chevrolet	93	75	Running
20	21	11	George Parrish	W.H. Pontress '53 Studebaker	91	75	Running
21	28	32	Ted Cannady	'53 Ford 6	90	50	Running
22	15	42	Lee Petty	Petty Engineering '55 Dodge	88	50	Running
23	26	53	Elmo Langley	'53 Oldsmobile	84	50	Running
24	27	94	Clarence DeZalia	DeZalia '54 Ford 6	79	50	Running
25	22	19	Gordon Smith	'55 Chevrolet	68	50	Crash
26	7	78	Jim Paschal	Ernest Woods '55 Oldsmobile	67	---	Bearing
27	29	59	Blackie Pitt	Pitt '54 Oldsmobile	47	---	Piston
28	25	5	Richard Brownlee	Joe Blair '54 Mercury	36	---	Crash
29	17	56	Fred Johnson	'55 Cadillac	27	200	Piston

Time of Race: 1 hour, 18 minutes, 32 seconds.
Average Speed: 76.400 mph.
Pole Winner: Tim Flock - 78.722 mph
Lap Leaders: Tim Flock 1-2, Fonty Flock 3-35, Herb Thomas 36, F. Flock 37-75, Herb Thomas 76-100.
Cautions: None   Margin of Victory: 3/4 lap   Attendance: 9,500.

Grand National Race No. 35
366 Laps at Darlington Raceway
Darlington, SC
"Southern 500"
500 Miles on 1.375-mile Paved Track
September 5, 1955

Fin	St	No.	Driver	Team / Car	Laps	Money	Status
1	8	92	Herb Thomas	Thomas '55 Chevrolet	366	$7,480	Running
2	21	7	Jim Reed	Reed '55 Chevrolet	365	1,550	Running
3	6	16	Tim Flock	Carl Kiekhaefer '55 Chrysler	363	2,500	Running
4	24	2	Gwyn Staley	Westmoreland '55 Chevrolet	359	1,300	Running
5	30	96	Larry Flynn	'55 Ford	359	1,175	Running
6	2	89	Buck Baker	Baker '55 Buick	359	1,055	Running
7	26	93	Lou Spear	'55 Chevrolet	354	700	Running
8	27	70	Cotton Owens	'55 Chevrolet	354	600	Running
9	4	25	Bill Widenhouse	Sam McCuthen '55 Chevrolet	353	445	Wheel
10	41	4	Jimmy Massey	Westmoreland '55 Chevrolet	352	400	Trans
11	20	20	Banks Simpson	Waldron & Co. '55 Buick	352	475	Running
12	5	82	Joe Eubanks	Phil Oates '55 Olds	351	550	Running
13	45	44	Marvin Panch	Bob Welborn '55 Chevrolet	351	300	Running
14	33	54	Nace Mattingly	Mattingly '55 Ford	349	350	Running
15	44	88	Jimmie Lewallen	Ernest Woods '55 Olds	348	335	Running
16	35	6	Ralph Liguori	Al Wheatley '55 Mercury	348	400	Running
17	13	84	Banjo Matthews	Paper Hangers '55 Olds	348	245	Running
18	37	98	Dave Terrell	Terrell '55 Olds	346	165	Running
19	29	17	Russ 'Bud' Graham	Earl Wright '55 Chevrolet	346	155	Running
20	18	51	Bill Champion	Leland Colvin '55 Buick	246	195	Running
21	25	42	Lee Petty	Petty Eng. '55 Olds	343	335	Running
22	46	68	Johnny Patterson	'55 Mercury	342	225	Running
23	34	46	Billy Myers	Westmoreland '55 Chevrolet	342	115	Running
24	48	95	Lloyd Moore	Julian Buesink '55 Ford	342	160	Running
25	32	35	Ray Platte	Harry Parry '55 Chevrolet	339	100	Running
26	38	22	Bill Blair	Blair '55 Olds	332	90	Running
27	43	24	Bobby Waddell	James Pardue '55 Chevrolet	331	75	Running
28	31	59	Blackie Pitt	Brownie Pitt '55 Ford	329	75	Running
29	52	12	Jimmy Thompson (NC)	'55 Plymouth	328	275	Running
30	69	49	Bob Welborn	Welborn '55 Chevrolet	327	75	Running
31	61	62	Ewell Hatfield	'55 Chevrolet	319	60	Running
32	50	50	Roy Bentley	Marion Cox Garage '55 Chev	317	60	Running
33	7	2	Joe Weatherly	Schwam Motors '55 Ford	317	1,500	Crash
34	10	78	Jim Paschal	Ernest Woods '55 Olds	317	60	Running
35	59	58	Bill Bowman	'54 Nash	311	260	Running
36	17	55	Junior Johnson	B & L Motors '55 Olds	308	60	Running
37	47	30	Ned Jarrett	Mellie Bernard '55 Pontiac	305	260	Running
38	57	61	Ed Bergin	M.C. Barlow '54 Dodge	302	160	Running
39	9	8	Billy Carden	Bishop Bros. '55 Buick	298	60	Running
40	55	78	Tojo Stephens	'55 Chevrolet	291	60	Running
41	62	43	Possum Jones	Steve Pearce '55 Chevrolet	276	60	Steering
42	42	28	Eddie Skinner	Frank Dodge '53 Olds	256	60	Running
43	51	71	Harold Kite	'55 Olds	256	60	Running
44	36	10	Van Van Wey	Ray Fletcher '55 Ford	247	60	Crash
45	3	87	Speedy Thompson	Griffin Motors '54 Olds	235	80	Vapor Lk
46	22	56	Fred Johnson	B & L Motors '55 Cadillac	231	260	Tires
47	53	37	Dutch Cox	Claude Porter '55 Pontiac	225	150	Trans
48	58	81	Gene Comstock	Mounts '54 Hudson	220	250	Running
49	66	94	Clarence DeZalia	DeZalia '54 Ford	210	50	Rear End
50	23	3	Dick Allwine	Earl Wright '55 Chevrolet	202	50	Crash
51	11	36	Fonty Flock	Carl Kiekhaefer '55 Chrysler	190	1,040	Crash
52	16	40	Gene Simpson	Bud Harbaugh '55 Buick	188	50	Trans
53	19	34	Dick Beaty	'55 Ford	184	50	Crash
54	67	32	Jim Thompson (WV)	'53 Hudson Hornet	184	150	Crash
55	40	23	Don Duckworth	Woodruff Motors '55 Chev	147	50	Crash
56	49	18	Arden Mounts	Mounts '54 Hudson	143	100	Crash
57	54	15	Jimmy Roland	R.C. Rollings '55 Chevrolet	137	50	Rear End
58	15	99	Curtis Turner	Schwam Motors '55 Ford	133	190	Tie Rod
59	54	76	Elmo Langley	'55 Dodge	79	100	Oil Press
60	14	91	Donald Thomas	Herb Thomas '55 Buick	78	50	Steering
61	39	14	Slick Smith	Frank Christian '55 Chevrolet	77	50	Gasket
62	12	3	Dick Rathmann	John Ditz '55 Chrysler	50	130	Trans
63	60	21	Bud Rackley	'54 Olds	44	50	Connect.
64	65	41	Tommy Thompson	Julian Buesink '55 Ford	41	50	Fuel Pmp
65	58	19	Gordon Smith	'55 Chevrolet	39	50	Rod Brng
66	1	M-1	Fireball Roberts	Fish Carburetor '55 Buick	30	140	Crash
67	63	33	Pop McGinnis	Owen Cox '55 Chevrolet	18	50	Crash
68	56	460	Ed Cole	Clarence DeZalia '55 Plym	12	150	Rod Brng
69	64	11	George Parrish	W.H. Pontress '53 Studebaker	11	250	Heating

drivers in the caution-free event. Tim Flock, after leading the first two laps from the pole, gave way to Fonty. Fonty then led the next 73 laps except when Thomas forged ahead by a bumper on the 36th. Thomas, who started third, passed Fonty for good in the 76th lap.

Flock was holding down second place on lap 88 when his Chrysler popped a tire and lost a lap in the pits. He eventually wound up ninth in the field of 29.

Tim Flock got by Welborn in the 94th lap to move into second place.

Lee Petty struggled to a 22nd place finish, twelve laps behind the winner.

Thomas averaged 76.400 mph before 9,500 spectators.

Race No. 35

Thomas Makes Promise Good; Snares 3rd Southern 500

DARLINGTON, SC (Sept. 5) -- Just as he promised from his hospital bed four months earlier, Herb Thomas bagged his third Southern 500 triumph at Darlington Raceway, an event which marked a "New Beginning" in NASCAR Grand National racing.

For the first time in the history of this six year classic, the Southern 500 was a complete sell-out. All 50,000 printed tickets had been sold 24 hours before race time. The intense competition between different brands of cars had spurred the interest of fans well beyond the imagination of everybody connected with the sport. The traffic jams on the roads leading to Darlington were still 10 miles long at the time the green flag was waved.

Thousands were turned away. Some fans sliced the fencing in order to sneak in the speedway. Others passed cash to the guards to gain admittance.

Over 50,000 jammed the humid flats of Darlington for the World Series of Stock Car Racing.

Inside the Darlington Raceway at precisely 11 a.m. 69 cars, lined up three-abreast, roared past the starting line with Fireball Roberts gaining the upper hand. Tim and Fonty Flock, both starting their heavily favored Kiekhaefer Chryslers from the front row, dominated the first 109 laps, leading all but the opening four trips around, which Roberts led from his pole position.

Time of Race: 5 hours, 25 minutes, 25 seconds
Average Speed: 92.281 mph
Pole Winner: Fireball Roberts - 110.682 mph
Fastest Qualifier: Fonty Flock -112.781 mph
Lap Leaders: Fireball Roberts 1-4, Tim Flock 5-10, Fonty Flock 11-94, T. Flock 95-109,
Curtis Turner 110-123, T. Flock 124-147, Bill Widenhouse 148-149,
Joe Weatherly 150-278, Herb Thomas 279-306, Weatherly 307-317,
H. Thomas 318-366.
Cautions: 8 for 51 laps   Margin of Victory: 1 lap plus   Attendance: 50,000

But the heavier Chryslers encountered tire problems before the first round of scheduled pit stops and began to lose ground to the lighter Fords and Chevrolets.

As mechanical problems and countless crashes depleted the field, Joe Weatherly, ex-motorcycle champ, wheeling a factory Ford and Thomas, driving a Smokey Yunick prepared Chevy, found themselves dueling for top honors in the $34,303 event.

Weatherly, who had led for 129 consecutive laps, made his last pit stop on lap 278. Thomas paced the field until lap 306 when he made his fourth and final pit stop. In the final stretch dash, Weatherly had built up a full lap lead in his purple, Schwam Motor Co. Ford tooled by ex-racer Buddy Shuman.

But as Weatherly was motoring along in the shadow of the checkered flag, his left front wheel collapsed on lap 317, sending him into the guard rail. Thomas assumed command and led the final 49 laps to collect the $7,480 first prize.

Jim Reed was a lap back in second, making it a one-two sweep for Chevrolet products. Tim Flock finished third, three laps back, Gwyn Staley's Chevrolet was fourth, seven laps behind, and Larry Flynn's Ford rounded out the top five driving in the same lap as Staley.

Weatherly's 317 laps completed gave him 33rd in the final rundown. He sat on pit wall in a dejected muse in the final laps watching Thomas cruise home first.

The other factory backed Ford, driven by Curtis Turner, had led for 14 laps; but as he lit a cigarette under the caution flag, he bumped into Fonty Flock bending a tie rod. Mr. Turner was out of action.

Fonty Flock climbs out of his wrecked Chrysler at Darlington.

Dick Beaty and Jim Graham spin in Southern 500.

Wrecks claimed many on the muggy overcast afternoon. Arden Mounts of Gilbert, WV and Don Duckworth of Woodruff, SC crashed heavily in the 155th lap. Mounts was shaken up, and Duckworth suffered extremely serious injuries. Doctors said they did not expect Duckworth to survive the first night, but after months of hospitalization, he eventually recovered.

Van Van Wey was involved in four crashes. He finally parked his Ford after 247 laps when he tore the front of his car off in a bout with the wall.

Others taken out by accidents were Fonty Flock, Fireball Roberts, Pop McGinnis, Dick Beaty, Dick Allwine and Jimmy Thompson.

Thomas covered the 500 miles at a 92.281 mph clip. His greenish-blue Chevrolet made the entire 500 miles without a tire change. He was using the new Firestone 170 SuperSport tire which was designed and tested in sports car racing.

Tim Flock took a big lead in the point standings, upping his margin to 416 over Buck Baker. Petty fell to third, 1,466 points behind as he limped to a 21st place finish.

Race No. 36

Flock Outruns Thomas for Montgomery Victory

MONTGOMERY, AL (Sept. 11) -- Tim Flock led the entire distance and racked up his 14th win of the season in the 100-mile Grand National race at Montgomery Speedway.

Flock's Chrysler was a lap up on second place Herb Thomas at the finish of the 200 lapper. Third place went to Bob Welborn, Lee Petty was fourth and Buck Baker fifth.

Fonty Flock switched to a Chevrolet, but crashed his new mount after 40 laps. Flock plunged through the protective barrier and landed in a sparsely populated area of the grandstands. No injuries were reported in the freak mishap.

Welborn, beneficiary in the Chevrolet factory sponsorship, entered two cars. Marvin Panch qualified second quickest in Welborn's back-up car. Panch was running third when the right front hub broke, putting him out after fifty laps.

Flock averaged 63.773 mph for his 31st career victory.

Grand National Race No. 36
200 Laps at Montgomery Speedway
Montgomery, AL
100 Miles on Half-mile Dirt Track
September 11, 1955

Fin	St	No.	Driver	Team / Car	Laps	Money	Status
1	1	300	Tim Flock	Carl Kiekhaefer '55 Chrysler	200	$1,100	Running
2	3	92	Herb Thomas	Thomas '55 Chevrolet	199	700	Running
3	5	49	Bob Welborn	Welborn '55 Chevrolet	197	475	Running
4	8	42	Lee Petty	Petty Eng.'55 Dodge	196	365	Running
5	6	89	Buck Baker	Baker '55 Buick	195	310	Running
6	15	1	Jack Smith	H. Rakestraw '55 Chevrolet	193	250	Running
7	12	14	Slick Smith	Frank Christian '55 Chevrolet	192	200	Running
8	4	2	Gwyn Staley	Westmoreland '55 Chevrolet	189	150	Running
9	16	88	Jimmie Lewallen	Ernest Woods '55 Olds	187	100	Running
10	7	55	Junior Johnson	B & L Motors '55 Olds	185	100	Running
11	21	80	Fred Harb	'53 Plymouth	183	75	Running
12	17	28	Eddie Skinner	Frank Dodge '53 Olds	182	60	Running
13	14	99	Sonny Black	'55 Olds	181	50	Running
14	20	75	Max Berrier	'53 Plymouth	177	50	Running
15	23	33	Al Watkins	'54 Dodge	177	50	Running
16	13	8	Billy Carden	Bishop Bros. '55 Buick	173	50	Running
17	18	27	John McVitty	'55 Chevrolet	167	50	Running
18	24	10	Bo Fields	'53 Plymouth	160	50	Running
19	9	04	Jimmy Massey	Westmoreland '55 Chevrolet	130	50	Rear End
20	22	3	Jimmy Ayers	'55 Ford	124	50	Tires
21	2	44	Marvin Panch	Bob Welborn '55 Chevrolet	50	---	RF Hub
22	10	78	Jim Paschal	Ernest Woods '55 Olds	41	---	Bearing
23	11	91	Fonty Flock	Thomas '55 Chevrolet	40	---	Crash
24	19	9	C.H. Dingler	'53 Hudson Hornet	8	---	Gas Tank

Time of Race: 1 hour, 34 minutes, 5 seconds
Average Speed: 63.773 mph
Pole Winner: Tim Flock - 68.728 mph
Lap Leaders: Tim Flock 1-200.
Cautions: Margin of Victory: 1 lap plus   Attendance:

Race No. 37

25,000 Watch Flock
Take Langhorne 250

LANGHORNE, PA Sept. 18) -- Tim Flock drove his Chrysler into the lead in the 81st lap and never looked back as he notched his 15th win of the year in the 250-miler at Langhorne Speedway.

Herb Thomas finished second, Fonty Flock third and Marvin Panch fourth. Fifth place went to Jimmy Massey.

Tim Flock led the first three laps after starting on the pole. Dick Rathmann, whose career had been in decline for almost a year, took the lead for three laps.

Dave Terrell, who started second in perhaps the biggest upset in qualifying all year, hustled past Rathmann on lap seven. He was holding a narrow lead on lap 15 when his Oldsmobile was knocked out as a rock went through his radiator.

Rathmann took the lead and was padding his advantage when his Chrysler blew an engine on lap 80. Flock took command at that point and was never threatened.

A crowd of 25,000 termed "the largest crowd in Langhorne history" by a track representative, watched Flock average 77.888 mph.

Three caution flags broke the action.   The most

Grand National Race No. 37
250 Laps at Langhorne Speedway
Langhorne, PA
250 Miles on 1-mile Dirt Track
September 18, 1955

Fin	St	No.	Driver	Team / Car	Laps	Money	Status
1	1	300	Tim Flock	Carl Kiekhaefer '55 Chrysler	250	$2,250	Running
2	3	92	Herb Thomas	Thomas '55 Chevrolet	249	1,525	Running
3	6	301	Fonty Flock	Carl Kiekhaefer '55 Chrysler	246	950	Running
4	13	44	Marvin Panch	Bob Welborn '5 Chevrolet	245	750	Running
5	32	04	Jimmy Massey	Westmoreland '55 Chevrolet	244	600	Running
6	15	89	Buck Baker	Baker '55 Buick	239	550	Running
7	17	49	Bob Welborn	Welborn '55 Chevrolet	234	350	Running
8	7	2	Gwyn Staley	Westmoreland '55 Chevrolet	233	300	Running
9	21	302	Mario Rossi	Carl Krueger '55 Chrysler	223	200	Running
10	42	70	Joe Eubanks	'55 Chevrolet	220	175	Running
11	35	178	John Lindsay	'55 Chevrolet	220	150	Running
12	39	20	Banks Simpson	Waldron & Co. '55 Buick	217	100	Running
13	18	900	Johnny Roberts	'55 Chevrolet	212	100	Running
14	26	101	Clayton Danello	'54 Hudson	212	200	Running
15	22	28	Eddie Skinner	Frank Dodge '53 Olds	208	200	Running
16	30	L-2	Art MacBurney	'55 Ford	204	175	Running
17	40	47	Harvey Eakin	Eakin '54 Nash	203	175	Running
18	23	121	Harvey Henderson	'53 Hudson Hornet	201	75	Running
19	19	26	Russ Truelove	Truelove '55 Ford	196	75	V-Joint
20	29	77	Walt Schubert	Dave Everett '55 Ford	196	75	Running
21	38	38	E.J. Turner	'53 Ford	194	50	Running
22	33	79	Leon Lundy	'53 Plymouth	193	150	Running
23	8	87	Speedy Thompson	Griffin Motors '54 Olds	186	50	C-Shaft
24	14	63	Bill Tanner	Al Liberty '55 Chevrolet	183	50	Running
25	36	93	Lou Spears	'54 Chevrolet	169	50	Heating
26	9	55	Junior Johnson	B & L Motors '55 Olds	166	50	RF Hub
27	27	136	Dick Hallock	'53 Hudson Hornet	154	50	RF Wheel
28	25	303	Lee Petty	Henry Ford '55 Chrysler	116	50	Crash
29	37	777	Axel Anderson	'55 Mercury	115	150	Crash
30	4	3	Dick Rathmann	John Ditz '55 Chrysler	80	50	Piston
31	31	88	Jimmie Lewallen	Ernest Woods '55 Olds	76	50	Gasket
32	11	40	Gene Simpson	Bud Harbaugh '55 Buick	75	50	RR Axle
33	20	14	Jerry Banjamin	'55 Chevrolet	71	50	Heating
34	41	141	Ted Chamberlain	'55 Chevrolet	67	50	Spindle
35	16	5	Fred Krebs	'55 Chevrolet	50	50	Tie Rod
36	5	78	Jim Paschal	Ernest Woods '55 Olds	32	50	Crash
37	24	32	Ted Cannady	'53 Ford 6	20	50	Tie Rod
38	12	17	Bud Graham	Earl Wright '55 Chevrolet	19	50	Gasket
39	10	22	Bill Blair	'55 Olds	17	50	Piston
40	28	75	Ed Paskovich	'53 Dodge	17	150	Oil Press
41	2	98	Dave Terrell	Terrell '55 Olds	15	50	Radiator
42	34	1	Elton Hildreth	Hildreth '54 Nash	10	---	Piston

Time of Race: 3 hours, 12 minutes, 35 seconds
Average Speed: 77.888 mph
Pole Winner: Tim Flock - 92.095 mph
Lap Leaders: Tim Flock 1-3, Dick Rathmann 4-6, Dave Terrell 7-15, Rathmann 16-80,
   T. Flock 81-250.
Cautions: 3   Margin of Victory: 1 lap plus   Attendance: 25,000

Axel Anderson's thundering crash at Langhorne.

Three caution flags held the winner's speed to 73.289 mph. Junior Johnson, Joe Eubanks and Jim Paschal were eliminated by crashes on the 1-mile paved track.

Veteran Curtis Turner and newcomer Ned Jarrett were among the early retirees. Of the 36 cars that started the race, 24 were running at the finish.

Fonty Flock

serious mishap occurred in the 137th lap when Axel Anderson, running 22 laps down, lost control of his Mercury. The car darted into the outside guard rail, vaulted into a series of flips and landed in a smoking heap.

Anderson was transported to Lower Bucks County Hospital with a fractured skull, a concussion, multiple-lacerations and a broken nose.

Joe Eubanks started last in the 42-car field but made a gallant charge into 10th place when the checkered flag fell.

Race No. 38

Fonty Flock Noses Out Herb Thomas at Raleigh

RALEIGH, NC (Sept. 30) -- The Flock brothers and the Thomas brothers squared off in a 100-mile Grand National race under the lights at Raleigh Speedway and Fonty Flock prevailed before a crowd of 6,000.

Fonty whipped his Mercury Outboards Chrysler around Herb Thomas in the 69th lap and held on for a six car length victory. It was his third win of the season.

Thomas was second in a Chevrolet. Tim Flock took third and Donald Thomas was fourth. Fifth place went to Modified driver Bill Widenhouse.

It was the third straight runner-up finish for the elder Thomas. He has won twice in seven starts since his May accident in Charlotte.

Grand National Race No. 38
100 Laps at Raleigh Speedway
Raleigh, NC
100 Miles on 1-mile Paved Track
September 30, 1955

Fin	St	No.	Driver	Team / Car	Laps	Money	Status
1	1	301	Fonty Flock	Carl Kiekhaefer '55 Chrysler	100	$1,100	Running
2	3	92	Herb Thomas	Thomas '55 Chevrolet	100	700	Running
3	2	300	Tim Flock	Carl Kiekhaefer '55 Chrysler	100	475	Running
4	5	91	Donald Thomas	Herb Thomas '55 Buick	100	365	Running
5	15	25	Bill Widenhouse	Sam McCuthen '55 Chevrolet	100	310	Running
6	11	49	Bob Welborn	Welborn '55 Chevrolet	100	250	Running
7	6	87	Buck Baker	DePaolo Eng.'55 Ford	97	200	Running
8	14	5	Ralph Liguori	Liguori '55 Buick	97	150	Running
9	20	42	Lee Petty	Petty Eng.'55 Dodge	96	100	Running
10	12	2	Gwyn Staley	Westmoreland'55 Chevrolet	95	100	Running
11	25	24	Bobby Waddell	Jimmy Pardue '55 Chevrolet	95	75	Running
12	28	32	Ted Cannady	'53 Ford	94	60	Running
13	22	27	John McVitty	'55 Chevrolet	94	50	Running
14	21	178	John Lindsay	'55 Chevrolet	93	50	Running
15	33	28	Eddie Skinner	Frank Dodge '53 Olds	93	50	Running
16	30	19	Gordon Smith	'55 Chevrolet	89	50	Running
17	3	34	Speedy Thompson	DePaolo Eng. '55 Ford	88	50	Running
18	18	20	Banks Simpson	Waldron & Co. '55 Buick	87	50	Running
19	32	94	Clarence DeZalia	DeZalia '54 Ford 6	82	50	Running
20	36	69	Volney Schulze	'54 Dodge	79	50	Running
21	35	59	Blackie Pitt	Brownie Pitt '54 Olds	77	---	Running
22	34	44	Harvey Eakin	Eakin '54 Nash	69	---	Running
23	26	65	Joe Sykes	'55 Ford	69	---	Running
24	29	41	Bob Beck	Beck '55 Chevrolet	65	---	Running
25	8	55	Junior Johnson	B & L Motors '55 Olds	63	---	Crash
26	17	44	Jimmie Lewallen	Bob Welborn '55 Chevrolet	60	---	Spindle
27	16	04	Jimmy Massey	Westmoreland '55 Chevrolet	50	---	Wheel
28	7	70	Joe Eubanks	'55 Chevrolet	55	---	Crash
29	9	78	Jim Paschal	Ernest Woods '55 Olds	55	---	Crash
30	19	29	Dink Widenhouse	'55 Chevrolet	53	---	Brakes
31	10	7	Jim Reed	Reed '55 Chevrolet	53	---	Gas Line
32	23	98	Dave Terrell	Terrell '55 Olds	43	---	Trans
33	27	30	Ned Jarrett	Mellie Bernard '55 Pontiac	28	---	Rear End
34	31	460	Ed Cole, Jr.	Brooks Bros. '55 Plymouth	21	---	Spindle
35	13	99	Curtis Turner	Schwam Motor Co 55 Ford	19	---	Handling
36	24	11	George Parrish	W.H. Pontress '53 Studebaker	9	---	Piston

Time of Race: 1 hour, 21 minutes, 52 seconds
  Average Speed: 73.289 mph
  Pole Winner: Fonty Flock - 82.098 mph
  Lap Leaders: Tim Flock 1-14, Fonty Flock 15-46, Herb Thomas 47-68, F Flock 69-100.
  Cautions: 3   Margin of Victory: 6 car lengths   Attendance: 6,000

Race No. 39

Reed Takes Flag at Greenville in Illegal Chevy; Flock Declared Winner

GREENVILLE, SC (Oct. 6) -- Jim Reed, a short track wizard, ran down Tim Flock in the late going and was flagged the winner in the 100-miler at Greenville-Pickens Speedway. However, the Peekskill, NY driver had little time to celebrate.

Carl Kiekhaefer, owner of the Chrysler which Tim Flock drove to second place honors, protested Reed's 'home-made' Chevrolet. NASCAR officials checked under the hood of Reed's car and discovered non-stock cylinder heads. Reed was disqualified and Flock was elevated to the winner's platform.

It was the third time a Grand National race winner had been disqualified in NASCAR's Grand National history. Ironically, one of the previous victims was Tim Flock.

Flock, who completed 199 of the scheduled 200 laps, wound up two laps ahead of second place finisher Junior Johnson. Bob Welborn was third, Jimmy Massey fourth and Buck Baker fifth.

A crowd of 8,000 watched Flock average 57.942 mph for the 99.5-mile race. Only one caution flag broke the brisk-paced event.

Jim Reed was disqualified after winning Greenville race.

Grand National Race No. 39
200 Laps at Greenville-Pickens Speedway
Greenville, SC
100 Miles on Half-mile Dirt Track
October 6, 1955

Fin	St	No.	Driver	Team / Car	Laps	Money	Status
1	2	300	Tim Flock	Carl Kiekhaefer '55 Chrysler	199	$1,100	Running
2	13	44	Junior Johnson	Bob Welborn '55 Chevrolet	197	700	Running
3	1	49	Bob Welborn	Welborn '55 Chevrolet	197	475	Running
4	4	04	Jimmy Massey	Westmoreland '55 Chevrolet	197	365	Running
5	15	87	Buck Baker	DePaolo Eng. '55 Ford	197	310	Running
6	18	34	Jimmy Thompson	DePaolo Eng. '55 Ford	196	250	Running
7	6	25	Bill Widenhouse	Sam McCuthen '55 Chevrolet	195	200	Running
8	5	1	Jack Smith	H. Rakestraw '55 Chevrolet	193	150	Running
9	12	88	Jimmie Lewallen	Ernest Woods '55 Olds	189	100	Running
10	16	42	Lee Petty	Petty Eng. '55 Dodge	189	100	Running
11	10	B-29	Dink Widenhouse	'55 Chevrolet	188	75	Running
12	14	22	Willard Stamey	'55 Chevrolet	187	60	Running
13	25	20	Bunk Moore	Waldron & Co. '55 Buick	185	50	Running
14	24	37	Doug Cox	'55 Pontiac	181	50	Running
15	19	27	John McVitty	'55 Chevrolet	179	50	Running
16	23	28	Eddie Skinner	Frank Dodge '53 Olds	176	50	Running
17	28	32	Ted Cannady	'55 Ford 6	166	50	Wheel
18	17	17	Bud Graham	Earl Wright '55 Chevrolet	166	60	Running
19	22	3-A	Bud Geiselman	'53 Hudson Hornet	164	50	Running
20	27	59	Blackie Pitt	Brownie Pitt '54 Olds	162	50	Running
21	26	19	Gordon Smith	'55 Chevrolet	156	---	Running
22	21	78	Jim Paschal	Ernest Woods '55 Olds	116	---	Heating
23	3	70	Joe Eubanks	'55 Chevrolet	104	---	Wheel
24	20	24	Bobby Waddell	Jimmy Pardue '55 Chevrolet	57	---	Tie Rod
25	8	91	Fonty Flock	Thomas '55 Chevrolet	45	---	Heating
26	7	44-X	Chester Brown	'55 Chevrolet	20	---	Spindle
27	11	2	Gwyn Staley	Westmoreland '55 Chevrolet	0	---	Trans
28	9	7	Jim Reed *	Reed '55 Chevrolet	200	---	Disqual.

* Jim Reed was flagged the winner, but was disqualified for not using stock cylindery heads
Time of Race: 1 hour, 43 minutes, 2 seconds
Average Speed: 57.942 mph
Pole Winner: Bob Welborn - 58.037 mph
Lap Leaders: Tim Flock 1-199.
Cautions: 1   Margin of Victory: 2 laps plus   Attendance: 8,000

Race No. 40

Thompson Ends Famine With Big Memphis-Arkansas Win

LeHi, AR (Oct. 9) -- Speedy Thompson of Monroe, NC ended a two-year famine on the Grand National trail by driving a factory backed Ford to victory in the 300-miler at Memphis-Arkansas Speedway.

When Thompson drove his car under the checkered flag at dusk, it was his first Grand National win since October 22, 1953, when he won at North Wilkesboro, NC. Marvin Panch, driving in the same lap as the winner, finished second in a Ford.

Third place went to Jimmy Massey whose Chevrolet was four laps off the pace. Tim Flock virtually

Lee Petty leads Dink Widenhouse through 4th turn at the Memphis-Arkansas Speedway.

wrapped up his second driving title by taking fourth in a Chrysler as Brother Bob took fifth in another Chrysler.

DeWayne "Tiny" Lund, making his first NASCAR start, was injured when his Chevrolet flipped an untold number of times in the 67th lap. The seat belts broke loose, throwing the Harlan, IA rookie out of the car onto the middle of the track. Several drivers came close to running over him.

Lund was taken to Crittenden County Hospital suffering from a broken arm,

Norm Nelson #299 and Speedy Thompson race side-by-side down front stretch at Memphis-Arkansas Speedway.

bruises and shock. Ironically, Lund's car was sponsored by Rupert Safety Belts, a manufacturer of seat belts for automobiles.

Carl Kiekhaefer entered four Mercury Outboard Chryslers, and he sponsored three other automobiles, including race winner Thompson. It was the first Grand National win for Ford since Jimmy Florian won at Dayton, OH on June 25, 1950.

Thompson's average speed for the 300 miles was 83.948 mph. Fonty Flock had won the pole at 100.390 mph, the first time the 100 mile barrier had been broken on the 1.5-mile dirt track.

A disappointing crowd of 8,500 turned out to watch the event. Attendance figures were off due to the recent troubles at the oval.

Grand National Race No. 40
200 Laps at Memphis-Arkansas Speedway
LeHi, AR
300 Miles on 1.5-mile Dirt Track
October 9, 1955

Fin	St	No.	Driver	Team / Car	Laps	Money	Status
1	10	297	Speedy Thompson	DePaolo Eng '55 Ford	200	$2,900	Running
2	6	98	Marvin Panch	DePaolo Eng '55 Ford	200	1,450	Running
3	12	04	Jimmy Massey	Westmoreland '55 Chevrolet	196	1,000	Running
4	2	300	Tim Flock	Carl Kiekhaefer '55 Chrysler	195	850	Running
5	8	308	Bob Flock	Carl Kiekhaefer '55 Chrysler	195	650	Running
6	3	87	Buck Baker	DePaolo Eng '55 Ford	194	525	Running
7	18	88	Jimmie Lewallen	Ernest Woods '55 Olds	190	400	Running
8	25	44	Ralph Liguori	Bob Welborn '55 Chevrolet	189	350	Running
9	14	B-29	Dink Widenhouse	'55 Ford	185	250	Running
10	20	49	Bob Welborn	Welborn '55 Chevrolet	183	225	Running
11	24	42	Lee Petty	Petty Eng.'55 Dodge	183	150	Running
12	35	22	Bill Blair	Blair '55 Olds	182	125	Running
13	22	188	Hooker Hood	Hood '54 Olds	177	125	Running
14	40	12	Al Hager	'55 Chevrolet	176	125	Running
15	27	51-X	Leland Sowell	'55 Ford	176	125	Running
16	42	89	Banks Simpson	Buck Baker '55 Buick	172	95	Running
17	31	64	Johnny Allen	Spook Crawford '55 Plymouth	169	195	Running
18	39	299	Norm Nelson	Carl Kiekhaefer '55 Chrysler	162	95	Engine
19	32	84	Gene Rose	'55 Chrysler	160	95	Running
20	30	5	Bob Coleman	'55 Ford	152	95	Running
21	20	155	Roscoe Rann	'54 Chrysler	146	60	Running
22	7	92	Herb Thomas	Thomas '55 Chevrolet	132	60	Rear End
23	26	52	Joe Guide, Jr.	Sally Guide '53 Hudson	125	160	Running
24	41	1	Bill Morton	'55 Buick	123	60	Crash
25	23	37	Tiny Lund	Carl Rupert '55 Chevrolet	65	60	Crash
26	37	46	Jim Murray	'55 Buick	63	60	Fuel Pmp
27	4	99	Billy Carden	Schwam Motor Co '55 Ford	55	60	Crash
28	17	70	Joe Eubanks	'55 Chevrolet	46	60	Steering
29	21	15	Johnny Mantz	DePaolo Eng. '55 Ford	46	60	Vapor Lk
30	15	68	Chuck Stevenson	DePaolo Eng '55 Ford	43	60	Vapor Lk
31	13	2	Gwyn Staley	Westmoreland'55 Chevrolet	38	60	Fuel Pmp
32	8	86	Joe Weatherly	DePaolo Eng '55 Ford	29	60	Vapor Lk
33	19	198	Dave Terrell	Terrell '55 Olds	27	60	Crash
34	16	17	Bud Graham	Earl Wright '55 Chevrolet	22	60	Heating
35	11	25	Bill Widenhouse	Sam McCuthen '55 Chevrolet	22	60	Radiator
36	5	95	Curtis Turner	Schwam Motors '55 Ford	19	40	Vapor Lk
37	38	28	Eddie Skinner	Frank Dodge '53 Olds	13	40	Gasket
38	36	112	Floyd Curtis	'55 Ford	10	40	Radiator
39	1	301	Fonty Flock	Carl Kiekhaefer '55 Chrysler	5	40	Radiator
40	29	32	Ted Cannady	'53 Ford 6	3	40	Piston
41	33	7	Jim Reed	Reed '55 Chevrolet	8	---	Disqual.

Time of Race: 3 hours, 34 minutes, 25 seconds
Average Speed: 83.948 mph
Pole Winner: Fonty Flock - 100.390 mph
Lap Leaders: Tim Flock 1-42, Speedy Thompson 43-200.
Cautions: Margin of Victory: 3/4 lap   Attendance: 8,500

Race No. 41

Flock Takes Columbia Event In Final Six Miles

COLUMBIA, SC (Oct. 15) -- Buck Baker suffered a heartbreaker, and Tim Flock was the opportunist who came home first in the 100-mile Grand National event at Columbia Speedway.

Baker, now a member of Peter DePaolo's factory Ford team, got around Flock in the 12th lap and led most of the way on the half-mile dirt oval. Running short of fuel, the Charlotte, NC veteran ducked into the pits with twelve laps to go allowing Flock to grab the lead. Baker finished second.

Herb Thomas came in third, with Gwyn Staley fourth and Jimmy Massey fifth.

Joe Weatherly was holding down third place in the

Lee Petty's Dodge lies in a crumpled heap after colliding with Joe Eubanks #70 at Columbia.

final five laps when his Ford broke an axle causing the car to flip upside down in the inside of the track. Weatherly was unhurt.

Lee Petty and Joe Eubanks crashed together in the 35th lap, putting both out of action. Petty, who led the point standings through the 32nd race of the year, has been utterly snake-bitten in the last four months.

Flock covered the 100 miles at an average speed of 55.393 mph.

Race No. 42

Thompson Joins Kiekhaefer Team; Wins Martinsville

MARTINSVILLE, VA (Oct. 16) -- Speedy Thompson got a driving assignment in the Kiekhaefer Chrysler, and he didn't let the opportunity go to waste as he guided his new machine to victory in the 100-mile event at Martinsville Speedway.

Thompson sped past Bob Welborn in the 138th lap and led the rest of the way to post his fourth career win on the Grand National trail. Welborn finished second, Jim Paschal was third, Herb Thomas fourth and Jim Reed fifth. It was Reed's first start since being disqualified for two straight events.

The race was held up for over an hour due to a stubborn rain, but it didn't thwart the 12,000 spectators who waited in their cars until the weather broke. Since the time trials were washed out, a blind draw determined the grid.

The lead changed hands seven times among five

Grand National Race No. 41
200 Laps at Columbia Speedway
Columbia, SC
100 Miles on Half-mile Dirt Track
October 15, 1955

Fin	St	No.	Driver	Team / Car	Laps	Money	Status
1	2	300	Tim Flock	Carl Kiekhaefer '55 Chrysler	200	$1,100	Running
2	5	87	Buck Baker	DePaolo Eng. '56 Ford	200	700	Running
3	6	92	Herb Thomas	Thomas '55 Chevrolet	197	475	Running
4	9	2	Gwyn Staley	Westmoreland '55 Chevrolet	194	365	Running
5	21	04	Jimmy Massey	Westmoreland '55 Chevrolet	194	310	Running
6	15	49	Bob Welborn	Welborn '55 Chevrolet	193	250	Running
7	1	55	Junior Johnson	B & L Motors '55 Olds	193	200	Running
8	13	9	Joe Weatherly	Schwam Motor Co. '56 Ford	191	150	Crash
9	10	88	Jimmie Lewallen	Ernest Woods '55 Olds	189	100	Running
10	12	15	Jim Roland	'55 Chevrolet	187	100	Rear End
11	14	44	Jim Paschal	Bob Welborn '55 Chevrolet	181	75	Running
12	19	460	Ed Cole, Jr.	Brooks Bros. '55 Plymouth	168	60	Running
13	18	1	Bill Morton	'55 Buick	165	50	Running
14	20	94	Clarence DeZalia	DeZalia '54 Ford 6	160	50	Running
15	16	28	Eddie Skinner	Frank Dodge '53 Olds	137	50	Running
16	4	25	Bill Widenhouse	Sam McCuthen '55 Chevrolet	129	50	Crash
17	3	B-29	Dink Widenhouse	'56 Ford	110	50	Wheel
18	11	34	Jimmy Thompson	DePaolo Eng. '55 Ford	58	50	Throttle
19	7	42	Lee Petty	Petty Eng. '55 Dodge	35	50	Crash
20	8	70	Joe Eubanks	'55 Chevrolet	34	50	Bearing
21	17	20	Bunk Moore	Waldron & Co. '55 Buick	14	---	Carb

Time of Race: 1 hour, 49 minutes, 19 seconds
Average Speed: 55.393 mph
Pole Winner: Junior Johnson - 61.728 mph
Lap Leaders: Tim Flock 1-11, Buck Baker 12-188, T. Flock 189-200.
Cautions: Margin of Victory: Attendance:

Grand National Race No. 42
200 Laps at Martinsville Speedway
Martinsville, VA
100 Miles on Half-mile Paved Track
October 16, 1955

Fin	St	No.	Driver	Team / Car	Laps	Money	Status
1	17	30	Speedy Thompson	Carl Kiekhaefer '55 Chrysler	200	$1,100	Running
2	11	49	Bob Welborn	Welborn '55 Chevrolet	200	700	Running
3	18	44	Jim Paschal	Bob Welborn '55 Chevrolet	200	475	Running
4	2	92	Herb Thomas	Thomas '55 Chevrolet	199	365	Running
5	9	7	Jim Reed	Reed '55 Chevrolet	198	310	Running
6	22	9	Joe Weatherly	Schwam Motor Co. '56 Ford	198	250	Running
7	1	2	Gwyn Staley	Westmoreland '55 Chevrolet	198	200	Running
8	4	42	Lee Petty	Petty Eng. '55 Dodge	198	150	Running
9	15	04	Jimmy Massey	Westmoreland '55 Chevrolet	194	100	Running
10	20	87	Buck Baker	DePaolo Eng.'56 Ford	194	100	Running
11	25	98	Marvin Panch	DePaolo Eng. '56 Ford	192	75	Running
12	13	55	Bobby Waddell	'55 Olds	187	60	Running
13	10	22	Bill Blair	Blair '55 Olds	186	50	Running
14	14	33	Pop McGinnis	Owen Cox '55 Chevrolet	183	50	Running
15	19	17	Bud Graham	Earl Wright '55 Chevrolet	182	50	Running
16	6	71	Ted Cannady	'55 Olds	178	50	Crash
17	5	28	Eddie Skinner	Frank Dodge '53 Olds	177	50	Running
18	12	24	Jimmy Thompson (NC)	'55 Ford	176	50	Running
19	8	32	Jim Thompson (WV)	'53 Hudson Hornet	173	50	Running
20	26	460	Ed Cole, Jr.	'55 Plymouth	172	50	Running
21	27	94	Clarence DeZalia	DeZalia '54 Ford 6	160	---	Running
22	21	70	Joe Eubanks	'55 Chevrolet	156	---	Wheel
23	24	91	Donald Thomas	Herb Thomas '55 Buick	155	---	Running
24	7	300	Tim Flock	Carl Kiekhaefer '55 Chrysler	70	---	Trans
25	3	301	Fonty Flock	Carl Kelkhaefer '55 Chrysler	62	---	Trans
26	23	22-A	Glen Wood	Wood Brothers '55 Ford	55	---	Bearing
27	28	B-29	Dink Widenhouse	'56 Ford	26	---	Brakes
28	16	24	Jimmy Pardue	Pardue '55 Chevrolet	10	---	Hub

Time of Race: 1 hour, 40 minutes, 40 seconds
Pole Winner: Drew For Position - Gwyn Staley drew pole
Lap Leaders: Herb Thomas 1-7, Tim Flock 8-73, Jim Reed 74-105, Bob Welborn 106-120, Speedy Thompson 121, Welborn 122-137, S. Thompson 138-200.
Cautions: 3   Margin of Victory: Attendance: 12,000

drivers. Thompson was on top twice for a total of 64 laps. His Chrysler win goes with two Oldsmobile and one Ford victories.

Tim Flock led for 66 laps. It was the 14th straight Grand National race in which Flock had led at least one lap, an all time record.

Race No. 43

Nelson Avoids 12-Car Crash; Rolls Winning Dice at Vegas

LAS VEGAS, NV (Oct. 16) -- The Grand National stock cars replaced the AAA Championship cars at the new Las Vegas Speedway, and Norm Nelson avoided a 12-car smash-up to score a two lap victory in the scheduled 100-miler.

The race was shortened from 200 laps to 111 when darkness set in. The race had been red flagged in the 74th lap so that wrecker crews could clean up the debris from the multi-car accident.

Virgil Martin, who was a dozen laps behind, lost control of his Ford. A pack of closely knit cars piled into Martin, completely blocking the track. Those involved included Danny Letner, John Lansaw, Johnny Mantz, Allen Adkins, Herb Hill, Ed Brown, Eddie Pagan, Sherman Clark, John Kieper, Ernie Young and Martin. Seven cars were sidelined in the wreck.

Lloyd Dane, who started fourth, got a good jump on the field, leading the first five laps.   Pole sitter Nelson then charged to the front and was leading when officials declared the race complete.

Bill Hyde, Bill West, Clark and Jim Murray rounded out the top five.

Nelson, who won in his second Grand National start, averaged a slow 44.449 mph.

Gwyn Staley #2 passes Bobby Waddell #24 at North Wilkesboro Speedway.

Race No. 44

Baker Takes Third Win of Year at N. Wilkesboro

N. WILKESBORO, NC. (Oct. 23) -- Buck Baker won his third victory of the year as he put his Ford into the lead at the start and led all the way to win the 100-miler at North Wilkesboro Speedway. Ironically, each victory came in a different make of car. Previously he had won in a Buick and an Oldsmobile.

Lee Petty drove his Dodge into second place, 5.0 seconds behind Baker at the finish. Gwyn Staley came in third with Joe Weatherly fourth. Tim Flock clinched the 1955 Point Championship by finishing fifth.

Herb Thomas brought out one of the day's three caution flags when his Chevrolet broke an idler arm and plunged over the north turn. He was running third at the time.

Grand National Race No. 43
200 Laps at Las Vegas Park Speedway
Las Vegas, NV
200 Miles on 1-mile Dirt Track
October 16, 1955

Fin	St	No.	Driver	Team / Car	Laps	Money	Status
1	1	299	Norm Nelson	Carld Kiekhaefer '55 Chrysler	111	$1,325	Running
2	2	96	Bill Hyde	'53 Olds	109	820	Running
3	8	33	Bill West	Jim Dane '53 Hudson Hornet	107	560	Running
4	9	34	Sherman Clark	Clark '55 Chevrolet	104	340	Running
5	19	46	Jim Murray	'55 Buick	102	270	Running
6	12	49	Bob Ruppert	Ellingham Body '55 Chevrolet	102	200	Running
7	6	5	Johnny Mantz	Bill Stroppe '55 Mercury	102	185	Running
8	16	12	Bill Stammer	Stammer '55 Chevrolet	100	150	Running
9	18	41	Ernie Young	Walt Palozi '52 Plymouth	99	100	Running
10	26	29	Bob Stanclift	'53 Olds	99	100	Running
11	25	210	Tom Francis	'54 Ford	95	90	Running
12	15	30	Fred Steinbroner	Steinbroner '55 Chevrolet	84	80	Running
13	24	53	Herb Crawford	'53 Studebaker	84	50	Running
14	3	6	Danny Letner	Coz Cancilla '54 Olds	74	55	Crash
15	17	91	John Lansaw	'55 Plymouth	74	50	Crash
16	5	2	Allen Adkins	Gus Davis '55 Dodge	72	50	Crash
17	14	11	Johnny Kieper	Kieper '55 Olds	72	50	Crash
18	7	26	Ed Brown	'55 Chevrolet	71	50	Crash
19	22	36	Herb Hill	'54 Studebaker	70	40	Heating
20	27	37	Virgil Martin	'56 Ford	62	20	Crash
21	11	9	Eddie Pagan	'55 Chevrolet	62	20	Crash
22	10	25	Erick Erickson	Erickson '54 Buick	59	30	Crash
23	20	7	Clyde Palmer	'54 Dodge	56	20	Crash
24	13	20	Bill Amick	'55 Olds	39	20	Heating
25	21	95	Carl Hoover	'53 Olds	35	20	Piston
26	4	47	Lloyd Dane	'55 Mercury	14	30	Unexpl
27	23	31	Britton Jones	'55 Dodge	11	20	Heating

Time of Race: 2 hours, 29 minutes, 50 seconds
  Average Speed: 44.449 mph
  Pole Winner: Norm Nelson - 74.518 mph
  Lap Leaders: Lloyd Dane 1-5, Norm Nelson 6-111.
  Cautions: Margin of Victory: 2 laps plus   Attendance:
  * Race shortened from 200 laps to 111 laps due to darkness

Baker secured second place in the point standings with his 72.347 mph victory.

Weatherly, who had been a front runner with absolutely no luck at all, painted his Ford a deep purple and tagged it the "Purple Pig". Apparently the new paint scheme worked as he enjoyed his best finish of the year.

Grand National Race No. 44
160 Laps at N. Wilkesboro Speedway
North Wilkesboro, NC
100 Miles on .625-mile Dirt Track
October 23, 1955

Fin	St	No.	Driver	Team / Car	Laps	Money	Status
1	1	87	Buck Baker	DePaolo Eng.'56 Ford	160	$1,100	Running
2	4	42	Lee Petty	Petty Eng.'55 Dodge	160	700	Running
3	12	2	Gwyn Staley	Westmoreland'55 Chevrolet	159	475	Running
4	9	9	Joe Weatherly	Schwam Motors '56 Ford	159	365	Running
5	11	300	Tim Flock	Carl Kiekhaefer '55 Chrysler	159	310	Running
6	6	301	Fonty Flock	Carl Kiekhaefer'55 Chrysler	159	250	Running
7	10	20	Speedy Thompson	Carl Kiekhaefer '55 Chrysler	157	200	Running
8	5	B-29	Dink Widenhouse	'56 Ford	157	150	Running
9	8	198	Dave Terrell	Terrell '55 Olds	156	100	Running
10	16	44	Jim Paschal	Bob Welborn '55 Clhevrolet	154	100	Running
11	17	04	Jimmy Massey	Westmoreland '55 Chevrolet	154	75	Running
12	18	88	Jimmie Lewallen	Ernest Woods '55 Olds	151	60	Running
13	16	49	Bob Welborn	Welborn '55 Chevrolet	145	50	Running
14	23	24	Bobby Waddell	Jimmy Pardue '55 Chevrolet	138	50	Running
15	27	460	Ed Cole, Jr.	Brooks Bros '55 Plymouth	136	50	Running
16	24	28	Eddie Skinner	Frank Dodge '53 Olds	132	50	Running
17	25	27	John McVitty	'55 Chevrolet	128	50	Wheel
18	15	5	Ralph Liguori	Liguori '55 Buick	127	50	Stalled
19	13	22	Bill Blair	Blair '55 Olds	127	50	RF Hub
20	7	99	Curtis Turner	Schwam Motor Co. '56 Ford	103	50	RF Hub
21	2	92	Herb Thomas	Thomas '55 Chevrolet	90	---	Crash
22	21	89	Ned Jarrett	Jarrett '55 Buick	70	---	Fuel Pmp
23	3	98	Marvin Panch	DePaolo Eng '56 Ford	50	---	Heating
24	14	70	Joe Eubanks	'55 Chevrolet	40	---	Steering
25	22	20	Banks Simpson	Waldron & Co. '55 Buick	40	---	Radiator
26	20	55	Junior Johnson	B & L Motors '55 Olds	35	---	Bumper
27	28	9-A	Tom Pistone	'55 Chevrolet	28	---	Heating
28	26	71	Ted Cannady	'55 Olds	25	---	Steering

Time of Race: 1 hour, 21 minutes, 16 seconds
Average Speed: 72.347 mph
Pole Winner: Buck Baker - 79.815 mph
Lap Leaders: Buck Baker 1-160.
Cautions: 3   Margin of Victory: 5 seconds   Attendance: 10,000

Race No. 45

Flock Caps Off Incredible Year With Hillsboro Win

HILLSBORO, NC (Oct. 30) -- Tim Flock sealed his record-shattering season with another flag-to-flag triumph in the 1955 Grand National finale at Orange Speedway. It was the 16th win of the year for the Atlanta ace and gave him a 508 point lead over Buck

Baker in the NASCAR championship point standings. He was also the 1952 champion.

Flock started on the pole for the 18th time this season and led from flag to flag for the 11th time. All are records.

He also amassed $37,779.60 in Grand National prize and point money, another record.

Curtis Turner finished second with Buck Baker third, Herb Thomas fourth and Dave Terrell fifth. Joe Weatherly was sixth as the first six cars were all running in the lead lap at the finish.

Flock's pole winning qualification was timed at 81.673 mph and his run for the 100 miles at 70.465 mph.

Speedy Thompson, winner of two late season events, drove a Hudson Hornet in the race, but a ruptured fuel tank sent him to the showers after 70 laps. He finished 21st in the 25 car field.

Grand National Race No. 45
100 Laps at Orange Speedway
Hillsboro, NC
100 Miles on 1-mile Dirt Track
October 30, 1955

Fin	St	No.	Driver	Team / Car	Laps	Money	Status
1	1	301	Tim Flock	Carl Kiekhaefer '55 Chrysler	100	$1,100	Running
2	9	99	Curtis Turner	Schwam Motor Co. '56 Ford	100	700	Running
3	12	87	Buck Baker	DePaolo Eng.'56 Ford	100	475	Running
4	14	92	Herb Thomas	Thomas '55 Chevrolet	100	365	Running
5	15	198	Dave Terrell	Terrell '55 Olds	100	310	Running
6	8	9	Joe Weatherly	Schwam Motor Co. '56 Ford	100	250	Running
7	7	B-29	Dink Widenhouse	'56 Ford	98	200	Running
8	16	2	Gwyn Staley	Westmoreland'55 Chevrolet	98	150	Running
9	6	04	Jimmy Massey	Westmoreland '55 Chevrolet	97	100	Running
10	10	44	Bob Welborn	Welborn '55 Chevrolet	95	100	Running
11	13	98	Marvin Panch	DePaolo Eng '56 Ford	93	75	Running
12	24	88	Fred Harb	Ernest Woods '55 Olds	93	60	Running
13	17	32	Ted Cannady	'53 Ford 6	91	50	Running
14	19	24	Bobby Waddell	Jimmy Pardue '55 Chevrolet	91	50	Running
15	3	78	Jimmie Lewallen	Ernest Woods '55 Olds	90	50	Running
16	25	28	Eddie Skinner	Frank Dodge '53 Olds	89	50	Running
17	20	121	Bill Gross	'53 Hudson Wasp	87	50	Running
18	22	460	Ed Cole, Jr.	Brooks Bros '55 Plymouth	83	50	Running
19	11	22	Jim Paschal	Bill Blair '55 Olds	83	50	RF Hub
20	18	5	Ralph Liguori	Liguori '55 Buick	70	50	Rear End
21	2	297	Speedy Thompson	DePaolo Eng. '55 Ford	70	---	Gas Tank
22	5	91	Donald Thomas	Herb Thomas '55 Buick	74	---	Gas Tank
23	4	42	Lee Petty	Petty Eng. '55 Dodge	14	---	Gas Tank
24	23	136	Dick Hallock	'53 Hudson Hornet	14	---	RR Hub
25	21	94	Woodie Arrington	Clarence DeZalia '54 Ford 6	4	---	Crash

Time of Race: 1 hour, 16 minutes, 38 seconds
Average Speed: 70.465 mph
Pole Winner: Tim Flock - 81.673 mph
Lap Leaders: Tim Flock 1-100.
Cautions: 3   Margin of Victory: Attendance: 6,000

1955 NASCAR Season
Final Point Standings Grand National Division

Rank	Driver	Points	Starts	Wins	Top 5	Top 10	Winnings
1	Tim Flock	9,596	38	18	32	33	$37,779.60
2	Buck Baker	8,088	42	3	24	34	19,770.90
3	Lee Petty	7,194	42	6	20	30	18,919.29
4	Bob Welborn	5,460	32	0	12	24	10,146.76
5	Herb Thomas	5,186	23	3	14	15	18,023.47
6	Junior Johnson	4,810	36	5	12	18	13,802.78
7	Eddie Skinner	4,652	38	0	4	15	4,736.85
8	Jim Paschal	4,572	36	3	12	20	10,585.88
9	Jimmie Lewallen	4,526	33	0	8	16	6,439.51
10	Gwyn Staley	4,360	24	0	7	14	6,546.43
11	Fonty Flock	4,266	31	3	12	14	13,099.11
12	Dave Terrell	3,170	25	0	3	10	3,654.11
13	Jimmy Massey	2,924	11	0	4	8	3,509.11
14	Marvin Panch	2,812	10	0	4	4	4,384.11
15	Speedy Thompson	2,452	15	2	3	5	7,089.11
16	Jim Reed	2,416	14	0	4	4	2,702.74
17	Gene Simpson	2,388	22	0	1	7	2,157.74
18	Dick Rathmann	2,298	20	0	7	8	4,367.74
19	Ralph Liguori	2,124	12	0	0	7	1,972.74
20	Joe Eubanks	2,028	14	0	0	4	2,007.74
21	Blackie Pitt	1,992	20	0	0	7	1,785.00
22	Harvey Henderson	1,930	17	0	1	6	1,810.00
23	Banks Simpson	1,852	7	0	0	0	870.00
24	Dink Widenhouse	1,752	15	0	0	6	1,660.00
25	Johnny Dodd, Jr.	1,496	13	0	1	7	1,695.00
26	Bill Widenhouse	1,444	5	0	1	3	1,065.00
27	Lou Spears	1,272	3	0	0	1	810.00
28	Larry Flynn	1,260	1	0	1	1	1,175.00
29	Cotton Owens	1,248	2	0	1	2	900.00
30	Gordon Smith	1,212	15	0	0	2	975.00
31	Billy Carden	1,172	13	0	2	3	1,340.00
32	Arden Mounts	1,170	12	0	0	4	1,025.00
33	Joel Million	1,136	8	0	2	6	1,685.00
34	Curtis Turner	1,120	9	0	4	4	2,605.00
35	John Lindsay	1,052	6	0	0	3	575.00
36	Nace Mattingly	992	3	0	1	1	700.00
37	Bill Blair	974	9	0	0	0	440.00
38	Donald Thomas	932	10	0	2	4	1,240.00
39	Ed Cole, Jr.	924	12	0	0	0	645.00
40	Mack Hanbury	900	8	0	0	2	575.00
41	Danny Letner	892	4	1	2	2	1,780.00
42	George Parrish	880	12	0	0	1	750.00
43	Banjo Matthews	860	3	0	0	2	745.00
44	Carl Krueger	748	7	0	0	1	585.00
45	Ted Cannady	744	9	0	0	0	450.00
46	Allen Adkins	740	4	0	2	2	1,160.00
47	Joe Weatherly	724	6	0	1	4	2,575.00
48	John McVitty	684	7	0	0	2	550.00
49	Lloyd Dane	674	5	0	1	2	780.00
50	Fred Dove	668	7	0	1	2	750.00

The 1956 Season
Kiekhaefer Wins 30
Races -- Then Vanishes

Volume one of a four volume series . . . . The Beginning 1949 - 1958

1956

At Daytona in 1955 Carl Kiekhaefer suddenly emerged as one of the most influential figures in NAS-CAR Grand National racing. Having made millions in the Mercury Outboard Motor Company, the Fond du Lac, WI entrepreneur ventured to NASCAR under the assumption that winning cars adorned with his business logo would increase sales of his boat motors.

Kiekhaefer entered stock car racing as a strictly business venture.

During the first six years of the sport the main artery in Grand National racing, from the competitors standpoint, was enjoyment. It was a game the contestants could thoroughly enjoy. Everyone was on equal terms and a wide variety of teams raced competitively. It was an era tinted with optimism.

Kiekhaefer changed all that.

In 1955, the irrepressible Kiekhaefer Chryslers were just getting warmed up. His cars won *only* 22 races in 40 starts. Principal driver, Tim Flock, won eighteen races and captured the championship.

Kiekhaefer compiled an enviable track record while more or less warming up. In 1956 Mr. K. would get serious.

His first step was to hire Buck Baker to take the wheel of one of his Chryslers. Baker, a hard-nosed

competitor who relished close quarter racing, had been one of Flock's formidable opponents in 1955. The veteran campaigner also had a reputation a mile long for on-track antics.

Kiekhaefer phoned Baker in January of 1956 and made his pitch. "If you are as big a son-of-a-bitch as everybody says you are, I'm curious. Would you like to drive for me?"

Baker wondered if a prankster was on the other end of the line. "I didn't know who that could be," Baker recalled. "I had run hard against his cars in 1955, and I had beaten him a few times. I figured I'd be the last to be asked to drive one of his cars."

The stage was set.

Kiekhaefer was a perfectionist who demanded perfection from all of his employees. That included his drivers. He had certain ideas about how things would operate in his domain - no ands, ifs or buts.

He employed a weatherman to travel with the team, taking readings on humidity and other meterological data. All his drivers were required to fill out a report on what type of gear was used, oil temperature readings during the race, tire wear and finish position. Samples of each of the dirt tracks were taken and placed in a plastic cylinder. All data was analyzed so the team could be better the next time they encountered a track of similar texture.

Carl Kiekhaefer makes point with drivers Herb Thomas, Buck Baker and Speedy Thompson.

Kiekhaefer had other ideas. He would often rent an entire 40 or 50 unit motel, leaving most of the rooms vacant. He would instruct the men to occupy one side of the motel with wives or girlfriends confined to the other. No "extra curricular activity" was permitted between the men and the women the night before a race.

Curfews were closely scrutinized. Bed checks were frequent. Kiekhaefer's rules and regulations were not unlike those of the armed forces.

One thing was different. Kiekhaefer

The Kiekhaefer team won 16 Grand National races in a row and 30 during the 1956 season.

paid his drivers a lot more than the armed forces did - up to $40,000 per year.

In the first 25 Grand National races Kiekhaefer entered in 1956, his cars won 21 of them. The Chrysler and Dodge automobiles also finished second eleven times.

Records tumbled. Kiekhaefer established a mark that is likely to stand for eternity -- his cars won 16 consecutive Grand National events from March 25 through May 30.

The unmitigated success of Kiekhaefer's squad brought king-sized headaches to Bill France, who did not particularly savor the utter domination by one team.

Car owners were airing complaints. They felt that any car *that fast* must be equipped with illegal additives. NASCAR inspectors were eye-balling the Kiekhaefer cars with unwavering regularity. "Not once were we able to find any of Carl's cars illegal," remembered France. "And, brother, did we try!"

France was not the only one who cared little for one team mopping up the premier stock car racing series. The spectators, who were paying anywhere from $2.50 to $10 to watch the Grand Nationals perform, got bored at viewing a private Kiekhaefer car battle

Herb Thomas' Chevrolet. A late season wreck denied him the championship.

for top honors.

They voiced their disapproval in the form of jeers. A chorus of boos and an occasional thrown bottle puzzled Kiekhaefer immensely. Meticulous preparation, the finest mechanics and high quality drivers had delivered success never before seen. Kiekhaefer felt observers would appreciate work of that nature.

In mid-1956, the handwriting was on the wall.

"Mr. K felt all the booing was detrimental to his Mercury Outboard business," says Baker, who had won nine of the first 21 first half races. "His main concern was to increase sales, and he really couldn't understand the fan reaction. He almost pulled out in the middle of the year. But he felt some sort of obligation to his drivers and finished the season out."

After his incredible winning streak, the Kiekhaefer team went into a tail-spin. After winning 21 of 25, they won only four of their next 20 starts.

Compounding the plight was the defection of two drivers. Tim Flock, who had won 22 of 47 starts for Kiekhaefer, suddenly quit after winning the April 8 event at North Wilkesboro, NC. Kiekhaefer was stunned that Flock would walk away from his team. "I needed a break," said Flock. "My ulcers were tearing me up. I was always on stand-by. Never had any time for myself. One time he phoned me and said a private jet would pick me up at the airport in an hour. He said he needed me to come up to Wisconsin for something important.

"I went to the airport and flew up to his office," Flock continued. "When I got there, he said I could go back home. I flew all the way up there just so he could tell me to go back home. He just wanted to know where I was."

After Flock quit, he had to settle on picking up rides at most of the races. He did land a driving assignment for Bill

Stroppe's Mercury team later in the year.

Herb Thomas, NASCAR's winningest driver, was hired to replace Flock. He joined Baker and Speedy Thompson as part of the powerful three-car punch.

At several points in the season, NASCAR would sanction same day Grand Nationals - one on the East coast and one on the West coast. While Baker and Thompson concentrated on the eastern shows, Kiekhaefer sent Thomas out West.

Convertible circuit was immediate off-spring from NASCAR-SAFE merger.

"I didn't really like having to go all the way out west when there were races near home," remarked Thomas, "but at least I did win some races. I won three in a row out west at one point in the year."

In late July, Thomas quit Kiekhaefer's team and cranked up his own Chevrolet to finish the season. He was second in the point race. "I felt all along that I was getting the worst equipment from Kiekhaefer," said Thomas. "He didn't want me to win the championship. He'd prefer that Buck win since he had driven for him all year. I felt I could do better in my car, so that's what I did."

It set the stage for one of the closest battles for the

Grand National title.

Thomas took the point lead from Baker at Langhorne on September 23. As the season wound down, it appeared Thomas would win his third Grand National title. But Kiekhaefer leased the Cleveland County Fairgrounds in Shelby, NC on October 23rd, arranged for an eleventh hour NASCAR sanction, and squeezed another event into the fall schedule. It gave Baker one more opportunity to shave the point deficit.

The 100-miler at Shelby got off on the wrong foot for Thomas. "I had a rear end go out in practice, and I had to change it," said Thomas. "The race officials held up the start of the race so I could get my car fixed."

Thomas had earned the 13th spot in qualifying, but he started at the rear of the 26-car field. He came charging through the pack. By the half-way point, he had worked his way into third place. For several laps, he tried to get around second place Speedy Thompson. Baker was a quarter lap ahead, leading.

On lap 109, Thomas made his bid to pass Thompson. "I don't remember much about it," Thomas said. "I remember passing Speedy. The last thing I remember is going straight into the wall. That's all I remember about that night."

Thompson's front bumper hooked Thomas' rear quarter panel. Thomas' Chevrolet shot into the wall. The steel rail broke and held Thomas' Chevy in front of an onrushing pack of cars.

Jack Smith, Billy Myers, Ralph Moody and Lee Petty plowed into Thomas. Also involved were Tiny Lund, George Green and Billy Carden.

Thomas was lifted from his car and placed on the track surface unconscious. He was transported to the hospital with a fractured skull, a badly lacerated scalp, a ruptured ear drum and internal injuries. Dr. John Hamrick, who treated Thomas, said he was in a coma, critically injured and in possible need of brain surgery.

Four of the Carl Kiekhaefer cars lined up on the sands of Daytona Beach.

Baker went on to win the race and Thomas was credited with a 17th finish position. Thomas still led the points, just 118 points ahead of Baker.

Baker was shaken by the turn of events. Initially, he said he was not going to enter the final three races of the year in respect for his fallen comrade.

But others convinced the Charlotte driver that the accident was not of his making, and accidents are part of the sport. Baker drove in the last three 1956 events and won the championship by 586 points. Thomas was second.

Baker, who won the first of two consecutive championships in 1956, said he caught flak from the Shelby race. "Some people blamed me for the crash, but I was on the other side of the track and didn't see it, Baker pointed out. "I don't know to this day what exactly happened. I didn't see it."

Kiekhaefer's team won the last five races of 1956. After conclusion of the season, he quit, virtually never

Tin Flock quit the Kiekhaefer team in April. He won only one more race in the 1956 season.

Kiekhaefer won 30 Grand National races out of 50 starts in 1956. For his brief two-year career he won 52 of 90 events records which will remain unapproachable for decades to come.

NASCAR President France paid Kiekhaefer a tribute when he packed up and left - almost as suddenly as he entered the sport. "Carl has done a great deal for stock car racing," said France. "He has provided excellent equipment on the tracks, top drivers, a lot of color and he has improved the engineering on the cars he raced."

While Kiekhaefer made most of the news for the season, there were other headlines. Most notable was the merger of NASCAR and SAFE. SAFE, the Society of Autosport and Fellowship Education, was a midwestern based outfit under the direction of President Charles E. Scharf and Secretary Harry Redkey. The merger was completed in January 1956. Offspring of the merger was the Convertible circuit of NASCAR, a late-model class for ragtops. Bob Welborn won the championship in 1956 on the strength of consistency and three victories. Curtis Turner wound up second, winning 22 of the 48 events.

On the lighter side, there was one Grand National event which got the green flag, but never became an official chapter in NASCAR history. That occurred at Tulsa, OK on August 4, 1956.

A 100-mile Grand National event was scheduled and 32 laps went into the record books when dust conditions became unbearable. Lee Petty, driving in the race, parked

Carl Kiekhaefer was light years ahead of his time. In the days of driving race cars to the track or dragging them behind a pick-up with a tow bar, Kiekhaefer brought his fleet of cars to the tracks in big transporters.

to be heard from again until he was inducted into the National Motorsports Press Association Hall of Fame some 25 years later.

his car in the pits, sprinted across the track and climbed into the flagstand. He took the red flag from the starter and red flagged the race himself. The spectators received a refund and the race was never rescheduled.

Ned Jarrett #X, Dave Terrell #97 and Herb Thomas duel at Hickory. Jarrett's car number was 89, but NASCAR officials re-lettered all cars in order to serial score using a typewriter.

chauffeurs who failed to finish.

Four caution periods for a total of 23 laps slowed Flock's average speed to 56.962 mph. A crowd of 7,500 spectators were on hand.

Racing great Lewis "Buddy" Shuman, recently appointed to head Ford Motor Company's factory effort, died early Sunday morning in a hotel fire. Police said the blaze originated in Shuman's room and that he died of smoke inhalation.

Shuman, a veteran of 27 Grand National races in his career, won one time on NASCAR's major

Race No. 1

Flock Wins '56 Opener; Shuman Dies in Hotel Fire

HICKORY, NC (Nov. 13) -- Tim Flock of Atlanta overcame a spinout and drove his Kiekhaefer Chrysler to victory in the 1956 season opening 80-miler at Hickory Speedway.

Flock led the first 121 laps from the pole slot. He spun out in the third turn while leading, giving the front spot to Lee Petty. Flock whipped his Chrysler in the right direction and chased down Petty in the 139th lap. The 27 year-old was never headed. Curtis Turner finished second, 7.0 seconds behind the winner. Petty wound up third, Dink Widenhouse was fourth and Jim Paschal fifth.

Tom Pistone finished sixth, but his Chevrolet was disqualified when a post race inspection revealed illegal engine parts. Pistone was dropped to the bottom of the 31 car order.

Buddy Shuman died in a Hickory hotel fire.

Factory-backed cars were plentiful, but they could not handle the independent, but potent, Flock/Kiekhaefer combination. Speedy Thompson, Joe Weatherly and Bob Flock were among factory

Grand National Race No. 1
200 Laps at Hickory Speedway
Hickory, NC
80 Miles on .4-mile Dirt Track
November 13, 1955

Fin	St	No.	Driver	Team / Car	Laps	Money	Status
1	1	301	Tim Flock	Carl Kiekhaefer '55 Chrysler	200	$1,150	Running
2	3	99	Curtis Turner	Schwam Motor Co '56 Ford	200	720	Running
3	2	42	Lee Petty	Petty Engineering '56 Dodge	200	505	Running
4	4	B-29	Dink Widenhouse	Widenhouse '56 Ford	199	365	Running
5	10	44	Jim Paschal	Bob Welborn '55 Chevrolet	199	360	Running
6	12	2	Gwyn Staley	Westmoreland '55 Chevrolet	199	360	Running
7	5	87	Buck Baker	Satcher Motors '56 Ford	198	200	Running
8	17	297	Fonty Flock	DePaolo Eng '56 Ford	194	150	Running
9	27	98	Marvin Panch	Tom Harbison '55 Olds	194	100	Running
10	15	46	Billy Myers	Hugh Babb '55 Chevrolet	193	100	Running
11	13	04	Jimmy Massey	Westmoreland '55 Chevrolet	193	75	Running
12	24	141	Reds Kagle	'55 Chevrolet	191	60	Running
13	8	49	Bob Welborn	Welborn '55 Chevrolet	191	50	Running
14	26	6	Ralph Liguori	Liguori '55 Mercury	189	50	Running
15	9	70	Cotton Owens	'55 Chevrolet	188	50	Running
16	30	92	Herb Thomas	Thomas '56 Chevrolet	187	50	RR Axle
17	25	16	Fred Harb	'54 Dodge	185	50	Running
18	28	32	Ted Canady	'53 Ford	185	50	Running
19	31	28	Eddie Skinner	Frank Dodge '53 Olds 88	183	50	Running
20	23	900	Johnny Roberts	'55 Chevrolet	155	50	Running
21	20	89	Ned Jarrett	Jarrett '55 Buick	123	--	Rear End
22	22	97	Dave Terrell	Terrell '56 Ford	115	--	RF Hub
23	14	72	John Dodd, Jr	Dodd '55 Ford	106	--	LR Axle
24	18	88	Jimmie Lewallen	Ernest Woods '55 Olds	100	--	Gasket
25	6	7	Jim Reed	Reed '55 Chevrolet	79	--	Crash
26	29	5	Blackie Pitt	Brownie Pitt '55 Buick	77	--	Crash
27	16	296	Bob Flock	Mauri Rose Eng '55 Chevrolet	45	--	Crash
28	7	9	Joe Weatherly	Schwam Motor Co. '56 Ford	35	--	Radiator
29	19	24	Bobby Waddell	Jimmy Pardue '55 Chevrolet	24	--	Coil
30	21	25	Speedy Thompson	Mauri Rose Eng '55 Chevrolet	23	--	Heating
31	11	91	Tom Pistone	'55 Chevrolet	199	--	Disqual

Time of Race: 1 hour, 24 minutes, 16 seconds
Average Speed: 56.962 mph
Pole Winner: Time Flock -
Fastest Qualifier: Jim Paschal - 68.965 mph
Lap Leaders: Tim Flock 1-121, Lee Petty 122-138, T. Flock 139-200.
Cautions: 4 for 23 laps   Margin of Victory: 7 seconds   Attendance: 7,500

league tour - a 100 miler at Niagara Falls, Ontario, on July 1, 1952. His forte was the old Modified circuit, where he won more than 100 races.

Race No. 2

Fonty Edges Tim at Charlotte

CHARLOTTE, NC (Nov. 20, 1955) -- The statistics will indicate that Fonty Flock enjoyed an easy triumph in the 100-mile Grand National race at Charlotte Speedway. The Chrysler driving Decatur, GA veteran led from start to finish to post his 19th career victory.

However, the finish was one of the closest climaxes in NASCAR history. Fonty held off a last ditch surge

Fonty (on the inside) and Tim Flock cross the finish line side-by-side at Charlotte. Fonty won by a half car length.

from brother Tim to take the $1,100 first prize. Officials called the final margin of victory a half-car length.

Lee Petty came in third. Joe Weatherly was fourth and Buck Baker fifth.

Flock's victory gave the Kiekhaefer cars 10 wins in the last 12 Grand National events dating back into the 1955 season.

A crowd of 10,500 were on their feet for the conclusion of the Bruton Smith promoted affaiar.

Two caution flags lowered Flock's average speed to 61.825 mph. One of the yellow flags came in the 24th lap when Don Oldenberg's Buick lost its gas tank. Bob Welborn, following closely, ran over the loose fuel tank. There was no fire, but Welborn took a trip into a dirt embankment and flipped his Chevrolet. There were no injuries.

Grand National Race No. 2
134 Laps at Charlotte Speedway
Charlotte, NC
100 Miles on .75-mile Dirt Track
November 20, 1955

Fin	St	No.	Driver	Team / Car	Laps	Money	Status
1	1	301	Fonty Flock	Carl Kiekhaefer '55 Chrysler	134	$1,100	Running
2	2	300	Tim Flock	Carl Kiekhaefer '55 Chrysler	134	700	Running
3	3	42	Lee Petty	Petty Engineering '56 Dodge	134	475	Running
4	8	9	Joe Weatherly	Schwam '56 Ford	133	365	Running
5	6	87	Buck Baker	Satcher Motors '56 Ford	133	310	Running
6	5	B29	Dink Widenhouse	Widenhouse '56 Ford	131	250	Running
7	7	99	Curtis Turner	Schwam '56 Ford	130	200	Running
8	13	97	Dave Terrell	Terrell '56 Ford	127	150	Running
9	16	2	Gwyn Staley	Westmoreland '55 Chevrolet	128	100	Running
10	20	70	Cotton Owens	Ernest Woods '55 Olds	111	50	Running
11	10	92	Herb Thomas	Thomas '56 Chevrolet	124	75	Running
12	12	89	Ned Jarrett	Jarrett '55 Buick	121	60	Running
13	25	460	Ed Cole, Jr	'55 Plymouth	115	50	Running
14	26	32	Ted Cannady	'53 Ford 6	114	50	Running
15	23	88	Blackie Pitt	Ernest Woods '55 Olds	111	50	Running
16	14	78	Jimmie Lewallen	Ernest Woods '55 Olds	92	50	Spring
17	21	25	Speedy Thompson	Mauri Rose '55 Chevrolet	86	50	Heating
18	11	22	Bill Blair	Blair '55 Olds	76	50	Radiator
19	18	04	Jimmy Massey	Westmoreland '55 Chevrolet	20	50	Radiator
20	15	49	Bob Welborn	Welborn '55 Chevrolet	25	50	Crash
21	19	14	Don Oldenberg	'55 Buick	24	--	Gas Tank
22	4	20	Bunk Moore	'55 Buick	20	--	Spindle
23	17	44	Jim Paschal	Welborn '55 Chevrolet	20	--	Carb
24	9	72	John Dodd, Jr	'55 Ford	20	--	Wheel
25	24	16	Fred Harb	'54 Dodge	15	--	Rear End
26	22	141	Reds Kagle	'55 Chevrolet	11	--	Rear End
27	27	28	Eddie Skinner	Frank Dodge '53 Olds	2	--	Mount

Time of Race: 1 hour, 35 minutes, 32 seconds
Average Speed: 61.825 mph
Pole Winner: Fonty Flock - 70.496 mph
Lap Leaders: Fonty Flock 1-134.
Cautions: 2 for 7 laps   Margin of Victory: 1/2 car length   Attendance: 10,500

Race No. 3

Stevenson First in Willow Springs Road Race

LANCASTER, CA (Nov. 20, 1955) -- The NASCAR Grand National tour performed on a road course for the second time, and former AAA champion Chuck Stevenson drove a Ford to victory.

Stevenson motored past Marvin Panch in the 63rd lap of the 80 lap contest on the 2.5-mile oiled dirt road course. He managed to beat Panch by 500 feet to nail down the first place check of $1,570.

Third place went to Johnny Mantz. Short track

specialist Jim Reed ws fourth with Allen Adkins fifth.

A crowd of 17,000 watched from the hillsides of the rolling course to watch Stevenson and Panch swap the lead seven times. The remainder of the 37 car field had to settle for leftovers.

Several cars spun off the course, but there were no accidents serious enough to warrant a caution flag. Stevenson averaged 66.512 mph for his first Grand National win. It came in his second start.

Panch took the lead in the point standings by 20 points over Stevenson.

Grand National cars on the pace lap at Palm Beach Speedway.

Grand National Race No. 3
80 Laps at Willow Springs Speedway
Lancaster, CA
200 Miles on 2.5-mile Dirt Road Course
November 20, 1955

Fin	St	No.	Driver	Team / Car	Laps	Money	Status
1	2	22	Chuck Stevenson	Carl Dane '56 Ford	80	$1,570	Running
2	3	98	Marvin Panch	Tom Harbison '56 Ford	80	1,130	Running
3	5	15	Johnny Mantz	Bill Stroppe '56 Mercury	79	1,130	Running
4	1	7	Jim Reed	Reed '56 Chevrolet	79	580	Running
5	4	2	Allen Adkins	Gus Davis '55 Dodge	78	445	Running
6	24	99	George Seeger	Oscar Maples '56 Ford	78	350	Running
7	12	10	Scotty Cain	Cain '56 Ford	77	260	Running
8	8	34	Sherman Clark	Clark '55 Chevrolet	77	215	Running
9	10	56	Chuck Meekins	Jim Rush '56 Chevrolet	77	165	Running
10	32	47	Lloyd Dane	'55 Mercury	76	150	Running
11	23	8	Jim Sills	'55 Mercury	76	150	Running
12	18	89	Jim Blomgren	'54 Mercury	76	160	Running
13	9	49	Bob Ruppert	Ellingham Body '55 Chevy	76	115	Running
14	11	33	Bill West	Jim Dane '53 Hudson	76	110	Running
15	16	96	Danny Letner	Coz Cancilla '56 Olds	75	110	Running
16	14	45	Eddie Pagan	Pagan '55 Chevrolet	75	110	Running
17	25	5	Gordon Campbell	'53 Olds	74	75	Running
18	6	25	Erick Erickson	Erickson '54 Buick	74	90	Running
19	29	55	Mel Larson	Larson '56 Ford	74	75	Running
20	17	12	Bill Stammer	Stammer '55 Chevrolet	73	85	Running
21	27	30	Fred Steinbroner	Steinbroner '55 Chevrolet	72	40	Running
22	34	77	Bob Stanclift	Fred Bince '54 Dodge	72	40	Running
23	7	26	Ed Brown	'55 Chevrolet	72	55	Running
24	35	40	Elgin Holmes	'55 Olds	71	50	Running
25	26	27	Don Stanyer	'55 Plymouth	70	40	Running
26	13	37	Bill Stacey	'55 Ford	70	50	Running
27	21	91	Jim Cook	Art Krebs '55 Plymouth	70	40	Running
28	31	210	Tom Francis	'54 Ford	68	40	Running
29	19	6	Bill Hyde	'54 Olds	67	50	Running
30	36	53	Herb Crawford	'53 Studebaker	63	40	Running
31	33	90	Dick Getty	Betty Getty '51 Ford	62	30	Running
32	15	95	Clyde Palmer	'54 Olds	61	40	Running
33	28	48	Bill Moore	Moore '56 Ford	46	30	Head
34	22	41	Ernie Young	Walt Palozi '52 Plymouth	25	30	Heating
35	20	43	Len Fraker	Floyd Johnson '51 Hudson	10	30	Crnk Shft
36	37	80	Arley Scranton	Western Auto Salv '51 Ford	9	20	Brakes
37	30	71	Sam Lamm	Ralph Briggs '53 Hudson	3	30	Rod

Time of Race: 3 hours, 25 seconds
Average Speed: 66.512 mph
Pole Winner: Jim Reed - 76.556 mph
Lap Leaders: Chuck Stevenson 1-19, Marvin Panch 20-25, Stevenson 26-38, Panch 39-43, Stevenson 44-46, Panch 47-61, Stevenson 62-80.
Cautions: 0   Margin of Victory: 500 feet   Attendance: 17,000

Race No. 4

Weatherly, Reed Disqualified; Thomas Named Winner

WEST PALM BEACH, FL (Dec. 11, 1955) -- Herb Thomas finished over a lap behind Joe Weatherly and Jim Reed, but he was elevated to first place when the top two finishers were disqualified in Palm Beach Speedway's 100-miler. It was the 44th career Grand National win for Thomas.

With the advent of factory participation, NASCAR officials were taking the necessary steps to assure that the "stock" stayed in stock car racing.

Weatherly's Schwam Motor Co. Ford outran Reed's Chevrolet in a stirring duel for what was apparently the first Grand National win for the former motorcycle champ. But NASCAR inspectors discovered a non-stock camshaft in Weatherly's purple Ford and disqualified the machine two days later.

Reed's Chevy was equipped with illegal valves, so he joined Weatherly at the bottom of the rundown.

Thomas' Chevrolet was thoroughly inspected and was declared to be the first finishing car to comply with the NASCAR rule book. Al Keller wound up second, Billy Myers was third, Buck Baker fourth and Lee Petty fifth.

After the race, NASCAR President Bill France announced that future rule busters would not only lose money earned in the race, but would be stripped of all championship points won up to that date.

Thomas averaged 65.009 mph for what turned out to be a 99.5-mile race. A crowd of 4,500 was on hand in overcast weather.

Grand National Race No. 4
200 Laps at Palm Beach Speedway
West Palm Beach, FL
100 Miles on Half-mile Paved Track
December 11, 1955

Fin	St	No.	Driver	Team / Car	Laps	Money	Status
1	3	92	Herb Thomas	Thomas '56 Chevrolet	199	$1,100	Running
2	4	64	Al Keller	Keller '56 Chevrolet	198	700	Running
3	6	46	Bill Myers	Hugh Babb '55 Chevrolet	197	475	Running
4	8	87	Buck Baker	Satcher Motors '56 Ford	195	365	Running
5	13	42	Lee Petty	Petty Engineering '56 Dodge	193	310	Running
6	22	44	Bob Welborn	Welborn '55 Chevrolet	191	250	Running
7	17	33	Johnny Patterson	'55 Chevrolet	191	200	Running
8	15	88	Blackie Pitt	Ernest Woods '55 Olds	180	150	Running
9	14	91	Jack Choquette	'54 Olds	173	100	Running
10	10	1	Bobby Myers	H. Rakestraw '55 Chevrolet	177	100	Running
11	23	31	Bill Thurber	'55 Studebaker	173	75	Running
12	16	900	Johnny Roberts	'55 Chevrolet	172	60	Running
13	9	98	Marvin Panch	Tom Harbison '56 Ford	148	50	Gasket
14	19	18	Dick Burns	'53 Olds	148	50	Running
15	11	C97	Red Farmer	J M Fitzgibbons '56 Chevrolet	147	50	Crash
16	7	99	Curtis Turner	Schwam Motors '56 Ford	117	50	Bearing
17	20	3	Al Watkins	'55 Ford	89	50	Bearing
18	18	28	Eddie Skinner	Frank Dodge '53 Olds	67	50	Heating
19	1	301	Fonty Flock	Kiekhaefer '55 Chrysler	65	50	Crash
20	21	27	John McVitty	'55 Chevrolet	62	50	Radiator
21	12	97	Dave Terrell	Terrell '56 Ford	25	50	Engine
22	2	9	Joe Weatherly*	Schwam Motors '56 Ford	200	--	Disqual
23	5	7	Jim Reed**	Reed '55 Chevrolet	200	--	Disqual

Time of Race: 1 hour, 31 minutes, 50 seconds
Average Speed: 65.009 mph
Pole Winner: Fonty Flock - 78.912 mph
Lap Leaders: - - - - - - - - - - Herb Thomas   -199
Cautions: Margin of Victory: 1 lap plus   Attendance: 4,500
 * Joe Weatherly was the race winner, driving a 1956 Ford, but his car was disqualified
   in a post race inspection because the cam shaft did not meet specifications and there
   was evidence of grinding and polishing of the intake manifold.
**Jim Reed finished second in a 1956 Chevrolet, but his car was disqualified in a post
   race inspection because the valves were light and not meeting specifications.

Bruton Smith interviews Buck Baker. Baker won the 150-miler at Phoenix.

was in the 150-miler at the Arizona State Fairgrounds. The Charlotte, NC driver responded as Kiekhaefer might have imagined -- with a victory.

Baker outran new running mate Frank Mundy by about a half-lap to win the $1,500 top prize. Mundy, who had quit the NASCAR tour to race in AAA competition in 1952, had to post a $1,000 bond in order to be reinstated.

Third place went to Tim Flock, giving the Kiekhaefer Chryslers a 1-2-3 finish. Marvin Panch finished fourth with Lee Petty fifth.

There was a rash of heart-stopping accidents during the course of the 150-miler. Howard Phillippi, Bob Ruppert, Bill Stammer and Sherman Clark all flipped their cars in separate crashes. Jim Stampley tumbled through the wooden barrier and landed upside down in a clump of shrubbery. No driver injuries were reported.

Joe Weatherly started on the pole and finished seventh.

Race No. 5

Baker Wins in 1st Start For Kiekhaefer Team

PHOENIX, AZ (Jan 22) -- In the latter half of the 1955 season, eccentric car owner Carl Kiekhaefer noticed that Buck Baker was giving his powerful Chrysler team a run for its money. "There's only one thing to do with a man like that," puffed Kiekhaefer. "And that is to hire him!"

Baker's first assignment with the Kiekhaefer Outboard team

Herb Thomas steers clear of debris littered front stretch after Sherman Clark knocked down the fence at Phoenix.

Grand National Race No. 5
150 Laps at Arizona State Fairgrounds
Phoenix, AZ
150 Miles on 1-mile Dirt Track
January 22, 1956

Fin	St	No.	Driver	Team / Car	Laps	Money	Status
1	12	301	Buck Baker	Carl Kiekhaefer '55 Chrysler	150	$1,500	Running
2	5	30	Frank Mundy	Carl Kiekhaefer '55 Chrysler	150	970	Running
3	6	300	Tim Flock	Carl Kiekhaefer '55 Chrysler	150	710	Running
4	3	98	Marvin Panch	Tom Harbison '56 Ford	149	560	Running
5	4	42	Lee Petty	Petty Engineering '56 Dodge	149	415	Running
6	18	10	Scotty Cain	Cain '56 Ford	147	275	Running
7	1	11	Joe Weatherly	Schwam Motors '56 Ford	148	275	Running
8	9	5	Clyde Palmer	'55 Mercury	144	185	Running
9	10	92	Herb Thomas	Thomas '56 Chevrolet	142	135	Running
10	11	55	Mel Larson	Larson '56 Ford	142	100	Running
11	24	56	Chuck Meekins	Jim Rush '55 Chevrolet	141	100	Running
12	21	99	Jiim Blomgren	Oscar Maples '56 Mercury	141	75	Running
13	16	2	Allen Adkins	Gus Davis '55 Dodge	137	50	Running
14	22	45	Eddie Pagan	Pagan '55 Chevrolet	135	50	Running
15	23	225	Lloyd Dane	'56 Mercury	134	50	Crash
16	13	32	Ted Cannady	'55 Chevrolet	134	50	Running
17	27	50	Blackie Pitt	'55 Olds	132	50	Running
18	14	22	George Seeger	'56 Ford	127	50	Running
19	30	41	Ernie Young	Walt Palozi '53 Pontiac	127	50	Running
20	26	66	Jack D McCoy	'56 Nash	125	50	Running
21	8	48	Bill Moore	Moore '56 Ford	118	35	Piston
22	29	91	John Lansaw	'55 Plymouth	114	35	Heating
23	20	20	Howard Phillippi	'55 Chevrolet	99	35	Crash
24	25	49	Bob Ruppert	Ellingham Body '55 Chevrolet	88	35	Crash
25	28	66	Leroy DeShields	'56 Buick	75	35	Heating
26	17	76	Dutch Munsinger	'56 Buick	69	25	Heating
27	2	12	Bill Stammer	Stammer '55 Chevrolet	58	55	Crash
28	15	9	Jim Cook	Art Krebs '56 Pontiac	51	25	Wheel
29	19	11X	Jim Stapley	'56 Ford	51	--	Crash
30	7	34	Sherman Clark	Clark '55 Chevrolet	33	10	Crash

Time of Race: 2 hours, 19 minutes, 44 seconds
Average Speed: 64.408 mph
Pole Winner: Joe Weatherly - 71.315 mph
Lap Leaders: - - - - - - - - - Buck Baker -150.
Cautions: Margin of Victory: Attendance:

Junior Johnson scrambles out of the rear window of his Pontiac after he flipped in Daytona Grand National.

Billy Myers' Mercury wound up in second place followed by Ralph Moody, Jimmie Lewallen and Jim Reed. Paschal departed late in the race and wound up 33rd in the 76 car field.

Flock led all but three laps in the 151.7-mile event. Paschal took the lead briefly when Flock pitted for fuel.

Flock had qualified at 135.747 mph. His time was six mph faster than the next quickest qualifier, Speedy Thompson. Both were in Kiekhaefer Chryslers. In all there were six entries from the Kiekhaefer camp, one driven by a black driver, Charlie Scott of Forrest Park, GA. He finished a respectable 19th.

There were a number of crack-ups on the cool, overcast afternoon. Junior Johnson's Pontiac hooked a tire in the loose sand and turned over several times along the beach. The portly Johnson scrambled out the back window unhurt.

Russ Truelove, whose father-in-law Bert Parks -- emcee of the Miss America Pageant -- was in the grand

Race No. 6

High Tide Fails to Stop Flock at Daytona

DAYTONA BEACH, FL (Feb. 26) -- Tim Flock had his Kiekhaefer Outboards Chrysler in front when race officials flagged the seventh annual SpeedWeek Grand National to a halt two laps shy of the scheduled distance at the Daytona Beach and Road Course.

Flock raced around Jim Paschal in the 27th lap and was 57 seconds ahead of the field when a high tide forced officials to call off the race.

Ralph Moody #12 begins rollover at Daytona as Lee Petty #42 narrowly misses.

Grand National Race No. 6
39 Laps at Beach & Road Course
Daytona Beach, FL
160 Miles on 4.1-mile Beach & Road Course
February 26, 1956

Fin	St	No.	Driver	Team / Car	Laps	Money	Status
1	1	300A	Tim Flock	Carl Kiekhaefer '56 Chrysler	37	$4,025	Running
2	24	14W	Billy Myers	Guy Wilson '56 Mercury	37	2,375	Running
3	22	12	Ralph Moody	DePaolo Eng '56 Ford	37	1,450	Running
4	16	88	Jimmie Lewallen	Ernest Woods '56 Olds		900	Running
5	27	7	Jim Reed	Reed '56 Chevrolet		700	Running
6	40	64	Al Keller	Keller '56 Chevrolet		600	Running
7	38	204	Darvin Randahl	Randahl '56 Ford		500	Running
8	6	15W	Bob Korf	Bill Stroppe '56 Mercury		400	Running
9	10	92	Herb Thomas	Thomas '56 Chevrolet		250	Running
10	12	500B	Fonty Flock	Carl Kiekhaefer '56 Dodge		200	Running
11	25	2	Gwyn Staley	Westmoreland '56 Chevrolet		160	Running
12	18	42	Lee Petty	Petty Eng '56 Dodge		135	Running
13	58	342	Jack Radtke	Hanlon Motors '56 Ford		110	Running
14	49	16	Ray Chaike	Gus Holzmeuller '56 Chevrolet		100	Running
15	55	40	Gene Simpson	Bud Harbaugh '55 Buick		100	Running
16	60	100	Ken Milligan	Dave Everett '56 Chevrolet		90	Running
17		5	Bill Blair	Joe Blair '56 Dodge		80	Running
18	35	91	Donald Thomas	Thomas '56 Ford		75	Running
19	14	300	Charlie Scott	Carl Kiekhaefer '55 Chrysler		75	Running
20	9	301	Buck Baker	Carl Kiekhaefer '55 Chrysler		75	Running
21	66	396	Dave Lundman	'56 Chevrolet		60	
22	30	X	Rex White	Max Welborn '56 Chevrolet		60	
23	19	63	Lyle Scott	Scott '56 Chrysler		60	
24	50	155	Mel Larson	Larson '56 Ford		60	
25		411	Pat Zocanno	'56 Chevrolet		60	
26		390	Ray Thompson	Johnny McCoy '56 Studebaker		50	
27	44	10	Jim Cushman	Cushman '56 Ford		50	
28	75	96	Eddie Skinner	Curtis Reid '55 Olds		50	
29	74	640	Ken Love	'56 Ford		50	
30	54	761	David Ezell	S G Russell '56 Chevrolet		50	
31	73	230	Benny DeRosier	Adelmo Tiezzi '54 Hudson		25	
32	70	34	Dick Beaty	Beaty '56 Ford		25	
33	8	75	Jim Paschal	Frank Hayworth '56 Mercury		25	
34	59	B-29	Dink Widenhouse	Widenhouse '56 Ford		25	
35	41	330	Don Bailey	'56 Ford		25	
36	52	C97	Red Farmer	J M Fitzgibbons '56 Chevrolet		25	
37	61	123	Charles Oldham	Oldham '56 Chevrolet		25	
38	71	77	Walt Shubert	Bob Bunselmeyer '55 Ford		25	
39	68	19	Harvey Henderson	'55 Chevrolet		25	
40	26	55	Junior Johnson	Brushy Mtn Mtr '56 Pontiac		25	Crash
41	57	84	Ken Wagner	Lawson & Netti '56 Ford		--	
42	67	264	Johnny Allen	Spook Crawford '55 Plymouth		--	
43	11	300B	Frank Mundy	Carl Kiekhaefer '56 Chrysler		--	
44	37	9	Joe Weatherly	Schwam Motor Co '56 Ford		--	
45	69	166	Bud Palmer	W E Campbell '55 Chevrolet		--	
46	63	1	Bobby Myers	H Rakestraw '55 Chevrolet		--	
47	5	226	Russ Truelove	Bob White '56 Mercury		--	Crash
48	45	68	Bill Widenhouse	Fred Sheibert '56 Ford		--	
49	62	108	Tom Herzbert	Len Svajian '55 Chevrolet		--	
50	56	203	Pete Yow	Strickland Motor Co '55 Buick		--	
51	48	265	H W Atkinson	Atkinson '56 Ford		--	
52	36	99	Curtis Turner	Schwam Motor Co '56 Ford		--	
53	42	8	Gene White	'56 Buick		--	
54	28	505	Charlie Cregar	Cregar '56 Chevrolet		--	
55	15	6	Ralph Liguori	Liguori '56 Dodge		--	
56		271	Dick Blackwell	'56 Mercury		--	
57	53	59	Blackie Pitt	Brownie Pitt '55 Olds		--	
58	33	M-1	Tommy Thompson	Fish Carburetor '55 Buick		--	
59	32	22	Fireball Roberts	DePaolo Eng '56 Ford		--	
60	4	285	Ed Kretz	Jim Stephens '55 Pontiac		--	
61	3	286	Cotton Owens	Jim Stephens '56 Pontiac		--	
62	51	56	Joe Eubanks	Satcher Motor Co '56 Ford		--	
63	29	97	Danny Letner	Ed Hastings '56 Ford		--	
64	43	719	Joy Fair	Russell Wainscott '56 Dodge		--	
65	14	49	Bob Welborn	Welborn '56 Chevrolet		--	
66	72	424	Johnny Osteen	'54 Olds		--	
67	31	78	Joel Million	Ernest Woods '56 Olds		--	
68	7	290	Jack Choquette	Bob Osiecki '56 Dodge		--	
69	34	157	Dick Linder	'56 Ford		--	
70	46	999	Jack Smith	B J Jones '56 Ford		--	
71	2	500B	Speedy Thompson	Carl Kiekhaefer '56 Dodge		--	
72	21	98	Marvin Panch	Tom Harbison '56 Dodge		--	

Fonty Flock #500-B passes Harvey Henderson #19 at Daytona Beach. Flock finished 10th, Henderson 39th.

Russ Truelove's Mercury comes apart during Daytona crash.

Fin	St	No.	Driver	Team / Car	Laps	Money	Status
73	17	576	Jim Wilson	Harvey Walters '56 Dodge		--	Crash
74	20	321	Buddy Krebs	Harvey Walters '56 Dodge		--	Crash
75	64	206	Jimmy Mairs	'55 Buick		--	Crash
76		113	Emanuel Zervakis	'56 Chevrolet		--	Crash

Time of Race: 1 hour, 40 minutes, 24 seconds
Average Speed: 90.657 mph
Pole Winner: Tim Flock - 135.747 mph
Lap Leaders: Tim Flock 1-23, Jim Paschal 24-26, T. Flock 27-37.
Cautions: 2 for 2 laps   Margin of Victory: 57 seconds   Attendance: 29,000
* Race cut 2 laps short of scheduled distance due to incoming tide

Billy Myers #14 heads onto the 2-mile A-1-A straightaway at Daytona. The Germanton, NC driver finished 2nd.

winner. The triumph came in his 17th start on NASCAR's major league stock car tour.

Buck Baker finished second, Herb Thomas was third, Joe Weatherly fourth and Fireball Roberts fifth.

With the disqualification of Keller, Myers' Big M Mercury took the lead from Jim Reed in the 142nd lap and led the

stands, flipped an uncountable number of times. His Mercury was wiped out, but Truelove was unhurt.

Third place finisher Moody flipped his Ford in the soft sand. The car landed on all four wheels and Moody raced on, not losing a single position in the mishap.

Buddy Krebs and Jim Wilson, driving identical Dodges from the Harvey Walters stable, flipped together on the south end of the highway in the opening laps. Neither driver was seriously injured.

The caution flag was out twice for two laps. A crowd of 29,000 watched the event on a cool winter afternoon.

Race No. 7

Controversy Flares at Palm Beach; Keller Disqualified

W. PALM BEACH, FL (Mar. 4) -- Al Keller of Buffalo, NY nosed out Billy Myers for an apparent victory, but for the second time in three months controversy flared at the Palm Beach Speedway.

On December 11th, Joe Weatherly and Jim Reed were disqualified from their 1-2 finish at this half-mile paved track. In a post race inspection Keller's Chevrolet was found to have been equipped with pistons which had been altered. He was disqualified and denied his third Grand National victory.

Myers, of Winston-Salem, NC, was declared the

Grand National Race No. 7
200 Laps at Palm Beach Speedway
West Palm Beach, FL
100 Miles on Half-mile Paved Track
March 4, 1956

Fin	St	No.	Driver	Team / Car	Laps	Money	Status
1	2	14W	Billy Myers	Guy Wilson '56 Mercury	199	$900	Running
2	1	500B	Buck Baker	Carl Kiekhaefer '56 Dodge	199	600	Running
3	2	92	Herb Thomas	Thomas '56 Chevrolet	195	425	Running
4	11	9	Joe Weatherly	Schwam '56 Ford	191	335	Running
5	27	22	Fireball Roberts	DePaolo '56 Ford	191	290	Running
6	20	12	Ralph Moody	DePaolo Eng '56 Ford	191	250	Running
7	4	501	Tim Flock	Carl Kiekhaefer '56 Dodge	191	200	Running
8	12	X	Rex White	Max Welborn '56 Chevrolet	189	150	Running
9	8	49	Bob Welborn	Welborn '56 Chevrolet	189	100	Running
10	29	27	John McVitty	'55 Chevrolet	187	100	Running
11	17	55	Mel Larson	Larson '56 Ford	183	75	Running
12	30	42	Lee Petty	Petty Engineering '56 Dodge	181	60	Running
13	16	576	Jim Wilson	Harvey Walters '56 Dodge	180	50	Running
14	21	32	Ted Cannady	'55 Chevrolet	179	50	Running
15	23	88	Jimmie Lewallen	Ernest Woods '56 Olds	178	50	Running
16	15	97	Millard Wright	Wright '54 Ford	178	50	Running
17	10	C97	Red Farmer	J M Fitzgibbons '56 Chevrolet	177	50	Running
18	24	78	Joel Million	Ernest Woods '56 Olds	175	50	Running
19	25	19	Harvey Henderson	'55 Chevrolet	174	50	Running
20	9	99	Curtis Turner	Schwam '56 Ford	168	50	Tire
21	5	7	Jim Reed	Reed '56 Chevrolet	141	--	Tire
22	22	96	Eddie Skinner	Frank Dodge '55 Olds	83	--	Shift Lev
23	18	999	Jack Smith	B J Jones '56 Ford	61	--	RF Hub
24	14	59	Blackie Pitt	Brownie Pitt '55 Olds	60	--	Rear End
25	7	98	Marvin Panch	Tom Harbison '56 Dodge	42	--	Wheel
26	13	33	Johnny Patterson	'55 Chevrolet	29	--	Crash
27	19	72	John Dodd, Sr	Dodd '55 Ford	28	--	Crash
28	26	75	Jim Paschal	Frank Hayworth '56 Mercury	22	--	Carb
29	28	424	Ralph Murray	'54 Olds	2	--	Steering
30	6	64	Al Keller	Keller '56 Chevrolet	200	--	Disqual

Time of Race: 1 hour, 26 minutes, 32 seconds
Average Speed: 68.990 mph
Pole Winner: Buck Baker - 81.081 mph
Lap Leaders: Buck Baker 1-32, Jim Reed 33-141, Billy Myers 142-300.
Cautions: 1 for 3 laps   Margin of Victory: Attendance: 5,200
* Al Keller finished first but was disqualified because pistons had been altered

rest of the way. He became the sixth different winner in the seven events staged during the 1956 season.

John Dodd, Sr. broke an axle on his Ford and flipped in the 29th lap. He was not hurt in the accident.

Race No. 8

Rain-shortened Wilson Event to Thomas

WILSON, NC (Mar. 18) -- Herb Thomas notched his 45th career win in the rain-shortened Grand National event at Wilson Speedway.

The scheduled 100-miler was curtailed just after the half-way point -- 106 laps -- with Thomas' Chevrolet out in front. Buck Baker and Tim Flock got credit for

Grand National Race No. 8
200 Laps at Wilson Speedway
Wilson, NC
100 Miles on Half-mile Dirt Track
March 18, 1956

Fin	St	No.	Driver	Team / Car	Laps	Money	Status
1	1	92	Herb Thomas	Thomas '56 Chevrolet	106	$1,100	Running
2	4	500B	Buck Baker	Carl Kiekhaefer '56 Dodge	106	700	Running
3	6	300B	Tim Flock	Carl Kiekhaefer '56 Chrysler	106	475	Running
4	15	75	Jim Paschal	Frank Hayworth '56 Mercury	105	365	Running
5	18	68	Bill Widenhouse	'56 Ford	105	310	Running
6	23	6	Ralph Liguori	Liguori '56 Dodge 500	104	250	Running
7	24	1	Bobby Myers	H. Rakestraw '55 Chevrolet	104	200	Running
8	13	X	Rex White	Max Welborn '56 Chevrolet	103	150	Running
9	10	91	Donald Thomas	'56 Ford	103	100	Running
10	2	500	Speedy Thompson	Carl Kiekhaefer '55 Dodge	103	100	Running
11	21	37	Tiny Lund	'56 Pontiac	99	75	Running
12	28	84	Ken Wagner	Larnson & Nitti '56 Ford	96	60	Running
13	11	42	Lee Petty	Petty Engineering '56 Dodge	95	50	Bearing
14	14	999	Jack Smith	B.J. Jones '56 Ford	92	50	Running
15	29	264	Johnny Allen	Spook Crawford '55 Plymouth	90	50	Running
16	26	203	Pete Yow	Strickland Motors '55 Buick	88	50	Running
17	16	96	Bobby Keck	'55 Chevrolet	87	50	Running
18	17	204	Darvin Randahl	Randahl '56 Ford	81	50	Fan Blt
19	8	27	John McVitty	'55 Chevrolet	80	50	Running
20	25	900	Johnny Roberts	'55 Chevrolet	74	50	Running
21	19	505	Charlie Cregar	Cregar '56 Chevrolet	74	--	Trans
22	12	19	Harvey Henderson	'55 Chevrolet	74	--	Tie Rod
23	7	25	Pee Wee Jones	Sam McCuthen '55 Chevrolet	70	--	Fan Blt
24	9	55	Junior Johnson	Brushy Mtn Motors '56 Pontiac	63	--	Suspen
25	27	73	John Dodd, Jr	Dodd '55 Olds	61	--	Gasket
26	3	14	Billy Myers	Guy Wilson '56 Mercury	57	--	Bearing
27	20	63	Johnny Zeke	'56 Chrysler	49	--	Push Rod
28	32	32	Ted Cannady	'55 Chevrolet	46	--	Crash
29	30	82	Joe Eubanks	Satcher Mtr '55 Chevrolet	45	--	Engine
30	22	2	Gwyn Staley	Westmoreland '56 Chevrolet	43	--	Brakes
31	31	20	George Mantooth	Waldron & Co. '55 Buick	43	--	Engine
32	5	49	Jimmie Lewallen	Bob Welborn '56 Chevrolet	40	--	Trans

Time of Race: 1 hour, 8 minutes, 42 seconds
Average Speed: 46.287 mph
Pole Winner: Herb Thomas - 57.197 mph
Lap Leaders: - - - - - - - - - Herb Thomas -106.
Cautions: Margin of Victory: Attendance: 5,000
* Shortened to 106 laps because of rain

second and third in Kiekhaefer cars. Jim Paschal finished fourth, and fifth at the stripe was Bill Widenhouse.

A crowd of 5,000 braved threatening weather to watch Thomas average 46.287 mph for the 53 miles completed. The Olivia, NC two-time champ also moved into second place in the point standings, 176 points behind Tim Flock.

Ted Cannady was involved in the only crash. He parked his Chevrolet in the fence in the 50th lap.

Lee Petty and Junior Johnson were two other favorites who failed to finish.

Grand National Race No. 9
100 Laps at Lakewood Speedway
Atlanta, GA
100 Miles on 1-mile Dirt Track
March 25, 1956

Fin	St	No.	Driver	Team / Car	Laps	Money	Status
1	23	300c	Buck Baker	Carl Kiekhaefer '56 Chrysler	100	$1,400	Running
2	5	500	Speedy Thompson	Carl Kiekhaefer '56 Dodge	100	800	Running
3	17	92	Herb Thomas	Thomas '56 Chevrolet	99	550	Running
4	15	2	Jimmy Massey	Westmoreland '56 Chevrolet	99	365	Running
5	4	42	Lee Petty	Petty Engineering '56 Dodge	99	310	Running
6	14	12	Ralph Moody	DePaolo Eng '56 Ford	99	250	Running
7	3	55	Fonty Flock	Brushy Mtn Mtr '56 Pontiac	97	200	Running
8	21	75	Jim Paschal	Frank Hayworth '56 Mercury	97	150	Running
9	22	44	Chester Barron	'56 Chevrolet	96	100	Running
10	25	100	Ken Miligan	Dave Everett '56 Chevrolet	92	100	Running
11	19	8	Charley Mincey	Bishop Bros. '55 Buick	91	75	Running
12	26	271	Dick Blackwell	'56 Mercury	90	60	Running
13	2	99	Billy Carden	Schwam Motors '56 Ford	86	50	RF Hub
14	27	999	Sonny Black	B.J. Jones '56 Ford	79	50	Running
15	20	204	Darvin Randahl	Randahl '56 Ford	76	50	Running
16	9	300B	Frank Mundy	Carl Kiekhaefer '56 Chrysler	72	50	Oil Pan
17	12	286	Junior Johnson	Jim Stephens '56 Pontiac	64	50	Trans
18	1	300A	Tim Flock	Kiekhaefer '56 Chrysler	55	50	Engine
19	28	63	Ray Baxter	'56 Chrysler	55	50	Steering
20	6	9	Bob Flock	DePaolo Eng '56 Ford	52	50	Steering
21	13	82	Joe Eubanks	Satcher Mtrs '56 Ford	50	---	Gasket
22	11	64	Al Keller	Keller '56 Chevrolet	48	---	Gas Tank
23	7	3	Paul Goldsmith	Smokey Yunick '56 Chevrolet	36	---	Crash
24	10	14	Billy Myers	Guy Wilson '56 Mercury	33	---	Gasket
25	18	68	Bill Widenhouse	'56 Ford	33	---	Brakes
26	16	285	Jimmie Lewallen	Jim Stephens '56 Pontiac	15	---	Engine
27	24	390	Ray Thompson	'56 Studebaker	12	---	Axle
28	8	6	Ralph Liguori	Liguori '56 Dodge	3	---	Crash

Time of Race: 1 hour, 24 minutes, 56 seconds
Average Speed: 70.643 mph
Pole Winner: Tim Flock - 82.154 mph
Lap Leaders: Tim Flock 1-51, Buck Baker 52-100.
Cautions: Margin of Victory: Attendance: 17,812

Race No. 9

Lou Moore Death Mars Baker Win at Lakewood

ATLANTA, GA (Mar. 25) -- Buck Baker whipped his Kiekhaefer Chrysler past a hobbling Tim Flock in the 52nd lap and went on to win the 100-miler at Lakewood Speedway for his second win of the year. The event was marred by the death of Lou Moore, who built or owned five Indianapolis 500 winning cars.

The 52 year-old Moore, on hand to supervise the Pontiac factory team effort, was stricken by an intra-cerebral hemorrhage at the one-mile dirt track just before the start of the race. He died at Grady Memorial Hospital by the time the checkered flag fell.

Fonty Flock and Jimmie Lewallen, pilots of the Pontiacs Moore was heading at Lakewood, competed in the race. Flock finished seventh and Lewallen blew an engine after 15 laps.

Speedy Thompson finished second to give the K-cars another 1-2 finish. Third place went to Herb Thomas, Jimmy Massey was fourth and Lee Petty fifth.

Baker averaged 70.643 mph before 17,812 on the balmy spring afternoon.

Tim Flock fell out of the race four laps after he lost the lead to Baker. He lost a large chunk of his point lead as Thomas moved to within 56 points.

Race No. 10

Flock Wins N. Wilkesboro; Then Quits Kiekhaefer Team

N. WILKESBORO, NC (Apr. 8) -- Tim Flock passed teammate Speedy Thompson in the 115th lap and outran Billy Myers to win the 100-mile Grand National race at North Wilkesboro Speedway.

After the 160-lap event on the .625-mile track, Flock dropped a bombshell by announcing he was quitting the highly successful Carl Kiekhaefer team.

Flock, 27, current leader in the NASCAR point standings, had won 21 races for the Kiekhaefer team in 14 months. He said his decision to give up Grand National racing's most enviable bucket seat stemmed from Kiekhaefer's Marine drill-sergeant attitude. Flock added that stomach ulcers, which he had for several years had worsened during his tenure with Kiekhaefer.

The millionaire car owner spoke with Flock in private quarters after the race, trying to get the defending champion to reconsider. Flock stuck to his decision and said he would join the Chevrolet team.

Myers' Mercury wound up second. Jim Paschal was third, Herb Thomas fourth and Ralph Moody fifth. Thompson had a ruptured fuel line on lap 127 which put him out of the running.

Junior Johnson put a Pontiac on the pole and led for the first 17 laps. A blown engine ended his day and

allowed Thompson to pick up first place. Flock, who started third, bided his time until well past the half-way point.

A crowd of 7,500 watched Flock average 71.034 mph for his 38th career win.

Grand National Race No. 10
160 Laps at N. Wilkesboro Speedway
North Wilkesboro, NC
100 Miles on .625-mile Dirt Track
April 8, 1956

Fin	St	No.	Driver	Team / Car	Laps	Money	Status
1	3	300A	Tim Flock	Carl Kiekhaefer '56 Chrysler	160	$1,100	Running
2	17	14	Billy Myers	Guy Wilson '56 Mercury	160	700	Running
3	8	75	Jim Paschal	Frank Hayworth '56 Mercury	160	475	Running
4	7	92	Herb Thomas	Thomas '56 Chevrolet	160	365	Running
5	5	12	Ralph Moody	DePaolo Eng '56 Ford	159	310	Running
6	12	B29	Dink Widenhouse	Widenhouse '56 Ford	158	250	Running
7	10	98	Allen Adkins	Tom Harbison '56 Ford	158	200	Running
8	18	42	Lee Petty	Petty Engineering '56 Dodge	158	150	Running
9	14	5	Bill Blair	Joe Blair '56 Dodge	151	100	Running
10	24	1	Whitey Norman	H. Rakestraw '55 Chevrolet	150	100	Running
11	19	300c	Buck Baker	Carl Kiekhaefer '56 Chrysler	148	75	Running
12	25	34	Dick Beaty	Beaty '56 Ford	147	60	Running
13	23	94	Ed Cole, Jr	'55 Mercury	145	50	Running
14	15	37	Tiny Lund	'56 Pontiac	142	50	Running
15	9	2	Gwyn Staley	Westmoreland '56 Chevrolet	134	50	Trans
16	11	100	Ken Milligan	Dave Everett '56 Chevrolet	1l34	50	Running
17	16	82	Joe Eubanks	Satcher Motors '56 Ford	133	50	Axle
18	2	501	Speedy Thompson	Carl Kiekhaefer '56 Dodge	127	50	Gas Line
19	4	X	Rex White	Max Welborn '56 Chevrolet	112	50	A Frame
20	13	27	John McVitty	'55 Chevrolet	102	50	Fuel Pmp
21	20	271	Dick Blackwell	'56 Mercury	102	---	Running
22	22	25	Jimmie Lewallen	Sam McCuthen '55 Chevrolet	93	---	Engine
23	29	54	Lou Spears	'55 Ford	83	---	Heating
24	21	6	Ralph Liguori	Liguori '56 Dodge	45	---	Tire
25	6	22	Fireball Roberts	DePaolo Eng '56 Ford	38	---	Drv Shft
26	26	264	Johnny Allen	Spook Crawford '55 Plymouth	22	---	Crash
27	27	96	Bobby Keck	'55 Chevrolet	22	---	Piston
28	1	55	Junior Johnson	Brushy Mtn Motors '56 Pontiac	17	---	Piston
29	28	19	Harvey Henderson	'55 Chevrolet	13	---	Engine

Time of Race: 1 hour, 24 minutes, 28 seconds
Average Speed: 71.034 mph
Pole Winner: Junior Johnson - 78.370 mph
Lap Leaders: Junior Johnson 1-17, Speedy Thompson 18-114, Tim Flock 115-160.
Cautions: Margin of Victory: Attendance: 7,500

Race No. 11

Baker, Thomas 1-2 for Kiekhaefer; McVitty Killed

LANGHORNE, PA (Apr. 22) -- Buck Baker ran down Tim Flock with six laps remaining and went on to capture the 150-miler at Langhorne Speedway. It was Baker's third win of the year and the 15th of his career.

John McVitty, young driver out of Raleigh, NC, was

Lee Petty drives his Dodge around the Langhorne Speedway.

grounds. He also took the lead in the point standings as Tim Flock finished last in the 25-car field.

Herb Thomas finished second, a lap down. Speedy Thompson was third with Billy Myers fourth and Jimmy Massey fifth.

It was the second 1-2-3 finish for the Kiekhaefer cars in the young 1956 season. In the last 22 Grand Nationals events, Kiekhaefer drivers have won 16 times.

Baker started on the pole and led for 164 laps. The Charlotte chauffeur made a brief pit stop which allowed Thomas to lead two laps. When Thomas pitted on lap 167, Baker jumped back into the lead for good.

killed Saturday when his Chevrolet flipped in qualifying. He was thrown out of his car during the roll-over and died a short time later of massive internal injuries. McVitty was a veteran of 11 Grand National races and became the fourth fatality on NASCAR's premier series.

Herb Thomas got around Flock in the final two laps to take second spot. Thomas was selected by car owner Carl Kiekhaefer to replace Tim Flock who had quit the team.

Lee Petty finished fourth just behind Flock who was driving Smokey Yunick's Chevrolet. Fifth place went to Jimmy Massey.

A crowd of 24,000 watched Baker storm into an early lead, pacing the field for 53 laps. Flock took the lead when Baker pitted for new tires. Baker then spent 41 laps chasing down his former teammate.

Fireball Roberts rolled his Ford over the wall in the 59th lap. He was not hurt and his car suffered very little damage. Tiny Lund and Jim Reed crashed in separate incidents.

Jimmie Lewallen, hard luck driver out of Archdale, NC, finished 34th, a position which was out of the money. It was the fourth straight race in which Lewallen had failed to earn any prize money.

Race No. 12

Baker Takes Point Lead and Richmond 100

RICHMOND, VA (Apr. 29) -- Buck Baker and his Kiekhaefer Dodge took Richmond by storm, leading all but two laps in the 100-miler at the Atlantic Rural Fair-

Grand National Race No. 11
150 Laps at Langhorne Speedway
Langhorne, PA
150 Miles on 1-mile Dirt Track
April 22, 1956

Fin	St	No.	Driver	Team / Car	Laps	Money	Status
1	1	87	Buck Baker	Carl Kiekhaefer '56 Chrysler	150	$1,750	Running
2	5	92	Herb Thoarns	Carl Kiekhaefer '56 Chrysler	149	1,000	Running
3	6	3	Tim Flock	Smokey Yunick '56 Chevrolet	149	725	Running
4	3	42	Lee Petty	Petty Engineering '56 Dodge	149	530	Running
5	12	2	Jimmy Massey	Westmoreland '56 Chevrolet	146	345	Running
6	17	97	Allen Adkins	Tom Harbison '56 Ford	146	200	Running
7	18	86	Cotton Owens	Jim Stephens '56 Pontiac	143	150	Running
8	7	14W	Billy Myers	Guy Wilson '56 Mercury	140	135	Running
9	14	75	Jim Paschal	Frank Hayworth '56 Mercury	139	115	Running
10	40	5	Bill Blair	Joe Blair '56 Dodge	134	100	Running
11	38	48	Al Watkins	Don Holcomb '56 Ford	129	50	Running
12	24	03	Bud Graham	'55 Chrysler	127	50	Running
13	32	78	John Lindsay	'55 Chevrolet	124	50	Running
14	23	18	Ray Chaike	'56 Chevrolet	124	50	Running
15	34	77	Walt Schubert	Bob Bunselmeyer '55 Ford	120	50	Running
16	29	81	Buzz Woodward	'55 Chevrolet	120	50	Running
17	4	98	Danny Letner	'56 Dodge	119	50	Running
18	13	7	Jim Reed	Reed '56 Chevrolet	116	50	Crash
19	33	95	Bill Parks	'55 Packard	113	50	Running
20	25	33	Bud Geiselman	Chick Garno '55 Chevrolet	112	50	Heating
21	35	47	Harvey Eakin	Eakin '54 Nash	105	25	A Frame
22	9	12	Ralph Moody	DePaolo Eng '56 Ford	98	25	Battery
23	27	19	Harvey Henderson	'55 Chevrolet	93	25	Running
24	10	55	Junior Johnson	Brushy Mtn Mtrs '56 Pontiac	83	25	Windshld
25	19	10	Rex White	Max Welborn '56 Chevrolet	83	25	Trans
26	39	50	Fred Lorenzen	'56 Chevrolet	76	25	Fuel Pmp
27	22	6	Ralph Liguori	Liguori '56 Dodge	71	25	Rear End
28	31	23	Benny DeRosier	Adelmo Tiezzi '54 Hudson	64	25	H Gasket
29	41	51	Donald Thomas	'56 Dodge	62	25	Engine
30	11	37	Tiny Lund	'56 Pontiac	50	25	Steering
31	15	22	Fireball Roberts	DePaolo '56 Ford	59	---	Windshld
32	37	63	Bill Tanner	Al Liberty '55 Chevrolet	48	---	Trans
33	30	39	Buzz Auckland	Leslie Carr '56 Chevrolet	43	---	Crash
34	16	49	Jimmie Lewallen	Bob Welborn '56 Chevrolet	40	---	Frame
35	26	17	Dick Allwine	Earl Wright '55 Chevrolet	31	---	Heating
36	36	85	Don Carr	'56 Pontiac	30	---	Vapor Lk
37	2	00	Speedy Thompson	Carl Kiekhaefer '56 Chrysler	29	---	RF Tire
38	8	15W	Bobby Myers	Bill Stroppe '56 Mercury	28	---	Engine
39	20	34	Fonty Flock	Carl Kiekhaefer '56 Chrysler	22	---	Shocks
40	21	26	Russ Truelove	Bob White '56 Mercury	22	---	Shocks
41	28	84	Ken Wagner	Lamson & Nitti '56 Ford	16	---	Heating

Time of Race: 1 hour, 58 minutes, 32 seconds
Average Speed: 75.928 mph
Pole Winner: Buck Baker - 104.590 mph
Lap Leaders: Buck Baker 1-53, Time Flock 54-94, Baker 95-150.
Cautions: Margin of Victory: 1 lap plus   Attendance: 24,000

Grand National Race No. 12
200 Laps at Atlantic Rural Exposition Fairgrounds
Richmond, VA
100 Miles on Half-mile Dirt Track
April 29, 1956

Fin	St	No.	Driver	Team / Car	Laps	Money	Status
1	1	87	Buck Baker	Carl Kiekhaefer '56 Dodge	200	$1,100	Running
2	3	92	Herb Thomas	Carl Kiekhaefer '56 Dodge	199	700	Shift Lev
3	2	300	Speedy Thompson	Carl Kiekhaefer '56 Chrysler	199	475	Running
4	5	14	Billy Myers	Guy Wilson '56 Mercury	198	365	Running
5	10	2	Jimmy Massey	Westmoreland '56 Chevrolet	197	310	Running
6	7	82	Joe Eubanks	Satcher Motors '56 Ford	195	250	Running
7	4	42	Lee Petty	Petty Engineering '56 Dodge	193	200	Running
8	12	59	Blackie Pitt	Brownie Pitt '56 Plymouth	191	150	Running
9	11	X	Rex White	Max Welborn '56 Chevrolet	188	100	Running
10	14	5	Bill Champion	'55 Olds	187	100	Running
11	13	97	Allen Adkins	Tom Harbison '56 Dodge	182	75	Piston
12	17	19	Harvey Henderson	'56 Chevrolet	172	60	Running
13	19	55	Tiny Lund	Brushy Mt. Motors '56 Pontiac	168	50	Running
14	18	96	Bobby Keck	'55 Chevrolet	166	50	Running
15	6	12	Ralph Moody	DePaolo Eng '56 Ford	162	50	Crash
16	16	271	Billy Carden	'56 Mercury	162	50	Rear End
17	8	75	Jim Paschal	Frank Hayworth '56 Mercury	147	50	Engine
18	15	22	Fireball Roberts	DePaolo Eng '56 Ford	95	50	Crash
19	22	98	Danny Letner	Tom Harbison '56 Dodge	69	50	RR Axle
20	23	54	Nace Mattingly	Mattingly '55 Ford	53	50	Heating
21	21	264	Johnny Allen	Spook Crawford '55 Plymouth	31	---	Spindle
22	20	84	Dave Terrell	Terrell '56 Ford	30	---	Heating
23	24	6	Ralph Liguori	Liguori '56 Dodge	7	---	Coil
24	9	49	Tim Flock	Mauri Rose Eng '56 Chevrolet	2	--	Withdrew

Time of Race: 1 hour, 46 minutes, 42 seconds
Average Speed: 56.232 mph
Pole Winner: Buck Baker - 67.091 mph
Lap Leaders: Buck Baker 1-164, Herb Thomas 165-166, Baker 167-200.
Cautions: Margin of Victory: 1 lap plus   Attendance: 5,000

Race No. 13

Thompson Treats Columbia to Dazzling Display of Speed

COLUMBIA, SC (May 5) -- Speedy Thompson, regarded as one of the bright future stars of the Grand National circuit, grabbed his first win of the year in the Arclite 100 at Columbia Speedway. It was Thompson's fifth win during his brief tenure on the NASCAR tour.

Thompson, starting third, drove to the high side of Curtis Turner in the 121st lap and led the rest of the way. Buck Baker finished second, 25 seconds behind the speeding Speedy. Joe Weatherly was third, Tiny Lund fourth and Bob Flock fifth.

Turner went out of lap 120 with a broken exhaust manifold. Earlier, Lee Petty departed on lap 111 with steering problems.

Lund's fourth place effort was remarkable considering the fact that he spun and was hit broadside by Bobby Johns. Johns was out for the evening, but Lund

made it back into the race after quick surgical work in the pits.

Ralph Liguori crashed his Dodge in the second lap, bringing out the first of two caution flags. Thompson averaged 54.545 mph before 5,000 spectators.

Grand National Race No. 13
200 Laps at Columbia Speedway
Columbia, SC
100 Miles on Half-mile Dirt Track
May 5, 1956

Fin	St	No.	Driver	Team / Car	Laps	Money	Status
1	2	500	Speedy Thompson	Carl Kiekhaefer '56 Dodge	200	$1,100	Running
2	1	500b	Buck Baker	Carl Kiekhaefer '56 Dodge	198	700	Running
3	12	9	Joe Weatherly	Schwam Mtr '56 Ford	196	475	Running
4	10	37	Tiny Lund	'56 Pontiac	192	365	Running
5	19	49	Bob Flock	Mauri Rose Eng '56 Chevrolet	191	310	Running
6	5	501	Herb Thomas	Kiekhaefer '56 Dodge	190	250	Running
7	22	34	Dick Beaty	Beaty '56 Ford	189	200	Running
8	11	X	Rex White	Max Welborn '56 Chevrolet	186	150	Running
9	17	59	Blackie Pitt	Brownie Pitt '56 Plymouth	178	100	Running
10	21	47	Al Watkins	Don Holcomb '56 Ford	177	100	Running
11	23	264	Johnny Allen	Spook Crawford '55 Plymouth	173	75	Running
12	16	34A	Charles Jackson	'55 Olds	166	60	RF Hub
13	13	75	Jim Paschal	Frank Hayworth '56 Mercury	166	50	Engine
14	25	94	Ed Cole Jr	'55 Mercury	161	50	Running
15	26	1R	Tim Flock	Mauri Rose Eng '56 Chevrolet	161	50	Running
16	8	2	Gwyn Staley	Westmoreland '56 Chevrolet	154	50	A Frame
17	4	99	Curtis Turner	Schwam Mtr '56 Ford	142	50	Tie Rod
18	20	760	Brownie King	'56 Chevrolet	120	50	Manifold
19	7	42	Lee Petty	Petty Engineering '56 Dodge	111	50	Steering
20	18	150	Fred Lorenzen	'56 Chevrolet	96	50	Steering
21	14	1	Jimmie Lewallen	H. Rakestraw '56 Chevrolet	71	---	Engine
22	6	14	Billy Myers	Guy Wilson '56 Mercury	47	---	Hose
23	15	7A	Bobby Johns	Johns '56 Chevrolet	40	---	Crash
24	3	82	Joe Eubanks	Satcher Motors '56 Ford	19	---	Steering
25	9	55	Junior Johnson	Brushy Mtn Mtrs '56 Pontiac	3	---	Piston
26	24	6	Ralph Liguori	Liguori '56 Dodge	1	---	Steering

Time of Race: 1 hour, 50 Minutes
Average Speed: 54.545 mph
Pole Winner: Buck Baker - 63.274 mph
Lap Leaders: Lee Petty 1-59, Curtis Turner 60-120, Speedy Thompson 121-200.
Cautions: 2   Margin of Victory: 25 seconds   Attendance: 5,000

Race No. 14

Thompson Leads All But One Lap in Concord Victory

CONCORD, NC (May 6) -- Speedy Thompson of Monroe, NC, notched his second straight win in the 100-miler at Harris Speedway in Concord. Buck Baker and Herb Thomas, who finished second and third, gave the Kiekhaefer team its second 1-2-3 finish of the season.

Thompson led all but the fifth lap in the 100-miler on

the half-mile dirt track. Baker was 18 seconds behind the winnner when the checkered flag fell. Tim Flock borrowed a Pontiac and finished fourth. Rex White, rookie out of Silver Spring, MD, was fifth.

Thomas came away from Concord with a four point lead over Baker in the Grand National point standings.

Only one caution flag was waved during the course of the race. Jim Paschal and Bobby Johns ran into each other in the 209th lap. Johns was sidelined, but Paschal took one full lap backwards in order to lose a minimum distance. He eventually finished ninth.

Marvin Panch took his lumps on the high banked half-mile oval. He flipped his Ford in qualifying but was able to make repairs before the race. Panch started 26th in the 30 car field, but crashed on lap 183 when he broke an axle.

Thompson averaged 61.633 mph for his sixth career win.

Race No. 15

Protests Fly as Baker Grabs Greenville 100

GREENVILLE, SC (May 10) -- Buck Baker gave car owner Carl Kiekhaefer his seventh straight win in the 100-miler at Greenville-Pickens Speedway, but the white Dodge D-500 had to survive a post-race tear-down.

After the race the Schwam Motor Co. team, which fields Fords driven by Joe Weatherly and Curtis Turner, filed a protest against the Kiekhaefer Dodge's fuel tank. Baker had run the entire 200 laps without a pit stop and finished a lap ahead of runner-up Turner.

When informed that his Dodge had to go to the "bull pen" to be torn down, an angered Kiekhaefer countered with a protest of "the hopped up engine and illegal rear end" used by both Schwam Fords.

NASCAR technical inspector Jim Ross supervised the lengthy inspection. After careful calculations, both cars were declared 'legal'. Finishing positions were upheld.

Grand National Race No. 14
200 Laps at Harris Speedway
Concord, NC
100 Miles on Half-mile Dirt Track
May 6, 1956

Fin	St	No.	Driver	Team / Car	Laps	Money	Status
1	1	300c	Speedy Thompson	Carl Kiekhaefer '56 Chrysler	200	$1,100	Running
2	6	300	Buck Baker	Carl Kiekhaefer '56 Chrysler	200	700	Running
3	3	300B	Herb Thomas	Carl Kiekhaefer '56 Chrysler	198	475	Running
4	9	285	Tim Flock	Jim Stephens '56 Pontiac	197	365	Running
5	8	X	Rex White	Max Welborn '56 Chevrolet	195	310	Running
6	29	37	Tiny Lund	'56 Pontiac	188	250	Running
7	13	2	Gwyn Staley	Westmoreland '56 Chevrolet	185	200	Running
8	25	264	Johnny Allen	Spook Crawford '55 Plymouth	182	150	Running
9	5	49	Jim Paschal	Bob Welborn '56 Chevrolet	181	100	Running
10	18	34A	Charles Jackson	'55 Olds	179	100	Running
11	28	209	Pete Stewart	'56 Chevrolet	179	75	Running
12	30	48	Al Watkins	Don Holcomb '56 Ford	174	60	Running
13	19	96	Bobby Keck	'55 Chevrolet	172	50	Running
14	20	19	Harvey Henderson	'56 Ford	158	50	Running
15	26	9	Marvin Panch	Tom Harbison '56 Ford	149	50	RR Axle
16	4	286	Cotton Owens	Jim Stephens '56 Pontiac	146	50	RF Hub
17	13	99	Billy Carden	DePaolo Eng '56 Ford	137	50	RR Axle
18	24	94	Ed Cole, Jr	'55 Mercury	128	50	Spindle
19	10	59	Blackie Pitt	Brownie Pitt '56 Buick	127	50	Hose
20	21	34	Dick Beaty	Beaty '56 Ford	122	50	RR Axle
21	22	760	Brownie King	'56 Chevrolet	120	---	Vapor Lk
22	15	150	Fred Lorenzen	'56 Chevrolet	89	---	Running
23	27	42	Lee Petty	Petty Engineering '56 Dodge	77	---	Rear End
24	12	B-29	Dink Widenhouse	Mauri Rose Eng '56 Ford	64	---	Piston
25	17	20	Bill Widenhouse	Waldron & Co. '55 Buick	49	---	Heating
26	16	271	Ralph Liguori	'56 Mercury	27	---	Crash
27	14	5	Bill Blair	Joe Blair '56 Dodge	25	---	Wheel
28	7	7A	Bobby Johns	Johns '56 Ford	23	---	Crash
29	23	24	Bobby Waddell	Jimmy Pardue '55 Chevrolet	19	---	Engine
30	2	14	Billy Myers	Guy Wilson '56 Mercury	17	---	Engine

Time of Race: 1 hour, 37 minutes, 21 seconds
Average Speed: 61.633 mph
Pole Winner: Speedy Thompson - 65.241 mph
Lap Leaders: Speedy Thompson 1-4, Billy Myers 5, Thompson 6-200.
Cautions: 1 for 3 laps   Margin of Victory: 18 seconds   Attendance: 6,000

Grand National Race No. 15
200 Laps at Greenville-Pickens
Speedway
Greenville, SC
100 Miles on Half-mile Dirt Track
May 10, 1956

Fin	St	No.	Driver	Team / Car	Laps	Money	Status
1	2	500B	Buck Baker	Carl Kiekhaefer '56 Dodge	200	$1,100	Running
2	5	99	Curtis Turner	Schwam Mtrs '56 Ford	199	700	Running
3	4	82	Joe Eubanks	Satcher Motors '56 Ford	197	475	Running
4	18	2	Gwyn Staley	Westmoreland '56 Chevrolet	195	365	Running
5	10	9	Joe Weatherly	Schwam Mtrs. '56 Ford	192	310	Running
6	13	7A	Bobby Johns	Johns '56 Chevrolet	190	250	Running
7	1	X	Rex White	Max Welborn '56 Chevrolet	190	200	Running
8	8	19	Harvey Henderson	'56 Ford	189	150	Running
9	14	37	Tiny Lund	'56 Pontiac	183	100	Running
10	16	49	Jim Paschal	Bob Welborn '56 Chevrolet	172	100	Engine
11	15	271	Billy Carden	'56 Mercury	168	75	Running
12	19	24	Bobby Waddell	Jimmy Pardue '55 Chevrolet	167	60	Running
13	21	264	Johnny Allen	Spook Crawford '55 Plymouth	155	50	RF Hub
14	9	901	Herb Thomas	Carl Kiekhaefer '56 Dodge	154	50	Wheel
15	3	500	Speedy Thompson	Carl Kiekhaefer '56 Dodge	125	50	Bearing
16	23	670	Brownie King	'56 Chevrolet	124	50	Crash
17	11	44	Chester Barron	'56 Chevrolet	111	50	Heating
18	22	6	Ralph Liguori	Liguori '56 Dodge	104	50	Engine
19	6	14	Billy Myers	Guy Wilson '56 Mercury	83	50	Bearing
20	12	42	Lee Petty	Petty Engineering '56 Dodge	66	50	Steering
21	7	150	Fred Lorenzen	'56 Chevrolet	66	---	Coil
22	20	59	Blackie Pitt	Brownie Pitt '56 Plymouth	60	---	RR Axle
23	17	34	Dick Beaty	Beaty '56 Ford	16	---	Rear End

Time of Race: 1 hour, 39 minutes, 24 seconds
Average Speed: 60.362 mph
Pole Winner: Rex White - 61.100 mph
Lap Leaders: - - - - - - - - - Curtis Turner -180, Buck Baker 181-200.
Cautions: Margin of Victory: 1 lap plus   Attendance: 5,000

Joe Eubanks, Gwyn Staley and Weatherly rounded out the top five.

Baker took the point lead by 100 points over Herb Thomas, who wound up 14th in the field of 23 when a wheel broke on his Dodge.

A crowd of 5,000 watched Baker average 60.362 mph for his fifth win of the year. The 37 year-old Baker took the lead for good in the 181st lap when leader Turner pitted for fuel.

Race No. 16

Caution-filled Hickory Race to Thompson

HICKORY, NC (May 12) -- Alfred "Speedy" Thompson led from start to finish in a caution-marred 80-mile Grand National race at Hickory Speedway.

The frequent yellow flags allowed the first five finishers to complete all 200 laps. Thompson was a car length ahead of runner-up Billy Myers as the race end-

Grand National Race No. 16
200 Laps at Hickory Speedway
Hickory, NC
80 Miles on .4-mile Dirt Track
May 12, 1956

Fin	St	No.	Driver	Team / Car	Laps	Money	Status
1	1	300c	Speedy Thompson	Carl Kiekhaefer '56 Chrysler	200	$1,100	Running
2	10	14	Billy Myers	Guy Wilson '56 Mercury	200	700	Running
3	13	500B	Buck Baker	Carl Kiekhaefer '56 Dodge	200	475	Running
4	12	502	Herb Thomas	Carl Kiekhaefer '56 Dodge	200	365	Running
5	2	2	Gwyn Staley	Westmoreland '56 Chevrolet	200	310	Running
6	6	7A	Bobby Johns	Johns '56 Chevrolet	198	250	Running
7	5	286	Cotton Owens	Stephens '56 Pontiac	196	200	Running
8	21	48	Al Watkins	Don Holcomb '56 Ford	182	150	Running
9	20	34A	Charles Jackson	'54 Olds	180	100	Running
10	11	19	Harvey Henderson	'56 Ford	180	100	Running
11	23	760	Brownie King	'56 Chevrolet	174	75	Running
12	7	82	Joe Eubanks	Satcher Motors '56 Ford	172	60	RR Axle
13	19	96	Bobby Keck	'55 Chevrolet	171	50	Running
14	22	37	Tiny Lund	'56 Pontiac	168	50	Crash
15	4	42	Lee Petty	Petty Engineering '56 Dodge	164	50	Trans
16	9	271	Billy Carden	'56 Mercury	154	50	Spindle
17	18	1	Jimmie Lewallen	H. Rakestraw '55 Chevrolet	102	50	Crash
18	24	75	Jim Paschal	Frank Hayworth '56 Mercury	95	50	Electric
19	17	34	Dick Beaty	Beaty '56 Ford	81	50	Rear end
20	8	150	Fred Lorenzen	'56 Chevrolet	73	50	Crash
21	15	204	Darvin Randahl	Randahl '56 Ford	47	---	Bearing
22	16	B-29	Dink Widenhouse	Widenhouse '56 Ford	24	---	Crash
23	14	24	Bobby Waddell	Jimmy Pardue '55 Chevrolet	24	---	Crash
24	3	55	Junior Johnson	Brushy Mtn Mtrs '56 Pontiac	9	---	Piston

Time of Race: 1 hour, 20 minutes, 45 seconds
Average Speed: 59.442 mph
Pole Winner: Speedy Thompson - 67.447 mph
Lap Leaders: Speedy Thompson 1-200.
Cautions: 6   Margin of Victory: Under caution   Attendance: 4,500

ed under the caution flag. Buck Baker, Herb Thomas and Gwyn Staley finished third through fifth.

Thompson's triumph gave car owner Carl Kiekhaefer his eighth straight Grand National win.

A crowd of 4,500 saw Thompson average 59.442 mph for his seventh career victory.

A new face belonging to Fred Lorenzen brought out one of the caution flags when he crashed his Chevrolet in the 75th lap. He was not hurt.

Bobby Waddell and Dink Widenhouse wrecked together in the 25th lap. Both were sidelined. Jimmie Lewallen flipped his Chevrolet on lap 104, and Tiny Lund stuffed his Pontiac in the wall late in the race. There were no driver injuries.

Race No. 17

Baker-Thompson Finish in Near Dead Heat at Hillsboro

HILLSBORO, NC (May 13) -- Buck Baker nosed out Speedy Thompson by a couple of feet in a thrilling climax to the 90-mile event at Orange Speedway. It was the sixth win of the year for the Charlotte charger.

Baker also upped his point lead to 186 over Herb Thomas, who finished 11th in the field of 31. Baker got around Thompson in the 58th lap and held off his rugged teammate for the rest of the way. Thompson swung to the low side on the last lap and crossed the finish line less than a half car length behind Baker.

Lee Petty made a stab to pass both Baker and Thompson in the final lap but slid sideways off the second turn and had to settle for a 'distant' third, two car lengths behind. Fireball Roberts finished fourth and Cotton Owens was fifth.

A Mother's Day crowd of 7,500 was on its feet much of the way as the Kiekhaefer cars once again dominated. It was the team's ninth straight win, an all-time NASCAR record.

Dick Beaty, former motorcycle racer, started 15th but was involved in a cr ash on lap 84. The collision knocked him out of the race. Beaty was not injured.

Curtis Turner started in third spot, but failing brakes put his Ford behind the wall after 54 laps.

Thompson's recent flurry of success moved him to sixth place in the point standings, 1,576 behind leader Baker.

Grand National Race No. 17
100 Laps at Orange Speedway
Hillsboro, NC
90 Miles on .9-mile Dirt Track
May 13, 1956

Fin	St	No.	Driver	Team / Car	Laps	Money	Status
1	1	300	Buck Baker	Carl Kiekhaefer '56 Chrysler	100	$1,100	Running
2	2	300c	Speedy Thompson	Carl Kiekhaefer '56 Chrysler	100	700	Running
3	8	42	Lee Petty	Petty Engineering '56 Dodge	100	475	Running
4	4	22	Fireball Roberts	DePaolo Eng '56 Ford	100	365	Running
5	9	286	Cotton Owens	Jim Stephens '56 Pontiac	99	310	Running
6	11	2	Gwyn Staley	Westmoreland '56 Chevrolet	99	250	Running
7	12	9	Joe Weatherly	Schwam Mtrs '56 Ford	98	200	Running
8	10	12	Ralph Moody	DePaolo Eng '56 Ford	98	150	Running
9	23	49	Jimmy Massey	Bob Welborn '56 Chevrolet	96	100	Running
10	7	14	Billy Myers	Guy Wilson '56 Mercury	96	100	Running
11	6	300B	Herb Thomas	Carl Kiekhaefer '56 Chrysler	95	75	Running
12	5	82	Joe Eubanks	Satcher Motors '56 Ford	95	60	Running
13	19	X	Rex White	Max Welborn '56 Chevrolet	94	50	Running
14	17	113	Emanuel Zervakis	'56 Chevrolet	94	50	Running
15	24	7A	Bobby Johns	Johns '56 Chevrolet	93	50	Idler
16	16	19	Bobby Henderson	'56 Ford	92	50	Running
17	25	48	Al Watkins	Don Holcomb '56 Ford	92	50	Running
18	30	264	Johnny Allen	Spook Crawford '55 Plymouth	93	50	Running
19	31	96	Bobby Keck	'55 Chevrolet	91	50	Running
20	28	94	Ed Cole	'55 Mercury	50	50	Running
21	15	34	Dick Beaty	Beaty '56 Ford	81	---	Crash
22	29	760	Brownie King	'56 Chevrolet	81	---	Running
23	22	203	Pete Yow	Strickland Motors '55 Buick	80	---	Running
24	20	59	Blackie Pitt	Brownie Pitt '56 Plymouth	63	---	Rod
25	27	34A	Charlie Jackson	'54 Olds	57	---	Rear End
26	3	99	Curtis Turner	Schwam Motors '56 Ford	54	---	Brakes
27	26	204	Darvin Randahl	Randahl '56 Ford	53	---	Bearings
28	13	75	Jim Paschal	Frank Hayworth '56 Mercury	51	---	Battery
29	18	271	Billy Carden	'56 Mercury	48	---	Spindle
30	14	5	Bill Blair	Joe Blair '56 Dodge	43	---	Tire
31	21	285	Don Carr	Jim Stephens '56 Pontiac	10	---	RF Hub

Time of Race: 1 hour, 4 minutes, 30 seconds
Average Speed: 83.720 mph
Pole Winner: Buck Baker - 89.305 mph
Lap Leaders: Speedy Thompson 1-57, Buck Baker 58-100.
Cautions: Margin of Victory: 1/2 car length   Attendance: 7,500

Bill O'Dell's Nash up on 2 wheels at Martinsville.

Grand National Race No. 18
500 Laps at Martinsville Speedway
Martinsville, VA
"Virginia 500"
250 Miles on Half-mile Paved Track
May 20, 1956

Fin	St	No.	Driver	Team / Car	Laps	Money	Status
1	1	502	Buck Baker	Carl Kiekhaefer '56 Dodge	500	$3,100	Running
2	2	500	Speedy Thompson	Carl Kiekhaefer '56 Dodge	500	1,500	Running
3	5	42	Lee Petty	Petty Engineering '56 Dodge	497	1,025	Running
4	8	3	Paul Goldsmith	Smokey Yunick '56 Chevrolet	596	750	Running
5	9	2	Gwyn Staley	Westmoreland '56 Chevrolet	491	600	Running
6	7	X	Rex White	Max Welborn '56 Chevrolet	483	450	Running
7	19	418	Sherman Utsman	'56 Chevrolet	477	350	Running
8	13	14	Billy Myers	Guy Wilson '56 Mercury	475	300	Running
9	21	91	Jack Smith	'56 Chevrolet	475	200	Running
10	15	12	Ralph Moody	DePaolo Eng '56 Ford	467	175	Running
11	33	19	Harvey Henderson	'56 Ford	464	150	Running
12	22	55	Tiny Lund	Brushy Mtn Mtrs '56 Pontiac	463	100	Running
13	6	7A	Bobby Johns	Johns '56 Chevrolet	458	100	Running
14	34	240	Reitzel Darner	'56 Ford	441	100	RF Hub
15	12	1	Bobby Myers	'55 Chevrolet	436	100	RF Hub
16	18	22	Fireball Roberts	DePaolo Eng '56 Ford	435	75	Running
17	30	16	Ray Chaike	'56 Chevrolet	430	75	Running
18	25	9	Pee Wee Jones	'56 Ford	419	75	Running
19	32	211	George Cork	'55 Plymouth	405	75	Running
20	3	92	Herb Thomas	Thomas '56 Chevrolet	377	75	Engine
21	29	209	Pete Stewart	'56 Plymouth	356	60	RR Axle
22	28	18	Arden Mounts	Mounts '56 Pontiac	338	60	Running
23	10	285	Don Carr	Stephens '56 Pontiac	304	60	Lug Bolt
24	14	150	Fred Lorenzen	'56 Chevrolet	293	60	Running
25	4	75	Jim Paschal	Frank Hayworth '56 Mercury	293	60	Bearing
26	31	59	Blackie Pitt	Brownie Pitt '56 Buick	252	60	RF Hub
27	7	286	Cotton Owens	Jim Stephens '56 Pontiac	243	60	RF Hub
28	24	32	Ted Cannady	'56 Chevrolet	156	60	Trans
29	23	204	Darvin Randahl	Randahl '56 Ford	149	60	Piston
30	16	11	Tim Flock	Mauri Rose Eng '56 Chevrolet	69	69	Crash
31	26	264	Johnny Allen	Spook Crawford '55 Plymouth	37	60	Trans
32	35	35	Bill O'Dell	'55 Rambler	37	60	Crash
33	20	95	Bob Duell	Julian Buesink '56 Ford	29	60	Crash
34	27	195	Jim Rhoades	'55 Packard	25	60	Tire
35	17	6	Ralph Liguori	Liguori '56 Dodge	8	60	Piston

Time of Race: 4 hour, 6 minutes, 7 seconds
Average Speed: 60.824 mph
Pole Winner: Buck Baker - 66.103 mph
Lap Leaders: Speedy Thompson 1-215, Buck Baker 216-221, Herb Thomas 222-337,
        Thompson 338-381, Baker 382-500.
Cautions: 7 for 20 laps   Margin of Victory: 1/2 lap   Attendance: 20,000

Race No. 18

Kiekhaefer Squad Leads
All the Way in Virginia 500

MARTINSVILLE, VA (May 20) -- The potent combination of Baker, Thompson and Kiekhaefer continued its grip on the Grand National circuit in the Virginia 500 at Martinsville Speedway.

Buck Baker passed Speedy Thompson in the 382nd lap and led the rest of the way to win the inaugural 500-lapper on the half-mile paved oval. Thompson led twice for a total of 259 laps, but was a half-lap behind Baker when the checkered flag fell. Kiekhaefer Dodge D-500s were at the head of the leader board for the entire afternoon.

Lee Petty finished third, three lap behind. Paul

Goldsmith was fourth and Gwyn Staley fifth.

A crowd of 20,000 was on hand at Clay Earles' facility to witness Baker's 19th career Grand National win. Seven caution flags for a total of 20 laps held Baker's winning speed to 60.824 mph.

Billy Myers' team owner, Bill Stroppe, filed a protest against the first two finishing Dodges, claiming the Kiekhaefer team did not have the same size tires on all four wheels as required by NASCAR rules.

NASCAR's Johnny Bruner said the matter was a technical issue and turned the matter over to the National Stock Car Racing Commission, which ruled in favor of the Kiekhaefer team.

The only two accidents occurred early. Bill O'Dell drove his Nash Rambler onto the curbing in the fourth turn and flipped without injury. Tim Flock crashed in the 70th lap when he hit a slower car in the rear.

Grand National Race No. 19
200 Laps at Lincoln Speedway
Abbottstown, PA
100 Miles on Half-mile Dirt Track
May 25, 1956

Fin	St	No.	Driver	Team / Car	Laps	Money	Status
1	5	500B	Buck Baker	Carl Kiekhaefer '56 Dodge	200	$1,100	Running
2	8	75	Jim Paschal	Frank Hayworth '56 Mercury	200	700	Running
3	6	42	Lee Petty	Petty Engineering '56 Dodge	200	475	Running
4	2	502	Herb Thomas	Carl Kiekhaefer '56 Dodge	195	365	Running
5	4	54	Nace Mattingly	Mattingly '56 Ford	185	310	Running
6	10	81	Frank Jamison	'55 Chevrolet	173	250	Running
7	14	4	Carl Anderson	'55 Ford	173	200	Running
8	9	59	Blackie Pitt	Brownie Pitt '56 Buick	168	150	Running
9	16	195	Jim Rhoades	'55 Packard	148	100	Spindle
10	12	19	Harvey Henderson	'56 Ford	113	100	Steering
11	1	500	Speedy Thompson	Carl Kiekhaefer '56 Dodge	97	75	Radiator
12	3	14	Billy Myers	Guy Wilson '56 Mercury	86	60	Fuel Pmp
13	13	114	Hank Trice	'54 Hudson Hornet	73	50	Spindle
14	11	113	Emanuel Zervakis	'56 Chevrolet	71	50	Axle
15	15	3	Curley Hatfield	'55 Chevrolet	70	50	Hub
16	7	900	Johnny Roberts	'55 Chevrolet	60	50	Axle
17	17	420	Cy Spencer	'56 Chevrolet	34	50	Wheel

Time of Race: 1 hour, 26 minutes, 11 seconds
Average Speed: 69.619 mph
Pole Winner: Speedy Thompson
Lap Leaders: Billy Myers 1-43, Herb Thomas 44-181, Buck Baker 182-200.
Cautions: Margin of Victory: 1 car length   Attendance:

Race No. 19

Baker Ambushes Abbottstown Field for Third in Row

ABBOTTSTOWN, PA (May 25) -- Buck Baker took the lead with 19 laps to go and nipped Jim Paschal and Lee Petty in a near photo finish at Lincoln Speedway.

It was Baker's third Grand National win in a row and the eighth of the year for the former bus driver.

Paschal, driving his 'C U Later Alligator' Mercury, wound up a close second. Petty followed in third, right on Paschal's tail pipes. Herb Thomas, who had led until a late pit stop, wound up fourth and Nace Mattingly was fifth.

Petty made an impressive drive after spinning out in the 21st lap and losing a lap to the field. He roared back into the lead lap and with the aid of a caution flag, made up his deficit. It was one of the few times this season that a Kiekhaefer car was *not* the fastest car on the track.

Pole winner Speedy Thompson fell out on lap 97 with a hole in his radiator. Only eight cars finished the 100-mile race.

Baker extended his point lead to 672 points over Thomas.

Billy Myers, who led the first 43 laps, had to quit on lap 86 with a faulty fuel pump.

Race No. 20

Thompson Wins 12th in Row For Kiekhaefer

CHARLOTTE, NC (May 27) -- For the fourth time this year, the three Kiekhaefer Mercury Outboard entries walked away with the top three positions as Speedy Thompson led the parade in the 100-miler at Charlotte Speedway. It was the 12th consecutive Grand National victory for the formidable independent team.

Junior Johnson, most recent addition to the Kiekhaefer team, finished second to Thompson. Point leader Buck Baker was third. Jim Paschal came in fourth with Lee Petty fifth.

Baker and Thompson swapped the lead six times in the 133-lap contest. Baker was running first when he had to pit for fuel with just four laps left. His pit stop dropped him to a lap off the pace and allowed Johnson to pick up second place.

Nine laps were run under the caution flag. The most serious accident happened in the opening lap. Curtis Turner, Bobby Johns, Blackie Pitt and Rex White tangled in the third turn on the congested start. Johns' Chevrolet flipped over the outer rim of the track, smashed through the 12-foot high wooden fence and tumbled down a deep embankment. The Miami driver suffered a serious shoulder injury. He was taken to Charlotte Memorial Hospital for further treatment.

The other two caution flags were brought out by Dick Beaty, who spun his Ford into the wall on two separate occasions. He persevered, however, and finished in 11th place.

Grand National Race No. 20
133 Laps at Charlotte Speedway
Charlotte, NC
100 Miles on .75-mile Dirt Track
May 27, 1956

Fin	St	No.	Driver	Team / Car	Laps	Money	Status
1	1	300c	Speedy Thompson	Carl Kiekhaefer '56 Chrysler	133	$1,100	Running
2	2	502	Junior Johnson	Carl Kiekhaefer '56 Dodge	133	700	Running
3	25	300	Buck Baker	Carl Kiekhaefer '56 Chrysler	132	475	Running
4	7	75	Jim Paschal	Frank Hayworth '56 Mercury	131	465	Running
5	3	42	Lee Petty	Petty Engineering '56 Dodge	131	310	Running
6	5	9	Joe Weatherly	Schwam Motors '56 Ford	129	250	Running
7	4	82	Joe Eubanks	Satcher Motors '56 Ford	129	200	Running
8	8	2	Gwyn Staley	Westmoreland '56 Chevrolet	127	150	Running
9	17	55	Jack Smith	Brushy Mtn Mtr '56 Pontiac	127	100	Running
10	9	14	Billy Myers	Guy Wilson '56 Mercury	123	100	Running
11	15	34	Dick Beaty	Beaty '56 Ford	122	75	Running
12	18	100	Ken Milligan	Dave Everett '56 Chevrolet	121	60	Running
13	20	48	Al Watkins	Don Holcomb '56 Ford	120	50	Running
14	23	264	Johnny Allen	Spook Crawford '55 Plymouth	112	50	Running
15	19	94	Ed Cole	'55 Mercury	110	50	Running
16	13	24	Bobby Waddell	Jimmy Pardue '55 Chevrolet	103	50	Piston
17	24	760	Brownie King	'56 Chevrolet	83	50	Running
18	10	99	Curtis Turner	Schwam Motors '56 Ford	78	50	Electric
19	21	96	Bobby Keck	'55 Chevrolet	73	50	Piston
20	14	19	Harvey Henderson	'56 Ford	66	50	Push Rod
21	11	X	Rex White	Max Welborn '56 Chevrolet	53	---	Radiator
22	22	34A	Charles Jackson	'55 Olds	53	---	Gas Line
23	16	271	Billy Carden	'56 Mercury	48	---	Bearing
24	12	59	Blackie Pitt	Brownie Pitt '56 Buick	2	---	Radiator
25	6	7A	Bobby Johns	Johns '56 Chevrolet	---	---	Crashed

Time of Race: 1 hour, 32 minutes, 16 seconds
Average Speed: 64.866 mph
Pole Winner: Speedy Thompson - 76.966 mph
Lap Leaders: Speedy Thompson 1-47, Buck Baker 48-58, Thompson 59-82, Baker 83-98 Thompson 99-118, Baker 119-129, Thompson 130-133.
Cautions: 3 for 9 laps   Margin of Victory: Attendance: 4,000

Race No. 21

Thomas Wins at Portland For Kiekhaefer

PORTLAND, OR (May 27) -- Herb Thomas of Olivia, NC kept the Kiekhaefer winning streak intact with a triumph in the 75-miler at Portland Speedway. It was the third win of the season for Thomas and the 13th straight on the Grand National trail for the 'Kiekhaefer Krew'.

Thomas qualified fourth fastest, but had to start 18th in the 21 car field when promoters decided to invert the field. Slowest qualifier Lyle Matlock started on the pole but faded quickly and wound up 17th, 26 laps behind.

John Kieper finished second to Thomas. Clyde Palmer was third, Ed Negre came in fourth and Curley Barker fifth. Thomas was the only East coast regular to make the trip out West.

Bob Carroll, who started third despite having one of the slowest qualifying times blew a right front tire and flipped his Hudson on lap 65. He was not hurt.

Thomas averaged 63.815 mph for his 46th career win.

Herb Thomas won the Grand National race at Portland, OR.

Grand National Race No. 21
150 Laps at Portland Speedway
Portland, OR
75 Miles on Half-mile Paved Track
May 27, 1956

Fin	St	No.	Driver	Team / Car	Laps	Money	Status
1	18	300B	Herb Thomas	Carl Kiekhaefer '56 Chrysler	150	$1,000	Running
2	19	98	John Kieper	Kieper '55 Oldsmobile	150	700	Running
3	15	1C	Clyde Palmer	'56 Dodge	150	475	Running
4	11	88	Ed Negre	'56 Oldsmobile	149	365	Running
5	9	11	Curley Barker	'56 Chevrolet	148	310	Running
6	12	52	Harold Hardesty	'56 Chevrolet	148	250	Running
7	8	66	Bill Hyde	'56 Oldsmobile	148	200	Running
8	6	325	Lloyd Dane	'56 Mercury	148	150	Running
9	7	77	Gordon Haines	'56 Dodge	147	125	Running
10	14	56	Lou Sherman	'56 Mercury	147	110	Running
11	2	15	Royce Hagerty	'56 Dodge	145	100	Running
12	4	14	Bob Keele	'56 Ford	145	100	Running
13	17	1	Art Watts	'55 Dodge	142	50	Running
14	5	25	Erick Erickson	Erickson '54 Buick	142	50	Running
15	10	6	Don Hildreth	'54 Oldsmobile	140	50	Running
16	21	71	Ted Sweeney	'56 Oldsmobile	131	50	Running
17	1	5	Lyle Matlock	'55 Mercury	124	50	Running
18	3	22	Bob Caroll	'53 Hudson	62	50	Crash
19	13	27	Andy Wilson	'56 Ford	59	50	Crash
20	16	6	Harold Beal	'56 Ford	38	50	Axle
21	20	55	Don Hamilton	'56 Studebaker	17	---	Axle

Time of Race: 1 hour, 10 minutes, 31 seconds
Average Speed: 63.815 mph
Pole Winner: John Kieper - 67.239 mph
Lap Leaders: - - - - - - - - - - Herb Thomas   -150.
Cautions: Margin of Victory: Attendance:

Race No. 22

Thomas Survives to Win Redwood Speedway Fiasco

EUREKA, CA (May 30) -- Herb Thomas drove his Kiekhaefer Outboards Chrysler to the front on a terribly bumpy Redwood Speedway and was declared the winner when officials halted the scheduled 100-miler due to poor track conditions.

Holes dug deep into the .625-mile dirt track and thick swirling dust hampered the vision of the drivers. In the interest of safety, officials terminated the event after 78.1 miles.

Gordon Haines was a lap behind in second place. Lloyd Dane, Bob Keefe and Jim Cooke rounded out the top five.

It took nearly three hours to complete the 125 laps. Thomas' average speed was 38.814 mph. John Kieper, who eventually finished sixth, won the pole at 66.040 mph. Four cautions interrupted the event.

Accident-prone Howard Phillippi crashed his Chevrolet through the fence in the 46th lap.

Thomas' victory enabled him to creep closer to point leader Buck Baker, closing the gap to 976 points.

Grand National Race No. 22
160 Laps at Redwood Speedway
Eureka, CA
100 Miles on .625-mile Dirt Track
May 30, 1956

Fin	St	No.	Driver	Team / Car	Laps	Money	Status
1	6	300B	Herb Thomas	Carl Kiekhaefer '56 Chrysler	125	$1,000	Running
2	5	77	Gordon Haines	'56 Dodge	124	700	Running
3	16	225	Lloyd Dane	'56 Mercury	124	475	Running
4	8	14	Bob Keefe	'56 Ford	124	365	Running
5	10	9	Jim Cooke	'56 Pontiac	123	310	Running
6	1	88	John Kieper	'56 Oldsmobile	122	250	Running
7	7	52	Harold Hardesty	'56 Chevrolet	120	200	Running
8	13	15	Royce Hagerty	'56 Dodge	120	150	Running
9	4	47	Sam Speers	'56 Pontiac	119	125	Running
10	20	1	Art Watts	'55 Dodge	119	110	Running
11	15	30	Jim Graham	'56 Plymouth	117	100	Running
12	14	188	Jim Blomgren	'56 Ford	117	100	Heating
13	24	75	Bill Sullivan	'56 Ford 6	116	50	Running
14	3	25	Erick Erickson	Erickson '54 Buick	113	50	Running
15	12	98	Ed Negre	'55 Oldsmobile	111	50	Heating
16	17	134	Bob Havemann	'54 Dodge	106	50	Running
17	25	95	Jack Williams	'53 Oldsmobile	94	50	Running
18	23	71	Ted Sweeney	'56 Oldsmobile	62	50	Running
19	9	50	Harold Deal	'56 Ford	57	50	Crash
20	11	66	Bill Hyde	'56 Oldsmobile	54	50	Piston
21	21	78	Don Porter	'55 Studebaker	53	---	RR Axle
22	19	20	Howard Phillippi	'55 Chevrolet	45	---	Crash
23	2	1C	Clyde Palmer	'56 Dodge	38	---	Piston
24	18	41	Ernie Young	Walt Palozi '56 Pontiac	37	---	Crash
25	22	5	Lyle Matlock	'55 Mercury	18	---	Heating

Time of Race: 2 hours, 46 minutes
Average Speed: 38.814 mph
Pole Winner: John Kieper - 66.040 mph
Lap Leaders: - - - - - - - - - - Herb Thomas -125.
Cautions: Margin of Victory: 1 lap plus   Attendance:
* Race shortened to 125 laps due to dust

Grand National Race No. 23
150 Laps at New York State Fairgrounds
Syracuse, NY
150 Miles on 1.0-mile Dirt Track
May 30, 1956

Fin	St	No.	Driver	Team / Car	Laps	Money	Status
1	1	300	Buck Baker	Carl Kiekhaefer '56 Chrysler	150	$1,900	Running
2	6	75	Jim Paschal	Frank Hayworth '56 Mercury	147	1,300	Running
3	2	7	Jim Reed	Reed '56 Chevrolet	146	950	Running
4	4	42	Lee Petty	Petty Engineering '56 Dodge	145	700	Running
5	8	2	Gwyn Staley	Westmoreland '56 Chevrolet	145	535	Running
6	3	14	Billy Myers	Guy Wilson '56 Mercury	144	375	Fuel Pmp
7	23	300c	Speedy Thompson	Carl Kiekhaefer '56 Chrysler	144	325	Running
8	5	340	Ralph Liguori	Liguori '56 Chrysler	142	275	Running
9	24	226	Russ Truelove	Bob White '56 Mercury	141	150	Running
10	12	10	Nolan Swift	'56 Buick	137	125	Running
11	16	147	Hoss Kagle	'55 Chevrolet	135	100	Running
12	13	1	Ken Sebel		134	100	Running
13	14	230	Benny DeRosier	Adelmo Tiezzi '54 Hudson	129	100	Running
14	15	179	John Lindsay	'55 Chevrolet	126	100	Running
15	21	3	Curley Hatfield	'55 Chevrolet	121	100	Running
16	9	285	Don Carr	Jim Stephens '56 Pontiac	120	100	Engine
17	22	211	Guy Cork	'55 Plymouth	117	100	Running
18	18	77	Walt Schubert	Bob Bunselmeyer '55 Ford	114	100	Running
19	19	41	Billy Rafter	Rafter '55 Dodge	114	50	Running
20	11	81	Frank Jamison	'55 Chevrolet	88	50	Heating
21	17	195	Jim Rhoades	'55 Packard	83	50	Piston
22	7	95	Bob Duell	Julian Buesink '56 Ford	23	50	LR Tire
23	20	11	Sonny Walters		20	50	Heating
24	10	59	Blackie Pitt	Brownie Pitt '56 Buick	1	35	Crash

Time of Race: 1 hour, 44 minutes, 26 seconds
Average Speed: 86.179 mph
Pole Winner: Buck Baker - 83.975 mph
Lap Leaders: Buck Baker 1-102, Speedy Thompson 103-111, Baker 112-150.
Cautions: 1 for 3 laps   Margin of Victory: 3 laps plus   Attendance: 6,000

Race No. 23

Baker Outlasts Thompson To Win at Syracuse

SYRACUSE, NY (May 30) -- Buck Baker barged past Speedy Thompson in the 112th lap and led the rest of the way to win the 150-miler at the New York State Fairgrounds.

Baker's ninth win of the season netted his Carl Kiekhaefer team $1,900 and its 15th straight Grand National win. After an hour deliberation, NASCAR scorers awarded second place to Jim Paschal. Jim Reed got

Buck Baker leads Speedy Thompson by a car length in early running of 150-miler at Syracuse, NY.

third place, Lee Petty fourth and Gwyn Staley fifth.

Baker led the first 102 laps on the flat one-mile dirt track. Teammate Thompson arrived late and did not take a time trial. He was forced to start 23rd, but came charging through the pack to take the lead when Baker entered the pits to have fresh rubber placed on his Chrysler.

A miscue in the pits forced Thompson to make an extra pit stop late in the race, which dropped him to seventh in the final rundown.

Only one caution was waved. Blackie Pitt and Bob Duell crashed in the second lap.

Jim Reed finished 3rd in Syracuse 150.

Race No. 24

Thomas Continues Westward Round-up; Takes Merced

MERCED, CA (June 3) -- Herb Thomas made it three-for-four in the West Coast Grand Nationals by winning the 100-miler at the Merced Fairgrounds. It was the fourth win of the year and the 48th of his

career for the all-time NASCAR win leader.

Harold Hardesty finished second, with Jim Graham, Lloyd Dane and Eddie Pagan following in that order.

Thomas' victory in the Kiekhaefer Dodge was the 16th straight Grand National win for the Mercury Outboard team, a record that will probably never be approached. The Kiekhaefer team had not lost a race since March 18, a 100-miler at Wilson, NC. Ironically, that race was won by Herb Thomas when he was fielding his own Chevrolet.

Lucky Long wasn't so lucky in the 185th lap. His Chevrolet snapped an axle and flipped over. Al Pombo's Dodge left the race track and struck a utility pole. No injuries were reported.

Parnelli Jones started third in his Ford, but he lost a wheel while running with the leaders in the 181st lap. He was unable to get back in the running and had to settle for a 13th place finish. Jones won all of $60 for his efforts.

Grand National Race No. 24
200 Laps at Merced Fairgrounds
Merced, CA
100 Miles on Half-mile Dirt Track
June 3, 1956

Fin	St	No.	Driver	Team / Car	Laps	Money	Status
1	1	300B	Herb Thomas	Carl Kiekhaefer '56 Chrysler	200	$910	Running
2	5	52	Harold Hardesty	'56 Chevrolet	200	650	Running
3	8	30	Jim Graham	'56 Plymouth	200	495	Running
4	2	225	Lloyd Dane	'56 Mercury	198	375	Running
5	12	45	Eddie Pagan	Pagan '56 Ford	197	310	Running
6	10	88	John Kieper	Kieper '56 Olds	194	250	Running
7	20	56	Chuck Meekins	Jim Rush '56 Chevrolet	194	200	Running
8	7	43	Bob Ross	'56 Mercury	190	200	Running
9	27	25	Erick Erickson	Erickson '54 Buick	190	125	Running
10	11	34	Sherman Clark	Clark '55 Chevrolet	185	110	Running
11	17	188	Jim Blomgren	'56 Ford	183	100	Running
12	22	14	Bob Keefe	'56 Ford	183	100	Running
13	3	11	Parnelli Jones	Vel Miletich '56 Ford	181	60	Wheel
14	23	101	Lucky Long	'56 Chevrolet	180	50	Crash
15	19	20	Howard Phillippi	'55 Chevrolet	172	50	Running
16	16	9	Jim Cook	'56 Pontiac	168	50	Running
17	24	75	Bill Sullivan	'54 Ford	162	50	Running
18	25	47	Nick Larl	'56 Ford	155	50	Running
19	15	5	Clyde Palmer	'55 Mercury	149	50	Running
20	14	2	Al Pombo	'55 Dodge	122	50	Crash
21	21	352	Bob Fancy	'55 Chevrolet	91	---	Shocks
22	9	77	Gordy Haines	'56 Dodge	77	10	Heating
23	4	48	Bill Moore	Moore '56 Ford	66	30	Piston
24	6	00	Dick Getty	Betty Getty '56 Chevrolet	55	10	Heating
25	26	55	Don Hamilton	'56 Studebaker	53	---	Engine
26	18	12	John Lansaw	'56 Chevrolet	19	---	Radiator
27	13	551	Jack Richardson	'56 Pontiac	8	---	Piston
28	28	8	Owen Loggins	'54 Dodge	---	---	Rods

Time of Race: 2 hours, 6 minutes, 47 seconds
Average Speed: 47.325 mph
Pole Winner: Herb Thomas - 58.234 mph
Lap Leaders: - - - - - - - - - Herb Thomas   -200.
Cautions: Margin of Victory: Attendance:

Team owner Peter DePaolo greets Memphis-Arkansas Speedway winner Ralph Moody.

car and died of multiple injuries. He was competing in only his third Grand National event.

Officially, Moody was given credit for leading the final 15 laps in a race which saw five lead changes. Pat Kirkwood finished third, Tim Flock was fourth and Joe Eubanks fifth.

Moody, starting 23rd in the field of 29, averaged 74.313 mph after five caution flags interrupted the pace. His final margin of victory was 4.0 seconds.

Point leader Buck Baker finished ninth, 11 laps behind. A crowd of 15,000 was on hand at the high-banked 1.5-mile dirt oval.

Fonty Flock announced his retirement from stock car racing. The Decatur, GA vete-

Race No. 25

Ralph Moody Gets First Win; 2 Die at Memphis-Arkansas

LeHi, AR (June 10) -- In a 250-mile event at the Memphis-Arkansas Speedway -- rapidly becoming one of America's most dangerous high-banked ovals -- confusion and tragedy marred the running of the Grand National event.

Jim Paschal's Mercury had been flagged the winner, giving Mercury its second win of the season. However, five hours after he had gone home, Ralph Moody of Taunton, MA was given the nod by NASCAR officials.

Paschal had finished 54 seconds in front of Moody's Ford, but scorers allegedly missed one of Moody's laps. Paschal got credit for second.

Moody's victory, the second for Ford this season, ended the Carl Kiekhaefer's team streak of 16 straight Grand National wins. Herb Thomas' seventh place finish was the best effort for the Mercury Outboard team.

Moody's first win in big league competition came after two drivers had been killed. Clint McHugh, 28, of Biloxi, MS, was killed on Saturday while attempting to qualify for his first Grand National race. He had just been given the assignment of the Col. Ernest Woods' Oldsmobile.

McHugh's car flipped over the wall, throwing its driver out. The car rolled down a steep embankment and landed upside down in a lake.

Thomas "Cotton" Priddy, a 27 year-old driver out of Louisville, KY, sideswiped another car and flipped in the 39th lap of the race. He, too, was thrown from his

Grand National Race No. 25
167 Laps at Memphis-Arkansas Speedway
LeHi, Arkansas
250 Miles on 1.5-mile Dirt Track
June 10, 1956

Fin	St	No.	Driver	Team / Car	Laps	Money	Status
1	23	12	Ralph Moody	DePaolo Eng '56 Ford	167	$4,100	Running
2	9	75	Jim Paschal	Frank Hayworth '56 Mercury	167	2,100	Running
3	14	286	Pat Kirkwood	Jim Stephens '56 Pontiac	165	1,325	Running
4	4	11	Tim Flock	Mauri Rose Eng '56 Chevrolet	164	950	Running
5	7	82	Joe Eubanks	Satcher Motors '56 Ford	163	650	Running
6	8	42	Lee Petty	Petty Engineering '56 Dodge	163	600	Running
7	6	502	Herb Thomas	Carl Kiekhaefer '56 Dodge	162	350	Running
8	13	2	Gwyn Staley	Westmoreland '56 Chevrolet	159	300	Running
9	1	300	Buck Baker	Carl Kiekhaefer '56 Chrysler	156	300	Running
10	10	91	Jack Smith	'56 Chevrolet	156	150	Running
11	15	4	Bob Flock	Mauri Rose Eng '56 Chevrolet	154	125	Fuel Pmp
12	17	88	Banjo Matthews	Ernest Woods '56 Olds	149	200	Running
13	22	264	Johnny Allen	Spook Crawford '55 Plymouth	149	200	Running
14	20	291	C H Dingler	'56 Dodge	148	100	Running
15	29	52	Joe Guide, Jr	Sally Guide '54 Hudson	141	200	Running
16	26	1	Gene Goodman	'54 Olds	130	75	Running
17	19	205	Bill Osborne	'56 Ford	128	75	A Frame
18	27	48	Al Watkins	Don Holcomb '56 Ford	128	75	Running
19	2	300c	Speedy Thompson	Carl Kiekhaefer '56 Chrysler	115	125	Engine
20	3	3	Paul Goldsmith	Smokey Yunick '56 Chevrolet	115	100	Crash
21	5	22	Fireball Roberts	DePaolo Eng '56 Ford	88	50	Piston
22	28	59	Blackie Pitt	Brownie Pitt '56 Buick	60	50	A Frame
23	25	35	Joe Stewart	'55 Chrysler	57	50	Steering
24	21	16	Cotton Priddy	'56 Chevrolet	38	50	Crash
25	12	285	Don Carr	Jim Stephens '56 Pontiac	35	50	Crash
26	11	14	Billy Myers	Guy Wilson '56 Mercury	31	50	Hose
27	18	760	Harold Gibson	'56 Chevrolet	21	50	Engine
28	16	418	Sherman Utsman	'56 Chevrolet	17	50	Engine
29	24	21	Arnold Denley	'55 Studebaker	5	150	Shocks

Time of Race: 3 hours, 22 minutes, 15 seconds
Average Speed: 74.313 mph
Pole Winner: Buck Baker - 98.504 mph
Lap Leaders: Speedy Thompson 1-2, Buck Baker 3-89, Thompson 90-105, Jim Paschal 106-152, Ralph Moody 153-167.
Cautions: 5   Margin of Victory: 4.0 seconds   Attendance: 15,000

ran said his decision was "definite". It was brought on, he said, after losing his ride in Carl Kiekhaefer's Chryslers. "I always did say that when I left Kiekhaefer, I'd quit," said Flock, 35. "you step into one of his cars and you're almost a cinch. There I was on Saturday qualifying 15th in a car that wouldn't run."

Flock walked away from the Chevrolet he qualified 15th and brother Bob drove to an 11th place finish.

Fireball Roberts wound up fourth despite falling out with seven laps remaining. Fifth place went to Buck Baker whose car conked out 11 laps from the finish.

Thompson and Roberts battled in the early going, but Thompson was able to start pulling away near the quarter-mark in the race. When Roberts fell out late in the race, all Thompson had to worry about was keeping the wheels on his Chrysler.

Two caution flags for six laps kept the winner's average speed down to 56.022 mph. A crowd of 7,800 was on hand to view the action.

Race No. 26

Car-Killing Charlotte 100 Goes to Thompson

CHARLOTTE, NC (June 15) -- Speedy Thompson took the lead in the 28th lap and sped to victory in the 100-mile Grand National event at the Southern States Fairgrounds. It was Thompson's fifth win of the year.

Nineteen cars started the 200 lapper on the half-mile dirt track, but only four were running at the end. Curtis Turner finished second, five laps behind Thompson. Lee Petty was third, also five laps back. Pole sitter

Race No. 27

Two in Row for Thompson; 30 of 37 for Kiekhaefer

ROCHESTER, NY (June 22) -- Speedy Thompson skimmed past Jim Paschal in the 118th lap and went on to give the Carl Kiekhaefer team its 30th victory in the last 37 Grand National races in the 100-miler at the Monroe County Fairgrounds.

Grand National Race No. 26
200 Laps at Southern States Fairgrounds
Charlotte, NC
100 Miles on Half-mile Dirt Track
June 15, 1956

Fin	St	No.	Driver	Team / Car	Laps	Money	Status
1	2	300c	Speedy Thompson	Carl Kiekhaefer '56 Chrysler	200	$650	Running
2	8	99	Curtis Turner	Schwam Motors '56 Ford	195	525	Running
3	7	42	Lee Petty	Petty Engineering '56 Dodge	195	400	Running
4	1	22	Fireball Roberts	DePaolo Eng '56 Ford	193	320	Rear end
5	5	300	Buck Baker	Carl Kiekhaefer '56 Chrysler	189	290	Quit
6	10	500B	Herb Thomas	Carl Kiekhaefer '56 Dodge	186	250	Fuel
7	6	11	Tim Flock	Mauri Rose '56 Chevrolet	180	300	Engine
8	3	12	Ralph Moody	DePaolo Eng '56 Ford	150	150	Crash
9	19	203	Pete Yow	Strickland Motors '56 Buick	150	100	Carb
10	17	34A	Richard Riley	'56 Olds	141	100	Running
11	18	94	Ed Cole	'56 Mercury	134	100	Heating
12	11	75	Jim Paschal	Frank Hayworth '56 Mercury	115	100	Oil Pres
13	4	14	Billy Myers	Guy Wilson '56 Mercury	106	100	Piston
14	12	55	Junior Johnson	Brushy Mt Mtrs '56 Pontiac	69	100	Clutch
15	15	9	Joe Weatherly	Schwam Motors '56 Ford	66	100	Rear End
16	14	82	Joe Eubanks	Satcher Motors '56 Ford	30	100	Distrib
17	16	62	Bobby Waddell	'56 Chevrolet	30	100	Brakes
18	9	271	Billy Carden	'56 Mercury	24	100	Engine
19	13	34	Dick Beaty	Beaty '56 Ford	16	50	Spindle

Time of Race: 1 hour, 47 minutes, 06 seconds
Average Speed: 56.022 mph
Pole Winner: Fireball Roberts - 59.661 mph
Lap Leaders: Speedy Thompson 1, Fireball Roberts 2-27, Thompson 28-200.
Cautions: 2 for 6 laps   Margin of Victory: 5 laps plus   Attendance: 7,800

Grand National Race No. 27
200 Laps at Monroe County Fairgrounds
Rochester, NY
100 Miles on Half-mile Dirt Track
June 22, 1956

Fin	St	No.	Driver	Team / Car	Laps	Money	Status
1	11	300c	Speedy Thompson	Carl Kiekhaefer '56 Chrysler	200	$850	Running
2	1	75	Jim Paschal	Frank Hayworth '56 Mercury	199	625	Running
3	8	500B	Herb Thomas	Carl Kiekhaefer '56 Dodge	199	450	Running
4	6	300	Buck Baker	Carl Kiekhaefer '56 Chrysler	197	350	Running
5	2	95	Bob Duell	Julian Buesink '56 Ford	192	310	Running
6	18	83	Lennie Page	'55 Chevrolet	180	250	Running
7	16	77	Walt Schubert	Bob Bunselmeyer '55 Ford	179	200	Running
8	20	4	Bobby Keck	'56 Chevrolet	171	150	Running
9	15	179	John Lindsay	'55 Chevrolet	171	100	Running
10	17	1	Bill McGraw	'56 Ford	170	100	Running
11	14	3	Al White	'55 Ford	168	100	Clutch
12	21	4-11	Joe Sykes	'55 Chevrolet	166	100	Running
13	10	19	Harvey Henderson	'56 Ford	151	100	Running
14	7	36	Ken Johnson	'56 Ford	127	100	Springs
15	9	41	Billy Rafter	Rafter '56 Dodge	91	100	Fuel Pmp
16	13	66	Larry Marx	'56 Ford	78	100	RF Hub
17	7	40	Chuck Mahoney	'56 Dodge	57	100	Piston
18	3	14	Billy Myers	Guy Wilson '56 Mercury	42	100	Radiator
19	19	31	Dick Denise	'55 Chevrolet	41	50	Bearing
20	20	10	Nolan Swift	'56 Plymouth	37	50	Fuel Pmp
21	4	42	Lee Petty	Petty Engineering '56 Dodge	25	---	Bearing

Time of Race: 1 hour, 44 minutes, 44 seconds
Average Speed: 57.288 mph
Pole Winner: Jim Paschal - 57.434 mph
Lap Leaders: Jim Paschal 1-39, Speedy Thompson 40-103, Paschal 104-117, Thompson 118-200.
Cautions: 1 for 7 laps   Margin of Victory: 1 lap plus   Attendance: 6,000

Pole sitter Paschal, who led twice for 53 laps, finished in second place. Herb Thomas was third and Buck Baker fourth, both driving Kiekhaefer Outboard entries. Fifth place went to Bob Duell.

Duell, driving a Julian Buesink Ford, qualified a surprising second and ran well the entire distance.

Top contender Lee Petty finished last in the 21 car field. Billy Myers, another front runner, fell out after 42 laps. He finished 18th.

The caution flag was out once for seven laps when Ken Johnson ditched his Ford into a gully. He was dredged up and carried on to a 14th place finish.

Thompson averaged 57.288 mph before a crowd of 6,000.

Race No. 28

Kieper's Olds
Potent at Portland

PORTLAND, OR (June 24) -- John Kieper pushed his Oldsmobile across the finish line first and won the 100-miler at Portland Speedway. Kieper became the ninth different winner in the 1956 Grand National season.

Clyde Palmer wound up second in a Dodge. Lou

Sherman, Harold Beal and Ed Negre, all one lap down, filled positions three through five.

Herb Thomas posted the fastest lap in qualifications, but started last in the 20-car field on the inverted start. The Dodge driver finished 11th, four laps down as he was foiled by unscheduled pit stops.

Don Porter started on the pole by virtue of having the slowest time -- and he finished last. An axle bearing burned out on his Studebaker after 38 laps.

Kieper averaged 62.586 mph for his first Grand National win, which came on his seventh start.

Race No. 29

Petty Staves Off Paschal in Close Weaverville Finish

WEAVERVILLE, NC (July 1) -- Lee Petty took the lead late in the race and nosed out Jim Paschal by a single car length to win the 100-miler at Asheville-Weaverville Speedway.

It was Petty's first win of the year and the 25th of his eight year career. He is the only driver who has won in each of the first eight years of Grand National racing.

Paschal, who started beside Petty in the sixth row, made a stab to get past his friendly rival in the final lap, but came up short. Joe Eubanks was third, three laps off the pace. Gwyn Staley came in fourth and Herb Thomas fifth.

Point leader Buck Baker lost more ground in the point race. His Chrysler broke a spindle in the 126th lap,

Grand National Race No. 28
200 Laps at Portland Speedway
Portland, OR
100 Miles on Half-mile Paved Track
June 24, 1956

Fin	St	No.	Driver	Team / Car	Laps	Money	Status
1	12	98	John Kieper	Kieper '55 Olds	200	$950	Running
2	18	1C	Clyde Palmer	'56 Dodge	200	665	Running
3	14	56	Lou Sherman	Jim Rush '56 Mercury	199	500	Running
4	17	50	Harold Beal	'56 Ford	199	395	Running
5	2	6	Ed Negre	'54 Olds	199	310	Running
6	11	52	Harold Hardesty	'56 Chevrolet	198	250	Running
7	16	1	Art Watts	'55 Dodge	197	200	Running
8	4	225	Lloyd Dane	'56 Mercury	197	150	Running
9	19	11	Curly Barker	'56 Chevrolet	197	135	Running
10	14	88	Bill Hyde	'56 Olds	197	110	Running
11	20	300B	Herb Thomas	Carl Kiekhaefer '56 Chrysler	196	120	Running
12	10	45	Eddie Pagan	Pagan '56 Ford	194	100	Running
13	6	14	Bob Keefe	'56 Ford	187	50	Running
14	5	71	Ted Sweeney	'56 Olds	184	50	Running
15	9	47	Bob Haveman	'56 Pontiac	180	50	Running
16	8	77	Gordy Haines	'56 Dodge	170	50	Piston
17	13	27	Bud Emra	'56 Ford	116	50	RR Axle
18	7	15	Royce Hagerty	'56 Dodge	97	50	O-drive
19	3	26	Fred Hunt	'55 Chevrolet	39	50	RR Axle
20	1	78	Don Porter	'55 Studebaker	38	50	Axle

Time of Race: 1 hour, 35 minutes, 52 seconds
Average Speed: 62.586 mph
Fastest Qualifier: Herb Thomas 65.934 mph
Lap Leaders: - - - - - - - - John Kieper -200.
Cautions: Margin of Victory: Attendance:

Fireball Roberts and Speedy Thompson get the green flag at Asheville-Weaverville Speedway.

Lee Petty #42 leads Jim Paschal #75 by a single car length at finish of 100-miler at Asheville-Weaverville.

leaving him with a 21st place finish in the field of 29.

Pole sitter Fireball Roberts fell out on lap 142 when his Ford shredded a left rear tire.

A crowd of 8,000 watched Petty win at an average speed of 56.435 mph.

Grand National Race No. 29
200 Laps at Asheville-Weaverville Speedway
Weaverville, NC
100 Miles on Half-mile Dirt Track
July 1, 1956

Fin	St	No.	Driver	Team / Car	Lasp	Money	Status
1	11	42	Lee Petty	Petty Engineering '56 Dodge	200	$850	Running
2	12	75	Jim Paschal	Frank Hayworth '56 Mercury	200	625	Running
3	4	82	Joe Eubanks	Satcher Motors '56 Ford	197	450	Running
4	7	2	Gwyn Staley	Westmoreland '56 Chevrolet	194	350	Running
5	9	300B	Herb Thomas	Carl Kiekhaefer '56 Chrysler	193	310	Running
6	6	500B	Frank Mundy	Carl Kiakhaefer '56 Dodge	193	250	Running
7	14	41	Billy Rafter	Rafter '56 Dodge	187	200	Running
8	16	34	Dick Beaty	Beaty '56 Ford	186	150	Running
9	18	58	Bill Bowman	'56 Plymouth	181	100	Running
10	22	48	Al Watkins	Don Holcomb '56 Ford	179	100	Running
11	13	100	Herb Estes	Dave Everett '56 Chevrolet	178	100	Running
12	27	264	Johnny Allen	Spook Crawford '56 Plymouth	172	100	Running
13	25	96	Bobby Keck	'56 Chevrolet	170	100	Running
14	21	19	Harvey Henderson	'56 Ford	168	100	Engine
15	29	114	Joe McGraw	'56 Ford	163	100	Running
16	19	40	Chuck Mahoney	'56 Chevrolet	162	100	Engine
17	23	209	Billy Carden	'56 Plymouth	147	100	Heating
18	1	22	Fireball Roberts	DePaolo Eng '56 Ford	142	100	Tire
19	10	X	Rex White	Max Welborn '56 Chevrolet	139	50	A Frame
20	15	55	Junior Johnson	Brushy Mtn Mtr '56 Pontiac	137	50	Windshld
21	5	300	Buck Baker	Kiekhaefer '56 Chrysler	126	---	Spindle
22	8	14	Billy Myers	Guy Wilson '56 Mercury	102	---	Crash
23	3	12	Ralph Moody	DePaolo Eng '56 Ford	85	---	Bearing
24	20	418	Sherman Utsman	'56 Chevrolet	80	---	Heating
25	17	56	Ed Massey	'56 Ford	76	---	Heating
26	2	300c	Speedy Thompson	Carl Kiekhaefer '56 Chrysler	71	---	Wheel
27	24	760	Brownie King	'56 Chevrolet	54	---	Steering
28	28	59	Blackie Pitte	Brownie Pitt '56 Plymouth	36	---	Crash
29	26	91	Jack Smith	'56 Chevrolet	5	---	Carb

Time of Racew: 1 hour, 46 minutes, 19 seconds
Average Speed: 56.435 mph
Pole Winner: Fireball Roberts - 72.260 mph
Lap Leaders: - - - - - - - - - Lee Petty -200.
Cautions: Margin of Victory: 1 car length   Attendance: 8,000

Grand National Race No. 30
250 Laps at Raleigh Speedway
Raleigh, NC
"Raleigh 250"
250 Miles on 1-mile Paved Track
July 4, 1956

Fin	St	No.	Driver	Team / Car	Laps	Money	Status
1	32	22	Fireball Roberts	DePaolo Eng '56 Ford	250	$3,000	Running
2	2	500	Speedy Thompson	Carl Kiekhaefer '56 Dodge	248	2,000	Running
3	27	502	Frank Mundy	Carl Kiekhaefer '56 Dodge	247	1,275	Running
4	3	92	Herb Thomas	Thomas '56 Chevrolet	246	925	Running
5	10	11	Tim Flock	Mauri Rose Eng '56 Chevrolet	243	750	Running
6	4	3	Paul Goldsmith	Smokey Yunick '56 Chevrolet	242	650	Running
7	30	99	Marvin Panch	Tom Harbison '56 Ford	241	550	Running
8	18	5	Bill Walker	'56 Chevrolet	238	500	Running
9	25	X	Rex White	Max Welborn '56 Chevrolet	237	400	Running
10	29	91	Jack Smith	'56 Chevrolet	236	375	Running
11	28	300c	Buck Baker	Kiekhaefer '56 Chrysler	234	300	Running
12	6	75	Jim Paschal	Frank Hayworth '56 Mercury	231	275	Running
13	20	113	Emanuel Zervakis	'56 Chevrolet	222	225	Running
14	14	9	Billy Carden	Bishop Bros. '56 Ford	217	225	Running
15	13	240	Rat Garner	'56 Ford	216	225	Running
16	36	94	Ed Cole	'56 Mercury	216	100	Running
17	15	48	Al Watkins	Don Holcomb '56 Ford	213	100	Running
18	16	31	Bill Champion	Whitford Bros '56 Ford	212	100	Running
19	35	96	Bob Keck	'56 Chevrolet	206	100	Running
20	12	286	Pat Kirkwood	Jim Stephens '56 Pontiac	203	150	Oil Pres
21	19	18	Arden Mounts	Mounts '56 Pontiac	195	100	Running
22	5	264	Johnny Allen	Spook Crawford '56 Plymouth	181	150	Heating
23	8	2	Gwyn Staley	Westmoreland '56 Chevrolet	146	100	Bearing
24	34	640	Kenneth Love	'55 Ford	144	100	RF Hub
25	7	82	Joe Eubanks	Satcher Motors '56 Ford	136	150	Engine
26	31	14	Billy Myers	Guy Wilson '56 Mercury	91	100	Engine
27	17	88	Ralph Liguori	Ernest Woods '56 Olds	90	150	Engine
28	9	12	Ralph Moody	DePaolo Eng '56 Ford	82	100	Lifter
29	22	131	Johnny Dodson	Dodson '56 Chevrolet	77	100	Heating
30	21	95	Bob Duell	Julian Buesink '56 Ford	63	100	Bearing
31	26	3A	Bud Geiselman	'55 Chevrolet	61	---	Engine
32	11	418	Sherman Utsman	'56 Chevrolet	47	---	Engine
33	33	34	Dick Beaty	Beaty '56 Ford	45	---	Engine
34	24	59	Blackie Pitt	Brownie Pitt '56 Plymouth	43	---	Engine
35	23	29	Pat Grogan	'56 Mercury	21	---	LR Axle
36	1	42	Lee Petty	Petty Engineering '56 Dodge	9	50	Oil Pres

Time of Race: 3 hours, 7 minutes, 55 seconds
Average Speed: 79.822 mph
Pole Winner: Lee Petty - 82.587 mph
Lap Leaders: Lee Petty 1-5, Ralph Moody 6-8, Petty 9, Joe Eubanks 10-13,
   Fireball Roberts 14-64, Buck Baker 65-87, Roberts 88-161,
   Speedy Thompson 162-174, Roberts 175-250.
Cautions: 1   Margin of Victory: 2 laps, 10 seconds   Attendance: 13,600

Race No. 30
Roberts Claims First Superspeedway Win at Raleigh

RALEIGH, NC (July 4) -- Fireball Roberts of Daytona Beach, FL scored his first superspeedway victory in the Independence Day 250-miler at the Raleigh Speedway. It was also Roberts' first Grand National win since August 13, 1950, when he won at Hillsboro.

Speedy Thompson finished two laps behind to claim runner-up honors. Apparently, that was not good

Herb Thomas #92 takes the inside groove to get around Arden Mounts #18 during Raleigh 250. Thomas finished 4th; Mounts 21st.

Fireball Roberts gave chase to Petty most of the way, but had to settle for second place. Marvin Panch was third, Bill Amick fourth and Joe Eubanks fifth.

Buck Baker padded his point lead despite leaving the race after 129 laps. Herb Thomas crashed his Kiekhaefer Dodge in the 18th lap and wound up 17th in the 18 car field.

After the race, Thomas announced he was going back to his own operation. He became the second star driver to quit the Kiekhaefer team. Tim Flock pulled the vanishing act in April.

Flock also had a bout with the retaining wall in the 147th lap. His Chevrolet had to be parked for the rest of the day.

Average speed for the race, which had only seven finishers, was 50.483 mph.

enough for car owner Carl Kiekhaefer, who protested the weight of the fly wheel on Roberts' Ford.

The Speedway did not have a weigh scale to handle such matters, so the fly wheel was weighed at a local fish market. It proved to be within the specifications and was a 'stock' part, so Roberts' victory was upheld.

Frank Mundy finished in third place. Herb Thomas, driving his own Chevrolet was fourth and Tim Flock fifth.

Prior to race time, rumors were flying that a split between Thomas and Kiekhaefer was imminent. The fact that Thomas mounted his own car apparently meant the rumors were true.

Lee Petty started on the pole but failed to lead a lap. The Randleman speedster fell out on lap nine with no oil pressure in his Dodge.

Frank Mundy led the first 13 laps before Roberts took over. Roberts led on three occasions for a total of 201 laps en route to the $3,000 pay-off.

An audience of 13,600 watched Roberts average 79.822 mph as only one caution flag slowed the field.

Point leader Buck Baker finished 11th and saw his lead in the standings drop to 396 points over Thomas.

Grand National Race No. 31
200 Laps at Piedmont Interstate Fairgrounds
Spartanburg, SC
100 Miles on Half-mile Dirt Track
July 7, 1956

Fin	St	No.	Driver	Team / Car	Laps	Money	Status
1	8	42	Lee Petty	Petty Engineering '56 Dodge	200	$850	Running
2	1	22	Fireball Roberts	DePaolo Eng '56 Ford	200	625	Running
3	7	99	Marvin Panch	Tom Harbison '56 Ford	198	450	Running
4	13	66	Bill Amick	DePaolo Eng '56 Ford	189	350	Running
5	11	82	Joe Eulbanks	Satcher Motors '56 Ford	186	310	Drv Shft
6	6	14	Billy Myers	Guy Wilson '56 Mercury	171	250	Running
7	4	300c	Speedy Thompson	Carl Kiekhaefer '56 Chrysler	168	300	Crash
8	14	34	Dick Beaty	Beaty '56 Ford	156	150	Running
9	18	1	Bennie Rakestraw	H. Rakestraw '56 Ford	156	100	Running
10	10	11	Tim Flock	Mauri Rose Eng '56 Chevrolet	145	100	Crash
11	3	12	Ralph Moody	DePaolo Eng '56 Ford	138	100	Oil Line
12	17	760	Brownie King	'56 Chrysler	131	100	Crash
13	2	300	Buck Baker	Carl Kiekhaefer '56 Chrysler	129	100	Steering
14	16	48	Al Watkins	Don Holcomb '56 Ford	64	100	Valve
15	15	264	Johnny Allen	Spook Crawford '56 Plymouth	47	100	Drv Shaft
16	12	999	Wilbur Rakestraw	B.J. Jones '56 Ford	29	100	RR Hub
17	6	500d	Herb Thomas	Carl Kiekhaefer '56 Dodge	18	100	Crash
18	9	2	Gwyn Staley	Westmoreland '56 Chevrolet	18	100	Carb

Time of Race: 1 hour, 58 minutes, 51 seconds
Average Speed: 50.483 mph
Pole Winner: Fireball Roberts - 58.900 mph
Lap Leaders: - - - - - - - - - - Lee Petty   -200.
Cautions: Margin of Victory: Attendance:

Race No. 31

Rejuvenated Petty Captures Spartanburg 100

SPARTANBURG, SC (July 7) -- Lee Petty, born again front runner, grabbed his second win of the season in the 100-mile Grand National race at the Piedmont Interstate Fairgrounds.

Race No. 32

Dane Dashes to Victory at Sacramento

SACRAMENTO, CA (July 8) -- Lloyd Dane of Downey, CA drove his Mercury to a narrow win in the

100-miler at the Sacramento Fairgrounds. It was the first win on the Grand National circuit for Dane.

Chuck Meekins finished a close second in a Chevrolet. John Kieper was third, Gordon Haines fourth and Clyde Palmer fifth.

Dane's triumph came in his 22nd Grand National start.

Jim Graham, who started fourth, crashed hard in the fourth lap. The young driver suffered a fractured knee and was transported to Merritt Hospital in satisfactory condition.

Dane averaged 74.074 mph on the flat one-mile dirt track.

event at Soldier Field in Chicago.

It was Roberts' second win of the year and, more surprisingly, it was Carl Kiekhaefer's fifth consecutive loss.

Jim Paschal finished second with Ralph Moody third. Ford Motor Company products celebrated as Roberts and Moody were in Fords and Paschal was wheeling a Mercury. It was Ford's first 1-2-3 finish of the year.

Kiekhaefer cars took the next three spots. Speedy Thompson, Frank Mundy and Buck Baker finished in that order.

Herb Thomas crashed his Chevrolet when the brakes went out. Bill Vesler was the victim of a similar incident.

Pole sitter Billy Myers, who earned the first pole slot of his brief career, fell out after 140 laps when he lost his brakes. In all, seven cars went to the sidelines with brake related problems.

Roberts averaged 61.037 mph.

Baker left Chicago with a 224 point lead over Thomas in the Grand National point standings.

Grand National Race No. 32
100 Laps at Sacramento Fairgrounds
Sacramento, CA
100 Miles on 1-mile Dirt Track
July 8, 1956

Fin	St	No.	Driver	Team / Car	Laps	Money	Status
1	15	225	Lloyd Dane	'56 Mercury	100	$1,100	Running
2	14	56	Chuck Meekins	Jim Rush '56 Chevrolet	100	700	Running
3	3	88	Johnny Kieper	Kieper '56 Olds	100	475	Running
4	7	77	Gordon Haines	'56 Dodge	100	365	Running
5	10	1	Clyde Palmer	'56 Dodge	99	310	Running
6	9	52	Harold Hardesty	'56 Chevrolet	99	250	Running
7	5	14	Bob Keefe	'56 Ford	99	200	Running
8	2	27	Bob Havemann	'56 Pontiac	99	150	Running
9	8	561	Bill Moore	Moore '56 Pontiac	99	100	Running
10	11	180	Jim Blomgren	'56 Ford	98	100	Running
11	6	9	Jim Cook	Art Krebs '56 Pontiac	97	75	Running
12	13	33	Carl Hamill	'56 Chevrolet	95	60	Running
13	17	98	Chet Thomson	'56 Mercury	94	50	Running
14	21	55	Eddie Skinner	'54 Olds	92	50	Running
15	18	8	Jess Nelson	'54 Dodge	88	50	Running
16	19	78	Don Porter	'55 Studebaker	88	50	Running
17	12	26	Fred Hunt	'55 Chevrolet	79	50	Trans
18	1	45	Eddie Pagan	Pagan '56 Ford	31	50	Heating
19	16	34	Sherman Clark	Clark '55 Chevrolet	8	50	Crash
20	20	41	Ernie Young	Walt Palozi '56 Pontiac	2	50	Piston
21	4	30	Jim Graham	'56 Plymouth	---	---	Crash

Tim of Race: 1 hour, 21 minutes
Average Speed: 74.074 mph
Pole Winner: Eddie Pagan - 76.612 mph
Lap Leaders: - - - - - - - - - Lloyd Dane -100.
Cautions: Margin of Victory: Attendance:

Race No. 33

Roberts Marches to Soldier Field Victory

CHICAGO, IL (July 21) -- Fireball Roberts beat back a stellar field and dodged water puddles left by intermittent rain to win the 100-mile Grand National

---

Grand National Race No. 33
200 Laps at Soldier Field
Chicago, IL
100 Miles on Half-mile Paved Track
July 21, 1956

Fin	St	No.	Driver	Team / Car	Laps	Money	Status
1	3	22	Fireball Roberts	DePaolo Eng '56 Ford	200	$850	Running
2	14	75	Jim Paschal	Frank Hayworth '56 Mercury	200	625	Running
3	4	12	Ralph Moody	DePaolo Eng '56 Ford	200	450	Running
4	12	500	Speedy Thompson	Carl Kiekhaefer '56 Dodge	200	350	Running
5	8	500B	Frank Mundy	Carl Kiekhaefer '56 Dodge	200	310	Running
6	9	502	Buck Baker	Carl Kiekhaefer '56 Dodge	199	250	Running
7	13	31	Bill Champion	Whitford Bros '56 Ford	199	200	Running
8	6	32	Paul Goldsmith	Smokey Yunick '56 Chevrolet	198	150	Running
9	7	719	Joy Fair	'56 Dodge	192	100	Running
10	10	42	Lee Petty	Petty Engineering '56 Dodge	190	100	Running
11	20	7	Bob Esposito	'55 Olds	189	100	Running
12	23	33	Frank Edwards	'56 Chevrolet	182	100	Running
13	22	48	Bill Massey	'56 Ford	176	100	Running
14	21	38	Chuck Mesler	'56 Dodge	175	100	Running
15	15	66	Al Watkins	'56 Ford	164	100	Running
16	24	2	Sal Tovella	'56 Ford	142	100	Brakes
17	1	14	Billy Myers	Guy Wilson '56 Mercury	140	100	Brakes
18	2	92	Herb Thomas	Thomas '56 Chevrolet	98	150	Crash
19	17	204	Darvin Randahl	Randahl '56 Ford	86	50	Brakes
20	11	150	Fred Lorenzen	'56 Chevrolet	85	50	Brakes
21	16	40	Bob Chauncey	'56 Pontiac	78	50	Spindle
22	5	3	Tom Pistone	'56 Chevrolet	50	50	Brakes
23	19	44	Bill Vesler	'55 Chevrolet	50	41	Crash
24	18	165	Kenny Paulson	'55 Chevrolet	40	50	Engine
25	25	37	Ray Crowley	'56 Plymouth	36	100	Carb

Time of Race: 1 hour, 38 minutes, 18 seconds
Average Speed: 61.037 mph
Pole Winner: Billy Myers
Lap Leaders: - - - - - - - - - Fireball Roberts -200.
Cautions: Margin of Victory: Attendance:

Race No. 34

Shelby Speedfest to Speedy Thompson

SHELBY, NC (July 27) -- Speedy Thompson got back on the winning track by driving his Kiekhaefer Outboards Dodge to victory in the 100.5-mile race at the Cleveland County Fairgrounds. It was Thompson's seventh win of the year.

Ralph Moody finished second in the race, which actually ran 201 laps. Scorers were not sure which lap they were on mid-way through the race, so they ran an extra lap just to be sure.

Billy Myers came in third, Fireball Roberts was fourth and Buck Baker fifth.

Harold Kite, winner of the 1950 Daytona Beach race who has been in retirement for several years, returned and finished 11th in a Ford. He was 23 laps behind.

Thompson averaged 53.699 mph for his 11th career win.

Race No. 35

Panch's Ford First In Montgomery 100

MONTGOMERY, AL (July 29) -- Marvin Panch started on the pole and won the 100-mile Grand National race at Montgomery Speedway. It was Ford's third win in the last six races, indicating that the Pete DePaolo led team is beginning to jell together.

Marvin Panch

Buck Baker finished second in a Chrysler and Bill Amick was third. Speedy Thompson and Lee Petty rounded out the top five.

Fireball Roberts was running with the leaders, but blew a tire with 27 laps left. The Daytona Beach leadfoot was one of only three drivers to fall out of the race. Only 14 cars started.

Panch, an Oakland, CA native, scored his initial win in his 35th Grand National start, averaging 67.252 mph.

Herb Thomas finished sixth and fell 280 points behind Baker in the championship point standings.

Grand National Race No. 34
200 Laps at Cleveland County Fairgrounds
Shelby, NC
100 Miles on Half-mile Dirt Track
July 27, 1956

Fin	St	No.	Driver	Team / Car	Laps	Money	Status
1	2	500	Speedy Thompson	Carl Kiekhaefer '56 Dodge	201	$950	Running
2	1	12	Ralph Moody	DePaolo Eng '58 Ford	201	675	Running
3	9	14	Billy Myers	Guy Wilson '56 Mercury	200	475	Running
4	2	22	Fireball Roberts	DePaolo Eng '56 Ford	200	365	Running
5	10	500B	Buck Baker	Carl Kiekhaefer '56 Dodge	197	320	Running
6	7	X	Rex White	Max Welborn '56 Chevrolet	195	250	Running
7	4	2	Gwyn Staley	Westmoreland '56 Chevrolet	191	200	Running
8	5	92	Herb Thomas	Thomas '56 Chevrolet	189	150	Running
9	11	42	Lee Petty	Petty Engineering '56 Dodge	188	100	Running
10	14	131	Johnny Dodson	Dodson '56 Chevrolet	178	100	Running
11	13	66	Harold Kite	'56 Ford	178	110	Running
12	16	264	Johnny Allen	Spook Crawford '56 Plymouth	153	100	Axle
13	12	75	Jim Paschal	Frank Hayworth '56 Mercury	73	100	Radiator
14	6	31	Bill Champion	Whitford Bros '56 Ford	69	100	Shocks
15	15	59	Blackie Pitt	Brownie Pitt '56 Plymouth	21	100	Fan Belt
16	17	271	Billy Carden	'56 Mercury	13	100	RF Hub
17	8	82	Joe Eubanks	Satcher Motors '56 Ford	0	100	Rear End

Time of Race: 1 hour, 51 minutes, 44 seconds
Average Speed: 53.699 mph
Pole Winner: Ralph Moody - 55.658 mph
Lap Leaders: - - - - - - - - - Speedy Thompson - 201.
Cautions: Margin of Victory: Attendance:

Grand National Race No. 35
200 Laps at Montgomery Speedway
Montgomery, AL
100 Miles on Half-mile Paved Track
July 29, 1956

Fin	St	No.	Driver	Team / Car	Laps	Money	Status
1	1	98	Marvin Panch	Tom Harbison '56 Ford	200	$950	Running
2	7	300	Buck Baker	Carl Kiekhaefer '56 Chrysler	199	675	Running
3	3	97	Bill Amick	DePaolo Eng '56 Ford	197	475	Running
4	4	500	Speedy Thompson	Carl Kiekhaefer '56 Dodge	197	365	Running
5	5	42	Lee Petty	Petty Engineering '56 Dodge	195	320	Running
6	2	92	Herb Thomas	Thomas '56 Chevrolet	192	250	Running
7	9	91	Jack Smith	'56 Chevrolet	192	200	Running
8	8	12	Ralph Moody	DePaolo Eng '56 Ford	185	150	Running
9	12	48	Al Watkins	Don Holcomb '56 Ford	176	100	Running
10	6	22	Fireball Roberts	DePaolo Eng '56 Ford	172	100	Tire
11	13	20	Jack Hatcher	'56 Ford	172	100	Running
12	14	40	Bob Slensey	'56 Ford	117	100	Running
13	10	66	Billy Carden	'56 Ford	43	100	Bearing
14	11	291	C H Dingler	'56 Dodge	16	100	Bearing

Time of Race: 1 hour, 29 minutes, 13 seconds
Average Speed: 67.252 mph
Pole Winner: Marvin Panch - 69.444 mph
Lap Leaders: - - - - - - - - - Marvin Panch - 200.
Cautions: Margin of Victory: 1 lap plus   Attendance:

Grand National Race No. 36
200 Laps at Oklahoma State
Fairgrounds
Oklahoma City, OK
100 Miles on Half-mile Dirt Track
August 3, 1956

Fin	St	No.	Driver	Team / Car	Laps	Money	Status
1	8	75	Jim Paschal	Frank Hayworth '56 Mercury	200	$850	Running
2	3	12	Ralph Moody	DePaolo Eng '56 Ford	200	625	Running
3	5	22	Fireball Roberts	DePaolo Eng '56 Ford	198	450	Running
4	4	92	Herb Thomas	Thomas '56 Chevrolet	196	350	Running
5	2	42	Lee Petty	Petty Engineering '56 Dodge	193	310	Diff
6	9	551	Bill Moore	Moore '56 Pontiac	190	250	Running
7	11	264	Johnny Allen	Spook Crawford '56 Ford	189	200	Running
8	10	7	Angie Howerton	'56 Chevrolet	181	150	Running
9	6	300	Buck Baker	Carl Kiekhaefer '56 Chrysler	173	100	Coil
10	12	59	Blackie Pitt	Brownie Pitt '56 Ford	100	100	Fuel Pmp
11	1	500	Speedy Thompson	Carl Kiekhaefer '56 Dodge	25	100	Engine
12	7	88	Jack Zink	Zink '56 Pontiac	10	100	Handling

Time of Race: 1 hour, 39 minutes, 50 seconds
Average Speed: 60.100 mph
Pole Position: Speedy Thompson - 64.655 mph
Lap Leaders: Speedy Thompson 1-25, Lee Petty 26-193, Jim Paschal 194-200.
Cautions: None   Margin of Victory: 1/4 lap   Attendance: 7,500

Race No. 36

Petty Dropout Hands
Oklahoma Win to Paschal

OKLAHOMA CITY, OK (Aug. 3) -- Jim Paschal shook the bridesmaid role and took his first win of the season in the 100-miler at the Oklahoma State Fairgrounds.

The 29 year-old High Point, NC driver took the lead in the 194th lap when Lee Petty dropped out with a differential problem. Petty had led from the 26th lap. His 193 laps got him fifth place in the final order.

Ralph Moody came in second, a quarter lap behind Paschal. Fireball Roberts was third with Herb Thomas fourth. Point leader Buck Baker finished ninth.

A crowd of 7,500 watched the caution-free event.

Paschal averaged 60.100 mph in his first win of the season. He has finished second six times.

Race No. 37

Flock's Comeback Nets
Victory at Road America

ELKHART LAKE, WI (Aug. 12) -- On a rainy afternoon in Wisconsin, Tim Flock got sweet revenge by taking first place in the 258.3-mile event at Road America. It was Flock's first win since leaving the Carl Kiekhaefer team in April.

Flock started sixth and led in the early stages. After dropping back in the field during the middle stages, Flock came on strong and moved into second place just past the half-way point. When leader Speedy Thompson retired to the garage area with a blown engine in his Dodge, Flock was home free.

It ws the 39th career Grand National win for Flock, who finished 17 seconds ahead of runner-up Billy Myers. Both drove Mercurys from the Bill Stroppe garage.

Fireball Roberts came from 17th starting spot to nail down third place. Paul Goldsmith was fourth and Joe Eubanks fifth.

Herb Thomas came in sixth and moved to within 200 points of standings leader Buck Baker, who wound up eighth.

Buck Baker and Thompson held the hopes for the Kiekhaefer groomed cars, and both led at various stages. In an unusual ruling, cars were limited to 10 gallons of fuel at the start. Flock made two pit stops en route to the $2,950 pay-off.

Several of the oval track specialists had problems negotiating the slick, twisting course. Curtis Turner skidded off the course early and landed on top of some hay

Joe Weatherly #9 and Curtis Turner, teammates on the factory Ford team, run close at Road America.

Tim Flock's Mercury glides over the wet surface en route to victory at Road America.

Junior Johnson was added to the Peter DePaolo Engineering factory Ford team. The Ronda, NC charger qualified third, but went only one lap before clutch failure put him out.

Red Amick, also in a DePaolo Ford, suffered a similar fate after just 10 laps.

A crowd of 10,000 braved the terrible weather to watch Flock average 73.858 mph for his fourth win of the season.

For Flock, it was perhaps his most important Grand National victory. It was his first since leaving the powerful Kiekhaefer team -- and Flock and his former car owner have not exactly been on speaking terms since.

sales, "Get me a pitchfork and let me dig it out," growled Turner to a safety worker. The Roanoke lumberman couldn't get back into the race and retired after 21 laps.

"This is certainly one of my biggest wins," said Flock. "To come up here in Kiekhaefer's back yard and win this race is special to me. This was one he wanted badly, and I won it."

Grand National Race No. 37
63 Laps at Road America
Elkhart Lake, WI
258.3 Miles on 4.1-mile Road Course
August 12, 1956

Fin	St	No.	Drvier	Team / Car	Laps	Money	Status
1	6	15	Tim Flock	Bill Stroppe '56 Mercury	63	$2,950	Running
2	11	14	Billy Myers	Guy Wilson '56 Mercury	63	1,900	Running
3	17	22	Fireball Roberts	DePaolo Eng '56 Ford	63	1,275	Running
4	8	3	Paul Goldsmith	Smokey Yunick '56 Chevrolet	63	900	Running
5	9	56	Joe Eubanks	Satcher Motors '56 Ford	63	675	Running
6	20	92	Herb Thomas	Thomas '56 Chevrolet	62	500	Running
7	24	75	Jim Paschal	Frank Hayworth '56 Mercury	62	475	Running
8	1	502	Buck Baker	Kiekhaefer '56 Dodge	61	475	Engine
9	15	21	Fred Johnson	'56 Chevrolet	60	325	Running
10	16	131	Johnny Dodson	Dodson '56 Chevrolet	60	300	Running
11	25	X	Rex White	Max Welborn '56 Chevrolet	60	275	Running
12	19	2	Gwyn Staley	Westmoreland '56 Chevrolet	60	200	Running
13	10	42	Lee Petty	Petty Engineering '56 Dodge	59	200	Running
14	23	300	Frank Mundy	Carl Kiekhaefer '56 Chrysler	58	200	Running
15	21	36	Jack Goodwin	'56 Dodge	58	200	Engine
16	7	12	Ralph Moody	DePaolo Eng '56 Ford	56	100	Rear End
17	18	264	Johnny Allen	Spook Crawford '56 Plymouth	53	150	Clutch
18	5	500	Speedy Thompson	Carl Kiekhaefer '56 Dodge	53	100	Engine
19	26	5	Ansel Rakestraw	Jaguar	48	100	Running
20	23	9	Joe Weatherly	Schwam Mtrs '56 Ford	44	100	Rear End
21	14	4	Bobby Myers	Guy Wilson '56 Mercury	39	100	Crash
22	2	98	Marvin Panch	Tom Harbison '56 Ford	37	150	Rear End
23	12	7	Jim Reed	Reed '56 Chevrolet	25	100	Fuel Pmp
24	22	26	Curtis Turner	DePaolo Eng '56 Ford	21	100	Crash
25	4	97	Bill Amick	DePaolo Eng '56 Ford	10	100	Clutch
26	3	296	Junior Johnson	DePaolo Eng '56 Ford	1	100	Clutch

Time of Race: 3 hour, 29 minutes, 50 seconds
Average Speed: 73.858 mph
Pole Winner: Buck Baker -
Fastest Qualifier: Frank Mundy (3 laps) 9 minutes, 27.52 seconds, 78.000 mph
Lap Leaders: Buck Baker 1-5, Tim Flock 6-12, Marvin Panch 13-35,
Speedy Thompson 36-53, T Flock 54-63.
Cautions: None   Margin of Victory: 17 seconds   Attendance: 10,000

Grand National Race No. 38
200 Laps at Old Bridge Stadium
Old Bridge, NJ
100 Miles on Half-mile Paved Track
August 17, 1956

Fin	St	No.	Driver	Team / Car	Laps	Money	Status
1		12	Ralph Moody	DePaolo Eng '56 Ford	200	$650	Running
2	1	7	Jim Reed	Reed '56 Chevrolet	200	525	Running
3		4	Billy Myers	Guy Wilson '56 Mercury	199	400	Running
4		22	Fireball Roberts	DePaolo Eng '56 Ford	199	320	Running
5		75	Jim Paschal	Frank Hayworth '56 Mercury	197	290	Running
6		264	Johnny Allen	Spook Crawford '56 Plymouth	196	250	Running
7		92	Herb Thomas	Thomas '56 Chevrolet	196	200	Running
8		340	Ralph Liguori	Liguori '56 Chrysler	193	150	Running
9		31	Buck Baker	Whitford Bros '56 Ford	190	100	Running
10		73	John Dodd Jr	Dodd '56 Chevrolet	185	100	Running
11		192	Jerry Morese	'56 Chevrolet	184	100	Running
12		5	Billy Walker	'56 Ford	180	100	Running
13		274	Peck Peckham	'56 Chevrolet	173	100	Running
14		318	Chuck Bluett	'55 Plymouth	169	100	Running
15		211	Guy Cork	'56 Plymouth	168	100	Running
16		3	Al White	'55 Ford	162	100	Bearing
17		X	Rex White	Max Welborn '56 Chevrolet	144	100	Bearing
18		179	John Lindsay	'56 Chevrolet	90	100	Wheel
19		226	Russ Truelove	Bob White '56 Mercury	90	50	Bearing
20		195	Jim Rhoades	'56 Packard	55	50	Radiator
21		52	Dan Galullo	'56 Ford	34	25	Rear End
22		42	Lee Petty	Petty Engineering '56 Dodge	12	25	Crank Sh
23		82	Joe Eubanks	Satcher Motors '56 Ford	1	25	Radiator
24		131	Lou Spears	'55 Ford	1	25	
25		43	Louis Headley	'56 Plymouth	1	25	

Time of Race: 1 hour, 32 minutes, 4 seconds
Average Speed: 65.170 mph
Pole Winner: Jim Reed - 72.028 mph
Lap Leaders: Jim Reed 1-176, Ralph Moody 177-200.
Cautions: Margin of Victory: Attendance:

Race No. 38

Moody Passes Reed in Final Laps; Wins Old Bridge

OLD BRIDGE, NJ (Aug. 17) -- Ralph Moody hustled past Jim Reed in the 177th lap and went on to score a narrow victory in the 100-mile race at Old Bridge Stadium. It was the second win of the season for the leathery Taunton, MA veteran.

Conspicuously absent were the Carl Kiekhaefer cars, rumored to be withdrawn from the Grand National scene after the 1956 season. Kiekhaefer, who has seen his cars fall from the top rung of stock car racing's ladder, figured the $650 top prize was not worth the effort.

Herb Thomas finished seventh and moved to within 48 points of standings leader Buck Baker.

Reed finished second with Billy Myers third. Fireball Roberts took fourth and Jim Paschal fifth.

Freshman driver Rex White showed some muscle, starting third and running in the top five until a burned wheel bearing sent his Chevrolet to the pits. He wound up 17th after completing 144 laps.

Moody averaged 65.170 mph.

Race No. 39

Eddie Pagan Winner in Death-Marred Bay Meadows 250

SAN MATEO, CA (Aug. 19) -- Eddie Pagan was declared the winner of the 250-mile Grand National race at the Bay Meadows Race Course, an event which was flagged to a halt nine laps short of its scheduled distance when a safety worker was killed.

Police officer Steve Clark was run over by a speeding Scotty Cain and died instantly. Clark had started to run across the course to check on Al Pombo, who had spun off the track. Cain swerved his Ford, but could not avoid hitting Clark. Pombo was not injured in the mishap.

It was the fourth fatality on the Grand National trail in the 1956 season.

Parnelli Jones finished second and Chuck Meekins was third. Lloyd Dane and Cain rounded out the top five.

Buck Baker and Herb Thomas, locked in a tight battle for the Grand National championship suffered blown engines and finished 35th and 36th respectively.

Each earned 20 championship points, and the margin stood at 48 in Baker's favor.

Grand National Race No. 39
250 Laps at Bay Meadows Race Course
San Mateo, CA
250 Miles on 1-mile Dirt Track
August 19, 1956

Fin	St	No.	Driver	Team / Car	Laps	Money	Status
1	1	45	Eddie Pagan	Pagan '56 Ford	241	$1,475	Running
2	7	11	Parnelli Jones	Vel Miletich '56 Ford	241	1,575	Running
3	6	56	Chuck Meekins	Jim Rush '56 Chevrolet	239	1,100	Running
4	17	225	Lloyd Dane	'56 Mercury	239	750	Running
5	14	21	Scotty Cain	Cain '56 Ford	239	550	Running
6	2	31	Bill Hyde	'56 Dodge	237	450	Running
7	13	43	Boss Ross	'56 Mercury	235	300	Running
8	11	12	Fireball Roberts	DePaolo Eng '56 Ford	233	250	Running
9	12	77N	Gordon Haines	'56 Dodge	232	200	Running
10	8	88N	Ed Negre	'56 Olds	231	250	Running
11	15	41	Ernie Young	Walt Palozi '56 Pontiac	228	200	Running
12	35	14N	Bob Keefe	'56 Ford	227	150	Piston
13	25	33	Carl Hamill	'56 Chevrolet	226	100	Running
14	28	188	Jim Blomgren	'56 Ford	226	100	Running
15	9	98N	John Kieper	'56 Chevrolet	225	100	Running
16	26	71N	Clyde Palmer	'56 Dodge	225	100	Running
17	31	66N	Lou Sherman	'56 Mercury	224	100	Running
18	30	25	Erick Erickson	Erickson '56 Pontiac	217	50	Running
19	18	89	Clyde Mitchell	'56 Ford	216	50	Running
20	20	52N	Harold Hardesty	'56 Chevrolet	216	50	Running
21	33	55	Bill West	'54 Olds	215	40	Running
22	24	36	Bill Bade	'55 Chevrolet	214	40	Running
23	4	2	Al Pombo	'56 Dodge	212	40	Spun
24	23	68	Frank Decrist	'56 Chevrolet	207	40	Running
25	34	20	Howard Phillippi	'56 Chevrolet	185	40	Running
26	10	15N	Royce Hagerty	'56 Dodge	172	40	Crash
27	22	9	Jim Cook	Art Krebs '56 Pontiac	154	40	Piston
28	15	156	Art Watts	'56 Mercury	139	40	RF Hub
29	37	91	Reggie Ausmus	'55 Chevrolet	138	40	Heating
30	5	551	Bill Moore	Moore '56 Pontiac	114	40	Fan belt
31	21	47	Bob Havemann	'56 Pontiac	111	40	Engine
32	27	34	Sherman Clark	Clark '55 Chevrolet	102	40	Drive Sh
33	29	1	Ralph Moody	DePaolo Eng '56 Ford	75	40	Engine
34	32	75N	Wally Gervais	'56 Olds	53	40	Engine
35	3	300B	Buck Baker	Carl Kiekhaefer '56 Chrysler	35	40	Engine
36	10	30	Herb Thomas	'56 Plymouth	20	90	
37	36	83	Ole Anderson	'54 Ford	9	40	Heating

Time of Race: 3 hours, 31 minutes
Average Speed: 68.161 mph
Pole Winner: Eddie Pagan - 81.614 mph
Lap Leaders: - - - - - - - - - - Eddie Pagan   -241.
Cautions: Margin of Victory: Attendance:
** Race shortened to 241 laps due to death of safety worker

Race No. 40

Myers' Mercury Nimble In Norfolk Win

NORFOLK, VA (Aug. 22) -- Billy Myers of Germantown, NC came from near the rear of the field and nabbed his second win of the year in the 100-miler at Norfolk Speedway. The Mercury driver currently ranks sixth in the point standings.

Jim Paschal finished second for the seventh time this

*Billy Myers captured
Norfolk 100-miler.*

season, giving the surging Mercury products another number 1-2 finish. Rex White was third, Buck Baker fourth and Johnny Allen fifth.

Herb Thomas fell out after 154 laps with rear end problems and wound up 10th in the 14 car field. He fell 96 points behind Baker in the battle for the championship.

Lee Petty, who ranks third in the standings, crashed his Dodge in the 19th lap of the 250-lapper on the .4-mile oval. Pole sitter Ralph Moody lasted only 10 laps before he went out with a broken idler arm.

there's an old saying in stock car racing circles: *"To finish first, first you have to finish."*

Thompson was pulling away from the field when his Ford blew an engine just seven laps from the finish. Ralph Moody, who had started on the pole and never ran worse than second, was in a position to take over at Thompson's misfortune.

Moody's Ford finished two laps ahead of Jim Paschal to win the $850 first prize. Rex White came across the line in third place. Herb Thomas was fourth and Thompson got credit for fifth.

Buck Baker struggled to a seventh place finish. His point lead was cut to 18 over Herb Thomas.

Moody's third win of the year came at an average speed of 54.372 mph.

Grand National Race No. 40
250 Laps at Norfolk Speedway
Norfolk, VA
100 Miles on .4-mile Dirt Track
August 22, 1956

Fin	St	No.	Driver	Team / Car	Laps	Money	Status
1	9	4	Billy Myers	Guy Wilson '56 Mercury	250	$850	Running
2	8	75	Jim Paschal	Frank Hayworth '56 Mercury	249	625	Running
3	5	X	Rex White	Max Welborn '56 Chevrolet	246	450	Running
4	10	501	Buck Baker	Carl Kiekhaefer '56 Dodge	245	350	Running
5	11	264	Johnny Allen	Spook Crawford '56 Plymouth	241	310	Running
6	3	31	Bill Champion	Whitford Bros '56 Ford	227	250	Running
7	6	42	Lee Petty	Petty Engineering '56 Dodge	198	200	Crash
8	2	22	Fireball Roberts	DePaolo Eng '56 Ford	198	150	Running
9	4	35	Joe Weatherly	Whitford Bros. '56 Ford	170	100	Gas line
10	7	92	Herb Thomas	Thomas '56 Chevrolet	154	100	Rear End
11	1	12	Ralph Moody	DePaolo Eng '56 Ford	104	100	Idler Arm
12	13	28	Jim Watkins	'56 Chevrolet	86	100	Steering
13	12	41	Billy Rafter	Rafter '56 Dodge	36	100	Bearing
14	14	14	Joe McGraw	'56 Ford	7	100	Fire

Time of Race: 1 hour, 46 minutes, 22 seconds
Average Speed: 56.408 mph
Pole Winner: Ralph Moody - 58.631 mph
Lap Leaders: - - - - - - - - - Billy Myers   -250.
Cautions: Margin of Victory: 1 lap plus   Attendance:

Grand National Race No. 41
200 Laps at Piedmont Interstate Fairgrounds
Spartanburg, SC
100 Miles on Half-mile Dirt Track
August 23, 1956

Fin	St	No.	Driver	Team / Car	Laps	Money	Status
1	1	12	Ralph Moody	DePaolo Eng '56 Ford	200	$850	Running
2	10	75	Jim Paschal	Frank Hayworth '56 Mercury	198	625	Running
3	6	X	Rex White	Max Welborn '56 Chevrolet	198	450	Running
4	3	92	Herb Thomas	Thomas '56 Chevrolet	196	350	Running
5	8	296	Speedy Thompson	DePaolo Eng '56 Ford	193	310	Engine
6	7	82	Joe Eubanks	Satcher Motors '56 Ford	193	250	Running
7	18	300	Buck Baker	Carl Kiekhaefer '56 Chrysler	192	200	Running
8	5	22	Fireball Roberts	DePaolo Eng '56 Ford	192	150	Running
9	12	100	Wayne Fielden	'56 Chevrolet	190	100	Running
10	11	264	Johnny Allen	Spook Crawford '56 Plymouth	176	100	Rear End
11	9	41	Billy Rafter	Rafter '56 Dodge	148	100	Rear End
12	14	50	Roy Bentley	Marion Cox '56 Ford	142	100	Running
13	13	35	Fred Frazier	Whitford Bros. '56 Ford	104	100	Crash
14	4	42	Lee Petty	Petty Engineering '56 Dodge	97	100	A Frame
15	15	62	Jimmy Pardue	'55 Chevrolet	28	100	Wheel
16	17	28	Jim Watkins	'55 Chevrolet	27	100	Engine
17	16	14	Bill McGraw	'56 Ford	18	100	Fuel Pmp
18	2	4	Billy Myers	Guy Wilson '56 Mercury	10	100	Axle

Time of Race: 1 hour, 50 minutes, 21 seconds
Average Speed: 54.372 mph
Pole Winner: Ralph Moody - 61.433 mph
Lap Leaders: Ralph Moody 1-126, Speedy Thompson 127-193, Moody 194-200
Cautions: Margin of Victory: 2 laps plus   Attendance:

Race No. 41

Moody No Match at Spartanburg; Wins Anyway

SPARTANBURG, SC (Aug 23) -- Speedy Thompson had the fastest machine in the 100-mile Grand National race at the Piedmont Interstate Fairgrounds. But

Race No. 42

Roberts Wins Myrtle Beach; Thomas Disqualified

MYRTLE BEACH, SC (Aug. 25) -- Rising star Fireball Roberts nabbed his third win of the season as Herb Thomas' title hopes endured a set back after an unusual ruling in the 100-miler at Coastal Speedway.

Fireball Roberts drove his #22 Ford to victory in 100-mile Grand National event at Myrtle Beach's Coastal Speedway.

prohibit refueling under the yellow flag.

The idea behind the new NASCAR ruling was to limit caution flag pit stops. Officials of the sanctioning body felt that the spectators would rather see pit crews do their work while the green flag was out, which would place a premium on efficiency.

Thomas pitted for tires and his pit crew mistakenly added fuel -- just as they always had done.

Thomas was dropped to 13th in the final order, falling 90 points behind point leader Baker.

Pole sitter Ralph Moody was kayoed in a crash on lap 61. He got credit for 16th place in the 20 car field.

Roberts averaged 50.576 mph for his fourth career win.

Roberts' Ford outran the Mercury of Billy Myers to pick up the $950 first prize. Jim Paschal finished third, Buck Baker fourth and Speedy Thompson fifth.

Thomas had qualified his Chevrolet in second place. On lap 76 he pulled into the pits during a caution flag. His pit crew filled the car with gasoline and NASCAR officials promptly disqualified him. NASCAR rules

Grand National Race No. 42
200 Laps at Coastal Speedway
Myrtle Beach, SC
100 Miles on Half-mile Dirt Track
August 25, 1956

Fin	St	No.	Driver	Team / Car	Laps	Money	Status
1	3	22	Fireball Roberts	DePaolo Eng '56 Ford	200	$950	Running
2	7	4	Billy Myers	Guy Wilson '56 Mercury	200	675	Running
3	10	75	Jim Paschal	Frank Hayworth '56 Mercury	199	475	Running
4	6	300	Buck Baker	Carl Kiekhaefer '56 Chrysler	196	365	Running
5	19	501	Speedy Thompson	Carl Kiekhaefer '56 Dodge	196	320	Running
6	9	82	Joe Eubanks	Satcher Motors '56 Ford	196	250	Running
7	4	271	Billy Carden	'56 Mercury	191	200	Running
8	18	264	Johnny Allen	Spook Crawford '56 Plymouth	184	150	Running
9	12	35	Fred Frazier	Whitford Bros. '56 Ford	184	100	Running
10	13	203	Pete Yow	Strickland Motors '56 Ford	182	100	Running
11	16	54	Larry Flynn	B B Morris '55 Buick	180	100	Heating
12	8	31	Bill Champion	Whitford Bros. '56 Ford	90	100	Gasket
13	2	92	Herb Thomas	Thomas '56 Chevrolet	76	100	Disqual
14	15	14	Bill McGraw	'56 Ford	66	100	Vapor Lk
15	5	42	Lee Petty	Petty Engineering '56 Dodge	64	100	Axle
16	1	12	Ralph Moody	DePaolo Eng '56 Ford	61	100	Crash
17	14	94	Ed Cole	'55 Mercury	60	100	Engine
18	20	28	Jim Watkins	'55 Chevrolet	43	100	Fuel pmp
19	11	50	Roy Bentley	Marion Cox '56 Ford	41	50	Radiator
20	17	64	Spook Crawford	Crawford '55 Plymouth	13	50	Crash

Time of Race: 1 hour, 58 minutes, 38 seconds
Average Speed: 50.576 mph
Pole Winner: Ralph Moody - 58.346 mph
Lap Leaders: - - - - - - - - - Fireball Roberts   -200.
Cautions: Margin of Victory: Attendance:

Grand National Race No. 43
250 Laps at Portland Speedway
Portland, OR
125 Miles on Half-mile Paved Track
August 26, 1956

Fin	St	No.	Driver	Team / Car	Laps	Money	Status
1	8	15N	Royce Hagerty	'56 Dodge	246	$1,200	Running
2	2	1	Clyde Palmer	'56 Ford	246	730	Running
3	13	11	Curley Barker	'56 Chevrolet	246	500	Running
4	7	56	Chuck Meekins	'56 Chevrolet	245	400	Running
5	3	45	Eddie Pagan	Pagan '56 Ford	244	350	Running
6	4	50N	Harold Beal	'56 Ford	243	270	Running
7	11	52N	Herb Thomas	'56 Chevrolet	243	200	Running
8	19	88N	Lloyd Dane	'56 Olds	240	150	Running
9	1	98N	John Kieper	Kieper '55 Olds	240	155	Running
10	14	21	Scotty Cain	Cain '56 Ford	238	150	Running
11	9	27N	Len Sutton	'56 Ford	238	150	Running
12	18	21N	Pat Diviney	'56 Ford	231	100	Running
13	16	41N	Chub Williams	'55 Dodge	225	75	Running
14	5	56N	Art Watts	'56 Mercury	221	75	Running
15	15	77N	Gordy Haines	'56 Dodge	217	50	Running
16	12	66N	Lou Sherman	'56 Mercury	211	50	Running
17	6	6	Harold Hardesty	Beryl Jackson '54 Olds	194	50	Bearing
18	10	71N	Bill Hyde	'56 Dodge	67	50	Trans
19	17	75N	Wally Gervaise	'56 Olds	51	50	Running

** Race shortened to 246 laps due to scoring mix-up
Time of Race: None
Average Speed: None
Pole Winner: John Kieper - 65.861 mph
Lap Leaders: - - - - - - - - - Royce Hagerty   -246.
Cautions: Margin of Victory: Attendance:

Race No. 43

Royce Races Dodge to Portland Victory

PORTLAND, OR (Aug. 26) -- Royce Hagerty claimed his first Grand National win after an embarrassing scoring mix-up at Portland Speedway.

Hagerty, Clyde Palmer and Curley Barker were running in close quarters when the checkered flag was waved suddenly. Only 246 of the scheduled 250 laps had been completed.

None the less, Hagerty won the race with Palmer second and Barker third. Chuck Meekins was fourth and Eddie Pagan fifth. Hagerty's win came in only his sixth GN start.

Nineteen automobiles started the race and 17 of them finished, including last place Wally Gervaise, who completed 51 laps in his Oldsmobile.

John Kieper won his third career pole position, but he drifted to ninth in the final rundown.

There was no official time of the race due to the scoring foul-ups.

Dink Widenhouse crashed in the Southern 500. Despite this dire appearance, Widenhouse was only shaken up.

Race No. 44

Turner Finally Wins Southern 500 at Darlington

DARLINGTON, SC (Sept. 3) -- Curtis Turner, always a leader but never a winner in the Southern 500 Classic, came through and hit the jackpot in the seventh annual running of the famed 500-miler at Darlington Raceway.

An enormous crowd estimated at 70,000 jammed every seat available at the 1.375-mile oval to watch the biggest race staged for the Grand National stocks.

Turner's purple Wild Hog Ford passed Marvin Panch in the 202nd lap and led the rest of the way to pocket the $11,750 prize. It was his first major league victory since June 6, 1954, when he won at Columbia, SC.

Finishing second and leaping into contention for the championship was Speedy Thompson. He powered his Kiekhaefer Chrysler into runner-up honors after starting on the pole. Panch held on to finish third, Jim Reed was fourth and Paul Goldsmith fifth.

The lead changed hands 14 times among seven different drivers. Turner was in front four times for a total of 225 laps, including the last 163. In the late stages Turner had built up a two-lap lead and cruised the final 50 miles.

Buck Baker set a qualifying record of 119.659 mph in the Kiekhaefer Chrysler. However, the Grand National point leader never led and eventually wound up 26th, 34 laps behind the winner.

Herb Thomas was involved in three accidents, some termed "suspicious" by eye witnesses, and finished 49th in the 70 car field. Oddly, both Baker and Thomas received 60 points, so the margin between them remained at 90 points. Sixty points went to each finisher below 25th position.

Thompson earned 1,440 points and moved to within 720 of first place.

Dink Widenhouse was transported to the hospital with minor injuries when his Ford crashed with

Curtis Turner and lovely lady beside the Southern 500 winning Ford.

Grand National Race No. 44
364 Laps at Darlington Raceway
Darlington, SC
"Southern 500"
500 Miles on 1.375-mile Paved Track
September 3, 1956

Fin	St	No.	Driver	Team / Car	Laps	Money	Status
1	11	99	Curtis Turner	Schwam Mtrs '56 Ford	364	$11,750	Running
2	3	57	Speedy Thompson	Carl Kiekhaefer '56 Chrysler	362	5,000	Running
3	2	8	Marvin Panch	DePaolo Eng '56 Ford	359	3,370	Running
4	23	7	Jim Reed	Reed '56 Chevrolet	350	1,850	Running
5	4	3	Paul Goldsmith	Smokey Yunick '56 Chevrolet	358	1,300	Running
6	17	26	Jim Paschal	Bill Stroppe '56 Mercury	358	1,850	Running
7	3	97	Bill Amick	DePaolo Eng '56 Ford	357	1,020	Running
8	16	9	Joe Weatherly	Schwam Mtrs '56 Ford	352	900	Running
9	30	47	Bobby Johns	Fitzgibbons '56 Chevrolet	349	700	Running
10	20	93	Pat Kirkwood	Howard Moore '56 Pontiac	347	550	Running
11	28	10	Rex White	Max Welborn '56 Chevrolet	345	400	Running
12	15	86	Tim Flock	John Foster Mtr '56 Ford	345	490	Running
13	22	61	Roz Howard	Howard '56 Chevrolet	343	250	Running
14	25	38	Johnny Patterson	H B Ranier '56 Chevrolet	343	225	Running
15	35	32	Junior Johnson	'56 Chevrolet	342	200	Running
16	14	14	Billy Myers	Guy Wilson '56 Mercury	341	300	Running
17	68	35	Lee Petty	Fred Frazier '56 Ford	340	175	Running
18	39	80	Harold Hardesty	Beryl Jackson '56 Olds	339	350	Running
19	42	81	Elmo Langley	'56 Chevrolet	338	140	Running
20	46	43	Shorty York	'56 Ford	336	130	Running
21	19	31	Bill Champion	Whitford Bros '56 Ford	336	120	Running
22	65	69	Possum Jones	Warren Lee '56 Chevrolet	336	110	Running
23	57	11	Emanuel Zervakis	'56 Chevrolet	334	100	Running
24	54	16	Tiny Lund	Gus Holzmueller '56 Chevy	331	100	Running
25	45	64	Johnny Allen	Spook Crawford '56 Plymouth	330	300	Running
26	6	87	Buck Baker	Kiekhaefer '56 Chrysler	330	225	Running
27	53	91	Jack Smith	Elridge Motors '56 Chevrolet	329	75	Running
28	36	19	Billy Carden	Schwam Mtrs '56 Ford	329	75	Running
29	24	75	Bill Blair	Frank Hayworth '56 Mercury	327	125	Running
30	33	63	Sherman Utsman	McReynolds '56 Chevrolet	327	75	Running
31	64	65	Lou Spears	'56 Plymouth	322	150	Running
32	50	60	Brownie King	'56 Chevrolet	320	50	Running
33	9	82	Joe Eubanks	Satcher Mtrs '56 Ford	317	50	Gasket
34	66	48	Allen Adkins	Don Holcomb '56 Ford	315	50	Running
35	43	89	Tom Lupo	Granger Mtrs '56 Ford	313	50	Running
36	29	21	Gene Bergin	Malcomb Barlow '56 Dodge	308	250	Running
37	31	88	Ralph Liguori	Ernest Woods '56 Olds	300	150	Axle
38	7	27	Frank Mundy	Carl Kiekhaefer '56 Dodge	276	180	Engine
39	40	66	Harvey Henderson	'56 Ford	266	50	Running
40	61	34	Dick Beaty	Beaty '56 Ford	264	50	Crash
41	67	84	Judge Rider	Lamson & Nitti '56 Ford	258	50	Running
42	52	23	Wade Fields	'56 Ford	244	50	Running
43	56	54	Bill Brown	Leland Colvin '55 Buick	235	250	Crash
44	53	73	Larry Flynn	B B Morris '56 Buick	222	150	Crash
45	62	83	Johnny Dodson	Dodson '56 Ford	204	50	Wheel
46	63	59	Blackie Pitt	Brownie Pitt '56 Plymouth	202	100	Rear End
47	51	6	Pat Grogan	Grogan '56 Mercury	202	50	Gas Tank
48	47	30	Clyde Palmer	'56 Plymouth	177	50	Heating
49	5	92	Herb Thomas	Thomas '56 Chevrolet	173	50	Crash
50	18	1	Parnelli Jones	Vel Miletich '56 Ford	169	70	Crash
51	13	22	Fireball Roberts	DePaolo Eng '56 Ford	166	160	Crash
52	44	44	Ray Hendrick	'56 Chevrolet	163	50	Engine
53	10	52	Bill Widenhouse	'56 Ford	159	50	Engine
54	27	29	Dink Widenhouse	'56 Ford	158	50	Crash
55	48	50	Roy Bentley	Marion Cox '56 Ford	146	50	Crash
56	58	24	Ken Love	Richard Gallup '56 Ford	134	50	Running
57	8	12	Ralph Moody	DePaolo Eng '56 Ford	119	70	Crash
58	12	15	Fonty Flock	Bill Stroppe '56 Mercury	117	80	Spindle
59	32	98	Danny Letner	Tom Harbison '56 Dodge	113	100	Crash
60	37	40	Don Oldenberg	'56 Plymouth	100	50	Gas Tank
61	34	76	Bobby Myers	Bill Stroppe '56 Mercury	91	50	Gas Tank
62	21	95	Bob Duell	Julian Buesink '56 Ford	90	50	Rear End
63	60	51	Nace Mattingly	Mattingly '56 Ford	73	50	Engine
64	41	5	Pee Wee Jones	'56 Dodge	60	50	Throttle
65	26	2	Gwyn Staley	Westmoreland '56 Chevrolet	57	50	Crash
66	49	25	Doug Yates	Leland Colvin '56 Chevrolet	54	50	Crash
67	79	72	Peck Peckham	'55 Chevrolet	27	50	Gasket
68	38	17	Bud Graham	Earl Wright '56 Chevrolet	26	50	Crash
69	69	13	Jesse James Taylor	Jesse James Taylor '56 Ford	25	50	Engine
70	50	18	Arden Mounts	Mounts '56 Pontiac	12	50	Piston

Blackie Pitt spins his Plymouth at Darlington.

Fireball Roberts and Roy Bentley.

Seven cautions were waved, lowering Turner's average speed to 95.167 mph. There were numerous wrecks, the most frightening involving Larry Flynn and Bill Brown. Flynn's Buick struck the guard rail and flipped over. The car slid down the banking on its roof. Brown swerved to miss Flynn, but smashed through the inside guard rail, tearing up fifty feet of railing in the process. Neither driver was hurt seriously.

Race No. 45

Baker Beats Montgomery Field Before Only 2,000

MONTGOMERY, AL (Sept. 9) -- Buck Baker finally made it back to victory circle as he drove the Kiekhaefer Outboards Chrysler to victory in the 100-miler at Montgomery Speedway. It was Baker's first win in over three months, and it broke a dry spell for car owner Carl Kiekhaefer, whose cars had won only once in the previous 14 outings after winning 16 in a

Time of Race: 5 hours, 15 minutes, 33 seconds
Average Speed: 95.167 mph
Pole Winner: Buck Baker - 119.659 mph
Lap Leaders: Marvin Panch 1, Speedy Thompson 2-3, Panch 4-7, Thompson 8-19, Tim Flock 20-32, Curtis Turner 33-35, Flock 36-38, Turner 39-95, Panch 96-100, Jim Paschal 101-132, Fireball Roberts 133-166, Turner 167-168, Panch 169-201, Turner 202-364.
Cautions: 7 for 68 laps　　　Margin of Victory: 2 laps plus　　　Attendance: 70,000

Buck Baker got back on the winning track by driving his Chrysler to victory at Montgomery, AL.

row earlier in the year.

Ralph Moody finished second, Marvin Panch was third, Fireball Roberts fourth and Johnny Allen fifth.

Tim Flock led the first 50 laps from the pole position. Jack Smith led for 49 laps and Panch was in front for

41 trips around the half-mile dirt track before Baker took the lead for good.

Once again, the Grand National tour was hit with scoring problems. Roberts was flagged in eighth spot but later was elevated to fourth. Allen, Jim Paschal and Herb Thomas all dropped one spot in another pencil and paper shuffle.

Baker increased his point lead to 130 points as Thomas wound up seventh.

Race No. 46

Charlotte 100 To Ralph Moody's Ford

CHARLOTTE, NC (Sept. 12) -- Ralph Moody charged through the pack, took the lead in the 27th lap and sped to victory in the 100-miler at the Southern States

Grand National Race No. 45
200 Laps at Chisholm Speedway
Montgomery, AL
100 Miles on Half-mile Dirt Track
September 9, 1956

Fin	St	No.	Driver	Team / Car	Laps	Money	Status
1	14	87	Buck Baker	Carl Kiekhaefer '56 Chrysler	200	$950	Running
2	5	12	Ralph Moody	DePaolo Eng '56 Ford	200	675	Running
3	7	98	Marvin Panch	Tom Harbison '56 Ford	199	475	Running
4	16	22	Fireball Roberts	DePaolo Eng '56 Ford	195	365	Running
5	8	264	Johnny Allen	Spook Crawford '56 Plymouth	194	320	Running
6	6	92	Herb Thomas	Thomas '56 Chevrolet	194	250	Running
7	12	75	Jim Paschal	Frank Hayworth '56 Mercury	194	200	Running
8	11	97	Bill Amick	DePaolo Eng '56 Ford	192	150	Running
9	4	82	Joe Eubanks	Satcher Motors '56 Ford	191	100	Piston
10	19	X	Rex White	Max Welborn '56 Chevrolet	191	100	Running
11	10	91	Jack Smith	Elridge Motors '56 Chevrolet	189	100	Running
12	2	42	Lee Petty	Petty Engineering '56 Dodge	188	100	Running
13	9	7A	Bobby Johns	Johns '56 Chevrolet	186	100	Crash
14	15	66	Freddy Fryar	'56 Ford	183	100	Running
15	17	4	Billy Myers	Guy Wilson '56 Mercury	182	100	Running
16	20	48	Al Watkins	Don Holcomb '56 Ford	178	100	Running
17	18	16	Tiny Lund	Gus Holzmueller '56 Chevy	173	100	Running
18	1	86	Tim Flock	John Foster Motors '56 Ford	139	100	Brakes
19	3	57	Speedy Thompson	Carl Kiekhaefer '56 Chrysler	58	50	Crash
20	13	27	Billy Carden	'56 Mercury	50	50	Bearing
21	21	291	C H Dingler	'56 Dodge	17	---	Bearing

Time of Race: 1 hour, 38 minutes, 32 seconds
Average Speed: 60.893 mph
Pole Winner: Tim Flock - 64.864 mph
Lap Leaders: Tim Flock 1-50, Jack Smith 51-99, Marvin Panch 100-140,
   Buck Baker 141-200.
Cautions: Margin of Victory: Attendance: 2,000

Grand National Race No. 46
200 Laps at Southern States
Fairgrounds
Charlotte, NC
100 Miles on Half-mile Dirt Track
September 12, 1956

Fin	St	No.	Driver	Team / Car	Laps	Money	Status
1	11	12	Ralph Moody	DePaolo Eng '56 Ford	200	$850	Running
2	5	4	Billy Myers	Guy Wilson '56 Mercury	200	625	Running
3	1	82	Joe Eubanks	Satcher Motors '56 Ford	200	450	Running
4	9	98	Marvin Panch	Tom Harbison '56 Ford	199	350	Running
5	7	92	Herb Thomas	Thomas '56 Chevrolet	196	310	Running
6	8	16	Tiny Lund	Gus Holzmueller '56 Chevrolet	196	250	Running
7	4	57	Speedy Thompson	Carl Kiekhaefer '56 Dodge	191	300	Running
8	3	X	Rex White	Max Welborn '56 Chevrolet	186	150	Running
9	14	75	Jim Paschal	Frank Hayworth '56 Mercury	184	100	Running
10	15	42	Lee Petty	Petty Engineering '56 Dodge	183	100	Running
11	16	19	Bunk Moore	'56 Ford	179	100	Running
12	23	203	Pete Yow	Strickland Motors '56 Ford	178	100	Running
13	21	760	Brownie King	'56 Ford	173	100	Running
14	13	52	Bill Widenhouse	'56 Ford	165	100	Battery
15	24	94	Ed Cole	'55 Mercury	160	100	Running
16	20	59	Blackie Pitt	Brownie Pitt '56 Plymouth	146	100	Running
17	25	41	Billy Rafter	Rafter '56 Ford	141	100	Running
18	26	27	Billy Carden	'56 Mercury	105	100	Axle
19	2	22	Fireball Roberts	DePaolo Eng '56 Ford	96	50	Vapor Lk
20	6	31	Bill Champion	Whitford Bros '56 Ford	91	50	Crash
21	10	35	Glen Wood	Fred Frazier '56 Ford	67	50	Shocks
22	22	34	Dick Beaty	Beaty '56 Ford	58	50	Rear End
23	17	87	Buck Baker	Kiekhaefer '56 Dodge	51	50	Carb
24	18	5	Fred Harb	Joe Blair '56 Dodge	31	50	Crash
25	12	97	Bill Amick	DePaolo Eng '56 Ford	23	50	Gas Line
26	19	25	Ray Hendrick	Sam McCuthen '56 Chevrolet	14	50	Gas Line

Time of Race: 1 hour, 53 minutes, 32 seconds
Average Speed: 52.847 mph
Pole Winner: Joe Eubanks - 59.464 mph
Lap Leaders: Fireball Roberts 1-78, Ralph Moody 79-200.
Cautions: Margin of Victory: 10.0 seconds   Attendance: 7,300

Fairgrounds. It was the fourth win of the year for the Ford driver.

Billy Myers finished in second place, Joe Eubanks was third, Marvin Panch fourth and Herb Thomas fifth.

Point leader Buck Baker left the race after 51 laps when his Dodge developed carburetor trouble. His point lead was sliced to 90 points by Thomas.

Rookies Bill Champion and Fred Harb crashed in separate incidents. Neither driver was hurt.

Moody averaged 52.847 mph before 7,300 spectators.

Race No. 47

Goldsmith By Big Margin In Langhorne 300

LANGHORNE, PA (Sept. 23) -- Paul Goldsmith of St. Clair Shores, MI romped to a seven mile victory in the 300-mile Grand National race at Langhorne Speedway. It was the first win for Goldsmith, who picked up a Chevrolet wrenched by the famed mechanic Smokey Yunick.

Lee Petty's Dodge was a distant second, finishing

Paul Goldsmith pits at Langhorne. He went on to win 300-miler.

more than seven laps behind the winner. Speedy Thompson was third, Jim Paschal fourth. Herb Thomas climbed to the top of the point standings with a fifth place finish.

Previous leader Buck Baker started on the pole but went out on lap 51 with a broken oil line. He wound up 38th in the 44-car field.

The lead changed hands ten times, with Goldsmith leading 182 of the 300 laps. The former motorcycle champ got past Paschal in the 253rd lap and led the rest of the way. Paschal was forced to make several pit stops which allowed Petty to finish second and Thomp

Grand National Race No. 47
300 Laps at Langhorne Speedway
Langhorne, PA
300 Miles on 1-mile Dirt Track
September 23, 1956

Fin	St	No.	Driver	Team / Car	Laps	Money	Status
1	2	3	Paul Goldsmith	Smokey Yunick '56 Chevrolet	300	$4,150	Running
2	8	42	Lee Petty	Petty Engineering '56 Dodge	293	1,800	Running
3	10	67	Speedy Thompson	Carl Kiekhaefer '56 Dodge	292	1,175	Running
4	9	26	Jim Paschal	Bill Stroppe '56 Mercury	292	950	Running
5	11	92	Herb Thomas	Thomas '56 Chevrolet	290	700	Running
6	7	14	Billy Myers	Guy Wilson '56 Mercury	288	550	Running
7	42	5	Bill Blair	Blair '56 Mercury	284	450	Running
8	37	10	Rex White	Max Welborn '56 Chevrolet	280	400	Running
9	19	64	Johnny Allen	'56 Buick	274	400	Running
10	21	62	Russ Truelove	Bob White '56 Mercury	268	250	Running
11	25	17	Dick Allwine	Earl Wright '56 Chevrolet	263	200	Running
12	23	03	Vince Cougineri	'56 Chrysler	256	150	Running
13	20	84	Jack Tykarski	Larnson & Nitti '56 Ford	250	225	Running
14	28	20	Chuck Bluett	'55 Plymouth	242	100	Running
15	29	77	Cecil Lassiter	Bob Bunselmeyer '56 Ford	235	100	Runing
16	13	16	Tiny Lund	Gus Holzmueller '56 Chevy	232	100	Running
17	3	22	Fireball Roberts	DePaolo Eng '56 Ford	220	125	Oil Line
18	35	21	Guy Cork	'55 Plymouth	215	100	Engine
19	34	98	Danny Letner	Tom Harbison '56 Dodge	209	100	Engine
20	31	53	Jack Montrangelo	Montrangelo '56 Chevrolet	206	100	Running
21	41	79	John Lindsay	'55 Chevrolet	204	75	Trans
22	32	34	Johnny Coy	'56 Chrysler	197	175	Running
23	17	63	Bill Tanner	Al Liberty '55 Chevrolet	182	75	Running
24	39	47	Harvey Eakin	Eakin '54 Nash	173	75	Crash
25	14	7	Jim Reed	Reed '56 Chevrolet	169	75	Fire
26	33	31	Bill Champion	Whitford Bros '56 Ford	145	75	Trans
27	38	95	Jim Rhoades	'55 Packard	143	75	Steering
28	15	1	Elton Hildreth	Hildreth '56 Mercury	122	75	Spindle
29	12	97	Bill Amick	DePaolo Eng '56 Ford	104	75	Radiator
30	40	27	Peck Peckham	'55 Chevrolet	101	75	Running
31	24	02	Mario Rossi	'55 Chrysler	97	60	Rear End
32	16	38	Bill Parks	'56 Ford	92	60	Crash
33	36	24	Gene Bergin	'56 Dodge	76	60	Gasket
34	6	9	Marvin Panch	Tom Harbison '56 Ford	74	60	Engine
35	22	69	Dave Terrell	'56 Plymouth	66	60	Gasket
36	27	83	Chuck Hansen	'55 Olds	66	50	Gasket
37	18	81	Frank Jamison	'55 Clhevrolet	54	50	Crank Sh
38	1	87	Buck Baker	Carl Kiekhaefer '56 Chrysler	51	125	Oil Line
39	26	23	Benny DeRosier	Adelmo Tiezzi '54 Hudson	43	50	Steering
40	30	18	Ronnie Herra	'55 Plymouth	34	50	Head
41	43	4	Cory Benjamin	'55 Plymouth	34	50	Gasket
42	4	12	Ralph Moody	DePaolo Eng '56 Ford	3	50	Crash
43	5	66	Harvey Henderson	'56 Ford	3	50	Crash
44	44	11	Frances Dione	'56 Packard	2	150	Crash

Time of Race: 4 hours, 6 minutes, 34 seconds
Average Speed: 70.615 mph
Pole Winner: Buck Baker - 93.628 mph
Lap Leaders: Buck Baker 1-9, Paul Goldsmith 10-13, Fireball Roberts 19-42,
Goldsmith 43-74, Roberts 75-76, Jim Reed 77, Jim Paschal 78-116,
Goldsmith 117-209, Roberts 210-221, Paschal 222-252, Goldsmith 253-300.
Cautions: 9   Margin of Victory: 7 laps plus   Attendance: 31,000

son third.

A hefty crowd of 31,000 watched the race.

Nine caution flags slowed the brisk pace. Jim Reed's Chevrolet caught on fire in the 171st lap. The Peekskill, NY driver leaped out with minor burns. He was taken to Lower Bucks Memorial Hospital for treatment and was held overnight.

Harvey Eakins crashed his Nash in a series of rollovers. The car landed on its wheels with the driver unhurt.

Race No. 48

Dane Wins Second of Year At Portland

PORTLAND, OR (Sept. 23) -- Lloyd Dane hammered his Ford to his second win of the season in the 125-miler staged at Portland Speedway.

Scoring problems, which have been frequent at this half-mile paved oval, surfaced again as no one was able to record a running time of the race. No official qualifying speed was given for pole winner Royce Hagerty.

Eddie Pagan finished second and Curley Barker was third. Fourth place went to John Kieper and fifth to Harold Hardesty.

Barker appeared headed to victory when his Chevrolet ran out of gas in the final lap. His car crept to a halt as Dane made the final lap pass.

Pat Diviney crashed his Ford on lap 149 and retired from the race. Thirteen cars finished after 19 started.

Race No. 49

Baker Bounces Back To Take Columbia Flag

COLUMBIA, SC (Sept. 29) -- Buck Baker rebounded after a rash of sour luck and won the 100-miler at Columbia Speedway. It was the 11th win of the year for the Charlotte Dodge driver.

Baker took the lead for the final time in the 168th lap from Speedy Thompson. He was about 100 yards ahead of runner-up Ralph Moody when the checkered flag fell. Thompson came in third, Fireball Roberts was fourth and Billy Myers fifth.

Tim Flock won the pole for the 37th time in his career. The Atlanta driver pushed his Chevrolet out into an early lead, but crashed in the 68th lap. He got credit for 16th place in the 18 car field.

Point leader Herb Thomas finished eighth and escaped from Columbia with a 374 point lead.

Grand National Race No. 48
250 Laps at Portland Speedway
Portland, OR
125 Miles on Half-mile Paved Track
September 23, 1956

Fin	St	No.	Driver	Team / Car	Laps	Money	Status
1		1	Lloyd Dane	'56 Ford	250	$1,020	Running
2		45	Eddie Pagan	Pagan '56 Ford	249	650	Running
3		11N	Curley Barker	'56 Chevrolet	249	450	Fuel
4		57	John Kieper	Kieper '56 Chevrolet	248	370	Running
5		80N	Harold Hardesty	Beryl Jackson '56 Olds	247	330	Running
6		98N	Ed Negre	'55 Ford	246	250	Running
7		27N	Joe Prismo	'56 Ford	246	200	Running
8		56	Chuck Meekins	Jim Rush '56 Chevrolet	245	150	Running
9		50N	Harold Beal	'56 Ford	244	150	Running
10		30	Clyde Palmer	'56 Plymouth	241	150	Running
11		42N	Chuck Akerblade	'56 Chevrolet	238	100	Running
12		15N	Royce Hagerty	'56 Dodge	237	180	Running
13		14N	Bob Keefe	'56 Ford	235	75	Running
14		43	Bob Ross	'56 Mercury	176	75	Piston
15		21N	Pat Diviney	'56 Ford	147	50	Crash
16		56N	Art Watts	'56 Mercury	117	50	Conn Rd
17		00	Dick Getty	Betty Getty '56 Mercury	69	50	Piston
18		66N	Lou Sherman	'56 Mercury	56	50	Bearing
19		22N	Wally Gervais	'56 Olds	6	50	Leak

Tim of Race: Not Recorded
Average Speed: Not Recorded
Pole Winner: Royce Hagerty - Time not recorded
Lap Leaders: - - - - - - - - - Lloyd Dane -250.
Cautions: Margin of Victory: 1 lap plus   Attendance:

Grand National Race No. 49
200 Laps at Columbia Speedway
Columbia, SC
100 Miles on Half-mile Dirt Track
September 29, 1956

Fin	St	No.	Driver	Team / Car	Laps	Money	Status
1	6	500B	Buck Baker	Carl Kiekhaefer '56 Dodge	200	$950	Running
2	10	12	Ralph Moody	DePaolo Eng '56 Ford	200	675	Running
3	3	500	Speedy Thompson	Carl Kiekhaefer '56 Dodge	200	475	Running
4	5	22	Fireball Roberts	DePaolo Eng '56 Ford	200	360	Running
5	12	4	Billy Myers	Guy Wilson '56 Mercury	198	320	Running
6	2	27	Billy Carden	'56 Mercury	197	250	Running
7	4	42	Lee Petty	Petty Engineering '56 Dodge	196	200	Running
8	7	92	Herb Thomas	Thomas '56 Chevrolet	195	150	Running
9	9	75	Jim Paschal	Frank Hayworth '56 Mercury	192	100	Running
10	14	264	Johnny Allen	Spook Crawford '56 Plymouth	186	100	Running
11	17	203	Pete Yow	Strickland Motors '56 Ford	184	100	Running
12	13	418	George Green	'56 Chevrolet	179	100	Running
13	16	100	Wayne Fielden	'56 Chevrolet	171	100	Running
14	8	16	Tiny Lund	Gus Holzmeuller '56 Chevy	170	100	Bearing
15	18	111	John Fike	'55 Plymouth	146	100	Running
16	1	86	Tim Flock	DePaolo Eng '56 Ford	68	100	Crash
17	11	25	Doug Yates	Sam McCuthen '56 Chevrolet	32	100	Bearing
18	15	60	Brownie King	'56 Chevrolet	17	100	Gas Line

Time of Race: 1 hour, 38 minutes, 3 seconds
Average Speed: 61.193 mph
Pole Winner: Tim Flock - 61.940 mph
Lap Leaders: Tim Flock 1-7, Speedy Thompson 8-88, Buck Baker 89-113
     Thompson 114-167, Baker 168-200.
Cautions: Margin of Victory: 100 Yards   Attendance:

*Buck Baker's big Chrysler cutting the corners at Hillsboro's Orange Speedway.
Baker finished a close 2nd to Fireball Roberts in the 99-miler.*

Baker held on to finish second. Speedy Thompson came in third, Herb Thomas was fourth and Bunk Moore fifth.

The lead changed hands six times as Thompson and Baker diced for the lead much of the way. Roberts had led only two laps before he assumed command for good.

A crowd of 7,200 sat through four caution flags, which held Roberts' average speed to 72.734 mph. Billy Myers' Mercury ran over a loose wheel and lurched into the home chute wall. His Big M pit crew got him back on the track and he was running sixth when his car suddenly burst into flames. Myers jumped out unhurt.

Brownie King flipped his Chevrolet three times in a turn. The rookie driver crawled out without injury.

Herb Thomas and Buck Baker continued their battle for the Grand National driving championship. Going

Race No. 50

Roberts Takes First Place in Hillsboro 99

HILLSBORO, NC (Sept. 30) -- Fireball Roberts pushed his Ford around Buck Baker 26 laps from the finish and won the 99-mile Grand National event at Orange Speedway. It was the fourth win of the year for Roberts.

Ralph Moody rim-rides the .9-mile Orange Speedway.

Grand National Race No. 50
110 Laps at Orange Speedway
Hillsboro, NC
99 Miles on .9-mile Dirt Track
September 30, 1956

Fin	St	No.	Driver	Team / Car	Laps	Money	Status
1	6	22	Fireball Roberts	DePaolo Eng '56 Ford	110	$950	Running
2	3	300B	Buck Baker	Carl Kiekhaefer '56 Chrysler	110	675	Running
3	1	300	Speedy Thompson	Carl Kiekhaefer '56 Chrysler	108	475	Running
4	5	92	Herb Thomas	Thomas '56 Chevrolet	108	365	Running
5	13	35	Bunk Moore	Whitford Bros. '56 Ford	107	320	Running
6	14	19	Harvey Henderson	'56 Ford	101	250	Running
7	20	96	Bob Keck	'55 Chevrolet	99	200	Running
8	19	94	Ed Cole	'55 Mercury	97	150	Running
9	2	12	Ralph Moody	DePaolo Eng '56 Ford	88	100	Running
10	15	16	Tiny Lund	Gus Holzmueller '56 Chevy	84	100	Running
11	16	59	Blackie Pitt	Brownie Pitt '56 Plymouth	83	100	RR Axle
12	12	42	Lee Petty	Petty Engineering '56 Dodge	68	100	A Frame
13	18	418	George Green	'56 Chevrolet	68	100	Stalled
14	9	6	Earl Moss	'56 Merc	62	100	Engine
15	4	31	Bill Champion	Whitford Bros '56 Ford	59	100	A Frame
16	21	203	Pete Yow	Strickland Motors '56 Ford	53	100	Brakes
17	17	60	Brownie Pitt	'56 Chevrolet	49	100	Crash
18	10	83	Johnny Dodson	Dodson '56 Chevrolet	45	100	Steering
19	8	75	Jim Paschal	Frank Hayworth '56 Mercury	43	50	Engine
20	23	4	Billy Myers	Guy Wilson '56 Mercury	27	50	Fire
21	11	62	Bobby Waddell	'56 Chevrolet	18	25	Crash
22	22	20	Buck Hall	Waldron & Co. '55 Buick	11	25	Trans
23	7	264	Johnny Allen	Spook Crawford '56 Plymouth	6	25	Oil Pres

Time of Race: 1 hour, 21 minutes, 40 seconds
Average Speed: 72.734 mph
Pole Position: Speedy Thompson - 88.067 mph
Lap Leaders: Speedy Thompson 1-2, Buck Baker 3-34, Fireball Roberts 35,
   Baker 36-68, Roberts 69, Baker 70-84, Roberts 85-110.
Cautions: 4   Margin of Victory: Attendance: 7,200

into the Hillsboro race, Thomas held a lead of 318 points. Baker picked up 24 points on Thomas at Hillsboro, dropping his deficit to 294 points. With only six more races to go, the Charlotte driver will have to average a gain of 49 points per race to tie.

Johnny Allen #264 and Blackie Pitt race in close quarters at Newport.

Race No. 51

Roberts Outmuscles Baker in Caution-free Newport Race

NEWPORT, TN (Oct. 7) -- Fireball Roberts blazed past Buck Baker in the 150th lap and streaked to victory in the 100-miler at the Tennessee-Carolina Speedway. It was win number six for the former Modified hot-shot.

Baker finished second and chipped a few more points off Herb Thomas' point lead. Bill Amick was third, Joe Weatherly fourth and Thomas fifth. Baker pulled to within 294 points in the point race.

A crowd of 6,000 was on hand in cool autumn weather to watch the accident-free contest. Roberts averaged 61.475 mph for the 100-miler

Joe Eubanks started on the pole for the third time in his career. He did not lead a lap and faded to sixth place in the final order, six laps down.

Speedy Thompson started fourth, but a broken oil line put him out after 141 laps.

Tim Flock and Marvin Panch, in a pair of Fords, went to the sidelines early with brake and oil line problems. Ralph Moody and Jim Paschal were two other threats who failed to finish.

Grand National Race No. 51
200 Laps at Tennessee-Carolina Speedway
Newport, TN
100 Miles on Half-mile Dirt Track
October 7, 1956

Fin	St	No.	Driver	Team / Car	Laps	Money	Status
1	14	22	Fireball Roberts	DePaolo Eng '56 Ford	200	$850	Running
2	2	300B	Buck Baker	Carl Kiekhaefer '56 Chrysler	200	625	Running
3	8	97	Bill Amick	DePaolo Eng '56 Ford	199	450	Running
4	15	31	Joe Weatherly	Whitford Bros '56 Ford	197	350	Running
5	3	92	Herb Thomas	Thomas '56 Chevrolet	196	310	Running
6	1	82	Joe Eubanks	Satcher Motors '56 Ford	196	250	Running
7	11	264	Johnny Allen	Spook Crawford '56 Plymouth	196	200	Running
8	13	4	Billy Myers	Guy Wilson '56 Mercury	193	150	Running
9	9	42	Lee Petty	Petty Engineering '56 Dodge	192	100	Running
10	16	16	Tiny Lund	Gus Holzmueller '56 Chevy	189	100	Running
11	21	83	Johnny Dodson	Dodson '56 Chevrolet	188	100	Running
12	22	60	Brownie King	'56 Chevrolet	185	100	Running
13	10	27	Billy Carden	'56 Mercury	183	100	Running
14	18	418	George Green	'56 Chevrolet	178	100	Running
15	7	12	Ralph Moody	DePaolo Eng '56 Ford	162	100	Vapor Lk
16	17	59	Blackie Pitt	Brownie Pitt '56 Plymouth	158	100	Engine
17	20	111	John Fite	'55 Plymouth	146	100	Heating
18	4	300	Speedy Thompson	Carl Kiekhaefer '56 Chrysler	141	100	Oil Line
19	12	75	Jim Paschal	Frank Hayworth '56 Mercury	141	50	Oil Pres
20	5	86	Tim Flock	John Foster Motors '56 Ford	118	50	Brakes
21	6	98	Marvin Panch	Tom Harbison '56 Ford	99	25	Oil Pres
22	19	41	Billy Rafter	Rafter '56 Dodge	64	25	RR Axle

Time of Race: 1 hour, 37 minutes, 36 seconds
Average Speed: 61.475 mph
Pole Winner: Joe Eubanks - 65.597 mph
Lap Leaders: Buck Baker 1-149, Fireball Roberts 150-200.
Cautions: None   Margin of Victory: Attendance: 6,000

Race No. 52

Baker Bags 12th of Year At Charlotte

CHARLOTTE, NC (Oct.17) -- Buck Baker kept his title hopes alive with a big win in the 100-mile Grand National event at Charlotte Speedway. It was his 12th win, and he closed to within 246 points of leader Herb Thomas, who finished seventh.

Baker started second on the grid and followed leaders Speedy Thompson and Ralph Moody for 29 laps. On lap 30, he surged past Moody to take a lead he would never relinquish.

Moody finished second, with Marvin Panch third. Jim Paschal came in fourth and Bill Amick fifth.

Speedy Thompson, who led the first 14 laps, wound up in sixth place, one spot ahead of Thomas.

Baker gave car owner Carl Kiekhaefer his 26th win of the season, averaging 72.268 mph in the caution-free race.

Grand National Race No. 52
133 Laps at Charlotte Speedway
Charlotte, NC
100 Miles on .75-mile Dirt Track
October 17, 1956

Fin	St	No.	Driver	Team / Car	Laps	Money	Status
1	2	300B	Buck Baker	Carl Kiekhaefer '56 Chrysler	133	$950	Running
2	1	12	Ralph Moody	DePaolo Eng '56 Ford	133	675	Running
3	12	98	Marvin Panch	Tom Harbison '56 Ford	132	475	Running
4	8	75	Jim Paschal	Frank Hayworth '56 Mercury	132	365	Running
5	7	97	Bill Amick	DePaolo Eng '56 Ford	130	320	Running
6	3	300	Speedy Thompson	Carl Kiekhaefer '56 Chrysler	129	250	Running
7	6	92	Herb Thomas	Thomas '56 Chevrolet	127	200	Running
8	5	42	Lee Petty	Petty Engineering '56 Dodge	127	150	Running
9	26	16	Tiny Lund	Gus Holzmueller '56 Chevy	126	100	Running
10	4	22	Fireball Roberts	DePaolo Eng '56 Ford	126	100	Running
11	13	83	Johnny Dodson	Dodson '56 Chevrolet	125	100	Running
12	20	418	George Green	'56 Chevrolet	118	100	Running
13	17	60	Brownie King	'56 Chevrolet	118	100	Running
14	19	13	Jesse James Taylor	'56 Ford	118	100	Running
15	18	25	Jim Donovan	'56 Chevrolet	115	100	Runing
16	15	31	Bill Champion	Whitford Bros '56 Ford	110	100	Engine
17	23	94	Ed Cole	'55 Mercury	110	100	Running
18	22	62	Bobby Waddell	'55 Chevrolet	105	100	Running
19	24	209	Jim Mundy	'56 Plymouth	104	50	Running
20	21	96	Bob Keck	'55 Chevrolet	102	50	Running
21	26	203	Pete Yow	Strickland Motors '56 Ford	99	---	Running
22	10	264	Johnny Allen	Spook Crawford '56 Plymouth	97	---	Radiator
23	27	111	John Fite	'55 Plymouth	96	---	Running
24	9	4	Billy Myers	Guy Wilson '56 Mercury	92	---	A Frame
25	11	27	Billy Carden	'56 Mercury	44	---	Spindle
26	16	34	Dick Beaty	Beaty '56 Ford	30	---	RR Hub
27	14	59	Blackie Pitt	Brownie Pitt '56 Plymouth	21	---	Engine

Time of Race: 1 hour, 22 minutes, 49 seconds
Average Speed: 72.268 mph
Pole Winner: Ralph Moody - 75.041 mph
Lap Leaders: Speedy Thompson 1-14, Ralph Moody 15-29, Buck Baker 30-133.
Cautions: None   Margin of Victory: Attendance: 6,800

Jack Smith watches in horror as cars continue to crash at Shelby.

National Championship in his own independently financed team, was gravely injured in a 109th lap pileup.

Thomas had just taken second place from Speedy Thompson as the pack exited the second turn.

Grand National Race No. 53
200 Laps at Cleveland County
Fairgrounds
Shelby, NC
100 Miles on Half-mile Dirt Track
October 23, 1956

Fin	St	No.	Driver	Team / Car	Laps	Money	Status
1	5	300B	Buck Baker	Carl Kiekhaefer '56 Chrysler	200	$850	Running
2	7	97	Bill Amick	DePaolo Eng '56 Ford	200	625	Running
3	2	98	Marvin Panch	Tom Harbison '56 Ford	200	450	Running
4	4	500B	Speedy Thompson	Carl Kiekhaefer '56 Dodge	197	350	Running
5	12	82	Joe Eubanks	Satcher Motors '56 Ford	191	310	Running
6	8	297	Billy Carden	DePaolo Eng '56 Ford	191	250	Running
7	14	83	Johnny Dodson	Dodson '56 Chevrolet	189	200	Running
8	16	264	Johnny Allen	Spook Crawford '56 Plymouth	184	150	Running
9	26	96	Bobby Keck	'55 Chevrolet	175	100	Running
10	20	75	Jim Paschal	Frank Hayworth '56 Mercury	156	100	Engine
11	24	62	Jimmy Pardue	Pardue '55 Chevrolet	142	100	Running
12	9	22	Fireball Roberts	DePaolo Eng '56 Ford	142	100	Running
13	15	16	Tiny Lund	Gus Holzmueller '56 Chevy	132	100	Crash
14	18	25	Jim Donovan	'56 Chevrolet	132	100	Running
15	23	13	Jess James Taylor	'56 Ford	126	100	Running
16	25	203	Pete Yow	Strickland Motors '56 Ford	118	100	Running
17	13	92	Herb Thomas	Thomas '56 Chevrolet	109	100	Crash
18	3	296	Jack Smith	DePaolo Eng '56 Ford	109	100	Crash
19	10	4	Billy Myers	Guy Wilson '56 Mercury	109	50	Crash
20	6	12	Ralph Moody	DePaolo Eng '56 Ford	109	50	Crash
21	11	42	Lee Petty	Petty Engineering '56 Dodge	108	50	Crash
22	17	418	George Green	'56 Chevrolet	103	50	Crash
23	19	6	Ralph Liguori	Liguori '56 Dodge	98	50	Coil
24	21	60	Brownie King	'56 Chevrolet	94	50	Running
25	1	86	Doug Cox	'56 Ford	70	50	Fire
26	22	41	Billy Rafter	Rafter '56 Dodge	25	50	Engine

Time of Race: 1 hour, 51 minutes
Average Speed: 54.054 mph
Pole Winner: Doug Cox - 58.479 mph
Lap Leaders: - - - - - - - - - Bill Amick   -197, Buck Baker 198-200.
Cautions: 2 (Red Flags)   Margin of Victory: 2 car lengths   Attendance:

Race No. 53

Baker Wins Shelby; Stands to Win Title as Thomas is Badly Injured

SHELBY, NC (Oct. 23) -- Carl Kiekhaefer is a powerful man in many professions. His cars have dominated the 1956 Grand National circuit, but his principal driver, Buck Baker, was running second in the driver standings.

Kiekhaefer, in order to give Baker another chance of catching up in the point race, leased the Cleveland County Fairgrounds, arranged for a NASCAR sanction, and promoted a 100-miler. The race wasn't added to the 1956 schedule until 10 days before the race.

Baker captured the 200 lapper in another patented drive. But point leader Thomas, who had quit the Kiekhaefer team and was on the verge of his third Grand

Thompson, another Kiekhaefer driver, darted into the right rear quarter-panel of Thomas' Chevrolet as it made the pass. Thomas shot across the track, struck a wooden guard rail and was pancaked by the on-rushing pack of cars. Among those involved were Jack Smith, Billy Myers, Tiny Lund, Ralph Moody, Lee Petty, Billy Carden and George Green.

Thomas was removed on a stretcher and rushed to Charlotte Memorial Hospital with a fractured skull, a badly lacerated scalp, a ruptured ear drum and internal injuries. Dr. John Hamrick, who treated Thomas, said he was in a coma and critically injured. He was in possible need of brain surgery.

Bill Amick settled for second place after Baker made a picture perfect broadside into the lead just three laps from the finish. Marvin Panch came in third, Thompson was fourth and Joe Eubanks fifth.

The accident left Thomas with no hope of winning the championship. He still held a lead of 118 points, but three races were left on the schedule with 900 points up for grabs.

Controversy flared at epic proportions about the alleged "teaming up" on Thomas. Baker was cleared of any wrong doing, but Thompson got the wrath from stock car racing supporters for several weeks, as did Kiekhaefer.

Race No. 54

Jack Smith Becomes 19th Different Winner of '56

MARTINSVILLE, VA (Oct. 28) -- Martinsville Speedway and NASCAR promoters organized an auto racing first by staging the first annual "Mixed 400", a

Jack Smith won the Mixed 400 at Martinsville in Kiekhaefer Dodge.

Grand National Race No. 54
400 Laps at Martinsville Speedway
Martinsville, VA
"Mixed 400"
200 Miles on Half-mile Paved Track
October 28, 1956

Fin	St	No.	Driver	Team / Car	Laps	Money	Status
1	23	502	Jack Smith	C Kiekhaefer '56 Dodge GN	400	$2,275	Running
2	21	98	Marvin Panch	Tom Harbison '56 Ford GN	400	1,400	Running
3	5	97	Bill Amick	DePaolo Eng '56 Ford GN	400	950	Running
4	3	300	Speedy Thompson	C Kiekhaefer '56 Chrysler GN	396	700	Running
5	19	22	Fireball Roberts	DePaolo Eng '56 Ford GN	394	600	Running
6	12	72	Joe Weatherly	DePaolo Eng '56 Ford C	394	500	Running
7	1	00	Buck Baker	C Kiekhaefer '56 Chrysler GN	394	350	Running
8	37	35	Bunk Moore	Whitford Bros '56 Ford GN	394	400	Running
9	29	50	Frank Mundy	C Kiekhaefer '56 Dodge GN	393	350	Running
10	16	34	Gwyn Staley	Julian Petty '56 Chevrolet C	389	350	Running
11	20	33	Jimmy Massey	Julian Petty '56 Chevrolet C	389	300	Running
12	31	3	Paul Goldsmith	Smokey Yunick '56 Chevy GN	384	200	Running
13	15	4	Billy Myers	Guy Wilson '56 Mercury GN	383	250	Running
14	13	64	Johnny Allen	Spook Crawford '56 Plym GN	383	200	Running
15	14	49	Bob Welborn	Welborn '56 Chevrolet C	378	200	Running
16	8	86	Don Oldenberg	Oldenberg '55 Buick C	371	150	Running
17	30	71	Bill Poor	Poor '56 Chevrolet C	364	200	Running
18	40	99	Bun Emery	'56 Ford C	364	200	Running
19	18	7	Larry Odo	Odo '56 Chevrolet C	361	150	Running
20	39	16	Tiny Lund	G. Holzmueller '56 Chevy GN	357	200	Running
21	7	42	Lee Petty	Petty Eng '56 Dodge GN	356	100	Running
22	34	14	Bob Keck	Keck '56 Chevrolet C	352	150	Running
23	38	23	Norm Schihl	Schihl '56 Ford C	349	150	Running
24	36	44	Art Binkley	Binkley '55 Plymouth C	349	150	Running
25	27	83	Johnny Dodson	Dodson '56 Chevrolet GN	343	150	Running
26	32	41	Billy Rafter	Rafter '56 Dodge GN	334	250	Running
27	35	31	Bill Champion	Whitford Bros '56 Ford GN	299	150	Running
28	4	26	Curtis Turner	DePaolo Eng '56 Ford C	299	100	Engine
29	9	95	Bob Duell	Julian Buesink '56 Ford GN	245	100	Heating
30	11	12	Ralph Moody	DePaolo Eng '56 Ford GN	183	100	Rear End
31	33	75	Jim Paschal	Frank Hayworth '56 Merc GN	163	50	Engine
32	17	X	Rex White	Max Welborn '56 Ford GN	143	---	Engine
33	6	21	Glen Wood	Wood Bros '56 Ford C	110	---	Engine
34	24	15	Tom Pistone	Pistone '56 Chevrolet C	106	75	Conn Rd
35	2	82	Joe Eubanks	Satcher Motors '56 Ford C	103	---	RF Lugs
36	25	29	Billy Carden	DePaolo Eng '56 Ford GN	87	50	RF Hub
37	28	55	Mel Larson	Larson '56 Ford C	77	50	Piston
38	26	76	Larry Frank	Lonnie Fish '56 Chevrolet C	77	50	Oil Pres
39	10	2	Bill Lutz	'56 Ford C	63	50	Engine
40	22	48	Jimmie Lewallen	Bob Welborn '56 Ford C	11	100	Fuel Pmp

Time of Race: 3 hours, 16 minutes, 17 seconds
Average Speed: 61.136 mph
Pole Winner: Buck Baker - 67.643 mph
Lap Leaders: Joe Eubanks 1-103, Speedy Thompson 104-178, Jack Smith 179-188,
Fireball Roberts 189-200, Bill Amick 201-209, Marvin Panch 210-225, Smith 226-400.
Cautions: 4   Margin of Victory: Attendance: 9,500

unique combination of Grand National hardtops and Convertibles running in the same race. This form of racing would later take up the name "Sweepstakes".

Jack Smith, most recently appointed driver from the Kiekhaefer team, surprisingly came out on top of the 200-miler on the half-mile paved track. The Sandy Springs, GA driver pushed his Dodge to the front on lap 226 and never looked back. He earned $2,275 for his efforts. It was his first Grand National win.

The race was a decisive victory for hard-top sedans. Marvin Panch, Bill Amick, Speedy Thompson and Fireball Roberts rounded out the top five. Joe

Convertibles and Grand National hardtops run at Martinsville Speedway during Mixed 400. Bobby Keck, Bunk Moore and Jimmy Massey chase each other down the backstretch.

Thompson's Chrysler crossed the finish line a scant 4.0 seconds in front of Earnhardt, the fan's favorite. Thompson survived a pit stop with five laps to go. He ducked into the pits, got a splash of fuel and was on his way.

Most of the 3,500 fans in attendance booed Thompson as he accepted the winner's trophy. Track officials, thinking the crowd reaction was related to the Thompson-Earnhardt contest, called for a scoring recheck. Scoring problems had plagued the sanctioning body all season long. Scorecards revealed Thompson to be the winner.

Runner-up Earnhardt took the public address

Weatherly was sixth in the highest finishing convertible.

Joe Eubanks, driving a Ford convertible, led the first 103 laps. While leading, he wobbled down pit road with the lug nuts pulled through the rim on the right front tire. He was through for the day. Thompson, Roberts, Amick and Panch all took turns leading until Smith motored into the lead for good on lap 226.

Buck Baker started on the pole and ran conservatively into a seventh place finish. He took the lead in the point standings by 282 points over the hospitalized Herb Thomas.

Race No. 55

Thompson Edges Earnhardt at Hickory for 8th Win

HICKORY, NC (Nov. 11) -- Speedy Thompson nabbed his eighth win of the year in the Buddy Shuman Memorial 250 at Hickory Speedway.

Ralph Earnhardt, driving in his first Grand National race, got a chance to drive the factory backed Ford normally driven by Fireball Roberts. He did not let his FoMoCo officer down as he led for 15 laps and finished second. Third place went to Buck Baker, who clinched the Grand National driving championship. Ralph Moody was fourth and Doug Cox fifth.

Grand National Race No. 55
250 Laps at Hickory Speedway
Hickory, NC
"Buddy Shuman Memorial"
100 Miles on .4-mile Dirt Track
November 11, 1956

Fin	St	No.	Driver	Team / Car	Laps	Money	Status
1	9	300	Speedy Thompson	Carl Kiekhaefer '56 Chrysler	250	$850	Running
2	1	22	Ralph Earnhardt	DePaolo Eng '56 Ford	250	625	Running
3	2	300B	Buck Baker	Carl Kiekhaefer '56 Chrysler	249	450	Running
4	12	12	Ralph Moody	DePaolo Eng '56 Ford	249	350	Running
5	3	86	Doug Cox	'56 Ford	247	310	Running
6	8	97	Bill Amick	DePaolo Eng '56 Ford	246	250	Running
7	11	16	Tiny Lund	Gus Holzmueller '56 Chevy	244	200	Running
8	5	83	Johnny Dodson	Dodson '56 Chevrolet	241	150	Running
9	17	31	Bill Champion	Whitford Bros '56 Ford	237	100	Running
10	15	75	Bill Blair	Frank Hayworth '56 Mercury	235	100	Running
11	10	42	Lee Petty	Petty Engineering '56 Dodge	232	100	RR Axle
12	18	209	Pete Stewart	'56 Plymouth	221	100	Running
13	22	418	George Green	'56 Chevrolet	221	100	Running
14	14	64	Johnny Allen	'56 Ford	215	100	Running
15	4	2	Junior Johnson	DePaolo Eng '56 Ford	210	100	Vapor Lk
16	16	60	Brownie King	'56 Chevrolet	200	100	Running
17	21	96	Bobby Keck	'56 Chevrolet	179	100	Bearing
18	7	500	Jack Smith	Carl Kiekhaefer '56 Dodge	126	100	Radiator
19	6	4	Bobby Myers	Guy Wilson '56 Mercury	105	50	Radiator
20	19	203	Pete Yow	Strickland Motors '56 Ford	89	50	Trans
21	20	59	Blackie Pitt	Brownie Pitt '56 Plymouth	63	---	Engine
22	13	297	Billy Carden	DePaolo Eng '56 Ford	9	---	Clutch

Time of Race: 1 hour, 30 minutes, 20 seconds
Average Speed: 66.420 mph
Pole Winner: Ralph Earnhardt - 68.278 mph
Lap Leaders: Buck Baker 1-38, Junior Johnson 39-81, Ralph Earnhardt 82-96, Speedy Thompson 97-250.
Cautions: Margin of Victory: 4 seconds   Attendance: 3,500

Cars on the pace lap at Hickory Speedway.

microphone and told the throng he was satisfied with the NASCAR ruling.

Thompson averaged 66.420 mph for his 12th career win.

distance without a pit stop, took the white flag in first place. Thompson had to pit a second time for a few seconds which removed him from the hunt.

Weatherly's Ford ran out of gas on the backstretch on the final lap. He came off the fourth turn without power and beat an on-rushing Baker across the finish line by two car lengths.

Baker's car owner, Carl Kiekhaefer, protested. He had noticed that Baker's Chrysler had gotten to the scoring stand -- which was located to the first turn side of the finish line -- first and contended his car was first under the official clock.

For hours, NASCAR officials deliberated. No rule governing such an occurrence was in the NASCAR rule book. Finally, they decided in favor of Kiekhaefer and Baker, a ruling without precedent.

Weatherly got paid for second place. Thompson was third, Fireball Roberts fourth and Bill Amick fifth.

Baker wrapped up the championship by 586 points over hospitalized Herb Thomas. For the year, Kiekhaefer cars won 30 times, including the last five.

With trouble brewing on the horizon, Kiekhaefer retired from stock car racing and dispersed his outfit after the race. Turbulent waters were flowing in the aftermath of the Thomas/Thompson episode at Shelby, NC.

Race No. 56

Weatherly Finishes First; Baker Declared Wilson Winner

WILSON, NC (Nov. 18) -- the 1956 season finale at the Wilson Speedway ended on a bizarre note as Buck Baker was declared the winner although he clearly finished second.

The scenario went like this. Speedy Thompson led the first 184 laps on the half-mile dirt track. When he pitted for fuel on lap 185, he gave the lead to Baker. When Baker pitted after 197 laps, Weatherly took command. Weatherly, gambling on going the

Buck Baker declared winner at Wilson.

Grand National Race No. 56
200 Laps at Wilson Speedway
Wilson, NC
100 Miles on Half-mile Dirt Track
November 18, 1956

Fin	St	No.	Driver	Team / Car	Laps	Money	Status
1	1	300B	Buck Baker	Carl Kiekhaefer '56 Chrysler	200	$950	Running
2	6	112	Joe Weatherly	DePaolo Eng '56 Ford	200	675	Running
3	3	300	Speedy Thompson	Carl Kiekhaefer '56 Chrysler	200	475	Running
4	9	22	Fireball Roberts	DePaolo Eng '56 Ford	200	365	Running
5	5	97	Bill Amick	DePaolo Eng '56 Ford	199	320	Running
6	14	98	Marvin Panch	Tom Harbison '56 Ford	198	250	Running
7	7	297	Billy Carden	DePaolo Eng '56 Ford	198	200	Running
8	2	12	Ralph Moody	DePaolo Eng '56 Ford	197	150	Running
9	12	42	Lee Petty	Petty Engineering '56 Dodge	194	100	Running
10	15	86	Doug Cox	'56 Ford	194	100	Fuel
11	20	83	Johnny Dodson	Dodson '56 Chevrolet	192	100	Running
12	4	322	Gwyn Staley	'56 Ford	192	100	Running
13	19	64	Johnny Allen	Spook Crawford '56 Plymouth	187	100	Running
14	8	500	Jack Smith	Carl Kiekhaefer '56 Dodge	172	100	Running
15	21	19	James Jones	Jones '56 Ford	169	100	Running
16	10	4	Billy Myers	Guy Wilson '56 Mercury	167	100	Running
17	17	59	Blackie Pitt	Brownie Pitt '56 Plymouth	167	100	Running
18	16	75	Jim Paschal	Frank Hayworth '56 Mercury	156	100	Electric
19	13	16	Tiny Lund	Gus Holzmueller '56 Chevy	101	50	Bearing
20	24	11	Emanuel Zervakis	'56 Chevrolet	51	50	Engine
21	18	3	Bill Champion	Whitford Bros '56 Ford	36	25	Rear End
22	11	35	Bunk Moore	Whitford Bros '56 Ford	36	25	Disqual
23	22	49	Mel Larson	Larson '56 Ford	28	25	Crash
24	23	6	Earl Moss	'56 Mercury	22	25	RR Axle

Time of Race: 1 hour, 58 minutes, 35 seconds
Average Speed: 50.597 mph
Pole Winner: Buck Baker - 60.160 mph
Lap Leaders: Speedy Thompson 1-184, Buck Baker 185-197, Joe Weatherly 198-199, Baker 200.
Cautions: Margin of Victory: 1 foot   Attendance:

1956 NASCAR Season
Final Point Standings Grand National Division

Rank	Driver	Points	Starts	Wins	Top 5	Top 10	Winnings
1	Buck Baker	9,272	48	14	31	39	$34,076.35
2	Herb Thomas	8,568	48	5	22	36	19,351.19
3	Speedy Thompson	8,328	42	8	24	29	27,168.62
4	Lee Petty	8,324	46	2	17	27	15,337.08
5	Jim Paschal	7,878	42	1	16	27	17,203.08
6	Billy Myers	6,920	43	2	13	21	15,829.08
7	Fireball Roberts	5,794	33	5	17	22	14,741.27
8	Ralph Moody	5,548	35	4	13	21	15,492.27
9	Tim Flock	5,062	22	4	11	13	15,768.19
10	Marvin Panch	4,680	20	1	12	13	11,519.40
11	Rex White	4,642	24	0	3	14	5,333.27
12	Johnny Allen	3,924	32	0	2	11	4,558.19
13	Paul Goldsmith	3,788	9	1	4	6	8,568.19
14	Gwyn Staley	3,550	22	0	5	13	5,158.19
15	Joe Eubanks	3,292	26	0	6	13	5,583.19
16	Joe Weatherly	3,084	17	0	6	12	5,250.46
17	Bill Amick	3,048	13	0	7	10	5,380.46
18	Jim Reed	2,870	11	0	5	5	5,076.46
19	Tiny Lund	2,754	21	0	1	8	2,810.46
20	Curtis Turner	2,580	13	1	4	5	14,540.46
21	Jack Smith	2,320	15	1	1	6	3,825.00
22	Billy Carden	2,128	23	0	0	4	2,175.00
23	Lloyd Dane	2,106	10	2	5	9	4,370.00
24	Frank Mundy	1,856	9	0	3	5	3,585.00
25	Bobby Johns	1,832	9	0	0	3	1,450.00
26	Bill Champion	1,764	14	0	0	4	1,570.00
27	Blackie Pitt	1,760	27	0	0	5	1,545.00
28	Harold Hardesty	1,724	9	0	2	6	2,380.00
29	Al Watkins	1,710	14	0	0	4	1,185.00
30	Chuck Meekins	1,656	7	0	3	6	2,815.00
31	Harvey Henderson	1,638	17	0	0	4	1,310.00
32	Eddie Pagan	1,598	8	1	4	4	4,095.00
33	Pat Kirkwood	1,540	3	0	1	2	2,025.00
34	Clyde Palmer	1,516	11	0	4	6	2,755.00
35	Johnny Dodson	1,508	11	0	0	3	1,450.00
36	John Kieper	1,507	8	1	4	7	3,250.00
37	Junior Johnson	1,372	15	0	1	1	1,350.00
38	Bill Blair	1,264	9	0	0	4	1,005.00
39	Tom Harbison *	1,248	0	0	0	0	0
40	Ed Cole	1,200	12	0	0	1	950.00
41	Brownie King	1,140	15	0	0	0	925.00
42	Allen Adkins	1,104	7	0	2	4	1,465.00
43	Bobby Keck	1,076	13	0	0	2	950.00
44	Gordon Haines	1,066	7	0	2	4	1,500.00
	Bob Keefe	1,066	7	0	1	2	1,040.00
46	Dick Beaty	1,036	15	0	0	3	910.00
47	Jim Blomgren	992	5	0	0	1	475.00
48	Ed Negre	952	5	0	2	4	1,255.00
49	Jimmy Massey	950	7	0	3	4	1,545.00
50	Fonty Flock	946	7	1	1	3	1,780.00

* Tom Harbison did not drive in a race in 1956. However, he was credited with 1,248 championship points in the official NASCAR tabulation

The 1957 Season
Factory Teams Withdraw
-- France Picks Up Tab

Volume one of a four volume series . . . . . . The Beginning 1949 - 1958

1957

After spending a year and a half in the NASCAR stock car circles , the automotive manufacturers were set for an all out assault in 1957.

The automotive industry had suspected that the Grand National ranks of NASCAR might be a good marketing area. The heads of General Motors and Ford Motor Company reasoned that winning stock car races would increase sales. The popularity of stock car racing and its access to free publicity were too much of a temptation for Detroit to resist.

Their reasoning was not far off base.

Although it took both Chevrolet and Ford factory teams several months to become steady contenders, interest soared at an all-time high.

General Motors team manager Frankie Del Roy placed Hugh Babb of Atlanta in charge of maintaining a fleet of Chevrolets for the 1957 Grand National season. Some of the drivers on the Chevy pay-roll included Buck Baker, Speedy Thompson, Jack Smith,

Cotton Owens, in the factory backed #6 Pontiac, leads Buck Baker and Dick Foley out of the North turn during the Daytona Beach Grand National event. The manufacturers supported stock car racing until June of 1957 when they withdrew en masse.

NASCAR President Bill France (left) congratulates car owner Peter DePaolo, driver Fireball Roberts and
chief mechanic John Holman after a victory. When the factory support was pulled out of Grand National racing,
DePaolo resigned from Ford. Holman teamed with Ralph Moody to form one of auto racing's most dominant forces.

Rex White and Frankie Schneider.

Ford's effort was in the hands of Peter DePaolo, winner of the 1925 Indianapolis 500. The Ford team was powerful but disappointing -- looking much disorganized at times. Buddy Shuman, retired driver, had been appointed to organize DePaolo's team at the close of the 1956 season, but he lost his life in a Hickory, NC hotel fire on November 10, 1956.

DePaolo's next choice was a hefty, gravel-voiced mechanic named John Holman. It was his duty to smooth over the frayed ends of the Ford factory team. Under his command were drivers Fireball Roberts, Curtis Turner, Joe Weatherly, Bill Amick, Marvin Panch and Ralph Moody.

Pontiac's modest involvement was through the Ray Nichels shops in Highland, IN. Cotton Owens and Banjo Matthews started the year off with Pontiacs.

California's Bill Stroppe handled the Mercury teams with Guy Wilson doing the mechanical work for East Coast drivers. Modified champ Billy Myers and Jim Paschal accepted driving chores.

The Lee Petty team raced Oldsmobiles that were more independently flavored. Old Master Petty and Ralph Earnhardt were the drivers for the two-car team.

The Plymouth division of Chrysler had Ronney Householder heading a one-car effort operated by Ankrum "Spook" Crawford. Flashy Johnny Allen took the controls.

The remainder of the starting grids were formed by independent teams, who did not have access to the big

Jack Smith's factory Chevrolet #47 leads a pair of Pontiacs driven by Banjo Matthews #8 and Darel Dieringer #85 at Daytona Beach.

highly successful boat motors.

Some reporters indicated Mercury used the lettering to their advantage, accenting the name rather than the product. Kiekhaefer got wind of the situation and chamged the lettering on his cars to *'Kiekhaefer Outboards'* for 1956.

The horsepower race was in full gear as the 1957 campaign got underway. Fuel-injected engines and superchargers were eligible since each manufacturer said the high performance pieces could be purchased by the public.

The directors of the Automobile Manufacturers Association were disturbed about the excessive advertising of brute horsepower, even if the ads were being done in an ethical manner. The nation's highways were the scene of record-breaking fatal wrecks and the AMA was concerned at the astronomical rise of horsepower in passenger cars.

industry dollars. They were more or less scrapping for leftovers.

There was never any pretense about Detroit's interest in racing as a sporting competition or any other phase of the speed spectaculars. Being manufacturers of cars, Detroit had no sentiment about NASCAR as a sporting proposition. It was strictly big business. Their sole purpose was to boost the sale of new cars.

Each manufacturer had swarms of press agents and hacksters to beat the drums of publicity in newspapers, magazines, radio and television. The factories produced optimum equipment in souped up vehicles with power and durability lacking in the same models sold to John Q. Citizen.

Advertising values of the controlled performances became dubious. Each manufacturer was laying claims to victory and bragging rights about performances because they could not afford to do otherwise. The result was an avalanche of half-truths and untruths that finally forced NASCAR to adopt a 1957 rule requiring "honest" advertising and publicity.

It started in 1955 when Carl Kiekhaefer's Chryslers carried large letters that read *'Mercury Outboards'*. There were reports that Lincoln-Mercury division of Ford Motor Co. reaped the most profits because the name of their automobile was the same as Mr. K's

In an attempt to appease the AMA, NASCAR outlawed all fuel injectors and superchargers. The sanctioning body then went one step further and disallowed the use of any race results in media advertising. Violating car makers would lose manufacturer's points. Both Ford and Chevrolet violated the non-advertising law and both lost manufacturer's points in the early part of the 1957 season.

The entire picture changed on May 19, 1957. In a scheduled 500 lap Grand National race at Martinsville Speedway, Billy Myers' Mercury hurtled a retaining wall and hit a number of spectators, including an eight year-old boy.

The boy, Alvin Helsabeck, was gravely injured. Four other spectators required treatment at a hospital.

Headlines of the incident flashed across the sports pages nationwide. The Associated Press and United Press International picked up on the story and virtually every American was aware of the unfortunate Virginia 500 crash. It was the type of publicity that AMA directors did not like to see.

On Thursday, June 6, 1957, heads of several car

companies, sitting as directors of the Automobile Manufacturers Association, recommended unanimously that the industry take no part or assist in any way automobile races or other competitive events in which speed or horse power are emphasized.

The Assocation believed, the recommendation said, "That the automobile manufacturers should encourage owners and drivers to evaluate passenger cars in terms of useful power and ability to provide safe, reliable and comfortable transportation, rather than in terms of capacity of speed."

Whatever may have prompted the recommendation, the car makers called upon themsevles to get out of all competitive tests of cars involving or suggesting racing or speed, including acceleration tests.

They also recommended that the industry "should not advertise or publicize actual or comparative capabilities of passenger cars for speed, or specific engine size, torque, horsepower or ability to accelerate or perform, in any context that suggests speed."

The fleet of factory backed race cars were left in the hands of the drivers, who suddenly found themselves team owners. A heavy transition was already on the horizon.

When the AMA made its announcement, it was only a few hours before NASCAR President Bill France issued a prepared statement. *"Business will continue as usual,"* declared France. *"We are interested in giving mechanically-minded and competitively minded Americans an opportunity to test their automobiles in supervised off-the-highway areas and we are extending our operations in this direction in many sections of the country. As always, safety is the primary objective of the National Association of Stock Car Auto Racing.*

"We believe it is essential to provide areas where drivers can take part, not only in such events as acceleration tests but also tests which involve braking, parking, driver reflexes and so on," added France. *"We believe such areas are a definite need and that they willl go far in letting drivers give expression to their desires to test their cars and at the same time, promote safety by letting drivers operate under experienced supervision and in proper areas."*

France took the position of the politician. *"I think that when the industry was actively competing in NASCAR racing, it learned a lot about handling and performance. In fact, more about its own cars than it had known before, even though it had built them.*

"Consequently, I think the industry's participation will reflect favorably on cars to come. I feel that the automobile industry cannot divorce itself from the moral obligation which it owes to mechanically-minded, competitive American car owners.

"One thing I will say," noted France, *"the industry's powers sure did play hard while they were playing."*

France subscribed to the theory that the factory withdrawal would encourage more independent teams to come back to the tracks. To help the teams compensate for the lack of factory dollars, France convinced individual race promoters to raise the purse of their events, especially to the winner.

In the early part of 1957, winner's prizes were as low as $650. After the factories got out, first place went up to $1,000.

The first major event after the withdrawal was the Raleigh 250 at Raleigh's one-mile paved superspeedway. Posted awards were $14,300, and France felt he needed a huge field to prove to the stock car racing fans that it was 'business as usual'.

The field was open to 60 cars, but only the top 30 would get official prize money. In order to guarantee a large field, France made a guarantee to the car owners. The NASCAR Prexy promised he would make sure every competitor got at least $300 for coming to Raleigh in the form of 'travel money'.

Every team which finished below 30th got $300. Those drivers finishing 15th through 30th positions, which paid less than $300, would be given enough money to equal $300.

Fifty-three cars started the Raleigh 250, which was won by Paul Goldsmith in a Ford. He won $4,000. France, promoter and director of the 13th superspeedway race in NASCAR history, paid 39 teams some $8,850 in 'travel money'.

The 'travel money' cut deeply into France's profits. But his investment was not in the Raleigh 250 purse -- France's investment was in the sport and the NASCAR members.

Buck Baker won his second Grand National championship in Chevrolets he groomed himself. He won 10 times in 40 starts for a total of $30,763.40 in point and prize money. The Charlotte veteran finished 38 of the 40 starts in the top 10. At one stretch during the latter half of 1956 and the first eight months of 1957, Baker placed in the top 10 in 35 consecutive events -- a NASCAR record.

Ken Rush of High Point, who competed in both the Grand Nationals and Convertibles, was named Rookie of the Year by the sanctioning body. He was the first freshman driver so honored since 1954, when Blackie Pitt was named top freshman driver.

Race No. 1

Panch Leads Ford 1-2-3 Sweep at Willow Springs

LANCASTER, CA (Nov. 11) -- Marvin Panch led a 1-2-3 sweep for Ford automobiles with a flawless performance on the tricky 11-turn Willow Springs International Raceway. It was Panch's second Grand National victory, and it came in the 1957 season opener.

Fireball Roberts finished second, 11.8 seconds behind Panch at the finish of the 60-lap, 150-mile event over the oiled dirt road course. Third place went to George Seeger, with Jim Paschal fourth and Eddie Pagan fifth.

Panch started on the pole and led the first 31 laps. Seeger, wheeling a Ford entered by Oscar Maples, Inc., ran down Panch in the 32nd lap and paced the 34 car field for 57.5 miles. After pit stops had been completed, Panch drove his DePaolo Engineering Ford back to the front with 10 laps remaining. He led the rest of the way.

Chuck Meekins, Billy Myers, Danny Letner and Parnelli Jones, all considered co-favorites in the 150-mile chase, crashed in four separate incidents. No drivers were injured.

The first place finish paid Panch $1,550 for his 78.648 mph afternoon.

Race No. 2

Panch Leads 99 of 100 Miles; Wins at Concord

CONCORD, NC (Dec. 2) -- Marvin Panch made it two in a row in the 100-miler at Concord Speedway, giving the DePaolo-Holman Ford team a perfect start in the 1956 season. The event was postponed a week

Grand National Race No. 1
60 Laps at Willow Springs
International Raceway
Lancaster, CA
150 Miles on 2.5-mile Dirt Road Course
November 11, 1956

Fin	St	No.	Driver	Team / Car	Laps	Money	Status
1	1	98	Marvin Panch	DePaolo Eng '56 Ford	60	$1,550	Running
2	5	22	Fireball Roberts	DePaolo Eng '56 Ford	60	1,000	Running
3	4	12	George Seeger	Oscar Maples Inc '56 Ford	60	755	Running
4	8	75	Jim Paschal	Frank Hayworth '56 Mercury	59	570	Running
5	9	45	Eddie Pagan	Pagan '56 Ford	50	430	Running
6	14	43	Bob Ross	Ross '56 Mercury	58	320	Running
7	6	17	Lloyd Dane	Dane '56 Ford	57	325	Running
8	11	21	Scotty Cain	Cain '56 Ford	56	215	Running
9	2	3	Paul Goldsmith	Smokey Yunick '56 Ford	55	225	Running
10	18	00	Dick Getty	Betty Getty '56 Chevrolet	55	135	Running
11	20	98W	Mike McGreevy	'56 Dodge	55	135	Running
12	12	34	Sherman Clark	Clark '55 Chevrolet	54	115	Running
13	23	18	Eddie Gray	Charles Green '56 Chevrolet	54	110	Running
14	25	35	Billy Cantrell	'56 Mercury	53	110	Running
15	24	188	Jim Blomgren	'56 Ford	53	110	Running
16	21	33	Bob Osborne	'56 Dodge	52	110	Running
17	17	8	Ed Brown	'56 Chevrolet	52	115	Running
18	10	1	Chuck Mekins	James Rush '56 Chevrolet	51	115	Crash
19	27	9	Jim Cook	Art Krebs '56 Pontiac	51	85	Running
20	26	89	Clyde Mitchell	'56 Ford	50	60	Running
21	30	66	Dick Hoffman	'54 Mercury	50	60	Running
22	7	4	Billy Myers	Bill Stroppe '56 Mercury	49	90	Crash
23	32	54	Ray Franklin	'56 Dodge	42	60	Running
24	3	11	Parnelli Jones	Oscar Maples Inc '56 Ford	34	50	Steering
25	13	30	Clyde Palmer	Jack Chataney '56 Plymouth	33	80	Con Rod
26	15	68	Frank Secrist	'56 Chevrolet	24	45	Con Rod
27	16	88	Danny Letner	Tom Harbison '56 Dodge	22	65	Crash
28	19	26	Fred Hunt	'55 Chevrolet	20	50	Con Rod
29	22	125	Elgin Holmes	'54 Buick	14	35	Clutch
30	28	86	Walt James	'55 Mercury	14	35	Bearing
31	31	46	George Norton	'56 Chevrolet	10	35	RR axle
32	29	48	Bill Moore	Moore '56 Ford	7	35	Fuel Pmp
33	33	80	Ed Negre	'56 Olds	0	---	Engine
34	34	91	Russ Dohlem	'55 Plymouth	0	---	Engine

Time of Race: 1 hour, 54 minutes, 26 seconds
Average Speed: 78.648 mph
Pole Winner: Marvin Panch - 78.596 mph
Lap Leaders: Marvin Panch 1-31, George Seeger 32-50, Panch 51-60.
Cautions: Margin of Victory: 11.8 seconds   Attendance:

Grand National Race No. 2
200 Laps at Concord Speedway
Concord, NC
100 Miles on Half-mile Dirt Track
December 2, 1956

Fin	St	No.	Driver	Team / Car	Laps	Money	Status
1	3	98	Marvin Panch	DePaolo Eng '56 Ford	200	$650	Running
2	6	3	Paul Goldsmith	Smokey Yunick '56 Chevrolet	200	525	Running
3	5	97	Bill Amick	Oscar Maples '56 Ford	199	400	Running
4	10	16	Tiny Lund	Gus Holzmueller '56 Chevy	194	320	Running
5	9	42	Lee Petty	Petty Engineering '56 Dodge	193	290	Running
6	14	75	Jim Paschal	Frank Hayworth '56 Mercury	192	250	Running
7	17	79	Mel Larson	Larson '56 Ford	186	200	Running
8	2	J12	Joe Weatherly	DePaolo Eng '56 Ford	181	250	Running
9	8	82	Joe Eubanks	Satcher Motors '56 Ford	180	100	Running
10	25	100	Bill Morton	'56 Chevrolet	169	100	Running
11	23	60	Brownie King	Jess Potter '56 Ford	167	100	Running
12	22	22	Ralph Earnhardt	DePaolo Eng '56 Ford	164	100	Crash
13	21	94	Ed Cole	'55 Mercury	163	100	Running
14	19	4	Billy Myers	Guy Wilson '56 Mercury	153	100	Running
15	12	27	Billy Carden	'56 Mercury	142	100	Running
16	16	83	Johnny Dodson	Dodson '56 Chevrolet	141	100	Running
17	15	34	Dirk Beaty	Beaty '56 Ford	141	100	Running
18	4	12	Ralph Moody	DePaolo Eng '56 Ford	132	100	Engine
19	13	64	Johnny Allen	Spook Crawford '56 Plymouth	120	50	Crash
20	11	610	Jack Smith	'56 Chevrolet	97	50	
21	1	C22	Curtis Turner	DePaolo Eng '56 Ford	79	50	Crash
22	7	31	Bill Champion	Whitford Bros '56 Ford	64	50	
23	24	62	Bobby Waddell	'55 Chevrolet	39	50	
24	18	86	Doug Cox	'56 Ford	28	50	Disqual
25	20	203	Bill Hall	'56 Ford	25	50	

Time of Race: 1 hour, 47 minutes, 22 seconds
Average Speed: 55.883 mph
Pole Winner: Curtis Turner - 62.586 mph
Lap Leaders: Curtis Turner 1-2, Panch 3-200.
Cautions: Margin of Victory: Attendance:

when a cold snap left the half-mile dirt track 'frozen out', according to promoter Bruton Smith.

Paul Goldsmith, wheeling a Smokey Yunick Chevrolet under the new General Motors racing manager Frankie Del Roy, took second place. Bill Amick, in another DePaolo-Holman entry, copped third place. Fourth and fifth were Tiny Lund and Lee Petty.

Curtis Turner started on the pole and led the first two laps. Panch sailed into the lead on lap three and led the rest of the way. Only Goldsmith was in the same lap with Panch at the finish.

Turner crashed in the 79th lap while battling for second place. He wound up 21st in the field of 25.

Johnny Allen spun his Plymouth into a telegraph pole on lap 122. The pole toppled into the grandstands, but fortunately it was an area with few spectators. No injuries were reported.

Ralph Earnhardt, subbing for Fireball Roberts who missed a plane connection and did not arrive in time to compete, went over a dirt embankment in the 167th lap. He was not hurt.

Panch won $650 for his efforts and moved to a 64 point lead in the standings over Jim Paschal, who finished sixth in the 100-miler.

Race No. 3

Holman-led Ford Team Sweeps Titusville Road Race

TITUSVILLE, FL (Dec. 30) -- Fireball Roberts took the lead in the 28th lap and led a 1-2-3-4 sweep for the DePaolo-Holman Ford factory team in the 89.6-mile Grand National race at Titusville-Cocoa Speedway.

It was Roberts' seventh career win and his first on a road course. John Holman, recently appointed to direct Peter DePaolo's factory Ford team on the NAS-CAR tour, had a 'Carl Kiekhaefer' type of afternoon as his Fords took the first four places. Curtis Turner came in second, Marvin Panch was third with Ralph Moody fourth. The independent Ford of Doug Cox was fifth.

A disappointing slim field of 15 entered NASCAR's fifth road race. Paul Goldsmith took Smokey Yunick's Chevrolet around the 1.6-mile course at an average speed of 69.106 mph. The St. Clair Shores, MI driver took the lead at the outset and led for 27 laps. Roberts motored past in lap 28 and led to the finish of the 56-lap contest.

Goldsmith departed on lap 34 with a mechanical problem and wound up 13th. Only three cars failed to go the distance.

A crowd of 16,000 was on hand to watch the event, which was staged at the Titusville-Cocoa Airport.

Grand National Race No. 3
56 Laps at Titusville-Cocoa Speedway
Titusville, FL
89.6 Miles on 1.6-mile Paved Road Course
December 30, 1956

Fin	St	No.	Driver	Team / Car	Laps	Money	Status
1	2	22	Fireball Roberts	DePaolo Eng '56 Ford	56	$850	Running
2	3	C22	Curtis Turner	DePaolo Eng '56 Ford	56	625	Running
3	6	98	Marvin Panch	DePaolo Eng '56 Ford	56	450	Running
4	4	12	Ralph Moody	DePaolo Eng '56 Ford	56	350	Running
5	7	86	Doug Cox	'56 Ford	55	310	Running
6	9	42A	Tiny Lund	Petty Engineering '56 Dodge	54	250	Running
7	10	75	Jim Paschal	Frank Hayworth '56 Mercury	53	200	Running
8	12	64	Johnny Allen	Spook Crawford '56 Plymouth	53	150	Running
9	11	38	Mel Larson	'56 Dodge	51	100	Running
10	15	69	Dick Joslin	'56 Chevrolet	48	100	Running
11	8	42	Lee Petty	Petty Engineering '56 Dodge	47	100	Running
12	14	424	Chuck Thompson	'54 Olds	47	100	Running
13	1	3	Paul Goldsmith	Smokey Yunick '56 Chevrolet	34	100	Fan Belt
14	13	79	Jimmy Thompson	'56 Ford	24	100	Rear End
15	5	J12	Joe Weatherly	DePaolo Eng '56 Ford	17	100	Clutch

Time of Race: No Time Recorded
Average Speed: None Recorded
Pole Winner: Paul Goldsmith - 69.106 mph
Lap Leaders: Paul Goldsmih 1-27, Fireball Roberts 28-56.
Cautions: Margin of Victory: Attendance: 16,000

Race No. 4

Owens and Pontiac Get First Win at Daytona

DAYTONA BEACH, FL (Feb. 17) -- Cotton Owens of Spartanburg, SC, assigned to drive a factory backed Pontiac in the 160-mile Grand National spectacle on the sands of Daytona, responded with a brilliant victory.

It was Owens' first career victory in Grand National competition, and it was the first time the Pontiac nameplate has visited victory lane.

For the popular Owens, who has been a part time driver in Grand National racing since 1950, the victory came before 35,000 fans in his 20th big league

An aerial view of the North turn of the famous Daytona Beach & Road Course.

and Marvin Panch in the De-Paolo-Holman Ford fifth.

Banjo Matthews started on the pole, but he departed midway with mechanical problems. He wound up 41st in the 57 car field.

Owens had led all but one lap when he made his only pit stop on lap 23. Owens' Pontiac was serviced in 61 seconds. Goldsmith pitted eight laps later and his Yunick-led crew did the work in 47 seconds. Goldsmith had padded his advantage to 25 seconds when his engine came apart.

Everett Brashear's Plymouth stalled in a sand bank. The yellow was displayed to warn other drivers, but officials left the car on the edge of the track. Lee Petty plowed into the idle car late in

start.

In what was an all-out effort by the Detroit manufacturers, Owens and Chevy ace Paul Goldsmith treated the sell-out audience to a tremendous duel. Owens led on three occasions and Goldsmith on two. The final outcome was sealed when Goldsmith's engine blew with eight laps to go. Johnny Beauchamp, driving a factory backed Chevrolet set up by Georgian Hugh Babb, finished second, 55 seconds behind Owens' fleet Pontiac. Third place went to Fonty Flock, who was driving an industry-supported Mercury wrenched by Californian Bill Stroppe. Buck Baker in a Babb Chevrolet was fourth

Daytona winner Cotton Owens and sponsor Jim Stephens with the victorious '57 Pontiac.

the race, putting himself out of the event.

Owens averaged 101.541 mph, the first Grand National race to be run at more than 100 mph.

Joe Weatherly (on the inside), Don Oldenberg and Charlie Cregar make it three abreast in sandy North turn at Daytona.

Grand National Race No. 4
39 Laps at Beach & Road Course
Daytona Beach, FL
160 Miles on 4.1-mile Beach & Road Course
February 17, 1957

Fin	St	No.	Driver	Team / Car	Laps	Money	Status
1	3	6	Cotton Owens	Ray Nichels '57 Pontiac	39	$4,250	Running
2	13	50	Johnny Beauchamp	Hugh Babb '57 Chevrolet		2,450	Running
3	4	18	Fonty Flock	Bill Stroppe '57 Mercury		1,500	Running
4	18	87	Buck Baker	Hugh Babb '57 Chevrolet		900	Running
5	21	98	Marvin Panch	DePaolo Eng '57 Ford		700	Running
6	27	43	Bill Lutz	Petty Engineering '57 Olds		600	
7	39	99	Curtis Turner	DePaolo Eng '57 Ford		500	
8	50	46	Speedy Thompson	Hugh Babb '57 Chevrolet		400	
9	53	44	Rex White	Hugh Babb '57 Chevrolet		250	
10	36	505	Charlie Cregar	Cregar '57 Plymouth		200	
11	49	712	Glen Wood	Wood Bros '56 Ford		150	
12	10	15	Tim Flock	Bill Stroppe '57 Mercury		135	
13	22	500	Phil Orr	May Day Inc '57 Ford		110	
14	28	90	Don Oldenberg	Osiecki Racing '57 Plymouth		100	
15	29	112	Rod Perry	Robert Whitmire '56 Ford		100	
16	11	14	Billy Myers	Bill Stroppe '57 Mercury		90	
17	30	64	Johnny Allen	Spook Crawford '57 Plymouth		80	
18	42	9	Joe Weatherly	DePaolo Eng '57 Ford		75	
19	46	34	Dick Beaty	Beaty '56 Ford		75	
20	34	36	Jim Delaney	Tom Harbison '57 Plymouth		75	
21	45	411	Jack Goodwin	'57 Ford		60	
22	16	29	Russ Hepler	Howard Coulter '57 Pontiac		60	
23	38	28	Eddie Skinner	Skinner '57 Ford		60	
24	20	3	Paul Goldsmith	Smokey Yunick '57 Chevrolet	31	60	Engine
25	51	640	Ken Love	Richard Gallop '57 Ford		60	
26	47	121	Scotty Cain	Cain '56 Ford		50	
27	33	42	Lee Petty	Petty Engineering '57 Olds		50	Crash
28	25	37	Pat Kirkwood	Herschel White '57 Plymouth		50	
29	32	527	Lem Svajian	'57 Plymouth		50	
30	57	55	Mel Larson	Larson '56 Ford		50	
31	9	20	Fred Boggs	Floyd's Auto Sales '57 Ford		25	
32	55	441	Chuck Hobs	Hobbs '57 Chevrolet		25	Crash
33	24	310	Joe Lee Johnson	S T Campbell '56 Dodge		25	
34	2	47	Jack Smith	Hugh Babb '57 Chevrolet		25	
35	37	23	Hank Chapman	Chapman '56 Pontiac		25	
36	44	154	Nace Mattingly	Mattingly '57 Ford		25	
37	14	22	Fireball Roberts	DePaolo Eng '57 Ford		25	
38	26	25A	Everett Brashear	Osiecki Racing '57 Plymouth		25	Crash
39	31	248	Sonny Morgan	Morgan '57 Plymouth		25	
40	7	45	Frankie Schneider	Hugh Babb '57 Chevrolet		25	
41	1	8	Banjo Matthews	Ray Nichels '57 Pontiac		100	
42	52	74	L D Austin	Austin '56 Chevrolet		---	
43	17	97	Ralph Moody	DePaolo Eng '57 Ford		---	
44	5	188	Tiny Lund	Petty Engineering '57 Olds		---	
45	8	17	Jim Paschal	Bill Stroppe '57 Mercury		---	
46	6	85	Darel Dieringer	'57 Pontiac		---	Crash
47	54	76	George West	Lonnie Fish '56 Chevrolet		---	
48	56	61	Dick Foley	Canada '57 Chevrolet		---	
49	12	39	Ed Fiola	George Mallinger '57 Chevrolet		---	
50	43	32	Brownie King	Jess Potter '56 Chevrolet		---	
51	48	81	Bernie Hentges	'56 Dodge		---	
52	40	54	Al Tasnady	Romeo Gelsi '57 Plymouth		---	
53	41	12	Bill Amick	DePaolo Eng '57 Ford		---	
54	15	7	Jim Reed	DePaolo Eng '57 Ford		---	
55	35	226	Russ Truelove	Bill White '56 Mercury		---	
56	23	118	Jim Russell	Russell '57 Ford		---	
57	19	95	Bob Duell	Julian Buesink '57 Ford		---	

Time of Race: 1 hour, 34 minutes, 29 seconds
Average Speed: 101.541 mph
Pole Winner: Banjo Matthews - 134.382 mph
Lap Leaders: Cotton Owens 1-10, Paul Goldsmith 11, Owens 12-23, Goldsmith 24-31 Owens 32-39.
Cautions: 1   Margin of Victory: 55 seconds   Attendance: 35,000

Race No. 5

Jack Smith Wins Shootout at Concord

CONCORD, NC (Mar. 3) -- Jack Smith took the lead with 14 laps to go and held off Buck Baker to win the 100-mile thriller at Concord Speedway.

Mel Larson's independent Ford earned the pole position, but he quickly yielded to a battle of factory backed machines. Speedy Thompson's Chevrolet got the early lead, holding it for 30 laps. Fireball Roberts shoved his Ford in front for 54 laps before a round of pit stops changed the complexion of the race.

Roberts pitted on lap 84,

Jack Smith

giving the lead to Smith. Smith was in front only one lap before he pitted. Thompson led the 86th lap and then Smith was back in front.

Baker finished second, 6.0 seconds behind the winner. Thompson wound up third, giving Chevrolet factory backed cars and owner Hugh Babb a 1-2-3 sweep. Roberts experienced pit problems and fell to fourth. Larson salvaged fifth place.

A crowd of 11,000 showed up at the half-mile oval for the Carolinas opener. The race had to be held up 25 minutes to allow the large gathering to find their seats. By race time it was strictly standing room only.

Glen Wood brought out the only caution of the day. The Stuart, VA driver rolled his Ford in the 78th lap. He was not hurt.

Point leader Marvin Panch blew an engine after 57 laps. He still held a 488 point lead over Jim Paschal who lasted only 10 more laps than Panch. He lost the clutch in his Mercury.

Buck Baker #87 leads Jack Smith #47, Nace Mattingly #154 and Paul Goldsmith #97 through turn at Wilson Speedway.

Race No. 6

Moody Laps Field Twice in Wilson 100

WILSON, NC (Mar. 17) -- Ralph Moody, racing out of Dania, FL, passed Fireball Roberts in the 101st lap and led the rest of the way to win the 100 miler at Wilson Speedway. It was the fifth win of his career for the Ford 'racing executive'.

Buck Baker finished second in a Chevrolet, two laps behind Moody. Speedy Thompson came in third. Lee Petty and Tiny Lund, both in Petty Enginering Oldsmobiles finished fourth and fifth.

Roberts led the first half of the race from the pole. But shortly after losing the lead to Moody, his Ford developed a miss in the engine. He struggled to finish ninth, 18 laps behind the winner.

Once in the lead, Moody never looked back. It was the fifth career Grand National win for the native New Englander.

Billy Myers crashed his Mercury in the 40th lap. The first of two yellow flags was waved while a wrecker removed the car from the track.

Point leader Marvin Panch went out with clutch problems after 52 laps. His point lead stood at 416 over Baker, who moved into second place.

Moody averaged 55.079 mph in becoming the fifth different winner in the six Grand National races of 1957.

Grand National Race No. 5
200 Laps at Concord Speedway
Concord, NC
100 Miles on Half-mile Dirt Track
March 3, 1957

Fin	St	No.	Driver	Team / Car	Laps	Money	Status
1	9	47	Jack Smith	Hugh Babb '57 Chevrolet	200	$650	Running
2	10	87	Buck Baker	Hugh Babb '57 Chevrolet	200	525	Running
3	2	46	Speedy Thompson	Hugh Babb '57 Chevrolet	200	400	Running
4	5	22	Fireball Roberts	DePaolo Eng '57 Ford	200	320	Running
5	1	55	Mel Larson	Larson '56 Ford	189	290	Running
6	17	32	Brownie King	Jess Potter '56 Chevrolet	179	250	Running
7	16	34	Dick Beaty	Beaty '56 Ford	175	200	Running
8	15	505	Charlie Cregar	Cregar '57 Plymouth	173	150	Fan Belt
9	18	74	L D Austin	Austin '56 Chevrolet	165	100	Running
10	7	82	Cotton Owens	Satcher Motors '56 Ford	161	100	Gas Tank
11	20	86	Doug Cox	'56 Ford	147	100	Gas Tank
12	14	64	Johnny Allen	Spook Crawford '57 Plymouth	80	100	Clutch
13	6	112	Glen Wood	Wood Bros '56 Ford	77	100	Crash
14	3	14	Billy Myers	Bill Stroppe '57 Mercury	73	100	Clutch
15	8	17	Jim Paschal	Bill Stroppe '57 Mercury	67	100	Rear End
16	4	12	Marvin Panch	DePaolo Eng '57 Ford	57	100	Engine
17	11	97	Joe Weatherly	DePaolo Eng '57 Ford	50	100	Rear End
18	12	99	Curtis Turner	DePaolo Eng '57 Ford	41	100	Axle
19	19	23	Ned Jarrett	Jarrett '56 Ford	7	50	Engine
20	13	188	Tiny Lund	Petty Engineering '57 Olds	6	50	Engine

Time of Race: 1 hour, 40 minutes, 14 seconds
Average Speed: 59.860 mph
Pole Winner: Mel Larson - 62.225 mph
Lap Leaders: Speedy Thompson 1-30, Fireball Roberts 31-84, Jack Smith 85, Thompson 86, Smith 87-200.
Cautions: 1   Margin of Victory: 6 seconds   Attendance: 11,000

Grand National Race No. 6
200 Laps at Wilson Speedway
Wilson, NC
100 Miles on Half-mile Dirt Track
March 17, 1957

Fin	St	No.	Driver	Team / Car	Laps	Money	Status
1	4	12	Ralph Moody	DePaolo Eng '57 Ford	200	$850	Running
2	5	87	Buck Baker	Hugh Babb '57 Chevrolet	198	625	Running
3	9	46	Speedy Thompson	Hugh Babb '57 Chevrolet	196	450	Running
4	8	42	Lee Petty	Petty Engineering '57 Olds	195	350	Running
5	17	188	Tiny Lund	Petty Engineering '57 Olds	195	310	Running
6	15	97	Paul Goldsmith	DePaolo Eng '57 Ford	194	250	Running
7	14	32	Brownie King	Jess Potter '56 Chevrolet	183	200	Running
8	10	505	Charlie Cregar	Cregar '57 Plymouth	183	150	Running
9	1	22	Fireball Roberts	DePaolo Eng '57 Ford	182	100	Running
10	3	47	Jack Smith	Hugh Babb '57 Chevrolet	174	100	Running
11	13	154	Nace Mattingly	Mattingly '57 Ford	172	100	Running
12	19	76	George Green	Lonnie Fish '56 Chevrolet	171	100	Running
13	20	74	L D Austin	Austin '56 Chevrolet	160	100	Running
14	21	94	Clarence DeZalia	DeZalia '56 Ford	157	100	Running
15	18	112	Bob Whitmire	Whitmire '56 Ford	153	100	Running
16	16	11	Emanuel Zervakis	'56 Chevrolet	133	100	Shocks
17	12	35	Bill Champion	Whitford Bros. '56 Ford	113	100	Gas Line
18	7	17	Jim Paschal	Bill Stroppe '57 Mercury	98	100	Steering
19	2	98	Marvin Panch	DePaolo Eng '57 Ford	52	50	Clutch
20	11	64	Johnny Allen	Spook Crawford '57 Plymouth	43	50	Head
21	6	14	Billy Myers	Bill Stroppe '57 Mercury	40	---	Crash

Time of Race: 1 hour, 48 minutes, 56 seconds
Average Speed: 55.079 mph
Pole Winner: Fireball Roberts - 59.269 mph
Lap Leaders: Fireball Roberts 1-100, Ralph Moody 101-200.
Cautions: Margin of Victory: 2 laps   Attendance: 10,000

Grand National Race No. 7
110 Laps at Orange Speedway
Hillsboro, NC
99 Miles on .9-mile Dirt Track
March 24, 1957

Fin	St	No.	Driver	Team / Car	Laps	Money	Status
1	3	87	Buck Baker	Hugh Babb '57 Chevrolet	110	$650	Running
2	4	46	Speedy Thompson	Hugh Babb '57 Chevrolet	110	525	Running
3	5	47	Jack Smith	Hugh Babb '57 Chevrolet	109	400	Running
4	8	99	Paul Goldsmith	Smokey Yunick '57 Ford	109	320	Running
5	10	42	Lee Petty	Petty Engineering '57 Olds	107	290	Running
6	18	74	L D Austin	Austin '56 Chevrolet	98	250	Running
7	14	32	Brownie King	Jess Potter '56 Chevrolet	97	200	Running
8	17	176	George Green	Lonnie Fish '56 Chevrolet	95	150	Running
9	15	64	Johnny Allen	Spook Crawford '57 Plymouth	93	100	Heating
10	19	94	Clarence DeZalia	DeZalia '56 Ford	93	100	Running
11	2	98	Marvin Panch	DePaolo Eng '57 Ford	92	100	Running
12	9	17	Jim Paschal	Bill Stroppe '57 Mercury	88	100	Cylinder
13	12	188	Tiny Lund	Petty Engineering '57 Olds	80	100	Running
14	16	34	Dick Beaty	Beaty '56 Ford	80	100	Running
15	11	80	Frank Jamison	'57 Chevrolet	65	100	Running
16	6	14	Bill Myers	Bill Stroppe '57 Mercury	57	100	Engine
17	1	22	Fireball Roberts	DePaolo Eng '57 Ford	41	100	Wheel
18	13	35	Bill Champion	Whitford Bros. '56 Ford	18	100	Crash
19	7	12	Ralph Moody	DePaolo Eng '57 Ford	1	50	Crash

Time of Race: 1 hour, 12 minutes, 14 seconds
Average Speed: 82.233 mph
Pole Winner: Fireball Roberts - 87.828 mph
Lap Leaders: Buck Baker 1-3, Fireball Roberts 4-41,   Baker 42-56, Marvin Panch 57-89,
   Baker 89-110.
Cautions: Margin of Victory: 3/4 lap   Attendance: 8,000

Race No. 7

Baker Grabs
First of Year in
Hillsboro 99

HILLSBORO, NC (Mar.24) --
Defending Grand National champion Buck Baker nailed down his
first win of the season with a victory in the 99-miler at Orange Speedway. Baker's triumph was a pleasant gift for General Motors
President Ed Cole, who was on
hand for the event to evaluate his
Chevrolet effort.

Baker took the lead from Marvin
Panch with 12 laps remaining. He
was three-quarters of a lap ahead of
runner-up Speedy Thompson at the
end of the 110-lap affair on the .9-
mile dirt oval.

Jack Smith finished third and Paul Goldsmith was
fourth. Fifth place went to Lee Petty.

Panch, who had led for 33 laps, encountered engine
problems and limped to an 11th place finish.

A crowd of 8,000 watched Baker, Panch and Roberts swap the lead five times. Roberts, who started on
the pole, left the race on lap 41 with a broken right
front wheel. He was pulling away when the mishap
occurred.

Buck Baker #87 zips his Chevrolet past Fireball Roberts' Ford to take the lead at Hillsboro.

Jim Paschal #17 and Billy Myers #14 pair up on the gently banked turns at Hillsboro's Orange Speedway. Paschal and Myers both fell victim to mechanical problems.

son and proceeded to lead the first 54 laps. Rear gearing failure put his Ford on the sidelines and left him with a 16th place finish in the 18 car field.

Speedy Thompson finished second, a lap behind his teammate Baker. Jim Paschal was third, Jack Smith fourth and independent Dick Beaty fifth.

Fireball Roberts took first place at Panch's departure, but he too was bitten by mechanical gremlins. His Ford belched a puff of smoke on lap 104. Roberts was left with a 14th place finish as the Ford went behind pit wall.

Baker closed his margin to 216 behind point leader Panch.

Ralph Earnhardt got an assignment in a Petty Engineering Oldsmobile, but overheating problems put him out after 71 laps.

Baker averaged 65.693 mph before 6,000 spectators.

Panch's point lead slipped to 336 with his late race misfortune. It was Hugh Babb's second 1-2-3 finish of the young 1957 season.

Baker averaged 82.233 mph for his 27th career Grand National win.

Following the race, Chevrolet division of General Motors advertised its recent stock car racing accomplishments in national publications. NASCAR had issued a new rule, which forbade manufacturers from advertising horsepower features. President Bill France announced that Chevrolet had lost all manufacturer's points for the Hillsboro win.

Race No. 8

Panch Falls Out Again; Baker Wins Again

WEAVERVILLE, NC (Mar 31) -- For the fourth consecutive race, point leader Marvin Panch was foiled by sour luck and Buck Baker was in position to capitalize in the 100-miler at Asheville-Weaverville Speedway.

Panch started on the pole for the second time this sea-

Grand National Race No. 8
200 Laps at Asheville-Weaverville
Weaverville, NC
100 Miles on Half-mile Dirt Track
March 31, 1957

Fin	St	No.	Driver	Team / Car	Laps	Money	Status
1	3	87	Buck Baker	Hugh Babb '57 Chevrolet	200	$850	Running
2	7	46	Speedy Thompson	Hugh Babb '57 Chevrolet	199	625	Running
3	4	17	Jim Paschal	Bill Stroppe '57 Mercury	198	350	Running
5	13	34	Dick Beaty	Beaty '56 Ford	188	310	Running
6	14	64	Johnny Allen	Spook Crawford '57 Plymouth	182	250	Running
7	12	100	Bill Morton	'56 Chevrolet	180	100	Running
8	10	14	Billy Myers	Bill Stroppe '57 Mercury	165	150	Running
9	17	74	L D Austin	Austin '56 Chevrolet	162	100	Running
10	11	42	Lee Petty	Petty Engineering '57 Olds	141	100	Running
11	15	32	Brownie King	Jess Potter '56 Chevrolet	130	100	Running
12	18	94	Clarence DeZalia	DeZalia '56 Ford	128	100	Acceler
13	2	22	Fireball Roberts	DePaolo Eng '57 Ford	104	100	Piston
14	9	188	Ralph Earnhardt	Petty Engineering '57 Olds	71	100	Heating
15	5	99	Paul Goldsmith	DePaolo Eng '57 Ford	68	100	Rear End
16	1	98	Marvin Panch	DePaolo Eng '57 Ford	54	100	Rear End
17	8	12	Ralph Moody	DePaolo Eng '57 Ford	17	100	Engine
18	16	76	George Green	Lonnie Fish '56 Chevrolet	9	100	Piston

Time of Race: 1 hour, 31 minuts, 20 seconds
Average Speed: 65.693 mph
Pole Winner: Marvin Panch - 73.649 mph
Lap Leaders: Marvin Panch 1-54, Fireball Roberts 55-104, Buck Baker 105-200.
Cautions: Margin of Victory: 1 lap plus   Attendance: 6,000

Race No. 9

Fireball's Ford Leads All The Way at Wilkesboro

N. Wilkesboro, NC (Apr. 7) -- Glenn "Fireball" Roberts started on the pole and led all the way to win the 100-mile event at North Wilkesboro Speedway. The 75.015 mph triumph enabled the Daytona Beach Ford driver to move from fifth to third in the Grand National point standings.

Paul Goldsmith, who shifted from Smokey Yunick's Chevrolet team to a DePaolo Engineering Ford, finished second. Ralph Moody and Marvin Panch were third and fourth, giving DePaolo's John Holman-led outfit a 1-2-3-4 sweep. Fifth place went to Chevrolet driver Buck Baker.

Top contenders Speedy Thompson, Jim Paschal, Jack Smith, Ralph Earnhardt and Billy Myers all failed to finish due to a variety of problems. The rest of the 20 car field finished the race.

A crowd of 8,000 watched as Roberts' uncontested victory was slowed only twice by caution flags. The yellow light was out for a total of five laps.

Dick Beaty brought out the first caution when he hit the guard rail. He returned to the race and placed 13th.

Thompson was responsible for the second caution when the A-frame broke on his Chevrolet.

Grand National Race No. 9
160 Laps at N. Wilkesboro Speedway
North Wilkesboro, NC
100 MIles on .625-mile Dirt Track
April 7, 1957

Fin	St	No.	Driver	Team / Car	Laps	Money	Status
1	1	22	Fireball Roberts	DePaolo Eng '57 Ford	160	$850	Running
2	2	97	Paul Goldsmith	DePaolo Eng '57 Ford	160	625	Running
3	9	12	Ralph Moody	DePaolo Eng '57 Ford	160	450	Running
4	5	98	Marvin Panch	DePaolo Eng '57 Ford	159	350	Running
5	3	87	Buck Baker	Hugh Babb '57 Chevrolet	149	310	Running
6	10	99	Allen Adkins	DePaolo Eng '57 Forrd	158	250	Running
7	7	42	Lee Petty	Petty Engineering '57 Olds	155	200	Running
8	15	55	Mel Larson	Larson '56 Ford	154	150	Running
9	13	64	Johnny Allen	Spook Crawford '57 Plymouth	153	100	Running
10	17	32	Brownie King	Jess Potter '56 Chevrolet	150	100	Running
11	11	421	Tiny Lund	C M Julian '56 Dodge	148	100	Running
12	16	100	Bill Morton	'56 Chevrolet	145	100	Running
13	18	34	Dick Beaty	Beaty '56 Ford	142	100	Running
14	19	74	L D Austin	Austin '56 Chevrolet	140	100	Running
15	20	94	Clarence DeZalia	DeZalia '56 Ford	132	100	Running
16	4	46	Speedy Thompson	Hugh Babb '57 Chevrolet	130	100	A Frame
17	12	14	Billy Myers	Bill Stroppe '57 Mercury	119	100	Fan
18	6	47	Jack Smith	Hugh Babb '57 Che;vrolet	52	100	Piston
19	14	188	Ralph Earnhardt	Petty Engineering '57 Olds	36	50	Rear End
20	8	17	Jim Paschal	Bill Stroppe '57 Mercury	34	50	Piston

Time of Race: 1 hour, 19 minutes, 59 seconds
Average Speed: 75.015 mph
Pole Winner: Fireball Roberts - 81.500 mph
Lap Leaders: Fireball Roberts 1-160.
Cautions: 2 for 5 laps   Margin of Victory: Attendance: 8,000

Grand National Race No. 10
150 Laps at Langhorne Speedway
Langhorne, PA
150 Miles on 1-mile Dirt Track
April 14, 1957

Fin	St	No.	Driver	Team / Car	Laps	Money	Status
1	2	22	Fireball Roberts	DePaolo Eng. '57 Ford	150	$1,890	Running
2	1	3	Paul Goldsmith	Smokey Yunick '57 Ford	150	1,125	Running
3	22	46	Speedy Thompson	Hugh Babb '57 Chevrolet	147	750	Running
4	10	14	Billy Myers	Bill Stroppe '57 Mercury	146	540	Running
5	21	87	Buck Baker	Hugh Babb '57 Chevrolet	145	345	Fuel
6	9	17	Jim Paschal	Bill Stroppe '57 Mercury	145	210	Running
7	8	47	Jack Smith	Hugh Babb '57 Chevrolet	140	160	Fuel
8	24	71	Bill Bowman	'56 Chevrolet	137	135	Running
9	6	42	Lee Petty	Petty Engineering '57 Olds	132	125	Crash
10	12	55	Mel Larson	Larson '56 Ford	130	110	Running
11	20	79	Tiny Lund	'56 Ford	129	75	Running
12	16	39	Ed Fiola	George Mellinger '57 Chevy	127	75	Running
13	27	88	Chuck Hanson	Hanson '56 Olds	126	75	Running
14	5	188	Ralph Earnhardt	Petty Engineering '57 Olds	123	90	Crash
15	18	74	L D Austin	Austin '56 Chevrolet	121	75	Running
16	17	26	Buzz Wilson	'56 Chevrolet	114	75	Running
17	4	98	Marvin Panch	DePaolo Eng '57 Ford	113	95	Crash
18	26	19	Johnny Frank	'56 Chevrolet	111	75	Running
19	19	32	Brownie King	Jess Potter '56 Chevrolet	69	75	Engine
20	15	421	Don Bailey	C M Julian '56 Dodge	62	75	Engine
21	23	81	Jim Linke	'57 Olds	58	50	Piston
22	7	29	Russ Hepler	Howard Coulter '57 Pontiac	46	60	Piston
23	11	64	Johnny Allen	Spook Crawford '57 Plymouth	26	60	Fan
24	13	80	Frank Jamison	'57 Chevrolet	22	50	Piston
25	28	78	Lucky Sawyer	'56 Ford	16	50	Engine
26	14	1	Elton Hildreth	Hildreth '56 Mercury	11	50	Bearing
27	25	31	Chuck Bluett	'56 Plymouth	8	50	Gas Tank
28	3	97	Bill Amick	DePaolo Eng. '57 Ford	0	80	Stalled

Time of Race: 1 hour, 44 minutes, 50 seconds
Average Speed: 85.850 mph
Pole Winner: Paul Goldsmith, 93.701 mph
Lap Leaders: Fireball Roberts 1-26, Paul Goldsmith 27-74, Roberts 75-82, Marvin Panch 83-85, Roberts 86-150.
Cautions: 1 for 3 laps   Margin of Victory: Attendance: 17,000

Race No. 10

Roberts Runs Away At Langhorne

LANGHORNE, PA (Apr. 14) -- Fireball Roberts pushed his Ford around Marvin Panch in the 86th lap and sped to victory in a tire-popping episode at Langhorne Speedway. It was his third win of the year and the ninth of his career in the Grand National ranks of NASCAR.

Paul Goldsmith finished second, Speedy Thompson was third, Billy Myers fourth and Buck Baker fifth.

Baker's Chevrolet ran out of gas in the closing laps.

Flat tires and wrecks were plentiful, although only three of the 150 laps were run under the caution flag. Lee Petty popped a tire in the 135th lap and whacked the guard rail, putting him out. Ralph Earnhardt, in the second Petty Engineering Oldsmobile suffered a similar fate on lap 124. Panch blew a tire and crashed on lap 113. He managed to leave Langhorne with an 80 point lead over Baker.

A crowd of 17,000 was on hand to watch the lead change hands five times between Roberts, Goldsmith and Panch. Roberts, who won at an average speed of 85.850 mph, was on top for 99 of the 150 laps.

Thirteen cars in the field of 28 finished the race. Three of the top 10 were not running at the end.

Fireball Roberts won his 3rd straight Grand National race at Charlotte.

Fairgrounds.

The victory pulled the Daytona Beach lead- foot to within 220 points of leader Marvin Panch, who finished second.

Third place at the stripe was Buck Baker. Lee Petty was fourth and Jim Paschal fifth. Independent Dick Beaty came in sixth and Ralph Earnhardt was seventh in a Petty Olds.

Baker started second on the grid and led the first 165 laps. When he pitted, Panch took the lead and held it for 14 laps. Roberts, who had pitted earlier in the race, got out of the pits quickly and took the lead when Panch came in for gasoline.

Speedy Thompson's Chevrolet pitted under caution and his crew added fuel. Under NASCAR rules, a car can not take on fuel during a yellow flag, so Thompson was disqualified. He was placed last in the 20 car field.

A crowd of 7,200 sat in balmy weather to watch Roberts average 52.083 mph for his fourth win of the season.

Grand National Race No. 11
200 Laps at Southern States Fairgrounds
Charlotte, NC
100 Miles on Half-mile Dirt Track
April 19, 1957

Fin	St	No.	Driver	Team / Car	Laps	Money	Status
1	4	22	Fireball Roberts	DePaolo Eng '57 Ford	200	$700	Running
2	1	98	Marvin Panch	DePaolo Eng '57 Ford	200	595	Running
3	2	87	Buck Baker	Hugh Babb '57 Chevrolet	200	400	Running
4	8	42	Lee Petty	Petty Enterprises '57 Olds	191	300	Running
5	12	17	Jim Paschal	Bill Stroppe '57 Mercury	190	270	Running
6	14	34	Dick Beaty	Beaty '56 Ford	184	225	Running
7	10	188	Ralph Earnhardt	Petty Engineering '57 Olds	183	185	Running
8	19	32	Brownie King	Jess Potter '56 Chevrolet	171	165	Running
9	17	74	L D Austin	Austin '56 Chevrolet	171	150	Running
10	15	76	George Green	Lonnie Fish '56 Chevrolet	169	150	Running
11	16	94	Clarence DeZalia	DeZalia '56 Ford	165	150	Running
12	9	64	Johnny Allen	Spook Crawford '57 Plymouth	149	150	Fan Belt
13	11	35	Bill Champion	Whitford Bros. '56 Ford	156	135	Tie Rod
14	18	421	T A Toomes	C M Julian '56 Dodge	144	125	Running
15	7	47	Jack Smith	Hugh Babb '57 Chevrolet	131	100	Shift
16	6	14	Billy Myers	Bill Stroppe '57 Mercury	97	100	RR Axle
17	5	97	Paul Goldsmith	DePaolo Eng'57 Ford	51	100	RR Axle
18	20	55	Tiny Lund	Brushy Mtn Mtrs '57 Pontiac	21	100	Rear End
19	13	2	Hal Gibson	'56 Ford	0	75	Crash
20	3	46	Speedy Thompson	Hugh Babb '57 Chevrolet	39	---	Disqual

Time of Race: 1 hour, 56 minutes, 12 seconds
Average Speed: 52.083 mph
Pole Winner: Marvin Panch - 60.060 mph
Lap Leaders: Buck Baker 1-165, Marvin Panch 166-179, Roberts 180-200.
Cautions: 3   Margin of Victory: Attendance: 7,200

Race No. 11

Fireball Fetches Third Straight at Charlotte

CHARLOTTE, NC (Apr. 19) --- Fireball Roberts seized his third straight win with a late charge in the 100-mile Grand National race at the Southern States

Race No. 12

Panch's Ford Holds Together; Takes Third Win of Year

SPARTANBURG, SC (Apr. 27) -- Marvin Panch, victimized by trouble in five of the last eight races, avoided the misfortune and won the 100-miler at Hub City Speedway. It was the third win of the year for the Oakland Ford driver.

Fireball Roberts finished in second place and Ralph Moody was third. Each of the first three finishers was driving DePaolo Engineering Fords. Lee Petty was fourth in an Oldsmobile as Johnny Allen, driving a Plymouth took fifth spot.

Cotton Owens, Daytona winner, entered his Ray Nichels Pontiac for the first time since SpeedWeek and fell out of the race with an oil leak after 27 laps. He had qualified third.

Pole winner Speedy Thompson encountered engine troubles and went behind pit wall just past the halfway point. He got credit for 15th in the field of 20. Ralph Earnhardt broke the axle on his Petty Olds on lap 121 and left the race.

Panch averaged 55.130 mph for his fourth career win.

NASCAR official Ike Isenhower (left), mechanic Norman Pruitt and driver Ralph Earnhardt. Earnhardt finished 10th in a Petty Engineering Oldsmobile at Greensboro.

CAR, outlawed super charged and fuel injected equipment. France had figured the horsepower race was getting out of hand.

Goldsmith's Smokey Yunick Ford held off Jack Smith by 5.0 seconds to win the 83.25-mile race on the .333-mile dirt oval. Buck Baker came in third with Ralph Moody and Fireball Roberts fourth and fifth.

Goldsmith was on top for 178 of the 250 laps. He took the lead for the final time from Baker in the 173rd

Grand National Race No. 12
200 Laps at Hub City Speedway
Spartanburg, SC
100 Miles on Half-mile Dirt Track
April 27, 1957

Fin	St	No.	Driver	Team / Car	Laps	Money	Status
1	5	98	Marvin Panch	DePaolo Eng '57 Ford	200	$700	Running
2	6	22	Fireball Roberts	DePaolo Eng '57 Ford	200	525	Running
3	4	12	Ralph Moody	DePaolo Eng '57 Ford	200	500	Running
4	12	42	Lee Petty	Petty Engineering '57 Olds	199	330	Running
5	14	64	Johnny Allen	Spook Crawford '57 Plymouth	191	320	Running
6	2	55	Tiny Lund	Brushy Mtn Mtrs '57 Pontiac	190	225	Running
7	16	5	Mel Larson	Larson '56 Ford	190	185	Running
8	15	34	Dick Beaty	Beaty '56 Ford	188	215	Running
9	18	74	L D Austin	Austin '56 Chevrolet	177	150	Running
10	7	87	Buck Baker	Hugh Babb '57 Chevrolet	165	250	Running
11	20	421	T A Toomes	C M Julian '56 Dodge	162	150	Wheel
12	9	47	Jack Smith	Hugh Babb '57 Chevrolet	157	150	Dist Sh
13	8	3	Paul Goldsmith	Smokey Yunick '57 Ford	143	135	Rear End
14	11	188	Ralph Earnhardt	Petty Engineering '57 Olds	119	125	RR Axle
15	1	46	Speedy Thompson	Hugh Babb '57 Chevrolet	105	100	Engine
16	19	94	Clarence DeZalia	DeZalia '56 Ford	100	150	Running
17	10	14	Billy Myers	Bill Stroppe '57 Mercury	96	125	Rear End
18	17	32	Brownie King	Jess Potter '56 Chevrolet	88	125	Oil Pan
19	3	6	Cotton Owens	Ray Nichels '57 Pontiac	27	75	Oil Leak
20	13	17	Jim Paschal	Bill Stroppe '57 Mercury	26	50	Oil Pres

Time of Race: 1 hour, 48 minutes, 50 seconds
Average Speed: 55.130 mph
Pole Winner: Speedy Thompson - 61.538 mph
Lap Leaders: - - - - - - - - - Marvin Panch   -200.
Cautions: Margin of Victory: Attendance:

Race No. 13

Goldsmith Noses out Smith In Greensboro Finish

GREENSBORO, NC (Apr. 28) -- Paul Goldsmith posted his first win of the season at the Greensboro Agricultural Fairgrounds as the Fords and Chevrolets bid farewell to optional high performance equipment

After feeling the pressure from the Automobile Manufacturers Association, Bill France, President of NAS-

Grand National Race No. 13
250 Laps at Greensboro Agricultural Fairgrounds
Greensboro, NC
83.25 Miles on .333-mile Dirt Track
April 28, 1957

Fin	St	No.	Driver	Team / Car	Laps	Money	Status
1	2	3	Paul Goldsmith	Smokey Yunick '57 Ford	250	$700	Running
2	5	47	Jack Smith	Hugh Babb '57 Chevrolet	250	525	Running
3	1	87	Buck Baker	Hugh Babb '57 Chevrolet	249	400	Running
4	7	12	Ralph Moody	DePaolo Eng '57 Ford	248	430	Running
5	3	22	Fireball Roberts	DePaolo Eng '57 Ford	247	270	Running
6	4	42	Lee Petty	Petty Engineering '57 Olds	244	225	Running
7	12	64	Johnny Allen	Spook Crawford '57 Plymouth	228	235	Running
8	16	74	L D Austin	Austin '56 Chevrolet	220	165	Running
9	17	94	Clarence DeZalia	DeZalia '56 Ford	209	200	Running
10	6	188	Ralph Earnhardt	Petty Engineering '57 Olds	204	150	Running
11	18	421	T A Toomes	C M Julian '56 Dodge	203	150	Running
12	11	17	Jim Paschal	Bill Stroppe '57 Mercury	199	150	Exhaust
13	10	55	Tiny Lund	Brushy Mtn Mtrs '57 Pontiac	172	135	Running
14	15	46	Speedy Thompson	Hugh Babb '57 Chevrolet	164	125	Ball Jnt
15	13	5	Mel Larson	Larson '56 Ford	159	100	Spindle
16	14	34	Dick Beaty	Beaty '56 Ford	150	150	Running
17	8	14	Billy Myers	Bill Stroppe '57 Mercury	56	150	Fuel Pmp
18	19	32	Brownie King	Jess Potter '56 Chevrolet	34	125	Steering
19	9	98	Marvin Panch	DePaolo Eng '57 Ford	25	75	Crash

Time of Race: 1 hour, 51 minutes, 34 seconds
Average Speed: 49.905 mph
Pole Winner: Buck Baker - 50.120 mph
Lap Leaders: Buck Baker 1-35, Goldsmith 36-135, Baker 136-172, Goldsmith 173-250.
Cautions: 4   Margin of Victory: 5.0 seconds   Attendance:

lap. Smith passed Baker in the late stages and was closing on Goldsmith when the checkered flag fell.

Four caution periods held Goldsmith's winning speed to 49.905 mph.

Grand National Race No. 14
100 Laps at Portland Speedway
Portland, OR
50 Miles on Half-mile Paved Track
April 28, 1957

Fin	St	No.	Driver	Team / Car	Laps	Money	Status
1	1	22N	Art Watts	Al Schmidhamer '56 Ford	100	$940	Running
2	2	45	Eddie Pagan	Pagan '57 Ford	100	635	Running
3	3	12	George Seeger	Oscar Maples Inc '57 Ford	100	480	Running
4	12	1	Chuck Meekins	James Rush '57 Chevrolet	99	340	Running
5	7	22	Jack D McCoy	'56 Ford	99	270	Running
6	15	14N	Bob Keefe	'57 Chevrolet	99	215	Running
7	9	11	Parnelli Jones	Oscar Maples Inc '57 Ford	97	215	Running
8	7	00	Dick Getty	Betty Getty '56 Chevrolet	97	150	Running
9	13	77	Jack Oldenhage	'56 Chevrolet	96	125	Running
10	4	44	Lloyd Dane	Dane '57 Ford	96	125	Running
11	11	14	Scotty Cain	Cain '56 Mercury	95	100	Running
12	15	50	Harold Beal	'56 Ford	94	75	Running
13	10	66	Bud Emra	'56 Mercury	67	95	Wheel
14	5	98	Ed Negre	'55 Olds	51	95	Piston
15	16	15	Royce Hagerty	'54 Lincoln	10	75	Heating
16	8	88	Johnny Kieper	Kieper '56 Olds	6	50	Con Rod

Time of Race: 46 minutes, 19.75 seconds
Average Speed: 64.754 mph
Pole Winner: Art Watts - 65.813 mph
Lap Leaders: Art Watts 1-100
Cautions: None   Margin of Victory: Attendance:

Race No. 14

Watts' First at Portland; Sixth Straight for Ford

PORTLAND, OR (Apr. 28) -- Art Watts led from start to finish to win the 50-mile Grand National race at Portland Speedway. It was the first Grand National win for the West Coast regular. It came in his 11th start.

Eddie Pagan wound up second and George Seeger was third. Chuck Meekins finished fourth and Jack D. McCoy was fifth.

Watts started his Al Schmidhamer Ford on the pole and was never headed in the caution free event. It was the sixth straight win for Ford automobiles.

Ed Negre, newcomer out of Kelso, WA, qualified fifth, but was the only front runner who failed to finish. His Oldsmobile blew an engine after 51 laps. He wound up 14th in the slim 16 car field.

Watts averaged 64.754 mph in the 46 minute, 19 second event.

Race No. 15

Fireball Wins Shelby; Lund Swallows Bitter Pill

SHELBY, NC (May 4) -- Tiny Lund of Harlan, IA was dealt a 'joker' in Shelby, NC. With the race seemingly well in hand, the 'joker' enabled Fireball Roberts to score his fifth win of the season in the 100-miler at Cleveland County Fairgrounds.

Lund earned the pole position and put his Pontiac out front for the first 115 laps. Speedy Thompson, Roberts and Marvin Panch all took turns leading for short stints before Lund got back on top in lap 166. He had led for 21 laps and was pulling away when his rear axle snapped, putting him out. He was left with a 10th place finish.

Roberts led the final 14 laps to score his fourth win in his last six starts on NASCAR's premier stock car racing series.

An audience of just 3,800 was on hand to see Roberts win at an average speed of 54.861 mph. It was his 11th career win.

Fourteen of the 18 cars that started the race finished. Lund, Billy Myers, Johnny Allen and Dick Beaty were the only four drivers not running at the finish.

Grand National Race No. 15
200 Laps at Cleveland County Fairgrounds
Shelby, NC
100 Miles on Half-mile Dirt Track
May 4, 1957

Fin	St	No.	Driver	Team / Car	Laps	Money	Status
1	2	22	Fireball Roberts	DePaolo Eng '57 Ford	200	$700	Running
2	5	3	Paul Goldsmith	Smokey Yunick '57 Ford	200	525	Running
3	4	98	Marvin Panch	DePaolo Eng '57 Ford	200	400	Running
4	6	17	Jim Paschal	Bill Stroppe '57 Mercury	197	330	Running
5	8	47	Jack Smith	Hugh Babb '57 Chevrolet	196	270	Running
6	7	87	Buck Baker	Hugh Babb '57 Chevrolet	196	225	Running
7	10	6	Cotton Owens	Ray Nichels '57 Pontiac	195	185	Running
8	11	42	Lee Petty	Petty Engineering '57 Olds	191	165	Running
9	3	46	Speedy Thompson	Hugh Babb '57 Chevrolet	190	150	Running
10	1	55	Tiny Lund	Brushy Mtn Mtr '57 Pontiac	186	150	RR Axle
11	12	76	George Green	Lonnie Fish '56 Chevrolet	180	150	Running
12	15	32	Brownie King	Jess Potter '56 Chevrolet	175	150	Running
13	14	94	Clarence DeZalia	DeZalia '56 Ford	160	135	Running
14	17	74	L D Austin	Austin '56 Chevrolet	160	125	Running
15	13	64	Johnny Allen	Spook Crawford '57 Plymouth	157	100	Spring
16	16	421	T A Toomes	C M Julian '56 Dodge	153	100	Running
17	9	14	Billy Myers	Bill Stroppe '57 Mercury	130	100	Bearing
18	18	34	Dick Beaty	Beaty '56 Ford	1	100	Steering

Timne of Race: 1 hour, 49 minutes, 22 seconds
Average Speed: 54.861 mph
Pole Winner: Tiny Lund - 57.544 mph
Lap Leaders: Tiny Lund 1-115, Speedy Thompson 116-139, Fireball Roberts 140-159, Marvin Panch 160-165, Lund 166-186, Roberts 187-200.
Cautions: 2   Margin of Victory: Attendance: 3,800

Race No. 16

Goldsmith Outduels Roberts at Richmond

RICHMOND, VA (May 5) -- Paul Goldsmith of St. Clair Shores, MI gave Ford its eighth straight Grand National win by taking first place in the 100-miler at the Atlantic Rural Exposition Fairgrounds.

Goldsmith passed Fireball Roberts in the 160th lap and won by over a lap as a fleet of red and white Fords took the first three spots. Roberts held on to finish second with Marvin Panch third. Frankie Schneider, recently appointed to drive a factory backed Chevrolet based out of Hugh Babb's shops, was fourth. Fifth place went to Jim Pascal.

Roberts moved into second place in the point standings, 92 behind Panch. Panch has led the standings from the first race of the 1957 season.

Russ Hepler put his Pontiac on the pole, but never led. He went only 49 laps before retiring with throttle linkage problems. He got credit for 18th place.

A crowd of 4,000 watched Goldsmith average 62.445 mph for his third career win.

Grand National Race No. 16
200 Laps at Atlantic Rural Exposition Fairgrounds
Richmond, VA
100 Miles on Half-mile Dirt Track
May 5, 1957

Fin	St	No.	Driver	Team / Car	Laps	Money	Status
1	7	12	Paul Goldsmith	DePaolo Eng '57 Ford	200	$700	Running
2	3	22	Fireball Roberts	DePaolo Eng '57 Ford	199	525	Running
3	2	98	Marvin Panch	DePaolo Eng '57 Ford	199	400	Running
4	12	45	Frankie Schneider	Hugh Babb '57 Chevrolet	194	330	Running
5	15	17	Jim Paschal	Bill Stroppe '57 Mercury	188	270	Running
6	16	64	Johnny Allen	Spook Crawford '57 Plymouth	184	225	Running
7	19	74	L D Austin	Austin '56 Chevrolet	181	185	Running
8	20	32	Brownie King	Jess Potter '56 Chevrolet	178	165	Running
9	11	188	Ralph Earnhardt	Petty Engineering '57 Olds	174	150	Running
10	5	87	Buck Baker	Hugh Babb '57 Chevrolet	172	150	Rear End
11	9	55	Tiny Lund	Brushy Mtn Mtr '57 Pontiac	160	150	Running
12	18	76	George Green	Lonnie Fish '56 Chevrolet	160	150	Running
13	8	50	Tom Pistone	Hugh Babb '57 Chevrolet	147	135	Steering
14	14	47	Jack Smith	Hugh Babb '57 Chevrolet	107	125	Rear End
15	22	70	Harvey Eakin	Eakin '56 Ford	97	100	Gasket
16	21	79	Dick Klank	'56 Ford	92	100	Running
17	13	46	Speedy Thompson	Hugh Babb '57 Chevrolet	60	100	Pistion
18	1	29	Russ Hepler	Howard Coulter '57 Pontiac	49	100	Throttle
19	10	3	Ralph Moody	Smokey Yunick '57 Ford	25	75	Engine
20	4	44	Rex White	Hugh Babb '57 Chevrolet	24	50	Piston
21	6	6	Cotton Owens	Ray Nichels '57 Pontiac	23	50	Crash
22	17	11	Emanuel Zervakis	'56 Chevrolet	7	50	Oil Line

Time of Race: 1 hour, 36 minutes, 5 seconds
Average Speed 62.445 mph
Pole Winner: Russ Helper - 64.239 mph
Lap Leaders: Fireball Roberts 1-159 ,Paul Goldsmith 160-200.
Cautions: Margin of Victory: 1 lap plus   Attendance: 4,000

Race No. 17

Baker Declared Martinsville Winner; Car Goes Into Crowd

MARTINSVILLE, VA (May 19) -- Buck Baker of Spartanburg, SC failed to lead the final lap but was declared the winner of the tragic Virginia 500 at Martinsville Speedway. Baker's third win of the year put him on top of the point standings by a 28 point margin over Marvin Panch, who finished eighth.

Buck Baker won Virginia 500 although he did not lead the final lap.

On lap 441, leader Billy Myers was trying to lap Tom Pistone when the two vehicles tangled wheels. Myers Mercury crashed through the guard rail, hurtled the wall and landed in an area plainly marked "No Spectators Allowed".

But several spectators were standing along the edge of the track.

Alvin Helsabeck, 8 years old, was among those in the path of Myers errant Mercury. Helsabeck was gravely injured when hit directly by Myers; the child underwent immediate brain surgery at Roanoke General Hospital. The race, of course, was immediately red-flagged and brought to a halt.

James Franklin and Rylon Jones, both of Patrick Springs, VA were seriously injured. Franklin, 19, suffered severe head and facial lacerations. Dalton, 29, suffered head and internal injuries. They were transported to Martinsville General Hospital.

Spectators Aubrey Riser, 44, of Hazel, VA and Wayne Braughn, 24 of Dobson, NC, were treated and released.

As ambulances carted the injured away, rain began pelting the half mile paved track. Although Myers led the final 113 laps, he did not win the race according to NASCAR scoring. Rules stipulate the final order will be based on positions held for the restart. Myers, after having brought out the red flag, was given fourth place, behind the other three cars in the lead lap.

Billy Myers' Mercury sailed over the wall at Martinsville and injured several spectators.

Baker was running a half lap behind Myers when the red flag came out. He was lined up first for the restart, which never came, and was awarded first place.

Curtis Turner got credit for second and Tom Pistone, who continued after his skirmish with Myers, got third. Lee Petty, a lap behind the leaders, was fifth.

Baker's victory ended the Ford streak at eight. He and his Hugh Babb Chevrolet team won $3,170 for his third win of the year. The Charlotte veteran was driving with a swollen ankle, which had required 19 stitches in a Modified wreck three days earlier.

Hard-luck Tiny Lund led the race for 73 laps, but a blown engine put his Pontiac out after 281 laps. He wound up 20th in the 24 car field.

A crowd of 16,000 was on hand for the scheduled 250-miler.

Spectator Virgil Hartgrove of Rural Hall, NC, won a Mercury automobile in a pre-race drawing.

Race No. 18

Pagan Prevails in Portland 75-miler

PORTLAND, OR (May 26) -- Eddie Pagan outran Lloyd Dane in a battle of Fords and won the 75-mile race at Portland Speedway. The Lynwood, CA driver became the ninth different winner in the 18 events staged during the '57 season.

Clyde Palmer finished third, a lap behind the leader. Scotty Cain came in fourth with Dick Getty fifth.

Art Watts started on the pole and fell to 11th, 11 laps behind Pagan.

Eddie Pagan

Two of the hot Western stars bowed out early. Third fastest qualifier Ed Negre went out with transmission failure on lap 60. Parnelli Jones departed on lap 37 when his Ford overheated.

Pagan averaged 64.732 mph for his second career Grand National win.

Grand National Race No. 17
500 Laps at Martinsville Speedway
Martinsville, VA
"Virginia 500"
250 Miles on Half-mile Paved Track
May 19, 1957

Fin	St	No.	Driver	Team / Car	Laps	Money	Status
1	14	87	Buck Baker	Hugh Babb '57 Chevrolet	441	$3,170	Running
2	10	99	Curtis Turner	DePaolo Eng '57 Ford	441	1,770	Running
3	4	50	Tom Pistone	Hugh Babb '57 Chevrolet	441	1,125	Crash
4	6	14	Billy Myers	Bill Stroppe '57 Mercury	441	980	Crash
5	8	42	Lee Petty	Petty Engineering '57 Olds	440	675	Running
6	12	47	Jack Smith	Hugh Babb '57 Chevrolet	436	500	Running
7	1	3	Paul Goldsmith	Smokey Yunick '57 Ford	432	475	Running
8	5	98	Marvin Panch	DePaolo Eng '57 Ford	431	400	Running
9	7	22	Fireball Roberts	DePaolo Eng '57 Ford	427	300	Running
10	23	17	Jim Paschal	Bil Stroppe '57 Mercury	416	300	Running
11	2	46	Speedy Thompson	Hugh Babb '57 Chevrolet	409	275	Running
12	16	32	Brownie King	Jess Potter '56 Chevrolet	404	200	Running
13	9	88	Ralph Earnhardt	Petty Engineering '57 Olds	391	200	Running
14	19	74	L D Austin	Austin '56 Chevrolet	391	200	Running
15	18	76	George Green	Lonnie Fish '56 Chevrolet	388	200	Running
16	11	64	Johnny Allen	Spook Crawford '57 Plymouth	377	200	Clutch
17	24	71	Bill Bowman	'56 Chevrolet	363	175	Running
18	22	24	Barney Oldfield	'56 Ford	356	150	Running
19	20	94	Clarence DeZalia	DeZalia '56 Ford	351	150	Running
20	3	55	Tiny Lund	Brushy Mtn Mtrs '57 Pontiac	281	295	Engine
21	13	29	Russ Hepler	Howard Coulter '57 Pontiac	270	125	Bearing
22	15	6	Cotton Owens	Ray Nichels '57 Pontiac	211	125	Crash
23	21	28	Eddie Skinner	Skinner '57 Ford	146	125	Rear End
24	17	421	T A Toomes	C M Julian '56 Dodge	121	125	Gasket

Time of Race: 3 hours, 50 minutes, 49 seconds.
Average Speed: 57.318 mph
Pole Winner: Paul Goldsmith - 65.693 mph
Lap Leaders: Paul Goldsmith 1-54, Tiny Lund 55-127, Buck Baker 128-144,
  Billy Myers 145-232, Baker 233-328, Myers 329-441.
Cautions: 3 for 51 laps   Margin of Victory: Attendance: 16,000
* Race shortened to 441 laps due to wreck and rain

Grand National Race No. 18
150 Laps at Portland Speedway
Portland, OR
75 Miles on Half-mile Paved Track
May 26, 1957

Fin	St	No.	Driver	Team / Car	Laps	Money	Status
1	6	45	Eddie Pagan	Pagan '57 Ford	150	$930	Running
2	2	44	Lloyd Dane	Dane '57 Ford	150	600	Running
3	5	82	Clyde Palmer	Hugh Babb '57 Chevrolet	149	470	Running
4	19	44	Scotty Cain	Cain '56 Mercury	147	345	Running
5	7	00	Dick Getty	Betty Getty '56 Chevrolet	146	270	Running
6	18	66N	Bud Emra	'56 Mercury	145	210	Running
7	12	39	Danny Letner	James Rush '57 Chevrolet	144	185	Running
8	20	99	Don Porter	Nick Porter '56 Ford	143	150	Running
9	16	30	Marvin Porter	Jack Chatenay '56 Plymouth	142	145	Running
10	15	80N	Chuck Meekins	'56 Oldsmobile	140	100	Running
11	1	22N	Art Watts	Al Schmidhamer '56 Ford	139	115	Running
12	17	77	Jack Oldenhage	'56 Chevrolet	138	75	Running
13	22	55	Marshall Sargent	'56 Chevrolet	137	75	Running
14	11	12	George Seeger	Oscar Maples, Inc. '57 Ford	112	75	Running
15	14	14N	Bob Keefe	'57 Chevrolet	89	100	Piston
16	9	50N	Harold Beal	'56 Ford	89	50	Piston
17	10	22	Jack D McCoy	'56 Ford	86	50	Piston
18	13	52N	Harold Hardesty	'57 Pontiac	86	80	Engine
19	3	98N	Ed Negre	'55 Oldsmobile	60	75	Trans.
20	23	83N	Bill Hidden	'56 Dodge	49	50	RF Tire
21	21	39N	Ben Eyerly	'57 Rambler	41	50	Wheel
22	4	11	Parnelli Jones	Oscar Maples, Inc. '57 Ford	37	85	Heating
23	8	81	Danny Graves	Hugh Babb '57 Chevrolet	17	50	Engine

Time of race: 1 hour, 9 minutes, 31 seconds.
Average Speed: 64.732 mph
Pole Winner: Art Watts - 66.732 mph
Lap Leaders: - - - - - - - - - - Eddie Pagan   -150.
Cautions: Margin of Victory: Attendance:

Race No. 19

Crash Halted Eureka Event to Lloyd Dane

EUREKA, CA (May 30) -- Lloyd Dane drove his Ford to his first win of the season in the 100-miler at Eureka Speedway.

Lloyd Dane

The race was called off 47 laps early when George Seeger, who was running second, crashed through the fence on lap 153. Officials determined the track's retaining barrier could not be repaired safely, so it was terminated at that point.

Oddly, Seeger wound up second to Dane, even though he was six laps behind when the red flag came out. Third place went to Eddie Pagan, with Cliff Yiskis fourth. Ed Negre came in fifth. Nine cars in the starting field of 15 finished.

Parnelli Jones started on the pole for the first time in his NASCAR career. However, the Torrance, CA speedster fell out with a blown engine after 129 laps. He still got credit for eighth place in the final order.

Dane averaged 55.957 mph for his third career Grand National win.

Grand National Race No. 19
160 Laps at Eureka Speedway
Eureka, CA
100 Miles on .625-mile Dirt Track
May 30, 1957

Fin	St	No.	Driver	Team / Car	Laps	Money	Status
1	5	44	Lloyd Dane	Dane '57 Ford	153	$900	Running
2	3	12	George Seeger	Oscar Maples '57 Ford	147	650	Crash
3	4	45	Eddie Pagan	Pagan '57 Ford	146	475	Running
4	10	25	Cliff Yiskis	'56 Ford	140	365	Running
5	9	98	Ed Negre	'55 Oldsmobile	139	310	Running
6	8	99	Don Porter	Nick Porter '56 Ford	134	250	Running
7	11	55	Marshall Sargent	'56 Chevrolet	130	200	Running
8	1	11	Parnelli Jones	Oscar Maples '57 Ford	129	150	Engine
9	2	37	Lemoine Frey	'57 Ford	122	125	Tie Rod
10	14	80	Norman McGriff	'56 Oldsmobile	122	110	Running
11	7	14	Scotty Cain	Cain '56 Mercury	120	100	Running
12	6	47	Bob Havemann	'56 Pontiac	117	100	Rear End
13	15	52	Harold Hardesty	'57 Pontiac	116	75	Running
14	12	00	Dick Getty	Betty Getty '56 Chevrolet	64	75	Brakes
15	13	30	Marvin Porter	Jack Chatenay '56 Plymouth	27	75	Axle

Time of Race: 1 hour, 42 minutes, 32 seconds.
Average Speed: 55.957 mph
Pole Winner: Parnelli Jones - 63.920 mph
Lap Leaders: - - - - - - - - - Lloyd Dane -153.
Cautions: Margin of Victory: 6 laps plus   Attendance:
* Race shortened to 153 laps due to crash

Race No. 20

Baker Takes Fourth of Year at New Oxford

NEW OXFORD, PA (May 30) -- Buck Baker drove his Hugh Babb-factory backed Chevrolet to victory in the dash for cash at Lincoln Speedway. It was his fourth win of the season.

Fireball Roberts was a close second and Paul Goldsmith was third. Marvin Panch finished fourth and Speedy Thompson fifth. All of the first five finishers completed the 200 laps around the half-mile clay track.

Twenty-eight cars started the 100-miler and 20 were running at the finish. Johnny Mackison, making his debut in the Grand National ranks, drove his Ford through the fence in the ninth lap and flipped into a wooded area. He was not hurt, but his new Ford looked as if it had gone through the 'crusher'.

Baker upped his point lead to 52 over Panch. He averaged 76.126 mph for his 30th career win.

Grand National Race No. 20
200 Laps at Lincoln Speedway
New Oxford, PA
100 Miles on Half-mile Dirt Track
May 30, 1957

Fin	St	No.	Driver	Team / Car	Laps	Money	Status
1	2	87	Buck Baker	Hugh Babb '57 Chevrolet	200	$700	Running
2	8	22	Fireball Roberts	DePaolo Eng '57 Ford	200	525	Running
3	5	3	Paul Goldsmith	Smokey Yunick '57 Ford	200	400	Running
4	1	98	Marvin Panch	DePaolo Eng '57 Ford	200	330	Running
5	3	46	Speedy Thompson	Hugh Babb '57 Chevrolet	200	270	Running
6	4	47	Jack Smith	Hugh Babb '57 Chevrolet	196	225	Running
7	14	17	Jim Paschal	Bill Stroppe '57 Mercury	196	185	Running
8	7	55	Tiny Lund	Brushy Mt. Motors '57 Pontiac	194	165	Running
9	13	64	Johnny Allen	Spook Crawford '56 Plymouth	194	150	Running
10	9	42	Lee Petty	Petty Engineering '57 Olds	193	150	Running
11	19	8	Elmo Langley	Langley '56 Chevrolet	189	150	Running
12	15	32	Brownie King	Jess Potter '56 Chevrolet	186	150	Running
13	10	888	Charles Hanson	Hanson '57 Chevrolet	185	135	Running
14	23	881	Peck Peckham	'57 Olds	180	125	Running
15	22	74	L D Austin	Austin '56 Chevrolet	178	100	Running
16	28	71	Bill Bowman	'56 Chevrolet	177	100	Running
17	27	70	Harvey Eakin	Eakin '56 Ford	173	100	Running
18	25	900	Gus Wilson	'56 Chevrolet	162	100	Running
19	11	54	Nace Mattingly	Mattingly '57 Ford	160	75	Spindle
20	16	69	Volney Schulze	'56 Chevrolet	124	50	Running
21	6	4	Billy Myers	Bill Stroppe '56 Mercury	109	50	Rear End
22	26	79	Dick Klank	'56 Ford	80	50	Running
23	17	181	Lucky Sawyer	'54 Oldsmobile	65	--	Trans.
24	18	81	Jerry Benjamin	'56 Ford	57	--	RF Hub
25	20	26	Carl Anderson	'56 Ford	56	--	Throttle
26	24	318	Charles Bluett	'56 Plymouth	26	--	Engine
27	21	100	John Findley	'56 Chevrolet	13	--	Shocks
28	12	104	Johnny Mackison	Camp Hill Spl. '57 Ford	9	--	Crash

Time of Race: 1 hour, 18 minutes, 49 seconds
Average Speed: 76.126 mph
Pole Winner: Marvin Panch - 78.238 mph
Lap Leaders: - - - - - - - - - - Buck Baker   -200.
Cautions: 1   Margin of Victory: Attendance:

Race No. 21

Goldsmith Grabs Gold In Lancaster 100

LANCASTER, SC   (June 1) -- Paul Goldsmith ran down Buck Baker late in the race and won the 100-mile event at Lancaster Speedway. It was the third win of the year for the Ford driving speedster.

Goldsmith's 61.622 mph triumph came just as there was much speculation of a massive pull-out by factory racing teams. Auto manufacturers were considering a 100 percent retreat following the Martinsville tragedy on May 19, and a more recent short track Modified race at Clarion, PA in which two children, age 8 and 12, were killed by a flying wheel from a race car.

Baker finished second to Goldsmith and Lee Petty was third. Marvin Panch took fourth spot. Speedy Thompson came in fifth.

Baker's point lead grew to 68 over Panch through 21 races on the NASCAR Grand National calendar.

Only two cars fell out of the race. Fireball Roberts' potent Ford blew its engine on lap 169. Jimmie Lewallen's Pontiac lasted only four laps before it lost oil pressure. Only 17 cars started the race.

Grand National Race No. 21
200 Laps at Lancaster Speedway
Lancaster, SC
100 Miles on Half-mile Dirt Track
June 1, 1957

Fin	St	No.	Driver	Team / Car	Laps	Money	Status
1	7	3	Paul Goldsmith	Smokey Yunick '57 Ford	200	$700	Running
2	1	87	Buck Baker	Hugh Babb '57 Chevrolet	200	525	Running
3	9	42	Lee Petty	Petty Engineering '57 Olds	199	400	Running
4	8	98	Marvin Panch	DePaolo Eng. '57 Ford	198	330	Running
5	4	46	Speedy Thompson	Hugh Babb '57 Chevrolet	198	270	Running
6	3	47	Jack Smith	Hugh Babb '57 Chevrolet	197	225	Running
7	10	17	Jim Paschal	Bill Stroppe '57 Mercury	194	185	Running
8	12	34	Dick Beaty	Beaty '56 Ford	185	165	Running
9	16	32	Brownie King	Jess Potter '56 Chevrolet	183	150	Running
10	15	94	Clarence DeZalia	DeZalia '56 Ford	176	150	Running
11	17	74	L D Austin	Austin '56 Chevrolet	175	150	Running
12	5	55	Tiny Lund	Brushy Mtn Motors '57 Pont	175	150	Running
13	6	6	Cotton Owens	Ray Nichels '57 Pontiac	172	135	Running
14	2	22	Fireball Roberts	DePaolo Eng. '57 Ford	169	125	Engine
15	13	14	Billy Myers	Bill Stroppe '56 Mercury	168	100	Running
16	11	64	Johnny Allen	Spook Crawford '57 Plymouth	158	100	Running
17	14	80	Jimmie Lewallen	J.S. Rice '57 Pontiac	4	100	Oil Pres

Time of Race: 1 hour, 37 minutes, 22 seconds
Average Speed: 61.622 mph
Pole Winner: Buck Baker - 67.365 mph
Lap Leaders: - - - - - - - - - Paul Goldsmith   -200.
Cautions: Margin of Victory: Attendance:

Race No. 22

Pagan First at Dusty Los Angeles Fairgrounds

LOS ANGELES, CA (June 8) -- Eddie Pagan of Lynwood, CA started on the pole and held a 28 car field in check most of the way as he won the scheduled 200-lapper at the Los Angeles Fairgrounds. The event was flagged to a halt after 150 laps due to poor and unsafe track conditions. Dust was billowing nearly as high as the adjacent ferris wheel on the Fairgrounds site.

The event was presented two days after the Automobile Manufacturers Association voted unanimously to withdraw from all forms of auto racing.

Lloyd Dane was flagged in second place. He was a lap behind Pagan when officials threw the red flag. Chuck Meekins was third, George Seeger fourth and Eddie Gray fifth.

Grand National Race No. 22
200 Laps at Los Angeles Fairgrounds
Los Angeles, CA
100 Miles on Half-Mile Dirt Track
June 8, 1957

Fin	St	No.	Driver	Team / Car	Laps	Money	Status
1	1	45	Eddie Pagan	Pagan '57 Ford	150	800	Running
2	6	44	Lloyd Dane	Dane '57 Ford	149	550	Running
3	12	1	Chuck Meekins	James Rush '57 Chevrolet	148	400	Running
4	9	12	George Seeger	Oscar Maples '57 Ford	148	305	Running
5	18	18	Eddie Gray	Chuck Green '56 Chevrolet	147	270	Running
6	14	14	Scotty Cain	Cain '56 Mercury	145	200	Running
7	4	97	Bill Amick	Amick '57 Ford	145	200	Running
8	26	8	Don Johns	Walt Palozle '57 Pontiac	144	175	Running
9	19	55	Marshall Sargent	'56 Chevrolet	142	150	Running
10	10	43	Bob Ross	Ross '56 Mercury	142	150	Running
11	21	00	Dick Getty	Betty Getty '56 Chevrolet	142	130	Running
12	3	82	Clyde Palmer	'57 Chevrolet	142	120	Ignition
13	7	56	Jim Hurtubise	'56 Chevrolet	138	110	Flagged
14	17	29	Danny Letner	'57 Chevrolet	136	100	Running
15	24	55 X	Bill Bade	Sam Arena '56 Chevrolet	134	90	Running
16	8	6	Jim Cook	H.B. Bassett '57 Pontiac	110	80	Heating
17	11	15	Bud Vaughn	'56 Mercury	100	70	Spindle
18	2	81	Danny Graves	Graves '57 Chevrolet	97	50	A Frame
19	5	11	Parnelli Jones	Oscar Maples '57 Ford	87	50	Crash
20	20	25	Reggie Ausmus	'56 Ford	80	50	Running
21	15	3	Frank Secrist	'56 Chevrolet	80	50	Brakes
22	28	16	Barry Knowlton	'56 Ford	73	50	Crash
23	25	47	George Norton	'56 Chevrolet	72	50	Flagged
24	27	52	Harold Hardesty	'56 Ford	68	50	Rear End
25	13	32	Howard Phillippi	'57 Pontiac	50	--	Tie Rod
26	16	22	Jack D McCoy	'56 Ford	34	--	Hose
27	22	101	Lucky Long	William Long '56 Chevrolet	24	--	Wiring
28	23	24	Bill Jarlick	'57 Ford	19	--	Heating

Time of Race: No Time Recorded
Average Speed: None
Pole Winner: Eddie Pagan - 67.290 mph
Lap Leaders: - - - - - - - - - Eddie Pagan   -150.
Cautions: Margin of Victory: Attendance:
* Race shortened to 150 laps due to unsafe track conditions

Parnelli Jones crashed his Ford after 87 laps. Young Jim Hurtubise was flagged off the course in the 138th lap. The newcomer had exercised reckless abandon on the pot-holed course, which thrilled the crowd but it didn't amuse the officials. Hurtubise got credit for 13th place in the final order, which was worth $110.

Race officials were unable to keep an accurate time of the race since it was red flagged to a halt 50 laps from its scheduled distance.

NASCAR raised the first place awards to $1,000 to help the independent front-runners. The only former factory backed driver not on hand was Paul Goldsmith.

Roberts averaged 60.687 mph for his first win as a car owner.

Baker led the point standings by a 60 point cushion over Panch. Roberts was third in the point tally, 168 markers behind Panch.

Race No. 23

Roberts Wins 'All Independent' Newport 100

NEWPORT, TN (June 15) -- Fireball Roberts drove his own Ford to victory in the 100-mile Grand National race at Newport Speedway for his sixth win of the year. Roberts was one of many former factory backed drivers who suddenly had the rug pulled out from under them by the auto manufacturers.

Marvin Panch and Buck Baker finished second and third, both completing the prescribed 200 lap distance on the half mile dirt track. Jack Smith finished fourth and Jim Paschal was fifth.

Race No. 24

Smith Ends Famine With Columbia Victory

COLUMBIA, SC (June 20) -- Jack Smith of Sandy Springs, GA ended a three month slump with a big win in the 100-miler at Columbia Speedway. It was his second win of the year and the third of his career.

Smith's Chevrolet nosed out Buck Baker for the $1,000 top prize. Marvin Panch was third, Jim

Grand National Race No. 23
200 Laps at Newport Speedway
Newport, TN
100 Miles on Half-mile Dirt Track
June 15, 1957

Fin	St	No.	Driver	Team / Car	Laps	Money	Status
1	5	22	Fireball Roberts	Roberts '57 Ford	200	$1,000	Running
2	2	98	Marvin Panch	Panch '57 Ford	200	625	Running
3	3	87	Buck Baker	Baker '57 Chevrolet	200	400	Running
4	6	47	Jack Smith	Smith '57 Chevrolet	199	295	Running
5	11	17	Jim Paschal	Paschal '57 Mercury	190	255	Running
6	12	75	Ken Rush	Frank Hayworth '56 Mercury	190	210	Running
7	4	55	Tiny Lund	Brushy Mtn Motors '57 Pontiac	187	175	Running
8	1	46	Speedy Thompson	Thompson '57 Chevrolet	186	165	Running
9	14	71	George Green	'56 Chevrolet	182	150	Running
10	9	42	Lee Petty	Petty Engineering '57 Olds	180	140	Running
11	10	64	Johnny Allen	Spook Crawford '57 Plymouth	180	135	Running
12	8	14	Billy Myers	Myers '57 Mercury	175	125	Throttle
13	13	32	Brownie King	Jess Potter '56 Chevrolet	175	110	Running
14	17	74	L D Austin	Austin '56 Chevrolet	171	100	Running
15	7	35	Darel Dieringer	Whitford Bros '57 Ford	94	100	Oil Pres
16	16	94	Clarence DeZalia	DeZalia '56 Ford	93	100	Steering
17	15	96	Bobby Keck	Keck '57 Chevrolet	18	100	Gas Line

Time of Race: 1 hour 38 minutes, 52 seconds
Average Speed: 60.687 mph
Pole Winner: Speedy Thompson - 61.813 mph
Lap Leaders: - - - - - - - - - - - Fireball Roberts   -200.
Cautions: Margin of Victory: Attendance:

Grand National Race No. 24
200 Laps at Columbia Speedway
Columbia, SC
100 Miles on Half-mile Dirt Track
June 20, 1957

Fin	St	No.	Driver	Team / Car	Laps	Money	Status
1	3	47	Jack Smith	Smith '57 Chevrolet	200	$1,000	Running
2	1	87	Buck Baker	Baker '57 Chevrolet	200	625	Running
3	6	98	Marvin Panch	Panch '57 Ford	200	400	Running
4	5	17	Jim Paschal	Paschal '57 Mercury	199	295	Running
5	2	46	Speedy Thompson	Thompson '57 Chevrolet	199	255	Running
6	11	35	Darel Dieringer	Whitford Bros '57 Ford	192	210	Running
7	8	14	Billy Myers	Myers '57 Mercury	190	175	Running
8	13	55	Tiny Lund	Brushy Mtn Motors '57 Pontiac	189	165	Crash
9	18	74	L D Austin	Austin '56 Chevrolet	189	150	Running
10	20	32	Brownie King	Jess Potter '56 Chevrolet	189	140	Running
11	16	400	Huck Spaulding	Spaulding '56 Dodge	188	135	Running
12	14	34	Dick Beaty	Beaty '56 Ford	185	125	Running
13	4	42	Lee Petty	Petty Engineering '57 Olds	177	110	Axle
14	15	94	Clarence DeZalia	DeZalia '56 Ford	158	100	Radiator
15	12	64	Johnny Allen	Spook Crawford '57 Plymouth	157	100	Engine
16	7	22	Fireball Roberts	Roberts '57 Ford	71	100	Crash
17	10	80	Jimmie Lewallen	J.S. Rice '57 Pontiac	69	100	Exhaust
18	17	5	Neil Castles	Bill Champion '56 Ford	51	100	Engine
19	9	75	Ken Rush	Frank Hayworth '56 Mercury	32	50	Trans
20	19	33	George Green	Jess Potter '56 Chevrolet	2	50	T Chain
--	--	49	Bob Welborn	Welborn '57 Chevrolet	--	50	DNS

Time of Race: 1 hour, 43 minutes, 22 seconds
Average Speed: 58.045 mph
Pole Winner: Buck Baker - 64.585 mph
Lap Leaders: - - - - - - - - - - Jack Smith   -200.
Cautions: Margin of Victory: Attendance:

Paschal came in fourth and Speedy Thompson was fifth.

Snake-bitten Tiny Lund was denied a chance for victory when his Pontiac blew a tire with just 11 laps remaining. The car wobbled and struck the retaining wall. Lund was out of the race and got credit for eighth in the final order.

Fireball Roberts' Ford was eliminated when an idler arm broke, causing him to hit the wall in the 71st lap. He was not injured in the mishap.

Smith toured the 200 laps on the half-mile dirt track at an average speed of 58.045 mph.

Bill Amick enjoys victory lane at Sacramento.

Race No. 25

Amick Drives Ford To Win at Sacramento

SACRAMENTO, CA (June 22) -- Bill Amick of Portland, OR won the 100-miler at Capitol Speedway in Sacramento for his first career Grand National victory. The race was flagged at 199 laps due to a scoring mix-up.

Lloyd Dane finished a lap behind in second place. George Seeger was third, Scotty Cain fourth and Danny Graves fifth.

Thirty-one cars took the green flag and 17 were running at the finish. Chuck Meekins, Bill Bade, Lyle Matlock and Harold Hardesty were victims of accidents. Hardesty's Pontiac flipped over the hood of another car in the 33rd lap. No injuries were reported.

Matlock rolled his Mercury three times on lap 50. He too, escaped injury.

Bade's Chevrolet tumbled end-over-end on lap 64. Bade was taken to the hospital for observation.

Amick, the 11th different driver to win during the 1957 season, averaged 59.580 mph for the 99.5-mile race.

Grand National No. 25
200 Laps at Capitol Speedway
Sacramento, CA
100 Miles on Half-mile Dirt Track
June 22, 1957

Fin	St	No.	Driver	Team / Car	Laps	Money	Status
1	3	97	Bill Amick	Amick '57 Ford	199	$900	Running
2	7	44	Lloyd Dane	Dane '57 Ford	198	600	Running
3	5	12	George Seeger	Oscar Maples '57 Ford	197	475	Running
4	9	14	Scotty Cain	Cain '56 Mercury	196	365	Running
5	4	81	Danny Graves	Graves '57 Chevrolet	196	320	Running
6	11	43	Bob Ross	Ross '56 Mercury	196	250	Running
7	16	37	Lemoine Frey	'57 Ford	191	200	Running
8	21	00	Dick Getty	Betty Getty '56 Chevrolet	188	150	Running
9	1	22N	Art Watts	Al Schmidhamer '56 Ford	183	100	Running
10	19	33	Howard Phillippi	'57 Pontiac	182	100	Running
11	18	39	Danny Letner	James Rush '57 Chevrolet	179	100	Engine
12	15	25	Reggie Ausmus	'56 Ford	176	100	Running
13	29	22	Jack D McCoy	'56 Ford	175	100	Running
14	17	30	Marvin Porter	Jack Chatenay '56 Plymouth	165	100	Running
15	23	15	Bud Vaughn	'56 Mercury	165	75	Running
16	25	99	Don Porter	Nick Porter '56 Ford	165	50	Running
17	14	45	Eddie Pagan	Pagan '56 Ford	157	50	Running
18	13	11	Parnelli Jones	Oscar Maples '57 Ford	130	50	Rear End
19	27	5	Jim Blomgren	Bob Smith '57 Ford	120	50	Battery
20	30	77	Jack Oldenhage	'56 Chevrolet	120	50	Running
21	6	18	Eddie Gray	Chuck Green '56 Chevrolet	118	25	Heating
22	2	82	Clyde Palmer	'57 Chevrolet	114	25	Heating
23	22	8	Don Johns	Walt Palozi '57 Pontiac	111	25	Heating
24	20	35	Bob Connor	'56 Mercury	88	25	Steering
25	26	21N	Bob Rauscher	'57 Ford	65	25	Heating
26	28	65	Bill Bade	Sam Arena '56 Chevrolet	60	--	Crash
27	24	225	Lyle Matlock	Ed Chann '56 Mercury	47	--	Crash
28	12	52N	Harold Hardesty	'57 Pontiac	33	--	Crash
29	31	98	Mike McGreevy	'56 Dodge	28	--	Heating
30	8	1	Chuck Meekins	James Rush '57 Chevrolet	25	--	Crash
31	10	6	Jim Cook	H B Bassett '57 Pontiac	23	--	Radiator

Time of Race: 1 hour, 40 minutes, 12 seconds
Average Speed: 59.580 mph
Pole Winner: Art Watts - 69.337 mph
Lap Leaders: - - - - - - - - - - Bill Amick -199 .
Cautions: Margin of Victory: 1-lap-plus   Attendance:

Race No. 26

Petty Wins Spartanburg As Baker and Thompson Crash

SPARTANBURG, SC (June 29) Lee Petty was declared the winner of the scheduled 100-mile race at Hub City Speedway when leaders Buck Baker and Speedy Thompson locked horns and plowed into the guard rail.

Petty was running third behind the lead duo when the red flag came out. Officials determined that the race

Lee Petty drove his Oldsmobile to victory in 100-miler at Spartanburg.

would not be restarted and red flagged the event.

In a scoring decision similar to the May 19 race at Martinsville, Petty was declared the winner although he did not lead the last completed lap.

He was lined up first for the restart and was given the first place money of $1,000. It was Petty's first win since July 7, 1956, which came at this same half-mile dirt facility.

Bill Amick got credit for second place, in the same lap with winner Petty. Baker, who led the final 94 laps, got credit for third place. Thompson got fourth

and Jack Smith was fifth.

Officials decided against attempting to restart the race since the guard rail had been damaged and there was a curfew to comply with. Petty started on the pole and led the first 93 laps.

Marvin Panch wrecked his Ford in the 95th lap. Cotton Owens' blew the engine in his Pontiac after 156 laps. Brownie King and Dick Beaty got tangled up in the Baker-Thompson affair and got credit for 10th and 11th respectively.

Petty averaged 46.287 mph for the 93.5 mile race.

Race No. 27

Baker Survival of the Fittest at Jacksonville

JACKSONVILLE, NC (June 30) -- Buck Baker's Chevrolet survived the rugged 100-miler at Speedway Park and gained his fifth victory of the year. Baker extended his point lead to 396 when Marvin Panch, second place runner in the standings, did not enter. Panch had crashed his Ford the night before in Spartanburg.

Jim Paschal wound up second, three laps behind. Tiny Lund was third, George Green fourth and Jack Smith fifth. Smith was 21 laps behind.

Grand National Race No. 26
200 Laps at Hub City Speedway
Spartanburg, SC
100 Miles on Half-mile Dirt Track
June 29, 1957

Fin	St	No.	Driver	Team / Car	Laps	Money	Status
1	1	42	Lee Petty	Petty Engineering '57 Olds	187	$1,000	Running
2	9	97	Bill Amick	Amick '57 Ford	187	575	Running
3	2	87	Buck Baker	Baker '57 Chevrolet	187	400	Crash
4	5	46	Speedy Thompson	Thompson '57 Chevrolet	187	295	Crash
5	12	47	Jack Smith	Smith '57 Chevrolet	186	255	Running
6	15	64	Johnny Allen	Spook Crawford '57 Plymouth	182	210	Running
7	3	14	Billy Myers	Myers '57 Mercury	182	175	Running
8	14	17	Jim Paschal	Paschal '57 Mercury	179	165	Running
9	7	22	Fireball Roberts	Roberts '57 Ford	178	150	Running
10	17	32	Brownie King	Jess Potter '56 Chevrolet	171	140	Crash
11	11	34	Dick Beaty	Beaty '56 Ford	170	135	Crash
12	10	1A	Whitey Norman	Norman '56 Ford	170	125	Running
13	18	33	George Green	Jess Potter '56 Chevrolet	168	110	Running
14	22	74	L D Austin	Austin '56 Chevrolet	165	100	Running
15	19	94	Clarence DeZalia	DeZalia '56 Ford	162	100	Running
16	20	21	T A Toomes	C M Julian '56 Dodge	158	100	Running
17	4	6	Cotton Owens	Ray Nichels '57 Pontiac	156	100	Engine
18	16	96	Bobby Keck	Keck '57 Chevrolet	143	100	Running
19	13	98	Marvin Panch	Panch '57 Ford	93	50	Crash
20	8	80	Jimmie Lewallen	J.S. Rice '57 Pontiac	51	50	Exhaust
21	6	55	Tiny Lund	Brushy Mt Motors '57 Pontiac	20	50	Radiator
22	21	13	Peck Peckham	William Meyer '56 Chevrolet	0	50	Clutch

Time of race: 2 hours, 1 minute, 12 seconds
Average Speed: 46.287 mph
Pole Winner: Lee Petty - 59.642 mph   Lap Leaders: Lee Petty 1-83, Buck Baker 84-187.
Cautions: 3   Margin of Victory: Red Flag   Attendance:
* Race was stopped at 187 laps due to crash and curfew

Grand National Race No. 27
200 Laps at Speedway Park
Jacksonville, NC
100 Miles on Half-mile Dirt Track
June 30, 1957

Fin	St	No.	Driver	Team / Car	Laps	Money	Status
1	3	87	Buck Baker	Baker '57 Chevrolet	200	$1,000	Running
2	7	17	Jim Paschal	Paschal '57 Mercury	197	575	Running
3	2	80	Tiny Lund	J.S. Rice '57 Pontiac	191	400	Running
4	17	33	George Green	Jess Potter '56 Chevrolet	187	295	Running
6	4	47	Jack Smith	Smith '57 Chevrolet	179	255	Running
6	16	94	Clarence DeZalia	DeZalia '56 Ford	176	210	Running
7	13	400	Huck Spaulding	Spaulding '56 Dodge	168	175	Spindle
8	1	42	Lee Petty	Petty Engineering '57 Olds	166	165	Running
9	18	21	T A Toomes	C M Julian '56 Dodge	151	150	Carb.
10	11	35	Bill Champion	Whitford Bros '56 Ford	146	140	Running
11	6	5	Darel Dieringer	Whitford Bros '57 Ford	121	135	Rear End
12	5	22	Fireball Roberts	Roberts '57 Ford	108	125	Running
13	8	1A	Speedy Thompson	Whitey Norman '56 Ford	101	100	Heating
17	12	32	Brownie King	Jess Potter '56 Chevrolet	89	100	Running
15	10	14	Billy Myers	Myers '57 Mercury	81	100	A Frame
16	15	74	L D Austin	Austin '56 Chevrolet	58	100	Electr.
17	19	13	Peck Peckham	William Meyer '56 Chevrolet	30	100	Engine
18	14	96	Bobby Keck	Keck '57 Chevrolet	14	100	Piston
19	9	64	Johnny Allen	Spook Crawford '57 Plymouth	12	50	Engine

Time of Race: 1 hour, 48 minutes, 25 seconds
Average Speed: 55.342 mph
Pole Winner: Lee Petty - 61.328 mph
Lap Leaders: - - - - - - - - - Buck Baker   -200.
Cautions: Margin of Victory: 3 laps plus   Attendance: 3,600

Lee Petty started on the pole for the second straight race but faded to eighth, 34 laps behind the winner.

A crowd of 3,600 watched Baker take his 31st career win at an average speed of 55.342 mph.

Fireball Roberts started fifth but encountered suspension problems on the rough track and wound up 12th, 92 laps behind Baker. Speedy Thompson borrowed a Ford and wound up 13th after overheating problems forced him to the showers.

Race No. 28

Goldsmith Grabs Raleigh 250 Before 15,500

RALEIGH, NC   (JULY 4) -- Paul Goldsmith made his return to the NASCAR wars by taking the Raleigh Sweepstakes event for Grand National hardtops and Convertible rag-tops at Raleigh Speedway.

Goldsmith drove his Ford into the lead on lap 213 during the day's second and final caution flag. For the final 38 trips around the high-banked one-mile paved oval, Goldsmith kept Frankie Schneider's Chevrolet at

bay and came home with the $4,000 victory. Joe Weatherly finished third in a Ford Convertible. Speedy Thompson was fourth in a Chevy Grand National, and Bob Welborn took fifth in a rag-top Chevy.

Point leader Buck Baker finished seventh and Marvin

The 1-mile superspeedway at Raleigh, NC.
The track had long straights and terribly tight turns.

Grand National Race No. 28
250 Laps at Raleigh Speedway
Raleigh, NC
"Raleigh 250"
250 Miles on 1-mile Paved Track
July 4, 1957

Fin	St	No.	Driver	Team / Car	Laps	Money	Status
1	7	3	Paul Goldsmith	Smokey Yunick '57 Ford GN	250	$4,000	Running
2	1	44	Frankie Schneider	Westmoreland '57 Chevy GN	250	2,475	Running
3	10	12	Joe Weatherly	Holman-Moody '57 Ford C	249	1,575	Running
4	11	46	Speedy Thompson	Thompson '57 Chevrolet GN	249	1,050	Running
5	2	49	Bob Welborn	Welborn '57 Chevrolet C	248	850	Running
6	12	21	Glen Wood	Wood Bros '57 Ford C	246	725	Running
7	3	87	Buck Baker	Baker '57 Chevrolet GN	245	650	Running
8	31	98	Marvin Panch	Panch '57 Ford GN	245	600	Running
9	4	48	Possum Jones	Bob Welborn '57 Chevrolet C	245	475	Running
10	29	150	Bill Walker	'57 Ford GN	244	450	Running
11	6	2	Johnny Dodson	Petty Eng '57 Olds C	244	425	Running
12	18	149	Gwyn Staley	Welborn '57 Chevrolet C	243	400	Running
13	25	11	Fireball Roberts	Roberts '57 Ford GN	242	350	Running
14	8	26	Curtis Turner	Turner '57 Ford C	240	300	Running
15	13	42	Lee Petty	Petty Eng '57 Olds GN	240	275	Running
16	30	80	Jimmie Lewallen	J S Rice '57 Pontiac GN	239	260	Running
17	27	47	Jack Smith	Smith '57 Chevrolet GN	238	250	Running
18	19	64	Johnny Allen	Spook Crawford '56 Plym GN	237	240	Running
19	14	39	Dick Beaty	Beaty '56 Ford C	236	230	Running
20	20	76	Larry Frank	Lonnie Fish '56 Chevrolet C	236	220	Running
21	32	28	Eddie Skinner	Skinner '57 Ford GN	234	210	Running
22	16	75	Ken Rush	Frank Hayworth '56 Mercury C	232	200	Running
23	38	35	Bill Champion	Whitford Bros '56 Ford GN	231	175	Running
24	22	90	Emanuel Zervakis	Junie Donlavey '57 Ford C	230	150	Running
25	41	69	Volney Schulze	'56 Ford GN	229	140	Running
26	44	32	Brownie King	Jess Potter '56 Chevrolet GN	228	100	Running
28	35	74	L D Austin	Austin '56 Chevrolet GN	227	100	Running
28	49	33	George Green	Jess Potter '56 Chevrolet GN	225	100	Running
29	33	4	Bill Morgan	'56 Ford GN	223	100	Running
30	28	7	Bill Taylor	"56 Ford C	223	100	Running
31	50	71	Bill O'Dell	'56 Chevrolet GN	222	---	Running
32	40	94	Clarence DeZalia	DeZalia '56 Ford GN	222	---	Running
33	36	421	T A Toomes	C M Julian '56 Dodge GN	222	---	Running
34	47	888	Chuck Hanson	Hanson '57 Chevrolet GN	219	---	Engine
35	42	5	Darel Dieringer	Whitford Bros '57 Ford C	218	---	Running
36	26	78	Shep Langdon	Lonnie Fish '56 Chevrolet C	216	---	Running
37	52	1A	Whitey Norman	Norman '56 Ford C	208	---	Running
38	43	96	Bob Keck	Keck '57 Chevrolet C	204	---	Running
39	34	79	Dick Klank	'56 Ford C	198	---	Running
40	24	77	Don Gray	Lonnie Fish '56 Chevrolet C	194	---	Running
41	37	88	Charles DiBrizzi	'57 Oldsmobile GN	190	---	Running
42	51	70	Harvey Eakin	Eakin '56 Ford GN	179	---	Running
43	21	97	Bill Amick	Amick '57 Ford GN	173	---	T Chain
44	23	95	Bob Duell	Julian Buesink '57 Ford GN	155	---	Lug Nuts
45	45	83	Lennie Page	'56 Chevrolet C	124	---	Oil Pres
46	9	92	Herb Thomas	Thomas '57 Pontiac GN	100	---	Brakes
47	46	10	Roger Baldwin	Baldwin '56 Ford C	78	---	Crash
48	17	17	Jim Paschal	Paschal '57 Mercury GN	78	---	Pit Crash
49	39	93	Ted Chamberlain	Chamberlain '56 Plymouth C	63	---	Fuel Pmp
50	5	6	Cotton Owens	Ray Nichels '57 Pontiac GN	54	---	Fan
51	53	55	Tiny Lund	Brushy Mt. Motors '57 Pont GN	28	---	Heating
52	15	14	Billy Myers	Myers '57 Mercury GN	6	---	Fuel Pmp
53	48	9	Dave Terrell	Terrell '57 Plymouth C	3	---	Trans

Time of Race: 3 hours, 18 minutes, 10 seconds
Average Speed: 75.693 mph
Pole Winner: Frankie Schneider - 83.371 mph
Lap Leaders: Bob Welborn 1-3, Frankie Schneider 4-11, Paul Goldsmith 12-86, Welborn 87-102, Goldsmith 103-180, Welborn 181-183, Schneider 184-212, Goldsmith 213-250.

Cautions: 2 for 14 laps   Margin of Victory: Attendance: 15,500

Panch eighth. Baker stretched his point lead slightly to 424 points over Panch.

Herb Thomas of Olivia, NC made his first start since being critically injured on October 23, 1956 at Shelby NC. The two-time Grand National champ qualified ninth in the field of 53, but wound up 46th when his Pontiac lost a brake cylinder.

The lead changed hands eight times among three drivers. Goldsmith was in front on three occasions for a total of 191 laps.

Four pit crewmen for Jim Paschal's Mercury team were injured in the 78th lap when the cars of Roger Baldwin and Bobby Keck crashed into the pits. Paschal's Mercury was being serviced at the time, and the spinning cars knocked it off the jacks. Injured most seriously were Harry Payne and Charlie Furr, both of whom fractured their pelvis.

Welborn led the first three laps from the outside pole, then gave way to Schneider. Welborn's short tenure at the top of the leader board was the only time a Convertible had the lead.

Of the 53 cars that entered, 41 were running at the finish.

Promoter Bill France announced that he would pay 'travel money' to any contestant who won less than $300. In the wake of the factory pull-out, France made sure every team went home with at least $300. The NASCAR President, who was directing the holiday 250-miler, paid out some $8,850 in travel money. The posted purse was $14,300.

Paul Goldsmith's Ford blazes down Raleigh home stretch.

Race No. 29

Baker's Bid Falls Short; Panch Wins at Charlotte

CHARLOTTE,NC (July 12) -- Marvin Panch edged Buck Baker by 2.0-seconds to win the 100-mile Grand National race at the Southern States Fairgrounds. It was the fourth win of the year for the good-natured Oakland, CA native.

Panch drove his Ford into the lead in the 135th lap

and held off Baker, who never led but made a bold charge near the end. Third place went to Lee Petty. Speedy Thompson got fourth place and Fireball Roberts took fifth.

NASCAR chief scorer Joe Epton with the new Bulova timing equipment.

Tiny Lund started on the pole, but his Pontiac succumbed to a broken gas line in the first lap. He wound up last in the 21 car field.

Thompson led twice for 42 laps before he fell a lap off the pace in the closing stages. Jack Smith was holding down first place when the transmission broke in his Chevrolet on lap 117. He got credit for 13th place.

A crowd of 7,800 watched Panch average 56.302 mph after four caution periods slowed the action for 12 laps.

Grand National Race No. 29
200 Laps at Southern States Fairgrounds
Charlotte, NC
100 Miles on Half-mile Dirt Track
July 12, 1957

Fin	St	No.	Driver	Team / Car	Laps	Money	Status
1	7	98	Marvin Panch	Panch '57 Ford	200	$700	Running
2	5	87	Buck Baker	Baker '57 Chevrolet	200	525	Running
3	4	42	Lee Petty	Petty Engineering '57 Olds	200	400	Running
4	2	46	Speedy Thompson	Thompson '57 Chevrolet	199	330	Running
5	13	34	Fireball Roberts	Dick Beaty '56 Ford	195	270	Running
6	10	14	Billy Myers	Myers '57 Mercury	194	225	Running
7	15	17	Jim Paschal	Paschal '57 Mercury	191	185	Running
8	8	75	Ken Rush	Frank Hayworth '56 Mercury	190	165	Running
9	14	32	Brownie King	Jess Potter '56 Chevrolet	183	150	Running
10	21	96	Bobby Keck	Keck '57 Chevrolet	180	150	Running
11	20	13	Peck Peckham	William Meyer '56 Chevrolet	166	150	Running
12	19	74	L D Austin	Austin '56 Chevrolet	157	150	Dist
13	3	47	Jack Smith	Smith '57 Chevrolet	117	135	Trans
14	17	94	Clarence DeZalia	DeZalia '56 Ford	111	125	Radiator
15	18	2	Ansel Rakestraw	'56 Chevrolet	110	100	Running
16	16	400	Huck Spaulding	Spaulding '56 Dodge	103	100	RF Whee
17	9	64	Johnny Allen	Spook Crawford '57 Plymouth	61	100	Axle
18	12	5	Darel Dieringer	Whitford Bros '57 Ford	53	100	Rock Arm
19	6	1A	Bobby Myers	Whitey Norman '56 Ford	26	75	Engine
20	11	97	Bill Amick	Amick '57 Ford	6	50	H Gasket
21	1	55	Tiny Lund	Brushy Mt. Motors '57 Pontiac	1	50	Gas Line

Time of Race: 1 hour , 46 minutes, 34 seconds
Average Speed: 56.302 mph
Pole Winner: Tiny Lund - 60.913 mph
Lap Leaders: Speedy Thompson 1-25, Jack Smith 26-74, Lee Petty 75, Smith 76-117, Thompson 118-134, Marvin Panch 135-200.
Cautions: 4 for 12 laps   Margin of Victory: 2.0 seconds   Attendance: 7,800

Race No. 30

Panch Drives Thomas Pontiac To Memphis-Arkansas Victory

LeHi, AR (July 14) -- Marvin Panch drove past Jack Smith in the 126th lap and held off a hard charging Bill Amick to win the 200-mile Sweepstakes race at Memphis-Arkansas Speedway.

The event was a big disappointment for the 9,500 spectators as many left half way through when blinding dust became an unbearable problem. Two caution flags totaling 56 minutes were used to dampen the billowing dust of the 1.5-mile superspeedway.

Panch was driving the Herb Thomas Pontiac to maintain second place in the point standings. He stood 344 points behind Buck Baker, who finished fourth in the

200-miler open to both Grand National hardtops and NASCAR Convertibles.

Grand National automobiles took the first four spots. Amick was second in the 134-lap chase and Fireball Roberts was third. Bob Welborn took fifth in a Convertible behind Baker.

Paul Goldsmith led the first 36 laps after starting second. Curtis Turner took the lead in his Ford Convertible and led through the 72nd lap when Smith took command. Smith had the race sewed up until the engine in his Chevrolet cut loose with nine laps to go.

Disgusted with the turn of events, Smith announced his retirement from auto racing. "I can't keep buying engines," he growled, accenting the plight of many drivers who turned car owners after the mass factory withdrawl on June 6. "I quit. I have run my last race."

Marvin Panch won big Memphis-Arkansas race.

Other than the two "dust cautions", there were no yellow flags -- and very little interest for the spectators. Panch collected $3,500 for his 67.167 mph triumph.

Goldsmith blew the engine in his Ford on lap 38, leaving him with a 27th place effort in the field of 28.

Grand National Race No. 30
134 Laps at Memphis-Arkansas Speedway
LeHi, AR
200 Miles on 1.5-mile Dirt Track
July 14, 1957

Fin	St	No.	Driver	Team / Car	Laps	Money	Status
1	10	92	Marvin Panch	Herb Thomas '57 Pontiac GN	134	$3,500	Running
2	5	97	Bill Amick	Amick '57 Ford GN	134	2,075	Running
3	6	11	Fireball Roberts	Paul Spaulding '57 Ford GN	134	1,375	Running
4	3	87	Buck Baker	Baker '57 Chevrolet GN	132	950	Running
5	13	49	Bob Welborn	Welborn '57 Chevrolet C	131	750	Running
6	9	42	Lee Petty	Petty Engineering '57 Olds GN	131	600	Running
7	11	6	Cotton Owens	Ray Nichels '57 Pontiac GN	131	500	Running
8	17	48	Possum Jones	Welborn '57 Chevrolet C	131	450	Running
9	15	2	Billy Carden	Westmoreland '57 Chevrolet GN	129	350	Running
10	4	26	Curtis Turner	Holman-Moody '57 Ford C	128	325	Running
11	12	21	Glen Wood	Wood Brothers '57 Ford C	127	275	Running
12	21	64	Johnny Allen	Spook Crawford '57 Plym GN	126	275	Running
13	8	47	Jack Smith	Smith '57 Chevrolet GN	125	250	Engine
14	20	76	Larry Frank	Lonnie Fish '56 Chevrolet C	124	225	Running
15	22	32	Brownie King	Jess Potter '56 Chevrolet GN	116	225	Running
16	26	74	L D Austin	Austin '56 Chevrolet GN	112	200	Running
17	19	41	Billy Rafter	C M Julian '56 Dodge C	111	200	Running
18	24	77	Don Gray	Lonnie Fish '56 Chevrolet C	109	175	Running
19	18	75	Ken Rush	Frank Hayworth Mercury C	102	200	Cont Arm
20	14	4F	Bill Hazel	'56 Ford GN	96	175	Engine
21	28	93	Ted Chamberlain	Chamberlain '56 Plym GN	90	150	Heating
22	1	46	Speedy Thompson	Thompson '57 Chevrolet GN	73	175	Carb
23	7	80	Jim Paschal	J S Rice '57 Pontiac GN	64	175	Fan
24	16	310	Joe Lee Johnson	S T Campbell '56 Dodge GN	63	150	Engine
25	23	13	Peck Peckham	William Meyer '56 Chevry GN	57	125	Oil Pres
26	25	12	Joe Weatherly	Holman-Moody '57 Ford C	52	125	Push Rod
27	2	3	Paul Goldsmith	Smokey Yunick '57 Ford GN	38	150	Engine
28	27	4	Art Binkley	Binkley '56 Plymouth C	33	125	Timing

Time of Race: 2 hours, 59 minutes, 33 seconds
Average Speed: 67.167 mph
Pole Winner: Speedy Thompson - 98.991 mph
Lap Leaders: Paul Goldsmith 1-36, Curtis Turner 37-72, Jack Smith 73-125,
Marvin Panch 126-134
Cautions: 2 for Dust Condition - 56 minutes   Margin of Victory: Attendance: 9,500

Race No. 31

Powerful Pagan Takes Portland 100

PORTLAND, OR (July 14) -- Eddie Pagan delivered his third win of the year in the 100-mile contest at Portland Speedway. The Lynwood, CA Ford driver was able to maintain 20th place in the Grand National point standings despite running only the West coast events.

Pagan outran Lloyd Dane to win the 200 lap event on the half-mile paved track. Danny Graves finished third, Scotty Cain was fourth and Dick Getty fifth.

Art Watts started on the pole for the fourth time in his career, but he lost ground in the pits and wound up 11th, 13 laps behind.

Pagan, who started second in the field of 18, led most of the way. He averaged 64.539 mph for his fourth career Grand National win.

Grand National Race No. 31
200 Laps at Portland Speedway
Portland, OR
100 Miles on Half-mile Paved Track
July 14, 1957

Fin	St	No.	Driver	Team / Car	Laps	Money	Status
1	2	45	Eddie Pagan	Pagan '57 Ford	200	$1,000	Running
2	4	44	Lloyd Dane	Dane '57 Ford	198	625	Running
3	3	81	Danny Graves	'57 Chevrolet	198	400	Running
4	14	14	Scotty Cain	Cain '56 Mercury	197	295	Running
5		00	Dick Getty	Betty Getty '56 Chevrolet	194	255	Running
6		66	Bud Emra	'56 Mercury	193	210	Running
7		98	Ed Negre	'55 Oldsmobile	193	175	Running
8		50	Harold Beal	'56 Ford	192	165	Running
9		80	Norman McGriff	'56 Oldsmobile	191	150	Running
10		21N	Bob Rauscher	'57 Ford	187	140	Running
11	1	22N	Art Watts	'56 Ford	187	135	Running
12		14N	Bob Keefe	'54 Ford	179	125	Running
13		83	Royce Haggerty	'56 Dodge	162	110	Running
14		22	Jack D McCoy	'56 Ford	159	100	Running
15		17	Rick Simon	'55 Plymouth	23	100	H Gasket
16		26	Carl Joiner	'54 Oldsmobile	18	100	Handling
17		21	Bob Wood	'54 Oldsmobile	18	100	Piston
18		15	Keith Olson	David Vaughn '54 Lincoln	17	100	Heating

Time of Race: 1 hour, 32 minutes, 58 seconds
Average Speed: 64.539 mph
Pole Winner: Art Watts - 66.396 mph
Lap Leaders: - - - - - - - - - - Eddie Pagan -200.
Cautions: Margin of Victory: 2 laps plus   Attendance:

Race No. 32

Jack Smith 'Unretires' And Wins at Hickory

HICKORY, NC (July 20,) -- Recently retired Jack Smith made a celebrated return to the stock car circuit by winning the 100-mile Grand National race at Hickory Speedway. It was the third win of the season for the Sandy Spring, GA veteran.

Jack Smith ended a brief retirement and won at Hickory.

The event was punctuated by a wild on-track brawl between Curtis Turner and Speedy Thompson, who fought with their cars like there was no tomorrow. Turner, who started eighth, slashed his way through the pack in the early going. He moved to second place by lap 38 and began pressuring Thompson, who was leading. Thompson blocked every Turner move and led through the first 46 laps.

On lap 47, Turner got under Thompson and shoved him aside as he took the lead. Turner then quickly applied the brakes to his Ford and Thompson rear-ended him.

Thompson was forced to retreat to the pits so that his pit crew could repair a damaged radiator.

Thompson returned to the track on lap 66 just in front of Turner. Thompson jammed his brakes and Turner plowed into the rear of his machine. Both were sidelined after the second altercation. After each had gone to the pits for good, harsh words and threatening gestures were exchanged.

Both Turner and Thompson were fined $50 by NASCAR's Bill France, who said in no uncertain terms, "This sort of activity has no place in any sports contest and NASCAR intends to do everything possible to see that a code of good sportsmanship is enforced."

Smith passed Lee Petty for good in the 214th lap and led the rest of the way in the 250-lapper on the .4-mile

Grand National Race No. 32
250 Laps at Hickory Speedway
Hickory, NC
100 Miles on .4-mile Dirt Track
July 20, 1957

Fin	St	No.	Driver	Team / Car	Laps	Money	Status
1	3	47	Jack Smith	Smith '57 Chevrolet	250	$1,000	Running
2	13	42	Lee Petty	Petty Engineering '57 Olds	250	625	Running
3	14	12	Joe Weatherly	Holman-Moody '57 Ford	250	400	Running
4	1	38	Gwyn Staley	Julian Petty '57 Chevrolet	250	280	Running
5	7	22	Fireball Roberts	Roberts '57 Ford	250	245	Running
6	18	97	Bill Amick	Amick '57 Ford	250	210	Running
7	6	87	Buck Baker	Baker '57 Chevrolet	244	175	Running
8	21	5	Darel Dieringer	Whitford Bros '57 Ford	243	165	Running
9	15	32	Brownie King	Jess Potter '56 Chevrolet	229	150	Running
10	12	1A	Whitey Norman	Norman '56 Ford	227	140	Running
11	23	74	L D Austin	Austin '56 Chevrolet	225	135	Running
12	17	98	Marvin Panch	Panch '57 Ford	220	125	Running
13	25	94	Clarence DeZalia	DeZalia '56 Ford	217	110	Running
14	22	13	Peck Peckham	William Myer '56 Chevrolet	212	100	Running
15	24	88	Duke DiBrizzi	'57 Oldsmobile	207	100	Running
16	11	96	Bobby Keck	Keck '57 Chevrolet	204	100	Steering
17	16	55	Tiny Lund	Brushy Mtn Motors '57 Pontiac	190	100	Running
18	20	6	Cotton Owens	Ray Nichels '57 Pontiac	156	100	Lug Nuts
19	4	64	Johnny Allen	Spook Crawford '57 Plymouth	120	50	Ball Jnt
20	5	92	Paul Goldsmith	Herb Thomas '57 Pontiac	83	50	Axle
21	10	14	Billy Myers	Myers '57 Mercury	67	50	Engine
22	8	26	Curtis Turner	Holman-Moody '57 Ford	66	50	Crash
23	2	46	Speedy Thompson	Thompson '57 Chevrolet	60	50	Crash
24	9	75	Ken Rush	Frank Hayworth '56 Mercury	51	50	Fuel Pmp
25	19	17	Jim Paschal	Paschal '57 Mercury	31	50	Oil Leak

Time of Race: 1 hour, 42 minutes, 9 seconds
Average Speed: 58.737
Pole Winner: Gwyn Staley - 66.085
Lap Leaders: Speedy Thompson 1-46, Curtis Turner 47-66, Gwyn Staley 67-170, Jack Smith 171-190, Lee Petty 191-198, Joe Weatherly 199-201, Petty 202-213, Smith 214-250.
Cautions: Margin of Victory: Attendance: 8,200

dirt track. Petty was second, followed by Joe Weatherly, Gwyn Staley and Fireball Roberts.

A crowd of 8,200 watched Smith average 58.737 mph for his fourth career victory.

Race No. 33

Baker Bags Norfolk 100; Stretches Point Lead to 472

NORFOLK, VA (July 24) -- Buck Baker upped his point lead to 472 points with his sixth win of the year in the 100-mile Grand National race at Norfolk Speedway. Baker's Chevrolet beat Joe Weatherly's Ford to the finish line by a full lap to take the $900 first prize.

Jim Paschal finished in third place with Billy Myers fourth and Jack Smith fifth. It was the first top five finish for Myers since May

Pole sitter Bill Amick finished last in the 23 car field. Distributor problems sidelined his Ford after just 29 laps.

Marvin Panch, driving Herb Thomas' Pontiac, qualified fifth but departed with a broken axle after 170 laps. It was the second straight race the Thomas car has been foiled by a broken axle.

Tiny Lund, hard charger who has been bitten by bad luck all season, started third and managed to finish sixth, five laps in arrears.

Baker averaged 47.987 mph for his 32nd career victory.

Grand National Race No. 33
250 Laps at Norfolk Speedway
Norfolk, VA
100 Miles on .4-mile Dirt Track
July 24, 1957

Fin	St	No.	Driver	Team / Car	Laps	Money	Status
1	8	87	Buck Baker	Baker '57 Chevrolet	250	$900	Running
2	12	12	Joe Weatherly	Holman-Moody '57 Ford	249	575	Running
3	15	75	Jim Paschal	Frank Hayworth '56 Mercury	249	375	Running
4	14	14	Billy Myers	Myers '57 Mercury	248	280	Running
5	2	47	Jack Smith	Smith '57 Chevrolet	245	245	Running
6	3	55	Tiny Lund	Brushy Mtn Motors '57 Pontiac	245	210	Running
7	9	38	Gwyn Staley	Julian Petty '57 Chevrolet	243	175	Running
8	6	42	Lee Petty	Petty Engineering '57 Olds	241	165	Running
9	11	46	Speedy Thompson	Thompson '57 Chevrolet	234	150	Running
10	16	1A	Whitey Norman	Norman '56 Ford	230	140	Running
11	23	74	L D Austin	Austin '56 Chevrolet	227	135	Running
12	21	88	Duke DiBrizzi	'57 Oldsmobile	225	125	Running
13	20	26	Wally Gore	J S Rice '56 Ford	203	110	Running
14	22	94	Clarence DeZalia	DeZalia '56 Ford	188	100	Running
15	17	35	Bill Champion	Whitford Bros. '56 Ford	173	100	A Frame
16	5	92	Marvin Panch	Herb Thomas '57 Pontiac	170	100	Axle
17	7	71	Bill Bowman	'56 Chevrolet	140	100	Piston
18	18	400	Huck Spaulding	Spaulding '56 Dodge	114	100	Steering
19	13	64	Johnny Allen	Spook Crawford '57 Plymouth	81	50	Engine
20	10	5	Darel Dieringer	Whitford Bros '57 Ford	62	50	Spindle
21	4	22	Fireball Roberts	Roberts '57 Ford	44	50	Radiator
22	19	15	Lou Spears	'56 Chevrolet	33	50	Oil Line
23	1	97	Bill Amick	Amick '57 Ford	29	50	Distrib'r

Time of Race: 2 hours, 5 minutes, 2 seconds
Average Speed: 47.987 mph
Pole Winner: Bill Amick - 56.338 mph
Lap Leaders: - - - - - - - - - - Buck Baker   -250.
Cautions: Margin of Victory: 1-lap-plus   Attendance:

Race No. 34

Thompson Unheaded in 100-Miler at Lancaster

LANCASTER, SC (July 30) -- Speedy Thompson of Monroe, NC ended a year-long famine with a flag-to-flag victory in the 100-mile event at Lancaster Speedway. It was his first triumph on the Grand National trail since Nov. 11, 1956 when he won at Hickory, NC.

Bill Amick finished second and Marvin Panch wasthird. Buck Baker placed fourth and Lee Petty was fifth.

Thompson started on the pole and led the entire 200 laps on the half-mile dirt oval. He averaged 66.543 mph in the caution-free race.

Biggest news of the week was the 'break' between NASC-

Speedy Thompson won at Lancaster, SC.

AR and Curtis Turner, who vowed never to race again unless the $50 fine for rough riding at Hickory a week earlier was lifted. The Roanoke, VA lumberman also announced that he and fellow racer Paul Goldsmith had purchased the Packard proving grounds near Detroit. The duo planned to convert the testing grounds over to a 2.5-mile super-speedway. They hoped the project could be completed by the 1958 season.

Curtis Turner was rumored to have split with NASCAR.

Grand National Race No. 34
200 Laps at Lancaster Speedway
Lancaster, SC
100 Miles on Half-mile Dirt Track
July 30, 1957

Fin	St	No.	Driver	Team / Car	Laps	Money	Status
1	1	46	Speedy Thompson	Thompson '57 Chevrolet	200	$1,000	Running
2	4	97	Bill Amick	Amick '57 Ford	200	625	Running
3	9	98	Marvin Panch	Panch '57 Ford	197	400	Running
4	3	87	Buck Baker	Baker '57 Chevrolet	194	295	Running
5	5	42	Lee Petty	Petty Engineering '57 Olds	192	255	Running
6	7	64	Johnny Allen	Spook Crawford '57 Plymouth	192	210	Running
7	2	22	Fireball Roberts	Roberts '57 Ford	188	175	Running
8	14	75	Ken Rush	Frank Hayworth '56 Mercury	182	165	Running
9	18	55	Tiny Lund	Brushy Mtn Motors '57 Pontiac	173	150	Fan Belt
10	16	74	L D Austin	Austin '56 Chevrolet	166	140	Running
11	13	96	Bobby Keck	Keck '57 Chevrolet	165	135	Running
12	19	47	Jack Smith	Smith '57 Chevrolet	148	125	Bearing
13	17	2	E J Brewer	'56 Ford	138	110	Engine
14	6	80	Jimmie Lewallen	J S Rice '57 Pontiac	135	100	Engine
15	15	94	Clarence DeZalia	DeZalia '56 Ford	126	100	Running
16	12	17	Jim Paschal	Paschal '57 Mercury	47	100	Rear End
17	10	1A	Whitey Norman	Norman '56 Ford	16	100	Radiator
18	11	38	Gwyn Staley	Julian Petty '57 Chevrolet	11	100	Oil Leak
19	8	6	Cotton Owens	Ray Nichels '57 Pontiac	3	50	Oil Pump

Time of Race: 1 hour, 30 minutes, 10 seconds
Average Speed: 66.543 mph
Pole Winner: Speedy Thompson - 67.694 mph
Lap Leaders: Speedy Thompson 1-200.
Cautions: None   Margin of Victory: Attendance:

Race No 35

Baker Best in Watkins Glen Road Race

WATKINS GLEN, NY (Aug. 4) -- The Grand National stockers made their first trip to the Watkins Glen complex and Buck Baker came home the winner for his seventh triumph of the season. The Charlotte, NC veteran was able to boost his point lead to 544 over Marvin Panch, who spun off the course and crashed into a retaining barrier in the 22nd lap.

Fireball Roberts finished second. Tiny Lund wound up in third place, Frankie Schneider was fourth and

Buck Baker won on the road course at Watkins Glen.

Johnny Allen fifth.

Baker started on the pole with a speed of 87.071 mph on the hilly road course. He got the jump at the green flag and led all 44 laps on the 2.3-mile lay-out.

Jim Reed was locked in a tight battle with Roberts for runner-up honors, but he crashed his Ford with two laps to go. The Peekskill, NY driver got credit for sixth place in the final rundown.

Baker averaged 83.064 mph in the caution free 101.2 mile event. It was his 33rd career Grand National victory.

Grand National Race No. 35
44 Laps at Watkins Glen
Watkins Glen, NY
101.2 Miles on 2.3-Mile Paved Road Course
August 4, 1957

Fin	St	No.	Driver	Team / Car	Laps	Money	Status
1	1	87	Buck Baker	Baker '57 Chevrolet	44	$1,000	Running
2	3	22	Fireball Roberts	Roberts '57 Ford	44	625	Running
3	7	55	Tiny Lund	Brushy Mtn Motors '57 Pontiac	44	400	Running
4	5	2	Frankie Schneider	Westmoreland '57 Chevrolet	43	295	Running
5	6	64	Johnny Allen	Spook Crawford '57 Plymouth	43	255	Running
6	2	7	Jim Reed	Reed '57 Chevrolet	42	210	Crash
7	8	88	Jim Linke	Ernest Woods '57 Olds	40	175	Running
8	10	42	Lee Petty	Petty Engineering '57 Olds	40	165	Running
9	13	65	Al White	'56 Ford	39	150	Running
10	17	41	Billy Rafter	C M Julian '56 Dodge	37	140	Running
11	15	4	Huck Spaulding	Spaulding '56 Chevrolet	35	145	Running
12	14	6	Spook Crawford	Crawford '56 Plymouth	34	125	Running
13	18	86	Gene Blair	'56 Pontiac	32	110	Running
14	4	92	Marvin Panch	Herb Thomas '57 Pontiac	22	100	Crash
16	16	19	Dick Walters	Walters '56 Ford	21	100	Running
16	20	14	Walt Mortz	'56 Ford	15	100	Heating
17	9	83	Lennie Page	'56 Ford	14	100	Fan Belt
18	11	150	Bill Walker	'57 Ford	12	100	Engine
19	19	11	Claude Holliday	'56 Dodge	12	50	Heating
20	12	74	L D Austin	Austin '56 Chevrolet	6	50	Distr

Time of Race: 1 hour, 13 minutes, 6 seconds
Average Speed: 83.064 mph
Pole Winner: Buck Baker - 87.071 mph
Lap Leaders: Buck Baker 1-44.
Cautions: None   Margin of Victory: .46 mile   Attendance:

Race No. 36

Parnelli Grabs First Win at Kitsap County Airport

BREMERTON, WA (Aug. 4) -- Rufus "Parnelli" Jones of Torrance, CA steered his Ford around the .9-mile road course on the runways of the Kitsap County Airport and won the 72-mile Grand National event. It was Jones' first big time NASCAR win and it came in his 10th start.

The season had been dismal for the former off-road racer. He had not finished once in the top five in six previous 1957 starts. Driving the Oscar Maples Ford, Jones was flawless.

Finshing second was Lloyd Dane and Art Watts was third. Eddie Pagan came in fourth and Bob Rauscher took fifth.

Fourteen cars started the event and 12 finished. Jones averaged only 38.959 mph on the flat, testy course, which required heavy braking in most of the turns.

Joltin' Johnny Mackison finished 5th at New Oxford.

Grand National Race No. 36
80 laps at Kitsap County Airport
Bremerton, WA
72 Miles on .9-mile Paved Road Course
August 4, 1957

Fin	St	No.	Driver	Team / Car	Laps	Money	Status
1	3	11	Parnelli Jones	Oscar Maples '57 Ford	80	$900	Running
2	5	44	Lloyd Dane	Dane '57 Ford	80	610	Running
3	1	22N	Art Watts	Schmidhamer '56 Ford	80	465	Running
4	4	45	Eddie Pagan	Pagan '57 Ford	79	315	Running
5	7	21N	Bob Rauscher	'57 Ford	77	270	Running
6	9	14	Scotty Cain	Cain '56 Mercury	77	210	Running
7	8	00	Dick Getty	Betty Getty '56 Chevrolet	77	200	Running
8	10	98N	Ed Negre	'55 Olds	76	170	Running
9	2	81	Danny Graves	'57 Chevrolet	74	175	Engine
10	11	66N	Bud Emra	'56 Mercury	74	114	Running
11	14	99	Don Porter	Nick Porter '56 Ford	73	110	Running
12	13	83N	Bill Hidden	'56 Dodge	72	100	Running
13	6	50N	Harold Beal	'56 Ford	54	110	Running
14	12	80N	Norman McGriff	'56 Olds	29	110	Trans

Time of Race: 1 hour, 50 minutes, 53 seconds
Average Speed: 38.959 mph
Pole Winner: Art Watts - 62.657 mph
Lap Leaders: - - - - - - - - - Parnelli Jones   -80.
Cautions: Margin of Victory: Attendance:

Race No. 37

Panch Outlasts Field; Wins at New Oxford

NEW OXFORD, PA (Aug. 10) -- Marvin Panch renewed his quest for the NASCAR Grand National championship with a victory in the 100-miler at Lincoln Speedway. It was his sixth win of the season and it pulled him to within 416 of point leader Buck Baker who wound up 26th in the field of 32

Speedy Thompson finished in second place. Pole winner Tiny Lund wound up third, Johnny Allen was fourth and Johnny Mackison was fifth.

Herb Thomas made his second start of the year. The 48-time winner started 18th and left the race after 46

laps with a broken hub. His Pontiac wound up 28th.

Other top drawing cards who failed to finish were Fireball Roberts, Lee Petty, Jim Paschal and hot-shot

Grand National Race No. 37
200 Laps at Lincoln Speedway
New Oxford, PA
100 Miles on Half-mile Dirt Track
August 10, 1957

Fin	St	No.	Driver	Team / Car	Laps	Money	Status
1	6	98	Marvin Panch	Panch '57 Ford	200	$1,000	Running
2	2	46	Speedy Thompson	Thompson '57 Chevrolet	200	625	Running
3	1	55	Tiny Lund	Brushy Mtn Motors '57 Pontiac	198	400	Running
4	8	64	Johnny Allen	Spook Crawford '57 Plymouth	191	295	Running
5	10	104	Johnny Mackison	Camp Hill Spl '57 Ford	188	255	Running
6	16	100	Jim Findley	'57 Chevrolet	187	210	Running
7	17	2	Frankie Schneider	Westmoreland '57 Chevrolet	185	175	Running
8	29	79	Dick Klank	'56 Ford	180	165	Running
9	20	69	Volney Schulze	'56 Chevrolet	177	150	Running
10	15	981	Fred Knapp	'56 Ford	177	140	Running
11	28	11	George Fleming	'56 Ford	174	135	Running
12	21	68	Jim Linke	Ernest Woods '57 Olds	173	125	Running
13	7	95	Bob Duell	Julian Buesink '57 Ford	171	110	Rear End
14	26	74	L D Austin	Austin '56 Chevrolet	168	100	Running
15	24	4X	Bill Lone	'56 Ford	167	100	Running
16	11	888	Charles Hanson	Hanson '57 Chevrolet	166	100	Running
17	23	83	Lennie Page	'56 Ford	165	100	Running
18	32	47	Jack Smith	Smith '57 Chevrolet	144	100	Crash
19	30	37	Bill Benson	'56 Mercury	136	50	Running
20	25	5	Lou Spears	'56 Chevrolet	132	50	Running
21	27	13	Peck Peckham	William Meyer '56 Chevrolet	126	50	Engine
22	31	70	Harvey Eakin	Eakin '56 Ford	106	50	Wheel
23	12	41	Billy Rafter	Rafter '56 Dodge	100	50	Brakes
24	22	900	Gus Wilson	'55 Chevrolet	98	50	Engine
25	5	42	Lee Petty	Petty Engineering '57 Olds	94	150	Wheel
26	4	87	Buck Baker	Baker '57 Chevrolet	91	25	Heating
27	19	73	John Dodd, Jr	Dodd '56 Chevrolet	67	25	Oil Leak
28	18	92	Herb Thomas	Thomas '57 Pontiac	46	25	Hub
29	13	81	Jerry Benjamin	'56 Ford	29	25	Engine
30	9	17	Jim Paschal	Paschal '57 Mercury	29	25	Crash
31	3	22	Fireball Roberts	Roberts '57 Ford	24	25	Hub
32	14	8	Reds Kagle	'57 Chevrolet	23	25	Wheel

Time of Race: 1 hour, 17 minutes, 21 seconds
Average Speed: 77.569 mph
Pole Winner: Tiny Lund - 80.971
Lap Leders: - - - - - - - - - Marvin Panch   -200.
Cautions: Margin of Victory: Attendance:

short track driver Reds Kagle.

Baker had finished in the top 10 in the last 35 races he had entered until his misfortune on this half-mile banked dirt track.

Panch averaged 77.569 mph for his seventh win of his career.

Race No. 38

Old Man Petty Wins At Old Bridge

OLD BRIDGE, NJ (Aug. 16) -- Lee Petty used a late race caution to close in on the rear bumper of leader Rex White, then dashed to victory in the 100-miler at Old Bridge Stadium. It was Petty's second win of the season and the 28th of his career.

White finished second, 2.0 seconds behind the Petty Oldsmobile. Third place went to Jim Reed. Marvin Panch came in fourth and Jack Smith finished fifth.

White, making a stab at his first Grand National win,

had taken the lead in the 15th lap and was holding nearly a lap lead when a three car crash involving Chuck Hansen, Dick Klank and Bill Benson brought out the only caution flag. The yellow light was on for four laps.

White led the charge when the green came out with 10 laps to go. But Petty muscled his way under White and led the final nine laps.

A crowd of 5,436 was on its feet for the finish.

Point leader Buck Baker finished seventh. His lead in the standings, which determine the national driving championship, was 392 points over Panch.

Race No. 39

Staley Comes Home First In Coastal Century

MYRTLE BEACH, SC (Aug. 26) -- Gwyn Staley drove his Julian Petty-owned Chevrolet to victory in the 100-mile grind at Myrtle Beach's Coastal Speedway. It was the first career Grand National victory for the Burlington, NC throttle stomper, and he became the season's 15th different winner.

Eddie Pagan, West coast driver who came East for the Darlington Southern 500, finished second. Fireball Roberts was third, Buck Baker fourth and L.D. Austin fifth.

Staley's victory came on the heels of a dramatic loss at the hands of Curtis Turner in a Convertible race at Charlotte less than 24 hours earlier Turner, who said he would boycott NASCAR until the sanctioning body lifted a $50 fine for rough-housing at Hickory. The Ford driver said he was back with NASCAR -- after having to pay the fine.

Gwyn Staley got 1st win at Myrtle Beach.

Staley and car owner Petty snapped a hard top on his Convertible racer and came home with the bacon at the Myrtle Beach track. He was ineligible for championship points because the car did not have a rear window, as required by NASCAR rules.

Johnny Allen startled everyone by taking his first career pole in a Plymouth. His A.M. Crawford entry was the first car out of the race, a victim of a broken fan pulley after running just 10 laps.

Grand National Race No. 38
200 Laps at Old Bridge Stadium
Old Bridge, NJ
100 Miles on Half-mile Paved Track
August 16, 1957

Fin	St	No.	Driver	Team / Car	Laps	Money	Status
1	3	42	Lee Petty	Petty Engineering '57 Olds	200	$1,000	Running
2	1	44	Rex White	Max Welborn '57 Chevrolet	200	625	Running
3	2	7	Jim Reed	Reed '57 Ford	200	400	Running
4	7	98	Marvin Panch	Panch '57 Ford	200	295	Running
5	6	47	Jack Smith	Smith '57 Chevrolet	199	255	Running
6	5	22	Fireball Roberts	Roberts '57 Ford	199	210	Running
7	9	87	Buck Baker	Baker '57 Chevrolet	197	175	Running
8	8	64	Johnny Allen	Spook Crawford '57 Plymouth	197	165	Running
9	4	2	Frankie Schneider	Westmoreland '57 Chevrolet	192	150	Running
10	10	73	John Dodd, Sr.	Dodd '56 Ford	189	140	Running
11	21	5	Lou Spears	'56 Chevrolet	186	135	Running
12	14	74	L D Austin	Austin '56 Chevrolet	184	125	Running
13	11	X	John Findley	'56 Chevrolet	182	110	Running
14	12	888	Chuck Hansen	Hansen '57 Chevrolet	178	100	Crash
15	13	69	Harvey Henderson	'56 Chevrolet	172	100	Running
16	22	318	Chuck Bluett	'56 Plymouth	171	100	Running
17	20	37	Bill Benson	'56 Mercury	170	100	Running
18	19	79	Dick Klank	'56 Ford	165	100	Crash
19	18	13	Peck Peckham	William Meyer '56 Chevrolet	105	50	Bearing
20	17	88	Jim Linke	'57 Oldsmobile	90	50	Piston
21	15	11	Ray Davis	'56 Ford	78	50	Bearing
22	16	65	Al White	'56 Ford	23	50	R F Hub
23	23	319	Tony Moretti	'56 Plymouth	19	50	Heating

Time of Race: 1 hour, 31 minutes, 10 seconds.
Average Speed: 65.813 mph
Pole Winner: Rex White - 71.599 mph
Lap Leaders: Jim Reed 1, Lee Petty 2-14, Rex White 15-191, Petty 192-200.
Cautions: 1 for 4 laps   Margin of Victory: 2.0 seconds   Attendance: 5,436

Grand National Race No. 39
200 Laps at Coastal Speedway
Myrtle Beach, SC
100 Miles on Half-mile Dirt Track
August 26, 1957

Fin	St	No.	Driver	Team / Car	Laps	Money	Status
1	3	38	Gwyn Staley	Julian Petty '57 Chevrolet	200	$1,000	Running
2	12	45	Eddie Pagan	Pagan '57 Ford	199	625	Running
3	2	22	Fireball Roberts	Roberts '57 Ford	198	400	Running
4	9	87	Buck Baker	Baker '57 Chevrolet	183	295	Running
5	10	74	L D Austin	Austin '56 Chevrolet	180	255	Running
6	4	42	Lee Petty	Petty Engineering '57 Olds	180	210	Running
7	15	94	Clarence DeZalia	DeZalia '56 Ford	170	175	Running
8	5	47	Jack Smith	Smith '57 Chevrolet	163	165	Running
9	11	51	Roy Tyner	Tyner '56 Ford	157	150	Running
10	14	37	Bill Benson	'56 Mercury	141	140	Running
11	6	32	Brownie King	Jess Potter '56 Chevrolet	123	135	A Frame
12	13	96	Speedy Thompson	Bobby Keck '57 Chevrolet	99	125	Fuel Line
13	7	98	Marvin Panch	Panch '57 Ford	68	110	Engine
14	8	75	Ken Rush	Frank Hayworth '56 Mercury	51	100	Steering
15	1	64	Johnny Allen	Spook Crawford '57 Plymouth	10	100	Fan

Time of Race: 1 hour, 58 minutes, 9 seconds
Average Speed: 50.782 mph
Pole Winner: Johnny Allen - 58.139 mph
Lap Leaders: - - - - - - - - - - Gwyn Staley   -200.
Cautions;   Margin of Victory: 1 lap plus   Attendance:

Bobby Myers died at the wheel of this Petty Engineering Oldsmobile in Southern 500.

Race No. 40

Speedy Thompson Hits Jackpot in Southern 500

DARLINGTON, SC (Sept. 2) -- Speedy Thompson of Monroe, NC passed Curtis Turner in the 216th lap and led the rest of the way to win the death-marred

Grand National Race No. 40
364 Laps at Darlington Raceway
Darlington, SC
"Southern 500"
500 Miles on 1.375-mile Paved Track
September 2, 1957

Fin	St	No.	Driver	Team / Car	Laps	Money	Status
1	7	46	Speedy Thompson	Thompson '57 Chevrolet	364	$13,590	Running
2	1	6	Cotton Owens	Ray Nichels '57 Pontiac	361	6,100	Running
3	32	98	Marvin Panch	Panch '57 Ford	360	3,745	Running
4	12	7	Jim Reed	Reed '57 Ford	356	2,155	Running
5	9	87	Buck Baker	Baker '57 Chevrolet	356	1,650	Running
6	45	2	Billy Carden	Westmoreland '57 Chevrolet	354	1,225	Running
7	29	14	Billy Myers	Myers '57 Ford	353	1,125	Running
8	25	40	Johnny Mackison	Camp Hill Spl. '57 Ford	352	975	Running
9	48	48	Possum Jones	Welborn '57 Chevrolet	350	775	Running
10	28	47	Jack Smith	Smith '57 Chevrolet	348	785	Crash
11	3	31	Curtis Turner	Smokey Yunick '57 Ford	346	1,060	Running
12	27	64	Johnny Allen	Spook Crawford '57 Plymouth	345	600	Running
13	17	34	Dick Beaty	Beaty '56 Ford	341	350	Running
14	4	80	Jimmie Lewallen	J S Rice '57 Pontiac	340	370	Running
15	34	45	Eddie Pagan	Pagan '57 Ford	339	250	Running
16	23	77	Bobby Johns	Shorty Johns '56 Chevrolet	335	225	Running
17	26	20	Jimmy Thompson	'56 Ford	328	225	Running
18	38	54	Nace Mattingly	Mattingly '57 Ford	326	200	Running
19	37	74	L D Austin	Austin '56 Chevrolet	312	200	Running
20	11	55	Tiny Lund	Brushy Mtn Motors '57 Pontiac	308	300	Running
21	31	32	Brownie King	Jess Potter '57 Chevrolet	307	150	Running
22	35	96	Bobby Keck	Keck '57 Chevrolet	283	150	Running
23	41	51	Roy Tyner	Tyner '56 Ford	282	150	Running
24	8	42	Lee Petty	Petty Engineering '57 Olds	281	750	Crash
25	42	71	George Parrish	Joe Frazier '56 Studebaker	263	350	Running
26	33	12	Marvin Porter	'57 Ford	221	100	Engine
27	30	10	Whitey Norman	Norman '56 Ford	215	100	Engine
28	20	44	Rex White	Max Welborn '57 Chevrolet	210	100	Axle
29	19	95	Bob Duell	Julian Buesink '57 Ford	156	100	Radiator
30	49	13	Peck Peckham	William Meyer '56 Chevrolet	155	100	Engine
31	39	35	Bill Champion	Whitford Bros '56 Ford	130	100	Rear End
32	18	97	Bill Amick	Amick '57 Ford	102	150	Crash
33	10	22	Fireball Roberts	Roberts '57 Ford	101	460	Crash
34	22	11	Parnelli Jones	Oscar Maples 57 Ford	99	100	Crash
35	50	75	Jim Paschal	Frank Hayworth '57 Ford	84	100	Piston
36	36	17	Shorty York	Jim Paschal '57 Mercury	79	300	Engine
37	16	89	Joe Caspolich	Pappy Crane '57 Ford	66	200	Crash
38	46	26	Bill Blair	J S Rice '57 Ford	63	100	Crash
39	24	90	Runt Harris	Junie Donlavey '57 Chevrolet	50	100	Clutch
40	14	9	Joe Weatherly	Weatherly '57 Ford	37	130	Crash
41	13	84	Banjo Matthews	'57 Ford	31	120	Engine
42	44	30	Cale Yarborough	'57 Pontiac	31	100	R F Hub
43	2	4	Bobby Myers	Petty Engineering '57 Olds	27	260	Crash
44	6	3	Paul Goldsmith	Smokey Yunick '57 Ford	27	200	Crash
45	43	88	Chuck Hansen	Hanson '57 Chevrolet	23	100	Piston
46	21	38	Gwyn Staley	Julian Petty '57 Chevrolet	22	100	Coil
47	5	62	Frankie Schneider	'57 Chevrolet	19	100	Engine
48	15	92	Fonty Flock	Herb Thomas '57 Pontiac	18	100	Crash
49	40	68	Neil Castles	Castles '56 Ford	13	100	Oil Pres
50	47	41	T A Toomes	C M Julian '56 Dodge	3	300	Brakes

Time of Race: 5 hours, 0 minutes, 1 second
Average Speed: 100.094 mph
Pole Winner: Cotton Owens - 117.416 mph
Fastest Qualifier: Paul Goldsmith - 119.291 mph
Lap Leaders: Cotton Owens 1-6, Curtis Turner 7-10, Paul Goldsmith 11-13,
Bobby Myers 14, Turner 15-16, Owens 17--28, Lee Petty 29-40, Fireball Roberts 41-69,
Petty 70-88, Roberts 89-100, Jack Smith 101-109, Speedy Thompson 110-170,
Turner 171-215, Thompson 216-364.
Cautions: 6 for 23 laps   Margin of Victory: 3-laps-plus   Attendance: 75,000

eighth annual Southern 500 at Darlington Raceway.
Bobby Myers, 33, of Winston-Salem was killed in the 27th lap when he crashed head-on into Fonty Flock's Pontiac, which had spun out. Flock, who was

a last minute replacement for Herb Thomas, looped his car down the backstretch. The car spun and came to a halt next to the guard rail at the entrance to the third turn. Myers, driving a Petty Engineering Oldsmobile, crashed full bore into Flock. Paul Goldsmith also hit Flock broadside.

Myers' white car lazily flipped over several times and it finally came to rest in the third turn. The engine was ripped out of the chassis. Rescue workers removed his limp body and rushed him to Florence's McLeod Hospital where he was pronounced dead on arrival.

Flock was in serious condition and Goldsmith was listed 'fair'.

Thompson started seventh in his Chevrolet and took the lead for the first time on lap 110. He held the front position for 61 laps until Turner took command. Thompson followed Turner for 45 laps before making his final bid.

Cotton Owens finished second in a Pontiac, three laps behind. Marvin Panch's Ford was third, Jim Reed's Ford came in fourth and the Chevrolet of point leader Buck Baker was fifth.

In the 67th lap, Joe Caspolich, driving in his first Grand National race, hit a spin-

Pit crews work on Grand National stockers in the pits at Darlington Raceway before the Southern 500.

ning Bill Blair and wrapped his Ford around the inside guard rail. The Gulf Port, MS driver climbed out and then collapsed. He suffered multiple fractures and a bruised heart. He was listed in critical condition. Blair was uninjured.

Lee Petty, who started eighth, emerged in a spirited duel with Turner in the middle stages. With Petty in close pursuit, the two cars touched and Turner's Ford shot into the retaining wall. He made a lengthy pit stop so his Smokey Yunick pit crew could repair a smashed radiator.

Joe Weatherly, Turner's side-kick on the Convertible circuit, peeled out of the pits and ran down Petty. He laid a thick bumper on Petty's quarter-panel, putting the former Grand National champ into the wall and out of the race. That incident took place on lap 282.

Turner got back in the race and wound up 11th, 18 laps behind winner Thompson.

Thompson, who pocketed the $13,590 first place jackpot, averaged 100.094 mph for his 14th career win. The caution flag was out six times for a total of 23 laps.

A pudgy kid named Cale

Smokey Yunick and pit crew quickly service Curtis Turner in Southern 500. Turner was involved in a scrape with Lee Petty. He eventually finished 11th.

Fonty Flock's Pontiac was torn up badly in fatal Darlington wreck.

Yarborough made his first Grand National start. The Timmonsville, SC youngster started a Pontiac in 44th spot and wound up 42nd after the right front hub broke after 31 laps.

There was no formal announcement concerning Myers' passing over the Public Address, but the rebel flag in the infield was lowered to half mast less than 100 miles into the event.

Race No. 41

Staley Stout at Syracuse; Wins 100-Miler

SYRACUSE, NY (Sept. 5) -- Gwyn Staley outlasted Jim Reed and won the 100-miler at the New York State Fairgrounds. It was the second win of the year for the Chevrolet driver.

Lee Petty finished in second place, over a lap behind the winner. Bill Walker came in third, Dean Layfield was fourth and Fireball Roberts was fifth.

Staley won the pole and led the first 62 laps on the one-mile flat oval. Reed, who started second, gave chase all the way until he forged to the front on lap 63. He was holding a narrow advantage when his Ford darted high and hit the guard rail. After a lengthy pit stop, Reed returned and finished 12th, 26 laps behind.

A crowd of 5,000 watched Staley win at an average speed of 80.591 mph.

Neither point leader Buck Baker or second place Marvin Panch entered the race.

Grand National Race No. 41
100 Laps at New York State Fairgrounds
Syracuse, NY
100 Miles on One-mile Dirt Track
September 5, 1957

Fin	St	No.	Driver	Team / Car	Laps	Money	Status
1	1	38	Gwyn Staley	Julian Petty '57 Chevrolet	100	$1,000	Running
2	3	42	Lee Petty	Petty Engineering '57 Olds	99	625	Running
3	7	150	Bill Walker	'57 Ford	99	400	Running
4	9	916	Dean Layfield	'56 Ford	97	295	Running
5	5	22	Fireball Roberts	Roberts '57 Ford	95	255	Running
6	13	83	Lennie Page	'56 Ford	93	210	Running
7	15	37	Bill Benson	'56 Mercury	89	175	Running
8	17	99	Buzz Woodward	'56 Ford	87	165	Running
9	20	93	Ted Chamberlain	Chamberlain '56 Plymouth	82	150	Running
10	16	19	Dick Walters	=Walters '56 Plymouth	80	140	Running
11	18	86	Ray Campbell	'56 Ford	77	135	Running
12	2	7	Jim Reed	Reed '57 Ford	74	125	Running
13	22	41	Ed Jacken	'56 Dodge	72	110	Spindle
14	19	319	Jake Jacobs	'56 Plymouth	58	100	Running
15	12	17	Al Stearn	'56 Chevrolet	57	100	Bearing
16	14	6	Ted Hauser	'56 Chevrolet	43	100	Heating
17	4	47	Jack Smith	Smith '57 Chevrolet	40	100	Bearing
18	11	98	Fred Knapp	'56 Chevrolet	39	100	Steering
19	24	13	Peck Peckham	William Meyer '56 Chevrolet	29	100	Piston
20	10	95	Bob Duell	Julian Buesink '57 Ford	21	50	Engine
21	21	9	Joe Saunder	'56 Ford	19	50	Oil Pres
22	8	30	Art Anderson	'56 Chevrolet	14	50	Piston
23	6	8	Emory Mahon	'56 Chevrolet	3	50	Axle
24	23	4	Billy Rafter	Rafter '56 Plymouth	2	50	Fuel Pmp

Time of Race: 1 hour, 14 minutes, 27 seconds
Average Speed: 80.591 mph
Pole Winner: Gwyn Stlaey - 83.045 mph
Lap Leaders Gwyn Staley 1-62, Jim Reed 63-72, Staley 73-100.
Cautions: Margin of Victory: 1 3/4 laps   Attendance: 5,000

Race No. 42

Petty Plays Waiting Game; Then Charges to Win at Asheville-Weaverville

WEAVERVILLE, NC (Sept. 8) -- Lee Petty passed Buck Baker with 45 laps to go and sped to victory in the 100-miler at Asheville-Weaverville Speedway. It was the third win of the season for the Oldsmobile driver.

Baker finished second with Bill Amick, Rex White and Jack Smith completing the top five.

Pole sitter Amick led the first nine laps. Cotton Owens, making an infrequent short track Grand National appearance, took the lead on lap 10 and was in front in the 141st lap when his Pontiac blew a tire and crashed into the wall.

Amick picked up the lead during the caution flag and Baker had the lead on the restart. Petty, playing the waiting game, moved into contention late in the race. He dogged Baker for 12 laps before making the decisive pass.

Petty's Oldsmobile nosed out Baker's Chevrolet by 10 feet to take the $1,000 first prize. It was his 29th career victory on NASCAR's major league circuit.

Grand National Race No. 42
200 Laps at Asheville-Weaverville Speedway
Weaverville, NC
100 Miles on Half-mile Paved Track
September 8, 1957

Fin	St	No.	Driver	Team / Car	Laps	Money	Status
1	2	42	Lee Petty	Petty Engineering '57 Olds	200	$1,000	Running
2	3	87	Buck Baker	Baker '57 Chevrolet	200	625	Runniing
3	1	97	Bill Amick	Amick '57 Ford	200	400	Running
4	7	44	Rex White	Max Welborn '57 Chevrolet	200	295	Running
5	11	47	Jack Smith	Smith '57 Chevrolet	199	255	Running
6	10	34	Dick Beaty	Beaty '56 Ford	198	210	Running
7	12	98	Marvin Panch	Panch '57 Ford	196	175	Running
8	8	62	Frankie Schneider	'57 Chevrolet	196	165	Running
9	13	64	Johnny Allen	Spook Crawford '57 Plymouth	196	150	Running
10	15	22	Fireball Roberts	Roberts '57 Ford	194	140	Running
11	9	84	Banjo Matthews	'57 Ford	188	135	Running
12	17	74	L D Austin	Austin '56 Chevrolet	185	125	Running
13	18	75	Jim Paschal	Frank Hayworth '57 Ford	185	110	Running
14	20	37	Bill Benson	'56 Mercury	150	100	Running
15	19	71	George Parrish	Joe Frazier '56 Studebaker	143	100	Wheel
16	4	6	Cotton Owens	Ray Nichels '57 Pontiac	140	100	Crash
17	16	96	Bobby Keck	Keck '57 Chevrolet	136	100	Vap Lock
18	6	46	Speedy Thompson	Thompson '57 Chevrolet	73	100	Bearing
19	5	80	Jimmie Lewallen	J S Rice '57 Pontiac	57	50	Crash
20	14	32	Brownie King	Jess Potter '57 Chevrolet	30	50	H Gasket

Time of Race: 1 hour, 28 minutes, 18 seconds
Average Speed: 67.950 mph
Pole Winner: Bill Amick - 77.687 mph
Lap Leaders: Bill Amick 1-9, Cotton Owens 10-140, Amick 141-142, Lee Petty 143,
 Buck Baker 144-155, Petty 156-200.
Cautions: 1 for 10 laps   Margin of Victory: 10 feet   Attendance:

Race No. 43

Graves Buries Field to Win Sacramento 100

SACRAMENTO,CA (Sept. 8) -- Danny Graves of Stockton, CA came home first in the 100-mile Grand National event at the California State Fairgrounds. It was his first Grand National victory. It came in only his sixth start.

Marvin Porter finished in second place, Eddie Pagan was third and Chuck Meekins fourth. Fifth place went to Dick Getty.

Graves started on the pole and kept his Chevrolet out front most of the way. Danny Letner crashed in the 65th lap, bringing out the caution flag. The field bunched up and seven cars were on the lead lap at the finish.

Danny Graves

Twenty-seven cars started the race and 18 finished. Graves averaged 68.663 mph on the one-mile dirt track.

Grand National Race No. 43
100 Laps at California State Fairgrounds
Sacramento, CA
100 Miles on 1-mile Dirt Track
September 8, 1957

Fin	St	No.	Driver	Team / Car	Laps	Money	Status
1	1	81	Danny Graves	'57 Chevrolet	100	$800	Running
2	10	12	Marvin Porter	'57 Ford	100	550	Running
3	14	45	Eddie Pagan	Pagan '57 Ford	100	450	Running
4	3	1	Chuck Meekins	'57 Chevrolet	100	325	Running
5	16	00	Dick Getty	Getty '56 Chevrolet	100	325	Running
6	9	18	Eddie Gray	Charles Green '56 Chevrolet	100	250	Running
7	8	44	Lloyd Dane	Dane '57 Ford	100	200	Running
8	7	99	Don Porter	Nick Porter '56 Ford	98	150	Running
9	17	14	Scotty Cain	Cain '56 Mercury	97	100	Runninig
10	25	17	Bill Jarlick	'56 Ford	96	100	Running
11	12	16	Ron Hornaday	'56 Ford	95	100	Running
12	27	65	Bob Rose	'56 Chevrolet	94	100	Running
13	15	4	Allen Adkins	'56 Ford	94	100	Running
14	24	55	Marshall Sargent	'56 Chevrolet	94	100	Running
15	21	188	Jim Cook	'56 Ford	94	75	Running
16	26	225	Lee Humphers	'56 Mercury	91	50	Running
17	19	31	Bob Perry	'56 Dodge	71	50	Running
18	20	5	Jim Blomgren	Bob Smith '57 Ford	71	50	Running
19	4	39	Danny Letner	'57 Chevrolet	65	50	Crash
20	2	25	Clyde Palmer	'56 Ford	49	50	Piston
21	6	8	Ernie Young	Walt Palozi '57 Pontiac	40	25	Heating
22	13	56	Bob Osborne	'56 Chevrolet	28	25	Engine
23	11	82	Arley Scranton	'57 Chevrolet	25	25	Diff
24	18	37	Lemoin Frey	'57 Ford	17	25	Radiator
25	5	11	Parnelli Jones	Oscar Maples '57 Ford	16	---	Heating
26	22	21	Pat Diviney	'56 Ford	13	---	Engine
27	23	30	Pete Cardenas	Jack Chataney '56 Plymouth	9	---	Radiator

Time of Race: 1 hour, 27 minutes, 17 seconds
Average Speed: 68.663 mph
Pole Winner: Danny Graves - 78.007 mph
Lap Leaders: - - - - - - - - - - Danny Graves   -100.
Cautions: Margin of Victory: Attendance:

Race No. 44

Porter Drives Ford To Win at San Jose

SAN JOSE, CA (Sept. 15) -- Marvin Porter of Lakewood CA was declared the winner of the 100-mile race at the Santa Clara Fairgrounds when a nine-car pile-up depleted the field too much to continue.

Officials flagged the race to a halt after 116 laps had been completed. Only four cars in the starting field of 22 were still running.

Eddie Pagan was flagged in second place. Lloyd Dane, involved in the melee, got credit for third. Ernie

Marvin Porter

Young was fourth and Jim Blomgren fifth, both of whom were eliminated in the crash.

Howard Phillippi and Bob Rose were taken out by a crash in the 107th lap. Jim Cook crashed his Ford after 94 laps.

Eddie Gray spun in the 116th lap and was collected by eight on-rushing cars. There were no serious injuries. Gray got credit for 11th in the final rundown

No official time was recorded and no time trials were held.

the 300-mile National Sweepstakes event at Langhorne Speedway.

Staley, of Burlington, NC, nipped Whitey Norman by 0.753 seconds as a crowd of 20,000 stood on their collective feet. After the score cards had been counted, Norman was found to have been two laps behind, yet still retained runner-up honors.

Johnny Allen's Plymouth finished third. Rex White came in fourth and Buck Baker was fifth.

Grand National Race No. 44
200 Laps at Santa Clara Fairgrounds
San Jose, CA
100 Miles on Half-mile Dirt Track
September 15, 1957

Fin	St	No.	Driver	Team / Car	Laps	Money	Status
1	12	12	Marvin Porter	'57 Ford	116	$800	Running
2	2	45	Ed Pagan	Pagan' '57 Ford	116	550	Running
3	1	44	Lloyd Dane	Dane '57 Ford	115	450	Crash
4	21	8	Ernie Young	Walt Palozi '57 Pontiac	113	350	Crash
5	10	5	Jim Blomgren	Bob Smith '57 Ford	112	310	Crash
6	11	101	Gene Long	'56 Chevrolet	112	250	Running
7	4	225	Dick Getty	Betty Getty '56 Mercury	111	200	Crash
8	14	47	George Norton	'56 Chevrolet	110	150	Engine
9	13	99	Don Porter	Nick Porter '56 Ford	109	100	Crash
10	22	56	Jim Hurtubise	'56 Chevrolet	106	100	Heating
11	5	18	Eddie Gray	Charles Green '56 Chevrolet	106	100	Crash
12	18	98	Mike McGreevy	'56 Dodge	106	100	Running
13	7	81	Danny Graves	'57 Chevrolet	105	100	Engine
14	19	43	Howard Phillippi	'56 Mercury	102	100	Crash
15	16	65	Bob Rose	'56 Chevrolet	101	75	Crash
16	8	188	Jim Cook	'56 Ford	93	50	Crash
17	9	4	Clyde Palmer	'56 Ford	91	50	Running
18	17	55	John Smith	'56 Chevrolet	61	50	Engine
19	20	33	Earl Mosbach	'57 Pontiac	55	50	Crash
20	15	82	Marshall Sargent	'57 Chevrolet	38	50	Engine
21	6	11	Parnelli Jones	Oscar Maples '56 Ford	34	25	Heating
22	3	14	Scotty Cain	Cain '56 Mercury	21	25	Gasket

Time of Race: None Recorded
Average Speed: None
Pole Winner: Lloyd Dane - No Time
Lap Leader:- - - - - - - - - Marvin Porter   -116.
Cautions: Margin of Victory: Attendance:
* Race shortened due to small number of cars still running

Race No. 45

Staley's Convertible Takes Langhorne Sweepstakes 300

LANGHORNE, PA (Sept. 15) -- Gwyn Staley led a trio of comparatively unknown drivers to top honors in

---

Grand National Race No. 45
300 Laps at Langhorne Speedway
Langhorne, PA
300 Miles on 1-Mile Dirt Track
September 15, 1957

Fin	St	No.	Driver	Team / Car	Laps	Money	Status
1	25	38	Gwyn Staley	Julian Petty '57 Chevrolet C	300	$4,500	Running
2	24	0	Whitey Norman	Norman '57 Ford GN	298	2,350	Running
3	22	64	Johnny Allen	Spook Crawford '57 Plym GN	295	1,700	Running
4	16	44	Rex White	Max Welborn '57 Chevrolet GN	295	1,135	Running
5	12	87	Buck Baker	Baker '57 Chevrolet GN	295	960	Running
6	23	9	Dave Terrell	Terrell '57 Chevrolet C	287	750	Running
7	7	12	Joe Weatherly	Holman-Moody '57 Ford C	286	660	Running
8	27	43	Ken Marriott	'57 Plymouth C	281	600	Running
9	41	2	Tommy Elliott	'57 Ford C	281	500	Running
10	19	14	Darel Dieringer	Slim Rominger '56 Ford C	279	450	Running
11	20	62	Frankie Schneider	'57 Chevrolet GN	276	400	Running
12	5	49	Bob Welborn	Welborn '57 Chevrolet C	273	300	Running
13	29	76	Larry Frank	Lonnie Fish '56 Chevrolet C	273	300	Running
14	4	42	Lee Petty	Petty Eng. '57 Olds GN	268	280	Running
15	13	35	Pee Wee Jones	Whitford Bros '57 Ford C	262	225	Running
16	31	10	Roger Baldwin	Baldwin '56 Ford C	259	200	Running
17	2	22	Fireball Roberts	Roberts '57 Ford GN	247	225	Running
18	42	93	Ted Chamberlain	Chamberlain '56 Chevrolet C	247	150	Running
19	37	37	Don Gray	Lonnie Fish '56 Chevrolet C	246	150	Running
20	36	37	Bill Benson	'56 Mercury GN	245	150	Running
21	38	4	Art Binkley	Binkley '56 Plymouth C	233	125	Running
22	21	5	Bill Champion	Whitford Bros '56 Ford C	233	125	Running
23	9	48	Possum Jones	Welborn '57 Chevrolet C	227	125	Gas Tank
24	6	7	Jim Reed	Reed '57 Ford GN	220	145	Piston
25	40	74	L D Austin	Austin '56 Chevrolet GN	219	125	Idler Arm
26	15	90	Emanuel Zervakis	Junie Donlavey '57 Chev C	215	125	Running
27	28	34	Huck Spaulding	'56 Dodge GN	209	125	Gas Line
28	45	70	Harvey Eakin	Eakin '56 Ford GN	208	125	Running
29	14	97	Bill Amick	Amick '57 Ford GN	206	135	Engine
30	17	68	Neil Castles	Castles '56 Ford C	203	125	Gas Tank
31	10	46	Speedy Thompson	Thompson '57 Chevrolet GN	280	110	Crash
32	8	55	Tiny Lund	Brushy Mtn Mtrs '57 Pont GN	167	120	Crash
33	1	3	Paul Goldsmith	Smokey Yunick '57 Ford C	162	200	Gas Line
34	18	98	Marvin Panch	Panch '57 Ford GN	146	100	A Frame
35	46	1	Elton Hildreth	Hildreth '56 Mercury GN	142	100	Oil Pres
36	3	21	Glen Wood	Wood Brothers '57 Ford C	131	120	Gas Tank
37	47	79	Dick Klank	'56 Ford GN	122	100	R F Hub
38	26	47	Jack Smith	Smith '57 Chevrolet GN	114	100	Shocks
39	48	81	Jerry Benjamin	'56 Ford GN	114	100	Heating
40	33	45	George Burngardner	Lyle Sokoll '57 Ford C	111	100	A Frame
41	11	75	Ken Rush	Frank Hayworth '56 Mercury C	103	---	Rear End
42	39	65	Al White	'56 Ford GN	99	---	Crash
43	32	88	Chuck Hansen	Hanson '57 Chevrolet GN	93	---	Running
44	44	6	Jim Paschal	'57 Ford GN	87	---	Idler Arm
45	34	86	Dutch Hoag	'55 Pontiac	85	---	A Frame
46	30	23	Bobby Abel	'56 Chevrolet GN	57	---	Engine
47	35	78	Shep Langdon	Lonnie Fish '56 Chevrolet C	52	---	Trans
48	43	32	Brownie King	Jess Potter '57 Chevrolet GN	10	---	Engine

Time of Race: 4 hours, 4 minutes, 3 seconds
Average Speed 72.759 mph
Pole Winner: Paul Goldsmith - 92.072 mph
Lap Leaders:- - - - - - - - - Gwyn Staley   -300
Cautions: Margin of Victory: 2 laps and 0.753 seconds   Attendance: 20,000

For Staley, driver of the Julian Petty-owned Chevrolet, it was a hard fought victory. He had to come from 25th starting position, and he was driving the only Convertible that placed in the top five.

It was the first time a Convertible had prevailed in a Sweepstakes race mixing Grand Nationals and ragtops.

Speedy Thompson, Tiny Lund and Al White were taken out by wrecks.

Staley averaged 72.759 mph for his third win of the season.

Race No. 46

Baker Takes 8th of Year in Columbia 100

COLUMBIA, SC (Sept. 19) -- Buck Baker snared his eighth win of the season in the 100-mile Grand National event at Columbia Speedway.

Baker's Chevrolet finished a lap in front of runner-up Gwyn Staley. Bill Amick was third, Billy Myers fourth and Brownie King fifth.

Speedy Thompson went out early after blowing an engine in his Chevrolet. It continued a sour string of

Grand National Race No. 46
200 Laps at Columbia Speedway
Columbia, SC
100 Miles on Half-mile Dirt Track
September 19, 1957

Fin	St	No.	Driver	Team / Car	Laps	Money	Status
1	1	87	Buck Baker	Baker' 57 Chevrolet	200	$900	Running
2	9	38	Gwyn Staley	Julian Petty '57 Chevrolet	199	575	Running
3	5	97	Bill Amick	Amick '57 Ford	198	375	Running
4	3	26	Billy Myers	J S Rice '57 Ford	196	280	Running
5	12	32	Brownie King	Jess Potter '57 Chevrolet	194	245	Running
6	7	98	Marvin Panch	Panch '57 Ford	190	210	Running
7	8	34	Dick Beaty	Beaty '56 Ford	189	175	Running
8	2	42	Lee Petty	Petty Engineering '57 Olds	186	165	Running
9	17	74	L D Austin	Austin '56 Chevrolet	181	150	Running
10	15	94	Clarence DeZalia	DeZalia '56 Ford	179	140	Running
11	14	51	Roy Tyner	Tyner '56 Ford	175	135	Running
12	16	37	Bill Benson	'56 Mercury	154	125	Running
13	4	47	Jack Smith	Smith '57 Chevrolet	134	110	H Gasket
14	13	17	Jim Paschal	Paschal '57 Ford	121	100	Carb
15	6	22	Fireball Roberts	Roberts '57 Ford	92	100	Bearing
16	19	96	Bobby Keck	Keck '57 Chevrolet	84	100	Fuel Pmp
17	11	64	Johnny Allen	Spook Crawford '57 Plymouth	68	100	Hub
18	18	75	Ken Rush	Frank Hayworth '56 Mercury	57	100	Coil
19	10	46	Speedy Thompson	Thompson '57 Chevrolet	7	50	Engine

Time of Race: 1 hour, 39 minutes, 9 seconds
Average Speed: 60.514 mph
Pole Winner: Buck Baker - 63.649 mph
Lap Leaders: - - - - - - - - - - Buck Baker   -200.
Cautions: Margin of Victory: 1-lap-plus   Attendance:

luck for the Monroe, NC driver since his triumph in the Southern 500.

Other top contenders who went to the sidelines early included Fireball Roberts, Jim Paschal and Johnny Allen.

Baker started on the pole and proceeded to win the race at an average speed of 60.514 mph.

Baker moved closer to his second straight Grand National championship, stretching his point lead over Marvin Panch to 760 points. Panch finished sixth in the 100 miler.

Race No. 47

Baker Nabs Panch With Late Race Pass; Wins at Shelby

SHELBY, NC (Sept. 21) -- Buck Baker moved one step closer to the Grand National title by taking the lead late in the race at winning for the ninth time of the year at the Cleveland County Fairgrounds.

The lead changed hands six times among four drivers in the 100-miler on the half mile dirt oval. Baker started on the pole and led four times for a total of 125 laps. He had to wait for the stroke of good luck as Panch was forced to make a pit stop with 12 laps from the finish while leading. Baker drove his Chevrolet into the lead for the final time and led the rest of the way.

Herb Thomas, NASCAR's winningest driver, announced his retirement at Shelby.

Panch wound up second with Bill Amick third. Fourth place went to Gwyn Staley and Lee Petty was fifth.

Baker extended his point lead to 768 over Panch.

Four caution flags for 19 laps held Baker's winning speed to 53.699 mph.

Fireball Roberts, who has been struggling since the

factory withdrawl, passed Baker for the lead midway through the 200 lapper. However, a tire let go, putting his Ford into the wall with 51 laps to go. Roberts got credit for 14th in the final order

Herb Thomas announced his retirement from the sport of stock car racing. It was a year earlier that the Olivia, NC driver was critically hurt in a multi car crash at this half-mile facility. The two-time Grand National champ had driven in only two races in 1957.

Grand National Race No. 47
200 Laps at Cleveland County
Fairgrounds
Shelby, NC
100 Miles on Half-mile Dirt Track
September 21, 1957

Fin	St	No	Driver	Team / Car	Laps	Money	Status
1	1	87	Buck Baker	Baker '57 Chevrolet	200	$900	Running
2	13	98	Marvin Panch	Panch '57 Ford	200	575	Running
3	10	97	Bill Amick	Amick '57 Ford	198	375	Running
4	3	38	Gwyn Staley	Julian Petty '57 Chevrolet	198	280	Running
5	5	42	Lee Petty	Petty Engineering '57 Olds	195	245	Running
6	12	64	Johnny Allen	Spook Crawford '57 Plymouth	190	210	Engine
7	7	3	Paul Goldsmith	Smokey Yunick '57 Ford	188	175	Running
8	6	96	Bobby Keck	Keck '57 Chevrolet	181	165	Running
9	17	51	Roy Tyner	Tyner '56 Ford	175	150	Running
10	11	32	Brownie King	Jess Potter '57 Chevrolet	172	140	Running
11	18	74	L D Austin	Austin '56 Chevrolet	169	135	Running
12	8	2	Joe Weatherly	Holman - Moody ' 57 Ford	167	125	Vap Lock
13	15	10	Whitey Norman	Norman '57 Ford	165	110	Engine
14	9	22	Fireball Roberts	Roberts '57 Ford	149	100	Crash
15	4	34	Speedy Thompson	Dick Beaty '56 Ford	144	100	Engine
16	2	37	Bill Benson	'56 Mercury	139	100	Fuel Pmp
17	20	21	George Green	'56 Dodge	125	100	Engine
18	16	321	Gene Glover	'56 Chevrolet	104	100	Shackle
19	19	94	Clarence DeZalia	DeZalia '56 Ford	103	50	Spindle
20	21	75	Ken Rush	Frank Hayworth '56 Mercury	103	50	Crash
21	14	17	Jim Paschal	Paschal '57 Ford	58	50	Dist

Time of Race: 1 hour, 51 minutes, 44 seconds
Average Speed: 53.699 mph
Pole Winner: Buck Baker - 58.177 mph
Lap Leaders: Buck Baker 1-65, Lee Petty 66-82, Baker 83-115, Fireball Roberts 116-149, Baker 150-164, Marvin Panch 165-188, Baker 189-200.
Cautions: 4 for 19 laps   Margin of Victory: 1/3-lap   Attendance: 5,000

Race No. 48

Petty's Oldsmobile Wings to Victory in Charlotte 100

CHARLOTTE, NC (Oct. 5) -- Lee Petty, the crafty veteran out of Randleman, NC, drove his Oldsmobile to victory in the 100-mile event at the Southern States Fairgrounds. It was the fourth win of the year for the Randleman, NC driver.

Fireball Roberts finished a close second and Eddie Pagan was third. Both were driving Fords. Buck Baker came in fourth in his Chevrolet and Tiny Lund was fifth.

Marvin Panch crashed his Ford in the 132nd lap and apparently lost all hope for the Grand National championship.

Joe Weatherly started third on the grid in his Holman-Moody Ford, but exited on lap 28 with steering problems. Second fastest qualifier Speedy Thompson had a rock go through his radiator and departed after 138 laps.

Johnny Allen qualified fourth in his Plymouth but rear end failure put him behind the wall after 128 laps.

Petty was the pole winner for the eighth time in his nine-year career. His win was the 30th time he reached victory lane.

Average speed for the race was 51.583 mph.

Grand National Race No. 48
200 Laps at Southern States
Fairgrounds
Charlotte, NC
100 Miles on Half-mile Dirt Track
October 5, 1957

Fin	St	No.	Driver	Team / Car	Laps	Money	Status
1	1	42	Lee Petty	Petty Engineering '57 Olds	200	$900	Running
2	5	22	Fireball Roberts	Roberts '57 Ford	200	575	Running
3	9	45	Eddie Pagan	Pagan '57 Ford	199	375	Running
4	7	87	Buck Baker	Baker '57 Chevrolet	195	280	Running
5	11	48	Tiny Lund	Welborn '57 Chevrolet	192	245	Running
6	12	34	Bill Amick	Dick Beaty '56 Ford	189	210	Running
7	15	32	Brownie King	Jess Potter '57 Chevrolet	183	175	Running
8	8	75	Ken Rush	Frank Hayworth '56 Mercury	180	165	Running
9	6	47	Jack Smith	Smith '56 Chevrolet	180	150	Running
10	23	74	L D Austin	Austin '56 Chevrolet	176	140	Running
11	24	76	George Green	Lonnie Fish '56 Chevrolet	173	135	Running
12	18	14	Billy Myers	Myers '57 Mercury	172	125	Engine
13	28	711	Bill Poor	Poor '56 Chevrolet	167	110	Running
14	26	2	Ansel Rakestraw	'56 Chevrolet	166	100	Running
15	25	94	Clarence DeZalia	DeZalia '56 Ford	160	100	Running
16	21	51	Roy Tyner	Tyner '56 Ford	147	100	Running
17	2	46	Speedy Thompson	Thompson '57 Chevrolet	138	100	Radiator
18	14	98	Marvin Panch	Panch '57 Ford	130	100	Crash
19	17	96	Bobby Keck	Keck '57 Chevrolet	130	50	Running
20	4	64	Johnny Allen	Spook Crawford '57 Plymouth	128	50	Rear End
21	10	17	Shorty York	Fred Harb '57 Mercury	109	50	Rear End
22	20	79	Dick Klank	'56 Ford	105	50	A Frame
23	13	40	Johnny Mackison	Camp Hill Spl. '57 Ford	87	50	Rear End
24	19	1A	Whitey Norman	Norman '56 Ford	70	50	Engine
25	16	55	Mel Larson	Larson '56 Ford	55	---	Brakes
26	3	2X	Joe Weatherly	Holman - Moody '57 Ford	28	---	Steering
27	27	18	Pete Stewart	'56 Plymouth	25	---	Radiator
28	22	11	Jim Russell	'56 Ford	9	---	Electrical

Time of Race: 1 hour, 56 minutes, 19 seconds
Average Speed: 51.583 mph
Pole Winner: Lee Petty - 60.585 mph
Lap Leaders: - - - - - - - - - - Lee Petty   -200.
Cautions: Margin of Victory: Attendance:

Race No. 49

Welborn-Jones Tandem Wins Martinsville Sweepstakes

MARTINSVILLE, VA (Oct. 6) -- Lewis "Possum" Jones, an old pro out of Mango, FL, relieved Bob Welborn shortly after the half-way point and cruised to victory in the 250-mile Sweepstakes race at Martinsville Speedway.

Welborn got credit for the victory, his first in Grand

National competition. His Convertible Chevrolet nipped runner-up Jimmy Massey by 14 seconds to claim the $3,100 winner's prize. Massey was in a Ford Convertible.

Lee Petty's Grand National Oldsmobile was third, Rex White was fourth and Joe Weatherly fifth.

The lead changed hands six times among four drivers with the Welborn-Jones team leading the final 251 laps.

Point leader Buck Baker struggled to finish 23rd in the field of 40. His Chevrolet was skipping badly when he took the checkered flag 71 laps behind the winner.

Johnny Mackison qualified third fastest, but he left the race after 133 laps with rear gearing fail-

Bob Welborn drove a Chevy Convertible to victory in the Sweepstakes 500 at Martinsville.

ure. Paul Goldsmith crashed his Ford on lap 334. Speedy Thompson was also sidelined by a wreck.

Eddie Pagan won the pole, but never got his Ford up to speed. He finished 19th, 39 laps behind.

Welborn and Jones averaged 63.025 mph for the 250-mile chase.

Grand National Race No. 49
500 Laps at Martinsville Speedway
Martinsville, VA
"Sweepstakes 500"
250 Miles on Half-mile Paved Track
October 6, 1957

Fin	St	No.	Driver	Team / Car	Laps	Money	Status
1	2	49	Bob Welborn	Welborn '57 Chevrolet C	500	$3,100	Running
2	16	11	Jimmy Massey	Wood Bros '56 Ford C	500	1,975	Running
3	15	42	Lee Petty	Petty Eng. '57 Olds GN	498	1,425	Running
4	27	44	Rex White	Max Welborn '57 Chevrolet GN	497	1,150	Running
5	4	12	Joe Weatherly	Holman - Moody '57 Ford C	493	850	Running
6	33	97	Bill Amick	Amick '57 Ford GN	491	750	Running
8	10	48	Possum Jones	Welborn '57 Chevrolet C	490	500	Running
9	12	38	Gwyn Staley	Julian Petty '57 Chevrolet C	489	425	Running
10	37	8	Tiny Lund	Bishop Bros. '57 Chevy GN	486	450	Running
11	35	10	Whitey Norman	Norman '57 Ford GN	485	525	Running
12	13	7	Fireball Roberts	Buck Baker '57 Chevrolet GN	482	350	Running
13	6	21	Glen Wood	Wood Brothers '57 Ford C	481	300	Running
14	8	76	Larry Frank	Frank '56 Chevrolet C	480	250	Running
15	25	32	Brownie King	Jess Potter '57 Chevrolet GN	477	225	Running
16	9	22	Marvin Panch	Fireball Roberts '57 Ford GN	473	210	Running
17	38	41	T A Toomes	C M Julian '56 Dodge GN	473	200	Running
18	23	26	Jim Paschal	J S Rice '57 Ford GN	470	190	Running
19	1	45	Eddie Pagan	Pagan '57 Ford GN	461	180	Running
20	21	74	L D Austin	Austin '56 Chevrolet GN	455	170	Running
21	36	28	Eddie Skinner	Skinner '57 Ford GN	453	210	Running
22	20	90	Emanuel Zervakis	Junie Donlavey '57 Chev C	447	250	Axle
23	7	87	Buck Baker	Baker '57 Chevrolet GN	429	125	Running
24	5	62	Frankie Schneider	'57 Chevrolet GN	426	100	Running
25	28	4	Art Binkley	Binkley '56 Plymouth C	424	140	Running
26	26	93	Ted Chamberlain	Chamberlain '56 Chevrolet C	421	100	Running
27	40	51	Roy Tyner	Tyner '56 Ford GN	417	100	Running
28	11	46	Speedy Thompson	Thompson '57 Chevrolet GN	416	50	Crash
29	14	75	Ken Rush	Frank Hayworth '56 Merc C	405	50	Running
30	30	5	Bill Champion	Champion '56 Ford C	399	100	Running
31	18	19	Dick Walters	Walters '56 Plymouth C	398	50	Running
32	22	3	Paul Goldsmith	Smokey Yunick '57 Ford C	334	125	Crash
33	29	84	Banjo Matthews	'57 Ford GN	334	125	Rear End
34	34	78	George Green	Lonnie Fish '56 Chevrolet GN	292	100	Running
35	19	64	Johnny Allen	Spook Crawford '57 Plym GN	242	50	Rear End
36	32	68	Neil Castles	Castles '56 Ford C	225	100	Coil
37	39	17	Billy Myers	Harb '57 Mercury GN	160	100	Rear End
38	31	6	Cotton Owens	Jim Stephens '57 Pontiac GN	144	100	Engine
39	3	40	Johnny Mackison	Camp Hills Spl '57 Ford GN	133	50	Rear End
40	24	1A	Bill Massey	Whitey Norman '56 Ford C	86	100	Trans

Time of Race: 3 hours, 58 minutes, 0 seconds
Average Speed: 63.025 mph
Pole Winner: Eddie Pagan - 65.837 mph
Lap Leaders: Bob Welborn 1-183, Lee Petty 184-198, Jimmy Massey 199-205,
   Rex White 206-221, Petty 222-248, Welborn 249-500.
Cautions: 4 for 14 laps   Margin of Victory: 14 seconds   Attendance: 5,000

Race No. 50

Roberts Wins at Newberry Before Only 900 Spectators

NEWBERRY, SC (Oct. 12) -- Fireball Roberts secured his seventh win of the season by outrunning Buck Baker by a full lap to win the 100-miler at Newberry Speedway. The race was seen by only 900 spectators, an all-time Grand National low.

Roberts started 10th on the grid and spent most of the evening dodging chuck-holes in the half-mile dirt track. He patiently worked his way into contention and took the lead from Baker with just 18 laps left.

Third place went to Jack Smith. Marvin Panch finished fourth and Gwyn Staley was fifth.

The track was in ragged condition. Driver Mel Larson, who failed to finish, said "This is the furthest thing from a race track I have ever seen. And I've seen some dandies!"

Lee Petty started 12th but fell out first with a broken oil line. Larson lost the oil pressure in his Ford on lap 140.

Roberts averaged 50.398 mph for his 13th career Grand National win.

led for six laps before Roberts pushed his Ford to the front for good. Lee Petty wound up second, Ken Rush was third, Marvin Panch fourth and the Smith-Lund team was fifth.

Baker's ride into ninth was eventful. Petty tagged the rear bumper of Baker's Chevrolet, knocking it into a turnover. It landed on all four wheels and Baker continued on to a top 10 finish with the help of relief driver Jimmy Thompson.

Petty also continued and finished 15 seconds behind Roberts.

A crowd of 3,800 was on hand to see the lead change hands six times. Five caution flags slowed the average speed to 59.553 mph.

Only five cars in the starting field of 26 failed to go the distance. Johnny Allen and Bill Amick, both of whom qualified in the top 10, fell by the wayside with mechanical problems.

Baker's point lead stood at 664 with only two races left on the 1957 slate.

Grand National Race No. 50
200 Laps at Newberry Speedway
Newberry, SC
100 Miles on Half-mile Dirt Track
October 12, 1957

Fin	St	No.	Driver	Team / Car	Laps	Money	Status
1	10	22	Fireball Roberts	Roberts '57 Ford	200	$900	Running
2	5	87	Buck Baker	Baker '57 Chevrolet	199	575	Running
3	1	47	Jack Smith	Smith '57 Chevrolet	198	375	Running
4	11	98	Marvin Panch	Panch '57 Ford	197	280	Running
5	4	38	Gwyn Staley	Julian Petty '57 Chevrolet	194	245	Running
6	3	46	Speedy Thompson	Thompson '57 Chevrolet	194	210	Running
7	2	64	Johnny Allen	Spook Crawford '57 Plymouth	193	175	Running
8	9	26	Ken Rush	J S Rice '57 Ford	191	165	Running
9	6	10	Whitey Norman	Norman '57 Ford	189	150	Running
10	7	32	Brownie King	Jess Potter '57 Chevrolet	188	140	Running
11	13	34	Dick Beaty	Beaty '56 Ford	178	135	Running
12	21	17	Fred Harb	Harb '57 Mercury	177	125	Running
13	16	51	Roy Tyner	Tyner '56 Ford	175	110	Running
14	8	2	Bill Amick	Holman - Moody '57 Ford	171	100	Running
15	20	74	L D Austin	Austin '56 Chevrolet	166	100	Running
16	19	45	Eddie Pagan	Pagan '57 Ford	165	100	Idler Arm
17	14	100	Jack Marsh	'56 Chevrolet	165	100	Running
18	18	94	Clarence DeZalia	DeZalia '56 Mercury	164	100	Running
19	17	55	Mel Larson	Larson '56 Ford	140	50	Oil Pres
20	15	11	Jim Russell	'56 Ford	119	50	Battery
21	23	96	Bobby Keck	Keck '57 Chevrolet	88	50	Coil
22	22	37	Bill Benson	'56 Mercury	75	50	Heating
23	12	42	Lee Petty	Petty Engineering '57 Olds	74	50	Oil Line

Time of Race: 1 hour, 59 minuters, 3 seconds
Average Speed 50.398 mph
Pole Winner: Jack Smith - 56.514 mph
Lap Leaders: Jack Smith 1-18, Speedy Thompson 19-65, Buck Baker 66-82, Fireball Roberts 83-200.
Cautions: Margin of Victory: 1 lap plus   Attendance: 900

Race No. 51

Roberts Wins Wild Battle of Concord

CONCORD, NC (Oct. 13) -- Fireball Roberts took the lead from Tiny Lund in the 93rd lap and breezed to victory in the 100-mile race at New Concord Speedway. Buck Baker clinched the 1957 NASCAR Grand National championship by taking ninth place.

Lund, who was driving in relief of Jack Smith, had

Grand National Race No. 51
200 Laps at New Concord Speedway
Concord, NC
100 Miles on Half-mile Dirt Track
October 13, 1957

Fin	St	No.	Driver	Team / Car	Laps	Money	Status
1	5	22	Fireball Roberts	Roberts '57 Ford	200	$900	Running
2	4	42	Lee Petty	Petty Engineering '57 Olds	200	575	Running
3	7	26	Ken Rush	J S Rice '57 Ford	197	375	Running
4	10	98	Marvin Panch	Panch '57 Ford	193	280	Running
5	1	47	Jack Smith	Smith '57 Chevrolet	192	245	Running
6	2	46	Speedy Thompson	Thompson '57 Chevrolet	191	210	Running
7	14	400	Huck Spaulding	Spaulding '56 Dodge	189	175	Running
8	15	100	Jack Marsh	'56 Chevrolet	188	165	Running
9	3	87	Buck Baker	Baker '57 Chevrolet	182	150	Running
10	19	74	L D Austin	Austin '56 Chevrolet	178	140	Running
11	25	51	Roy Tyner	Tyner '56 Ford	177	135	Running
12	20	96	Bobby Keck	Keck '57 Chevrolet	172	125	Running
13	6	6	Cotton Owens	Jim Stephens '57 Pontiac	167	110	Running
14	23	10	Whitey Norman	Norman '57 Ford	164	100	Running
15	21	94	Clarence DeZalia	DeZalia '56 Ford	159	100	Running
16	11	32	Brownie King	Jess Potter '57 Chevrolet	147	100	Running
17	24	17	Fred Harb	Harb '57 Mercury	145	100	Running
18	16	76	George Green	Lonnie Fish '56 Chevrolet	142	100	Running
19	22	41	T A Toomes	C M Julina '56 Dodge	130	50	Running
20	17	23	R L Combs	'56 Ford	122	50	Running
21	13	34	Dick Beaty	Beaty '56 Ford	122	50	Running
22	9	2	Bill Amick	Holman - Moody '57 Ford	87	50	Engine
23	18	71	George Parrish	Joe Frazier '56 Studebaker	77	50	Axle
24	8	64	Johnny Allen	Spook Crawford '57 Plymouth	51	50	Steering
25	12	55	Mel Larson	Larson '56 Ford	41	---	Engine
26	26	37	Bill Benson	'56 Mercury	21	---	LF Whee

Time of Race: 1 hour , 40 minutes, 45 seconds
Average Speed: 59.553 mph
Pole Winner: Jack Smith - 65.052 mph
Lap Leaders: Speedy Thompson 1-31, Jack Smith 32-67, Lee Petty 68-69, Thompson 70-86, Smith 87-92, Fireball Roberts 93-200.
Cautions: 5   Margin of Victory 15 seconds   Attendance: 3,800

Speedy Thompson pulls his Chevrolet into the pits during 100-miler at North Wilkesboro. Thompson finished in 4th place.

Race No. 52

Smith Takes Wilkesboro Thriller; Spectator Killed In Freak Mishap

N.WILKESBORO, NC (Oct. 20) -- Jack Smith prevailed in one of the most thrilling races of the year in the 100-miler at North Wilkesboro Speedway, an event which had tragic undercurrents.

A left rear axle snapped on Tiny Lund's Pontiac in the second half of the race, and a loose wheel bounced over the fence. It landed in the grandstands, killing spectator W.R.Thomason of Mt. Holly, NC.

Smith pushed his Chevrolet past Banjo Matthews' Ford with 10 laps to go and beat Lee Petty to the wire by 4.0-seconds. It was Smith's fourth win of the year.

Matthews fell to third in the waning laps. Speedy Thompson was fourth and Cotton Owens fifth.

Fireball Roberts started on the pole and led for 61 laps before crashing over the north turn. His Ford landed upside down well outside the speedway. The Daytona Beach driver was shaken but not seriously injured.

Smith and Matthews traded the lead five times after Robert's departure.

Junior Johnson, making his first start of the year, wound up 20th in a Pontiac. Johnson had been away from racing, serving a 12 month sentence in Chillicothe, OH for moonshine involvement.

Grand National Race No. 52
160 Laps at N. Wilkesboro Speedway
North Wilkesboro, NC
100 Miles on .625-mile Paved Track
October 20, 1957

Fin	St	No.	Driver	Team / Car	Laps	Money	Status
1	4	47	Jack Smith	Smith '57 Chevrolet	160	$900	Running
2	8	42	Lee Petty	Petty Engineering '57 Olds	160	575	Running
3	2	84	Banjo Matthews	'57 Ford	160	375	Running
4	7	46	Speedy Thompson	Thompson '57 Chevrolet	160	280	Running
5	6	6	Cotton Owens	Jim Stephens '57 Pontiac	160	245	Running
6	12	87	Buck Baker	Baker '57 Chevrolet	160	210	Running
7	3	98	Marvin Panch	Panch '57 Ford	160	175	Running
8	17	44	Rex White	Max Welborn '57 Chevrolet	159	165	Running
9	14	36	Bill Morton	'56 Ford	159	150	Running
10	5	21	Jimmy Massey	Wood Brothers '56 Ford	152	140	Running
11	10	32	Brownie King	Jess Potter '57 Chevrolet	151	135	Running
12	16	34	Dick Beaty	Beaty '56 Ford	149	125	Running
13	13	64	Johnny Allen	Spook Crawford '57 Plymouth	148	110	Running
14	22	74	L D Austin	Austin '56 Chevrolet	145	100	Running
15	20	96	Bobby Keck	Keck '57 Chevrolet	142	100	Running
16	19	100	Jack Marsh	'56 Chevrolet	136	100	Running
17	23	11	Jim Russell	'56 Ford	135	100	Running
18	26	2	Bill Massey	'56 Chevrolet	129	100	Radiator
19	9	80	Tiny Lund	J S Rice '57 Pontiac	118	50	Axle
20	11	55	Junior Johnson	Brushy Mtn Motors '57 Pontiac	102	50	Engine
21	1	22	Fireball Roberts	Roberts '57 Ford	61	50	Crash
22	25	41	Johnny Dodson	C M Julian '56 Dodge	19	50	Engine
23	15	63	R L Combs	'56 Ford	1	50	Trans
24	21	75	Max Berrier	Frank Hayworth '56 Mercury	0	50	Crash
25	24	71	George Parrish	Joe Frazier '56 Studebaker	0	25	Crash
26	18	51	Roy Tyner	Tyner '56 Ford	0	25	Crash

Time of Race: 1 hour, 29 minutes, 10 seconds
Average Speed: 69.902 mph
Pole Winner: Fireball Roberts - 81.640 mph
Lap Leaders: Fireball Roberts 1-61, Jack Smith 62-93, Banjo Matthews 94-111, Smith 112, Matthews 113-150, Smith 151-160.
Cautions: 2   Margin of Victory: 4 seconds   Attendance: 5,000

Two caution flags and a complete restart following a five car crash in the opening lap held Smith's winning speed to 69.902 mph.

Race No. 53

Baker Tops Off Season With Greensboro Victory

GREENSBORO, NC (Oct. 27) -- The 1957 season came to a close with Grand National champion Buck Baker topping off another fine year by winning the 83.25-mile race at the Central Carolina Fairgrounds. It was the 10th win of the year for the Charlotte Chevrolet driver.

The event was punctuated by several bone-jarring crashes. The most spectacular came in the 34th lap when rookie pole sitter Ken Rush spun his Ford on the backstretch. Possum Jones, Speedy Thompson, Gwyn Staley and Marvin Panch were among those who piled into Rush. Panch's Ford performed a complete end-over-end flip, then continued on its way.

Roy Tyner of Red Springs, NC lost control of his Ford and plowed into the judges stand. Tyner and the tower occupants were not injured.

Curtis Turner showed up without a ride and persuaded Bob Welborn to let him drive his Chevrolet. Welborn refused at first, then gave in. "Just bring me the steering wheel back," Welborn told Turner.

Turner failed to finish, but he did bring the steering wheel back to Welborn with the rest of the car attached.

The lead changed hands four times with Baker and Lee Petty leading all the way.

Speedy Thompson finished second to Baker. Third place went to Joe Weatherly, Jack Smith was fourth and Petty fifth.

Baker won his second straight Grand National title by a margin of 760 points over Panch.

Grand National Race No. 53
250 Laps at Central Carolina Fairgrounds
Greensboro, NC
83.25-Miles on .333-Mile Dirt Track
October 27, 1957

Fin	St	No.	Driver	Team / Car	Laps	Money	Status
1		87	Buck Baker	Baker '57 Chevrolet	250	$900	Running
2		46	Speedy Thompson	Thompson '57 Chevrolet		575	Running
3		12	Joe Weatherly	Holman - Moody '57 Ford		375	Running
4		47	Jack Smith	Smith '57 Chevrolet		280	Running
5		42	Lee Petty	Petty Engineering '57 Olds		245	Running
6		3	Paul Goldsmith	Smokey Yunick '57 Ford		210	
7		400	Huck Spaulding	Spaulding '56 Dodge		175	
8		32	Brownie King	Jess Potter '57 Chevrolet		165	
9		36	Bill Morton	'57 Ford		150	
10		41	Johnny Dodson	Dodson '57 Ford		140	
11		17	Fred Harb	Harb '57 Mercury		135	
12		64	Johnny Allen	A M Crawford '57 Plymouth		125	
13		63	R L Combs	'56 Ford		110	
14		74	L D Austin	Austin '56 Chevrolet		100	
15		10	Whitey Norman	Norman '56 Ford		100	
16		76	George Green	Lonnie Fish '56 Chevrolet		100	
17		37	Bill Benson	'56 Mercury		100	
18		44	Rex White	Max Welborn '57 Chevrolet		100	
19		711	Bill Poor	Poor '56 Ford		50	
20		19	Herman Beam	Beam '57 Chevrolet		50	
21		98	Marvin Panch	Panch '57 Ford		50	
22		48	Possum Jones	Welborn '57 Chevrolet		50	
23		49	Curtis Turner	Welborn '57 Chevrolet		50	
24		68	Neil Castles	Castles '56 Ford		50	
25		71	George Parrish	Joe Frazier '56 Studebaker		---	
26		51	Roy Tyner	Tyner '56 Ford		---	
27		96	Bobby Keck	Keck '57 Chevrolet		---	
28	1	26	Ken Rush	J S Rice '57 Ford		---	Crash
29		38	Gwyn Staley	Julian Petty '57 Chevrolet		---	Crash
30			Roger Clemmens	'56 Chevrolet		---	Crash
31		75	Max Berrier	Frank Hayworth '56 Mercury		---	Crash

Time of Race: 2 hours, 8 minutes, 19 seconds.
Average Speed: 38.927 mph
Pole Winner: Ken Rush - 48.358 mph
Lap Leaders: Lee Petty 1-154, Buck Baker 155-160, Petty 161-190, Baker 191-250.
Cautions: Margin of Victory: Attendance:

1957 NASCAR Season
Final Point Standings Grand National Division

Rank	Driver	Points	Starts	Wins	Top 5	Top 10	Winnings
1	Buck Baker	10,716	40	10	30	38	$30,763.40
2	Marvin Panch	9,956	42	6	22	27	24,306.60
3	Speedy Thompson	8,580	38	2	16	22	26,840.58
4	Lee Petty	8,528	41	4	20	33	18,325.28
5	Jack Smith	8,464	40	4	16	26	14,561.10
6	Fireball Roberts	8,268	42	8	21	27	19,828.04
7	Johnny Allen	7,068	42	0	4	17	9,814.01
8	L D Austin	6,532	40	0	1	13	6,484.68
9	Brownie King	5,740	36	0	1	16	5,588.68
10	Jim Paschal	5,136	35	0	9	17	7,078.68
11	Tiny Lund	4,848	32	0	6	15	6,423.68
12	Billy Myers	4,682	28	0	4	9	6,565.52
13	Paul Goldsmith	4,224	25	4	10	15	12,733.68
14	Cotton Owens	4,200	17	1	3	6	12,783.68
15	Eddie Pagan	3,624	15	3	11	11	7,273.58
16	Bill Amick	3,512	21	1	8	12	8,072.44
17	Dick Beaty	3,220	20	0	1	7	3,647.44
18	Jim Reed	2,836	6	0	2	3	3,407.44
19	Clarence DeZalia	2,828	25	0	0	6	3,307.44
20	Frankie Schneider	2,516	10	0	3	6	4,587.44
21	Rex White	2,508	9	0	4	6	3,870.00
22	Curtis Turner	2,356	10	0	2	4	4,830.00
23	George Green	2,216	17	0	1	4	2,240.00
24	Whitey Norman	1,920	13	0	1	4	3,990.00
25	Lloyd Dane	1,864	10	1	7	10	4,985.00
26	Jimmie Lewallen	1,796	7	0	0	0	1,030.00
27	Johnny Mackison	1,764	5	0	1	2	1,330.00
28	Bobby Keck	1,740	16	0	0	2	1,525.00
29	Billy Carden	1,600	3	0	0	2	1,675.00
30	Bill Benson	1,592	11	0	0	2	1,090.00
31	Dick Getty	1,520	10	0	3	8	1,890.00
32	Scotty Cain	1,504	10	0	2	6	1,165.00
33	Roy Tyner	1,468	10	0	0	2	1,020.00
34	T A Toomes	1,404	11	0	0	1	1,450.00
35	Possum Jones	1,360	6	0	0	4	2,375.00
36	Huck Spaulding	1,240	8	0	0	3	1,120.00
37	Ralph Earnhardt	1,180	9	0	0	3	1,150.00
38	Ken Rush	1,104	16	0	1	6	2,045.00
39	Bill Champion	956	10	0	0	1	1,125.00
40	Joe Weatherly	920	14	0	5	7	5,240.00
41	Danny Graves	880	7	1	3	4	1,895.00
42	Marvin Porter	872	6	1	2	3	1,770.00
43	George Seeger	832	6	0	5	5	2,740.00
44	Parnelli Jones	812	10	1	1	3	1,625.00
45	Don Porter	784	6	0	0	4	810.00
46	Chuck Meekins	776	6	0	3	4	1,280.00
47	Art Watts	760	5	1	2	3	1,755.00
48	Darel Dieringer	684	9	0	0	3	1,210.00
49	Bill Walker	664	3	0	1	2	950.00
50	Eddie Gray	656	5	0	1	2	755.00

The 1958 Season
NASCAR Needs Superstar
and Finds a Fireball

Volume one of a four volume series . . . . The Beginning 1949 - 1958

1958

As the 1957 Grand National season came to a close, NASCAR was experiencing one of its most difficult transitional periods. The sport had caught the fancy of American auto enthusiasts and American car builders who were largely responsible for pulling stock car racing out of the backwoods and onto the threshold of acceptability. The sport and its athletes were crossing into another mainstream.

Factory backed teams were plentiful as the 1957 season got underway. But as of June, they were gone -- leaving drivers with equipment but no incoming dollars. The drivers -- many who had suddenly become car owners -- played the year out. Figuratively, NASCAR made it to the end of the year -- on wobbly knees.

The heroic drivers of the early 50s were rapidly decreasing in numbers. The pioneers -- men like Herb Thomas, Tim Flock, Fonty Flock, Dick Rathmann, Marshall Teague, Frank Mundy, Hershel McGriff, Curtis Turner, Al Keller, Bob Flock and Bill Blair had collectively won 152 of the first 277 races through the 1956 season. Now they were fading fast. Not one of those crowd-pleasing stars won a race in 1957.

Statistically, the 1957 season didn't live up to 1956. There were 33 events which

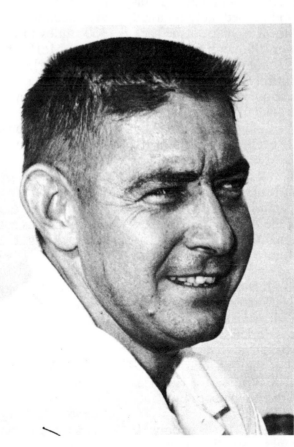
Fireball Roberts -- A year to be proud of

were conducted in both years. In 20 of these the qualifying speeds were faster in 1956. Speeds had increased each and every year -- until 1957. Twice at Langhorne and Martinsville, and at Darlington and Daytona -- all major events -- pole winning speeds were faster in 1956 than in 1957.

The jury was still out on whether stock car racing could maintain its public appeal while speeds were leveling off.

In Darlington's Southern 500, 50 cars started in 1957 -- a significant drop from the 70 which started the annual biggie in 1956.

Fewer cars, new faces and relatively inexperienced drivers were coming out of the woodwork. Fonty Flock, who was seriously injured in the 1957 Southern 500 and never to race again, said "amateur" drivers were cluttering up stock car racing's major league tour.

Flock contended that "two amateur drivers forced me into a spin" in the early stages of the Darlington race. Bobby Myers and Paul Goldsmith crashed full bore into Flock. Myers died in the accident.

NASCAR badly needed a new star to replace the dozens who had vanished -- a fresh face who could draw admiration from the fans and take the sport to a higher plateau. A single creator, it has been said, gives

All the leaders missed the spinning Don Kimberling in the Southern 500, including Fireball Roberts, who went on to win by five laps

a show its characteristic look, sound and momentum.

Edward Glenn "Fireball" Roberts was NASCAR's savior in 1958.

Roberts, who lost the 1950 Grand National championship by a narrow margin and immediately returned to the speedy Modified wars for five years, came back to NASCAR's premier series in 1956 with the blessing of Ford Motor Co. When the Automobile Manufacturers Association withdrew entirely on June 6, 1957, Roberts became driver and car owner. Having no intention of paying the bills, he sold all of his equipment at the end of the year.

The 29 year-old Daytona Beach driver was in the market for a full time ride. After finishing ninth at Daytona's Beach-Road finale in a Bob Fish Buick and then running third in a Beau Morgan-owned Ford at Atlanta, Roberts hooked up with Frank Strickland of Atlanta. Strickland, owner of the Atlanta Tune-up Service, had a 1957 Grand National Chevrolet which had been carefully groomed by future Hall of Famer Paul McDuffie.

The Strickland, Roberts and McDuffie team went on a rampage. In eight Grand National starts for Strickland in 1958, Roberts won six times, including all three superspeedway events. He led 380 of the 500 laps on Trenton's one-mile paved oval, led the final 57 laps to win the Raleigh 250 at the banked one-mile track, and took the Southern 500, leading for 196 laps. Roberts lapped the field in all three superspeedway races and was five laps in front at Darlington.

Earnings for the year came to $32,218.20 in only 10 starts. In 1958 dollars, that was a small fortune. He finished 11th in the final Grand National point standings despite missing 41 of the 51 races. Of the 2,601 laps he drove, he led over 1,200 of them.

For his deeds, the Florida Sports Writers voted Roberts the Professional Athlete of the Year for 1958, the first time the coveted award went to a race car driver. The trophy he received would be one of Roberts' most prized possessions until the day he died. He felt the award helped stock car racing finally make the mark in the sporting world.

Fireball Roberts became the first driver to become the most talked about competitor without having run most of the races.

Roberts' prowess took up the slack in other areas. Memphis-Arkansas Speedway, at a mile-and-a-half the biggest oval track to host the Grand Nationals for four years, failed to open for the 1958 season. Track owners Clarence Camp, Nat Epstein and Harold Woolridge opted to close the often troubled facility when the Arkansas Highway Dept. began construction of a major expressway on the outskirts of the speedway.

Located at LeHi, AR, Memphis-Arkansas Speedway hosted five Grand National events. Buck Baker, Fonty Flock, Speedy Thompson, Ralph Moody and Marvin Panch won each of the races, ranging from 200 to 300 miles in length. Clint McHugh and Cotton Priddy died trying to do so.

Original plans called for a 1.5-mile paved oval. But construction costs and delays tapped the financial resources and paving was continually postponed. Recurring dust problems haunted the track. In the final NASCAR event staged at the track on July 14, 1957, almost half the crowd walked out during a 56-minute yellow flag while a utility vehicle

Billy Myers died of a heart attack in a Modified race

watered down the track. Its days were numbered. The Arkansas Highway Dept. simply drilled the last nail into the coffin.

Riverside International Raceway, a massive road course in Southern California, conducted a NASCAR race on June 1, 1958. It was a much celebrated presentation.

Three 500-milers were on tap for the weekend -- a 500-mile Big Car race, a 500-mile event for Sprint cars and the 500 for NASCAR's Grand National stocks. Promoters Gelard "Al" Slonaker and Charles A. Curryer invested some $60,000 in the project. They lost about $50,000.

In 1958 it was difficult to attract an audience out in the desert in the summertime -- the kaleidoscope of 500-milers notwithstanding. In a bold promotion, the 190-lap contest on the 2.631-mile, 11-turn course was open to 75 cars, including foreign makes. Also eligible were Continentals, Imperials, Mercedes Benz and Rolls Royce.

The "Crown America International Stock Car Race" attracted 46 cars, including four foreign cars. No one attempted to qualify a Rolls Royce.

The start of the race was held up by Bill France for over an hour. France, who had flown West to protect the best interests of his drivers, noticed that the sparse crowd wouldn't generate enough gate receipts to cover the $20,000 purse. He insisted that promoters Sloanaker and Curryer post the purse before the race got underway. All the money from the ticket booths surrounding the track was collected. It came to $16,570 -- right down to the last quarter. France accepted a personal check from Sloanaker for $3,430 to cover the balance and the race got underway.

Eddie Gray won the event after Parnelli Jones crashed with 43 laps to go.

There were plenty of happenings in the Modified and Sportsman races in NASCAR. On April 12, 1958, Billy Myers, the 1955 NASCAR Sportsman champion and winner of two events in his 1956 rookie season on the Grand National trail, died of a heart attack during a race at Winston-Salem's Bowman-Gray Stadium. Myers was leading the race when the seizure occurred. He was able to slow the car and aimed it safely off the track. He was slumped over the wheel when rescue workers reached him.

Curtis Turner survived a violent spill in a Modified race at the Charlotte Fairgrounds. The throttle of his Ford hung open and Turner sailed through the fence. He suffered seven broken ribs and was out of action over a month.

Finally, a pudgy kid named Cale Yarborough had an anxious moment at Ashwood Speedway in Bishopville, SC in May. The 18 year-old farm boy flipped his Limited Sportsman car outside the track and it happened to land in a lake. Cale stood on top of the car and dove in -- making it to the shoreline with waterlogged shoes. "I got wet when I flipped," remarked Yarborough, "so I figured I might as well have a swim. I'll get 'em next time."

Rex White receives trophy for taking 1958 season opener at Fayetteville's Champion Speedway. It was the first Grand National win for White.

sixth.

Grand National events at Hickory, NC and Bishopville, SC, scheduled in late November, were cancelled. The annual Buddy Shuman Memorial at Hickory was cancelled on Nov. 10 due to a widespread outbreak of the flu in Catawba County. A 100-miler at Ashwood Speedway in Bishopville was replaced by Sportsman and Hobby events.

Race No. 1

Rex White Takes '58 Opener For First Career Win

FAYETTEVILLE, NC (Nov. 3, 1957) -- Rex White inherited the lead five laps from the finish and nailed down his first Grand National victory in the 50-mile race at Champion Speedway.

The first Grand National win for the Silver Spring, MD Chevrolet driver came in his 34th start.

Jack Smith, who won the pole position, led for 117 laps. He appeared to have things well in hand until bad luck reared up and struck him down with less than two miles remaining. Smith's Chevrolet hit the wall after a wheel bearing burned out. He was left with a disappointing seventh place finish.

White led the final five laps to take the $630 first prize. Lee Petty came in second, Tiny Lund was third, Gwyn Staley fourth and Jimmy Massey was fifth.

Possum Jones, who led the first 28 laps, finished

Grand National Race No. 1
150 Laps at Champion Speedway
Fayetteville, NC
50 Miles on .333-mile Paved Track
November 3, 1957

Fin	St	No.	Driver	Team / Car	Laps	Money	Status
1	5	44	Rex White	Max Welborn '57 Chevrolet	150	$630	Running
2	3	42	Lee Petty	Petty Engineering '57 Olds	150	500	Running
3	4	76	Tiny Lund	Lonnie Fish '57 Chevrolet	149	380	Running
4	10	38	Gwyn Staley	Julian Petty '57 Chevrolet	148	310	Running
5	6	21	Jimmy Massey	Wood Brothers '56 Ford	148	255	Running
6	2	49	Possum Jones	Bob Welborn '57 Chevrolet	147	220	Running
7	1	47	Jack Smith	Smith '57 Chevrolet	145	195	Crash
8	7	87	Buck Baker	Baker '57 Chevrolet	145	210	Running
9	8	46	Speedy Thompson	Thompson '57 Chevrolet	144	165	Running
10	11	3	Paul Goldsmith	Slim Rominger '57 Ford	139	140	Running
11	14	28	Eddie Skinner	Skinner '57 Ford	136	145	Running
12	21	711	Bill Poor	Poor '56 Chevrolet	131	120	Running
13	15	17	Fred Harb	Harb '57 Mercury	130	100	Running
14	20	94	Clarence DeZalia	DeZalia '56 Mercury	127	100	Running
15	16	51	Roy Tyner	Tyner '56 Ford	126	110	Running
16	12	32	Brownie King	Jess Potter '57 Chevrolet	125	115	Running
17	9	64	Johnny Allen	Spook Crawford '57 Plymouth	119	90	Running
18	18	74	L D Austin	Austin '56 Chevrolet	118	60	Running
19	17	37	Bill Benson	Benson '56 Ford	98	60	Running
20	13	63	R L Combs	'56 Ford	79	65	Engine
21	19	71	George Parrish	Joe Frazier '56 Studebaker	7	50	Fan Belt
22	22	26	Ken Rush	J S Rice '57 Ford	0	---	Engine

Time of Race: 50 minutes, 39 seconds
Average Speed: 59.170 mph
Pole Winner: Jack Smith - 62.665 mph
Lap Leaders: Possum Jones 1-28, Jack Smith 29-145, Rex White 146-150.
Cautions: None   Margin of Victory: Half-lap   Attendance: 3,500

Race No. 2

Goldsmith's Pontiac First in Daytona Beach-Road Finale

DAYTONA BEACH, FL (Feb. 23) -- Paul Goldsmith of St. Clair Shores, MI and Roanoke, VA rabbit Curtis Turner treated the crowd of 35,000 to a memor-

able farewell to the famous Beach-Road course in the 160-mile Grand National race at Daytona.

Goldsmith, carrying the colors of famed mechanic Smokey Yunick, nipped Turner's Holman - Moody Ford by five car lengths at the finish line after an unexpected and exciting climax to the beachside racing facility.

Turner and Goldsmith were locked in a ferocious duel for top honors when Goldsmith got a break with nine laps remaining. Turner got trapped behind the Plymouth of Johnny Allen and spun around in the

Paul Goldsmith streaks his Smokey Yunick Pontiac past the finish line in the final stock car race at the historic Beach & Road Course at Daytona.

*Curtis Turner spins into the surf as Charlie Stone #54
passes late in the Daytona Beach Grand National.*

surf. His brief mishap allowed Goldsmith to open a
10 second lead.

But the ending caught everyone off guard as Goldsmith, who had lost the use of his windshield wipers,
sped past the North turn on the final lap and drove up
the beach. The Indianapolis 500 veteran quickly realized his mistake, cut a 180-degree turn and recovered
to cross the finish line a few feet ahead of the speeding
Turner.

Third place went to Jack Smith while Joe Weatherly
took fourth and Gwyn Staley grabbed fifth.

The swan song for the Beach & Road course was

Paul Goldsmith #3 leads Curtis Turner and Jack Smith at Daytona.

Grand National Race No. 2
39 Laps at Beach & Road Course
Daytona Beach, FL
160 Miles on 4.1-mile Beach & Road Course
February 23, 1958

Fin	St	No.	Driver	Team / Car	Laps	Money	Status
1	1	3	Paul Goldsmith	Smokey Yunick '58 Pontiac	39	$4,550	Running
2	8	26	Curtis Turner	Holman - Moody '58 Ford	39	2,600	Running
3	6	47	Jack Smith	Smith '57 Pontiac	39	1,575	Running
4	23	12	Joe Weatherly	Holman - Moody '58 Ford	39	900	Running
5	20	187	Gwyn Staley	Buck Baker '57 Chevrolet	38	700	Running
6	5	42	Lee Petty	Petty Enginnering '57 Olds	38	600	Running
7	18	87	Buck Baker	Baker '58 Chevrolet	37	500	Rear End
8	4	45	Eddie Pagan	Pagan '57 Ford	37	400	Running
9	7	M-1	Fireball Roberts	Fish Carburetor '58 Buick	37	250	Running
10	3	6	Cotton Owens	Jim Stephens '57 Pontiac	37	200	Running
11	2	55	Jimmy Thompson	Brushy Mtn Motors '57 Pontiac	36	150	Running
12	22	916	Dean Layfield	William Dickenson '58 Chevy	36	135	Running
13	31	56	Bill Morton	James Lowery '57 Ford	36	110	Running
14	12	98	Marvin Panch	John Whitford '57 Ford	35	100	Running
15	39	54	Charlie Stone	Tom Pine's Cafe '57 Chevrolet	35	100	Running
16	40	99	Ward Towers	Towers '57 Ford	34	90	Running
17	15	11	Lloyd Ragon	Paul Spaulding '57 Ford	34	80	Running
18	38	83	Cecil Wray	Paul Craig, Jr. '57 Olds	34	75	Running
19	13	61	Dick Foley	'56 Chevrolet	34	75	Running
20	9	5	Dick Bailey	'58 Pontiac	33	75	Running
21	34	310	Joe Lee Johnson	S T Campbell '57 Chevrolet	32	60	Engine
22	35	85	Carl Tyler	Tyler '57 Ford	32	60	Engine
23	21	10	Whitey Norman	Norman '56 Ford	32	60	Running
24	33	90	Buzz Woodward	'56 Ford	32	60	Running
25	25	28	Eddie Skinner	Skinner '57 Ford	31	60	Running
26	41	74	L D Austin	Austin '56 Chevrolet	31	50	Running
27	16	500	Phil Orr	Orlando, Fla Spl. '58 Ford	31	50	Running
28	43	52	Bob Walden	Walden '57 Pontiac	30	50	Running
29	10	2	Frankie Schneider	'57 Chevrolet	29	50	Engine
30	28	14	Billy Myers	Myers '57 Mercury	28	50	Engine
31	37	64	Johnny Allen	Spook Crawford '57 Plymouth	28	25	Running
32	36	62	Bobby Lee	Horne Motors '58 Ford	28	25	Engine
33	26	123	Johnny Mackison	Ken Corman '57 Mercury	28	25	H Gasket
34	44	145	Kenny Love	'57 Ford	26	25	Running
35	42	32	Brownie King	Jess Potter '57 Chevrolet	24	25	Engine
36	19	1	Banjo Matthews	Jim Rathmann '58 Chevrolet	17	25	Rear End
37	45	73	Bob Pronger	'57 Ford	16	25	Wheel
38	32	31	Doug Yates	Monroe Shook '58 Chevrolet	16	25	Engine
39	27	999	Wilbur Rakestraw	Joe Jones '57 Ford	11	25	Crash
40	46	49	Darel Dieringer	Bob Welborn '57 Chevrolet	11	25	Fuel Pm
41	47	48	Tiny Lund	Bob Welborn '57 Chevrolet	9	---	Battery
42	24	89	Bill Corley	Pappy Crane '57 Ford	7	---	Engine
43	29	71	Dick Joslin	Doc White '57 Dodge	6	---	Hose
44	30	40	Frank Thompson	Camp Hill Spl. '57 Ford	5	---	Engine
45	48	444	Axel Anderson	George Augustine '58 Pontiac	3	---	Crash
46	11	15	Tim Flock	Flock '57 Mercury	3	---	Steering
47	49	53	Carl Burris	'57 Chevrolet	3	---	Engine
48	17	46	Speedy Thompson	Thompson '57 Chevrolet	0	---	Engine
49	14	120	Bennie Rakestraw	Talmadge Cochrane '57 Merc	0	---	Engine

Time of Race: 1 hour, 34 minutes, 53 seconds
Average Speed: 101.113 mph
Pole Winner: Paul Goldsmith - 140.570 mph
Lap Leaders: Paul Goldsmith 1-39.
Cautions: None   Margin of Victory: 5 car lengths   Attendance: 35,000

completed in heavily overcast skies at nearly 5:00 pm.
A late afternoon low tide forced a 3:00 pm start.

Pit stops played a major role in the outcome as Turner spent 44 seconds on his lone stop. Goldsmith was
in the pits for only 38 seconds while Yunick's troops
serviced the car.

Forty-nine automobiles started the race and 31 were
running at the finish.

Buck Baker ran with the leaders in his '58 Chevrolet,

out rear end problems knocked him out in the final two laps. Tim Flock lasted only three laps before steering problems forced his Mercury out of action. Speedy Thompson lost an engine in the opening lap and wound up 48th. Frankie Schneider, Banjo Matthews and Billy Myers were other top rated drivers who failed to go the distance.

Goldsmith averaged 101.113 mph for his $4,550 victory.

Race No. 3

Petty Declared Winner in Concord Uproar

CONCORD, NC (March 2) -- In one of the most controversial events in the history of NASCAR Grand National racing, Lee Petty was declared the winner of a 100-mile race at Concord Speedway four days after he was flagged in third place.

Curtis Turner started in the front row and jumped out to an early lead. His Holman - Moody Ford was clearly the class of the field as he lapped most of his rivals. Witnesses said Petty was one of the drivers Turner had lapped on the half-mile dirt track.

After a late caution period, Petty passed Turner coming off the second turn on lap 198. Turner let his rival go and concentrated on beating runner-up Speedy Thompson. Petty was flagged in third place.

The Petty camp said they had won the race, leading the final three laps. Turner's Holman - Moody team claimed they led every lap.

NASCAR officials examined the score cards for four days. Finally, they announced that on the basis of the score cars, Petty was the winner. Turner got second and Thompson third. Gwyn Staley took fourth and Eddie Pagan was fifth.

The decision did not sit well with Turner, who said the entire audience of 12,000 and the other competitors knew the real outcome. "That Mama Elizabeth (Petty's wife and scorekeeper) has the fastest pencil in NAS-CAR," he said.

Thompson, who was dropped from second to third, threatened to quit the NASCAR tour. "The whole scoring system could stand revising," said the Monroe, NC veteran. "Mistakes are always popping up. It's not the money here (a difference of $175). But if they can whip you once like this and get by with it, they'll do it again. It's not worth it. I called Bill France and told him that if this is the way things are going to be, then racing is on the way out. And I feel like going be-

Grand National Race No.3
200 Laps at Concord Speedway
Concord, NC
100 Miles on Half-mile Dirt Track
March 2, 1958

Fin	St	No.	Driver	Team / Car	Laps	Money	Status
1		42	Lee Petty	Petty Engineering '57 Olds	200	$800	Running
2		21	Curtis Turner	Holman - Moody '58 Ford	200	525	Running
3	1	46	Speedy Thompson	Thompson '57 Chevrolet	200	350	Running
4		38	Gwyn Staley	Julian Petty '57 Chevrolet		250	Running
5		45	Eddie Pagan	Pagan '57 Ford		225	Running
6		47	Jack Smith	Smith '57 Chevrolet		200	
7		6	Cotton Owens	Jim Stephens '57 Pontiac		165	
8		11	Lloyd Ragon	Paul Spaulding '57 Ford		150	
9		32	Brownie King	Jess Potter '56 Chevrolet		140	
10		26	Bob Walden	Walden '57 Ford		130	
11		90	Buzz Woodward	'56 Ford		125	
12			Jim Paschal	'57 Ford		110	
13		96	Bobby Keck	Keck '56 Chevrolet		100	
14		94	Clarence DeZalia	DeZalia '56 Ford		85	
15		916	Dean Layfield	William Dickenson '58 Chevy		75	
16		74	L D Austin	Austin '56 Chevrolet		60	
17		145	Kenny Love	'57 Ford		50	
18		17	Fred Harb	Harb '57 Mercury		50	
19		66	Roy Tyner	Spook Crawford '57 Plymouth		50	
20		56	Bill Morton	James Lowery '57 Ford		50	
21		19	Herman Beam	Beam '56 Chevrolet		50	
22		711	Bill Poor	Poor '56 Chevrolet		50	
23		64	Johnny Allen	Spook Crawford '57 Plymouth		50	
24		400	Huck Spaulding	Spaulding '56 Dodge		50	
25		14	Billy Myers	Myers '57 Mercury		---	
26		86	Neil Castles	Castles '56 Ford		---	
27		73	Bob Pronger	'57 Ford		---	
28		202	Johnny Gardner	'56 Ford		---	
29		87	Buck Baker	Baker '58 Chevrolet		---	
30		55	Jimmy Thompson	Brushy Mtn Motors '57 Pontiac		---	

Time of Race: 1 hour, 42 minutes, 28 seconds
Average Speed: 58.555 mph
Pole Winner: Speedy Thompson -
Lap Leaders: Curtis Turner 1-197, Lee Petty 198-200.
Cautions: 1   Margin of Victory: 3 car lengths   Attendance : 12,000

fore it does. It's got me all shooked."

Petty claimed the score cards proved he was the winner and declined to elaborate.

Race No. 4

Turner Rebounds; Takes Fayetteville 150-Lapper

FAYETTEVILLE, NC (March 15) -- Curtis Turner hopped into his powerful Ford and held off three hungry challengers in a spine-tingling 50-mile Grand National race at Champion Speedway. It was Turner's first official win of the year.

At the finish of the 150-lapper on the .333-mile paved oval, Turner nipped Gwyn Staley's Chevrolet by a single car length. Buck Baker was third, Frankie Schneider came in fourth and Fred Harb was fifth.

Pole sitter Lee Petty led the opening lap, but Turner charged past and led for 34 laps. Little Rex White, winner of the 1958 season opener on this same track, moved past Turner on lap 35 and was leading when he crashed with Harvey Henderson on lap 38. Turner moved back on top and held off Staley in the stretch duel. White came in sixth.

Turner averaged 56.141 mph for his 12th career Grand National win.

Grand National Race No. 4
150 Laps at Champion Speedway
Fayetteville, NC
50-Miles on .333-mile Paved Track
March 15, 1958

Fin	St	No.	Driver	Team / Car	Laps	Money	Status
1		21	Curtis Turner	Holman - Moody'57 Ford	150	$600	Running
2		38	Gwyn Staley	Julian Petty '57 Chevrolet	150	470	Running
3		87	Buck Baker	Baker '57 Chevrolet	150	350	Running
4		62	Frankie Schneider	'57 Chevrolet	150	275	Running
5		17	Fred Harb	Harb '57 Mercury	225		
6	2	44	Rex White	J H Petty '57 Chevrolet	205		
7		26	Bob Walden	Walden '57 Ford	175		
8		49	Bob Welborn	J H Petty '57 Chevrolet	165		
9	1	42	Lee Petty	Petty Engineering '57 Olds	150		
10			Richard Haygood	'57 Chevrolet	140		
11		74	L D Austin	Austin '57 Chevrolet	130		
12		96	Bobby Keck	Keck '57 Chevrolet	125		
13			Barney Shore	Shore '57 Chevrolet	110		
14		32	Brownie King	Jess Potter '57 Chevrolet	100		
15		94	Clarence DeZalia	DeZalia '56 Mercury	85		
16		78	Shep Langdon	Langdon '56 Ford	70		
17		12	Joe Weatherly	Holman - Moody '57 Ford	60		
18		X	Volney Schulze	'56 Chevrolet	50		
19		46	Speedy Thompson	Thompson '57 Chevrolet	50		
20		53	Carl Burris	'57 Chevrolet	50		
21		64	Johnny Allen	Spook Crawford '57 Plymouth	50	50	
22		45	Eddie Pagan	Pagan '57 Ford		50	
23		23	Harvey Henderson	Henderson '57 Ford	38	50	Crash
24		59	Blackie Pitt	Pitt '58 Studebaker		50	
25		47	Jack Smith	Smith '57 Chevrolet		---	
26		54	Nace Mattingly	Mattingly '57 Ford		---	

Time of Race: 53 minutes, 23 seconds
Average Speed: 56.141 mph
Pole Winner: Lee Petty - 62.600 mph
Lap Leaders: Lee Petty 1, Curtis Turner 2-34, Rex White 35-38, Turner 39-150.
Cautions: 1   Margin of Victory: 1 car length   Attendance: 5,200

Race No. 5

Turner Breaks Down; Leaves Petty With Wilson Win

WILSON, NC (March 16) -- Lee Petty became the first repeat winner of the young 1958 Grand National season by lapping the field four times in the 100-miler at Wilson Speedway.

Buck Baker finished a distant second and pole sitter

Grand National Race No. 5
200 Laps at Wilson Speedway
Wilson, NC
100-Miles on Half-mile Dirt Track
March 16, 1958

Fin	St	No	Driver	Team / Car	Laps	Money	Status
1	6	42	Lee Petty	Petty Engineering '57 Olds	200	$800	Running
2	9	87	Buck Baker	Baker '57 Chevrolet	196	525	Running
3	1	98	Marvin Panch	John Whitford '57 Ford	193	350	Running
4	4	47	Jack Smith	Smith '57 Chevrolet	192	250	Running
5	15	88	Reds Kagle	'57 Chevrolet	191	225	Running
6	13	96	Bobby Keck	Keck '56 Ford	190	200	Running
7	12	126	Bob Walden	Walden '57 Ford	187	165	Running
8	14	74	L D Austin	Austin '56 Chevrolet	182	150	Running
9	18	961	Jack Lawrence	'57 Chevrolet	177	140	Running
10	16	94	Clarence DeZalia	DeZalia '56 Ford	176	130	Running
11	20	85	Carl Tyler	Tyler '57 Ford	167	125	Running
12	22	X	Volney Schulze	'57 Chevrolet	167	110	Running
13	2	21	Curtis Turner	Holman - Moody '57 Ford	160	100	D Shaft
14	17	90	Buzz Woodward	'57 Ford	158	85	Running
15	21	32	Brownie King	Jess Potter '57 Chevrolet	150	70	Engine
16	5	64	Johnny Allen	Spook Crawford '57 Plymouth	120	60	Engine
17	19	9	Dave Terrell	Terrell '57 Chevrolet	113	50	Running
18	11	54	Nace Mattingly	Mattingly '57 Ford	105	50	Heating
19	7	123	Buzz Wilson	'57 Chevrolet	87	50	Engine
20	8	46	Speedy Thompson	Thompson '57 Chevrolet	71	50	Ball Jt
21	10	2	Bobby Lee	Horne Motors '58 Ford	30	50	Wheel
22	3	55	Jerry Draper	Brushy Mtn Motors '57 Pontiac	10	50	Oil Pres

Time of Race: 2 hours, 3 minutes, 49 seconds
Average Speed: 48.459 mph
Pole Winner: Marvin Panch - 58.901 mph
Lap Leaders: Curtis Turner 1, Marvin Panch 2-73, Turner 74-160, Lee Petty 161-200.
Cautions: Margin of Victory: 4-laps-plus   Attendance: 3,400

Marvin Panch was third. Jack Smith came in fourth and Reds Kagle was fifth.

Curtis Turner started second and led the opening lap. The Roanoke, VA wild-man spun out as the lead cars jockeyed for position on lap two. Turner recovered without losing a lap.

Panch took the lead and held it through lap 74 when Turner charged into the lead once again. His Ford was pulling away from the field when the drive shaft broke with 40 laps to go.

Petty, the great calculator, eased into the lead and coasted to his 32nd career Grand National victory.

A crowd of 3,400 watched Petty average 48.459 mph on the half-mile dirt track.

Race No. 6

Baker's Flawless Drive Nets Victory in Hillsboro 99

HILLSBORO, NC (March 23) -- Buck Baker rang the victory bell for the first time in the 1958 campaign with a come from behind triumph in the 99-mile event at Orange Speedway.

Johnny Allen qualified 3rd and finished 6th at Hillsboro.

The Chevrolet driver started on the pole and led the first 69 laps. When Johnny Nave lost a wheel and brought out the day's only caution flag, Baker pitted for fresh tires. He rejoined the fray in fourth place. He ran down Speedy Thompson and Lee Petty, then set out for leader Marvin Panch. Baker made the final pass with 15 laps to go.

Panch finished second, Thompson was third and Petty fourth. Curtis Turner took fifth place.

Grand National Race No. 6
110 Laps at Orange Speedway
Hillsboro, NC
99 Miles on .9-mile Dirt Track
March 23, 1958

Fin	St	No	Driver	Team / Car	Laps	Money	Status
1	1	87	Buck Baker	Baker '57 Chevrolet	110	$800	Running
2	4	98	Marvin Panch	John Whitford "57 Ford	110	525	Running
3	5	46	Speedy Thompson	Thompson '57 Chevrolet	110	350	Running
4	2	42	Lee Petty	Petty Engineering '57 Olds	110	250	Running
5	7	21	Curtis Turner	Holman - Moody '57 Ford	108	225	Running
6	3	64	Johnny Allen	Spook Crawford '57 Plymouth	108	200	
7	10	10	E J Brewer	'56 Ford	103	165	
8	12	74	L D Austin	Austin '56 Chevrolet	103	150	
9	9	96	Bobby Keck	Keck '57 Chevrolet	101	140	
10	15	59	Blackie Pitt	Pitt '58 Studebaker	93	130	
11	18	94	Clarence DeZalia	DeZalia '56 Ford	89	125	
12	6	47	Jack Smith	Smith '57 Chevrolet	82	110	
13	8	45	Eddie Pagan	Pagan '57 Ford	82	100	
14	17	X	Volney Schulze	'56 Chevrolet	73	85	
15	14	561	Johnny Nave	'56 Ford	70	70	Wheel
16	13	19	Herman Beam	Beam '57 Chevrolet	55	60	
17	16	88	Reds Kagle	'57 Chevrolet	18	50	
18	11	32	Brownie King	Jess Potter '57 Chevrolet	15	50	

Time of Race: 1 hour, 15 minutes, 40 seconds
Average Speed: 78.502 mph
Pole Winner: Buck Baker - 83.076 mph
Lap Leaders Buck Baker 1-69, Marvin Panch 70-95, Baker 96-110.
Cautions: 1   Margin of Victory: Attendance: 8,000

The world of racing suffered a major loss with the death of Gwyn Staley, who died in a crash at Richmond, VA in a same day Convertible race.

A crowd of 8,000 watched Baker average 78.502 mph for his 37th career win.

Grand National Race No. 7
150 Laps at Champion Speedway
Fayetteville, NC
50 Miles on .333-Mile Paved Track
April 5, 1958

Fin	St	No	Driver	Team/Car	Laps	Money	Status
1	2	38	Bob Welborn	Julian Petty '57 Chevrolet	150	$600	Running
2	7	62	Frankie Schneider	'57 Chevrolet	150	470	Running
3	6	46	Speedy Thompson	Thompson '57 Chevrolet	150	350	Running
4	16	126	Curtis Turner	Holman - Moody '58 Ford	150	275	Running
5	14	45	Eddie Pagan	Pagan '57 Ford	149	225	Running
6	9	88	Reds Kagle	'57 Chevrolet	148	205	Running
7	11	87	Buck Baker	Baker '57 Chevrolet	147	220	Running
8	12	76	Larry Frank	Frank '57 Chevrolet	147	165	Running
9	10	17	Fred Harb	Harb '57 Mercury	144	150	Running
10	22	99	Barney Shore	Shore '57 Chevrolet	144	155	Running
11	13	150	Billy Rafter	\Rafter '57 Ford	141	130	Running
12	5	64	Johnny Allen	Spook Crawford '57 Plymouth	138	135	Running
13	15	28	Eddie Skinner	Skinner ' 57 Ford	136	100	Running
14	28	32	Brownie King	Jess Potter '57 Chevrolet	135	100	Running
15	19	123	Johnny Mackison	Ken Corman '57 Chevrolet	135	90	Running
16	18	74	Shep Langdon	Langdon '56 Ford	132	75	Running
17	24	74	L D Austin	Austin '56 Chevrolet	129	75	Running
18	26	X	Volney Schulze	'56 Chevrolet	123	60	Running
19	29	67	Roy Tyner	Spook Crawford '57 Plymouth	120	50	Flat Tire
20	17	56	Bill Morton	James Lowery '57 Ford	116	50	Steering
21	27	96	Bobby Keck	Keck '57 Chevrolet	114	35	Running
22	21	94	Clarence DeZalia	DeZalia '56 Ford	102	25	Crank
23	8	99	Shorty Rollins	Rollins '58 Ford	62	45	Engine
24	20	8	Elmo Langley	'57 Chevrolet	46	25	Brakes
25	1	42	Lee Petty	Petty Engineering '57 Olds	27	30	Axle
26	4	44	Rex White	J H Petty '57 Chevrolet	17	30	Crash
27	3	47	Jack Smith	Smith '57 Chevrolet	17	--	Crash
28	23	10	E J Brewer	'56 Ford	16	15	Crash
29	25	59	Blackie Pitt	Pitt '58 Studebaker	5	--	Engine

Time of Race: 59 minutes, 40 seconds
Average Speed: 50.229 mph
Pole Winner: Lee Petty - 60.576 mph
Lap Leaders: Lee Petty 1-24, Buck Baker 25-76, Bob Welborn 77-150.
Cautions: 2   Margin of Victory: Attendance: 4,000

Race No. 7
Welborn Drives Chevrolet To Victory at Fayetteville

FAYETTEVILLE, NC (Apr. 5) -- Bob Welborn, new replacement for the late Gwyn Staley in Julian Petty's Chevrolet, edged past Buck Baker in the 77th lap and went on to score his first win of the season in the 50-miler at Champion Speedway.

It was the third Grand National event NASCAR has sanctioned at the .333-mile paved track in the 1958 season.

Welborn, a two-time Convertible champion, started second on the grid. He followed Lee Petty and Buck Baker who had traded the lead in the first half of the race. Welborn, of Summerfield, NC, passed Baker with 73 laps to go.

Frankie Schneider finished second and Speedy Thompson was third. Curtis Turner came in fourth and Eddie Pagan was fifth.

While battling for the lead, Petty and Baker engaged in a fender bending duel. Petty fell out on lap 27 with a broken axle and Baker struggled to a seventh place finish.

Rex White and Jack Smith were eliminated in a 17th lap crash as the pair were battling for second place.

Race No. 8

Thompson Outduels Smith In Columbia Century

COLUMBIA, SC (April 10) -- Speedy Thompson outdueled Jack Smith and registered his first win of the year in the 100-miler at Columbia Speedway. It was the 15th career win for the Chevrolet driver.

Smith finished a close second and took second place in the point standings. Tiny Lund came from 19th starting spot to finish third. Lee Petty wound up fourth and moved to a 188 point lead in the Grand National standings. Fifth place went to Eddie Pagan.

Thirty-three cars started the race and with the crowded track conditions, it was a wreck-strewn affair. Rookie Shorty Rollins was knocked out in an opening lap crash. Marvin Panch and Billy Rafter were put out in another wreck two laps later.

Panch and Rafter, starting second and third, crashed through the steel retaining wall, resulting in a red flag condition. There were no injuries.

Other drivers taken out by accidents included Junior Johnson, Roy Tyner, Gene Hege and Doug Cox.

Possum Jones outran the favorites in qualifying and earned his first Grand National pole. His Chevrolet went out of the race on lap 54 with wheel bearing problems.

Grand National Race No. 8
200 Laps at Columbia Speedway
Columbia, SC
100-Miles on Half-mile Dirt Track
April 10, 1958

Fin	St	No.	Driver	Team / Car	Laps	Money	Status
1	7	46	Speedy Thompson	Thompson '57 Chevrolet	200	$800	Running
2	5	47	Jack Smith	Smith '57 Chevrolet	200	525	Running
3	19	37	Tiny Lund	Don Angel '56 Ford	199	350	Running
4	9	42	Lee Petty	Petty Engineering '57 Olds	199	250	Running
5	11	45	Eddie Pagan	Pagan '57 Ford	198	225	Running
6	13	88	Reds Kagle	'57 Chevrolet	193	200	Running
7	6	25	Roz Howard	Howard '57 Chevrolet	192	165	Running
8	22	30	Doug Cox	'56 Ford	185	150	Crash
9	26	94	Clarence DeZalia	DeZalia '56 Ford	184	140	Running
10	30	74	L D Austin	Austin '56 Chevrolet	180	130	Running
11	20	26	Bob Walden	'57 Ford	179	125	Running
12	21	19	Herman Beam	Beam '57 Chevrolet	175	110	Running
13	28	96	Bobby Keck	Keck '57 Chevrolet	173	100	Running
14	23	32	Brownie King	Jess Potter '57 Chevrolet	165	85	Running
15	14	86	Neil Castles	Castles '56 Ford	153	70	Running
16	15	123	Johnny Mackison	Ken Corman '57 Mercury	151	60	Rear End
17	4	64	Johnny Allen	Spook Crawford '57 Plymouth	150	50	Engine
18	27	85	Carl Tyler	Tyler '56 Ford	148	50	Spindle
19	25	33	George Green	Green '56 Chevrolet	132	50	Piston
20	33	711	Richard Spittle	Bill Poor '57 Chevrolet	125	50	Running
21	10	9	Billy Carden	Bishop Bros. '57 Chevrolet	119	50	Axle
22	32	202	Johnny Gardner	'56 Ford	117	50	Running
23	29	78	Shep Langdon	Langdon '56 Ford	99	50	Carb
24	16	87	Buck Baker	Baker '57 Chevrolet	92	50	Valve
25	31	1	Gene Hege	'57 Ford	85	---	Crash
26	18	2	Bobby Lee	Horne Motors '58 Ford	81	---	Lug Nuts
27	24	916	Dean Layfield	William Dickenson '58 Chevy	80	---	Engine
28	17	66	Roy Tyner	Spook Crawford '57 Plymouth	74	---	Crash
29	1	2B	Possum Jones	Max Welborn '57 Chevrolet	54	---	Bearing
30	12	11	Junior Johnson	Paul Spaulding '57 Ford	11	---	Crash
31	2	98	Marvin Panch	John Whitford '57 Ford	3	---	Crash
32	3	50	Billy Rafter	Rafter '57 Ford	3	---	Crash
33	8	99	Shorty Rollins	Rollins '58 Ford	1	---	Crash

Time of Race: No time recorded
Average Speed: None
Pole Winner: Possum Jones - 66.201 mph
Lap Leaders: --------- Speedy Thompson   -200.
Cautions: Margin of Victory: Attendance:

Race No. 9

Speedy Hustles to Hub City Speedway Win

SPARTANBURG, SC (April 12) -- Speedy Thompson and Jack Smith engaged in a personal duel for the second day in a row -- and the results were the same in Hub City Speedway's 100-miler.

Thompson's second straight victory moved him to fifth place in the point standings

Smith wound up a close second. Junior Johnson came in third, showing his one year "vacation" in Chillicothe, OH hadn't dulled his skills. Eddie Pagan and Possum Jones were fourth and fifth.

Thompson started his Chevrolet on the pole and led most of the way. Second fastest qualifier Cotton Owens was only around 14 laps before he departed with a broken fan belt. Other top drivers on the sidelines when the checkered flag fell were Buck Baker, Tiny Lund and Jimmy Thompson.

Thompson's 16th career win came at a speed of 56.613 mph.

Grand National Race No. 9
200 Laps at Hub City Speedway
Spartanburg, SC
100 Miles on Half-mile Dirt Track
April 12, 1958

Fin	St	No	Driver	Team / Car	Laps	Money	Status
1	1	46	Speedy Thompson	Thompson '57 Chevrolet	200	$800	Running
2	4	47	Jack Smith	Smith '57 Chevrolet	200	525	Running
3	8	11	Junior Johnson	Paul Spaulding '57 Ford	196	350	Running
4	7	45	Eddie Pagan	Pagan '57 Ford	196	250	Running
5	12	2B	Possum Jones	Welborn '57 Chevrolet	193	225	Running
6	19	123	Johnny Mackison	Ken Corman '57 Mercury	185	200	Running
7	21	88	Reds Kagle	'57 Chevrolet	185	165	Running
8	16	32	Brownie King	Jess Potter '57 Chevrolet	184	150	Running
9	15	96	Bobby Keck	Keck '57 Chevrolet	180	140	Running
10	27	50	Billy Rafter	Rafter '57 Ford	178	130	Running
11	20	94	Clarence DeZalia	DeZalia '56 Ford	175	125	Running
12	3	42	Lee Petty	Petty Engineering '57 Olds	172	110	Running
13	24	74	L D Austin	Austin '56 Chevrolet	166	100	Running
14	25	19	Herman Beam	Beam '57 Chevrolet	163	85	Running
15	23	78	Shep Langdon	Langdon '56 Ford	157	70	Running
16	22	59	Blackie Pitt	Pitt '58 Studebaker	154	60	Running
17	14	916	Dean Layfield	William Dickenson '58 Chevy	153	50	Running
18	13	66	Roy Tyner	Spook Crawford '57 Plymouth	153	50	Running
19	9	37	Tiny Lund	Don Angel '56 Ford	140	50	Distrib
20	10	17	Fred Harb	Harb '57 Mercury	126	50	Distrib
21	26	25	Roz Howard	Howard '57 Chevrolet	108	50	Oil Press
22	6	87	Buck Baker	Baker '57 Chevrolet	78	50	Ball Jt
23	5	55	Jimmy Thompson	Brushy Mtn Motors '57 Pontiac	49	50	Oil Press
24	11	9	Billy Carden	Bishop Bros. '57 Chevrolet	44	50	Axle
25	18	85	Carl Tyler	Tyler '57 Ford	31	---	Spk Plug
26	2	6	Cortton Owens	Jim Stephens '57 Pontiac	14	---	Fan Belt
27	17	86	Neil Castles	Castles '56 Ford	6	---	Oil Line

Time of Race: 1 hour, 45 minutes, 59 seconds.
Average Speed: 56.613 mph
Pole Winner: Speedy Thompson - 61.412 mph
Lap Leaders: - - - - - - - - - Speedy Thompson -200.
Cautions: Margin of Victory: Attendance:

Race No. 10

'Stardust Twins' Star in Lakewood's 100-Miler

ATLANTA, GA (April 13) -- Curtis Turner and Joe Weatherly wheeled their Holman - Moody Fords relentlessly over Lakewood Speedway's rutted surface and came away with a 1-2 finish in the 100-miler.

Turner led the first 41 laps on the one-mile dirt track. Tim Flock, seeking to regain the winning touch, surged to the front and led for 26 laps. He was holding down first place when a broken ball joint put his

Mercury out of action.

Turner took the lead on lap 67 and led the rest of the way. He outran Weatherly by three-quarters of a lap and pocketed the $1,540 top prize.

Fireball Roberts, making his first start since Daytona, finished third. Marvin Panch was fourth and Joe Lee Johnson came in fifth.

The original race date was March 30, but heavy rains forced postponement. In the following two weeks, Turner and Weatherly did their own promotional work and promised a 1-2 finish. A crowd of 18,000 showed up to cheer them on.

Point leader Lee Petty finished dead last but still held a lead of 36 points over Jack Smith, who wound up 13th in the field of 25.

Curtis Turner won Lakewood event.

Grand National Race No. 10
100 Laps at Lakewood Speedway
Atlanta, GA
100 miles on 1-Mile Dirt Track
April 13, 1958

Fin	St	No	Driver	Team / Car	Laps	Money	Status
1	2	26	Curtis Turner	Holman - Moody '58 Ford	100	$1,540	Running
2	1	12	Joe Weatherly	Holman - Moody '58 Ford	100	545	Running
3	6	494	Fireball Roberts	Beau Morgan '57 Ford	100	400	Running
4	11	98	Marvin Panch	John Whitford '57 Ford	100	250	Running
5	16	310	Joe Lee Johnson	S T Campbell '57 Chevrolet	99	225	Running
6	14	87	Buck Baker	Baker '57 Chevrolet	98	200	Running
7	4	9	Billy Carden	Bishop Bros. '57 Chevrolet	98	190	Running
8	12	147	Johnny Allen	Spook Crawford '57 Plymouth	97	150	Running
9	17	999	Wilbur Rakestraw	Joe Jones '57 Ford	95	165	Running
10	13	45	Eddie Pagan	Pagan '57 Ford	94	130	Running
11	5	6	Cotton Owens	Jim Stephens '57 Pontiac	93	125	Running
12	19	54	Thomas Aiken	Nace Mattingly '57 Ford	93	110	Running
13	8	47	Jack Smith	Smith '57 Chevrolet	89	100	Suspens
14	23	74	L D Austin	Austin '56 Chevrolet	88	85	Running
15	25	50	Billy Rafter	Rafter '57 Ford	85	70	Running
16	22	916	Dean Layfield	William Dickenson '58 Chevy	85	60	Running
17	24	96	Bobby Keck	Keck '57 Chevrolet	75	50	Running
18	3	15	Tim Flock	Flock '57 Mercury	66	310	Ball Jt
19	7	46	Speedy Thompson	Thompson '57 Chevrolet	51	50	Ball Jt
20	10	11	Junior Johnson	Paul Spaulding '58 Ford	28	50	Ball Jt
21	18	88	Reds Kagle	'57 Chevrolet	22	50	Oil Press
22	21	59	Blackie Pitt	Pitt '58 Studebaker	20	50	Bearing
23	20	85	Carl Tyler	Tyler '57 Ford	15	50	Clutch
24	15	123	Johnny Mackison	Ken Corman '57 Mercury	9	50	Axle
25	9	42	Lee Petty	Petty Engineering '57 Olds	1	--	Axle

Time of Race: 1 hour, 15 minutes, 56 seconds.
Average Speed: 79.016 mph
Pole Winner: Joe Weatherly - 81.577 mph
Lap Leaders: Curtis Turner 1-41, Tim Flock 42-66, Turner 67-100.
Cautions: None   Margin of Victory: 3/4 lap   Attendance: 18,000

Race No. 11

Curtis Turner
Romps at Charlotte

CHARLOTTE, NC (April 18) -- Curtis Turner provided a one man show at Southern States Fairgrounds Speedway, romping to victory in the 100-miler.

Turner's Holman - Moody Ford was the class of the field. He started on the pole and led every lap to score his third win of the season. Jack Smith finished second, a lap behind. Johnny Allen came in third, Lee Petty was fourth and Joe Weatherly fifth.

The crowd of 8,100 watched a boring series of left hand turns. Turner jumped away at the start, performed his patented powerslide and ran away from his rivals. He was never challenged.

Three caution flags for a total of eight laps allowed the field to close in on the Roanoke rabbit, but he was still four laps ahead of the third and fourth place finishers.

Only one potential front runner was sidelined. Marvin Panch, who qualified fourth fastest in the 21 car field, fell out after 59 laps when a ball joint broke on his Ford.

Turner averaged 53.254 mph for his 14th career Grand National victory.

Bob Welborn gets the checkered flag at finish of Virginia 500 at Martinsville Speedway.

			Grand National Race No. 11			
			200 Laps at Southern States			
			Fairgrounds			
			Charlotte, NC			
			100 Miles on Half-mile Dirt Track			
			April 18, 1958			
Fin	St	No	Driver	Team / Car	Laps	Money	Status
---	---	---	---	---	---	---	---
1	1	26	Curtis Turner	Holman - Moody '58 Ford	200	$800	Running
2	5	47	Jack Smith	Smith '57 Chevrolet	199	525	Running
3	12	64	Johnny Allen	Spook Crawford '57 Plymouth	196	350	Running
4	3	42	Lee Petty	Petty Engineering '57 Olds	196	250	Running
5	2	12	Joe Weatherly	Holman - Moody '58 Ford	195	225	Running
6	8	87	Buck Baker	Baker '57 Chevrolet	191	200	Running
7	9	6	Cotton Owens	Jim Stephens '57 Pontiac	191	165	Running
8	21	50	Billy Rafter	Rafter '57 Ford	178	150	Running
9	16	74	L D Austin	Austin '56 Chevrolet	176	140	Running
10	13	94	Clarence DeZalia	DeZalia '56 Ford	174	130	Running
11	7	126	Possum Jones	Holman - Moody '57 Ford	169	125	Running
12	6	45	Eddie Pagan	Pagan '57 Ford	165	110	Ball Jt
13	14	63	R L Combs	'56 Ford	155	100	Fuel Pmp
14	19	711	Darel Dieringer	Bill Poor '56 Chevrolet	114	85	Shocks
15	10	81	Buck Brigance	'57 Ford	109	70	Crash
16	11	39	Billy Carden	Bishop Bros. '57 Chevrolet	71	60	Piston
17	4	98	Marvin Panch	John Whitford '57 Ford	59	50	Ball Jt
18	18	78	Shep Langdon	Langdon '56 Ford	27	50	Shocks
19	17	198	Dick Beaty	Beaty '57 Ford	7	50	Engine
20	20	33	George Green	Green '56 Chevrolet	5	50	Engine
21	15	86	Neil Castles	Castles '56 Ford	2	50	Brakes

Time of Race: 1 hour, 52 minutes, 40 seconds
Average Speed: 53.254 mph
Pole Winner: Curtis Turner - 57.471 mph
Lap Leaders: Curtis Turner 1-200.
Cautions: 3 for 8 laps   Margin of Victory: 1-plus-laps   Attendance: 8,100

Race No. 12

Welborn Survives Spin;
Snares Virginia 500

MARTINSVILLE, VA (April 20) -- Bob Welborn started deep in the field, grabbed the lead past the half way point, survived a late race scare and rode home first in the Virginia 500 at Martinsville Speedway.

Welborn's Chevrolet was 12 car lengths ahead of Rex White when the checkered flag fell. Jim Reed was a close third, Whitey Norman was fourth and Marvin Panch fifth.

Welborn started 20th in the 47 car field and spent most of the early stages working his way into contention. Buck Baker, Glen Wood and Lee Petty led most of the way in the 250-miler.

Wood's Ford, with relief driver Jimmy Massey at the helm, blew a tire a n d crashed while leading on lap 396. The mishap allowed Welborn to take over first place for good.

Welborn had built a four laps lead with just 30 laps to go, but he very nearly lost it all. A tire blew on his

Julian Petty Chevrolet and he spun out. The Summerfield, NC short track specialist got his car restarted and went to the pits for fresh rubber. Four laps later, he returned to the track just in front of White. Welborn was able to stretch his lead slightly in the final laps.

Four cautions held Welborn's average speed for the 500 laps to 61.166 mph.

Jack Smith heads his '58 Pontiac into the first turn at Martinsville.

Clarence DeZalia of Aberdeen, NC flipped his Ford with about 50 miles to go. DeZalia, in his second full season in the Grand National ranks, calmly dismounted, uprighted his bent automobile and hopped back in. He cranked up the car and continued to a 28th place finish.

Grand National Race No. 12
500 Laps at Martinsville Speedway
Martinsville, VA
"Virginia 500"
250 Miles on Half-mile Paved Track
April 20, 1958

Fin	St	No	Driver	Team / Car	Laps	Money	Status
1	20	4	Bob Welborn	J H Petty '57 Chevrolet	500	$3,640	Running
2	12	44	Rex White	J H Petty '57 Chevrolet	500	1,675	Running
3	11	7	Jim Reed	Reed '57 Ford	500	1,125	Running
4	15	41	Whitey Norman	Norman '57 Chevrolet	495	800	Running
5	21	98	Marvin Panch	John Whitford '57 Ford	494	675	Running
6	34	26	Curtis Turner	Holman - Moody '58 Ford	488	550	Running
7	34	39	Billy Carden	Bishop Bros. '57 Chevrolet	485	425	Running
8	4	46	Jimmy Thompson*	Speedy Thompson '57 Chevy	483	375	Running
9	17	53	Carl Burris	'57 Chevrolet	479	300	Running
10	2	21	Glen Wood**	Wood Brothers '57 Ford	474	460	Running
11	10	42	Lee Petty	Petty Engineering '57 Olds	471	260	Running
12	26	310	Joe Lee Johnson	S T Campbell '57 Chevrolet	465	150	Running
13	30	78	Shep Langdon	Langdon '56 Ford	460	135	Running
14	5	99	Shorty Rollins	Rollins '58 Ford	458	125	Running
15	19	30	Doug Cox	'57 Ford	457	125	Running
16	28	19	Herman Beam	Beam '57 Chevrolet	457	110	Running
17	32	32	Brownie King	Jess Potter '57 Chevrolet	456	110	Running
18	25	57	Billy Rafter	'57 Ford	453	100	Running
19	16	37	Tiny Lund	Don Angel '56 Ford	449	100	Running
20	31	74	L D Austin	Austin '56 Chevrolet	448	100	Running
21	13	47	Jack Smith	Smith '58 Pontiac	446	100	Oil Press
22	42	198	Dick Beaty	Beaty '57 Ford	441	100	Running
23	14	28	Eddie Skinner	Skinner '57 Ford	437	90	Engine
24	27	86	Neil Castles	Castles '56 Ford	437	90	Engine
25	44	52	Bob Walden	Walden '57 Ford	425	85	Engine
26	24	50	Ben Benz	Billy Rafter '57 Chevrolet	424	80	Running
27	3	62	Frankie Schneider	'57 Chevrolet	404	75	Running
28	39	94	Clarence DeZalia	DeZalia '56 Ford	404	75	Running
29	18	88	Reds Kagle	'57 Chevrolet	329	75	Carb
30	9	11	Junior Johnson	Paul Spaulding '57 Ford	325	75	Engine
31	35	12	Joe Weatherly	Holman - Moody '58 Ford	312	140	Engine
32	23	64	Johnny Allen	Spook Crawford '57 Plymouth	282	50	Oil Press
33	6	76	Larry Frank	Frank '57 Chevrolet	267	50	Oil Press
34	36	63	R L Combs	'56 Ford	198	50	Oil Press
35	1	87	Buck Baker	Baker '57 Chevrolet	156	50	Wiring
36	7	97	Barney Shore	Shore '57 Chevrolet	154	---	Gen'tor
37	37	33	George Green	Green '56 Chevrolet	130	---	Trans
38	8	3	Cotton Owens	Smokey Yunick '58 Pontiac	126	---	Brakes
39	22	17	Fred Harb	Harb '57 Mercury	117	---	Rear End
40	29	31	Jerry Draper	Monroe Shook '58 Chevrolet	107	---	Rear End
41	46	89	Chuck Hansen	Hanson '57 Chevrolet	77	---	Engine
42	33	10	E J Brewer	'56 Ford	69	---	Oil Press
43	45	8	Elmo Langley	'57 Chevrolet	55	---	Gas Tank
44	41	83	Lennie Page	'56 Ford	14	---	Brakes
45	43	81	Eddie Pagan	'57 Ford	4	---	Trans
46	40	96	Bobby Keck	Keck '57 Chevrolet	3	---	Gas Line
47	47	66	Roy Tyner	Spook Crawford '57 Plymouth	0	---	Engine

Time of Race: 4 hours, 5 minutes, 27.27 seconds
Average Speed: 66.166 mph
Pole Winner: Buck Baker - 66.007 mph
Lap Leaders: Buck Baker 1, Glen Wood 2-139, Lee Petty 140-197, Bob Welborn 198-297, Wood 298-326, Welborn 327-500.
Cautions: 4   Margin of Victory: 12 car lengths   Attendance: 15,000
*Relieved by Buck Baker   **Relieved by Jimmy Massey

Race No. 13

Schneider Gets $600 For First Grand National Win

MANASSAS, VA (April 25) -- Frankie Schneider of Lambertville, NJ notched his first Grand National victory in the 56.25-mile event at Old Dominion Speedway. The wily veteran became the eighth different driver to post a victory on NASCAR's premier series in the 1958 season.

Schneider started fourth in the field of 25 and took over the lead on lap 45. He held off Jack Smith in the final few laps

Frankie Schneider won at Manassas.

on the .375-mile paved track.

Rex White finished in third and Lee Petty was fourth. Fifth place went to Johnny Allen.

Eddie Pagan started on the pole but his Ford encountered a number of problems in the 150-lapper. He eventually finished 19th, 30 laps behind winner Schneider.

Schneider averaged 67.590 mph in the 49 minute race.

Stadium.

Reed put his Ford on the pole, got off to a good start and was never headed. He was a lap in front of the field when officials red flagged the event after 187 of the scheduled 200 laps had been completed. It had begun to rain 102 laps earlier.

Eddie Pagan was flagged in second place. Rex White got credit for third, Frankie Schneider was fourth and Elmo Langley fifth.

Lee Petty was running in fourth place when he spun off the course in the 184th lap. Petty said he lost it on the wet track. He got credit for eighth place.

The race started out under gray skies and rain began falling after 85 laps. Officials determined the rain was not heavy enough to warrant a yellow flag, so the cars continued to race at top speed.

Pete Frazee, Modified champion at the half-mile facility, suffered engine problems in the early stages but came back to finish 15th in the field of 27.

Reed averaged 68.438 mph for his first Grand National win.

Grand National Race No. 13
150 Laps at Old Dominion Speedway
Manassas, VA
56.25-miles on .375-Mile Paved Track
April 25, 1958

Fin	St	No.	Driver	Team/Car	Laps	Money	Status
1	4	62	Frankie Schneider	'57 Chevrolet	150	$600	Running
2	3	47	Jack Smith	Smith '57 Chevrolet	150	475	Running
3	2	44	Rex White	Max Welborn '57 Chevrolet	148	355	Running
4	5	42	Lee Petty	Petty Engineering '57 Olds	148	280	Running
5	6	64	Johnny Allen	Spook Crawford '57 Plymouth	147	240	Running
6	11	88	Reds Kagle	'57 Chevrolet	146	215	Running
7	10	8	Elmo Langley	'56 Chevrolet	144	170	Running
8	9	11	Junior Johnson	Paul Spaulding '57 Ford	141	170	Running
9	15	54	Nace Mattingly	Mattingly '57 Ford	140	165	Running
10	14	888	Charles Hansen	Hanson '57 Chevrolet	139	155	Running
11	8	90X	Buz Woodward	'56 Ford	139	130	Running
12	13	25	Bailey Wynekoop	'56 Ford	138	120	Running
13	17	100	Jim Findley	'57 Chevrolet	137	120	Running
14	25	96	Bobby Keck	Keck '56 Chevrolet	134	115	Running
15	20	70	Jim Parsley	'56 Chevrolet	134	85	Running
16	19	74	L D Austin	Austin '56 Chevrolet	132	85	Running
17	21	900	Gus Wilson	'56 Chevrolet	130	75	Running
18	12	23	Harvey Henderson	Henderson '56 Ford	122	75	Bearing
19	1	45	Eddie Pagan	Pagan '57 Ford	120	100	Running
20	16	30	Don Gray	'57 Chevrolet	95	65	Heating
21	24	59	Blackie Pitt	Pitt '58 Studebaker	81	25	Heating
22	7	90	Emanuel Zervakis	Junie Donlavey '57 Chevrolet	39	25	Trans
23	23	123	Buzz Wilson	'56 Chevrolet	29	25	Ignition
24	22	28	Eddie Skinner	Skinner '57 Ford	10	25	Springs
25	18	X	Volney Schulze	'57 Chevrolet	10	25	Engine

Time of Race: 49 minutes, 56 seconds
Average Speed: 67.590
Pole Winner: Eddie Pagan - 69.018
Lap Leaders: ------------------ Frankie Schneider 45-150.
Cautions: Margin of Victory :   Attendance:

Race No. 14

Reed Sloshes to Victory
At Rainy Old Bridge

OLD BRIDGE, NJ (April 27) -- Jim Reed stormed out of the starting blocks, led for 85 laps then 'skated' to victory on a rain slickened track at Old Bridge

---

Grand National Race No. 14
200 Laps at Old Bridge Stadium
Old Bridge, NJ
100-miles on Half-mile Paved Track
April 27, 1958

Fin	St	No.	Driver	Team / Car	Laps	Money	Status
1	1	7	Jim Reed	Reed '57 Ford	187	$800	Running
2	4	45	Eddie Pagan	Pagan '57 Ford	186	525	Running
3	3	44	Rex White	J H Petty '57 Chevrolet	185	350	Running
4	6	62	Frankie Schneider	'57 Chevrolet	184	250	Running
5		8	Elmo Langley	'56 Chevrolet	184	225	Running
6	5	47	Jack Smith	Smith '57 Chevrolet	184	200	Running
7		11	Junior Johnson	Paul Spaulding '57 Ford	184	165	Running
8	2	42	Lee Petty	Petty Engineering '57 Olds	184	150	Crash
9		48	Ben Benz	'57 Chevrolet	180	140	Running
10		64	Johnny Allen	Spook Crawford '57 Plymouth	180	130	Running
11		100	Jim Findley	'57 Chevrolet	179	125	
12		90	Buzz Woodward	'56 Ford	177	110	
13		40	Frank Thompson	'57 Ford	172	100	
14		444	Axel Anderson	George Augustine '58 Pontiac	172	85	
15		41	Pete Frazee	'58 Ford	171	70	
16		74	L D Austin	Austin '56 Chevrolet	169	60	
17		30	Don Gray	'57 Chevrolet	169	50	
18		916	Dean Layfield	William Dickenson '58 Chevy	168	50	
19		X	John Lindsay	'56 Chevrolet	167	50	
20		900	Gus Wilson	'56 Chevrolet	163	50	
21		411	Barney Hatchell	'56 Chevrolet	155	50	
22		85	Carl Tyler	Tyler '57 Ford	132	50	
23		13	Peck Peckham	Peckham '56 Chevrolet	123	50	
24		70	Jim Parsley	'56 Chevrolet	121	50	
25		88	Reds Kagle	'57 Chevrolet	53	---	
26		888	Chuck Hansen	Hanson '57 Chevrolet	11	---	
27		59	Blackie Pitt	Pitt '58 Studebaker	8	---	

Time of Race: 1 hour, 21 minutes, 32 seconds.
Average Speed: 68.438 mph
Pole Winner: Jim Reed - 71.371 mph
Lap Leaders: Jim Reed 1-187.
Cautions: Margin of Victory: 1-lap-plus   Attendance: 5,000
* Race shortened to 187 laps due to rain

Race No. 15

Jack Smith Bags First Of Year at Greenville

GREENVILLE, SC (May 3) -- Jack Smith of Sandy Springs, GA moved to within 88 points of standings leader Lee Petty with a triumph in the 100-mile Grand National event at Greenville-Pickens Speedway. It was Smith's first win of the year and he became the 10th different winner in the 15 events staged in 1958.

Buck Baker finished in second place on the half-mile dirt oval. Junior Johnson came in third, Doug Cox was fourth and Eddie Pagan fifth.

Lee Petty was hounding Smith for first place most of the way, but a blown engine knocked his Oldsmobile from the hunt with 18 laps to go. He got credit for sixth place in the field of 19.

Curtis Turner, Cotton Owens, Speedy Thompson and Billy Carden, all regarded as pre-race favorites, fell out of the race. Fourteen cars finished the 100-miler.

Race No. 16

Hometown Favorite Welborn Grabs Greensboro Victory

GREENSBORO, NC (May 11) -- Bob Welborn fended off Jack Smith in an early duel then sprinted to an easy victory in the 50-mile Grand National event at the Central Carolina Fairgrounds. It was Welborn's third Grand National win of the year and his sixth in the last eight starts including Convertible races.

Car owner Julian Petty with Bob Welborn.

Lee Petty finished in second place and moved to a 192-point lead in the driver standings. Junior Johnson took third place money, Speedy Thompson was fourth and

Grand National Race No. 15
200 Laps at Greenville-Pickens
Speedway
Greenville, SC
100 Miles on Half-mile Dirt Track
May 3, 1958

Fin	St	No	Driver	Team / Car	Laps	Money	Status
1	1	47	Jack Smith	Smith '57 Chevrolet	200	$800	Running
2	3	87	Buck Baker	Baker '57 Chevrolet	199	525	Running
3	15	11	Junior Johnson	Paul Spaulding '57 Ford	197	350	Running
4	2	30	Doug Cox	'57 Ford	196	250	Running
5	4	45	Eddie Pagan	Pagan '57 Ford	192	225	Running
6	6	42	Lee Petty	Petty Engineering '57 Olds	183	200	Engine
7	19	37	Tiny Lund	Don Angel '56 Ford	183	165	Running
8	9	57	Billy Rafter	Rafter '57 Ford	181	150	Running
9	17	96	Bobby Keck	Keck '57 Chevrolet	178	140	Running
10	11	74	L D Austin	Austin '56 Chevrolet	171	130	Running
11	12	94	Clarence DeZalia	DeZalia '56 Ford	169	125	Running
12	16	64	Johnny Allen	Spook Crawford '57 Plymouth	165	110	Running
13	14	19	Herman Beam	Beam '57 Chevrolet	158	100	Running
14	13	67	Spook Crawford	Crawford '57 Plymouth	152	85	Running
15	10	33	George Green	Green '57 Chevrolet	132	70	Running
16	8	9	Billy Carden	Bishop Bros. '57 Chevrolet	88	60	Rear End
17	7	46	Speedy Thompson	Thompson '57 Chevrolet	87	50	Trans
18	5	6	Cotton Owens	Stephens '57 Pontiac	84	50	Axle
19	18	2	Curtis Turner	'58 Ford	81	50	Heating

Time of Race: 1 hour, 36 minutes, 19 seconds
Average Speed: 62.295 mph
Pole Winner: Jack Smith - 60.484 mph
Lap Leaders: - - - - - - - - - - Jack Smith -200.
Cautions: Margin of Victory: 1-lap-plus   Attendance:

Grand National Race No. 16
150 Laps at Central Carolina
Fairgrounds
Greensboro, NC
50 Miles on .333-mile Dirt Track
May 11, 1958

Fin	St	No	Driver	Team / Car	Laps	Money	Status
1	1	44	Bob Welborn	J H Petty '57 Chevrolet	150	$600	Running
2	3	42	Lee Petty	Petty Engineering '57 Olds	149	500	Running
3	11	11	Junior Johnson	Paul Spaulding '57 Ford	148	355	Running
4	5	46	Speedy Thompson	Thompson '57 Chevrolet	147	260	Running
5	4	30	Doug Cox	'57 ford	147	240	Running
6	6	87	Buck Baker	Baker '57 Chevrolet	145	220	Running
7	8	52	Eddie Pagan	Bob Walden '57 Ford	143	185	Running
8	14	57	Billy Rafter	Rafter '57 Ford	142	170	Running
9	12	74	L D Austin	Austin '56 Chevrolet	137	165	Running
10	19	32	Brownie King	Jess Potter '57 Chevrolet	136	160	Running
11	17	19	Herman Beam	Beam '57 Chevrolet	135	130	Running
12	7	48	Possum Jones	J H Petty '57 Chevrolet	134	120	Carb.
13	18	94	Clarence DeZalia	DeZalia '56 Ford	133	100	Running
14	10	17	Fred Harb	Harb '57 Mercury	131	115	Running
15	13	96	Bobby Keck	Keck '56 Chevrolet	130	90	Running
16	20	63	R L Combs	'56 Ford	130	90	Running
17	15	33	George Green	Green '57 Chevrolet	85	85	Gas Line
18	16	10	E J Brewer	'56 Ford	61	60	Engine
19	2	47	Jack Smith	Smith '57 Chevrolet	57	75	Spindle
19	9	81	Harvey Hege	Hege '56 Ford	50	65	Radiator

Time of Race: 1 hour, 5 minutes, 41 seconds
Average Speed: 45.628 mph
Pole Winner: Bob Welborn - 46.250 mph
Lap Leaders: Jack Smith 1-25, Bob Welborn 26-150.
Cautions: Margin of Victory: 1 lap plus   Attendance:

fifth place went to Doug Cox.

Smith led the first 25 laps on the .333-mile dirt track. Welborn took the lead on lap 26 and led the rest of the way. Smith was challenging Welborn for top honors when his Chevrolet broke a spindle on lap 57. He wound up 19th in the field of 20.

Welborn won $600 for his 45.628 mph victory.

Race No. 17

Reed's Ford First at Starkey Speedway

ROANOKE, VA (May 15) -- Jim Reed, five-time Short Track champion, proved he is among the best on small ovals with a flag-to-flag victory in the 150-lapper at Starkey Speedway. It was Reed's second win of the year.

Reed started on the pole and led all the way in the 37.5-mile Grand National event. Rex White chased Reed for the entire distance but had to settle for second

Jim Reed bagged 2nd Grand National win at Roanoke, VA.

place. Eddie Pagan finished third, Frankie Schneider was fourth and Curtis Turner fifth.

Turner, suffering from a dislocated disc in his back, was determined to perform before his hometown fans. Driving a Holman - Moody Ford, Turner won the first heat race but was never a factor in the feature. Following the event, crew members had to lift him out of the car.

There was little passing in the 45 minute contest. The first 10 starters gained the top 10 finishing positions.

Reed averaged 49.504 mph in his Ford on the quarter mile track.

Grand National Race No. 17
150 Laps at Starkey Speedway
Roanoke, VA
37.5-Miles on Quarter-mile Paved Track
May 15, 1958

Fin	St	No.	Driver	Team / Car	Laps	Money	Status
1	1	7	Jim Reed	Reed '57 Ford	150	$550	Running
2	3	44	Rex White	J H Petty '57 Chevrolet	150	450	Running
3	2	45	Eddie Pagan	Pagan '57 Ford	149	325	Running
4	4	62	Frankie Schneider	'57 Chevrolet	148	250	Running
5	5	26	Curtis Turner	Holman - Moody '58 Ford	148	215	Running
6	6	21	Glen Wood	Wood Brothers '57 Ford	148	190	Running
7	7	42	Lee Petty	Petty Engineering '57 Olds	148	170	Running
8	9	47	Jack Smith	Smith '57 Chevrolet	147	150	Running
9	10	99	Shorty Rollins	Rollins '58 Ford	147	150	Running
10	8	87	Buck Baker	Baker '57 Chevrolet	147	140	Running
11	12	57	Billy Rafter	Rafter '57 Ford	144	130	Running
12	18	34	Joe Weatherly	Dick Beaty '57 Ford	144	120	Running
13	13	17	Fred Harb	Harb '57 Mercury	143	100	Running
14	21	48	Possum Jones	J H Petty '57 Chevrolet	142	100	Running
15	14	888	Chuck Hansen	Hanson '57 Chevrolet	139	75	Running
16	22	96	Bobby Keck	Keck '56 Chevrolet	134	75	Running
17	20	33	George Green	Green '57 Chevrolet	133	75	Running
18	19	74	L D Austin	Austin '56 Chevrolet	131	50	Running
19	15	81	Hervey Hege	Hege '56 Ford	131	50	Running
20	17	70	Jim Parsley	'56 Chevrolet	127	50	Tires
21	11	144	Ken Rush	J H Petty '57 Chevrolet	115	25	Piston
22	16	53	Carl Burris	'57 Ford	20	25	H Gasket

Time of Race: 45 minutes, 27 seconds
Average Speed: 49.504 mph
Pole Winner: Jim Reed - 51.963 mph
Lap Leades: Jim Reed 1-150.
Cautions: Margin of Victory: Attendance:

Race No. 18

Johnson Ends Three Year Drought With Wilkesboro Win

N.WILKESBORO, NC (May 18) -- Junior Johnson scored his first win in three years with a narrow triumph in the 100-miler at North Wilkesboro Speedway. It was Johnson's sixth win on NASCAR's pre-

Junior Johnson takes checkered flag at North Wilkesboro.

mier stock car racing circuit, but his first since July 29, 1955 when he won at Altamont, NY.

Johnson grabbed the lead from Jack Smith in the 79th lap of the 160-lapper and led the rest of the way to stake claim to the $800 first prize. His Paul Spaulding Ford was 6.0 seconds ahead of Smith when the checkered flag fell.

Eddie Pagan's Ford left the track in practice at North Wilkesboro and broke down the wooden fence. He came back to finish 5th in the 100-miler.

Rex White took third place with Buck Baker fourth and Eddie Pagan fifth. Pagan came back from a practice mishap in which his Ford plowed through the wooden fence.

The race was originally scheduled three weeks earlier, but rain forced postponement. Speedy Thompson had won the pole but did not return on the rescheduled date. Qualifying trials were held again and Smith won

the pole at 82.056 mph. Since the entire program was rescheduled, Thompson lost credit for winning the pole on the original race date.

Johnson had a half lap lead in the closing stages. He also blew it when he went into the third turn too hard and went over the embankment. The Ronda, NC charger held the throttle down, ran through some high weeds and managed to get back on the track just ahead of Smith.

A crowd of 5,800 watched Johnson average 78.636 mph for the 100-miles.

Race No. 19

Welborn Class of the Field At Winston-Salem

WINSTON-SALEM, NC (May 24) -- Bob Welborn skimmed past Rex White in the 102nd lap and went on to score his fourth win of the season in the 37.5-mile Grand National event at Bowman Gray Stadium.

Welborn started 10th on the grid, but his Chevrolet was the class of the field. It took the Summerfield, NC driver just 25.5-miles to get to the front on the tight quarter-mile oval.

White finished in second place after starting on the pole. He led for the first 101 laps.

Jim Reed wound up third in his Ford. Rookie Fred Harb finished a strong fourth and Barney Shore was fifth.

Point leader Lee Petty started third but his Oldsmobile suffered engine failure after 49 laps. He wound up 23rd in the field of 24. He still managed to come away with a 128 point lead over Jack Smith, who also departed early.

Eleven of the cars, including six of the top 10 finishers, were Convertible cars with Grand National hardtops bolted in place. The drivers of the Convertible cars did not earn points. Welborn was one of those, so he stood still in the Grand National point chase.

Eddie Pagan started on the front row but wrecked his Ford after 77 laps. Another top contender, Buck Baker, left the race early with rear end problems.

Welborn averaged 40.407 mph for his fifth career Grand National win.

Grand National Race No. 18
160 Laps at N. Wilkesboro Speedway
North Wilkesboro, NC
100 Miles on .625-Mile Paved Track
May 18 , 1958

Fin	St	No	Driver	Team / Car	Laps	Money	Status
1	3	11	Junior Johnson	Paul Spaulding '57 Ford	160	$800	Running
2	1	47	Jack Smith	Smith '57 Chevrolet	160	525	Running
3	6	44	Rex White	J H Petty '57 Chevrolet	160	350	Running
4	9	87	Buck Baker	Baker '57 Chevrolet	159	250	Running
5	4	45	Eddie Pagan	Pagan '57 Ford	157	225	Running
6	7	6	Cotton Owens	Jim Stephens '57 Pontiac	155	200	Running
7	13	26	Curtis Turner	Holman - Moody '58 Ford	154	165	Running
8	15	30	Doug Cox	'57 Ford	154	150	Running
9	11	21	Glen Wood	Wood Brothers '57 Ford	152	140	Running
10	10	99	Shorty Rollins	Rollins '58 Ford	152	135	Running
11	2	42	Lee Petty	Petty Engineering '57 Olds	151	125	Running
12	12	19	Herman Beam	Beam '57 Chevrolet	148	110	Running
13	17	17	Fred Harb	Harb '57 Mercury	147	100	Running
14	5	46	Speedy Thompson	Thompson '57 Chevrolet	145	85	Running
15	14	32	Brownie King	Jess Potter '57 Chevrolet	142	70	Running
16	16	96	Bobby Keck	Keck '56 Chevrolet	139	60	Running
17	18	70	Jim Parsley	'56 Chevrolet	132	50	Running
18	22	711	Bill Poor	Poor '56 Chevrolet	125	50	Running
19	23	81	Harvey Hege	'56 Ford	118	50	Running
20	20	33	George Green	Jess Potter '57 Chevrolet	115	50	Running
21	19	202	John Gardner	'56 Ford	111	50	Accel.
22	8	41	Whitey Norman	'57 Chevrolet	110	50	Engine
23	21	74	L D Austin	Austin '56 Chevrolet	105	50	Running
24	24	10	Cecil Grubbs*	'56 Ford	79	50	Engine

Time of Race: 1 hour, 16 minutes, 18 seconds
Average Speed: 78.636 mph
Pole Winner: Jack Smith - 82.056 mph
Lap Leaders: Jack Smith 1-3, Lee Petty 4-41, Smith 42-78, Junior Johnson 79-160.
Cautions: Margin of Victory: 6.0 seconds   Attendance: 5,800
*Relieved by E J Brewer.

Grand National Race No. 19
150 Laps at Bowman Gray Stadium
Winston-Salem, NC
37.5-miles on .25-Mile Paved Track
May 24, 1958

Fin	St	No	Driver	Team / Car	Laps	Money	Status
1	10	49	Bob Welborn	J H Petty '57 Chevrolet	150	$600	Running
2	1	44	Rex White	J H Petty '57 Chevrolet	150	475	Running
3	6	7	Jim Reed	Reed '57 Ford	150	355	Running
4	4	17	Fred Harb	Harb '57 Mercury	149	275	Running
5	8	97	Barney Shore	Shore '57 Chevrolet	148	230	Running
6	7	44A	Ken Rush	J H Petty '57 Chevrolet	147	240	Running
7	5	21	Glen Wood	Wood Brothers '57 Ford	146	185	Running
8	11	6	Cotton Owens	Jim Stephens '57 Pontiac	146	170	Running
9	14	14	George Dunn	Manley Britt '57 Mercury	144	150	Running
10	24	67	Shorty Rollins	'56 Pontiac	144	170	Running
11	21	52	Paul Walton	Walden '57 Ford	144	130	Running
12	18	96	Bobby Keck	Keck '56 Chevrolet	143	135	Running
13	23	32	Brownie King	Jess Potter '57 Chevrolet	141	100	Running
14	16	66	Roy Tyner	Spook Crawford '57 Plymouth	139	100	Running
15	20	711	Bill Poor	Poor '56 Chevrolet	139	75	Running
16	22	33	George Green	Jess Potter '57 Chevrolet	136	90	Running
17	19	81	Harvey Hege	Hege '56 Ford	132	85	Running
18	15	19	Herman Beam	Beam '57 Chevrolet	126	60	Running
19	17	78	Shep Langdon	Langdon '56 Ford	116	50	Running
20	13	64	Johnny Allen	Spook Crawford '57 Plymouth	101	65	Heating
21	2	37	Eddie Pagan	Don Angel '56 Ford	77	45	Crash
22	12	48	Jack Smith	Smith '57 Chevrolet	68	35	Bearing
23	3	42	Lee Petty	Petty Engineering '57 Olds	49	25	Engine
24	9	87	Buck Baker	Baker '57 Chevrolet	8	40	Rear End

Time of Race: 55 minutes, 41 seconds
Average Speed: 40.407 mph
Pole Winner: Rex White - 46.851 mph
Lap Leaders: Rex White 1-101, Bob Welborn 102-150.
Cautions: Margin of Victory: Attendance:

Race No. 20

Roberts Gets First '58 Win In Northern 500 at Trenton

TRENTON, NJ (May 30) -- Fireball Roberts motored into the lead in the 121st lap and breezed to an easy victory in the Northern 500 Memorial Day event at the New Jersey State Fairgrounds. It was Roberts' first win of the year and the 15th of his career. The 500-lapper on the one-mile oval was also the third superspeedway win for the Daytona Beach Chevrolet driver.

Junior Johnson, who led for 20 laps before Roberts took over for good, finished second, two laps behind. Third place went to Lee Petty, who was eight laps back. Jim Reed and Eddie Pagan rounded out the top five.

Frankie Schneider had earned the pole position, but withdrew from the $26,000 event and was suspended indefinitely by sanctioning NASCAR. Executive

Manager Pat Purcell said the Lambertville, NJ hot-shot was suspended for "actions detrimental to the best interests of stock car racing and for unsportsmanlike conduct." Purcell added that Schneider had requested a large sum of "appearance" money and when it was refused, he pulled his Chevrolet out of the garage.

A crowd of 12,582 showed up on the hot summer-like day and watched Roberts set a stock car record of 84.522

Frankie Schneider was suspended by NASCAR after Trenton episode.

Grand National Race No. 20
500 Laps at New Jersey State
Fairgrounds
Trenton, NJ
"Northern 500"
500 Miles on 1-Mile Paved Track
May 30, 1958

Fin	St	No	Driver	Team / Car	Laps	Money	Status
1	17	22	Fireball Roberts	Frank Strickland '57 Chevrolet	500	$6,500	Running
2	3	11	Junior Johnson	Paul Spaulding '57 Ford	498	3,160	Running
3	15	42	Lee Petty	Petty Engineering '57 Olds	492	2,125	Running
4	9	7	Jim Reed	Reed '57 Ford	489	1,510	Running
5	14	45	Eddie Pagan	Pagan '57 Ford	488	1,225	Running
6	19	87	Buck Baker	Baker '57 Chevrolet	488	800	Running
7	8	99	Shorty Rollins	Rollins '58 Ford	478	775	Running
8	20	12	Joe Weatherly	Holman - Moody '58 Ford	477	625	Running
9	2	46	Speedy Thompson	Thompson '57 Chevrolet	475	650	Running
10	7	198	Jimmy Massey	John Whitford '57 Ford	458	500	Running
11	30	30	Herb Estes	Estes '57 Ford	457	425	Running
12	18	26	Curtis Turner	Holman - Moody '58 Ford	455	325	Running
13	32	8	Elmo Langley	'57 Chevrolet	454	275	Running
14	26	4	Johnny Mackison	Camp Hill Spl. '57 Ford	452	270	Engine
15	31	888	Chuck Hansen	Hanson '57 Chevrolet	451	250	Running
16	33	9	Buzz Woodward	'57 Chevrolet	450	225	Running
17	11	50	Mario Rossi	'57 Chevrolet	449	200	Running
18	29	13	Peck Peckham	Peckham '56 Chevrolet	391	200	Running
19	13	66	Jerry Draper	'56 Plymouth	371	200	Piston
20	10	41	Pete Frazee	'58 Ford	346	240	H Gasket
21	28	33	Al White	'58 Ford	317	150	RF Hub
22	21	72	John Dodd, Sr.	'58 Ford	290	150	Crash
23	1	98	Marvin Panch	John Whitford '57 Ford	254	180	Clutch
24	4	90	Emanuel Zervakis	Junie Donlavey '58 Chevy	220	190	Engine
25	25	60	Jim Rhoades	'58 Chevrolet	208	150	RF Hub
26	16	3	Cotton Owens	Jim Stephens '57 Pontiac	196	150	Valve
27	12	88	Jim Linke	Petty Engineering '57 Olds	195	100	Engine
28	24	74	L D Austin	Austin '56 Chevrolet	141	100	Piston
29	5	5	Mel Larson	Larson '57 Mercury	138	100	Rear End
30	6	27	Charlie Cregar	Cregar '57 Ford	127	100	Engine
31	23	28	Reds Kagle	'57 Ford	93	100	Engine
32	34	93	Jack Russell	'56 Chevrolet	74	100	Electrical
33	22	47	Jack Smith	Smith '57 Chevrolet	63	100	Engine
34	27	78	Frank Lies	'58 Ford	33	100	Engine

Time of Race: 5 hours, 54 minutes, 56 seconds
Average Speed: 84.522 mph
Pole Winner: Marvin Panch - 89.02 mph
Fastest Qualifier: Speedy Thompson - 89.933 mph
Lap Leaders: Marvin Panch 1-59, Speedy Thompson 60-100, Junior Johnson 101-120, Fireball Roberts 121-500.
Cautions: 3 for 15 laps   Margin of Victory: 2-laps plus   Attendance: 12,582

Fireball Roberts blazes down the front chute at Trenton. The Daytona Beach, FL driver won the 500-miler on the 1-mile superspeedway by 2 laps.

mph on the one-mile track. He collected $6,500 as three cautions slowed the action for 15 laps.

Charlie Cregar purchased a Smokey Yunick Ford and ran as high as second before departing with a blown engine after 127 laps.

Marvin Panch started on the pole and led for 59 laps. Clutch problems put his Ford out after 254 miles.

Race No 21

Eddie Gray Nabs Crown America 500 at Riverside

RIVERSIDE, CA (June 1) -- Eddie Gray of Gardena, CA, who had earned most of his racing laurels in Jalopy cars, cashed in on the biggest prize of his career by taking the Crown America 500 at Riverside International Raceway.

Eddie Gray won Riverside 500-miler.

Promoters Galard Sloanaker and Charles Curryer staged a trio of 500 mile events at the 2.631-mile road cours and lost about $50,000 on the fiasco.

Parnelli Jones won the pole and led the first 147 laps. But the Torrance, CA driver crashed his Ford in turn six, allowing Gray to take the lead.

Gray started sixth on the grid and stayed in contention for the entire endless afternoon. It took over six hours to complete the 500 miles.

Lloyd Dane finished second, a mile and a half behind Gray's winning Ford. Jack Smith finished third, Lee Petty was fourth and Bob Keefe came in fifth.

The event was open to foreign cars and Bill Jones, driving a Citreon came in 18th to lead the four overseas entries.

A crowd of 4,000 was on hand to watch Gray triumph at an average speed of 79.481 mph.

Grand National Race No. 21
190 Laps at Riverside International Raceway
Riverside, CA
"Crown America 500"
500 Miles on 2.631-mile Paved Road Course
June 1, 1958

Fin	St	No.	Driver	Team / Car	Laps	Money	Status
1	6	98	Eddie Gray	'57 Ford	190	$3,225	Running
2	5	44	Lloyd Dane	'58 Ford	190	1,850	Running
3	40	47	Jack Smith	Smith '58 Pontiac	186	1,375	Running
4	4	42	Lee Petty	Petty Engineering '57 Olds	184	1,100	Running
5	44	15	Bob Keefe	'56 Ford	181	725	Running
6	43	22	Jack D McCoy	'56 Ford	181	550	Running
7	15	46	Otis Skinner	'56 Ford	178	325	Running
8	17	3	Scotty Cain	'56 Mercury	176	275	Running
9	14	21	Dave James	'56 Chevrolet	169	200	Running
10	45	45	Paul Aars	'56 Ford	168	200	Running
11	24	10	Lucky Long	'57 Chevrolet	167	250	Running
12	46	38	Jack Round	'57 Chevrolet	167	150	Running
13	36	12	Mike Batinick	'57 Ford	166	140	Running
14	20	22N	Art Watts	'56 Ford	165	140	Diff
15	8	37	Ernie Young	'57 Pontiac	165	130	Running
16	27	36	Bill Oldson	'56 Ford	162	130	Running
17	39	47W	George Norton	'56 Chevrolet	162	120	Running
18	31	100	Bill Jones	'58 Citreon	160	195	Running
19	30	101	Ralph Robert	'58 Citreon	160	120	Running
20	35	5	Jim Cook	'57 Ford	160	120	Running
21	19	7	Jim Reed	Reed '57 Ford	158	110	Crash
22	21	17	Bill Thorp	'56 Ford	154	110	Running
23	26	55	Chuck Townsen	'56 Ford	152	110	Running
24	41	85	Kirby Miller	'56 Ford	152	110	Running
25	3	4	Bill Boldt	'56 Ford	151	110	Crash
26	1	97	Parnelli Jones	Vel Miletich '56 Ford	147	110	Crash
27	32	102	Danny Eames	'58 Goliath	147	185	Running
28	38	9	Bob Price	'56 Chevrolet	145	110	Running
29	7	82	Marshall Sargent	'57 Chevrolet	135	110	Running
30	12	75	Jim McCorkindale	'56 Mercury	120	110	Rods
31	18	31	Bob Perry	'56 Chrysler	120	100	Unknown
32	16	43	Bill Mitchell	'56 Mercury	107	100	Cam Shft
33	25	29	Bill Hasley	'56 Mercury	103	100	Engine
34	11	95	Peck Markota	'56 Mercury	98	100	Heating
35	2	57	Danny Graves	'57 Chevrolet	66	100	Con Rod
36	33	106	Hilan Micka	'58 Renault	66	150	Piston
37	23	18	Ruben Thrash	'57 Chevrolet	42	100	Engine
38	28	20	Eddie Pagan	'56 Chevrolet	36	100	Trans
39	20	65	Bob Ross	'56 Chevrolet	35	100	Con Rod
40	29	99	Marvin Porter	Porter '57 Ford	32	100	Cam Shft
41	37	11	Owen Loggins	'58 Plymouth	25	175	Con Rod
42	42	42W	Jim Dunn	'57 Pontiac	21	100	Con Rod
43	22	66	Bob Osborne	'56 Chevrolet	16	100	Engine
44	29	16	Bill Jarick	'56 Ford	16	100	Gasket
45	13	2	Ron Hornaday	'56 Chevrolet	4	100	Clutch
46	9	33	Arley Scranton	'57 Pontiac	0	100	Crash

Time of Race: 6 hour, 17 minutes
Average Speed: 79.481 mph
Pole Winner: Parnelli Jones - 85.569 mph
Lap Leaders: Parnelli Jones 1-147, Eddie Gray 148-190.
Cautions: Margin of Victory: 1 1/2 miles   Attendance: 4,000

Race No. 22

Johnson Wins Columbia by 8 Laps

COLUMBIA, SC (June 5) -- Junior Johnson drove an uncharacteristically cautious race, avoiding a number of wrecks, and cruised to an eight lap victory at Columbia Speedway. It was the second Grand National win of the year for the Ronda, NC Ford driver.

Johnson started sixth and did not move into the lead until the 156th lap of the 200 lap contest on the half-mile dirt track. George Dunn wound up second and Fred Harb was third. Wilbur Rakestraw finished fourth and Short Rollins was fifth.

Eight caution flags reduced Johnson's winning speed to 54.752 mph.

Pole sitter Buck Baker led the first 70 laps, but frequent pit stops relegated the two-time Grand National champ to an 18th place finish in the field of 23. Jack Smith took the lead on lap 71 and appeared to be heading for a runaway victory when the fan belt slipped off the engine of his Chevrolet on lap 155. He made a

seven minute pit stop and came back to finish sixth.

Bennie Rakestraw finished eighth, but officials disqualified his Mercury after a post race inspection.

Point leader Lee Petty was involved in a 67th lap crash with Marvin Panch, but continued to a ninth place finish. He held a 202 point lead over Smith after 22 events.

Junior Johnson won 100-miler at Columbia by 8 laps.

Grand National Race No. 22
200 Laps at Columbia Speedway
Columbia, SC
100 Miles on Half-mile Dirt Track
June 5, 1958

Fin	St	No.	Driver	Team /Car	Laps	Money	Status
1	6	11	Junior Johnson	Paul Spaulding '57 Ford	200	$800	Running
2	8	14	George Dunn	Manley Britt '57 Mercury	192	525	Running
3	14	17	Fred Harb	Harb '57 Mercury	192	350	Running
4	20	999	Wilbur Rakestraw	Joe Jones '57 Ford	190	250	Running
5	12	67	Shorty Rollins	Spook Crawford '57 Plymouth	189	225	Running
6	4	47	Jack Smith	Smith '57 Chevrolet	185	200	Running
7	10	96	Bobby Keck	Keck '57 Chevrolet	184	165	Running
8	13	125	J V Hamby	Leland Colvin '56 Chevrolet	180	150	Running
9	21	42	Lee Petty	Petty Engineering '57 Olds	173	140	Running
10	17	94	Clarence DeZalia	DeZalia '56 Ford	171	130	Running
11	5	46	Speedy Thompson	Thompson '57 Chevrolet	165	125	Spindle
12	9	2	Bobby Lee	Horne Motors '58 Ford	163	110	Running
13	16	78	Shep Langdon	Langdon '56 Ford	160	100	Running
14	19	33	George Green	Jess Potter '56 Chevrolet	154	85	Running
15	7	39	Billy Carden	Bishop Bros. '57 Chevrolet	151	70	Crash
16	15	74	L D Austin	Austin '56 Chevrolet	150	50	Running
17	2	45	Eddie Pagan	Pagan '57 Ford	133	50	Running
18	1	87	Buck Baker	Baker '56 Chevrolet	118	50	Running
19	3	98	Marvin Panch	John Whitford '57 Ford	67	50	Crash
20	23	30	Doug Cox	'57 Ford	39	50	Crank
21	18	711	Bill Poor	Poor '57 Chevrolet	26	50	H Gasket
22	11	202	John Gardner	'56 Ford	11	50	Spindle
23	22	12	Bennie Rakestraw	Talmadge Cochrane '57 Merc	183	---	Disq.

Time of Race: 1 hour, 49 minutes, 35 seconds
Average Speed: 54.752 mph
Pole Winner: Buck Baker - 64.308 mph
Lap Leaders: Buck Baker 1-70, Jack Smith 71-155, Junior Johnson 156-200.
Cautions: 8   Margin of Victory: 8-laps-plus   Attendance:

Race No. 23

Johnson Wins at Bradford; Three Drivers Disqualified

BRADFORD, PA (June 12) -- Junior Johnson bagged his second straight win in the 50-mile event at Bradford Speedway. The 150-lap Grand National race was the grand opening for the .333-mile dirt track.

Lee Petty finished second and pole sitter Bob Duell was third. Fourth place went to Jack Smith and Billy Rafter was fifth.

Three drivers were disqualified in a post race inspection. Dean Layfield, Squirt Johns and Emory Mahan were all placed at the rear of the order with no pay as NASCAR began a crack-down on rule benders. It was the second race in a row in which at least one driver has been disqualified.

Jim Reed started eighth but got caught up in an opening lap scramble on a congested start. He stuffed his Ford into the wall and had to retire from the race.

Buck Baker, winner of the 1956 and 1957 NASCAR Grand National championships, has had a run of sout luck in the 1958 season. He started third at Bradford, but fell out on lap 112 when his Chevrolet snapped a spindle.

Al White, Buffalo policeman, finished ninth in a Ford.

Johnson's eighth career Grand National win came at an average speed of 59.840 mph.

Grand National Race No. 23
150 Laps at New Bradford Speedway
Bradford, PA
50 Miles on .333-mile Dirt Track
June 12, 1958

Fin	St	No.	Driver	Team / Car	Laps	Money	Status
1	6	11	Junior Johnson	Paul Spaulding '57 Ford	150	$550	Running
2	4	42	Lee Petty	Petty Engineering '57 Olds	150	450	Running
3	1	95	Bob Duell	Julian Buesink '57 Ford	148	325	Running
4	7	47	Jack Smith	Smith '57 Chevrolet	148	250	Running
5	13	57	Billy Rafter	'57 Ford	147	215	Running
6	2	46	Speedy Thompson	Thompson '57 Chevrolet	142	190	Running
7	9	45	Eddie Pagan	Pagan '57 Ford	140	170	Running
8	21	70	Jim Parsley	'56 Chevrolet	136	150	Running
9	17	3	Al White	'58 Ford	132	150	Running
10	11	93	Ted Chamberlain	Chamberlain '57 Chevrolet	130	140	Running
11	10	52	Bob Walden	Walden '57 Ford	125	130	Running
12	14	83	Lennie Page	'56 Ford	125	120	Running
13	20	13	Peck Peckham	Peckham '56 Ford	121	100	Running
14	15	80	Chuck Hansen	Hanson '57 Chevrolet	119	100	Running
15	3	87	Buck Baker	Baker '57 Chevrolet	112	75	Running
16	19	74	L D Austin	Austin '56 Chevrolet	42	75	Distr.
17	12	64	Johnny Allen	Spook Crawford '57 Plymouth	39	75	Heating
18	8	7	Jim Reed	Reed '57 Ford	1	60	Crash
19	16	916	Dean Layfield	William Dickenson '58 Chevy	---	---	Disq.
20	5	511	Squirt Johns	'57 Chevrolet	---	---	Disq.
21	18	8	Emory Mahan	'57 Chevrolet	---	---	Disq.

Time of Race: 50 minutes, 5 seconds.
Average Speed: 59.840 mph
Pole Winner: Bob Duell - 65.831 mph
Lap Leaders: - - - - - - - - - - Junior Johnson -150.
Cautions: Margin of Victory: Attendance:

Grand National Race No. 24
200 Laps at Reading Fairgrounds
Reading, PA
100 Miles on Half-Mile Dirt Track
June 15, 1958

Fin	St	No.	Driver	Team / Car	Laps	Money	Status
1	2	11	Junior Johnson	Paul Spaulding '57 Ford	200	$800	Running
2	3	45	Eddie Pagan	Pagan '57 Ford	200	525	Running
3	7	87	Buck Baker	Baker '57 Chevrolet	199	350	Running
4	4	42	Lee Petty	Petty Engineering '57 Olds	199	250	Running
5	1	46	Speedy Thompson	Thompson '57 Chevrolet	198	225	Running
6	24	90	Buzz Woodward	'57 Ford	190	200	Running
7	22	83	Lennie Page	'57 Ford	188	165	Running
8	23	52	Bob Walden	Walden '57 Ford	187	150	Running
9	17	70	Jim Parsley	'56 Ford	185	140	Running
10	13	50	Ben Benz	'57 Chevrolet	184	130	Running
11	8	23	Buzz Wilson	'57 Mercury	184	125	Running
12	18	69	Volney Schulze	'56 Ford	184	110	Running
13	25	3	Al White	'58 Ford	182	100	Running
14	9	57	Billy Rafter	'57 Ford	180	85	Running
15	16	64	Johnny Allen	Spook Crawford '57 Plymouth	176	70	Running
16	28	19	Dick Walters	Walters '56 Ford	164	60	Running
17	29	37	Bill Benson	'56 Mercury	154	50	Running
18	20	400	Bill Wimble	Lyle Sokoll '57 Ford	147	50	Running
19	12	79	Tiny Benson	'57 Chevrolet	135	50	Running
20	10	7	Jim Reed	Reed '57 Ford	125	50	Fuel pmp
21	5	47	Jack Smith	Smith '57 Chevrolet	122	50	Piston
22	11	123	Frank Thompson	'57 Chevrolet	108	50	Crash
23	26	13	Peck Peckham	Peckham '57 Ford	103	50	Spindle
24	21	5	Mel Larson	Larson '57 Mercury	77	50	Rear End
25	30	80	Chuck Hansen	Hanson '57 Chevrolet	75	---	Gas Tank
26	14	40	Johnny Mackison	Camp Hill Spl. '57 Ford	43	---	Rear End
27	6	41	Tommy Elliott	'58 Ford	40	---	Heating
28	27	93	Ted Chamberlain	Chamberlain '57 Chevrolet	40	---	RF Whee
29	15	74	L D Austlin	Austin '56 Chevrolet	19	---	Engine
30	19	30	Herb Estes	Estes '57 Ford	11	---	Brakes

Time of Race: 1 hour, 51 minutes, 36 seconds
Average Speed: 53.763 mph
Pole Winner: Speedy Thompson - 60.687 mph
Lap Leaders: Speedy Thompson 1-28, Junior Johnson 29-33, Eddie Pagan 34-77,
    Thompson 78-89, Buck Baker 90-115, Johnson 116-200.
Cautions: Margin of Victory: 10 car lengths   Attendance: 4,000

Race No. 24

Red-Hot Johnson Wins
Third in Row at Reading

READING, PA (June 15) -- Junior Johnson of Ronda, NC got hooked up just past the half-way point, throttled past Buck Baker in the 116th lap and held off Eddie Pagan's late surge to win the 100-mile event at the Reading Fairgrounds. It was the third win in a row for the burly chicken farmer.

Pagan finished second, 10 car lengths behind Johnson. Baker's Chevrolet came home third and Lee Petty was fourth. Fifth place went to Speedy Thompson.

Thompson started on the pole and led the first 28 laps. Johnson, who started second, led for five laps before Pagan roared to the front. Pagan, Thompson and Baker all swapped the lead before Johnson took the lead for good.

Jack Smith blew an engine after 122 laps and wound up 21st. Petty moved out to a commanding 1,122 point lead in the Grand National point standings.

A crowd of 4,000 watched Johnson win at an average speed of 53.763 mph.

Race No. 25

Petty Wins Third of Year
At New Oxford

NEW OXFORD, PA (June 25) -- Lee Petty continued his determined bid for the Grand National championship by winning the 100-miler at Lincoln Speedway. Buck Baker finished second, Bob Welborn was third, Shorty Rollins fourth and Reds Kagle fifth.

Ken Rush, the 1957 NASCAR Rookie of the Year, won his second career pole position, but could only manage a 12th place finish, 16 laps behind winner Petty.

Junior Johnson was bidding for his fourth straight win, but his day ended early. During an early caution period, Johnson tangled with Jack Smith. Johnson's

Lee Petty

Ford flipped over and was out of the race.

Curiously, Johnson relieved Smith and flipped his car in the first turn on lap 146. Johnson sat out the remainder of the race.

Jim Reed, Speedy Thompson and Johnny Allen also failed to finish.

Petty earned $800 for the 69.726 mph victory. It was his third win of the season.

Oldsmobile across the finish line a single car length ahead of Junior Johnson to win the 100-mile race at Hickory Speedway. Speedy Thompson came in third, right on Johnson's bumper.

Jack Smith finished fourth and leading rookie Shorty Rollins had another strong run that netted him fifth place.

The crowd of 10,000 was on its feet for the exciting finish. The three contenders toured the .4-mile dirt track in close quarters for the second half of the race.

Petty averaged 62.413 mph for his 34th career Grand National triumph.

Officials were forced to wave the red flag in the 25th lap when heavy dust conditions made driving unsafe. After utility trucks toured the .4-mile oval for 15 minutes, the race was restarted.

Curtis Turner started sixth in a Ford and ran 181 laps before he ran out of tires. He got credit for 24th place in the field of 31.

Grand National Race No. 25
200 Laps at Lincoln Speedway
New Oxford, PA
100 Miles on Half-Mile Dirt Track
June 25, 1958

Fin	St	No.	Driver	Team / Car	Laps	Money	Status
1	2	42	Lee Petty	Petty Engineering '57 Olds	200	$800	Running
2	3	87	Buck Baker	Baker '57 Chevrolet	200	525	Running
3	8	49	Bob Welborn	J H Petty '57 Chevrolet	199	350	Running
4	4	99	Shorty Rollins	Rollins '58 Ford	196	250	Running
5	26	88	Reds Kagle	' 57 Chevrolet	194	225	Running
6	9	45	Eddie Pagan	Pagan '57 Ford	193	200	Running
7	28	37	Jim Paschal	Don Angel '56 Ford	193	165	Running
8	15	57	Billy Rafter	Rafter '57 Ford	193	150	Running
9	13	52	Bob Walden	Walden '57 Ford	192	140	Running
10	12	5	Mel Larson	Larson '57 Mercury	192	130	Running
11	17	70	Rex White	'56 Chevrolet	187	125	Running
12	1	44	Ken Rush	J H Petty '57 Chevrolet	184	110	Running
13	16	96	Bobby Keck	Keck '57 Chevrolet	182	100	Running
14	18	74	L D Austin	Austin '56 Chevrolet	180	85	Running
15	23	881	Jim Linke	'57 Oldsmobile	178	70	Running
16	19	100	Jim Findley	'57 Chevrolet	169	60	Running
17	20	69	Volney Schulze	'56 Chevrolet	168	50	Running
18	27	64	Johnny Allen	Spook Crawford '57 Plymouth	168	50	Frame
19	6	7	Jim Reed	Reed '57 Ford	155	50	LF Hub
20	7	47	Jack Smith*	Smith '57 Chevrolet	146	50	Crash
21	24	13	Peck Peckham	Peckham '56 Chevrolet	92	50	Axle
22	21	123	Buzz Wilson	'56 Chevrolet	86	50	RF Hub
23	10	60	Troy Funk	'58 Chevrolet	64	50	Rear End
24	14	8	Elmo Langley	'57 Chevrolet	59	50	A Frame
25	30	50	Mario Rossi	'57 Chevrolet	52	20	RF Whee
26	22	46	Speedy Thompson	Thompson '57 Chevrolet	48	20	Brakes
27	25	93	Ted Chamberlain	Chamberlain '57 Chevrolet	41	20	Engine
28	11	40	Johnny Mackison	Camp Hill Spl '57 Ford	31	20	Trans
29	31	181	Jerry Benjamin	'56 Ford	26	10	Piston
30	29	170	Lucky Sawyer	'56 Ford	12	10	Oil Press
31	5	11	Junior Johnson	Paul Spaulding '57 Ford	3	20	Crash

Time of Race: 1 hour, 26 minutes, 3 seconds.
Average Speed: 69.726 mph
Pole Winner: Ken Rush - 82.796 mph
Lap Leaders: - - - - - - - - - - - Lee Petty -200.
Cautions: Margin of Victory: Attendance:

Race No. 26

Lee Edges Junior and Speedy In 3-Car Hickory Finish

HICKORY, NC (June 28) -- Lee Petty pushed his

Grand National Race No. 26
250 Laps at Hickory Speedway
Hickory, NC
100 Miles on .4-mile Dirt Track
June 28, 1958

Fin	St	No.	Driver	Team / Car	Laps	Money	Status
1	9	42	Lee Petty	Petty Engineering '57 Olds	250	$800	Running
2	10	11	Junior Johnson	Paul Spaulding '57 Ford	250	525	Running
3	1	46	Speedy Thompson	Thompson '57 Chevrolet	250	350	Running
4	4	47	Jack Smith	Smith '57 Chevrolet	248	250	Running
5	3	99	Shorty Rollins	Rollins '58 Ford	247	225	Running
6	2	87	Buck Baker	Baker '57 Chevrolet	246	200	Running
7	14	45	Eddie Pagan	Pagan '57 Ford	245	165	Running
8	19	6	Cotton Owens	Jim Stephens '57 Pontiac	244	150	Running
9	13	30	Doug Cox	'57 Ford	242	140	Running
10	5	25	Gene White	White '57 Chevrolet	242	130	Running
11	12	57	Billy Rafter	Rafter '57 Ford	237	125	Running
12	18	52	Johnny Allen	Bob Walden '57 Ford	235	110	Running
13	7	17	Fred Harb	Harb '57 Mercury	235	100	Running
14	25	37	Tiny Lund	Don Angel '56 Ford	232	85	Running
15	22	66	Roy Tyner	Spook Crawford '57 Plymouth	229	70	Running
16	20	202	Johnny Gardner	'56 Ford	218	60	Running
17	23	33	George Green	Jess Potter '56 Chevrolet	216	50	Running
18	24	74	L D Austin	Austin '56 Chevrolet	214	50	Running
19	29	48	Possum Jones	J H Petty '57 Chevrolet	207	50	Running
20	30	711	Bill Poor	Poor '57 Chevrolet	207	50	Running
21	17	19	Herman Beam	Beam '57 Chevrolet	197	50	Running
22	26	78	Shep Langdon	Langdon '56 Ford	194	50	Running
23	16	32	Brownie King	Jess Potter '56 Chevrolet	188	50	Steering
24	6	98	Curtis Turner	John Whitford '57 Ford	181	50	Tires
25	21	96	Bobby Keck	Keck '57 Chevrolet	160	25	Running
26	28	94	Clarence DeZalia	DeZalla '56 Ford	89	25	Spindle
27	11	49	Bob Welborn	J H Petty '57 Chevrolet	80	25	Axle
28	27	34	Red Kalajainen	'57 Chevrolet	68	25	
29	8	44	Ken Rush	J H Petty '57 Chevrolet	66	25	Engine
30	15	97	Barney Shore	Shore '57 Chevrolet	51	25	Trans
31	31	39	Billy Carden	Bishop Bros. '57 Chevrolet	48	---	Heating

Time of Race: 1 hour, 36 minutes, 8 seconds
Average Speed: 62.413 mph
Pole Winner: Speedy Thompson - 68.768 mph
Lap Leaders - - - - - - - - - - Lee Petty -250.
Cautions: 3 for 11 Laps   Margin of Victory: 1 car length   Attendance: 10,000

Race No. 27

White Ends Dry Spell With Asheville-Weaverville Win

WEAVERVILLE, NC (June 29) -- Rex White of Silver Spring, MD ended his seven month dry spell with a convincing victory in the 100-miler at Asheville-Weaverville Speedway. It was the first Grand National triumph for White since he bagged the 1958 season opener at Fayetteville, NC on Nov. 3, 1957.

Buck Baker, Speedy Thompson, Jim Paschal and Eddie Pagan rounded out the top five.

White started on the pole and led only two laps before Cotton Owens moved atop the leader board. Owens' lead was short lived as White was back on top by lap four. Owens drilled his Pontiac into the lead once again on lap five and had built up a slight lead over the next 35 miles.

White chased Owens until the 77th lap when the 5'4" Chevrolet driver grabbed the lead for good. Owens

eventually fell out after 172 laps with wheel bearing trouble.

A crowd of 9,000 jammed the grandstands to watch White average 73.892 mph.

Grand National Race No. 27
200 Laps at Asheville-Weaverville Speedway
Weaverville, NC
100 Miles on Half-mile Paved Track
June 29, 1958

Fin	St	No.	Driver	Team / Car	Laps	Money	Status
1	1	44	Rex White	J H Petty '57 Chevrolet	200	$800	Running
2	8	87	Buck Baker	Baker '57 Chevrolet	199	525	Running
3	4	46	Speedy Thompson	Thompson '57 Chevrolet	196	350	Running
4	9	4	Jim Paschal	J H Petty '57 Chevrolet	196	250	Running
5	10	45	Eddie Pagan	Pagan '57 Ford	196	225	Running
6	5	42	Lee Petty	Petty Engineering '57 Olds	196	200	Running
7	12	49	Bob Welborn	Julian Petty '57 Chevrolet	196	165	Running
8	6	16	Herb Estes	'58 Ford	192	150	Running
9	7	99	Shorty Rollins	Rollins '58 Ford	184	140	Running
10	15	19	Herman Beam	Beam '57 Chevrolet	182	130	Running
11	25	32	Brownie King	Jess Potter '57 Chevrolet	178	125	Running
12	3	11	Junior Johnson	Paul Spaulding '57 Ford	175	110	Crash
13	24	57	Billy Rafter	Rafter '57 Ford	173	100	Running
14	2	6	Cotton Owens	Jim Stephens '57 Pontiac	172	85	Bearing
15	11	25	Gene White	White '57 Chevrolet	171	70	Running
16	21	96	Bobby Keck	Keck '57 Chevrolet	169	60	Running
17	18	74	L D Austin	Austin '56 Chevrolet	159	50	Running
18	17	97	Barney Shore	Shore '57 Chevrolet	154	50	Rear End
19	22	66	Roy Tyner	Spook Crawford '57 Plymouth	103	50	Heating
20	16	202	Johnny Gardner	'56 Ford	92	50	Engine
21	13	30	Doug Cox	'57 Ford	85	50	Oil Press
22	23	48	Possum Jones	J H Petty '57 Chevrolet	54	50	H Gasket
23	20	711	Bill Poor	Poor '57 Chevrolet	48	50	Trans
24	19	33	George Green	Green '56 Chevrolet	33	50	Steering
25	14	47	Jack Smith	Smith '57 Chevrolet	28	---	Oil Press

Time of Race: 1 hour, 21 minutes 12 seconds
Average Speed: 73.892 mph
Pole Winner: Rex White - 76.857 mph
Lap Leaders: Rex White 1-2, Cotton Owens 3, White 4, Owens 5-76, White 77-200.
Cautions: Margin of Victory: 1-lap-plus   Attendance: 9,000

Race No. 28

Roberts Survives Late Scare; Wins Raleigh Sweepstakes 250

RALEIGH, NC (July 4) -- Fireball Roberts took the lead with 57 laps remaining, survived a late race scare and won his second 250-mile Sweepstakes race at Raleigh Speedway. It was Roberts' fourth win on a superspeedway, tying him with retired driver Herb Thomas for the most wins in major events on high-banked oval tracks.

Roberts finished a lap ahead of runner-up Buck Baker. Rex White took third place, Shorty Rollins was fourth and Speedy Thompson fifth.

Roberts had passed Baker in the 194th lap and was holding a comfortable one lap lead. With just 15 laps

Fireball Roberts won Independence Day Raleigh 250.

to go, Roberts hooked bumpers with Bob Welborn as the two darted high to avoid Bobby Keck's Chevrolet, which had just blown an engine. The two cars remained locked together until the pair reached the main straight. The cars separated and Roberts continued his way to the $3,800 pay-off.

Welborn finished seventh, three laps behind.

A crowd of 15,000 watched the lead change hands eight time among seven different drivers. One of the outstanding efforts was turned in by rookie Rollins, who led for 23 laps before having to make a pit stop. He was two laps off the pace when the race ended.

Cotton Owens won the pole and led the first 30 laps. But the Spartanburg, SC Pontiac driver succumbed to a broken crankshaft after 78 laps. He wound up 45th

in the final order.

Grand National hardtops swept the first six places. Welborn was the highest finisher of the 25 Convertibles that entered.

Victims of accidents on the one-mile banked oval were Curtis Turner, Fred Harb, Roy Tyner and Junior Johnson. There were no injuries.

Roberts averaged 73.691 mph as eight caution flags slowed the pace for 32 laps.

Race No. 29

Paschal Homers at McCormick Field; Petty Runs into Dugout

ASHEVILLE, NC (July 12) -- Jim Paschal, who has been in semi-retirement for most of the 1958 season, got a ride in Julian Petty's Chevrolet and scampered to a one car length victory at McCormick Field.

The High Point, NC driver was competing in only his fifth race in the 1958 season. Cotton Owens finished second. Rex White, who was tailing Paschal and Owens, encountered transmission problems with three laps to go and fell to a distant third. Lee Petty finished fourth and Jack Smith was fifth.

Petty was involved in an unusual accident in the preliminary heat race. The McCormick Field, which is located at a baseball park, provides a number of obstacles. One of them is a dugout, which Petty's Oldsmobile dived into after a bump from Owens.

Grand National Race No. 28
250 Laps at Raleigh Speedway
Raleigh, NC
"Raleigh 250"
250 Miles on 1-Mile Paved Track
July 4, 1958

Fin	St	No..	Driver	Team / Car	Laps	Money	Status
1	3	22	Fireball Roberts	Frank Strickland '57 Chevy GN	250	$3,800	Running
2	17	87	Buck Baker	Baker '57 Chevrolet GN	249	2,325	Running
3	5	44	Rex White	J H Petty '57 Chevy GN	248	1,575	Running
4	15	99	Shorty Rollins	Rollins '58 Ford GN	248	1,075	Running
5	21	46	Speedy Thompson	Thompson '57 Chevrolet GN	248	850	Running
6	7	42	Lee Petty	Petty Eng. '57 Olds GN	247	700	Running
7	4	49	Bob Welborn	J H Petty '57 Chevrolet C	247	625	Running
8	12	87A	Possum Jones	Buck Baker '57 Chevy C	246	575	Running
9	11	45	Eddie Pagan	Pagan '58 Ford GN	245	455	Running
10	8	4	Jim Paschal	J H Petty '57 Chevrolet C	245	425	Running
11	19	95	Bobby Johns	Shorty Johns '57 Chevy GN	243	400	Running
12	10	25	Gene White	White '57 Chevrolet GN	242	375	Running
13	2	21	Glen Wood	Wood Brothers '57 Ford C	242	325	Running
14	16	999	Wilbur Rakestraw	Joe Jones '57 Ford C	241	275	Running
15	9	95	Bob Duell	Julian Buesink '58 Ford GN	240	250	Running
16	36	41	E J Brewer	'57 Ford C	237	250	Running
17	45	19	Herman Beam	Beam '57 Chevrolet GN	235	250	Running
18	43	32	Brownie King	Jess Potter '57 Ford C	235	225	Running
19	40	98	Curtis Turner	John Whitford '58 Ford C	233	225	Crash
20	38	76	Larry Frank	Frank '57 Chevrolet C	233	220	Running
21	33	74	L D Austin	Austin '56 Chevrolet GN	233	210	Running
22	39	44A	Ken Rush	J H Petty '57 Chevy C	231	200	Running
23	26	711	Bill Poor	Poor '56 Chevrolet C	229	175	Running
24	29	57	Billy Rafter	Rafter '57 Chevrolet GN	227	150	Running
25	14	17	Fred Harb	Harb '57 Mercury C	222	140	Crash
26	24	78	Shep Langdon	Langdon '56 Ford C	220	100	Running
27	41	198	Joe Weatherly	Holman - Moody '57 Ford C	218	100	Running
28	22	66	Roy Tyner	Spook Crawford '58 Plym C	214	100	Crash
29	51	19A	James Jones	Jones '56 Ford C	212	100	Running
30	31	94	Clarence DeZalia	DeZalia '56 Ford GN	211	100	Running
31	30	96	Bobby Keck	Keck '57 Chevrolet GN	207	---	Engine
32	27	47	Jack Smith	Smith '58 Pontiac GN	203	---	Rear End
33	32	37	Bill Benson	'56 Mercury GN	200	---	Running
34	50	52	Bob Bullheimer	'57 Ford C	194	---	Running
35	48	23	Johnny Mackison	Ken Corman '57 Merc GN	190	---	H Gasket
36	42	202	Johnny Gardner	'56 Ford GN	180	---	Running
37	20	86	Neil Castles	Castles '56 Ford C	177	---	Gas Tank
38	25	40	Dave White	'58 Chevrolet GN	172	---	Rear End
39	6	14	George Dunn	Manley Britt '57 Mercury C	157	---	Running
40	34	5	Mel Larson	Larson '57 Mercury GN	139	---	Rear End
41	37	56	Bill Morton	James Lowery '57 Ford C	133	---	Rear End
42	49	97	Barney Shore	Shore '57 Chevrolet C	126	---	Piston
43	54	56A	Cannonball Brown	Brown '56 Chrysler C	93	---	Running
44	55	36	Herb Estes	Estes '56 Ford C	85	---	Engine
45	1	3	Cotton Owens	Jim Stephens '58 Pont GN	78	---	Crank
46	46	31	Johnny Allen	Monroe Shook '58 Chevy GN	56	---	RF Hub
47	28	81	Harvey Hege	Hege '57 Ford C	51	---	Piston
48	35	400	Bob Malzahn	'57 Ford C	33	---	Bearing
49	44	55	Tiny Lund	Brushy Mtn Motors '57 Pont GN	27	---	D Shaft
50	52	88	Jim Linke	Petty Eng '57 Oldsmobile GN	24	--	H Gasket
51	53	111	Dick Parran	'56 Ford GN	22	---	Brakes
52	13	00	Reds Kagle	'57 Ford GN	21	---	RF Hub
53	47	13	Peck Pekcham	Peckham '57 Chevrolet GN	19	---	H Gasket
54	23	11	Junior Johnson	Paul Spaulding '57 Ford GN	7	---	Crash
55	18	90	Emanuel Zervakis	Junie Donlavey '57 Chevy C	6	---	Heating

Time of Race: 3 hours, 23 minutes, 33 seconds
Average Speed: 73.691 mph
Pole Winner: Cotton Owens - 83.896 mph
Lap Leaders: Cotton Owens 1-30, Bob Welborn 31-39, Glen Wood 40-46, Lee Petty 47-62,
    Buck Baker 63-81, Fireball Roberts 82-157, Shorty Rollins 158-280, Baker 181-193, Roberts 194-250.
Cautions: 8 for 32 laps   Margin of Victory: 1-lap-plus   Attendance: 15,000

Grand National Race No. 29
150 Laps at McCormick Field
Asheville, NC
37.5 Miles on Quarter-mile Paved Track
July 12, 1958

Fin	St	No.	Driver	Team / Car	Laps	Money	Status
1	1	49	Jim Paschal	J H Petty '57 Chevrolet	150	$570	Running
2	2	6	Cotton Owens	Jim Stephens '57 Pontiac	150	465	Running
3	3	44	Rex White	J H Petty '57 Chevrolet	150	340	Running
4		42	Lee Petty	Petty Engineering '57 Olds	149	265	Running
5		47	Jack Smith	Smith '57 Chevrolet	148	235	Running
6		34	Junior Johnson	Dick Beaty '57 Ford	148	215	Running
7		87	Buck Baker	Baker '57 Chevrolet	148	270	Running
8		41	Whitey Norman	'57 Chevrolet	147	200	Running
9		99	Shorty Rollins	Rollins '58 Ford	144	175	Running
10		97	Barney Shore	Shore '57 Chevrolet	143	190	Running
11		57	Billy Rafter	Rafter '57 Ford	141	145	Running
12		63	R L Combs	'56 Ford	137	150	Running
13		37	Tiny Lund	Don Angel '56 Ford	81	130	Tires
14		55	Banjo Matthews	Brushy Mtn Mtrs '57 Pontiac	54	115	Crash
15		19	Herman Beam	Beam '57 Chevrolet	16	90	Handling

Time of Race:48 minutes, 27 seconds
Average Speed: 46.440 mph
Pole Winner: Jim Paschal - 50.336 mph
Lap Leaders: Jim Paschal 1-150.
Cautions: Margin of Victory: 1 car length   Attendance:

Jim Paschal

Jack Smith, Herman Beam and Banjo Matthews all crashed in the heat races, but were able to make the 150 lap feature on the quarter mile track.

Barney Shore and Whitey Norman won the heat races.

Paschal averaged 46.440 mph for his seventh career Grand National win.

Petty moved out to a 1,630 point lead over Smith in the standings.

Race No. 30

Rookie Rollins Leads Unknowns to Romp at Busti

BUSTI, NY (July 16) -- Lloyd "Shorty" Rollins of Corpus Christi, TX drove his Ford home first at State Line Speedway to win the 50-mile Grand National event. It was the first win on the NASCAR big league circuit for the Ford driver.

Finishing second was Bob Duell, who was driving a

Ford entered by Julian Buesink. Ken Johnson was third, Emory Mahan came in fourth and John Seeley was fifth.

Relative unknown drivers took the first seven spots. Eighth place finisher Lee Petty started on the pole but mechanical problems knocked him 11 laps off the pace.

Rollins became the 15th different driver to win in the 1958 campaign. The 29 year-old driver also put a lock on the Rookie of the Year title. Fred Harb is the other leading contestant for freshman honors.

Shorty Rollins

Grand National Race No. 30
150 Laps at State Line Speedway
Busti, NY
50 Miles on .333-Mile Dirt Track
July 16, 1958

Fin	St	No.	Driver	Team / Car	Laps	Money	Status
1	3	99	Shorty Rollins	Rollins '58 Ford	150	$600	Running
2	5	95	Bob Duell	Julian Buesink '57 Ford	150	470	Running
3	11	36	Ken Johnson	'56 Ford	149	375	Running
4	10	8	Emory Mahan	'57 Chevrolet	149	270	Running
5	8	16	John Seeley	'57 Ford	143	245	Running
6	2	74	L D Austin	Austin '56 Chevrolet	141	205	Running
7	6	711	Bill Poor	Poor '56 Chevrolet	140	170	Running
8	1	42	Lee Petty	Petty Engineering '57 Olds	139	175	Running
9	16	97	Bob Finale	'56 Chevrolet	138	165	Running
10	20	54	John Walker	'56 Ford	135	155	Running
11	19	9	Bob Seharns	'56 Chevrolet	131	130	Running
12	13	85	Carl Tyler	Tyler '57 Ford	130	150	Differen.
13	23	102	Bud Gardner	'56 Ford	127	100	Running
14	15	18	Dick Walters	Walters '56 Ford	119	100	Running
15	9	511	Squirt Johns	'57 Chevrolet	105	90	A Frame
16	22	133	Clyde Goons	'56 Ford	69	85	Lug Nut
17	14	1	Marv Thorpe	'56 Chevrolet	67	100	Running
18	12	28	Paul Wilson	'56 Pontiac	58	60	Tie Rod
19	18	F9	Jug Pierce	'56 Chevrolet	53	50	Trans
20	17	44	Tom Nundy	'57 Nash	34	65	Differen.
21	7	83	Lennie Page	'56 Ford	29	40	Steering
22	21	93	Ted Chamberlain	Chamberlain '56 Chevrolet	4	25	Fuel
23	4	33	Al White	'57 Ford	1	35	RF Hub

Time of Race: 1 hour, 3 minutes, 37 seconds
Average Speed: 47.110 mph
Pole Winner: Lee Petty -
Lap Leaders: - - - - - - - - - Shorty Rollins   -150.
Cautions: Margin of Victory: Attendance:

Grand National Race No. 31
100 Laps at Canadian National Exposition Speedway
Toronto, Canada
33.3 Miles on .333-Mile Paved Track
July 18, 1958

Fin	St	No.	Driver	Team / Car	Laps	Money	Status
1	3	42	Lee Petty	Petty Engineering '57 Olds	100	$575	Running
2	4	6	Cotton Owens	Jim Stephens '57 Pontiac	100	480	Running
3	2	7	Jim Reed	Reed '57 Ford	100	305	Running
4	5	99	Shorty Rollins	Rollins '58 Ford	100	275	Running
5	6	23	Johnny Mackison	Ken Corman '57 Mercury	99	220	Running
6	8	57	Billy Rafter	Rafter '57 Ford	99	210	Running
7	1	44	Rex White	J H Petty '57 Chevrolet	98	190	Running
8	12	79	Tiny Benson	'57 Chevrolet	98	175	Running
9	11	711	Bill Poor	Poor '56 Chevrolet	97	180	Running
10	17	95	Bob Duell	Julian Buesink '57 Ford	96	150	Running
11	10	17	Howard Phillippi	'57 Ford	94	160	Running
12	9	74	L D Austin	Austin '56 Chevrolet	93	120	Running
13	16	93	Ted Chamberlain	Chamberlain '57 Chevrolet	92	115	Running
14	14	33	Al White	'58 Ford	86	105	Running
15	18	13	Peck Peckham	Peckham '56 Chevrolet	86	95	Running
16	15	41	Neil Haight	'56 Chevrolet	69	105	Running
17	7	142	Richard Petty	Petty Engineering '57 Olds	55	115	Crash
18	13	83	Lennie Page	'56 Ford	22	90	Ignition
19	19	18	Dick Walters	Walters '56 Ford	18	65	Rear End

Time of Race: 46 minutes, 16 seconds
Average Speed: 43.184 mph
Pole Winner: Rex White - 51.406 mph
Lap Leaders: Rex White 1-71, Lee Petty 72-100.
Cautions: Margin of Victory: Attendance:

Race No. 31

Lee Wins at Toronto; Richard Petty Makes First Start

TORONTO, ONT. CAN. (July 18) -- Lee Petty drove past Rex White in the 72nd lap and led the rest

Lee Petty waves to the crowd as he takes the checkered flag in the 33.3-mile Grand National event at Toronto, Canada.

trimmed the 19 car field in the 25-miler at Civic Stadium. It was the shortest Grand National race in terms of distance in NASCAR history.

Cotton Owens finished in second place in his Pontiac. Johnny Mackison, surprise second fastest qualifier, wound up third in a lightly regarded Mercury. Shorty Rollins was fourth and pole sitter Rex White came in fifth.

Reed averaged 46.972 mph for the half-hour race. White had the pole position at a speed of 38.593 according to officials' stopwatches. It was the slowest pole time in NASCAR's history.

The father-son combination of Lee and Richard Petty finished sixth and 11th respectively in a pair of Oldsmobiles. Lee was a lap off the pace and Richard was four laps behind the winner.

Only two cars fell out of the race and a crowd of 7,750 was on hand.

of the way to win the 33.3-mile Grand National event at the Canadian National Exposition Speedway. It was his fifth win of the year.

Petty's young offspring Richard made his first Grand National start and wound up 17th in the field of 19. Richard, 21, hit the fence in the 55th lap, knocking him from the race.

The Toronto event came less than a week after young Richard made his professional debut in a Convertible event at Columbia, SC. "This was my first Grand National," said the younger Petty. "Cotton Owens was leading Daddy. They came up on me and I moved over to let them pass.

"Cotton went on by," Petty continued, "but Daddy bumped me in the rear and my car went right into the wall."

Owens finished second in the 100-lap event on the .333-mile paved oval. Jim Reed came in third, Shorty Rollins was fourth and Johnny Mackison fifth.

Sixteen of the 19 cars finished the race. Petty averaged 43.184 mph for his 35th career win.

Race No. 32

Reed Wins 25-Miler at Buffalo's Civic Stadium

BUFFALO, NY (July 19) --Jim Reed gunned his blue Ford around Rex White in the 46th lap and

Grand National Race No. 32
100 Laps at Civic Stadium
Buffalo, NY
25 Miles on Quarter-Mile Paved Track
July 19, 1958

Fin	St	No.	Driver	Team / Car	Laps	Money	Status
1	3	7	Jim Reed	Reed '57 Ford	100	$605	Running
2	4	6	Cotton Owens	Jim Stephens '57 Pontiac	100	450	Running
3	2	23	Johnny Mackison	Ken Corman '57 Mercury	100	320	Running
4	6	99	Shorty Rollins	Rollins '58 Ford	99	275	Running
5	1	44	Rex White	J H Petty '57 Chevrolet	99	250	Running
6	5	42	Lee Petty	Petty Engineering '57 Olds	99	195	Running
7	10	95	Bob Duell	Julian Buesink '57 Ford	98	220	Running
8	7	79	Tiny Benson	'57 Chevrolet	96	165	Running
9	8	57	Billy Rafter	Rafter '57 Ford	96	170	Running
10	9	17	Howard Phillippi	'57 Ford	96	160	Running
11	13	42A	Richard Petty	Petty Engineering '57 Olds	96	155	Running
12	12	74	L D Austin	Austin '56 Chevrolet	95	145	Running
13	14	83	Lennie Page	'56 Ford	93	115	Running
14	16	33	Al White	'58 Ford	91	95	Running
15	17	93	Ted Chamberlain	Chamberlain '57 Chevrooet	88	95	Running
16	18	13	Peck Peckham	Peckham '56 Chevrolet	88	95	Running
17	11	711	Bill Poor	Poor '56 Chevrolet	86	120	Running
18	15	41	Neil Haight	'56 Chevrolet	63	90	Heating
19	19	18	Dick Walters	'56 Ford	4	65	Ignition

Time of Race: 31 minutes, 56 seconds
Average Speed: 46.972 mph
Pole Winner: Rex White - 38.593 mph
Lap Leaders: Rex White 1-45, Jim Reed 46-100.
Cautions: None   Margin of Victory: Attendance: 7,750

Cotton Owens got his first Grand National win of the year in the 100-miler at Rochester, NY.

Grand National Race No. 33
200 Laps at Monroe County Fairgrounds
Rochester, NY
100 Miles on Half-Mile Dirt Track
July 25, 1958

Fin	St	No.	Driver	Team / Car	Laps	Money	Status
1	3	6	Cotton Owens	Jim Stephens '57 Pontiac	200	$800	Running
2	6	87	Buck Baker	Baker '57 Chevrolet	198	525	Running
3	5	46	Speedy Thompson	Thompson '57 Chevrolet	198	350	Running
4	7	42	Lee Petty	Petty Engineering '57 Olds	197	250	Running
5	8	95	Bob Duell	Julian Buesink '57 Ford	195	225	Running
6	12	70	Jim Parsley	'56 Chevrolet	181	200	Running
7	16	711	Bill Poor	Poor '56 Chevrolet	181	165	Running
8	13	94	Clarence DeZalia	DeZalia '56 Ford	178	150	Running
9	11	74	L D Austin	Austin '56 Chevrolet	176	140	Running
10	18	83	Lennie Page	'56 Ford	176	130	Running
11	17	93	Ted Chamberlain	Chamberlain '56 Chevrolet	171	125	Running
12	19	57	Billy Rafter	Rafter '57 Ford	162	110	Running
13	14	33	Al White	'57 Ford	162	100	Running
14	20	13	Peck Peckham	Peckham '56 Chevrolet	155	85	Running
15	21	4	Roy Campbell	'57 Chevrolet	150	70	Running
16	10	79	Tiny Benson	'57 Chevrolet	116	60	Rear End
17	4	47	Jack Smith	Smith '57 Chevrolet	95	50	Gas Tank
18	15	400	Bill Wimble	Lyle Sokoll '57 Chevrolet	94	50	Engine
19	9	471	Johnny Allen	Jack Smith '57 Chevrolet	77	50	Shocks
20	2	99	Shorty Rollins	Rollins '58 Ford	45	50	Piston
21	1	44	Rex White	J H Petty '57 Chevrolet	10	50	Heating

Time of Race: 1 hour, 40 minutes, 1 second
Average Speed: 59.990 mph
Pole Winner: Rex White - 62.871 mph
Lap Leaders: Shorty Rollins 1-7, Jack Smith 8-35, Rollins 36-45, Smith 46-95, Owens 96-200.
Cautions: Margin of Victory: 2 laps plus   Attendance: 4,513.

Race No. 33

Owens Overtakes Smith, Captures Rochester 100

ROCHESTER, NY (July 25) -- Everett "Cotton" Owens took the lead from Jack Smith in the 95th lap and hustled to his first win of the year in the 100-miler at the Monroe County Fairgrounds.

Buck Baker finished second, two laps behind. Third place went to Speedy Thompson with Lee Petty fourth and Bob Duell fifth.

Rookie Shorty Rollins qualified second and led the first seven laps. Smith passed Rollins on lap eight and held first place until lap 36 when Rollins went back in front.

Bidding for his second win of the year, Rollins was pulling away when the engine blew in his Ford on lap 45.

Smith went back in front and was holding a 220 yard lead over Owens when the plug came out of his fuel tank. He was unable to get back in the race and Owens was home free.

Rollins wound up 20th and Smith got 17th place.

A crowd of 4,513 watched Owens' Pontiac cover the 100 miles at a 59.990 mph clip. It was his second Grand National career triumph.

Race No. 34

Reed Runs Hard To Win At Wall Stadium

BELMAR, NJ (July 26) -- Jim Reed of Peekskill, NY nosed out Rex White by a car length to win the 300-lapper at Wall Stadium. It was the fourth win of the year for the former truck driver.

Buck Baker finished in third place with Lee Petty fourth. Petty's Olds was the fastest car on the track at the end of the race, but the Randleman, NC veteran was foiled by an unscheduled pit stop. Fifth place went to Jack Smith.

Reed started second on the grid and led all 300-laps on the .333-mile oval. The caution came out only once for five laps when Richard Petty's Oldsmobile stalled in the third turn. Young Petty got going again and finished ninth, the first time he has cracked the top 10 in Grand National competition.

Reed averaged 65.395 mph for the 100-miles.

Grand National Race No. 34
300 Laps at Wall Stadium
Belmar, NJ
100 Miles on .333-Mile Paved Track
July 26, 1958

Fin	St	No.	Driver	Team / Car	Laps	Money	Status
1	2	7	Jim Reed	Reed '57 Chevrolet	300	$800	Running
2	1	44	Rex White	J H Petty '57 Chevrolet	300	525	Running
3		87	Buck Baker	Baker '57 Chevrolet	300	350	Running
4		42	Lee Petty	Petty Engineering '57 Olds	300	250	Running
5		47	Jack Smith	Smith '57 Chevrolet	291	225	Running
6		90	Buzz Woodward	'56 Ford	290	200	Running
7		46	Speedy Thompson	Thompson '57 Chevrolet	284	165	Running
8		X	John Lindsay	'57 Chevrolet	279	150	Running
9		42A	Richard Petty	Petty Engineering '57 Olds	278	140	Running
10		711	Bill Poor	Poor '56 Ford	276	130	Running
11		74	L D Austin	Austin '56 Chevrolet	273	125	Running
12		70	Jim Parsley	'56 Chevrolet	273	110	Running
13		83	Lennie Page	'56 Ford	254	100	Running
14		33	Al White	'58 Ford	248	85	Running
15		94	Clarence DeZalia	DeZalia '56 Mercury	157	70	Brakes
16		37	Bill Benson	'56 Ford	84	60	Engine
17		17	Marvin Porter	'57 Ford	77	50	Engine
18		13	Peck Peckham	Peckham '56 Chevrolet	58	50	Bearing
19		50	Ben Benz	'56 Chevrolet	43	50	Clutch

Time of Race: 1 hour, 31 minutes, 45 seconds
Average Speed: 65.395 mph
Pole Winner: Rex White - 68.936 mph
Lap Leaders: Jim Reed 1-300.
Cautions: 1 for 5 laps   Margin of Victory: 1 car length   Attendance:

Race No. 35

Jack Smith Best at Bridgehampton

BRIDGEHAMPTON, NY (Aug.2) -- Jack Smith shoved his Chevrolet into the lead on the first turn of the first lap and led all 35 laps in winning the 100-mile Grand National contest at the Bridgehampton Raceway. It was the first time the NASCAR circuit had ventured into Long Island, NY

Jack Smith won on Bridgehampton's road course.

Cotton Owens finished second, 12 seconds behind Smith's Chevrolet. Jim Reed was third, Junior Johnson fourth and Buck Baker fifth.

Smith said he drove the 2.85-mile road course all the way in high gear, and he had a lead of a mile or more during the middle stages. Owens was

able to slice the deficit in the late laps when Smith backed off.

Axel Anderson, who was out of racing for nearly three years after he crashed violently at Langhorne in 1955, blew a tire on his Chevrolet on the final lap and flipped over. He was not hurt.

Smith averaged 80.696 mph for his seventh career Grand National win.

Grand National Race No. 35
35 Laps at Bridgehampton Raceway
Bridgehampton, NY
100 Miles on 2.85-Mile Paved Road Course
August 2, 1958

Fin	St	No.	Driver	Team / Car	Laps	Money	Status
1	1	47	Jack Smith	Smith '57 Chevrolet	35	$800	Running
2	5	3	Cotton Owens	Jim Stephens '58 Pontiac	35	525	Running
3	3	7	Jim Reed	Reed '57 Ford	35	350	Running
4	8	11	Junior Johnson	Paul Spaulding '57 Ford	35	250	Running
5	2	87	Buck Baker	Baker '57 Chevrolet	35	225	Running
6	7	42	Lee Petty	Petty Engineering '57 Olds	34	200	Running
7	6	46	Speedy Thompson	Thompson '57 Chevrolet	34	165	Running
8	9	40	Dave White	'58 Chevrolet	33	150	Running
9	4	17	Marvin Porter	'57 Ford	32	140	Running
10	10	147	Johnny Allen	Jack Smith '58 Pontiac	31	130	Running
11	12	74	L D Austin	Austin '56 Chevrolet	31	125	Running
12	11	X	John Lindsay	'56 Chevrolet	30	110	Running
13	15	94	Clarence DeZalia	DeZalia '56 Ford	29	100	Running
14	14	79	Irvin Blatt	'56 Ford	28	85	Running
15	17	444	Axel Anderson	George Augustine '56 Chevy	28	70	Crash
16	16	13	Peck Peckham	Peckham '56 Chevrolet	27	60	Running
17	13	37	Bill Benson	'56 Mercury	13	50	Ignition

Time of Race: 1 hour, 14 minutes, 10 seconds
Average Speed: 80.696 mph
Pole Winner: Jack Smith - 82.001 mph
Lap Leaders: Jack Smith 1-35.
Cautions: None   Margin of Victory 12 seconds   Attendance:

Race No. 36

Columbia Cash Goes to Speedy Thompson

COLUMBIA, SC   (Aug.7) -- Speedy Thompson outdueled Bob Welborn and won the 100-miler at Columbia Speedway for his third win of the season.

Thompson and Welborn were five laps ahead of third place finisher Cotton Owens. Shorty Rollins came in fourth and George Dunn nabbed fifth place.

Lee Petty finished seventh in the field of 21 and upped his point lead to 2,202 over Buck Baker, whose Chevrolet overheated on lap 132, leaving him with a

14th place finish.

Clarence DeZalia blew a tire and crashed late in the race. The Aberdeen, NC Ford driver still managed to finish in ninth place.

Thompson averaged 54.820 mph for his 17th career win.

winner's prize on a peculiar technical ruling.

The race ended under the caution flag. Jack Smith crashed his Chevrolet into the wall, forcing the fifth and final caution of the day. He was not injured.

Convertible cars grabbed the first four places. Bob Welborn finished second to Weatherly, with Larry Frank third, Jimmy Thompson fourth and Lee Petty fifth. Both Thompson and Petty were in Petty Engineering Oldsmobiles.

White led the first 118 laps before Weatherly sailed into the lead. White was holding down second place when his Chevrolet blew a tire and crashed on lap 162. He got credit for 23rd in the field of 32.

Weatherly's first 'official' win came in his 47th Grand National start. He averaged 59.269 mph as the Fairgrounds Speedway conducted its grand opening. A crowd of 13,998 was on hand.

Grand National Race No. 36
200 Laps at Columbia Speedway
Columbia, SC
100 Miles on Half-Mile Dirt Track
August 7, 1958

Fin	St	No	Driver	Team / Car	Laps	Money	Status
1	1	46	Speedy Thompson	Thompson '57 Chevrolet	200	$800	Running
2	7	49	Bob Welborn	J H Petty '57 Chevrolet	200	525	Running
3	10	6	Cotton Owens	Jim Stephens '57 Pontiac	195	350	Running
4	4	99	Shorty Rollins	Rollins '58 Ford	193	250	Running
5	9	14	George Dunn	Manley Britt '57 Mercury	183	225	Running
6	19	711	Bill Poor	Poor '56 Chevrolet	178	200	Running
7	3	42	Lee Petty	Petty Engineering '57 Olds	175	165	Running
8	15	74	L D Austin	Austin '56 Chevrolet	171	150	Running
9	17	94	Clarence DeZalia	DeZalia '56 Ford	169	140	Crash
10	16	78	Shep Langdon	Langdon '56 Ford	169	130	Running
11	20	81	Harvey Hege	Hege '57 Ford	167	125	Running
12	14	202	Johnny Gardner	'56 Ford	165	110	Running
13	12	30	Doug Cox	'57 Ford	158	100	Running
14	6	87	Buck Baker	Baker '57 Chevrolet	132	85	Heating
15	5	36	Herb Estes	Estes '58 Ford	130	70	Spindle
16	2	37	Tiny Lund	Don Angel '56 Ford	126	60	Rear End
17	8	17	Fred Harb	Harb '57 Mercury	119	50	Ball Jt
18	11	96	Bobby Keck	Keck '57 Chevrolet	79	50	Trans
19	21	67	Roy Tyner	Spook Crawford '56 Dodge	59	50	Spindle
20	18	86	Neil Castles	Castles '56 Ford	35	50	Heating
21	13	34	Don Angel	Angel '57 Ford	22	50	Oil Press

Time of Race: 1 hour, 49 minutes, 27 seconds
Average Speed: 54.820 mph
Pole Winner: Speedy Thompson 64.240 mph
Lap Leaders: - - - - - - - - - Speedy Thompson -200.
Cautions: Margin of Victory: Attendance:

Race No. 37

Weatherly Finishes First; and Keeps a Victory For a Change

NASHVILLE, TN (Aug. 10) -- Joe Weatherly whipped his Ford Convertible around Rex White in the 119th lap and led the rest of the way to win the Sweepstakes 100-miler at the Nashville Fairgrounds.

It was the third Grand National event which Weatherly had finished first, but the first one in which he was able to keep first place money. Previously, the Norfolk, VA driver had won at Palm Beach, FL in 1956, but his car was disqualified. He also finished first at Wilson, NC later that year but Buck Baker got the

Grand National Race No. 37
200 Laps at Fairgrounds Speedway
Nashville, TN
100 Miles on Half-Mile Paved Track
August 10, 1958

Fin	St	No	Driver	Team / Car	Laps	Money	Status
1	8	72	Joe Weatherly	'58 Ford C	200	$1,850	Running
2	6	49	Bob Welborn	J H Petty '57 Chevy C	200	1,050	Running
3	2	76	Larry Frank	Frank '57 Chevrolet C	200	800	Running
4	31	2	Jimmy Thompson	Petty Eng. '57 Olds C	198	575	Running
5	15	42	Lee Petty	Petty Eng '57 Olds GN	197	475	Running
6	3	87	Buck Baker	Baker '57 Chevrolet GN	193	400	Running
7	9	31	Joe Lee Johnson	'57 Chevrolet GN	193	350	Running
8	13	47	Jack Smith	Smith '57 Chevrolet GN	192	300	Crash
9	21	36	Herb Estes	Estes '58 Ford GN	192	250	Running
10	5	99	Shorty Rollins	Rollins '58 Ford GN	191	200	Running
11	20	32	Brownie King	Jess Potter '57 Chevy C	191	190	Running
12	12	21	Glen Wood	Wood Brothers '57 Ford C	191	170	Running
13	17	25	Gene White	White '57 Chevrolet GN	191	150	Running
14	14	56	Bill Morton	James Lowery '57 Ford C	189	130	Running
15	22	17	Fred Harb	Harb '57 Mercury C	188	120	Running
16	11	46	Speedy Thompson	Thompson '57 Chevy GN	187	105	Running
17	10	8	Possum Jones	'58 Chevrolet C	182	100	Running
18	18	9	Wilbur Rakestraw	Joe Jones '57 Ford C	179	100	Crash
19	25	82	Eddie McDonald	'57 Ford GN	177	100	Running
20	19	44	Lloyd Dane	'58 Ford GN	174	100	Running
21	29	74	L D Austin	Austin '56 Chevrolet GN	166	100	Running
22	27	19	Herman Beam	Beam '57 Chevrolet GN	162	95	Running
23	1	11	Rex White	'57 Chevrolet GN	162	85	Crash
24	30	81	Shep Langdon	Harvey Hege '57 Ford C	155	75	Running
25	26	24	Jerry Green	'58 Ford GN	154	65	Running
26	28	86	Neil Castles	Castles '56 Ford C	145	60	Running
27	23	45	Ken Love	'58 Ford GN	99	60	Running
28	16	39	Billy Carden	Bishop Bros. '57 Chevrolet C	67	60	Coil
29	7	6	Cotton Owens	Jim Stephens '57 Pontiac GN	61	60	Crash
30	4	22	Fireball Roberts	Frank Strickland '57 Chevy C	40	60	Gas Leak
31	24	97	Barney Shore	Shore '57 Chevrolet C	15	50	Engine
32	32	67	Roy Tyner	Spook Crawford '57 Dodge C	0	50	Engine

Time of Race: 1 hour, 41 minutes, 14 seconds
Average Speed: 59.269 mph
Pole Winner: Rex White - 71.315 mph
Lap Leaders: Rex White 1-118, Joe Weatherly 119-200.
Cautions: 5   Margin of Victorty: Under Caution   Attendance: 13,998

Race No. 38

Roberts-Matthews Team Wins Weaverville Sweepstakes

WEAVERVILLE, NC (Aug. 17) -- Fireball Roberts, with Banjo Matthews providing a crucial assist, won the Western North Carolina 500 at the Asheville-Weaverville Speedway.

It was the second Sweepstakes win in a row for the

<table>
<tr><td colspan="8">Grand National Race No. 38
500 Laps at Asheville-Weaverville
Speedway
Weaverville, NC
"Western North Carolina 500"
250 Miles on Half-mile Paved Track
August 17, 1958</td></tr>
<tr><th>Fin</th><th>St</th><th>No.</th><th>Driver</th><th>Team / Car</th><th>Laps</th><th>Money</th><th>Status</th></tr>
<tr><td>1</td><td>2</td><td>22</td><td>Fireball Roberts**</td><td>Frank Strickland '57 Chevy C</td><td>500</td><td>$2,650</td><td>Running</td></tr>
<tr><td>2</td><td>8</td><td>49</td><td>Bob Welborn</td><td>J H Petty '57 Chevy C</td><td>499</td><td>1,800</td><td>Running</td></tr>
<tr><td>3</td><td>3</td><td>42</td><td>Lee Petty</td><td>Petty Eng. '57 Olds GN</td><td>497</td><td>1,250</td><td>Running</td></tr>
<tr><td>4</td><td>7</td><td>46</td><td>Speedy Thompson*</td><td>Thompson '57 Chevy GN</td><td>494</td><td>925</td><td>Running</td></tr>
<tr><td>5</td><td>15</td><td>87</td><td>Buck Baker</td><td>Baker '57 Chevrolet GN</td><td>493</td><td>775</td><td>Running</td></tr>
<tr><td>6</td><td>12</td><td>44</td><td>Ken Rush</td><td>J H Petty '57 Chevy C</td><td>491</td><td>700</td><td>Running</td></tr>
<tr><td>7</td><td>11</td><td>7</td><td>Jim Reed</td><td>Reed '57 Ford GN</td><td>489</td><td>625</td><td>Running</td></tr>
<tr><td>8</td><td>14</td><td>2</td><td>Joe Weatherly</td><td>Petty Eng. '57 Olds C</td><td>489</td><td>575</td><td>Running</td></tr>
<tr><td>9</td><td>10</td><td>76</td><td>Larry Frank</td><td>Frank '57 Chevrolet C</td><td>484</td><td>455</td><td>Running</td></tr>
<tr><td>10</td><td>17</td><td>16</td><td>Tommy Irwin</td><td>'57 Ford GN</td><td>479</td><td>425</td><td>Running</td></tr>
<tr><td>11</td><td>18</td><td>37</td><td>Tiny Lund</td><td>Don Angel '56 Ford C</td><td>477</td><td>400</td><td>Running</td></tr>
<tr><td>12</td><td>20</td><td>66</td><td>Roy Tyner</td><td>Spook Crawford '58 Plym GN</td><td>462</td><td>375</td><td>Running</td></tr>
<tr><td>13</td><td>26</td><td>32</td><td>Brownie King</td><td>Jess Potter '57 Chevy C</td><td>456</td><td>325</td><td>Running</td></tr>
<tr><td>14</td><td>27</td><td>19</td><td>Herman Beam</td><td>Beam '57 Chevrolet GN</td><td>451</td><td>275</td><td>Running</td></tr>
<tr><td>15</td><td>6</td><td>56</td><td>Bill Morton</td><td>James Lowery '57 Ford C</td><td>447</td><td>250</td><td>Running</td></tr>
<tr><td>16</td><td>22</td><td>97</td><td>Barney Shore</td><td>Shore '57 Chevrolet C</td><td>444</td><td>250</td><td>Running</td></tr>
<tr><td>17</td><td>36</td><td>711</td><td>Bill Poor</td><td>Poor '56 Chevrolet C</td><td>444</td><td>250</td><td>Running</td></tr>
<tr><td>18</td><td>23</td><td>74</td><td>L D Austin</td><td>Austin '56 Chevrolet GN</td><td>437</td><td>225</td><td>Running</td></tr>
<tr><td>19</td><td>24</td><td>81</td><td>Shep Langdon</td><td>Harvey Hege '57 Ford C</td><td>431</td><td>225</td><td>Running</td></tr>
<tr><td>20</td><td>25</td><td>96</td><td>Bobby Keck</td><td>Keck '57 Chevrolet GN</td><td>419</td><td>220</td><td>Running</td></tr>
<tr><td>21</td><td>30</td><td>24</td><td>Jimmie Lewallen</td><td>'57 Chevrolet C</td><td>389</td><td>210</td><td>Oil Leak</td></tr>
<tr><td>22</td><td>38</td><td>12</td><td>Bennie Rakestraw</td><td>Tal Cochrane '57 Merc C</td><td>372</td><td>200</td><td>Oil Press</td></tr>
<tr><td>23</td><td>37</td><td>17</td><td>Fred Harb</td><td>Harb '57 Mercury C</td><td>369</td><td>175</td><td>Engine</td></tr>
<tr><td>24</td><td>4</td><td>21</td><td>Glen Wood</td><td>Wood Brothers '57 Ford C</td><td>354</td><td>150</td><td>Timing</td></tr>
<tr><td>25</td><td>28</td><td>86</td><td>Neil Castles</td><td>Castles '56 Ford C</td><td>324</td><td>140</td><td>Crash</td></tr>
<tr><td>26</td><td>29</td><td>70</td><td>Jim Parsley</td><td>'56 Chevrolet GN</td><td>249</td><td>100</td><td>Crash</td></tr>
<tr><td>27</td><td>31</td><td>41</td><td>Whitey Norman</td><td>'57 Chevrolet C</td><td>194</td><td>100</td><td>Spindle</td></tr>
<tr><td>28</td><td>19</td><td>36</td><td>Herb Estes</td><td>Estes '58 Ford GN</td><td>181</td><td>100</td><td>Steering</td></tr>
<tr><td>29</td><td>34</td><td>5</td><td>Lloyd Dane</td><td>'57 Ford GN</td><td>181</td><td>100</td><td>Crash</td></tr>
<tr><td>30</td><td>1</td><td>55</td><td>Jimmy Massey</td><td>Brushy Mt. Mtrs '57 Pont GN</td><td>181</td><td>100</td><td>Crash</td></tr>
<tr><td>31</td><td>13</td><td>99</td><td>Jack Smith</td><td>Shorty Rollins '58 Ford GN</td><td>171</td><td>---</td><td>Rear End</td></tr>
<tr><td>32</td><td>35</td><td>10</td><td>Harry Leake</td><td>'56 Ford C</td><td>154</td><td>---</td><td>Engine</td></tr>
<tr><td>33</td><td>21</td><td>25</td><td>Billy Carden</td><td>Gene White '57 Chevy GN</td><td>141</td><td>---</td><td>Bearing</td></tr>
<tr><td>34</td><td>16</td><td>14</td><td>George Dunn</td><td>Manley Britt '57 Merc GN</td><td>129</td><td>---</td><td>Steering</td></tr>
<tr><td>35</td><td>33</td><td>71</td><td>Marvin Porter</td><td>'57 Ford GN</td><td>113</td><td>---</td><td>Gener.</td></tr>
<tr><td>36</td><td>9</td><td>6</td><td>Cotton Owens</td><td>Stephens '57 Pontiac GN</td><td>59</td><td>---</td><td>Engine</td></tr>
<tr><td>37</td><td>5</td><td>11</td><td>Rex White</td><td>'57 Chevrolet GN</td><td>46</td><td>---</td><td>Engine</td></tr>
<tr><td>38</td><td>32</td><td>33</td><td>George Green</td><td>Jess Potter '56 Chevrolet GN</td><td>33</td><td>---</td><td>Crank</td></tr>
</table>

Time of Race: 3 hours, 44 minutes, 38 seconds.
Average Speed 66.780 mph
Pole Winner: Jimmy Massey - 76.596 mph
Lap Leaders: - - - - - - - - - - Fireball Roberts -500.
Cautions: Margin of Victory: 1-lap-plus   Attendance: 10,000
*Jack Smith relieved Speedy Thompson.
**Banjo Matthews relieved Fireball Roberts on lap 370.

ragtops of NASCAR's Convertible division. Robert started second on the grid and was among the leaders all the way.

On lap 370, the Daytona Beach driver pitted and his Frank Strickland team seated Matthews in the car. Roberts had become fatigued and did not return in the race.

Matthews performed excellently and beat runner-up Bob Welborn by over a lap. Lee Petty finished third, Speedy Thompson with relief help from Jack Smith, was fourth. Fifth place went to Buck Baker.

Thirty-eight cars started the 500-lapper on the banked half-mile paved track. Only 20 were running at the finish.

Pole sitter Jimmy Massey and Lloyd Dane crashed together in the 181st lap, knocking both out of action. Neil Castles stuffed his Ford into the wall on lap 336. No one was injured.

Roberts averaged 66.780 mph for his 16th career victory. Petty's point lead grew to 2,284 points over Baker.

Race No. 39

Thrilling Winston-Salem Sweepstakes to Petty's Olds

WINSTON-SALEM, NC (Aug. 22) -- Old pro Lee Petty eeked out a half car length victory over rookie Shorty Rollins in the exciting climax to the 50-mile Sweepstakes race at Bowman Gray Stadium.

It was Petty's sixth win of the season Jim Reed finished a close third, Fred Harb was fourth and Buck Baker fifth.

Petty took the lead from Rollins with 19 laps remaining on the quarter-mile paved oval. The two drivers treated the crowd of 12,000 to a spine-tingling conclusion. Rollins' last lap bid fell short by only a few feet.

George Dunn put his Mercury on the pole and led the first 10 laps. Petty, who started second, nosed to the front on lap 11 and stayed there for 126 laps. Rollins, who started sixth, found the 'groove' and began pressuring Petty at the half way point. He was able to push his Ford into the lead on lap 137 and led until Petty made the final pass.

Curtis Turner crashed his Ford in the 26th lap. In an effort to overtake Jim Reed, Turner got too close to his rival and walloped the wall. The left front fender of Turner's Ford was left hanging on Reed's car.

Bob Welborn qualified third, but his Chevrolet was

taken out with transmission failure after just one lap.

Petty won the 50-miler at an average speed of 39.258 mph.

the start and wrecked his Chevrolet. Young Petty, who qualified ninth, was running in the top 10 when his Oldsmobile sailed over the third turn and landed in a water pond. He got a thorough soaking in the 166th lap incident but was unhurt.

Pole sitter Speedy Thompson broke an axle on his Chevrolet and went out in the last half of the event.

Welborn, who has won five of 14 starts in the 1958 Grand National season, collected $800 for his 60.443 mph victory.

Grand National Race No. 39
200 Laps at Bowman Gray Stadium
Winston-Salem, NC
50 Miles on Quarter-Mile Paved Track
August 22, 1958

Fin	St	No.	Driver	Team / Car	Laps	Money	Status
1	2	42	Lee Petty	Petty Eng. '57 Olds GN	200	$765	Running
2	6	99	Shorty Rollins	Rollins '58 Ford GN	200	550	Running
3	4	7	Jim Reed	Reed '57 Ford GN	200	495	Running
4	9	17	Fred Harb	Harb '57 Mercury C	199	295	Running
5	8	87	Buck Baker	Baker '57 Chevrolet GN	199	250	Running
6	1	14	George Dunn	Manley Britt '57 Merc C	199	240	Running
7	15	67	Roy Tyner	Spook Crawford '57 Dodge C	197	190	Running
8	13	37	Tiny Lund	Don Angel '56 Ford C	196	170	Running
9	12	55	Lloyd Dane	'57 Ford GN	196	190	Running
10	10	71	Marvin Porter	'57 Ford GN	196	175	Running
11	14	711	Bill Poor	Poor '56 Chevrolet GN	195	165	Running
12	22	52	Shep Langdon	Bob Walden '57 Ford C	193	165	Running
13	16	74	L D Austin	Austin '56 Chevrolet GN	187	140	Running
14	5	44	Ken Rush	J H Petty '57 Chevy C	187	150	Running
15	20	96	Bobby Keck	Keck '57 Chevrolet GN	185	115	Running
16	19	32	Brownie King	Jess Potter '57 Chevy C	183	110	Running
17	21	10	Harry Leake	'56 Ford C	182	115	Running
18	17	76	Larry Frank	Frank '57 Chevy C	178	125	Running
19	18	63	R L Combs	'56 Ford GN	167	140	Running
20	11	2	Richard Petty	Petty Eng. '57 Olds C	165	115	Running
21	23	18	Neil Castles	'56 Ford C	54	85	Spindle
22	7	21	Curtis Turner	Wood Brothers '57 Ford C	26	125	Crash
23	3	49	Bob Welborn	J H Petty '57 Chevy C	1	210	Trans

Time of Race: 1 hour, 16 minutes, 25 seconds
Average Speed: 39.258 mph
Pole Winner: George Dunn - 46.680 mph
Lap Leaders: George Dunn 1-10, Lee Petty 11-136, Shorty Rollins 137-182, L. Petty 183-200.
Cautions: Margin of Victory: Half-Car length   Attendance: 12,000

Race No. 40

Weatherly, Petty Wreck; Welborn Wins at Myrtle Beach

Grand National Race No. 40
200 Laps at Rambi Race Track
Myrtle Beach, SC
100 Miles on Half-Mile Dirt Track
August 23, 1958

Fin	St	No.	Driver	Team / Car	Laps	Money	Status
1	8	49	Bob Welborn	J H Petty '57 Chevrolet	200	$800	Running
2	5	87	Buck Baker	Baker '57 Chevrolet	200	525	Running
3	2	99	Shorty Rollins	Rollins '58 Ford	200	350	Running
4	14	37	Tiny Lund	Don Angel '56 Ford	198	250	Running
5	6	42	Lee Petty	Petty Engineering '57 Olds	197	225	Running
6	11	17	Fred Harb	Harb '57 Mercury	196	200	Running
7	3	11	Junior Johnson	Paul Spaulding '57 Ford	196	165	Running
8	10	52	Bob Walden	Walden '57 Ford	194	150	Running
9	12	14	George Dunn	Manley Britt '57 Mercury	189	140	Running
10	16	711	Bill Poor	Poor '56 Chevrolet	185	130	Running
11	20	81	Harvey Hege	Hege '57 Ford	184	125	Running
12	17	74	L D Austin	Austin '56 Chevrolet	182	110	Running
13	18	94	Clarence DeZalia	DeZalia '56 Ford	181	100	Running
14	15	202	Johnny Gardner	'56 Ford	169	85	Running
15	1	46	Speedy Thompson	Thompson '57 Chevrolet	166	70	Axle
16	9	2	Richard Petty	Petty Engineering '57 Olds	166	60	Crash
17	13	67	Roy Tyner	Spook Crawford '58 Dodge	133	50	Crash
18	7	25	Gene White	White '57 Chevrolet	80	50	Engine
19	19	125	J V Hamby	Leland Colvin '56 Chevrolet	57	50	Engine
20	21	18	Neil Castles	'56 Ford	15	50	Engine
21	4	44	Joe Weatherly	J H Petty '57 Chevrolet	1	50	Crash

Time of Race: 1 hour 39 minutes, 16 seconds
Average Speed: 60.443 mph
Pole Winner: Speedy Thompson - 66.667 mph
Lap Leaders: - - - - - - - - - - Bob Welborn - 200.
Cautions: Margin of Victory: Attendance:

MYRTLE BEACH, SC (Aug. 23) -- The New Rambi Race Track opened its doors and Bob Welborn took home the bacon for his fifth win of the season. Top threats Joe Weatherly and Richard Petty were taken out by crashes on the new half-mile dirt track.

Buck Baker wound up a close second and Shorty Rollins was third. Tiny Lund came in fourth and Lee Petty was fifth.

Weatherly, who started in the second row, got caught up in traffic on

Fred Harb made another good run to finish 6th at Myrtle Beach.

Race No. 41

Roberts Wins Crash-Filled Southern 500 Before 80,000

DARLINGTON, SC (Sept. 1) -- Fireball Roberts drove his Frank Strickland Chevrolet into the lead in

Eddie Pagan's Ford smashes through the steel guard rail in Southern 500. He was not seriously injured in the frightful looking accident.

Grand National Race No. 41
364 Laps at Darlington Raceway
Darlington, SC
"Southern 500"
500 Miles on 1.375-Mile Paved Track
September 1, 1958

Fin	St	No.	Driver	Team / Car	Laps	Money	Status
1	2	22	Fireball Roberts	Frank Strickland '57 Chevrolet	364	$13,220	Running
2	7	87	Buck Baker	Baker '57 Chevrolet	359	5,750	Running
3	8	99	Shorty Rollins	Rollins '58 Ford	359	3,815	Running
4	17	46	Speedy Thompson	Thompson '57 Chevrolet	358	1,995	Running
5	20	98	Marvin Panch	John Whitford '58 Ford	357	1,525	Running
6	25	49	Bob Welborn	Julian Petty '57 Chevrolet	355	1,150	Running
7	13	40	Rex White	'58 Chevrolet	348	1,045	Running
8	34	30	Doug Cox	'57 Ford	348	925	Running
9	23	95	Bob Duell	Julian Buesink '57 Ford	346	775	Running
10	21	36	Herb Estes	Estes '57 Ford	346	675	Running
11	28	11	Junior Johnson	Paul Spaulding '57 Ford	345	500	Running
12	33	66	Roy Tyner	Spook Crawford '58 Plymouth	344	400	Running
13	29	92	Wilbur Rakestraw	Joe Jones '57 Ford	344	300	Running
14	19	1	Speedy Thompson	'58 Chevrolet	344	310	Running
15	30	44	Lloyd Dane	'57 Ford	343	250	Running
16	12	86	G C Spencer	'57 Chevrolet	343	315	Running
17	35	48	Possum Jones	J H Petty '57 Chevrolet	342	225	Runnniig
18	22	97	Parnelli Jones	Vel's '57 Ford	340	200	Running
19	5	42	Lee Petty	Petty Engineering '57 Olds	335	345	Running
20	36	25	Gene White	White '57 Chevrolet	326	200	Running
21	31	15	Jim Paschal	'57 Chevrolet	321	150	Engine
22	10	19	Herman Beam	Beam '57 Chevrolet	311	190	Running
23	15	77	Bobby Johns	Shorty Johns '57 Chevrolet	304	150	Engine
24	18	88	Tiny Lund	Jim Linke '58 Ford	285	230	Running
25	41	94	Clarence DeZalia	DeZalia '56 Ford	277	150	Running
26	48	33	Al White	'58 Ford	264	100	Running
27	43	85	Carl Tyler	Tyler '57 Ford	248	100	Running
28	27	2	Bobby Lee	Horne Motors '58 Ford	230	100	Running
29	3	12	Joe Weatherly	Holman - Moody '58 Ford	226	265	Engine
30	45	74	L D Austin	Austin '57 Ford	214	100	Running
31	14	47	Jack Smith	Smith '58 Pontiac	210	100	Crash
32	16	43	Jim Reed	Petty Engineering '57 Olds	207	315	Engine
33	4	26	Curtis Turner	Holman - Moody '58 Ford	195	1,350	Engine
34	24	8	Eddie Gray	Vel's '57 Ford	160	100	Crash
35	6	6	Joe Eubanks	Jim Stephens '57 Pontiac	146	380	Clutch
36	1	45	Eddie Pagan	Pagan '58 Ford	136	240	Crash
37	47	9	Jesse James Taylor	Jesse James '56 Ford	95	100	Crash
38	38	89	Marvin Porter	'57 Ford	92	100	Crash
39	11	24	Larry Frank	'57 Chevrolet	71	275	Crash
40	32	14	George Dunn	Manley Britt '57 Mercury	61	100	Engine
41	27	10	Reds Kagle	Kagle '57 Ford	49	100	Piston
42	26	90	Emanuel Zervakis	Junie Donlavey '57 Chevy	47	100	Heating
43	46	5	Cotton Owens	'57 Dodge	15	100	Piston
44	42	31	Bob Bolheimer	Monroe Shook '58 Chevy	15	100	Heating
45	44	81	Harvey Hege	Hege '57 Ford	8	100	Throttle
46	39	60	Don Kimberling	'58 Chevrolet	7	100	Crash
47	9	55	Jimmy Massey	Brushy Mt. Motors '57 Pontiac	5	100	Trans
48	40	84	Bob Perry	'57 Ford	1	100	Engine

Time of Race: 4 hours, 52 minutes, 44 seconds.
Average Speed: 102.585 mph
Pole Winner: Eddie Pagan - 116.952 mph
Fastest Qualifier: Fireball Roberts - 118.648 mph
Lap Leaders: Joe Weatherly 1, Eddie Pagan 2-12, Joe Eubanks 13-38, Curtis Turner 39-85, Pagan 86-87, Speedy Thompson 88-93, Turner 94-168, Fireball Roberts 169-364.
Cautions: 6 for 28 laps   Margin of Victory: 5-laps-plus   Attendance: 80,000

the 169th lap and led the rest of the way to win the ninth annual Southern 500 at Darlington Raceway. It was the third win of the year for the popular Daytona Beach star.

Buck Baker finished second, five laps behind. Shorty Rollins was third, 38 seconds behind Baker. Jimmy Thompson finished fourth and Marvin Panch was fifth.

The 364-lap, 500-mile event on the 1.375-mile egg-shaped oval was punctuated by a series of wild crashes. Don Kimberling lost control of his Chevrolet in the seventh lap. The car skidded backwards, rode the guard rail and burst into flames. The Tyronne, PA driver, making his first Grand National start, escaped injury.

Jesse James Taylor, making only his fourth start since life-threatening injuries suffered at Atlanta in 1951, rode the top of the guard rail in the first turn on lap 98. He, too, escaped harm.

The real fireworks started on lap 136 when pole winner Eddie Pagan blew a tire and blasted through the guard rail. Pagan's Ford was totally demolished and he suffered a broken nose.

The retaining barrier was destroyed in the crash. Race officials were unable to make repairs. NASCAR representatives warned the drivers to stay away from the unprotected upper groove in turn one.

Within 20 miles, Eddie Gray's Ford lost traction and sailed directly through the opening in the rail. Miraculously, he escaped injury.

On lap 202, Jack Smith tumbled over the first turn near the site of the Pagan and Gray wrecks. He was badly shaken but not hurt.

Roberts continued his brisk pace, riding the upper crest of the 'Lady in Black', virtually ignoring warnings of race officials. He padded his lead with every turn and cashed in on the $13,220 first prize. It was

Jack Smith's Pontiac nose-dives over the turn at Darlington.

down Welborn.

Lee Petty startred on the pole and led the first 44 laps.

After a series of pit stops, Petty wound up 10th.

Bobby Keck was having a fine run until the A Frame snapped on his Chevrolet. He still managed to place seventh.

Baker averaged 52.280 mph for his 38th career win.

Bob Welborn

Roberts' fifth superspeedway victory and his third in a row. Both are records.

The lead changed hands eight times among six drivers. Roberts led once for the final 196 laps. In all, Roberts has led 1,030 laps in superspeedway competition since 1950, more than any other driver.

The 500 miles was covered in just under five hours at an average speed of 102.585 mph. Point leader Lee Petty wound up 19th in the field of 48. His point lead was sliced to 1,184 points over Baker.

Race No. 42

Welborn Wrecks, Baker Beats Field at Charlotte

CHARLOTTE, NC (Sept. 5) -- Buck Baker cruised into the lead when a wreck forced Bob Welborn out of the race and won the 100-mile Grand National event at the Southern States Fairgrounds. It was only the second win of the year for the defending Grand National champion.

Speedy Thompson wound up second, a lap behind. Shorty Rolling, a cinch of win the Rookie of the Year honors, came in third. Bob Walden placed fourth and Bill Poor was fifth.

Welborn had taken the lead from Junior Johnson in the 56th lap and was leading by a half lap when his Chevrolet tagged the retaining wall. He was unable to return to the race an wound up 17th in the final order.

Johnson crashed in the 89th lap while trying to run

Grand National Race No. 42
200 Laps at Southern States Fairgrounds
Charlotte, NC
100 Miles on Half-Mile Dirt Track
September 5, 1958

Fin	St	No.	Driver	Team / Car	Laps	Money	Status
1	7	87	Buck Baker	Baker '57 Chevrolet	200	$800	Running
2	6	46	Speedy Thompson	Thompson '57 Chevrolet	199	525	Running
3	3	99	Shorty Rollins	Rollins ' 58 Ford	191	350	Running
4	24	52	Bob Walden	Walden '57 Ford	183	250	Running
5	17	711	Bill Poor	Poor '56 Chevrolet	179	225	Running
6	22	81	Harvey Hege	Hege '57 Ford	179	200	Running
7	16	96	Bobby Keck	Keck '57 Chevrolet	178	165	A Frame
8	20	36	Herb Estes	Estes '58 Ford	176	150	Running
9	23	30	Doug Cox	'57 Ford	174	140	Running
10	1	42	Lee Petty	Petty Engineering '57 Olds	174	130	Running
11	12	202	Johnny Gardner	'56 Ford	167	125	Running
12	8	67	Roy Tyner	Spook Crawford '58 Plymouth	166	110	Running
13	15	94	Clarence DeZalia	DeZalia '56 Ford	164	100	Running
14	13	55	Jimmy Massey	Brushy Mt. Motors '57 Pontiac	161	85	Spindle
15	4	6	Cotton Owens	Jim Stephens '57 Pontiac	159	70	Running
16	10	17	Fred Harb	Harb '57 Mercury	142	60	Running
17	2	49	Bob Welborn	J H Petty '57 Chevrolet	102	50	Crash
18	11	32	Brownie King	Jess Potter '57 Chevrolet	93	50	Running
19	5	11	Junior Johnson	Paul Spaulding '57 Ford	89	50	Crash
20	19	44	Ken Rush	J H Petty '57 Chevrolet	54	50	A Frame
21	21	74	L D Austin	Austin '56 Chevrolet	31	50	Axle
22	9	41	Whitey Norman	'57 Chevrolet	27	50	Clutch
23	14	48	Banjo Matthews	Julian Petty '57 Chevrolet	19	50	Axle
24	25	18	Neil Castles	'56 Ford	19	50	Heating
25	18	37	Tiny Lund	Don Angel '56 Ford	11	---	Engine

Time of Race: 1 hour, 54 minutes, 46 seconds
Average Speed: 52.280 mph
Pole Winner: Lee Petty - 576.897 mph
Lap Leaders: Lee Petty 1-44, Junior Johnson 45-55, Bob Welborn 56-102,
    Buck Baker 103-200.
Cautions: Margin of Victory : 1-lap-plus   Attendance: 8,700.

Race No. 43

Rare Short Track Appearance By Roberts Nets Victory

BIRMINGHAM, AL (Sept. 7) -- Fireball Roberts, concentrating on only 'major' NASCAR events in the

1958 season, showed up at the Birmingham Fairgrounds Speedway and walked away with top honors in the 100-miler. It was his fifth win of the year in only eight starts.

Roberts outdistanced Buck Baker to take the $800 first prize. Third place went to Lee Petty with Joe Eubanks fourth and Tiny Lund fifth.

Pole sitter Cotton Owens led in the early stages, but faded to a ninth place finish. Jack Smith ,who started fourth, wrecked his Chevrolet in the 155th lap.

A field of 18 took the starter's flag and only 10 were around at the finish.

Roberts averaged 60.678 mph for his 19th career Grand National win.

Bob Ross came in second, the only other driver in the 28 car field to complete the 100 lap distance on the one-mile dirt track. Danny Weinberg came in third. Jim Cook was fourth and fifth place went to Harold Hardesty.

Eddie Gray, who survived a spectacular crash in Darlington's Southern 500, wrecked his Ford in the 87th lap. He had started fourth and was running in the top five at the time.

Jones won the race at an average speed of 65.550 mph. His pole wining effort was 77.922 mph.

Grand National Race No. 43
200 Laps at Fairgrounds Speedway
Birmingham, AL
100 Miles on Half-mile Dirt Track
September 7, 1958

Fin	St	No.	Driver	Team / Car	Laps	Money	Status
1	3	22	Fireball Roberts	Frank Strickland '57 Chevy	200	$800	Running
2	6	87	Buck Baker	Baker '57 Chevrolet	200	525	Running
3	2	42	Lee Petty	Petty Engineering '57 Olds	199	450	Running
4	8	6	Joe Eubanks	Jim Stephens '57 Pontiac	194	325	Running
5	5	48	Tiny Lund	J H Petty '57 Chevrolet	194	225	Running
6	11	25	Gene White	White '57 Chevrolet	192	200	Engine
7	10	40	Rex White	'58 Chevrolet	192	165	Running
8	13	14	Bennie Rakestraw	'56 Chevrolet	189	150	Running
9	1	3	Cotton Owens	Jim Stephens '58 Pontiac	189	140	Running
10	7	50	Gober Sosebee	Sosebee '57 Chevrolet	187	130	Running
11	16	51	Sam Colvin	'57 Plymouth	185	125	Running
12	4	47	Jack Smith	Smith '57 Chevrolet	155	110	Crash
13	15	39	Charley Griffith	Bishop Bros '57 Chevrolet	123	100	Differ.
14	17	85	Carl Tyler	Tyler '57 Ford	78	85	Engine
15	14	54	George Alsobrook	'57 Chevrolet	54	70	Engine
16	12	92	Billy Carden	'57 Ford	54	60	Crank
17	9	310	Joe Lee Johnson	S T Campbell '57 Chevrolet	54	50	Crank
18	18	56	Cannonball Brown	Brown '56 Chrysler	11	50	Engine

Time of Race: 1 hour, 38 minutes, 53 seconds
Average Speed: 60.678 mph
Pole Winner: Cotton Owens - 64.034 mph
Lap Leaders: Cotton Owens 1- .... Fireball Roberts -200.
Cautions: Margin of Victory: Attendance:

Grand National Race No. 44
100 Laps at Sacramento Fairgrounds
Sacramento, CA
100 Miles on 1-Mile Dirt Track
September 7, 1958

Fin	St	No.	Driver	Team / Car	Laps	Money	Status
1	1	97	Parnelli Jones	Vel's '56 Ford	100	$700	Running
2	5	43	Bob Ross	'56 Mercury	100	500	Running
3	6	8	Danny Weinberg	'57 Ford	99	425	Running
4	9	5	Jim Cook	'57 Ford	98	335	Running
5	3	22N	Harold Hardesty	'56 Ford	98	300	Running
6	10	37	Charles Sanchez	'57 Ford	98	250	Running
7	8	14	Bob Keefe	'56 Ford	95	200	Running
8	26	17	Bill Jarlick	'56 Ford	95	150	Running
9	23	21	Dave James	'57 Chevrolet	93	100	Running
10	17	4	Bill Boldt	'56 Ford	93	100	Running
11	27	73	Jerry Johnson	'57 Chevrolet	93	100	Running
12	13	12	Mike Batinich	'57 Ford	91	100	Running
13	22	7	Bob Havenmann	'58 Pontiac	91	100	Running
14	18	18	Ruben Thrash	'57 Chevrolet	91	100	Running
15	12	23	Elgin Holmes	'56 Pontiac	91	75	Running
16	4	98	Eddie Gray	Vel's '57 Ford	87	50	Crash
17	11	47	George Norton	'56 Chevrolet	86	50	Running
18	20	90	Dick Carter	'56 Mercury	86	50	Running
19	35	36	Chauncey Crist	'56 Ford	85	50	Running
20	16	10	Lucky Long	'57 Chevrolet	85	50	Crash
21	24	29	Bill Hasley	'56 Mercury	51	25	Crash
22	21	2	Ron Hornaday	'56 Chevrolet	49	25	Fan Belt
23	15	100	Bill Bade	'57 Chevrolet	28	25	Heating
24	2	57	Danny Graves	'57 Chevrolet	24	25	Push Ro
25	7	22	Jack D McCoy	'56 Ford	17	---	Engine
26	19	33	Arley Scranton	'57 Pontiac	17	---	Radiator
27	28	0	Jim Blomgren	'57 Pontiac	8	---	Trans.
28	14	9	Bob Price	'56 Chevrolet	1	---	Engine

Time of Race: 1 hour, 31 minutes, 32 seconds
Average Speed: 65.550 mph
Pole Winner: Parnelli Jones - 77.922 mph
Lap Leaders: - - - - - - - - - Parnelli Jones   -100.
Cautions: Margin of Victory: Attendance:

Race No. 44

Parnelli Perfect in Sacramento 100

SACRAMENTO, CA (Sept. 7) -- Parnelli Jones of Torrance, CA started on the pole and finished first in the 100-mile Grand National event at the Sacramento Fairgrounds. It was the first win of the year the West Coast star.

Race No. 45

Baker Guides Chevy To Victory at Gastonia

GASTONIA, NC (Sept. 12) -- Buck Baker steered his Chevrolet to a close win over Lee Petty in the 66.7-mile Grand National event at the Gastonia Fairgrounds. It was Baker's third win of the year.

Petty finished about a straightaway behind Baker at the finish of the 200 lap event on the .333-mile dirt track. Bob Welborn came in third, Whitey Norman was fourth and Speedy Thompson fifth.

Tiny Lund, huge Harlan, IA native who is still looking for his first win, started on the pole but went only one lap before his Julian Petty Chevrolet broke an A Frame. He finished last in the 19 car field.

Roy Tyner qualified a Dodge third fastest, but a hole in his radiator knocked him out after 95 laps. He got credit for 17th in the final order.

Baker earned $800 for his 47.856 mph ride.

Tiny Lund started on the pole at Gastonia, but finished dead last.

at the Atlantic Rural Exposition Fairgrounds. It was the 18th career victory for the Chevrolet driver.

Petty, who led from lap 149 until the last 13 laps of the 200 lapper, finished in second place. Tommy Irwin came in third with Buck Baker fourth and Jim Findlay fifth.

Thompson won the pole and led the first 39 laps. Joe Weatherly pushed his Ford into the lead on lap 40 and led for 21 laps. A blown head gasket ended Weatherly's bid on lap 60.

Thompson grabbed first place at that point and led through lap 148 when Petty moved into the lead. Thompson remained in hot pursuit until making the decisive pass on lap 188.

Shorty Rollins qualified third but departed after 38 laps with a blown engine.

Junior Johnson started seventh but left after 88 laps with a burned out wheel bearing.

Local driver Emanuel Zervakis drove a Junie Donlavey Chevrolet din the 100-miler. Zervakis departed on lap 27 with overheating problems.

Thompson averaged 57.878 mph.

Grand National Race No. 45
200 Laps at Gastonia Fairgrounds
Gastonia, NC
66.7-Miles on .333-Mile Dirt Track
September 12, 1958

Fin	St	No.	Driver	Team/Car	Laps	Money	Status
1	2	87	Buck Baker	Baker '57 Chevrolet	200	$800	Running
2	7	42	Lee Petty	Petty Engineering '57 Olds	200	525	Running
3	5	49	Bob Welborn	J H Petty '57 Chevrolet	200	350	Running
4	8	41	Whitey Norman	'57 Chevrolet	196	250	Running
5	12	46	Speedy Thompson	Thompson '57 Chevrolet	193	225	Running
6	10	17	Fred Harb	Harb '57 Mercury	182	200	Running
7	11	96	Bobby Keck	Keck '57 Chevrolet	181	165	Running
8	4	99	Shorty Rollins	Rollins '58 Ford	181	150	Running
9	15	81	Harvey Hege	Hege '57 Ford	178	140	Running
10	9	52	Bob Walden	Walden '57 Ford	177	130	Running
11	17	711	Bill Poor	Poor '56 Ford	174	125	Running
12	14	74	L D Austin	Austin '56 Chevrolet	173	110	Running
13	18	78	Shep Langdon	Langdon '56 Ford	173	100	Running
14	19	18	Bill Walker	'56 Ford	160	85	Running
15	13	94	Clarence DeZalia	DeZalia '56 Ford	149	70	Carb.
16	6	36	Herb Estes	Estes '58 Ford	102	60	Valve
17	3	67	Roy Tyner	Spook Crawford '57 Dodge	95	50	Radiator
18	16	66	Vernon West	Spook Crawford '58 Plymouth	1	50	Engine
19	1	48	Tiny Lund	J H Petty '57 Chevrolet	1	50	A Frame

Time of Race: 1 hour, 23 minutes, 30 seconds
Average Speed: 47.856 mph
Pole Winner: Tiny Lund: 51.650 mph
Lap Leaders: - - - - - - - - - Buck Baker -200.
Cautions: Margin of Victory: Attendance:

Race No. 46

Thompson Nips Petty at Richmond

RICHMOND, VA (SEPT. 14) -- Speedy Thompson of Monroe, NC scampered around Lee Petty in the final laps and won the 100-mile Grand National event

Grand National Race No. 46
200 Laps at Atlantic Rural Exposition
Fairgrounds
Richmond, VA
100 Miles on Half-Mile Dirt Track
September 14, 1958

Fin	St	No.	Driver	Team / Car	Laps	Money	Status
1	1	46	Speedy Thompson	Thompson '57 Chevrolet	200	$800	Running
2	4	42	Lee Petty	Petty Engineering '57 Olds	200	525	Running
3	10	16	Tommy Irwin	'57 Ford	197	350	Running
4	2	87	Buck Baker	Baker '57 Chevrolet	195	250	Running
5	16	100	Jim Findley	'57 Chevrolet	189	225	Running
6	17	70	Jim Parsley	;56 Chevrolet	182	200	Running
7	5	3	Cotton Owens	Jim Stephens '58 Pontiac	179	165	Running
8	9	8	Elmo Langley	'57 Chevrolet	174	150	Running
9	18	74	L D Austin	Austin '56 Chevrolet	169	140	Engine
10	19	200	Ray Fanning	'56 Ford	157	130	Running
11	14	6	Joe Eubanks	Stephens '57 Pontiac	127	125	Oil Leak
12	21	41	Barney Hatchell	'56 Chevrolet	126	110	Running
13	22	4	J L McDaniel	'57 Chevrolet	123	100	Running
14	7	11	Junior Johnson	Paul Spaulding '57 Ford	88	85	Bearing
15	12	54	Nace Mattingly	Mattingly '57 Ford	80	70	Rock Arm
16	13	90	Buzz Woodward	Junie Donlavey '57 Chevrolet	72	60	Trans.
17	20	31	Gus Wilson	'56 Chevrolet	66	50	Engine
18	8	96	Bobby Keck	Keck '57 Chevrolet	63	50	Running
19	6	72	Joe Weatherly	'58 Ford	60	50	H Gasket
20	3	99	Shorty Rollins	Rollins '58 Ford	38	50	Engine
21	11	9	Emanuel Zervakis	Junie Donlavey '57 Chevy	27	50	Heating
22	15	5	Bailey Wynekoop	'56 Chevrolet	15	50	Engine

Time of Race: 1 hour, 43 minutes, 40 seconds
Average Speed: 57.878 mph
Pole Winner: Speedy Thompson - 62.915 mph
Lap Leaders: Speedy Thompson 1-39, Joe Weatherly 40-60, Thompson 61-148, Lee Petty 149-187, Thompson 188-200.
Cautions: Margin of Victory   Attendance:

Race No. 47

Un-retired Joe Eubanks Wins First Race at Hillsboro

HILLSBORO, NC (Sept. 28) -- Joe Eubanks of Spartanburg, SC, who ended his retirement in the Southern 500, finally made it to victory lane with a popular win in the 99-mile Grand National event at Orange Speedway.

It was Eubank's first win on NASCAR's Grand National circuit and it came in hs 133rd start.

Eubanks had retired following the 1957 season when no good rides were available. Good friend and neighbor Cotton Owens persuaded him to come back and give it a try. Owens provided a Pontiac for Eubanks to drive.

Buck Baker #86 leads Speedy Thompson in close battle at Hillsboro.

In the 110-lap event on the .9-mile dirt oval, Eubanks took the lead with just 12 laps to go when front-running Junior Johnson broke a tie-rod and crashed his Ford. Doug Cox finished second, a half-lap behind. Buck Baker finished third, Tommy Irwin was fourth and Lee Petty fifth.

Owens led the first 32 laps before being passed by Tiny Lund. Lund, wheeling a Buck Baker Chevrolet, started on the pole and was leading when the A Frame broke in his car. It was the second straight race in which Lund won the pole but was sidelined by suspension problems.

Baker, a good friend of Lund, said, "If I gave that boy an anvil, he'd have it in about six pieces before you'd know it."

Johnson moved into the lead when Lund faltered and led until he crashed. Owens was forced to make a long pit stop shortly after he relinquished the lead. He fell to 10th place but had moved back up to second when the engine let go in his Pontiac on lap 68.

Eubanks, who started seventh and bided his time most of the way, averaged 72.439 mph after four cautions slowed the action for 19 laps.

Grand National Race No. 47
110 Laps at Orange Speedway
Hillsboro, NC
99-Miles on .9-Mile Dirt Track
September 28, 1958

Fin	St	No.	Driver	Team / Car	Laps	Money	Status
1	7	6	Joe Eubanks	Jim Stephens '57 Pontiac	110	$800	Running
2	10	30	Doug Cox	'57 Ford	110	525	Running
3	9	87	Buck Baker	Baker '57 Chevrolet	109	350	Running
4	15	16	Tommy Irwin	'57 Ford	109	250	Running
5	13	42	Lee Petty	Petty Engineering '57 Olds	108	225	Running
6	4	99	Shorty Rollins	Rollins '58 Ford	108	200	Running
7	21	64	Roy Tyner	Spook Crawford '58 Plymouth	107	165	Running
8	3	50	Gober Sosebee	Sosebee '57 Chevrolet	106	150	Running
9	19	63	R L Combs	'56 Ford	105	140	Running
10	29	52	Bob Walden	Walden '57 Ford	105	130	Running
11	26	15	Bill Blair	'57 Ford	104	125	Running
12	28	93	Ted Chamberlain	Chamberlain '57 Chevrolet	103	110	Running
13	14	37	Don Angel	Angel '56 Ford	102	100	Running
14	32	711	Bill Poor	Poor '56 Chevrolet	100	85	Running
15	8	11	Junior Johnson	Paul Spaulding '57 Ford	98	70	Crash
16	25	19	Herman Beam	Beam '57 Chevrolet	98	60	Running
17	18	32	Brownie King	Jess Potter '57 Chevrolet	95	50	Running
18	17	96	Bobby Keck	Keck '57 Chevrolet	91	50	Running
19	11	46	Speedy Thompson	Thompson '57 Chevrolet	85	50	Rear End
20	5	55	Jimmy Massey	Brushy Mt. Motors '57 Pontiac	70	50	Fan Belt
21	30	202	Johnny Gardner	'56 Ford	69	50	Running
22	2	3	Cotton Owens	Jim Stephens '58 Pontiac	68	50	Engine
23	22	17	Fred Harb	Harb '57 Mercury	66	50	Engine
24	6	25	Gene White	White '57 Chevrolet	57	50	Axle
25	1	86	Tiny Lund	Buck Baker '58 Chevrolet	46	---	A Frame
26	31	74	L D Austin	Austin '56 Ford	39	---	Engine
27	24	4	J L McDaniel	'57 Chevrolet	30	---	Axle
28	20	14	Larry Frank	Manley Britt '57 Mercury	24	---	Tie Rod
29	23	94	Clarence DeZalia	DeZalia '56 Ford	23	---	Rear End
30	27	81	Harvey Hege	Hege '57 Ford	21	---	Con. Arm
31	16	2	Richard Petty	Petty Engineering '57 Olds	16	---	Engine
32	12	44	Ken Rush	J H Petty '57 Chevrolet	2	---	Engine
33	33	41	Whitey Norman	'57 Chevrolet	0	---	Engine

Time of Race: 1 hour, 22 minutes, 0 seconds.
Average Speed: 72.439 mph
Pole Winner: Tiny Lund - 87.308
Lap Leaders: Cotton Owens 1-32, Tiny Lund 33-46, Junior Johnson 47-98,
    Joe Eubanks 99-110.
Cautions: 4 for 19 laps   Margin of Victory: Half-lap   Attendance: 5,000.

Race No. 48

Petty Super at Salisbury Super Speedway

SALISBURY, NC (Oct. 5) -- Lee Petty outran Buck Baker to win the 100-mile event at Bruton Smith's Salisbury Super Speedway for his 37th career victory. Petty clinched the 1958 driving title as his point lead rose to 1,112 over Baker.

Baker finished in second place and Cotton Owens

was third. Fourth place went to George Dunn and Roy Tyner came in fifth.

Gober Sosebee, one of the pioneers of NASCAR racing, won the pole in a Chevrolet. The former moonshine hauler finished seventh, 11 laps behind Petty.

Fred Harb, rookie driver out of High Point, was running in the top 10 when a tie rod broke on his Mercury. He got credit for 14th in the field of 30.

Only five cars failed to go the route.

Petty averaged 58.271 mph for his seventh win of the season.

shortened Old Dominion 500 at Martinsville Speedway.

Roberts drove his Frank Strickland Chevrolet around Glen Wood in the 186th lap and was in front when officials flagged the race to a halt on lap 350. He had driven the final few laps on a flat tire and Roberts admitted the outcome might have been different if the race had gone the full 500 laps.

The race was held up almost an hour while officials tried to figure out who was to be in the 40 car starting field.

Speedy Thompson finished in second place, a lap behind. Rex White was third, Bobby Johns fourth and Buck Baker fifth. Wood, who led the first 185 laps in

Grand National Race No. 48
160 Laps at Salisbury Super Speedway
Salisbury, NC
100 Miles on .625-Mile Dirt Track
October 5, 1958

Fin	St	No.	Driver	Team / Car	Laps	Money	Status
1		42	Lee Petty	Petty Engineering '57 Olds	160	$800	Running
2		87	Buck Baker	Baker '57 Chevrolet	160	525	Running
3		3	Cotton Owens	Jim Stephens '58 Pontiac	157	350	Running
4		14	George Dunn	Manley Britt '57 Mercury	157	250	Running
5		49	Roy Tyner	J H Petty ' 57 Chevrolet	157	225	Running
6		30	Doug Cox	'57 Ford	157	200	Running
7	1	50	Gober Sosebee	Sosebee '57 Chevrolet	149	165	Running
8		6	Joe Eubanks	Jim Stephens '57 Pontiac	148	150	Running
9		44	Ken Rush	J H Petty '57 Chevrolet	148	140	Running
10		37	Tiny Lund	Don Angel '56 Ford	147	130	Running
11		41	Whitey Norman	'57 Chevrolet	147	125	Running
12		81	Harvey Hege	Hege '57 Ford	146	110	Running
13		16	Tommy Irwin	'57 Ford	146	100	Running
14		17	Fred Harb	Harb '57 Mercury	144	85	Tie Rod
15		711	Bill Poor	Poor '56 Chevrolet	144	70	Running
16		0	Jimmy Thompson	'57 Chevrolet	143	60	Running
17		94	Clarence DeZalia	DeZalia '56 Ford	142	50	Running
18		66	Neil Castles	Spook Crawford '58 Plymouth	141	50	Running
19		93	Ted Chamberlain	Chamberlain '57 Chevrolet	140	50	Running
20		74	L D Austin	Austin '56 Chevrolet	139	50	Running
21		64	Shorty Rollins	Spook Crawford '58 Dodge	138	50	Running
22		2	Richard Petty	Petty Engineering '57 Olds	137	50	Running
23		202	Johnny Gardner	'56 Ford	136	50	Running
24		96	Bobby Keck	Keck '57 Chevrolet	130	50	Running
25		19	Herman Beam	Beam '57 Chevrolet	129	---	Running
26		4	J L McDaniel	'57 Chevrolet	126	---	Running
27		52	Bob Walden	Walden '57 Ford	120	---	Spindle
28		78	Shep Langdon	Langdon '56 Ford	101	---	Spindle
29		46	Speedy Thompson	Thompson '57 Chevrolet	76	---	Oil Press
30		63	R L Combs	'56 Ford	12	---	Carb.

Time of Race: 1 hour, 42 minutes, 58 seconds
Average Speed: 58.271 mph
Pole Winner: Gober Sosebee - 72.162 mph
Lap Leaders: - - - - - - - - - - Lee Petty -160.
Cautions: Margin of Victory: Attendance:

Race No. 49

Roberts Wins At Martinsville on Flat Tire

MARTINSVILLE, VA (Oct. 12) -- Fireball Roberts won his sixth race in nine 1958 starts in the darkness

Grand National Race No. 49
500 Laps at Martinsville Speedway
Martinsville, VA
"Old Dominion 500"
250-Miles on Half-Mile Paved Track
October 12, 1958

Fin	St	No.	Driver	Team / Car	Laps	Money	Status
1	4	22	Fireball Roberts	Frank Strickland '57 Chev GN	350	$2,875	Running
2	2	46	Speedy Thompson	Thompson '57 Chevy GN	349	1,925	Running
3	16	40	Rex White	'58 Chevrolet GN	348	1,405	Running
4	12	77	Bobby Johns	Shorty Johns '57 Chevy GN	347	1,075	Running
5	38	87	Buck Baker	Baker '58 Chevrolet GN	347	850	Running
6	14	7	Jim Reed	Reed '57 Ford GN	347	690	Running
7	6	42	Lee Petty	Petty Eng. '57 Olds GN	346	655	Running
8	13	2	Bob Welborn	Petty Eng. '57 Olds C	341	565	Running
9	1	21	Glen Wood	Wood Brothers '58 Ford C	340	650	Running
10	40	3	Cotton Owens	Jim Stephens '58 Pontiac GN	339	400	Running
11	17	32	Brownie King	Jess Potter '57 Chevrolet C	338	380	Running
12	15	56	Bill Morton	James Lowery '57 Ford C	338	330	Running
13	22	25	Jack Smith	Gene White '57 Chevrolet GN	338	305	Running
14	21	50	Bill Poor	'57 Chevrolet C	336	280	Running
15	23	14	George Dunn	Manley Britt '57 Mercury C	336	250	Running
16	33	97	Barney Shore	Shore '57 Chevrolet C	336	210	Running
17	20	99	Shorty Rollins	Rollins '58 Ford C	335	210	Running
18	31	92	Wilbur Rakestraw	Joe Jones '57 Ford C	332	175	Running
19	36	36	Herb Estes	Estes '58 Ford GN	330	165	Running
20	8	55	Jimmy Massey	Brushy Mt. Mtrs '57 Pont GN	330	210	Running
21	24	16	Tommy Irwin	'57 Ford GN	324	155	Running
22	34	8	L D Austin	'57 Chevrolet GN	318	135	Running
23	30	19	Herman Beam	Beam '57 Chevrolet GN	313	120	Running
24	28	96	Bobby Keck	Keck '57 Chevrolet GN	311	115	Running
25	39	78	Shep Langdon	Langdon '56 Ford C	308	75	Running
26	37	86	Neil Castles	Castles '56 Ford C	286	60	Running
27	35	37	Don Angel	Angel '57 Ford C	277	60	Engine
28	32	94	Clarence DeZalia	DeZalia '56 Ford GN	264	60	Running
29	29	76	Larry Frank	Frank '57 Chevrolet C	204	65	Oil Press
30	7	48	Tiny Lund	J H Petty '57 Chevrolet C	204	110	Engine
31	11	98	Marvin Panch	John Whitford '58 Ford C	161	100	Dist.
32	5	66	Roy Tyner	Spook Crawford '58 Plym C	130	130	Running
33	9	90	Emanuel Zervakis	Junie Donlavey '57 Chev C	118	100	Fuel Pmp
34	10	6	Joe Eubanks	Jim Stephens '57 Pontiac GN	94	100	Crash
35	3	1	Joe Weatherly	Holman - Moody '57 Ford C	82	175	Engine
36	18	11	Junior Johnson	Paul Spaulding '57 Ford GN	62	80	Handling
37	19	39	Billy Carden	Bishop Bros. '57 Chevrolet C	53	80	Dist.
38	25	17	Fred Harb	Harb '57 Mercury C	31	75	Engine
39	26	10	Elmo Langley	'57 Ford GN	18	70	Rear End
40	27	0	Jimmy Thompson	'57 Chevrolet GN	14	70	Oil Press

Time of Race: 2 hours, 43 minutes, 11 seconds
Average Speed: 64.344 mph
Pole Winner: Glen Wood - 67.950 mph
Lap Leaders: Glen Wood 1-185, Fireball Roberts 186-350.
Cautions: Margin of Victory: 1-lap-plus   Attendance: 13,000
* Race shortened to 375 laps due to darkness

Fireball Roberts takes the high side at Martinsville.

his Ford Convertible wound up ninth.

Two 50-lap heats determined the starting field. Wood won the first 50-lapper for Convertible cars and Thompson grabbed top honors in the Grand National heat. However, there were many disputes on who finished in the top 20 in each qualifier and it took NASCAR officials some 45-50 minutes to determine the starting field.

In the Convertible heat, Bob Welborn's car caught on fire. The car was badly damaged. Lee Petty, new 1958 Grand National champ, stepped in to help his comrade and provided him a car to race in the 500. Welborn finished eighth, the highest among Convertible entries.

Roberts averaged 64.344 mph and the $2,875 he won pushed his yearly earnings to over $30,000.

A crowd of 13,000 watched the two hour, 43 minute show.

Race No. 50

Jumpin' Johnson Jaunts to Victory at N. Wilkesboro

N.WILKESBORO, NC (Oct. 19) -- Junior Johnson surged past Glen Wood midway through the race and won the 100-miler at North Wilkesboro Speedway. It was the fifth win of the year for the Ronda Roadrunner.

Wood finished in second place, a lap behind the winner. Speedy Thompson, Cotton Owens and Jack Smith rounded out the top five.

Point champion Lee Petty finished in ninth place. It

was Petty's 43 time in the top 10 in 49 starts during the 1958 season.

Petty's young son Richard went only 35 laps before his Oldsmobile overheated.

Johnson averaged 84.906 mph in the caution-free event. Eighteen of the 24 cars that went to the starting post finished the 160-lapper.

Grand National Race No. 50
160 Laps at N.Wilkesboro Speedway
N.Wilkesboro, NC
100-Miles on .625-Mile Paved Track
October 19, 1958

Fin	St	No.	Driver	Team / Car	Laps	Money	Status
1	2	11	Junior Johnson	Paul Spaulding '57 Ford	160	$800	Running
2	1	21	Glen Wood	Wood Brothers '58 Ford	159	525	Running
3	4	46	Speedy Thompson	Thompson '57 Chevrolet	158	350	Running
4	3	3	Cotton Owens	Jim Stephens '58 Pontiac	158	250	Running
5	11	86	Jack Smith	Buck Baker '57 Cherolet	155	225	Running
6	5	55	Jimmy Massey	Brushy Mt. Motors '57 Pontiac	154	200	Running
7	14	14A	Wilbur Rakestraw	'57 Chevrolet	154	165	Running
8	16	32	Brownie King	Jess Potter '57 Chevrolet	154	150	Running
9	7	42	Lee Petty	Petty Engineering '57 Olds	150	140	Running
10	8	87	Buck Baker	Baker '57 Chevrolet	150	130	Running
11	13	50	Gober Sosebee	Sosebee '57 Chevrolet	150	125	Running
12	12	14	Larry Frank	Manley Britt '57 Mercury	147	110	Running
13	18	17	Fred Harb	Harb '57 Mercury	144	100	Running
14	6	36	Tiny Lund	Herb Estes '58 Ford	141	85	Running
15	22	0	Bunk Moore	'57 Chevrolet	141	70	Running
16	17	19	Herman Beam	Beam '57 Chevrolet	140	60	Running
17	19	94	Clarence DeZalia	DeZalia '56 Ford	136	50	Out / gas
18	21	74	L D Austin	Austin '56 Chevrolet	132	50	Running
19	20	711	Bill Poor	Poor '56 Chevrolet	131	50	Running
20	18	96	Bobby Keck	Keck '57 Chevrolet	112	50	Electrical
21	23	63	R L Combs	'56 Ford	79	50	Piston
22	24	202	Johnny Gardner	'56 Ford	67	50	Fuel Pmp
23	10	2	Richard Petty	Petty Engineering '57 Olds	35	50	Heating
24	9	97	Barney Shore	Shore '57 Chevrolet	26	50	Radiator

Time of Race: 1 hour, 10 minutes, 40 seconds
Average Speed: 84.906 mph
Pole Winner: Glen Wood - 86.805 mph
Lap Leaders: Glen Wood 1- - - - - - - - - - - -Junior Johnson   - 160.
Cautions: None   Margin of Victory : 1-lap-plus   Attendance:

Race No. 51

Johnson Nails Roberts Near Finish to Take Lakewood 150

ATLANTA, GA (Oct.26) -- Junior Johnson passed Fireball Roberts with 15 laps to go and won the 150 mile Grand National event at Lakewood Speedway.

Roberts, the scourge of the 1958 season, led much of the way until Johnson's late charge. Third place at the stripe was Lee Petty, who drove an Olds Convertible. Fourth place went to Joe Weatherly and Charlie

Promoters at Lakewood Speedway in Atlanta put a tarpaulin over the open grandstand for "spectator comfort".

Mincey was fifth.

Petty failed to earn any Grand National points, but still wrapped up the 1958 title by 644 points over Buck Baker.

Bill Morton of Church Hill, TN was seriously injured when his Ford Convertible crashed on lap 112. The car turned over and Morton was thrown from his car. Fred Harb, rookie driver, approached the scene and stopped his car at an angle to protect Morton. Harb later continued and finished 16th.

Bill Morton was injured in Lakewood crack-up...

For his heroic deed, Harb was presented the John Naughton Sportsmanship award.

Johnson prevailed in a tough race on a rough race track. Charley Griffith, Elmo Langley and Jimmy Massey all crashed. Jack Smith, Speedy Thompson, Billy Carden, Roscoe Thompson and Tiny Lund were eliminated by broken axles. Tim Flock, making an infrequent appearance, had his steering damaged on the choppy dirt track.

Johnson averaged 69.570 mph for his 11th career victory. Glen Wood, who started on the pole for the third consecutive time, wound up 10th.

...Fred Harb came to Morton's rescue and won a sportsmanship award.

Grand National Race No. 51
150 Laps at Lakewood Speedway
Atlanta, GA
150 Miles on 1-Mile Dirt Track
October 26, 1958

Fin	St	No.	Driver	Team / Car	Laps	Money	Status
1	4	11	Junior Johnson	Paul Spaulding '57 Ford GN	150	$1,925	Running
2	12	22	Fireball Roberts	Frank Strickland '57 Chev GN	150	1,200	Running
3	7	2	Lee Petty	Petty Eng. '57 Olds C	150	950	Running
4	29	45	Joe Weatherly	Beau Morgan '58 Ford C	149	650	Running
5	24	29	Charlie Mincey	Bishop Bros. '57 Chevy GN	148	550	Running
6	22	99	Shorty Rollins	Rollins '58 Ford GN	146	450	Running
7	40	77	Joe Lee Johnson	Shorty Johns '57 Chevy GN	146	375	Running
8	5	14	Larry Frank	Manley Britt '57 Mercury C	144	325	Running
9	15	32	Brownie King	Jess Potter '57 Chevrolet C	142	275	Running
10	1	21	Glen Wood	Wood Brothers '58 Ford C	142	325	Running
11	13	92	Wilbur Rakestraw	Joe Jones '57 Ford C	142	200	Running
12	30	25	Gene White	White '57 Chevrolet GN	140	175	Running
13	28	87	Buck Baker	Baker '58 Chevrolet GN	140	175	Running
14	11	66	Roy Tyner	Spook Crawford '58 Plym C	140	175	Running
15	18	3	Joe Eubanks	Stephens '58 Pontiac GN	137	175	Running
16	19	17	Fred Harb	Harb '57 Mercury C	135	150	Running
17	17	81	Harvey Hege	Hege '57 Ford C	133	150	Running
18	37	74	L D Austin	Austin '56 Chevrolet C	132	150	Running
19	10	114	Buddy Ragsdale	'57 Chevrolet GN	130	150	Running
20	23	711	Bill Poor	Poor '56 Chevrolet C	129	150	Running
21	45	78	Shep Langdon	Langdon '56 Ford C	125	125	Running
22	9	56	Bill Morton	James Lowery '57 Ford C	111	125	Crash
23	36	10	Elmo Langley	Ratus Walters '57 Ford GN	106	125	Crash
24	14	55	Jimmy Massey	Brushy Mt. Motors '57 Pont GN	105	125	Crash
25	16	50	Gober Sosebee	Sosebee '57 Chevrolet GN	100	125	Radiator
26	20	15	Tim Flock	Beau Morgan '57 Mercury GN	98	100	Steering
27	6	14A	Charley Griffith	'57 Pontiac GN	88	115	Crash
28	8	8	Jack Smith	'57 Chevrolet GN	56	100	Axle
29	32	46	Speedy Thompson	Thompson '57 Chevrolet GN	56	100	Axle
30	3	39	Billy Carden	Bishop Bros. '57 Chevrolet C	50	110	Axle
31	26	44	Chester Barron	'57 Chevrolet GN	49	75	Gas Line
32	34	5	Roscoe Thompson	'57 Chevrolet GN	44	75	Axle
33	33	X	Bill Blair	'57 Ford GN	43	75	Engine
34	39	85	Carl Tyler	Tyler '58 Ford GN	35	75	Dist
35	35	42	Richard Petty	Petty Eng. '57 Olds GN	29	75	Piston
36	38	30	Doug Cox	'57 Ford GN	27	50	Piston
37	31	12	Benny Rakestraw	Tal Cochrane '57 Mercury C	12	50	Oil Press
38	2	36	Tiny Lund	Herb Estes '58 Ford GN	11	100	Axle
39	27	202	Johnny Gardner	'56 Ford C	8	50	Tie Rod
40	21	86	Neil Castles	Castles '56 Ford C	3	50	Engine

Time of Race: 2 hours, 9 minutes, 22 seconds.
Average Speed: 69.570 mph
Pole Winner: Glen Wood - 81.522 mph
Lap Leaders - - - - - - - - - - - - - - - Fireball Roberts - 135, Junior Johnson 136-150.
Cautions: Margin of Victory: Attendance:

1958 NASCAR Season
Final Point Standings Grand National Division

Rank	Driver	Points	Starts	Wins	Top 5	Top 10	Winnings
1	Lee Petty	12,232	50	7	28	44	$26,565.00
2	Buck Baker	11,588	44	3	23	35	25,840.20
3	Speedy Thompson	8,792	36	4	18	23	15,214.56
4	Shorty Rollins	8,124	29	1	12	22	13,398.08
5	Jack Smith	7,666	38	2	14	21	12,633.28
6	L D Austin	6,972	46	0	0	10	6,245.96
7	Rex White	6,552	22	2	13	17	12,232.40
8	Junior Johnson	6,380	27	6	12	16	13,808.40
9	Eddie Pagan	4,910	27	0	11	18	7,471.52
10	Jim Reed	4,762	17	4	10	12	9,643.60
11	Fireball Roberts	4,420	10	6	8	9	32,218.20
12	Bobby Keck	4,240	30	0	0	8	3,458.20
13	Herman Beam	4,224	20	0	0	1	2,598.20
14	Herb Estes	4,048	11	0	0	4	2,508.20
15	Clarence DeZalia	3,448	27	0	0	6	3,003.20
16	Doug Cox	3,736	14	0	3	9	3,403.80
17	Cotton Owens	3,716	29	1	8	16	6,578.80
18	Marvin Panch	3,424	11	0	5	5	4,113.80
19	Billy Rafter	2,916	19	0	1	8	2,798.80
20	Curtis Turner	2,856	17	3	8	10	10,028.80
21	Lloyd Dane	2,844	5	0	1	2	2,490.00
22	Bob Duell	2,740	7	0	3	6	2,415.00
23	Jimmy Thompson	2,540	8	0	2	3	3,275.00
24	Fred Harb	2,484	25	0	4	7	3,320.00
25	Tiny Lund	2,436	23	0	4	7	3,155.00
26	Bill Poor	2,292	24	0	1	7	3,115.00
27	Gene White	2,040	9	0	0	2	1,400.00
28	Joe Weatherly	2,032	15	1	5	7	6,330.00
29	Johnny Mackison	1,680	11	0	2	3	1,255.00
30	Jim Parsley	1,488	10	0	0	4	1,135.00
31	Al White	1,464	9	0	0	1	920.00
32	Jimmy Massey	1,300	9	0	1	3	1,625.00
33	Parnelli Jones	1,140	3	1	1	1	1,010.00
34	Joe Eubanks	1,120	7	1	2	3	2,070.00
35	Brownie King	1,116	23	0	0	4	3,045.00
36	Richard Petty	1,016	9	0	0	1	760.00
37	Billy Carden	1,012	13	0	0	2	815.00
38	Elmo Langley	980	9	0	1	3	1,090.00
39	Buzz Woodward	964	9	0	0	2	1,195.00
40	Possum Jones	960	11	0	1	3	1,790.00
41	Jim Paschal	928	6	1	2	4	1,670.00
42	Chuck Hansen	916	7	0	0	1	580.00
43	Eddie Gray	910	3	1	1	1	3,375.00
44	Lennie Page	836	8	0	0	2	760.00
45	Bob Keefe	782	2	0	1	2	925.00
46	R L Combs	760	9	0	0	1	805.00
47	Ted Chamberlain	656	8	0	0	1	585.00
48	Dave James	646	2	0	0	2	300.00
49	Jack D McCoy	608	2	0	0	1	550.00
50	Gwyn Staley	604	4	0	4	4	1,730.00